Cultures and Nations
of Central and Eastern Europe

Essays in Honor of Roman Szporluk

Harvard Ukrainian Research Institute
Publications

Robert A. De Lossa,
Director of Publications

Daria Yurchuk,
Assistant Editor

Claire Rosenson,
Editorial Assistant

Cambridge, Massachusetts

Cultures and Nations of Central and Eastern Europe

Essays in Honor of Roman Szporluk

Edited by

Zvi Gitelman
Lubomyr Hajda
John-Paul Himka
Roman Solchanyk

Distributed by Harvard University Press
for the
Ukrainian Research Institute, Harvard University

Support for the publication of this volume was provided by the Dr. Stefan and Olena Wojtowycz Fund in Ukrainian Studies at Harvard University.

Cover: <u>Background</u>: "Europe: Showing International Boundaries as They Were at the Beginning of the War of the Nations," 1914, New York Evening Post, Co. <u>Inset</u>: Detail from "Europe—Political," *Hammond Odyssey World Atlas* (1999), © Hammond World Atlas Corporation, NJ, Lic. No. 12505. Reproduced with permission. Cover design by R. De Lossa.

Library of Congress Cataloging-in-Publication Data

Cultures and nations of Central and Eastern Europe : essays in honor of Roman Szporluk / edited by Zvi Gitelman ... [et al.].

 p. cm. -- (Ukrainian Research Institute publications)
Includes bibliographical references.
 ISBN 0-916458-93-8 (alk. paper)

 1. Europe, Eastern--Civilization. 2. Europe, Central--Civilization. 3. Szporluk, Roman. I. Gitelman, Zvi Y. II. Szporluk, Roman. III. Title. IV. Publications (Harvard Ukrainian Research Institute)
 DJK24 .C85 2000
 943--dc21

00-008792

ISBN 0-916458-93-8 (paper)
Printed in the United States of America by Flagship Press, Inc.
This book is printed on acid-free paper

PUBLISHED SIMULTANEOUSLY AS VOL. 22 (1998) OF
HARVARD UKRAINIAN STUDIES

The Ukrainian Research Institute was established in 1973 as an integral part of Harvard University. It supports research associates and visiting scholars who are engaged in projects concerned with all aspects of Ukrainian studies. The Institute also works in close cooperation with the Committee on Ukrainian Studies, which supervises and coordinates the teaching of Ukrainian history, language, and literature at Harvard University.

TABULA GRATULATORIA

Olga Andriewsky
Vera Andrushkiw
John A. Armstrong
Jerzy Axer
Mark Baker
Margarita Balmaceda
Stanisław Barańczak
Morris and Reva Bornstein
Yevhen Bystrytsky
Stephan and Maria Chemych
Andrzej Chojnowski
Serge Cipko
James Clem
John and Patricia Coatsworth
Timothy Colton
Patrice Dabrowski
Robert De Lossa
Volodymyr Dibrova
Robert J. Donia
Jaroslaw and Olha Duzyj
Grzegorz Ekiert
Leonid Finberg
Jonathan Frankel
Benjamin Frommer
Sherman Garnett
Marshall and Merle Goldman
Andrea Graziosi
Raymond and Daphne Grew
Rev. Borys Gudziak
Andrei Harasymiak
Liliana Hentosh
Patricia Herlihy
Halyna Hryn
Samuel and Nancy Huntington
Iaroslav Isaievych
Petro Jacyk

Georgii Kasianov
Michael D. Kennedy
Nancy Kollman
Roman Koropeckyj
Bohdan Krawchenko
Marian Krzyzowski
Bohdan Kudryk
John LeDonne
Paulina Lewin
Eric Lohr
James E. Mace
Charles Maier
Terry Martin
Gudrun and Ladislav Matejka
Askold Melnyczuk
Jaroslaw and Nadia Mihaychuk
Rev. Iaroslav Nalysnyk
Hrihoriy Nemyria
Marysia Ostafin
Alexander Pivovarsky
Peter J. Potichnyj
Roman and Lydia Procyk
Myroslaw Prokop
Alexander and Anna Pryshlak
William Rosenberg
Jeffrey Sachs
Gwendolyn Sasse
Nadia Schadlow
Myroslav Shkandrij
Orest Subtelny
Mary Ann Szporluk
Oleksiy Tolochko
Themistocle Wirsta and Orysia
    Lagoshniak-Wirsta
Sharon L. Wolchik
Daria Yurchuk

Behold

Who sees us? Who knows us?
Today is a long way off,
a dot on a ghost meridian.
Who knows us? Who frames us?
A lemon breaks open—five fingers,
five lobes of a tight-knit blossom,
a lotus unfisting its fate.
Who works in the dark, who makes us?
Sometimes I think you're the tree,
all *vita* and *ombra*, the delicate roots
underneath. And I am an owl,
howling daughter, scouring fields
for things to steal. And then it's a different
hour. I'm yours, in your arms, a child.
You're teaching me how to sit still.
Territorial lines in script
take wing. The rind grows soft,
like walls to a yellowing city
that fall, like flesh, from grace, and yet
reveal a stellar core—its pulse
allays the loss, your timeless voice
my tired ear. You're young.
I'm old. The seed is in itself.
Behold the yield.

Larissa Szporluk

CONTENTS

CONTRIBUTORS

MARTHA BOHACHEVSKY-CHOMIAK is senior program officer in the Division of Preservation and Access at the National Endowment for the Humanities.

AUDREY HELFANT BUDDING is an Academy Scholar at the Harvard Academy for International and Area Studies.

WALTER D. CONNOR is professor and director of undergraduate studies in the Department of Political Science at Boston University.

STEVEN D. CORRSIN is acting head of acquisitions at Wayne State University Libraries.

JOHN V. A. FINE is professor of history at the University of Michigan, Ann Arbor.

MICHAEL S. FLIER is the Oleksandr Potebnja Professor of Ukrainian Philology in the Department of Slavic Languages and Literatures at Harvard University.

ZVI GITELMAN is professor of political science, director of the Jean and Samuel Frankel Center for Judaic Studies, Preston R. Tisch Professor of Judaic Studies, and research scientist at the Center for Russian and East European Studies at the University of Michigan, Ann Arbor.

GEORGE G. GRABOWICZ is the Dmytro Čyževs'kyj Professor of Ukrainian Literature in the Department of Slavic Languages and Literatures at Harvard University.

PATRICIA KENNEDY GRIMSTED is a research fellow at the Harvard Ukrainian Research Institute.

LUBOMYR A. HAJDA is associate director of the Harvard Ukrainian Research Institute and editor of *Harvard Ukrainian Studies*.

FIONA HILL is director of strategic planning at the Eurasia Foundation.

JOHN-PAUL HIMKA is professor of history in the Department of History and Classics at the University of Alberta.

YAROSLAV HRYTSAK is director of the Institute for Historical Research, Ivan Franko Lviv National University, and visiting professor, Central European University.

ASSYA HUMESKY is professor of Slavic Languages and Literatures at the University of Michigan, Ann Arbor, emerita.

OWEN V. JOHNSON is professor in the School of Journalism and adjunct professor in the Department of History at Indiana University, Bloomington.

EDWARD L. KEENAN is the Andrew W. Mellon Professor of History and director of the Dumbarton Oaks Research Library and Collection at Harvard University.

PADRAIC KENNEY is associate professor of East European history in the Department of History at the University of Colorado, Boulder.

KSENYA KIEBUZINSKI is the Petro Jacyk Bibliographer in Ukrainian Studies at the Harvard Ukrainian Research Institute and a doctoral candidate in the Interdisciplinary Program in Literary Studies at Brandeis University.

ZENON E. KOHUT is director of the Canadian Institute of Ukrainian Studies at the University of Alberta.

RITA KRUEGER is associate director of the Center for Russia, East Europe, and Central Asia at the University of Wisconsin, Madison.

HUGO LANE is assistant professor of history at Polytechnic University.

MICHAŁ ŁESIÓW is professor and director of the Department of Ukrainian Philology at Marie Curie-Skłodowska University, emeritus, and professor and director of the Department of Slavic Languages at Catholic University of Lublin, emeritus.

IRINA LIVEZEANU is professor in the Department of History at the University of Pittsburgh.

RICHARD PIPES is the Frank R. Baird, Jr. Research Professor of History at Harvard University, emeritus.

ANTONY POLONSKY is the Walter Stern Hilborn Professor of Judaic and Social Studies at Brandeis University.

OMELJAN PRITSAK is the Mykhailo S. Hryshevs′kyi Professor of Ukrainian History at Harvard University, emeritus.

TERESA RAKOWSKA-HARMSTONE is professor of political science at Carleton University, emerita.

KONRAD SADKOWSKI is assistant professor of history at the University of Northern Iowa.

IHOR ŠEVČENKO is the Dumbarton Oaks Professor of Byzantine History and Literature at Harvard University, emeritus.

ROMAN SOLCHANYK is a consultant at the Rand Corporation in Santa Monica, California.

KEELY STAUTER-HALSTED is assistant professor of history at Michigan State University.

RONALD GRIGOR SUNY is professor of political science at the University of Chicago.

FRANK E. SYSYN is director of the Peter Jacyk Centre for Ukrainian Historical Studies at the Canadian Institute of Ukrainian Studies, University of Alberta, Edmonton.

LARISSA SZPORLUK is assistant professor in the department of English at Bowling Green State University and the author, most recently, of a collection of poetry, *Isolato*.

ANDRZEJ WALICKI is professor of history at the University of Notre Dame, emeritus.

LARRY WOLFF is professor of history at Boston College.

WILLIAM ZIMMERMAN is professor of political science, director and research scientist at the Center for Political Studies, and research scientist at the Center for Russian and East European Studies at the University of Michigan, Ann Arbor.

PREFACE

Cultures and Nations of Central and Eastern Europe represents an *homage* to our esteemed colleague and friend, Roman Szporluk, the Mykhailo S. Hrushevs'kyi Professor of Ukrainian History. Roman came to Harvard nearly a decade ago, after an already distinguished and fruitful career at the University of Michigan. His association with Harvard and its Ukrainian Research Institute, however, has been much longer. Even before the Institute's inception, he was part of the intellectual group that was defining just what kind of a Ukrainian research center should exist at a major American university. His physical association with our Institute started with the very first years after its founding. Among his other professional connections, in 1972 he was the second professor of history to teach at the Institute's summer school. Since his permanent move to Harvard in the early 1990s, Roman has been a robust force in Ukrainian studies here, helping to guide those studies through the dramatic changes that have followed Ukrainian independence. He has been director of the Ukrainian Research Institute since 1996 and has overseen a broadening of its vision with a renewed interest in Ukraine's place within what is now commonly called "East Central Europe."

This volume represents the well-wishes and contributions of many of Roman's colleagues and students from both Michigan and Harvard. The variety and nature of the studies attest to the broad interests and deep intellectual influence of our honorand. The Executive Committee of the Institute would like to thank the volume's editors, with a special note of gratitude to Mary Ann Szporluk, who with patience and professionalism aided our Institute's staff in the preparation of the volume. Our Festschrift has been immeasurably enriched by her keen eye and deft editing pencil. We also would like to thank Larissa Szporluk, noted poet, for adding a daughter's voice to this tribute to her father.

To the object of this admiration and respect we add, "Вітаємо, дорогий Романе!"

Edward L. Keenan
Michael S. Flier
George G. Grabowicz

INTRODUCTION

Our honorand received his first lessons in history at an early age, growing up in a place and time that felt the brunt of the twentieth-century catastrophe. Roman Szporluk was born on 8 September 1933 in Hrymailiv (*Pol.* Grzymałów), Skalat County, in the Ukrainian-inhabited eastern borderlands of what was then, and remained for the next six years, the Second Polish Republic; his birthplace now is in Ternopil Oblast, Ukraine. Roman is the son of Vasyl Szporluk (1899–1973) and his wife Maria Mikhenko (1910–1971). His sister, Marta (b. 1936), lives in Warsaw. His brother, Yuri, died as a child (1940–1947).

Roman received his secondary education in Lublin, graduating from the Państwowe Gimnazjum i Liceum im. Hetmana Jana Zamojskiego in 1951. In 1951–1955 he went on to a higher education in the same city, in the faculty of law of the Uniwersytet im. Marii Curie-Skłodowskiej. He wrote his master's thesis on Plato's *Republic* under the supervision of an authority on political theory, Grzegorz Leopold Seidler. In the following years, until 1958, he worked as an instructor (*asystent*) in the university's department of theory of state and law.

During 1958–1960 Roman did graduate work at Oxford and earned the degree of B.Litt. in the history of political thought in 1961. He wrote his thesis on "The Political Ideas of Thomas Garrigue Masaryk." Here John Plamenatz was his supervisor at Nuffield College and Sir Isaiah Berlin, then Chichele Professor at All Souls College, was his university supervisor.

From Britain Roman moved to California. He studied under Anatole G. Mazour and Wayne Vucinich at Stanford (1962–1965) and wrote a doctoral thesis on "M. N. Pokrovsky's Interpretation of Russian History." While there he met Mary Ann Bridley, whom he married in 1963. Their son Benjamin was born a year later.

In 1965 Roman joined the faculty of the history department at the University of Michigan as assistant professor. His daughter Larissa was born in Ann Arbor in 1967. In 1968–1969 the Szporluks lived in Vienna, where Roman continued the research on Masaryk that he had begun at Oxford and where his son Michael was born (1968). Roman stayed in Ann Arbor until 1991, with promotions to associate professor in 1970 and professor in 1975. While at Michigan he published some of the fruits of his earlier graduate research, including the collection of Pokrovsky's writings on Russia in world history, with his own detailed introduction (Bibl. 36), and the book on Masaryk's political thought (Bibl. 83). It was also at Michigan that he prepared his pathbreaking study of communism and nationalism (Bibl. 127). It was a time, too, that was fruitful in graduate students. During the Michigan years he supervised the doctorates of

Stephen Corrsin, Steven Guthier, John-Paul Himka, Owen Johnson, Padraic Kenney, Irina Livezeanu, James Mace, Konrad Sadkowski, Roman Solchanyk, and Keely Stauter-Halsted. He also served as director of the University of Michigan's Center for Russian and East European Studies from 1986 until 1991.

In 1991 Roman was appointed Mykhailo S. Hrushevs'kyi Professor of Ukrainian History at Harvard University. He currently also serves as director of Harvard's Ukrainian Research Institute. The move to Harvard coincided with the collapse of the Soviet Union, and much of Roman's work there has focused on interpreting this momentous change in East European and, indeed, world, history (see esp. Bibl. 246). So far at Harvard he has supervised to completion the doctoral dissertations of Audrey H. Budding, Patrice Marie Dabrowski, Benjamin R. Frommer, Rita Krueger, and Eric Lohr. Several other dissertations are underway.

*   *
*

One of Roman's major achievements in Ukrainian history was his recontextualization of it. Those outside the field had tended to regard Ukrainian history, if they noticed it at all, as an appendage of Russian history, while many practitioners ignored any extra-Ukrainian context altogether. Roman's innovation was to insist on examining Ukrainian history as a component of East Central European history, to be studied particularly in connection with developments in Poland, Hungary, and Czechoslovakia. In his thoughts about Ukrainian history and politics, Roman was inspired by Ivan L. Rudnytsky, whom he had first read in Lublin and met personally shortly after his arrival in America.

More than any other historian of Ukraine Roman paid attention to connections with neighboring nations, including the Belarusians, who were almost invisible in the 1960s and 1970s when Roman began writing about them (Bibl. 28, 76), and the Czechs as well. It was not simply that Roman placed Ukraine in the full context of its neighbors, but, uniquely among historians of Ukraine, he made independent contributions to the history of Belarus, Czechoslovakia, Poland (esp. Bibl. 70), and Russia. He also supervised doctoral dissertations covering virtually the whole gamut of modern Eastern Europe, from the Balkans to the Baltic.

He articulated the conception that the Soviet westward expansion of 1939 had incorporated part of Eastern Europe, "Far Eastern Europe," into the Soviet Union. In general, he brought to his numerous studies of the Soviet nationality question a highly differentiated understanding of its many components.

More importantly, he insisted on the centrality of this question long before the implosion of the USSR convinced many other scholars how critical the issue really was. He was certainly not the only analyst working on Soviet nationalities, but few had worked on the question as long as he had or had brought to it the theoretical depth that he did. When the Sovietology field as a whole rethought its premises in the late 1980s and early 1990s, the rapidity of its reorientation owed a great deal to the preparatory work of those like Roman who had seen what was coming and had labored long and hard over the inferences. Roman in particular had the insight that a central nationality question in the USSR was the Russian identity question itself. This was a problem that he had already broached in his work on Pokrovsky in the 1960s and formulated more explicitly by the early 1970s (e.g., Bibl. 46); it continues to have significant ramifications for the field to this day. This is another theme he picked up early whose relevance only becomes clearer as the history of the new Russia continues to unfold.

His work on nationalism is deeply steeped in theory. As both his colleagues and students well know, he reads analyses of nationalism closely and intensely, working through them, pressing them on others, discussing them, perpetually weighing their merits against competing analyses. Over the years he has engaged a good many theorists of nationalism in this manner—his old teacher John Plamenatz, Anthony D. Smith, Gale Stokes, Miroslav Hroch, Benedict Anderson, Liah Greenfeld, Prasenjit Duara, and others. But there were two theorists, with very different approaches to nationalism, whom he found particularly useful in developing his own thought: Karl Deutsch and Ernest Gellner.

The encounter with Deutsch was prior, dating back to the late 1950s. Deutsch, the author of *Nationalism and Social Communication*, was the prophet of nationalism as social mobilization, dependent particularly on instruments of communication and on education and urbanization. Working along lines suggested by Deutsch, Roman produced numerous studies of the East European periodical press, especially of the Ukrainian press, from the early 1960s on. He communicated his interest in the press to his doctoral students, several of whom wrote theses and/or books based largely on newspapers and what they indicated about national identity and consciousness (Guthier, Himka, Stauter-Halsted). Also originally inspired by Deutsch was his long-term interest in urbanization and its effects, including his work on Kyiv as Ukraine's "primate city." Again, he established himself as the leading expert on the urban history of Ukraine. And once more, he communicated this interest in cities to his students, one of whom wrote a thesis on Poland's "primate city," Warsaw (Corrsin). Roman himself worked little on the history of education, which was also part of the Deutschian program, but he did interest one of his students in the history of education in Slovakia (Johnson). Roman's work on the press and demography was widely read and appreciated by social scientists.

Roman's study of Ernest Gellner began in the 1960s, during his intensive work on Masaryk. The intellectual encounter with Gellner has been engagingly recounted by Roman himself (Bibl. 240). It was Gellner who served as the catalyst for Roman's search for the quintessential nationalist thinker, the Marx of nationalism, whom Roman identified as Friedrich List in his 1988 book on

Communism and Nationalism.[1] His reading of Gellner also inspired Roman to develop in original ways his long-standing interest in the interrelationship of socialism and nationalism. More and more, he began to treat them as the dual aspects of a single global process of modernization.

The concern with socialism and nationalism, which went back at least to the study of Pokrovsky, but more probably back to personal experiences of the late 1930s and 1940s, had a powerful impact on his students, several of whom wrote their doctoral dissertations precisely on the intersection of the two political movements (Himka, Mace, Solchanyk). What particularly distinguishes Roman's approach to the interrelation of socialism and nationalism is its complexity: on the one hand, he treats them as two rival, alternative interpretations of and responses to the transition to modernity, but on the other, he sees them as becoming inextricably intertwined in the twentieth century, with the nationalist paradigm growing increasingly influential precisely within the socialist movement. These views find their fullest exposition in *Communism and Nationalism*.

The strong commitment to theory does not prevent Roman from an equally strong commitment to the practical application of scholarship. He sees his historical work as a tool for understanding the present as it overlaps into the future. Since the inception of his academic career, he has produced a steady stream of commentary on current events, beginning with his informative articles on contemporary Soviet Ukraine in *Suchasnist'* in the early 1960s and continuing on into his television appearances and op-ed pieces in *The New York Times* and elsewhere. His work in this sphere received additional stimulus in 1991, when he moved to America's most visible university, Harvard, and the Soviet Union collapsed precisely because of the national question on which he had worked so long and fruitfully. He made sense out of what were, for many, bewildering events, and he also served as an articulate and sympathetic interpreter of the new Ukraine that emerged from under the Soviet rubble. He serves frequently as a consultant to high-level government bodies and NGOs such as the Soros Foundation. His own practice of bringing to wider audiences the results of historically and theoretically informed scholarship has found reflection also in the work of some of his students, particularly Roman Solchanyk's contributions as a research analyst for Radio Liberty and James Mace's for the Ukrainian news agency UNIAN.

While wrestling with the theory of nationalism and writing constantly in several directions, Roman remains a superb teacher. Not only does he give his students a genuine sense that they are collaborating with him in working out

---

[1] List was obviously on Roman's mind earlier. In the 1981 book on Masaryk, in which List had not figured at all, Roman had written: "In between the individual and the human race stood the nations . . . " (Bibl. 83, p. 80). Later, in *Communism and Nationalism,* Roman cited List's axiom that "'between each individual and entire humanity . . . stands the NATION'" (Bibl. 159, p. 115).

fundamental questions of scholarship, and indeed of the modern human condition, but he manages to do this with extraordinary charm and wit. He has developed some excellent, constantly evolving courses, including his famous "Socialism and Nationalism" taught as both lecture course and seminar and offered both at Michigan and Harvard; also lecture courses on Eastern Europe and on Ukraine. The success of these courses may be measured by how many students so far have gone on to complete a doctorate under his supervision: fifteen.

In the light of such accomplishments what is there to say but "Vivat!" and "Sto lat!" and "Многая літа!"

THE BIBLIOGRAPHY OF ROMAN SZPORLUK

compiled by

KSENYA KIEBUZINSKI[*]

Entries in the bibliography are arranged by year of appearance, from 1956 through 2000. Under each year items appear in the following order: books, articles or chapters in edited volumes, reviews, commentaries, interviews, and letters. Books, both authored and edited, as well as articles and commentaries are given in alphabetical order by title; reviews are listed alphabetically by name of author. Interviews and articles reflecting conversations with Roman Szporluk are alphabetized by name of interlocutor. Under each entry additional information is provided when appropriate: references to subsequent editions, translations, or reprints. Listed under REV. are reviews of the relevant publication by Roman Szporluk, alphabetized by name of reviewer; not included are reviews of collected monographs in which Roman Szporluk's contribution is not discussed, and short bibliographical notices. Listed under DISC. are publications with extensive discussion of the particular work by Roman Szporluk. Works published under a pseudonym are given with the pseudonym in brackets.

1956

1. (with W. Skrzydło and J. Ziembiński). "Konstytucyjne podstawy przebudowy ustroju rolnego PRL." In *Rola prawa w przebudowie ustroju PRL.* Wydział Prawa UMCS. Lublin. 9–25.

REVIEW:

2. Foustka, Radim. *Petra Chelčického názory na stát a pravo* (Prague, 1955), in: *Państwo i Prawo* 11(8–9): 463.

1957

3. "W sprawie klasyfikacji państw." *Annales Universitatis Mariae Curie Skłodowska,* Sectio G, 4(2): 139–54.

---

[*] Jennifer Elaine Hedda (Harvard University History Department, Ph.D. 1998) worked on an earlier version of this bibliography and helped locate many of the references listed here.

1958

REVIEW:

4. *Radians'ke pravo* (Kyiv, 1958), in: *Państwo i Prawo* 13(8–9): 432–34.

1959

LETTER:

5. [A Kiev Traveller]. "Kiev's Theatres." *The Spectator* 6824 (10 April): 512.

1960

REVIEW:

6. Deutscher, Isaac. *The Great Contest: Russia and the West* (New York: Oxford University Press, 1960), in: [Pavlo Chernov]. *Suchasna Ukraïna* [Munich] 27 November: 9.

COMMENTARY:

7. "Dyskryminatsiia ukraïns'kykh periodykiv." *Suchasna Ukraïna* [Munich] 30 October: 9–10.

1961

8. [Pavlo Chernov]. "Mis'ki hazety v URSR: trokhy tsyfr i faktiv do pytannia pro misto i movu na Ukraïni." *Suchasnist'* 5: 11–21.
9. [Pavlo Chernov]. "Zamitky pro polityku peretryvannia i vik chesnosty." *Suchasnist'* 11: 34–41.

REVIEWS:

10. *The Europa Year Book*, vol. 1 (London: Europa Publications, 1960); and *Statistics of Newspapers and Other Periodicals* (Paris: UNESCO, 1959), in: [P.Ch.]. *Suchasnist'* 4: 117–18.
11. *Pechat' SSSR v 1960 godu* (Moscow: Vsesoiuznaia knizhnaia palata, 1961), in: [P. Chernov]. "Bahato tsyfr—ale pro nykh treba znaty." *Suchasnist'* 10: 102–106.

1962

12. *A List of Materials for the Study of the History of Poland, with a Note on Holdings in the Libraries of Stanford University.* Stanford: University Library. 32 pp.
13. [Pavlo Chernov]. "Do presovoï polityky v URSR." *Suchasnist'* 5: 69–79.
14. "Masaryk's Idea of Democracy." *The Slavonic and East European Review* 41(96): 31–49.
15. [Pavlo Chernov]. "Presa URSR za mynule desiatyrichchia." *Suchasnist'* 3: 73–84.

REVIEWS:
16. Dovifat, Emil. *Handbuch der Auslandspresse* (Bonn: Athenäum-Verlag, 1960), in: [P.Chernov]. "Pro radians′ku presu." *Suchasnist'* 3: 121–22.
17. Łopatka, Adam. *Kierownicza rola partii komunistycznej w stosunku do państwa socjalistycznego: Zasady leninowskie* (Poznań: Wydawnictwo Poznańskie, 1960), in: *Slavic Review* 21(4): 754–55.
18. *Pechat' SSSR v 1961 godu* (Moscow: Vsesoiuznaia knizhnaia palata), in: [Pavlo Chernov]. "Pro vydavnychu polityku v URSR." *Suchasnist'* 12: 117–20.

1963

19. [Pavlo Chernov]. "Shcho chytaiut′ u nas na Ukraïni?" *Suchasnist'* 11: 57–68.

1964

20. [Pavlo Chernov]. "Do natsional′nykh vidnosyn v URSR—misto, mova i presa skhidnikh oblastei." *Suchasnist'* 6: 73–89.
21. [Pavlo Chernov]. "Iak hovoriat′ i shcho vydaiut′ na pivdni URSR." *Suchasnist'* 9: 87–93.
22. "Pokrovsky and Russian History." *Survey* 53: 107–118.
23. [Pavlo Chernov]. "Z problematyky sil′s′koï chastyny URSR. 'Iugo-Zapadnyi Krai' u 1960-ykh rokakh." *Suchasnist'* 7: 70–79.

1965

24. "Masaryk in Search of Authority." *Canadian Slavonic Papers* 7: 235–52.

1966

25. [Pavlo Chernov]. "Chy ie v nas stolytsia?" *Suchasnist'* 9: 76–90.

LETTER:
26. "Rumania's Lost Lands." *The New York Times* 1 June.

1967

27. "Pokrovskii's View of the Russian Revolution." *Slavic Review* 26(1): 70–84.
28. "The Press in Belorussia, 1955–1965." *Soviet Studies* 18(4): 482–93.

REVIEW:
29. Hoensch, Jörg K. *Die Slowakei und Hitlers Ostpolitik: Hlinkas Slowakische Volkspartei zwischen Autonomie und Separation 1938/ 1939* (Cologne and Graz: Böhlau Verlag, 1965), in: *East European Quarterly* 1(3): 288–90.

LETTER:
30. [Pavlo Chernov]. "Potribnyi obmin dumok na storinkakh zhurnala." *Suchasnist'* 9: 126–27.

1968

31. [Pavlo Chernov]. "Iuvileine. Z pryvodu 2500 chysla 'Literaturnoï Ukraïny.'" *Suchasnist'* 4: 100–108.
32. [Pavlo Chernov]. "Kil'ka dumok pro nashi suchasni problemy." *Suchasnist'* 7: 59–75.
    For reprint of excerpts, see no. 33.
33. [Pavlo Chernov]. "Kil'ka dumok pro nashi suchasni problemy." *Ukraïns'ke slovo* [Paris] 18 August.
    (Excerpts of no. 32)

REVIEW:
34. McGuigan, Dorothy Gies. *The Hapsburgs* (Garden City, NY: Doubleday, 1966), in: *Michigan Quarterly Review* 7(2): 143–44.

1969

35. [Pavlo Chernov]. "Choho vchyt' pryklad Katal'oniï?" *Suchasnist'* 6: 87–92.

1970

36. (ed. and introd.). *Russia in World History: Selected Essays by M. N. Pokrovskii.* Trans. Roman and Mary Ann Szporluk. Ann Arbor: University of Michigan Press. 241 pp.

REV.:

Dorotich, D., in: *Canadian Slavonic Papers* 14(1) 1972: 117–18.

Engeldin, Eugene A., in: *RQ* 10(3) 1971: 276–77.

Gooding, J. E., in: *The English Historical Review* 87(345) 1972: 900–901.

Malia, Martin, in: "Backward History in a Backward Country." *The New York Review of Books* 7 October 1971: 36–37.

McCagg, William O., Jr., in: *Michigan Academician* 4 (1971–72): 129–30.

Mosse, W. E., in: *The Slavonic and East European Review* 49(116) 1971: 475–76.

TLS, The Times Literary Supplement 23 October 1970: 1228.

Wade, Rex A., in: *The Russian Review* 30(2) 1971: 208–209.

Weber, Walter, in: *Osteuropa* 24(5) 1974: 388–89.

37. "Periods and Problems in Polish History." *Polish Language and Heritage: A Study Guide for Students and Teachers.* Orchard Lake, MI: Orchard Lake Center for Polish Studies and Culture. 73–84.

38. [Pavlo Chernov]. "'Ukraïna iak profesiia.' Lyst do molodoho chytacha 'Suchasnosty.'" *Suchasnist'* 6: 100–108.

1971

39. "The Nations of the USSR in 1970." *Survey* 17(4): 67–100.

DISC:

Dunn, Ethel, in: Letter to the editor. *Survey* 18(1) 1972: 223–26.

Reply. *Survey* 18(1) 1972: 226–29.

REVIEW:

40. Pokrovsky, M. N. *Izbrannye proizvedeniia* (Moscow: Mysl', 1965–67), in: *Slavic Review* 30(3): 649–55.

1972

41. "Dissent and the Non-Russian Nationalities." *Dissent in the Soviet Union: Papers and Proceedings of the Fifth Annual Conference Organized by the Interdepartmental Committee on Communist and East European Affairs, McMaster University, Held at Hamilton, Ontario on October 22 and 23, 1971.* Ed. Peter J. Potichnyj. Hamilton, ON: Interdepartmental Committee on Communist and East European Affairs, McMaster University. 155–229.

Disc.:

> Hodnett, Grey, in: *Dissent in the Soviet Union: Papers and Proceedings of the Fifth Annual Conference . . . October 22 and 23, 1971.* 230–42.

42. "The Plight of the Minorities." *Problems of Communism* 21(5): 79–84. For Spanish translation, see no. 43.
43. "El Problema de las nacionalidades menores en la URSS." *Problemas Internacionales* 19(6): 83–88. (Translation of no. 42)

Reviews:

44. Kusín, Vladimír V. *The Intellectual Origins of the Prague Spring: The Development of Reformist Ideas in Czechoslovakia 1956–1967* (New York: Cambridge University Press, 1971); and Ivan Sviták, *The Czechoslovak Experiment: 1968–1969* (New York: Columbia University Press, 1971), in: *The American Historical Review* 77(4): 1161–62.
45. *Ukraine: A Concise Encyclopaedia.* 2 vols. (Toronto: University of Toronto Press, 1963–1971), in: *Canadian Slavonic Papers* 14(2): 353–56.

1973

46. "Nationalities and the Russian Problem in the USSR: An Historical Outline." *Journal of International Affairs* 27(1): 22–40.
47. "'Radians'ka Ukraïna.'" *Entsyklopediia ukraïnoznavstva.* Ed. Volodymyr Kubiiovych. 10 vols. Munich: Shevchenko Scientific Society, 1955–1984.

1974

48. "Deshcho pro amerykans'ki universytety. Zamitky z pryvodu dyskusiï pro 'Ukraïns'kyi Harvard.'" *Suchasnist'* 1: 107–114.

REVIEWS:
49. Bruegel, J. W. *Czechoslovakia before Munich: The German Minority Problem and British Appeasement Policy* (New York: Cambridge University Press, 1973), in: *The American Historical Review* 79(4): 1214–1215.
50. Sokolov, O. D. *M. N. Pokrovskii i sovetskaia istoricheskaia nauka* (Moscow: Mysl', 1970), in: *Slavic Review* 33(2): 354–55.
51. Stercho, Peter G. *Diplomacy of Double Morality: Europe's Crossroads in Carpatho-Ukraine, 1919–1939* (New York: Carpathian Research Center, 1971), in: *Slavic Review* 33(1): 163–64.
52. Wynot, Edward D., Jr. *Polish Politics in Transition: The Camp of National Unity and the Struggle for Power, 1935–1939* (Athens, GA: University of Georgia Press, 1974), in: *History: Reviews of New Books* 3(2): 29.

1975

53. (ed.). *The Influence of East Europe and the Soviet West on the USSR.* New York: Praeger. 258 pp.

REV.:

Brown, Archie, in: *International Affairs* 53(2) 1977: 309–311.
Chrypinski, V., in: *Canadian-American Slavic Studies* 10(4) 1976: 617–19.
Dallin, Alexander, in: *The Russian Review* 36(1) 1977: 100–101.
Dean, Robert W., in: *Problems of Communism* 26(4) 1977: 83–88.
Ezergailis, Andrew, in: *Slavic Review* 35(4) 1976: 754–55.
Gruhn, Werner, in: *Osteuropa* 27(9) 1977: 814.
McCagg, William O., Jr., in: *East Central Europe* 3 (1976): 118–19.

54. "Russians in Ukraine and Problems of Ukrainian Identity in the USSR." *Ukraine in the Seventies: Papers and Proceedings of the McMaster Conference on Contemporary Ukraine, October 1974.* Ed. Peter J. Potichnyj. Oakville, ON: Mosaic Press. 195–217.
55. "The Ukraine and the Ukrainians." *Handbook of Major Soviet Nationalities.* Eds. Zev Katz, Rosemarie Rogers, and Frederic Harned. New York: The Free Press. 21–48.
For Chinese translation, see no. 100.

REV.:

Matthews, Mervyn, in: *TLS, The Times Literary Supplement* 21 May 1976: 618.
Parming, Tönu, in: *The Annals of the Ukrainian Academy of Arts and Sciences in the U.S.* 14(37–38) 1978–1980: 276–78.
Vardys, V. Stanley, in: *The American Political Science Review* 72(2) 1978: 737–38.

1976

56. "Presa URSR s'ohodni." *Suchasnist'* 3: 71–82.
57. "Valentyn Moroz: His Political Ideas in Historical Perspective." *Canadian Slavonic Papers* 18(1): 80–90.

REVIEWS:

58. Kwilecki, Andrzej. *Łemkowie: Zagadnienie migracji i asymilacji* (Warsaw: Państwowe Wydawnictwo Naukowe, 1974), in: *Slavic Review* 35(2): 369–70.
59. Muszyński, Jerzy. *Socjalizm w państwach środkowej i południowo-wschodniej Europy* (Warsaw: Państwowe Wydawnictwo Naukowe, 1975), in: *Slavic Review* 35(3): 545–46.
60. Rothschild, Joseph. *East Central Europe Between the Two World Wars* (Seattle; London: University of Washington Press, 1974), in: *Slavic Review* 35(1): 146–48.

COMMENTARY:

61. "Holosy chytachiv pro oboronu pravdy." *Svoboda* [Jersey City] 21 January.

1977

62. "Aspects of T. G. Masaryk." *East Central Europe* 4(1): 67–76.
63. "Natsiï SRSR u perspektyvi 2000 roku." *Suchasnist'* 10: 76–80.

REVIEWS:

64. Beld, Antonie van den. *Humanity: The Political and Social Philosophy of Thomas G. Masaryk* (The Hague; Paris: Mouton, 1975), in: *Slavic Review* 36(3): 522–23.
65. Brock, Peter. *The Slovak National Awakening: An Essay in the Intellectual History of East Central Europe* (Buffalo: University of Toronto Press, 1976), in: *The American Historical Review* 82(4): 1022.
66. Kupchinskii, Roman. *Natsional'nyi vopros v SSSR* (New York: Suchasnist', 1975), in: *The Russian Review* 36(1): 98–99.
67. Pidhainy, Oleh S. and Olexandra I. *The Ukrainian Republic in the Great East-European Revolution: A Bibliography* (Toronto; New York: New Review Books, 1975), in: *The Russian Review* 36(3): 391.

COMMENTARY:

68. "Why Some Soviet Sociologists Are Alarmed." *The New York Times* 27 August. Also published in *International Herald Tribune* [Paris] 1 September.

Rev.:

>Bordewich, Fergus M., in: *Columbia Journalism Review* November/December 1977: 36–37.

1978

69. "Kiev's New Paper: A Status Guide." *Soviet Analyst* 7(5) 9 March: 6–7.
70. "Poland." *Crises of Political Development in Europe and the United States*. Ed. Raymond Grew. Princeton: Princeton University Press. 383–418.

Rev.:

>Herr, Richard, in: *The Journal of Modern History* 52(2) 1980: 302–305.
>
>Kiernan, V. G., in: *The English Historical Review* 96(379) 1981: 427.
>
>McCaughrin, Craig, in: *The American Political Science Review* 74 (1980): 546–47.
>
>Merkl, Peter H., in: *World Politics* 34(1) 1981: 114–35.
>
>Skocpol, Theda, in: *The American Historical Review* 85(1) 1980: 81.

Reviews:

71. Murdzek, Benjamin P. *Emigration in Polish Social-Political Thought, 1870–1914* (Boulder, CO: East European Quarterly, 1977), in: *History: Reviews of New Books* 6(9) July: 158–59.
72. Nekrich, Aleksandr M. *The Punished Peoples: The Deportation and Fate of Soviet Minorities at the End of the Second World War* (New York: Norton, 1978), in: *History: Reviews of New Books* 7(1) October: 6.

1979

73. *Ukraine: A Brief History*. Detroit: Ukrainian Festival Committee. 143 pp.
For second edition, see no. 97.
For Ukrainian translation, see no. 177.

Rev.:

>Dushnyck, Walter, in: *The Ukrainian Quarterly* 36(3) 1980: 290.
>
>*Forum* 46 (1980): 30.
>
>Heydenkorn, Benedykt, in: *Kultura* 6 (1989): 141–46.

74. "History and Russian Nationalism." *Survey* 24(3): 1–17.
For another version, see no. 77.
75. "Polityka 1978: Pohliad nazad—i vpered." *Suchasnist'* 3: 159–66.
For Polish translation, see no. 87.
76. "West Ukraine and West Belorussia: Historical Tradition, Social Communication, and Linguistic Assimilation." *Soviet Studies* 31(1): 76–98.

1980

77. "History and Russian Ethnocentrism." *Ethnic Russia in the USSR: The Dilemma of Dominance.* Ed. Edward Allworth. New York: Pergamon Press. 41–54.
    (Version of no. 74)

78. "Kiev as the Ukraine's Primate City." *Harvard Ukrainian Studies* 3–4 (1979–1980): 843–49 [=*Eucharisterion: Essays Presented to Omeljan Pritsak*].

79. "Masarykova republika: Nacionalismus s lidskou tváří." *Proměny* 17(2): 31–42.
    (Translation of no. 85)

80. "The Role of the Press in Polish-Ukrainian Relations." *Poland and Ukraine: Past and Present.* Ed. Peter J. Potichnyj. Edmonton: Canadian Institute of Ukrainian Studies. 212–27.

REV.:

Kulchycky, George P., in: *Canadian-American Slavic Studies* 16(2) 1982: 284–85.

Veryha, Wasyl, in: *Canadian Slavonic Papers* 24(1) 1982: 101–102.

81. "Zamistʹ obitsianoï statti." *Suchasnist'* 2: 26–33.
    For reprint, see no. 126.

REVIEW:

82. Hunczak, Taras, ed. *The Ukraine, 1917–1921: A Study in Revolution* (Cambridge, MA: Harvard Ukrainian Research Institute, 1977), in: *The Annals of the Ukrainian Academy of Arts and Sciences in the U.S.* 14(37–38) 1978–1980: 267–71.

1981

83. *The Political Thought of Thomas G. Masaryk.* Boulder, CO: East European Monographs. 244 pp.

REV.:

Barnard, Frederick M., in: *East Central Europe* 9(1–2) 1982: 162–67.

D.K., in: *Znak* 37(5) 1985: 157–58.

Freeze, Karen, in: *Slavic Review* 42(1) 1983: 140–41.

Garver, Bruce M., in: *The American Historical Review* 88(3) 1983: 713–14.

Hoensch, Jörg K., in: *Historische Zeitschrift* 238(2) 1984: 456–57.

Thomas, Trevor, in: *The Slavonic and East European Review* 64(3) 1986: 477–78.

Whisker, James B., in: *Perspective* 11(1) 1982: 69–70.

84. (ed., with Ivo Banac and John G. Ackerman). *Nation and Ideology: Essays in Honor of Wayne S. Vucinich.* Boulder, CO: East European Monographs. 479 pp.

REV.:

Augustinos, Gerasimos, in: *Canadian-American Slavic Studies* 16(3–4) 1982: 572–73.

Boczek, Boleslaw A., in: *Perspective* 12(1) 1983: 25–26.

Burks, R. V., in: *Slavic Review* 42(2) 1983: 315–16.

85. "Masaryk's Republic: Nationalism with a Human Face." *T. G. Masaryk in Perspective: Comments and Criticism.* Ed. Milic Čapek and Karel Hrubý. Ann Arbor, MI: SVU Press. 219–39.

For Czech translation, see no. 79.

REV.:

Zeman, Z.A.B., in: *The Slavonic and East European Review* 60(4) 1982: 629–30.

86. "The Pokrovskii-Trotsky Debate of 1922." *Nation and Ideology: Essays in Honor of Wayne S. Vucinich.* Ed. Ivo Banac, John G. Ackerman, and Roman Szporluk. Boulder, CO: East European Monographs. 369–86.

87. "Polityka 1978: Spojrzenie w przeszłość i w przyszłość." *Obóz: Niezależne pismo poświęcone problemam krajów ościennych* 1: 20–25.

(Translation of no. 75)

88. "Poľśki refleksiï." *Suchasnist'* 3–4: 154–65.

89. "Urbanization in Ukraine since the Second World War." *Rethinking Ukrainian History.* Ed. Ivan L. Rudnytsky. Edmonton: Canadian Institute of Ukrainian Studies. 180–202.

REV.:

Armstrong, John A., in: *Slavic Review* 44(1) 1985: 150–51.

Bohachevsky-Chomiak, Martha, in: *Russian History* 10(1) 1983: 132–33.

90. "Współczesna Ukraina: problemy i perspektywy." *Obóz: Niezależne pismo poświęcone problemam krajów ościennych* 3: 26–33.

(Translation of chapter 11, no. 97)

REVIEWS:

91. Kostiuk, Hryhory. *Okaianni roky: Vid Lukianivs'koï tiurmy do Vorkuts'koï trahediï, 1935–1940* (Toronto: Diyaloh, 1978), in: *The Russian Review* 40(2): 203.

92. Liebich, André. *Between Ideology and Utopia: The Politics and Philosophy of August Cieszkowski* (Dordrecht; Boston: D. Reidel, 1979); and André Liebich, ed. and trans., *Selected Writings of August*

Cieszkowski (Cambridge; New York: Cambridge University Press, 1979), in: *The American Historical Review* 86(1): 176–77.

93. Motyl, Alexander J. *The Turn to the Right: The Ideological Origins and Development of Ukrainian Nationalism, 1919–1929* (Boulder, CO: East European Monographs, 1980), in: *The Russian Review* 40(2): 202–203.

94. Serczyk, Władysław A. *Historia Ukrainy* (Wrocław: Zakład Narodowy im. Ossolińskich, 1979), in: *Journal of Ukrainian Studies* 6(1) 10: 99–101.

COMMENTARIES:

95. "Lenin Predicted Poland's Kind of Revolutionary Action." *The Capital Times* [Sacramento] 19 October. Also published under variant titles in *The Michigan Daily* 22 October, and other newspapers (Pacific News Service).

96. "A History of Polish Revolution." *The Michigan Daily* 29 March. Also published under variant titles in *Tribune* [Oakland] 1 April, *The Los Angeles Times* 2 April, *Sunday Star* [Toronto] 19 April, and other newspapers (Pacific News Service).

1982

97. *Ukraine: A Brief History.* 2nd rev. ed. Detroit: Ukrainian Festival Committee. 162 pp.
   (Second expanded edition of no. 73)
   For Polish translation of chapter 11, "Contemporary Ukraine: Problems and Prospects," see no. 90.

98. "Defining 'Central Europe': Power, Politics, and Culture." *Cross Currents* 1: 30–38.
   For Russian translation, see no. 107.

99. "Gdansk and Its Antecedents." *Studium News Abstracts* 6(2): 4–5.

100. "Wu-ke-lan he Wu-ke-lan ren." *Su-lian zhu yao min zu shou ce.* Ed. Zefu, Ka-ci. [Shanghai]: Ren min chu ban she. 27–66.
   (Translation of no. 55)

REVIEWS:

101. Barber, John. *Soviet Historians in Crisis, 1928–1932* (New York: Holmes and Meier, 1981), in: *The Russian Review* 41(4): 492–93.

102. Farmer, Kenneth C. *Ukrainian Nationalism in the Post-Stalin Era: Myth, Symbols and Ideology in Soviet Nationalities Policy* (The Hague: Martinus Nijhoff, 1980), in: *The Russian Review* 41(3): 338–39.

103. Kamiński, Leszek. *Romantyzm a ideologia: Główne ugrupowania polityczne Drugiej Rzeczypospolitej wobec tradycji romantycznej*

(Wrocław: Zakład Narodowy im. Ossolińskich, 1980), in: *The American Historical Review* 87(1): 219–20.

104. Yanov, Alexander. *The Origins of Autocracy: Ivan the Terrible in Russian History* (Berkeley: University of California Press, 1981), in: "Rosiis′ka al′ternatyva Oleksandra Ianova: Evropa chy Aziia?" *Suchasnist′* 3: 113–17.

COMMENTARIES:

105. "Polish Leaders Determined Not to Let Solidarity-Style Union Arise Again." *The San Francisco Sunday Examiner and Chronicle* 29 August. Also published under variant titles in *The Plain Dealer* [Cleveland] 3 September, *The Toronto Star, The Michigan Daily* 17 September, and other newspapers (Pacific News Service).

106. "Ukraïna i Rosiia." *Ukraïns′ke slovo* [Paris] 10 October; 17 October; 24 October.

1983

107. "K opredeleniiu 'Tsentral′noi Evropy': vlast′, politika i kul′tura." *Problemy Vostochnoi Evropy* 7–8: 74–86.
(Translation of no. 98)

REVIEW:

108. Horak, Stephan M., ed. *Guide to the Study of the Soviet Nationalities: Non-Russian Peoples of the USSR* (Littleton, CO: Libraries Unlimited, 1982), in: *Journal of Ukrainian Studies* 8(1) 14: 100–103.

COMMENTARY:

109. "Poles Anticipate Coming Papal Visit." *Sentinel* [Waterville, ME] 14 June. Also published in other newspapers (Pacific News Service).

1984

110. "Recent Trends in Soviet Policy towards Printed Media in the Non-Russian Languages." *Radio Liberty Research Bulletin* Suppl. 2(84) 7 November. 32 pp.
For reprint, see no. 111.

111. "Recent Trends in Soviet Policy towards Non-Russian Printed Media." *The Ukrainian Weekly* [Jersey City] 23 December; 30 December; 6 January 1985.
(Reprint of no. 110)

Reviews:

112. Walicki, Andrzej. *Philosophy and Romantic Nationalism: The Case of Poland* (New York: Clarendon Press of Oxford University Press, 1982), in: *The American Historical Review* 89(2): 484–86.

113. Zwick, Peter. *National Communism* (Boulder, CO: Westview Press, 1983), in: *Slavic Review* 43(3): 487–88.

Commentary:

114. "Soviets Will Maintain a Closed-Door Policy." *The Philadelphia Inquirer* 15 February. Also published in *The San Francisco Examiner* 16 February, *The Ann Arbor News* 9 March, and other newspapers (Pacific News Service).

1985

115. "National History as a Political Battleground: The Case of Ukraine and Belorussia." *Russian Empire: Some Aspects of Tsarist and Soviet Colonial Practices*. Ed. Michael S. Pap. Cleveland: Institute for Soviet and East European Studies, John Carroll University; Ukrainian Historical Association. 131–50.

Rev.:

Kristof, Ladis K. D., in: *Canadian Slavonic Papers* 29(1) 1987: 89–90.

Mark, Rudolf A., in: *Jahrbücher für Geschichte Osteuropas* 35(2) 1987: 271–73.

Rywkin, Michael, in: *Slavic Review* 46(3–4) 1987: 629–30.

116. "War by Other Means." Comment in discussion titled "Empty Pedestals?" with F. Gregory Campbell and Gale Stokes. *Slavic Review* 44(1): 20–26.

For Czech translation, see no. 122.

Other:

117. "Guidelines for Evaluation of RL Broadcasts to Ukrainian Speakers in the Soviet Union." Circulated, but unpublished, guide.

Disc:

Bedrii, A., in: *Homin Ukraïny* [Toronto] April 1985. Also published in *Shliakh peremohy* [New York] 25 August 1985.

Strutyns'kyi, Iu., in: "Za kulisamy podii dovkola Ukraïns'koï redaktsiï Radio 'Svoboda.'" *Shliakh peremohy* [New York] 19 January 1986.

1986

118. "Marx, List, Palacký: Nationalism in Central Europe." *Cross Currents* 5: 25–38.
     For Ukrainian translation, see no. 124.
119. "The Press and Soviet Nationalities: The Party Resolution of 1975 and Its Implementation." *Nationalities Papers* 14(1–2): 47–64.
120. (et al.). "Russia." *The World Book Encyclopedia*. Vol. 16. 488–528.
121. "The Ukraine and Russia." *The Last Empire: Nationality and the Soviet Future*. Ed. Robert Conquest. Stanford: Hoover Institution Press. 151–82.
     For Ukrainian translation, see no. 125.
REV.:

> Clive, Nigel, in: *International Studies* 63(2) 1987: 329–30.
> Duncan, Peter J. S., in: *Soviet Studies* 39(4) 1987: 686.
> Kanet, Robert E., et al., in: "Innenpolitische und militärische Determinanten der sowjetischen Aussenpolitik." *Osteuropa* 38(11) 1988: 1030–48.
> Kappeler, Andreas, in: *Osteuropa* 38(9) 1988: 867–68.
> Motyl, Alexander J., in: *Political Science Quarterly* 102(2) 1987: 331–32.

122. "Válka jinými prostředky." *150000 slov* 5(14): 13–17.
     (Czech translation of no. 116)

REVIEW:
123. Kubijovyč, Volodymyr, ed. *Encyclopedia of Ukraine*, vol. 1 A–F (Toronto: University of Toronto Press, 1984), in: *Russian Literature Triquarterly* 19: 435.

1987

124. "Marks—List—Palats'kyi. Natsionalizm u Tsentral'nii Evropi." *Suchasnist'* 4: 62–77.
     (Translation of no. 118)
125. "Ukraïna i Rosiia." *Vidnova* 6–7: 316–42.
     (Translation of no. 121)
REV.:

> N. G., in: *Kontinent* 58 (1988): 421–24.
> Moroz, Raïsa, in: *Svoboda* [Jersey City] 16 November 1988.

126. "Zamist' obitsianoï statti." *Suchasnist', 1961–1985: vybrane*. Munich: Suchasnist'. 338–46.
     (Reprint of no. 81)

1988

127. *Communism and Nationalism: Karl Marx Versus Friedrich List.* New York: Oxford University Press. 307 pp.

  For reprint, see no. 159.

  For Slovene translation of excerpts (pp. 225–40), see no. 163.

  For Ukrainian translation, see no. 237.

DISC.:

  Stokes, Gale, in: *ACLS Newsletter* 1(4) 1988: 13–14.

REV.:

  Armstrong, John A., in: "The Future of Eastern Europe." *Problems of Communism* 38(2–3) 1989: 121–26.

  Blackbourn, David, in: "Ways of Catching Up." *TLS, The Times Literary Supplement* 19–25 May 1989: 556.

  Englund, Stephen, in: *Commonweal* 115 (1988): 662–63.

  Gellner, Ernest, in: "The Dramatis Personae of History." *East European Politics and Societies* 4(1) 1990: 116–33.

  Hroch, Miroslav, in: "How Much Does Nation Formation Depend on Nationalism?" *East European Politics and Societies* 4(1) 1990: 101–115.

  Hrytsak, Iaroslav, in: *Zapysky Naukovoho tovarystva im. Shevchenka* 225 (1993): 473–79.

  Hughes, Michael, in: *The English Historical Review* 107(424) 1992: 740–41.

  Josh, Bhagwan, in: *Studies in History* 7(2) 1991: 353–57.

  Journal of Economic Literature 26(4) 1988: 1808.

  Kitchen, Martin, in: *The International History Review* 12(3) 1990: 589–91.

  Lassman, Peter, in: *Political Studies* 37(3) 1989: 711.

  Love, D. M., in: *Choice* 26 (1988): 370.

  Mitchinson, Paul G., in: "The 'Pig-Headed' Nation: Marxism Grapples with the National Question." *East European Quarterly* 25(2) 1991: 223–35.

  Sayers, Sean, in: *History of European Ideas* 12(4) 1990: 552–54.

  Senghaas, Dieter, in: *Das Historisch-politische Buch* 37(4) 1989: 108–109.

  Stillman, Peter G., in: *The Journal of Modern History* 62(3) 1990: 576–78.

  Stokes, Gale, in: "Class and Nation: Competing Explanatory Systems." *East European Politics and Societies* 4(1) 1990: 98–100.

  Stokes, Gale, in: *The American Historical Review* 95(2) 1990: 454.

  Wasiutyński, Wojciech, in: *Dziennik Związkowy* (6–7 January 1989): 4.

128. Prepared Statement. *United States-Soviet Relations: 1988.* Vol. 1. Hearings before the Subcommittee on Europe and the Middle East of the Committee on Foreign Affairs, House of Representatives, 100th Congress, 2nd session. Washington: Government Printing Office. 145–56. (See also pp. 191–209.)

INTERVIEW:
129. (by Zdzisław Najder). "Czarnobyl uzmysłowił Ukraińcom, że chodzi o ich kraj." *Kontakt* 9: 105–116.

1989

130. "Dilemmas of Russian Nationalism." *Problems of Communism* 38(4): 15–35.
   For reprints, see nos. 160 and 179.
131. (with W. G. Rosenberg). "Arthur P. Mendel, 1927–1988—Obituary." *Slavic Review* 48(2): 354.
132. "Poland Fifty Years After." *Studium Papers* 13(3): 152–53.
133. "The Ukraine." *Reform or Revolution? Nationalism in Eastern Europe.* Ed. Viktoria S. Herson and Carole R. Rogel. Columbus, OH: Center for Slavic and East European Studies. 21–28.

COMMENTARY:
134. "Slovo podiaky red. Tvardovs'komu—i kil'ka propozytsii." *Svoboda* [Jersey City] 31 January.

INTERVIEWS:
135. (by Jerzy Jastrzębowski). "Rozmowy o braciach." *Zeszyty Historyczne* 88: 3–33.
   For reprint of excerpts, see no. 136.
DISC.:
   Skaradziński, Bohdan, in: *Tygodnik Solidarność* [Warsaw] 8 September: 9.

136. (by Jerzy Jastrzębowski). "Czyj Lwów, czyj Przemyśl?" *Związkowiec* [Warsaw and Toronto] 22 August.
   (Excerpts of no. 135)
137. (by L. Morkunas). "Pralaužti izoliacijos sienas." *Akiračiai* 4: 4–5.

1990

138. "*Comment*—The Burden of History—Made Lighter by Geography?" *Problems of Communism* 39(4): 45–48.
   For Russian translation, see no. 178.
139. "Eurasia House: Problems of Identity in Russia and Eastern Europe." *Cross Currents* 9: 3–15.
   For Polish translation, see no. 161.
   For Ukrainian translation, see nos. 180 and 219.

140. "The Imperial Legacy and the Soviet Nationalities Problem." *The Nationalities Factor in Soviet Politics and Society*. Ed. Lubomyr Hajda and Mark Beissinger. Boulder, CO: Westview Press. 1–23.

REV.:

Batt, Judy, in: *International Affairs* 67(3) 1991: 616.
Bremmer, Ian, in: *Contemporary Sociology* 21(2) 1992: 205–206.
Ellison, Herbert J., in: *The Russian Review* 51(3) 1992: 438–39.
Noonan, Norma, in: *Perspectives on Political Science* 20(2) 1991: 118.

141. "In Search of the Drama of History: Or, National Roads to Modernity." *East European Politics and Society* 4(1): 134–50.
For Ukrainian translation, see no. 218.

142. "National Reawakening: Ukraine and Belorussia." *The Soviet Empire: The Challenge of National and Democratic Movements*. Ed. Uri Ra'anan. Lexington, MA: Lexington Books. 75–93.

143. "Poland and the Rise of the Theory and Practice of Nationalism 1770–1870." *Dialectics and Humanism* 17(2): 43–64.
For Polish translation, see no. 144.

144. "Polska: powstanie teorii i praktyki nowoczesnego narodu (1770–1879)." *Sens polskiej historii*. Ed. Andrzej Ajnenkiel, Janusz Kuczyński, and Andrzej Wohl. Proceedings from the conference, "Sens polskiej historii i współtworzenie przyszłości Polski." Warsaw, 4–11 November 1988. Warsaw: Uniwersytet Warszawski, Program Badań i Współtworzenia Filozofii Pokoju. 94–120.
(Translation of no. 143)

145. (with Dusan Bilandzic et al.). "Post-Communist Eastern Europe: A Survey of Opinion." Roundtable discussion. *East European Politics and Societies* 4(2): 153–207.

REVIEWS:

146. Jaworski, Rudolf. *Handel und Gewerbe im Nationalitätenkampf: Studien zur Wirtschaftsgesinnung der Polen in der Provinz Posen (1871–1914)* (Göttingen: Vandenhoeck und Ruprecht, 1986), in: *The American Historical Review* 95(2): 541–42.

147. Prymak, Thomas M. *Mykhailo Hrushevsky: The Politics of National Culture* (Toronto: University of Toronto Press, 1987), in: *Canadian Review of Studies in Nationalism* 17(1–2): 294–97.

COMMENTARIES:

148. "Commentary on Poland." *LSA Magazine* [University of Michigan] 13(2): 26.

149. "Gorbachev's Last Chance—Democracy." *The New York Times* 2 July.

150. "Gorbachev's Need: A Diminished Russia." *The New York Times* 5 April.
     Also published in *International Herald Tribune* [Paris] 7–8 April.
     For Estonian translation, see no. 151.
151. "Pidama pisemat venemaad." *Rahva Hääl* [Tallinn] 22 April.
     (Translation of no. 150)
152. "Turn toward Capitalism in Soviet Union Will Require a Rapid Roll of
     the Dice." *The Detroit News* 30 September.

INTERVIEWS:
153. "Pro perspektyvy ukraïns′koho natsional′noho vidrodzhennia." *Postup*
     [Lviv] May, no. 7: 6–7.
154. (by Kira Fomenko). "Kak dela, kollegi? Chto tantsuiut v angliiskom
     parke . . ." *Komsomol′skoe znamia* [Kyiv] 16 September: 6.
155. (by T. D. Holovko). "Balansuiuchy mizh mynulym i maibutnim."
     Trybuna 12: 22–23.
156. (by Ewa Juńczyk-Ziomecka). "W poszukiwaniu tożsamości: O Ukrainie,
     Rosji i Polsce." *Dziennik Polski* [Detroit] 18 April: 1+.
157. (by K. Kindras′). "Ia z toboiu, Ukraïno, hovoriu." *Radians′ka Ukraïna*
     [Kyiv] 31 August: 3.
158. (by Roman Solchanyk). "Roman Szporluk and Valerii Tishkov Talk
     about the National Question." *Report on the USSR* 2(22): 19–24.
     For reprint, see no. 191.

1991

159. *Communism and Nationalism: Karl Marx Versus Friedrich List.* 2nd ed.
     New York: Oxford University Press. 307 pp.
     For Ukrainian translation, see no. 237.
     (Reprint of no. 127)
REV.:
     Hryshchenko, Taras, in: *Harvard Ukrainian Studies* 16(3–4) 1992: 451–53.
     Levin, Michael, in: *Political Studies* 42(2) 1994: 360.
     Lovell, David W., in: *History of European Ideas* 21(1) 1995: 142–43.

160. "Dilemmas of Russian Nationalism." *The Soviet System in Crisis: A
     Reader of Western and Soviet Views.* Ed. Alexander Dallin and Gail
     W. Lapidus. Boulder, CO: Westview Press. 441–62.
     (Excerpts of no. 130)
161. "Euroazjatycki Dom: Problem tożsamości w Rosji i Europie Wschod-
     niej." *Zustriczi* 1: 86–96.
     (Translation of no. 139)

162. "Global Struggles for Democracy: Three Authors in Search of the Actors." *Rackham Reports* [University of Michigan]. Symposium "Emerging Concepts of Democracy: China, Eastern Europe, and the Soviet Union," 5–6 April 1990. 8–14.

163. "Komunizem in nacionalizem." *Študije o etnonacionalizmu: zbornik.* Ed. Rudi Rizman. Ljubljana: Knjižnica revolucionarne teorije. (Translation of excerpts from no. 127)

164. "The Soviet West—or Far Eastern Europe?" *East European Politics and Societies* 5(3): 466–82.

165. "Ukraïns'ke natsional'ne vidrodzhennia v konteksti ievropeis'koï istoriï kintsia XVIII–pochatku XIX stolit'." *Nauka i kul'tura, Ukraïna* 25: 159–67.
For reprints, see nos. 166 and 196.

166. "Ukraïns'ke natsional'ne vidrodzhennia v konteksti ievropeis'koï istoriï kintsia XVIII–pochatku XIX stolit'." *Slovo* [Kyiv] February, nos. 3 and 4.
(Reprint of no. 165)

COMMENTARIES:
167. "The Clever Ukrainians." *The New York Times* 1 August.

168. "Koniec imperialnej przeszłości ZSRR?" *Rzeczpospolita* [Warsaw] 27 August.
(Translation of no. 172)

169. "The Soviet Union Has Ceased to Exist." *The New York Times* 23 January. Also published in *Baltimore Evening Sun* 30 January.

DISC.:

Zacek, Jane Shapiro, in: "Gorbachev Won't Yield Baltic Republics." Letter. *The New York Times* 1 March.

170. "UdSSR: Ganz im Sinne Moskaus?" *Der Standard* [Vienna] 3 August.

171. "Ukraine Stands Up to Russia (The Jagged Pieces of the Soviet Empire)." *The New York Times* 29 August.

172. "The War between Two Russias: Yeltsin and the New Awakening." *The Washington Post* 25 August. Also published under a variant title in *The Washington Post National Weekly Edition* 2–8 September.
For Polish translation, see no. 168.

INTERVIEWS:
173. (by L. Briukhovets'ka). "Dopomahaty ukraïntsiam stavaty hromadianamy svitu." *Kyïv* 2: 153–59.

174. (by Jerzy Jastrzębowski). "Polska—Ukraina: szansa do wykorzystania." *Związkowiec* [Warsaw and Toronto] 10 December: 5+.
For reprint, see no. 190.

175. (by Ewa Juńczyk-Ziomecka). "Może być wojna domowa, mogą być rozruchy, może być zamach stanu . . . " *Tygodnik Świat Polski* [Hamtramck, MI] 14 February: 3+.
176. (by Oleh Strekal' and Ivan Bezsmertnyi). "Politolohiiu vam dovedet'sia pochynaty z nulia." *Molod' Ukraïny* [Kyiv] 24 January: 1+.

1992

177. *Ukraïna: korotka istoriia.* Kyiv: Taki Spravy. 60 pp.
(Translation of no. 73)

178. "Bremia istorii? Ne oblegchit li ego geografiia?" *Druzhba narodov* 11–12: 258–60.
(Translation of no. 138)

179. "Dilemmas of Russian Nationalism." *The Soviet Nationality Reader: The Disintegration in Context.* Ed. Rachel Denber. Boulder, CO: Westview Press. 509–43.
(Reprint of no. 130)

180. "Ievraziis'kyi dim. Problemy identychnosti v Rosiï ta Skhidnii Ievropi." *Suchasnist'* 5: 69–78.
(Translation of no. 139)
For reprint, see no. 219.

181. "The National Question." *After the Soviet Union: From Empire to Nations.* Ed. Timothy Colton and Robert Legvold. New York: W.W. Norton and Company. 84–112.

REV.:

Kincade, William H., in: *The Russian Review* 53(1) 1994: 150–52.

Sempa, Francis P., in: *Presidential Studies Quarterly* 23(4) 1993: 797–99.

Williams, David L., in: *Political Science Quarterly* 108(1) 1993: 166–67.

182. (with G. Breslauer et al.). "One Year after the Collapse of the USSR—A Panel of Specialists." *Post-Soviet Affairs* 8(4): 303–330.

183. "Polish-Ukrainian Relations in 1918: Notes for Discussion." *The Reconstruction of Poland, 1914–23.* Ed. Paul Latawski. London: Macmillan in Association with the School of Slavonic and East European Studies, University of London. 41–54.

REV.:

Miller, Stefania Szlek, in: *The International History Review* 15(3) 1993: 596–97.

Piekalkiewicz, Jaroslaw, in: *Slavic Review* 53(1) 1994: 286–87.

Sanford, George, in: *The Slavonic and East European Review* 71(3) 1993: 553–55.

184. "Rozdumy i refleksiï istoryka pro suchasnu Ukraïnu." *Quo vadis, Ukraïno? Materialy tret'oï (zymovoï) sesiï Mizhnarodnoï shkoly ukraïnistyky.* Ed. Ihor Ostash. Odesa: Maiak. 74–85.
185. "The Strange Politics of Lviv: An Essay in Search of an Explanation." *The Politics of Nationality and the Erosion of the USSR.* Ed. Zvi Gitelman. New York: St. Martin's Press. 215–31.

COMMENTARIES:
186. "Nash suchasnyk Hrushevs'kyi." *Svoboda* [Jersey City] 23 January.
187. "Shliakh do El'dorado lezhyt' cherez dolynu ekonomichnoï svobody." *Post-Postup* [Lviv] n.d. (no. 29).
188. "Ukraine's Independence and the New Social Covenant." *The Ukrainian Weekly* [Jersey City] 23 August.

INTERVIEWS:
189. (by Iaroslav Hrytsak). "U restoranakh ievropeis'kykh stolyts' til'ky i chuty pro Ukraïnu." *Post-Postup* (Lviv) n.d (no. 27).
190. (by Jerzy Jastrzębowski). "Polska—Ukraina: szansa do wykorzystania." *Obserwator Codzienny* (Warsaw) 16–17 May.
    (Reprint of no. 174)
191. (by Roman Solchanyk). "Roman Szporluk and Valerii Tishkov Talk about the National Question." *Ukraine: From Chernobyl' to Sovereignty: A Collection of Interviews.* Ed. Roman Solchanyk. Edmonton: Canadian Institute of Ukrainian Studies Press. 105–116.
    (Reprint of no. 158)

LETTER:
192. "Crimea Has Been Ukrainian Since 1954." *The New York Times* 15 April.
DISC.:
    Svoboda [Jersey City] 18 April.

1993

193. "Belarus', Ukraine, and the Russian Question: A Comment." *Post-Soviet Affairs* 9(4): 366–74.
194. "Conflict in Soviet Domestic and Foreign Policy: Universal Ideology and National Tradition." *Behavior, Culture, and Conflict in World Politics.* Ed. William Zimmerman and Harold K. Jacobson. Ann Arbor: University of Michigan Press. 275–90.
    For reprint, see no. 205.

195. "Independent Ukraine." *Russia, Ukraine and the U.S. Response.* Twelfth Conference. Aspen Institute, 9–14 January. Ed. Dick Clark. Queenstown, MD: Aspen Institute. 23–29.

196. "Natsional'ne vidrodzhennia v konteksti istorychnoho dosvidu." *Etnonatsional'nyi rozvytok Ukraïny: terminy, vyznachennia, personaliï.* Eds. Iu. I. Rymarenko et al. Kyiv: Instytut derzhavy i prava AN Ukraïny. 13–23.
   (Reprint of no. 165)

197. "Policy Implications of an Independent Ukraine." *Harvard Journal of World Affairs* Spring: 28–40.

198. "*Radians'ka Ukraina.*" *Encyclopedia of Ukraine.* Eds. Volodymyr Kubijovyč and Danylo Husar Struk. 5 vols. Toronto: University of Toronto Press, 1984–1993.

COMMENTARY:

199. "Kak za 5 let unichtozhit' Ukrainu." *Argumenty i fakty* [Moscow] 32 (669) August.

INTERVIEWS:

200. (by Ewa Juńczyk-Ziomecka). "Czyli na zachód od wschodu." *Gazeta Wyborcza* [Warsaw] 11 January.

201. (by Andrij Wynnyckyj). "Ukraine in International Arena." *The Ukrainian Weekly* [Jersey City] 22 August.

1994

202. (ed.) *National Identity and Ethnicity in Russia and the New States of Eurasia.* Armonk, NY: M.E. Sharpe. 328 pp. [=*The International Politics of Eurasia*, ed. Karen Dawisha and Bruce Parrott, 2].

REV.:

Aussenpolitik 46(4) 1995: 407.

Birch, Julian, in: *International Affairs* 71(4) 1995: 891–92.

British East–West Journal 100 (1995): 16.

Choice 32(11–12) 1995: 1795.

Décsy, Gy., in: *Eurasian Studies Yearbook* 69 (1997): 240–46.

Dunlop, John B., in: *The American Political Science Review* 89(4) 1995: 1065–1066.

Hickey, Michael C., in: *Journal of Baltic Studies* 26(2) 1995: 172–73.

Kanet, Roger E., et al., in: "Von Revolution zu Revolution." *Osteuropa* 45(9) 1995: 861–69.

Melvin, Neil, in: "Nationalism II: Memory, Myth and Diversity." *The World Today* 51(11) 1995: 224–25.

Pearson, Raymond, in: *Europe-Asia Studies* 48(3) 1996: 487–89.
Raymond, Ellsworth, in: *Perspectives on Political Science* 24(4) 1995: 236.

203. "After Empire: What?" *Daedalus* 123(3): 21–39.
204. "Reflections on Ukraine after 1994: The Dilemmas of Nationhood." *The Harriman Review* 7(7–9): 1–10.
205. "Soviet Domestic Foreign Policy: Universal Ideology and National Tradition." *Nationalities Papers* 22(1): 195–208.
(Reprint of no. 194)
206. "Statehood and Nation Building in Post-Soviet Space." Introduction. *National Identity and Ethnicity in Russia and the New States of Eurasia.* Ed. Roman Szporluk. Armonk, NY: M.E. Sharpe. 3–17.
207. "Ukraine dans l'Europe post-communiste." Roundtable with Aleksandr Arhangel'skij et al. Geneva, 28 May. *Cahiers du monde russe* 36(4): 481–97.

INTERVIEW:
208. (by Jerzy Jastrzębowski). "Kijów wciąż musi się tłumaczyć." *Rzeczpospolita* [Warsaw] 26–27 March.

LETTER:
209. *Foreign Policy* 97: 178–80.
DISC.:
Rumer, Eugene. Reply to letter. *Foreign Policy* 97: 180–81.

1995

210. "Des marches de l'empire à la construction d'une nation." *L'autre Europe* 30–31: 134–50.
(Translation of an earlier version of no. 228)
211. "Nation Building in Ukraine: Problems and Prospects." *The Successor States to the USSR.* Ed. John W. Blaney. Washington, DC: Congressional Quarterly Inc. 173–83.

INTERVIEWS:
212. (by Leonid Finberg). "Mizh 'het' vid Moskvy' ta 'naviky razom.'" *Vechirnii Kyïv* 3 January.
For reprint, see no. 213.
213. (by Leonid Finberg). "Mizh 'het' vid Moskvy' ta 'naviky razom.'" *Demokratychna Ukraïna* [Kyiv] 5 January.
(Reprint of no. 212)

214. (by Andrii Rybalt). "Bezsumnivno, amerykans'kyi pohliad na ukraïns'ku problematyku pominiavsia." *Nashe slovo* [Warsaw] 30 July.

LETTER:
215. "Francis Joseph I." *TLS, The Times Literary Supplement* [London] 31 March.

1996

216. "Dlaczego upadają imperia? (Cesarstwo Rosyjskie i Związek Radziecki)." *Eurazja* 3(2): 65–77.
     (Translation of no. 224)
217. Introduction. *Mala entsyklopediia etnoderzhavoznavstva.* Kyiv: Heneza; Dovira. 15–20.
218. "Natsional'ni shliakhy do modernizatsiï." *Mala entsyklopediia etnoderzhavoznavstva.* Kyiv: Heneza; Dovira. 772–75.
     (Translation of no. 141)
219. "Natsionalizm ievraziis'kyi." *Mala entsyklopediia etnoderzhavoznavstva.* Kyiv: Heneza; Dovira. 734–38.
     (Translation of no. 139; Reprint of no. 180)
220. "Propad carističnega imperija in ZSSR." *Teorija in praksa* [Ljubljana] 33(6): 1021–1046.
     (Translation of no. 224)
221. "Ukraïna: vid impers'koï peryferiï do suverennoï derzhavy." *Suchasnist'* 11: 74–87; 12: 53–65.
     (Translation of no. 228)

LECTURE:
222. "Renesans Ukrainy." Warsaw, 18–19 May. *Konteksty: polska sztuka ludowa* 3–4: 53–56.

ROUNDTABLE:
223. (with Lubomyr Hajda et al.). "The State of Ukrainian Independence: An Overview from Harvard. The Political Scene." *The Ukrainian Weekly* [Jersey City] 25 August.

1997

224. "The Fall of the Tsarist Empire and the USSR: The Russian Question and Imperial Overextension." *The End of Empire? The Transformation of the USSR in Comparative Perspective.* Ed. Karen Dawisha and Bruce

Parrott. Armonk, NY: M.E. Sharpe. 65–93 [=*The International Politics of Eurasia*, ed. Karen Dawisha and Bruce Parrott, 9].

For Ukrainian translation, see no. 226. For Polish translation, see no. 216. For Slovene translation, see no. 220.

225. "*Kultura*: Bridging Ukrainian–Polish Relations." *ACE: Analysis of Current Events* 9(8): 12, 15.

226. "Padinnia tsarysts'koï imperiï ta SRSR: rosiis'ke pytannia i nadmirne rozshyrennia imperiï." *Dukh i litera* 1–2: 100–136.

    (Translation of no. 224)

227. "Ukraina: ot periferii imperii k suverennomu gosudarstvu." *Ukraina i Rossiia: obshchestva i gosudarstva.* Ed. D. E. Furman. Moscow: Prava cheloveka. 41–70.

    (Translation of no. 228)

228. "Ukraine: From an Imperial Periphery to a Sovereign State." *Daedalus* 126(3): 85–119.

    For Ukrainian translation, see no. 221. For Russian translation, see no. 227. For French translation, see no. 210.

REVIEW:

229. Benner, Erica. *Really Existing Nationalisms: A Post-Communist View from Marx and Engels* (Oxford: Clarendon Press, 1995), in: *The American Journal of Sociology* 102(4): 1236–38.

INTERVIEWS:

230. "Zakhid nam dopomozhe iakshcho my bodai iomu ne zavazhatymemo." *Den'* [Kyiv] 8 July.

231. (by Jerzy Jastrzębowski). "Rozmowa braci po latach." *Rzeczpospolita. Plus Minus.* [Warsaw] 28–29 June.

    For reprint see no. 232.

232. (by Jerzy Jastrzębowski). "Rozmowa braci po latach." *Nowy Dziennik. Przegląd Polski.* [New York] 10 July.

    (Reprint of no. 231)

233. (by Bohdan Strumiński). "The Dialectics of Nations—Dialektyka narodów." *2B: Polish American Academic Quarterly* 11–12: 83–90.

234. (by Maria Wągrowska). "Kłopoty z tożsamością." *Rzeczpospolita* [Warsaw] 8 April.

COMMENTARY:

235. "Klucze do Wschodu." *Rzeczpospolita. Plus Minus.* [Warsaw] 4–5 October.

DISC.:

    Dziewanowski, Kazimierz, in: *Kultura* 11 (1997): 117–31.

236. "Na zakhyst Dzhefri Saksa: Zakhid Ukraïnu ne zanapastyt′, ale i ne poriatuie." *Den′* [Kyiv] 5 August.

1998

237. *Komunizm i natsionalizm: Karl Marks proty Fridrikha Lista.* Trans. Heorhii Kas'ianov. Kyiv: Osnovy. 479 pp. (Translation of no. 127)

REV.:

> Prokop, Myroslav, in: "Komunizm i natsionalizm: dvi svitohliadni systemy." *Suchasnist′* 6 (1999): 150–57.
>
> Zaiets′, Vasyl′, in: "Zhyva voda Fridrikha Lista." *Kul′tura i zhyttia* [Kyiv] 22 July (1998).

238. "Ernest Gellner ta istoriia natsionalizmu." *Krytyka* [Kyiv] 2(3): 8–13. (Translation of no. 240)

239. "Nationalism after Communism: Reflections on Russia, Ukraine, Belarus and Poland." *Nations and Nationalism* 4: 301–320 [=Ernest Gellner Nationalism Lecture of *Nations and Nationalism*. London School of Economics and Political Science, 27 March].

240. "Thoughts about Change: Ernest Gellner and the History of Nationalism." *The State of the Nation: Ernest Gellner and the Theory of Nationalism.* Ed. John A. Hall. Cambridge: Cambridge University Press. 23–39.

For Ukrainian translation, see no. 238.

REVIEWS:

241. Bollerup, Soren Rinder, and Christian Dons Christensen. *Nationalism in Eastern Europe. Causes and Consequences of the National Revivals and Conflicts in the Late–Twentieth-Century Eastern Europe* (Basingstoke: Macmillan, 1997), in: *Europe-Asia Studies* 50(6): 1086–1087.

242. Ishay, Micheline R. *Internationalism and Its Betrayal* (Minneapolis: University of Minnesota Press, 1995), in: *American Journal of Sociology* 104(2): 570–71.

1999

COMMENTARIES:

243. "Is Russia-Belarus Union a Danger?'" *The New York Times* 4 January.

DISC.:

> Dreyer, Edward L., in: *The New York Times* 6 January.

244. "Pol'shcha, Ievropa—i nova ukraïns'ka heohrafiia: 'Z moskaliamy chy z liakhamy?'" *Den'* [Kyiv] 26 January. Also published in *Zakordonna hazeta* [North Arlington, NJ] 1–15 February.

For Russian translation, see no. 245. For English translation, see no. 246.

245. "Pol'sha, Evropa—i novaia ukrainskaia geografiia: 'Z moskaliamy chy z liakhamy?'" *Den'* [Kyiv] 26 January.

(Translation of no. 244)

246. "Poland, Europe, and Ukraine's New Geography: 'With the Russians or the Poles?'" *The Day* [Kyiv] 2 February.

(Translation of no. 244)

INTERVIEW:

247. (by Diana Klochko). "Roman Shporliuk: 'V Ukraïny nemaie inshoho vyboru, krim solidarnosti.'" *Den'* [Kyiv] 22 October.

2000

248. *Russia, Ukraine, and the Breakup of the Soviet Union.* Stanford: Hoover Institution Press. 440 pp.

["Introduction"; Ch. 1, "Nationalities and the Russian Problem in the USSR: A Historical Outline"; Ch. 2, "The Nations of the USSR in 1970"; Ch. 3, "Russians in Ukraine and Problems of Ukrainian Identity in the USSR"; Ch. 4, "West Ukraine and West Belorussia: Historical Tradition, Social Communication, and Linguistic Assimilation"; Ch. 5, "Urbanization in Ukraine since the Second World War"; Ch. 6, "History and Russian Nationalism"; Ch. 7, "Dilemmas of Russian Nationalism"; Ch. 8, "The Imperial Legacy and the Soviet Nationalities Problem"; Ch. 9, "The Soviet West—or Far Eastern Europe"; Ch. 10, "The Press and Soviet Nationalities: The Party Resolution of 1975 and Its Implementation"; Ch. 11, "The Strange Politics of Lviv: An Essay in Search of an Explanation"; Ch. 12, "Nation-Building in Ukraine: Problems and Prospects"; Ch. 13, "Reflections on Ukraine after 1994: The Dilemmas of Nationhood"; Ch. 14, "After Empire: What?"; Ch. 15, "Ukraine: From Imperial Periphery to a Sovereign State"; Ch. 16, "The Fall of the Tsarist Empire and the USSR."]

Women in Ukraine:
The Political Potential of Community Organizations

MARTHA BOHACHEVSKY-CHOMIAK

Community organizations and informal social groups have defined, preserved, and transmitted a sense of local identity in Ukraine more effectively than Ukraine's political groupings. However, when community activists have reflected on their work, they have focused on popularly intellectualized justifications rather than on descriptions of what they did. Historians and political analysts have been equally ready to use ideological labels on the rare occasions when they have included community organizations in their analyses.

Political parties in Ukraine today exhibit the typical approach of the Eastern European intelligentsia—their members are united around an articulated program based on their interpretation of justified values rather than on tactically effective local policies. Ukraine has never produced an indigenous ideology, and its noncommunist ideological movements have played more of a ritual than a political or organizational role.[1]

In conducting research on community organizations in Ukraine, one repeatedly comes across a discrepancy between community actions and their written programs. Community activity begins with a practical agenda—literacy, trade schools, choirs, theater groups, underground math courses when entry to secondary and higher schools is banned—but because these measures are held suspect, the work is later defined in lofty principles. The principles, rather than the practical agenda, are considered the program. The concrete goal of the organization is thus misinterpreted by supporters and detractors alike. The community organizations that emerged initially with the collapse of communism appeared to be broad based and less ideological than the formal or informal political groupings. Community organizations were actively engaged in practical social and self-help outreach programs that had economic as much as national goals. Their political ideologies were not clearly formulated. When they did attempt a precise political determination, their broad base of support disintegrated.

Women in Ukraine historically have engaged in specific community-oriented projects. The goals of feminism—equal opportunity, self-definition, autonomy of one's self or group—were the goals of whatever oppressed group one might choose: workers, nationalities, students. Hence, women in Ukraine failed to realize that they were engaging in a feminist agenda, even while they behaved as feminists. In the interwar years, western Ukrainian women achieved political significance, ironically, as Poland's government moved toward authoritarianism. The economic self-help program of the Ukrainian Women's Union (Soiuz Ukraïnok) transformed the community organization into a significant pressure group within Ukrainian politics and in relations with the Polish authorities. That was feminism.[2] What was remembered, however, was the patriotism of the women, not their political or economic clout.

Women again emerged in the public arena during the disintegration of the USSR. Although ostensibly unwilling to become involved in issues beyond home and kin, they nevertheless played a public—if not necessarily a political—role between 1989 and 1992. In the last months of the existence of the USSR, women's organizations outside the control of the Party mounted mass demonstrations that challenged the Soviet political system, helped decentralize the army, and popularized public gatherings. The first public admission of the Terror Famine of 1932–1933 by a member of formal Soviet elite structures was by a woman.[3] Women organized the first parliamentary hearings in the Ukrainian Rada,[4] attempted to establish women's political parties, and increased the number as well as the power of women deputies in the Rada with each election. Most significantly, since Ukraine's independence, over 40 nationwide women's organizations were created, as well as countless local ones.

The disintegration of the USSR coincided with the UN Decade of Women— not that women claim the credit for the collapse. The thrust of the UN women's initiative had been an emphasis on the critical role of women in development programs. While Ukrainian women may still be unclear about their public function or their own goals, the Ukrainian government heard the UN message and became interested in women because of the contribution they could make to welfare and economic programs. The Ukrainian government has come to view women within the context of society, family, and children, as the first official governmental commission dealing with the UN mandated issues enunciated. So do most women. Both men and women consider that a democratic state should provide social and economic support for its citizens. Since the state is short of funds, it is relying upon women to provide many social services, such as the care of the aged and children, and even some rudimentary medical help. The rise of single-parent families and of illnesses among children, and the decline in multigenerational housing—all combined with an expectation of welfare support—impel the government to offer services it cannot well afford.

Demography contributes to the importance of women's issues for the government.[5] Women constitute more than half of the population of Ukraine, lead the rolls of the unemployed, and have a high level of poverty.[6] In their own estimation, Ukrainian women

> are the most vulnerable category of the population to the wave of exploitation, criminality and violence. Women suffer discrimination in the workplace. They constitute over 70 percent of the unemployed. The mean income level of women is a third less than the equivalent among males. These factors have a negative impact upon the health and welfare of the whole population [and] . . . are in great measure responsible for the catastrophic demographic situation in Ukraine.[7]

The birth rate in Ukraine by 1998 had fallen below the death rate. Ukraine has one of the highest abortion rates in the world, and most women cease child-bearing by their late twenties. Health conditions and prostitution are causing such heavy social problems that even international financial organizations are troubled by them.

Still, many women have a higher education, perform well in their jobs, exhibit less criminality, express more interest in stability, drink less, and live longer than men. In addition, women's community organizations have evolved programs for needy children. All of these are factors that suggest the potential of women to support development initiatives. The Ministry of Family and Youth, created in October 1996, and headed in sequence by the (then) only two women ministers, is a weak recognition of that potential, as much as it is another means to relegate some of the welfare activities to the private sector.[8] If women are to be the "welfare corps," the state must support women's awareness programs, even when it would rather introduce social reforms some other way.

The Soviet reality of a patriarchal society with little understanding of women's needs and a totalitarian regime obsessed with security vitiated the women's rights won in the first flush of the revolutions of 1917–1918. Hence, in the popular view today, feminism is either identified with communism or with frivolous Westernism; in both cases, it is discredited. The peculiarities of Soviet gender policy, lack of familiarity with modern sociological discourse on gender, and the attraction of the ostensible golden age of domesticity stand in the way of a mass resurgence of women's activism. The Soviet regime pro-duced a woman who expected that basic social services would be guaranteed by the state. All women's organizations in Ukraine have taken for granted the responsibility of the government for social welfare, extended maternity leave, child care, and health benefits.[9] The necessity of political—or at least public—action is raised on occasion, but remains mostly rhetorical. The notion of gender as the socially (rather than simply biologically) determined role of sex is only slowly gaining recognition among the intellectual elite in Ukraine. Women's organizations are hesitant in popularizing the usage. Indeed, the All-Ukrainian Women's Congress, sponsored by the Ministry for Families and Youth, with the cooperation of all major women's community organizations, passed a resolution in May 1998 specifically rejecting the term "feminism" in favor of "women's rights."

Women of postcommunist societies confront two extreme positions on women's issues—absolute gender equality on the one hand or separate spheres on the other. The idea of absolute parity of women and men is not popular. Most women consider that childbearing and child-rearing endow women with unique functions, a view that undermines societal changes on the division of labor in the family. Unmitigated equality is also suspect because it appears to be similar to the Soviet solution to the "woman question." An unregulated market economy places women, especially single mothers, unskilled laborers, and pensioners in a very vulnerable position and that vulnerability strengthens the case for special treatment of women. Democrats, socialists, nationalists, and feminists alike favor a system in which the needs of women and children for specific economic welfare provisions are recognized as rights secured by special considerations.

The "separate but equal" argument on women's rights, on the other hand, is justified in many ways in contemporary Ukraine. Thus, within the Ukrainian Women's Union the argument is made from a historical perspective: in historical Ukraine (when the country was free from foreign control) the position of women has always been characterized by reverence for the mother and the nobility of womanhood. This same argument is translated, within a more modern context, into the document drafted in preparation of the Beijing Conference on the Status of Women in 1996:

> ... we need to turn to the *ancient traditions of the Ukrainian nation,* to the depths of history, where we find that the role of woman—as a government activist, as a homemaker, as a mother, as a wife—was always the determining [factor] in the fate of the nation. The traditional approach in Ukraine is to weld patriarchal bases in societal relations with matriarchy within the family.[10]

Another popular notion is that women's psychological makeup, so different from men's, softens the rough edges of life and is thus a factor in raising society's cultural level. Most women in Ukraine agree that "the transition to market relations presupposes the growth of the active role of women,"[11] but how that is to be achieved is not clear. The only specifically women's party—the Women's Christian Party—founded by Ol'ha Horyn', a democratic political activist, in October 1992—failed to recruit members. A similar fate befell a later attempt to found a liberal women's party. When the Women's Union announced in 1998 that its members were to support exclusively one party, there was virtually no discussion of the relationship of that party to the Union.[12]

Within the Soviet Union, only those women's organizations authorized by the Communist Party had been permitted, and none of them was specifically Ukrainian.[13] In 1987, Mikhail Gorbachev, the last general secretary of the Communist Party of the Soviet Union, tried to muster active women's support for his cause by authorizing the establishment of a separate Council of Women of Ukraine (Rada Zhinok Ukraïny),[14] headed by Maria A. Orlyk and closely connected with the Party apparat. It failed to garner new support for Gorbachev or to serve as a focal point for women.[15]

Neither women's rights, nor equality, nor feminism motivated women activists in Ukraine.[16] Women became visible in the public arena at the end of the 1980s because their traditional interests—family, welfare, health care—had political repercussions and crossed existing social and ethnic divisions. Women first mobilized to defend their sons. Since soldiers found little recourse for their grievances about abuses perpetrated against them in the vast Soviet military establishment, women organized themselves into the Committee of Soldiers' Mothers (Komitet Soldats'kykh Materiv) to defend their sons.[17] The Committee originated in Moscow, and the first mass demonstrations were held there in 1989. The Mothers' Committee was strong in Ukraine, which had borne a heavy burden in the unpopular war in Afghanistan and the cleanup of nuclear waste at Chornobyl, but its activists were not connected to any of the so-called Ukrainian nationalist groups. Although the organization drew media coverage, it was not accused of nationalism or of political sabotage, so it could develop a network. This was the first step toward the independent activism of women.

Ecology was the next organizing issue. Ecological crises, of which Chornobyl was merely the most publicized example, made many mothers aware of the direct link between the policies of the regime and the welfare of their children.

By early 1990, women active within the emerging opposition movement, Rukh, established "Women's Community" (Zhinocha Hromada) that included representatives of organized minority women.[18] Concomitantly, Ukrainian women discovered the indigenous non-socialist women's movement in Ukraine, became conscious of the fact that they were resurrecting a women's movement that had been part of the world movement, and created local Women's Union organizations.[19] By January 1992, representatives of the Ukrainian Women's Union convened in Kyiv to claim formally to be "the heir to the democratic traditions of the Ukrainian Women's Union that functioned in Ukraine starting in 1917 and was liquidated as the result of Bolshevik occupation."[20] The reference to a women's organization of the pre-Soviet period drew the new women's movement into the historical framework of Ukraine and legitimized it as patriotic activity. The Women's Community in Kyiv used the socialist International Women's Day on 8 March 1991 to spearhead a major political demonstration aimed against socialist control.[21] In conjunction with the Committee of Soldiers' Mothers, the Union of Women of Ukraine, the newly formed "Committee of Families with Many Children" (a society of mothers who have more than five children) and "Mother-86" (a group of mothers whose children were born around the time of Chornobyl), the Women's Community organized the largest independent women's rally in Kyiv and the first one in 50 years that raised political issues.[22]

This marked another step in the political emergence of women. The initial coalition was broad, a zeal for action seemed to be present, and professional Ukrainian urban women were drawn to the Hromada. But the budding movement failed to articulate its goals effectively, and the coalition that put the demonstration together disintegrated.[23] Women seemed aware of the importance of political work, but not yet certain of its appropriateness as a major goal of a women's organization. The elections of 1998 led women to initiate a formal discussion on the establishment of a National Council of Women, but so far only an informal advisory committee of the major women's organizations functions under the aegis of the Ministry for Families and Youth. The Ministry suggested that Maria Orlyk's group chair this advisory committee, but other organizations insisted on rotation among the major groups.

The most influential women's organizations may be grouped into five clusters—the formerly communist organization, those based on national traditions (of whatever definition), philanthropic organizations, feminists, and professional networks. All view the situation in Ukraine from different perspectives.

After the proclamation of Ukraine's independence in August 1991, the official Council of Women of Ukraine restructured itself as the Confederation of Women of Ukraine (Spilka Zhinok Ukraïny) and distanced itself from the immediate past.[24] Its government subsidy severed, the Confederation encouraged its members to set up commercial enterprises and join the march to the market. The Confederation now supports cooperatives, joint ventures, and a Society of Ukrainian Businesswomen, and works with the Association of Independent Women Farmers of Ukraine.[25] It has done little to promote Ukraine's independence, but its conferences in 1992 and 1995 were heavily weighted toward addressing the history and culture of Ukraine.[26]

The organizations of the second cluster—those based on national traditions—span the political and ethnic gamut, but all stress children, welfare, and culture. There are organizations aimed at specific groups, such as the Jewish Women's Organization "Compassion" (Zhinoche Ievreis'ke Tovarystvo "Myloserdia," headed by Faina Neiman), and those that promote a heterogeneous organization of all women of Ukraine, such as the Association of Minority Women of Ukraine (Asosiatsiia Zhinok Natsional'nykh Menshostei Ukraïny, founded by a Korean Ukrainian, Svitlana Li, and part of the Women's Community). The aforementioned Ukrainian Women's Union has focused, primarily, although not exclusively, on issues relating to Ukraine's national independence from its inception. Local chapters and regional councils, however, show a more practical bent. In Lviv, for instance, the Women's Union initiated a program to train small-business entrepreneurs. In Kyiv, the local branch lobbied to establish a Center for the Study of Menopause.

There is a fair amount of overlap among these organizations and those whose purpose is purely philanthropic. One of the most openly patriotic women's organizations, the Olena Teliha Society, created on 9 June 1994, grew out of a project of the women on the editorial staff of the newspaper *Ukraïns'ke slovo* (Ukrainian Word) to distribute donated medicines.[27] The Society now "promotes the strengthening of national statehood and the consolidation of the Ukrainian people."[28] Indigenous philanthropic organizations try to draw on domestic sources of funding from the emerging wealthy class, but are more frequently conduits for foreign support.

There is no feminist movement as such, but centers for the study of gender in Kyiv, Odesa, and Kharkiv are initiating something of the kind. By far the most active is the Kharkiv Center for Gender Studies, directed by the philosopher Irina Zherebkina. With nine colleagues, she prepared an introductory textbook for gender studies and in 1998 began publishing *New Image: A Ukrainian Feminist Journal*.[29] In western Ukraine young scholars working on women's history are becoming aware of sexism. Articles on women's issues and firsthand exposure to gender relations outside the Soviet context promote greater self-awareness as well as involvement of women in public life.[30]

Women's professional interest networks appear to be the social groups most capable of mounting effective actions. The Organization of Women Cinematographers serves as a resource and a forum for its members. Librarians and teachers are beginning to be attracted to women's agenda.

The most important group politically is made up of women working in the middle management tiers of the government. Although they do not view themselves as any type of bloc, on occasion they raise issues relating to the status of women and receive active support from women parliamentary deputies. These women prepared the official Ukrainian delegation for the Fourth World Conference on Women in Beijing in July 1995.[31] They were responsible for the unprecedented parliamentary hearings on the status of women held in July 1995.[32] Some write about the need for gender-sensitive policies and for a system of democracy that incorporates a femininity capable of "rectifying the coarseness of our male culture."[33] Although this kind of overtly feminist language is rare, its use in print is significant. The women deputies in Parliament form an ad hoc bloc when issues of particular interest to women do arise. Among the women parliamentarians—in addition to the vocal democrats (Lilia Hryhorovych, for instance) and their opponents, the communists and socialists (e.g., Natalia Vitrenko)—increasingly one comes across pragmatic businesswomen of the type of Aleksandra Kuzhil' or Yulia Tymoshenko.[34]

While during the Soviet period women deputies constituted 50 percent of local soviets and 30 percent in the republican Supreme Soviet, "that high percentage of women in social and political life of Soviet Ukraine was created artificially, so that the free elections in 1994 returned only 17 women deputies among the 405 elected to the Supreme Council, 4 percent of the total."[35] In the 1998 elections the number was almost doubled—32 women were elected.[36] Only a minuscule number of women are in prestigious positions and even fewer are in positions of actual power. There is one woman ambassador, there are a few judges above the district level, and the newly created position in Parliament of ombudsman for human rights is held by a woman.[37] The fact that overall in government service women constitute about 68 percent of the labor force of which 48 percent work on the managerial level, may be a variant of feminization of the profession but also a portent of potential organization.

Ukrainian non-governmental organizations now play a more visible role on the overall NGO forum at the United Nations than previously. The existence of an independent Ukraine that encourages, and at times informally supports, these organizations is definitely a factor, but, for the most part, the organizations pursue independent policies. Outside support also helps the independent course of the non-governmental organizations. By early 1997 a Gender Center was set up in Kyiv to work with the UN and with the Ministry for Family and Youth. The United Nations Development Fund, with the aid of the British Council, supported the publication of a brochure on gender as an aid for "workers in the media and organizers of courses on gender issues."[38] Their first project was to prepare a critique of the new constitution of Ukraine (adopted in 1996) from the standpoint of gender relations.

The Institute of Government Management and Self-Administration, under the aegis of the Cabinet of Ministers of Ukraine and with the help of Canadian academic institutions, has actively recruited women since its inception in 1992. The alumnae association from this two-year program sponsors programs for women in business, with assistance from the International Renaissance Foundation, the Ministry of Foreign Affairs, and the Women's Community.[39]

Activist women conflate women's goals, social concerns, and public concerns. One Ukrainian scholar elaborated on women's organizations as follows:

> The future of the women's movement depends on whether it will . . . help a woman, ameliorate her condition, teach her how to function in a market economy, ensure her access to a better life, show her how to help her family, feed her children and so on. Women are not striving for a feminist society, but for a society free of sexism and patriarchy, where conditions for freedom for all men and women prevail, and where the issues that today are characterized as "women's" will involve the whole society. All this cannot be done without a deep structural transformation of the whole context of social relations.[40]

Although sociological polls taken in Ukraine in the last three years concur that most women show little inclination for political activism and little belief in its efficacy, openly political women's groups and petitions that protest the disregard of women in public appointments emerge sporadically.[41]

An International Women's Club of Kyiv, composed of non-Ukrainian women working and living in Kyiv, holds monthly meetings, social gatherings, cultural programs, and an annual major fundraising event for a Ukrainian charity. The scope of their work, the quality of the members, and the visible involvement of non-Ukrainian males in the fundraising serves as an example of community volunteerism.

Discourse on women in the last five years has progressed from trite rhetorical statements to a more practical hands-on approach. This area is where some of the most significant changes can take place. While in the early 1990s the discussion of women's issues was often limited to bombastic historical presentations, during the middle part of the decade women were analyzing what women's organizations can do to actively prevent and diffuse conflicts,[42] how gender relations influence economic development, and how feminist study of psychology can help overcome the legacy of terror and decrease family violence.[43] Of equal importance is the growth of interest among sociologists in gender relations in society, economy, and government.[44] Research institutes, especially private ones that function on grant money, even if they are not primarily geared toward women's issues, often focus on women. Scholars are helping to develop a language for feminist and women's studies. Sex education and the availability of more reliable birth control devices as well as awareness of sexually transmitted diseases including the AIDS virus are making society less reticent about the implications of gender relations. Violence, rape, and wife abuse are more openly discussed, and there is even some attempt to create homes for battered women. Sex trafficking is being addressed. The statements drafted at the various national conferences reflect the growth of feminist discourse. The fact that the All-Ukrainian Women's Congress on 21–23 May 1998 was addressed by President Leonid Kuchma, (then) Prime Minister Valeriy Pustovoitenko, and (then) Vice Premier for Culture Valeriy Smoliy is some indication of the growing realization of the importance of women.

The institutions that either existed under the Soviet regime or were inchoate are now emerging as fora for women's issues. Some of the old Soviet youth structures have been reorganized to serve new needs. The Scouting movement (Plast) is taking over the Komsomol social functions. The Ukrainian State Center of Social Services for Youth has moved with particular energy toward developing programs directed toward young women in the cities.[45] The agency finances local programs and provides informative materials on problems facing young women in a transitional society—sex, drugs, violence, and the need for job training.

Cultural patterns change slowly, but public usage reflects a slightly growing sensitivity to women. Such concepts as the feminization of poverty, the double burden of having full responsibility for household upkeep and family care *and* working a full-time job, violence against women, the need to develop legal outreach programs for women, and stress on the implementation (and not only on the enactment) of laws, offer further proof of the changed conditions. The government of Ukraine is working on a statement on women that even takes into consideration the need to actively promote overcoming sexual stereotypes through the media. Its practical program, with planned conferences, leadership workshops, special programs for women, and provisions for the keeping of current statistics on the employment and promotion of women is most commendable.[46] Increased openness to the outside world, a growing international community in Ukraine, and particularly the experience of students studying abroad can contribute to the changed attitudes toward gender relations.[47]

More women are now aware of the discrepancy between the relatively high educational level of women and their absence in "organs of power." Both specialists and women activists fault society, not women, for the discrepancy. That conviction may even strengthen women's activism, since societal change is more palatable as a cause than women's rights. The dissolution of daycare facilities that accompanied the decline of Soviet industrial enterprises and the growing dissatisfaction with communal child care are working at cross-purposes to women's involvement in the public sphere. Pressures of family are cited as the single most salient factor in keeping the women from participating more fully in political and public life—and those will not diminish. Lack of faith in the efficacy of any political changes and inability to discern the direction in which the various political parties are headed are also important factors in preventing women from finding time to become politically active.

The ambivalence of women toward exhibiting political aspirations is illustrated by the handsome booklet *Ukraine* prepared for the 1995 Beijing conference. It had the conventional introduction about the high status that women are supposed to have enjoyed throughout Ukraine's history as well as the soft focus photography that characterized Ukrainian Soviet women's publications. What is more, the Ukrainian delegation to Beijing was headed by a man, Ivan Kuras.[48] But the booklet also provided well-structured statistical data and an overview of what Ukraine has done since 1983 when it signed the UN Convention "On Eradicating All Forms of Discrimination against Women." Of greater importance, the document included among the specific desiderata the introduction of "feminology"—defined as the study of "the position of women in the family, the social role of the woman in the system of humanitarian education, in moral upbringing, in training, and in public life"—into the public school curriculum.[49] Perhaps the strongest condemnation of the position of women in Ukraine was provided by a male historian who had specialized in the history of the Communist Party. He was one of the few to note publicly the marginalization of women:

> The democratic changes in Ukraine again, now in the new historical era, pose the question of freedom and equality, the freeing of mankind not only from patriarchal but also vulgar norms and ideas. From this point of view the spiritual wellsprings and the traditions of the women's movement of the nineteenth and the beginning of the twentieth century are interesting and essential today. The few women's organizations that include women's issues in their program are not only not taken seriously by the regime, they themselves lack the political and juridical power necessary to affect a change in the position of women. An analysis of the programs of the political parties demonstrates that none of them address this question even as a remote possibility. Woman has found herself on the margins of state building. It is also sad that in a society with a longstanding domination of males, women have become so accustomed to male value systems that they themselves support the system, not noticing that it is unjust toward them.[50]

To sum up: in the years of modern Ukraine's independence we witness first of all the emergence of independent women's organizations that span the entire political and ideological spectrum. Whereas within the Soviet Union there had been one "solution" to the women's question, determined in 1930 and unchanged, now there is a veritable rainbow of solutions and non-solutions. The variety of women's organizations is proof of the societal differentiation that is occurring in the post-Soviet period. At the same time we see deeply conflicting tendencies among the women themselves. Along with the reemergence of feminist autonomy and the stress on individualism, the argument that the state owes the woman sustenance and support in the peculiarly female role of producing and nurturing the younger generation remains popular. The liberalism of the democratic state is thus tempered by the argument for the duty of the state to continue caring for its citizens, especially for women and children. Women are among the most vociferous proponents of this support. Security considerations, if nothing else, push the government to address issues of health and reproduction, but pro-natalist policies are offset by the protracted economic crisis. Women support grassroots activities and community welfare programs, but few take the step toward political or community power.

Next, the opening of society and the process that is making socioeconomic differences in lifestyles explicit both make the would-be ideal of the wife/mother cared for by a husband very attractive. The popularity of religious sentiment, especially of evangelical Christianity, has the same effect in a different manner. The other side of the coin is the equally growing proclivity among some young women to make full use of the opportunities of the free market economy to make their own lives more immediately satisfying regardless of risks to their own independence, safety, or morality.

Economic considerations, cultural pressures, and the relatively high level of education will keep women in the work force. If the economic and cultural modernization of the country continues, greater awareness of the role and potential of women will lead to their more active participation in public life, either in general or in women's movements. The level of political awareness of women will determine in which direction they will throw their support. It will also determine whether women will have a say in policies affecting them, or whether these decisions will be made for them.

At present, women's organizations are incapable of becoming a political force in Ukraine. They do not form a conscious interest group, so they cannot rally around a political platform. They need a charismatic leader able to articulate their needs, but at the same time they resent any leadership. The very nature of women's socialization militates against a strong organizational structure, and none of the contemporary women is able to voice a democratic women's ideal with sufficient clarity and force to rally women into a potent movement. In the foreseeable future there will be no Mothers' Movement and no Ukrainian Women's Union to elect members of Parliament.

If women were to emerge again as a political force in Ukraine, it would be from the ranks of government and those NGOs with a window to the outside world. They will not constitute a mass movement, but they might be able to rally the members of the larger women's organizations. NGOs and the government are now attracting women with drive, talent, and a sense of public awareness who had previously been the candidates for community organizations. Politically conscious women see the potential role of women, but do not see themselves as part of the women's movement.

If the women's organizations were able to expand their activities and attract the political activists as well, then women could act as an effective pressure group. But they should remember that, historically, their power in Ukraine lay not in rhetorical proclamations but in effective grass-roots organizational work.

NOTES

1. For the Ukrainian intelligentsia the major issues were not existential, but rather those of the sheer existence of the nation. In the face of denial of its existence, daily activities such as speaking one's language, attempting to publish in it, holding meetings, establishing daycare centers, and setting up student cafeterias took on an aura of exceptional achievement. In this context, the simplicity of such tasks is overlooked, the heroism remembered. Today, Ukrainian newspapers bristle with stories of historical personages and fantastic claims that sometimes rival medieval state-building myths. Scholarly works dwell with increasing frequency upon "the national character" or else discover a preternatural "mentalité." Pundits focus on political groupings and political statements, while even young historians update a hagiography of a linear national movement. Recent studies (such as those by Heorhiy Kasianov, Serhiy Yekelchyk, and Oleksiy Haran') also focus upon programmatic, national, and human rights aspects and appear to have little interest in the more practical facets of the work of individuals or organizations.

2. For a full discussion of this development, see Martha Bohachevsky-Chomiak, *Feminists Despite Themselves: Women in Ukrainian Community Life, 1884–1939* (Edmonton, 1988).

3. Nina Kovals'ka tearfully acknowledged the famine at a workshop held during the Forum meetings that preceded the official UN Conference on the Status of Women in Nairobi in July 1985. Today she is the only woman ambassador to represent Ukraine.

4. The hearings, held on 13 July 1995, marked a new level of public awareness of the role of women in society and in politics in Ukraine. All but one of the representatives of the women's organizations who testified raised genuine concerns about women's legal status and de facto opportunities in contemporary Ukraine. Their measured demands contrasted sharply with the cant of some socialist deputies, who presented the women during the hearings with a bouquet of flowers that jarred sharply with the tenor of the discussions before the packed chamber, galleries, and diplomatic and press sections. The parliamentary socialist majority, especially the speaker of the Rada, Oleksandr Moroz, had tried to dismiss, or at least to postpone, the hearings. The socialist women deputies, however, enlisted the support of the entire Parliament, especially of the democrats, and the hearings were held.

5. Because of the Chornobyl catastrophe, some couples are hesitant to have children at all. In general, women appear to be more pessimistic than men about their health prospects. The decline in the birth rate preceded Chornobyl. In the 1960s the average family was composed of 4 persons; in 1975 it was down to 3.4; in 1989 to 3.2; and in 1994 the average size of

the family was 3 persons—hence, 1 child per couple. In 1989 the average woman in Ukraine had 1.93 children; in 1993 it was down to 1.63 On the other hand, abortions declined from 85.4 per 1000 women of child-bearing age in 1989, to 68.6. See Predstavnytstvo OON v Ukraïni, Orhkomitet pry Kabineti Ministriv Ukraïny po pidhotovtsi do IV Vsesvitn'oï Konferentsiï zi stanovyshcha zhinok, *Zhinka v Ukraïni. Chetverta Vsesvitnia konferentsiia zi stanovyshcha zhinok (Pekin, 4–15 veresnia 1995 roku)* (n.p., 1995), p. 17.

6. In Kyiv alone the birth rate between 1990 and 1993 fell by 28 percent, in the whole country by 20 percent. The disproportion between the sexes is higher than in most other countries. Demographers suggest that this is due not only to the losses in Ukraine in the 1930s and 1940s, but also to the high rate of early mortality in males. See S. I. Pyrozhkov, N. M. Lakiza-Sachuk, I. V. Zapatirna, *Ukraïna v demohrafichnomu vymiri: mynule, suchasne, maibutn'e* (Kyiv, 1995), p. 15 [= Natsional'nyi instytut stratehichnykh doslidzen', *Naukovi dopovidi, 35*].

7. Quotation from "Recommendations of the Participants of the Parliamentary Hearings. Proposed by the Organizational Committee to Hold Parliamentary Hearings, the Committee on Human Rights, Rights of National Minorities and Interethnic Relations" (Kyiv, 1995), p. 3. See also N. M. Lakiza-Sachuk, *Deformiruiushchee vliianie sovremennogo planirovaniia sem'i v Ukraine na osnove demograficheskogo vosproizvodstva ee naseleniia* (Kyiv, 1993), p. 25 [=Natsional'nyi instytut stratehichnykh doslidzhen', *Naukovi dopovidi, 8*].

8. The ministry focuses on the immediate medical needs of children, such as vaccination and nutrition, on the regulation of foster care, and on care of the elderly, but little on the needs of women. Suzan Stanik was the only woman minister in Ukraine until August 1997, when she was replaced as Minister of Family and Youth by Valentyna Dovzhenko, and herself in turn replaced the reformist Serhiy Holovaty as Minister of Justice. Stanik's sex diffused some of the criticism for the removal of Holovaty, well known for his liberal reformist views. Both Stanik and Dovzhenko come from the Soviet youth movement.

9. The program of the renewed Ukrainian Women's Union reflects the changed nature of this organization from its interwar predecessor in Galicia. Where the interwar Women's Union stressed modernization of the village, the contemporary organization focuses upon the cultural and educational programs of its present middle-class constituency. It also expects outside support for its activities, placing the immediate welfare of small children at the top of its priorities. Among the smaller organizations one could name the League of Mothers and Sisters of the Soldiers of Ukraine, which took as its aim the amelioration of the spiritual and material conditions of the draftees; the International Association "Hope"

in Alushta, Crimea, headed by Nina Karpacheva, a deputy to the second Supreme Rada; the association of women workers "For the Future of the Children of Ukraine"; and the association of women "For the Genetic Fund of Ukraine" as examples of the diversity of the groups. Churches have also served as focal groups for religious and philanthropic organizations of women.

10.   Emphasis in the original. See *Zhinka v Ukraïni. Chetverta Vsesvitnia konferentsiia*, p. 4.

11.   Ibid., p. 9.

12.   The political party in question was Rukh, headed by V'iacheslav Chornovil, the husband of Atena Pashko, the head of the Ukrainian Women's Union (more in note 23, below). Very few women protested, and even fewer left the Union in protest of the Union's abandonment of an independent political stand. The Union argued it was an effective tactical move and that the organization did not become an affiliate of the party.

13.   Officially, feminism was branded as bourgeois and non-Soviet Ukrainian women's organizations as nationalist. Separate women's Party organizations were disbanded in 1930, when the woman question was considered solved. A new women's organization was established after the Second World War to facilitate participation on the international forum. The organization was all-Soviet, but a separate journal was published in Ukrainian.

14.   The resolution authorizing the new organizations tellingly illustrated what the elite of the former USSR expected: " . . . women [in the USSR], who continually experience the paternal care of the Party, will support its policy of speeding up the socioeconomic development of the country with all their heart." Quoted in *Visti z Ukraïny* 1987 (4): 2.

15.   A Council of Women of Ukraine, recognized by the International Council of Women, existed during the period of the Ukrainian National Republic and through a decade of exile in the 1920s. The Soviets opposed it, in much the same fashion as they boycotted the international women's movement outside the socialist camp.

16.   Feminism, in the sense of the assertion of women's rights and of self-liberation, is not easily understood in Ukraine, where women even more than men were raised in the tradition of service and self-dedication to others. The goal for women is not emancipation or liberation, but rather, as had been the goal of early American women activists, the welfare of their community, making life better for others. Ukrainian society is one in which family structures, personal relationships, and traditional social relations determine worldviews and expectations. Western democracy, with its stress on personal initiative and personal responsibility, with its

impersonal relations embedded in law, with its self-discipline and its work ethic, is understood by most former Soviet citizens as a system of mutual advantage, not of individual responsibility.

17. See, for instance, "I bude syn, i bude maty," by Oleksandr Kryvoshei and Liudmyla Chechel', in *Radians'ka zhinka* 1990 (11): 35. This journal, published monthly in a run of more than two and a half million copies and previously known for its bland toeing of the Party line, invited its readers to express their views on the demands of the mothers' committee. See also Bohdan Pyskir, "Materi dlia Bat'kivshchyny," in *Suchasnist'* 1994 (June): 70–82 [originally published as "Mothers for a Fatherland: Ukrainian Statehood, Motherhood, and National Security," *Journal of Slavic Military Studies* 7(1) March 1994: 50–66]. Mothers of draftees were the first activists in the late 1980s to form an effective pressure group. The high mortality rate of soldiers from Ukraine in the Afghan war made mothers acutely aware of the political issues in the country.

18. Russian women in Ukraine have not formed separate women's organizations.

19. Western publications in Ukrainian introduced some of the women to women's studies and to community activities. Rukh activists encouraged American women to talk to Ukrainian audiences at public meetings.

20. Text of the by-laws of the Ukrainian Women's Union (Soiuz Ukraïnok); copy in the possession of the author.

21. At the initiative of Klara Zetkin, the International Congress of Socialist Women, meeting in Copenhagen on 26–28 August 1910, proclaimed March 8 a day of celebration of progressive women in society. It was made a formal holiday in the Soviet Union, where it quickly became a formality—as Mothers' Day is in the West—having little connection to ideas of women's liberation. It was never widely accepted beyond the socialist spheres, and it is a contentious affair in Ukraine. Some women continue to support it as a day of recognition of the separate status of women. Other women and men are strongly opposed to celebrating the holiday even informally. The nationalists see it as a Soviet imposition; others see it as one more example of the duplicitous political rhetoric of the Soviets towards women repeated by the current government. For a personal view of the holiday as "an annual antifeminist ritual," see Solomiia Pavlychko, "Posttotalitarna kul'tura iak nosii znevahy do zhinok," in *Zhinka v derzhavotvorenni: materialy mizhnarodnoï naukovoï konferentsiï (Kyiv 29–31 May 1993),* ed. H. Skrypnyk et al. (Kyiv, 1993).

22. A cynical male reporter noted that "Ukrainian, Russian, Belarusian, Jewish, Bulgarian, and Korean women chanted how difficult it is to live in slavery, and in unison humbly repeated the words of 'Our Father'"

(Hennadiy Kyryndiasov, "Choho khoche zhinka, toho khoche Boh," *Vechirnii Kyïv* 11 March 1991: 2).

23. Maria Drach, the wife of the poet Ivan Drach, emerged as the voice of the organization. She succeeded in creating a coalition of various women's groups, including a fair number of former Komsomol activists. Personal politics spilled into the women's movement and stymied the formation of an effective women's bloc. Ivan Drach, the poet, community organizer, and a free man under the Soviet regime, was pitted against V'iacheslav Chornovil, a journalist who had received a series of gulag sentences. Chornovil emerged as the leader of the Rukh, with Drach a member but not the major leader. Chornovil's wife, the relatively unknown Atena Pashko, came to head the Women's Union, which originated in western Ukraine, but quickly established footholds in the east. The two democratic groups of women nominally cooperated, but both also moved from political action to welfare activities. The reformed communist bloc of women also failed to produce a leader other than Maria Orlyk or Valentyna S. Shevchenko, the former nominal president of the Ukrainian SSR, whose name was linked to the disastrous May Day parade in Kyiv five days after Chornobyl. *Visti z Ukraïny* 7 (1991): 2, published a statement of the Women's Union (Soiuz Ukraïnok) to the effect that its aim was the struggle for an independent Ukraine, and hence they found it impossible to cooperate with Orlyk's organization. The Women's Community in turn called in flowery terms for that cooperation.

24. "Respublikans'ka Rada Zhinok," *Visti z Ukraïny* 4 (1987): 2. Valentyna Shevchenko and Volodymyr Ivashko, the secretary of the Central Committee of the Communist Party of Ukraine and Gorbachev's Party stalwart, helped organize the Council. Later, charges were made that the Women's Councils were used to launder Party coffers; see *Samostiina Ukraïna* 13 (September 1991): 3. By the fall of 1991, with the approach of the referendum on independence and the presidential elections, Orlyk used the Council to revivify the old Party lines and to keep women in an organizational structure. The creation of the initial separate Ukrainian Women's Council was already a concession by Gorbachev.

25. Liudmyla Smoliar, "Feministychna tradytsiia Ukraïny i pytannia suchasnoho zhinochoho rukhu," *Zhinka i demokratiia. Materialy mizhnarodnoï naukovo-praktychnoï konferentsiï*, ed. Tamara Mel'nyk (Kyiv, 1995), pp. 45–51 (sponsored by the Mizhnarodna orhanizatsiia "Zhinocha hromada" with the original conference taking place in Kyiv on 2–5 June 1995).

26. During the three-day meetings, half of the sessions (held in either Ukrainian or Russian) dealt with some aspect of the historical development of women in Ukrainian history, culture, and spiritual life. Health and economy covered two sessions and only one session dealt with "the role

and place of women's organizations in the sociopolitical life of Ukraine."
Zhinky Ukraïny: suchasnyi status i perspektyvy (Kyiv and Odesa,
1995)—program notes.

27. Olena Teliha, a poet who lived in Prague in the interwar years, returned
to Kyiv in the wake of the invading German army. She worked for a time
at the newspaper *Ukraïns'ke slovo*, and was burned alive by the Nazis
along with other members of the Ukrainian intelligentsia in one of the
massacres near Baby Yar in Kyiv. A newspaper with the same title was
founded in Kyiv in the early 1990s, and it was the women working in its
editorial offices who were the initiators of the group.

28. First paragraph of point 2.3 of the by-laws.

29. *Teoriia i istoriia feminizma: kurs lektsii* (Kharkiv, 1996). Zherebkina
published a very critical study of Ukrainian women, *Zhenskoe
politicheskoe bessoznatel'noe: problema gendera i zhenskoe dvizhenie v
Ukraine* (Kharkiv, 1996), in which she draws heavily on the text of
Feminists Despite Themselves. See Martha Bohachevsky-Chomiak,
"Navkolo Genderu," *Krytyka* (Kyiv) 1998 (3) 5: 7–8.

30. See, for instance, Valentyna Zlenko and Natalia Napadovs'ka, "Zhinky v
polӥtytsi," *Molod' Ukraïny* 12 March 1990: 3.

31. Interview with Ella Lamakh, one of the Ukrainian representatives to the
March meeting on the Commission on the Status of Women.

32. Fuller discussion in Martha Bohachevsky-Chomiak, "Practical Concerns
and Political Protests in Post-Soviet Ukraine," *Transition* 16 (8 September 1995): 12–17.

33. *Zhinka v Ukraïni. Chetverta Vsesvitnia konferentsiia*, p. 3.

34. The latter, an executive in the private energy company that appeared to
be closely linked with Pavlo Lazarenko, is an extremely capable and
apparently independent person. In December 1999 she was named a vice-
premier in the government formed by Viktor Yuschenko.

35. *Zhinka v Ukraïni. Chetverta Vsesvitnia konferentsiia*, p. 11. The situation
in the government structures is not as dismal: in the Ministry of Statistics,
82 percent of the workers are women; in the Ministry of Health, 62
percent; in the Ministry of Education, 58 percent; in the Ministry of
Welfare, 60 percent; in the Ministry of Labor, 56 percent; in the Ministry
of Culture, 53 percent; in the Ministry of Youth and Sport, 52 percent; in
the Ministry of Nationalities and Religion, 46 percent; and in the Ministry of Foreign Affairs, 42 percent.

36. We should remember, however, that within the structure of the USSR
genuinely significant decisions were not made by the government, and
the Ukrainian organs of power in state and Party were subject to
Moscow's control.

37. The Ambassador to Switzerland is Nina Kovals´ka, formerly a frequent spokesperson for Soviet Ukrainian women. Nina Karpacheva (the ombudsman), a lawyer, was elected from Crimea. She has been active in promoting women's concerns.

38. *Henderni pytannia v zasobakh masovoï informatsiï*, ed. Iryna Ihnatova and Oksana Kuts, trans. Maksym Kononenko and Tetiana Moskvitina (Kyiv, 1997).

39. Liudmyla Hrebeniuk, "Zhinka v derzhavnomu upravlinni," in *Zhinka i demokratiia*, pp. 87–89. See also articles there by Karina Shumbatiuk, Taïssa Halina, Natalia Petrova, Ivanna Ibrahimova, et al. Analyzing the difficulties of reform of the Ukrainian economy—difficulties due in large measure to the "incompleteness of its economic structure"—Tamara Romaniuk emphasized the continued need for some welfare support in view of the inevitable continuing inflation. Lidia Kononko bemoaned the low participation of women in political parties. Larysa Kravchenko stressed the importance of women's participation in the development of a democratic society. See their contributions in *Zhinka v derzhavotvorenni*.

40. Liudmyla Smoliar, "Feministychna tradytsiia Ukraïny," p. 51.

41. Thus, in June 1997 "Diia" (Action) was formed to encourage women to work closely with the National Democratic Party. Meanwhile, reflecting the personal politics of its president, the Women's Union threw its support exclusively to Rukh. Another group—the League for Women Voters—founded in July 1997, focuses on the general goal of mobilizing women to vote. In December 1998, women leaders in Lviv publicly protested the disregard of their organizations in local political appointments. See Natalia Baliuk, "P'iemont demokratiï chy patriarkhatu," *Vysokyi zamok* 8 January 1999: 3.

42. See, for instance, the articles in *Zhinka i demokratiia*.

43. The work of Valentyna Bondarovs´ka in a social service consulting firm, Rozrada, in Kyiv is especially significant. See also her brief article "Psykholohichnyi status zhinky Ukraïny: shliakh do novykh psykholohichnykh modelei," in *Zhinka i demokratiia*, pp. 82–86.

44. Iurii Neimer, for instance, provided an exhaustive picture of working women in Ukraine in a series of three articles "Rabotaiushchie zhenshchiny (sotsial´nyi portret gruppy)," in *Sovremennoe obshchestvo* (Kharkiv) 1994 (nos. 1, 2, 3).

45. See *Dovira i nadiia* 3, edited by Halyna Laktionova and published in 1995 by the Ukrainian State Center of Social Services for Youth. Laktionova is also the driving force in establishing the first women's gymnasium with residential facilities in Kyiv.

46. The July 1997 working document of the proposed statement on government policy toward women includes the following " . . . although in its legislation Ukraine fully measures up to the statutes of the Convention against the discrimination of women . . . there is a clear discrepancy between the legislation on gender equality and practical reality. So far Ukraine still lacks a state mechanism to ensure the enforcement of laws relating to the welfare of families, motherhood and children, and to ensure the rights of women."

47. According to sociological studies carried out in Ukraine, gender equality brings greater satisfaction. Thus, in terms of overall contentment with their lives, professional women are basically more content than women in unskilled jobs who believe only marriage to a good provider will ensure a good life. There is also a new openness on matters of family and sexual violence, and articles providing information on available legal recourse for victims of sexual harassment are appearing with greater frequency. Aggression against the wife is the dominant form of abuse, with rape in the second place. Complaints about prostitution, forced sex, and sex with family members are less common. See *Zhinka v Ukraïni. Chetverta vsesvitnia konferentsiia*, p. 3. That does not necessarily mean that the cases may be rare, merely that complaints are not widespread.

48. It is interesting to note that during the interwar period the Ukrainian cooperatives in Poland sent a man to represent Ukrainian cooperatives to the International Women's Cooperative Guild, although even then there were qualified women capable of doing the job.

49. Valentyna Zlenko, "Politychnyi imidzh lidera," in *Zhinka i demokratiia*, pp. 38–43.

50. H. I. Tereshchenko, "Do pytannia istoriï zhinochoho rukhu," in *Zhinochyi rukh v Ukraïni: istoriia i suchasnist'. Mizhnarodna naukovo-metodychna konferentsiia (Odesa, zhovten' 1994): tezy dopovidei* (Odesa, 1994), p. 7.

Systemic Crisis and National Mobilization:
The Case of the "Memorandum of the Serbian Academy"

AUDREY HELFANT BUDDING

When members of a multinational state's most powerful nation turn from state-based and state-supporting internationalist ideologies to embrace national particularism, their choice appears paradoxical. What attracts them to an ideology that by its nature threatens the state in which they have enjoyed primacy? The emergence of an anti-Soviet Russian nationalism has raised this question in a particularly urgent form, and has called forth a broad array of interpretations in response. One of the most compelling is Roman Szporluk's contention that the rise of all the anti-Soviet nationalisms, and especially anti-Soviet *Russian* nationalism, "must be seen in connection with, and as a reaction to, the failure of 'Sovietism' broadly defined."[1] Anti-Soviet Russian nationalism, in other words, cannot be separated from its context of system failure. It represents a conscious response to the crisis of the communist system, and not simply the opportunistic resurgence of an ideology which that system had suppressed.

In this essay, I will take Szporluk's interpretation of anti-Soviet Russian nationalism as the starting point for a fresh look at a parallel phenomenon: the emergence of anti-Yugoslav Serbian nationalism. Specifically, I will examine the pivotal 1986 document known as the "Memorandum of the Serbian Academy" from a point of view informed by Szporluk's thought. Before turning to the Serbian case, however, it is worth emphasizing that there were important differences, as well as similarities, between the position of Russians in the Soviet Union and the position of Serbs in socialist Yugoslavia.[2] Indeed, a comparison with the position of Russians in the USSR may serve to illustrate some of the limits of Serbian "dominance."

Numerically speaking, Russians and the Russian Republic enjoyed a much more commanding position in the USSR than did Serbs and Serbia in Yugoslavia. While Russians in the USSR comprised an (admittedly bare) majority in the 1980s, Serbs were merely a plurality. They made up about 36 percent of the population, while Croats, the next largest group, made up just under 20 percent. Serbia (including the Autonomous Provinces of Kosovo and Vojvodina) was Yugoslavia's most populous republic, with approximately 9.3 million inhabitants, compared to Croatia's 4.6 million. Nevertheless, its relative "advantage" did not approach that of the RSFSR, whose population of 147.0 million left Ukraine's 51.5 million a distant second.[3]

A comparison of Soviet and Yugoslav institutions reveals equally striking differences. A merging of Serbian and federal institutions on the Russian-

Soviet model would have been inconceivable in socialist Yugoslavia.[4] Serbian and federal institutions were entirely separate, and in their complex relation to the latter, Serbs experienced both advantages and disadvantages. They were overrepresented among the cadres of some federal institutions: most importantly, almost 70 percent of the Yugoslav army's officers were Serbs and Montenegrins (who together made up 40 percent of the Yugoslav population). In the League of Communists of Yugoslavia (henceforth LCY), regional patterns were particularly significant: Serbs were overrepresented in the parties and the political structures of both Bosnia-Herzegovina and Croatia. (These patterns were due in part to Serbs' disproportionate participation in the Partisan movement.)[5] On the other hand, because most federal institutions—for example, the state and party presidencies and the federal legislature—were organized on the basis of republican parity, Yugoslavia's more populous republics, including Serbia, were also in a sense *underrepresented* at the federal level.

The difference between Russians' and Serbs' positions was perhaps most marked in the ideological sphere. In the USSR, the fusion of Russian and Soviet identities received a degree of official encouragement that had no counterpart in socialist Yugoslavia. As Veljko Vujačić has put it: "In sharp contrast to the official sponsorship of 'Soviet-Russian nationalism,' in Communist Yugoslavia 'Serbo-Yugoslavism' was not to be, and no toasts were ever raised to the special historic role played by the 'leading Serbian nation.'"[6] The Serbian content of "socialist Yugoslavism," in other words, was far weaker than the Russian content of "Soviet man."[7] Indeed, there was a complex and ambiguous relationship between Serbian national identity and "socialist Yugoslavism"—officially defined in carefully non-national terms as "a socialist Yugoslav consciousness, a Yugoslav socialist patriotism, which is not the opposite of but rather a necessary internationalist supplement to democratic national consciousness."[8] The victory of Tito's Partisans over the Serbian nationalist Chetniks during World War II represented (among other things) the victory of Yugoslav-oriented Serbs over Serbian-oriented ones. Throughout the socialist period, Serbian nationalism was tainted by its association with the defeated Chetniks. It is noteworthy, too, that Serb proponents of socialist Yugoslavism sometimes advocated renouncing elements of traditional Serbian identity such as the Cyrillic alphabet.[9]

In spite of these important differences, Russians and Serbs shared the basic dilemma that defined their positions within their multinational states. For both peoples, nation building and state building were conflicting imperatives: in asserting their own national identities, they risked undermining the legitimacy of the states they inhabited. (Hence Szporluk's widely cited distinction between Russian "nation-builders" and "empire-savers.")[10] Likewise, because both peoples had significant diasporas outside their "own" federal units, they had a structurally defined interest in maintaining their multinational states. The USSR for Russians, and Yugoslavia for Serbs, satisfied one of the main requirements of modern nationalism: that all the nation's members be included in one state. Twenty-four percent of Serbs lived outside Serbia—just over 40 percent if one counts as "outsiders" the Serb inhabitants of the Autonomous Provinces of Kosovo and Vojvodina, which had the de facto status of republics through much of the Titoist period. (By contrast, 22 percent of Croats and 19 percent of Muslims lived outside their "home" republics.)

The dispersal of Serbs among several of Yugoslavia's federal units was the central reason why, throughout most of the existence of both monarchist and socialist Yugoslavia, the majority of Serbs were convinced that as a group they had a unique interest in preserving the Yugoslav state. They believed in what Belgrade sociologist and opposition leader Vesna Pešić has called "a symbiosis between 'Serbianism' and 'Yugoslavism.'"[11] That belief was not significantly eroded until the mid-1980s. Even then (in fact, throughout the period of Yugoslavia's disintegration) Serbian nationalism in the radically anti-Yugoslav form that rejected *any* Yugoslav state remained a marginal phenomenon of little political significance.[12] What became decisive in Serbian politics was the line of thinking that held that the *existing* Yugoslav state was unendurable. Without this Serbian devaluation of Yugoslavia, and a concomitant willingness to risk its survival, Milošević could not have pursued his reckless brinkmanship—and in particular, his protracted confrontation with the Slovenes.[13] Without his aggressive actions and still more aggressive rhetoric, it would have been much harder for separatist forces in Slovenia and Croatia to move from marginal to dominant political positions.[14] The Serbian turn against Yugoslavism, therefore, was crucial to the collapse of the Yugoslav state. To put it another way, the phenomenon that is commonly called "the rise of Serbian nationalism" could just as accurately be labeled "the decline of Serbian Yugoslavism." Throughout the existence of both Yugoslavias, Serbian and Yugoslav modes of thought had coexisted, with the pendulum swinging sometimes toward one and sometimes toward the other.[15] Still, the *political* anti-Yugoslav Serbian nationalism that arose in the mid-1980s was a new phenomenon. To return to the question that opened this essay, how might Szporluk's interpretation of nationalism as a direct response to the crisis and failure of communism influence our understanding of the Serbian case?

By the mid-1980s, it was generally agreed that the Yugoslav system was in crisis. Indeed, discussions of the "crisis"—who or what was responsible for it, and what should be done about it—dominated political discourse in Yugoslavia.[16] The beginning of the crisis is difficult to date: 1979, when the economy began its eventually catastrophic decline; 1980, when Tito died; and 1981, when Kosovo exploded as Albanians sought republican status, are all reasonable starting points. Taken together, these events ushered in an era of political stalemate and economic hardship as Tito's successors fought to divide a shrinking economic pie. Although politicians had initially repudiated intellectuals' description of Yugoslavia's plight as a crisis, by early 1983 even the LCY president had accepted the term. Yugoslavia's leaders, working within a political system that required consensus for any major action at the federal level, proved quite unable to agree on how to find the "exit from the crisis." Meanwhile, the faltering economy was wreaking havoc on the daily lives of Yugoslavia's citizens. Inflation and unemployment both rose, real wages fell dramatically, and the consumer goods to which Yugoslavs had long been accustomed disappeared from store shelves.[17] A Western scholar writing in 1989 observed: "The decline in the standard of living has been so great that it is difficult to think of any other country that would not have responded with major political changes, or even revolution."[18]

The crisis is always included—more or less prominently—in general accounts of Yugoslavia's dissolution. In explanations of Serbian discontent with Yugoslavia, however, the crisis tends to recede into the background, or to be left out of the picture altogether. Overwhelmingly, Serbian mobilization is understood as a more or less manipulated response to specifically Serbian grievances connected with Yugoslavia's decentralization. Thus, Serbian nationalism is explained as a long-term consequence (an "unintended consequence," in the arguments of several scholars) of the postwar border decisions that left Serbs divided among several federal units, and Serbia itself divided into three parts; of the extensive devolution of power to Yugoslavia's federal units that culminated in the Constitution of 1974; or of the Titoist policies that encouraged nation building among other Yugoslav peoples.

A sampling of the large and growing literature on Yugoslavia's self-destruction will suffice to illustrate this point. Sabrina Petra Ramet, in a widely used text, has argued that "Milošević owes his rise, above all, to the growing Serbian bitterness about the demographic changes in Kosovo and Serbian fears that the province will be 'lost.'"[19] Paul Shoup has said: "Milošević's populist appeal reflects the deep feelings of frustration which built up in Serbia over the Kosovo question, and the fate of the Serbs, generally, in Tito's Yugoslavia . . ."[20] George Schöpflin has contended that Yugoslavia's decentralization and the encouragement of national self-assertion among its various groups "had a major unintended consequence—the rise of a Serbian separatist nationalism."[21] Veljko Vujačić articulates what appears to be the tacit theoretical understanding behind the dominant explanation when he argues that:

> In multinational contexts, "dominant nations" have no reason to develop a *particularist political nationalism* of their own. Both in the Soviet Union and Yugoslavia, Russian and Serbian nationalism developed largely as a reaction to peripheral nationalist movements threatening the larger state.[22]

There can be no question that the factors these authors cite—above all, Kosovo—were extremely important in shaping the content of the Serbian national movement. Kosovo has justly been called the catalyst of the Yugoslav tragedy, for the "Kosovo question"—the controversy over relations between the province's Albanian majority and its Serb minority, and over the reasons for Serbs' massive emigration—had repercussions far beyond the province.[23] With its potent tangle of myth-laden national history and present-day grievances, Kosovo became a prism through which *all* of Yugoslavia's Serbs could look, and see themselves as an endangered minority. Given that fewer than three percent of Yugoslavia's Serbs lived in Kosovo in the 1980s, this phenomenon offered remarkable proof of the power of intellectuals and the media to shape the "imagined community's" vision of itself. (The phrase, of course, is Benedict Anderson's.) But no matter how insistently Serbs might claim Kosovo as their historic heartland, the 1974 Yugoslav Constitution, which made Serbia's provinces "constituent parts of the federation" with representatives on every federal body, ensured that Kosovo was not simply an internal Serbian matter. When Milošević took up the cause of the Kosovo Serbs in the spring of 1987, he altered the dynamic of the Yugoslav crisis, pushing it from stagnation into the first stages of state collapse. To meet his pledge to reassert Serbian control over the provinces, Milošević had to restructure Yugoslavia— and his attempt to do so aroused the determined resistance of other republics.

It is this author's contention that analyses which present the rise of anti-Yugoslav Serbian nationalism simply as the result of Serbs' and Serbia's divisions within the Yugoslav state, although certainly not wrong, are incomplete. In positing this causal chain, even those scholars who are most critical of the Serbian national movement's goals appear to accept its premises, finding necessary and sufficient reasons for national mobilization in the grievances presented by the nationalists. Yugoslavia's systemic crisis, meanwhile, retreats into the background. At most, it is treated as a mass-level rather than an elite-level phenomenon—one that provided cannon fodder for nationalist ideologues rather than in any way shaping their thought.[24] One reason for this orientation is that most analysts of Yugoslavia's dissolution focus their interest on either the crisis or national ideologies, but not on both.[25] Another reason is that many scholars conceive of national ideologies as essentially static and unchanging— a point of view that clearly precludes investigation of how the crisis of communism might have shaped these ideologies' late-communist incarnations.[26]

Utilizing as a catalyst Szporluk's contention that dominant nations may turn from statism to particularism as a response to systemic crisis, rather than purely national grievances, I will now probe the connection between the Yugoslav crisis and anti-Yugoslav Serbian nationalism using one example of Serbian national ideology: the 1986 "Memorandum of the Serbian Academy." The Memorandum's oft-cited turn toward Serbian particularism was motivated as much by the crisis of Yugoslav self-managing socialism as by Serbian national grievances; it reflected not only preexisting national ideologies, but also the authors' conceptions of socialism and Yugoslavia's place in it.

The "Memorandum of the Serbian Academy" is by far the best-known document of the contemporary Serbian national movement.[27] It has been described (with considerable exaggeration) as the ultimate statement of exclusionary Serbian nationalism and as a "blueprint" for the Milošević movement and the post-Yugoslav wars.[28] Yet in spite of the Memorandum's notoriety, some basic facts about its provenance remain unknown. The outline of the story is well established. In May 1985, at the annual convention of the Serbian Academy of Sciences and Arts (SANU in its Serbian abbreviation), several speakers urged the Academy to become more involved in the search for solutions to the Yugoslav crisis. The economist Ivan Maksimović made the specific proposal that SANU should address "the most current . . . political, economic, social, scientific, and cultural problems in the form of a Memorandum, and that this Memorandum should be sent to all of those who are responsible for the conduct of public affairs in Serbia and in Yugoslavia."[29] Soon after the convention, the SANU presidency named a sixteen-member commission to prepare a "Memorandum on Current Social Questions." The commission in its turn appointed an eight-member working group.[30] No one has conclusively established specific responsibility for the various parts of the draft document that eventually emerged from the working group. Both internal and external evidence, however, suggests that key roles were played by economist Kosta Mihailović (b. 1917), historian Vasilije Krestić (b. 1932), novelist Antonije Isaković (b. 1923), and philosopher Mihailo Marković (b. 1923). Marković's role is the most pertinent to the present study.[31]

By late September 1986, the working group had produced the draft document that became known as the Memorandum, and the commission as a whole began its review of the draft.[32] At this point, however, the commission's work came to a halt. A Belgrade newspaper published a two-part article revealing the Memorandum's existence, and quoting some passages. (The full text of the Memorandum was not published in Yugoslavia until 1989.) These revelations set off a political firestorm; the Memorandum was denounced throughout Serbia and Yugoslavia. In the furor that followed the September revelations, the Academy based its defense mainly on the fact that the document was a draft and had never actually been approved by the committee.[33]

The Memorandum consists of two parts, each about 25 pages long: "The Crisis of the Yugoslav Economy and Society," and "The Position of Serbia and the Serbian People."[34] It is a rambling and repetitive document, clearly a draft, and the work of multiple authors. More a patchwork than a coherent whole, it can only be described, not summarized. The following description is necessarily incomplete, including only those parts of the Memorandum that are relevant to the present argument.

The Memorandum opens with a warning that the Yugoslav crisis has become so serious that it could lead to the collapse of the state—a prediction that, in 1986, still seemed apocalyptic:

> Stagnation in the development of society, economic difficulties, increased social tensions and open clashes between nations evoke deep concern in our country. A serious crisis has taken hold of not only the political and economic system, but also the entire public order of the country. Idleness and irresponsibility at work, corruption and nepotism, the absence of legal security, bureaucratic caprice . . . are all everyday phenomena. The collapse of moral values and of the reputation of the leading institutions of society, [and] lack of

confidence in the competence of those who make decisions result in the apathy and embitterment of the people, [and] alienation of the individual from all the holders and symbols of public order. An objective appraisal of Yugoslav reality allows for the possibility that the current crisis may finish in social disturbances with unforeseeable consequences, not even excluding a result as catastrophic as the collapse of the Yugoslav state unit.[35]

Much of the Memorandum's first section is devoted to explaining the Yugoslav economy's low productivity, seen as the underlying cause of all of Yugoslavia's economic woes. Some of the factors cited (for example, the blind adherence to the labor theory of value) imply a critique of Marxist economic principles in general, but most of the blame is assigned to the economic reforms of the mid-1960s. This is the first statement of a conviction that recurs throughout the Memorandum: that Yugoslavia followed a promising path from 1948 to the mid-1960s, and then took a catastrophic wrong turn. According to the Memorandum, the reforms—meant to downgrade planning in favor of market mechanisms—instead destroyed planning without liberating market forces. At the same time, the political leaders of each republic and province took over control of their own economies, running them not to promote economic development but to increase their own power.[36] The final result is the current economic crisis—a crisis that can only be resolved through fundamental political change.

The disintegration of the Yugoslav economy, the Memorandum argues, ultimately reflects the transformation of the Yugoslav federation founded by the Partisans in 1943 into the confederation embodied in the 1974 Constitution.[37] That constitution, and particularly its requirement that all major decisions be made by consensus, has made the Yugoslav political system "a textbook case of inefficiency."[38] In politics as in economics, the Memorandum traces the roots of disaster to the 1960s. It was in the 1960s that the process of democratization ended, to be replaced by "bureaucratic decentralization."[39] Now, democratization is essential to the resolution of the crisis. Here the Memorandum comes very close to endorsing multiparty democracy, and it does explicitly call for multicandidate elections.[40]

From Yugoslavia's economic and political crisis, the Memorandum turns to its moral and ideological one.[41] The morality of the revolution, it argues, has been defeated, and no other morality has replaced it: "The gap between socialist principles and reality is so great that it engenders apathy on a mass scale."[42] This failure is once again traced back to "the fatal turning point of 1965." Here, that turning point is described in terms highly reminiscent of the Marxist-humanist critique put forward in the 1960s and 1970s by the Praxis group to which Mihailo Marković belonged: "The project of political democratization was replaced by a project of economic liberalization. The idea of self-management—the essence of which is ending the alienation of politics—was replaced by the idea of decentralization which led to the establishment of regional centers of alienated power."[43]

Among the reasons cited for this wrong turn are the materialism of the "new middle class," domination of the Yugoslav political system by the more developed republics, and the revolutionary project's inherent over-reliance on violence and dictatorship. To find its way out of the crisis, the Memorandum continues, Yugoslavia must abandon the political and economic system based on the 1974 Constitution for one based on "the four great principles of modern society": sovereignty of the people, self-determination of the nation, human rights, and "rationality" (which, according to the Memorandum, requires that a modern state function as a unified whole).[44]

The Memorandum's second half, "The Position of Serbia and the Serbian People," begins with the assertion that Serbs, besides facing the same difficulties as everyone else in Yugoslavia, confront three additional problems: "the economic backwardness of Serbia, its unresolved state-legal relations with Yugoslavia and with the provinces, and the genocide in Kosovo."[45] As this list suggests, this section actually devotes much more attention to "the position of Serbia" (including the provinces) than to "the Serbian people" elsewhere in Yugoslavia. In this respect, it is typical of Serbian national discourse in the mid-1980s. Serbia's "economic subordination," the Memorandum claims, reflects its "politically inferior position" within Yugoslavia, which Slovenia and Croatia have tailored to suit themselves.[46] The Memorandum asserts: "it cannot be disputed that Slovenia and Croatia have established political and economic domination, through which they realize their national programs and economic aspirations."[47]

It is this section that includes the Memorandum's best-known assertions: that the Serb population in Kosovo is the victim of "physical, political, legal, and cultural genocide" carried out by Albanian nationalists determined to create an "ethnically pure" Kosovo, and that the very survival of Serbs in Croatia is threatened by assimilation. Regarding the latter, the Memorandum states that, "except during the existence of the Independent State of Croatia [the World War II fascist state that attempted genocide against its Serb population], Serbs in Croatia were never as endangered in the past as they are today."[48] Today, these claims ring with the tragic irony of self-fulfilling prophecies. It is very clear that the hyperbolic fears they embodied, by driving Serbs to acts of "defensive" aggression, helped set in motion the events that ultimately led to the destruction of Serb communities in both Kosovo and Croatia.

In its conclusion, the Memorandum makes explicit the assumption that unites its two halves: Yugoslavia's decentralization lies at the root of both the Yugoslav crisis and the problems of the Serbian nation. "By insisting on a federal [as opposed to confederal] order," it contends, "Serbia would contribute not only to the equality of all nations in Yugoslavia, but also to the resolution of the political and economic crisis."[49] The Serbian people must be allowed to realize its "historic and democratic right" to establish its "full national and cultural integrity . . . regardless of which republic or province it is in."[50] To this vague demand the Memorandum adds two specific proposals: at least one chamber of the federal legislature should be elected according to the one-man, one-vote principle, rather than republican parity; and the autonomy of Serbia's provinces should be reduced to a level that does not "destroy the integrity of the Republic."[51]

To this point—that is, until its last two pages—the Memorandum is a plea for a transformed Yugoslavia. Then, almost in passing, it returns to the possibility hinted at in its very first paragraph: the collapse of the Yugoslav state. Others in Yugoslavia, it says, are considering alternatives to the Yugoslav state, and so must Serbia. Serbia supports "AVNOJ Yugoslavia" (that is, a relatively centralized federation like the one the Partisans set up in 1943), but others may not. "Therefore, [Serbia] faces the task of looking clearly at its economic and national interests so as not to be surprised by events."[52]

This is as far as the Memorandum goes in envisioning a post-Yugoslav future. It obviously does not call for Yugoslavia's dissolution. In fact, compared to much of the anti-Yugoslav rhetoric rife in Serbia a few years later, the Memorandum's critique appears mild. Nevertheless, contemporaries (as well as later observers) were right to see in the Memorandum a turn toward "Serbian nationalism of the separatist type."[53] A more centralized Yugoslavia might be the Memorandum's first choice, but its second choice appears to be some form of Serbian state—not the highly decentralized, consensus-dependent Yugoslavia that existed in 1986. In fact, one might say that the Memorandum's authors wanted a more centralized state so much that they were prepared to leave Yugoslavia to get it.

Scholars who have discussed the Memorandum's turn away from Yugoslavia and toward Serbian particularism have interpreted it in exclusively national terms: the Yugoslav state was rejected because it had become a barrier to Serbian national unity. In other words, they have ignored or discounted the Memorandum's first section in favor of its second.[54] The Memorandum's authors, of course, claimed that the crisis as well as the Serbian question motivated their attack on Yugoslav decentralization. (Many observers both inside and outside Yugoslavia would have agreed that the Memorandum's argument that republican prerogatives and consensus requirements were stalemating the search for an "exit from the crisis" was quite correct as far as it went. The problem lay in its failure to recognize that at least some of Yugoslavia's nations saw in these same prerogatives and requirements the only safeguards for their national existence within the multinational state.)

How might our interpretation of the Memorandum change if we took seriously its authors' claim to be responding to the Yugoslav crisis as well as the Serbian national predicament, and tried to understand what factors (besides their national affiliation) shaped their understanding of the crisis? An analysis along these lines suggests that the authors' call for recentralization was based on their understanding of Yugoslav socialism as well as their understanding of the Serbian national problem. Simply put, their belief in the uniqueness of Yugoslav socialism was so strong that they saw the Yugoslav crisis entirely in state terms, as a result of the Constitution of 1974, and *not* as part of the broader crisis of Soviet and East European socialism. Most of the members of the Memorandum Commission, it should be noted, belonged to the Partisan generation (those in their teens or early twenties at the outbreak of the Second World War), and several had fought with the Partisans or otherwise taken part in the resistance. Their loyalty to Yugoslav socialism in what they considered its pristine form—as it developed after the 1948 break with Stalin and before the "wrong turn" of 1964–1965—was still very much in evidence in the mid-1980s.

An examination of the Memorandum's first paragraph (cited above) reveals some of the consequences of this orientation. By defining the Yugoslav crisis in predominantly social terms, with only a passing reference to "clashes between nations," this paragraph suggests that what it is describing is the failure of a communist system, rather than the breakdown of a multinational state. This impression is heightened by the Memorandum's first word—stagnation (*zastoj*)—a word associated with the problems of late communism, and specifically with Gorbachev's critique of Brezhnev. In February 1986, just a few months before the Memorandum's authors held their first meeting, Gorbachev had included a conspicuous attack on "phenomena of stagnation [*zastoinye iavleniia*]" in his speech to the 27th Congress of the CPSU.[55] And yet the Memorandum's authors, even while choosing this word to begin their critique of Yugoslav self-managing socialism, reveal no awareness of this echo, or of the possibility that Yugoslavia's crisis might form part of the broader crisis of socialism. Shaped by their experience of the Second World War and the 1948 break with Stalin, they were convinced that Yugoslavia had nothing in common with the countries of "real socialism." It was this belief in Yugoslav uniqueness—which they paradoxically maintained even while denouncing Tito and all his (post-1965) works—that gave their thinking about the Yugoslav crisis its strangely parochial quality, and allowed them to echo Gorbachev without making any connection between the Yugoslav crisis and the broader socialist one.

That this blinkered view of the Yugoslav crisis resulted from conviction, and not from any ignorance of contemporary events, could not be proved from the Memorandum itself. It emerges very clearly, however, from an article that Mihailo Marković wrote in August 1986 (during the period that he was involved in work on the Memorandum). This article, "Jugoslovenska kriza i nacionalno pitanje" (The Yugoslav Crisis and the National Question), offers analyses of both the crisis and the Serbian predicament that closely resemble the Memorandum's.[56] Like the Memorandum, it insists that some degree of state recentralization is necessary both to resolve the Yugoslav crisis and to give the Serbian people "national equality." Like the Memorandum (and like Marković's earlier Praxis critique), it maintains that Yugoslavia followed a promising path from 1948 to the mid-1960s and then took a wrong turn.[57] Finally, and more explicitly than the Memorandum, Marković argues that if

Yugoslavia's other peoples will not agree to reform the Yugoslav state in accordance with the Serbian critique, Serbs should acquiesce in those peoples' leaving Yugoslavia.[58]

Unlike the Memorandum, Marković's essay explicitly develops the idea of the uniqueness of Yugoslav socialism. Marković maintains that those who set up the dichotomy "Europe [or] Bolshevism," and blame Yugoslavia's ills on the latter, are mistaken. Socialism as such cannot be responsible for the crisis, he argues, for socialist systems have met with varying degrees of success in different countries (more, for instance, in East Germany than in Romania), and at different times (more in Yugoslavia before 1965 than after). Moreover, Yugoslav socialism is unique because it came to power through the Partisan struggle, because it broke with Stalin in 1948, and because it has been open to influences from the West.[59]

Marković's assumption that Yugoslavia's crisis is fundamentally one of the state rather than of socialism unites his article's two subjects, "the Yugoslav crisis" and "the [Serbian] national question." The same assumption—though here implicit rather than explicit—unites the Memorandum's two parts. Serb intellectuals who addressed the Yugoslav crisis without sharing the commitment to Yugoslavia's socialist system could come to very different conclusions. For instance, in a 1988 symposium with the provocative title "Yugoslavia—The Day Before Yesterday, Yesterday, Today. Tomorrow?" novelist Slobodan Selenić argued that because "Bolshevik dogmatism [had] contributed to compromising Yugoslavia as a state unit," it would be impossible to tell whether the Yugoslav *state* was worth keeping until the country tried a different *social system*.[60]

The commitment of the authors of the Memorandum to Yugoslav socialism had important political as well as theoretical consequences. When Slobodan Milošević formed his Socialist Party of Serbia in July 1990, Mihailo Marković became the Party's Vice President, and he and three other members of the Memorandum Commission were elected to its governing board.[61] Meanwhile, Kosta Mihailović became one of Milošević's top advisers.[62] These links lend support to the common contention that the Memorandum was in some sense a "blueprint" for Milošević. Yet what made it so was not its vaguely defined national program, which was simply the commitment to Serbian unity that all major Serbian parties shared in the period of Yugoslavia's dissolution. Rather, what was specific to the Memorandum *and* to the Milošević program was the conviction that the Yugoslav state, and not the Yugoslav social system, was at the root of the crisis. To be sure, both the Memorandum and Milošević advocated many systemic reforms, but they presented those reforms as a means of returning to an earlier, more authentic, version of self-managing socialism. Milošević's notoriously misleading 1990 campaign slogan—"With us, there is no uncertainty"—promised security to an electorate afraid that any change would be for the worse. When the anticommunist opposition insisted on the need for change, using the rhetoric of "1989" to identify Milošević's Socialist

Party with the East European regimes toppled by that year's revolutions, Milošević countered with "1948": that is, he maintained that Yugoslav socialism had nothing in common with the East Bloc model.[63]

The term crisis (derived from the Greek verb *krinein*, to separate) implies a point of decision, a metaphorical parting of the ways that forces the choice of one path or another. However badly this concept may fit a "crisis" of more than ten years' duration, it remains essential to understanding the significance of the national programs that emerged in Yugoslavia's last years. The programs put forward by Serbs, Croats, Slovenes, and others were not simply responses to particular nationally defined grievances. They were also the respective elites' bids to rescue their own peoples from the crisis that had engulfed Yugoslavia.

Moreover, these programs engendered conflict and ultimately violence not only because they made incompatible demands on the Yugoslav state, but also because competition between them occurred in a context in which the status quo was considered unendurable, and action—in one direction or another— essential. This point is emphasized because it challenges the view that considers Yugoslavia's dissolution as a more or less inevitable consequence of the incompatibility of its peoples' national ideologies.[64] Serbian, Croatian, and Slovene nation-state ideologies were always incompatible with a multinational Yugoslav state—but it was systemic failure that catapulted these ideologies from relative insignificance to political prominence.[65] In the case of the Memorandum, it was the authors' commitment to state centralization as a means of resolving the crisis, as much as their commitment to Serbian national unity, that made them willing to sacrifice Yugoslavia in order to obtain a more centralized state. Their anti-Yugoslav Serbian nationalism was, to paraphrase Szporluk, "a reaction to the failure of Yugoslavism, broadly defined."

NOTES

The scholars and institutions who assisted me in the doctoral research on which this essay is based are too numerous to acknowledge here. Special thanks are due, however, to Roman Szporluk, who guided me through my dissertation and inspired the present essay, and to the Harvard Academy for International and Area Studies for its generous support.

1. Roman Szporluk, "The National Question," in *After the Soviet Union: From Empire to Nations*, ed. Timothy J. Colton and Robert Legvold (New York, 1992), p. 88. In this passage, after arguing that "a reasonably successful economic reform under Gorbachev might conceivably have prevented the emergence of a mass-scale nationalist challenge to Moscow's rule in Ukraine," Szporluk goes on to say: "Even less probably would an anti-Soviet *Russian* nationalism have risen without a growing realization that not only Gorbachev but the October Revolution itself had failed to deliver on *its* promises."

2. Veljko Vujačić makes a compelling distinction between Russians' "imperial" and Serbs' "dominant" position in his elegant "Historical Legacies, Nationalist Mobilization, and Political Outcomes in Russia and Serbia: A Weberian View," *Theory and Society* 25 (1996): 763–801. Cf. Reneo Lukic and Allen Lynch, *Europe from the Balkans to the Urals: The Disintegration of Yugoslavia and the Soviet Union* (Oxford, 1996). Lukic and Lynch assert that "Serbia—and Serbs—never dominated Communist Yugoslavia to the extent that Russians dominated the USSR" (p. 4). See also Bogdan Denitch, "Dilemma of the Dominant Ethnic Group," in *Ethnic Russia in the USSR: The Dilemma of Dominance,* ed. Edward Allworth (New York, 1980), pp. 315–24. Portions of this section are adapted from the introduction to my dissertation, "Serb Intellectuals and the National Question, 1961–1991," Ph.D. dissertation, Harvard University, 1998.

3. For the Yugoslav population figures, see Ruža Petrović, *Migracije u Jugoslaviji i etnički aspekt* (Belgrade, 1990), pp. 31, 50.

4. For the impact of the merging of Russian and Soviet institutions, see Edward Allworth, part 5, "RSFSR or USSR: Confusing a Part with the Whole," in *Ethnic Russia*, pp. 178–204. Cf. Vujačić, "Historical Legacies," pp. 779–80.

5. See Lenard Cohen, *The Socialist Pyramid: Elites and Power in Yugoslavia* (Oakville, ON, 1989), particularly chapter 7; and, for the 1980s, John R. Lampe, *Yugoslavia as History: Twice There Was a Country* (Cambridge, 1996), p. 337.

6. Vujačić, "Historical Legacies," p. 781.

7.   Two useful essays on the Russian content of "Soviet man" are Oleh S. Fedyshyn, "The Role of Russians among the New, Unified 'Soviet People,'" and Rusian O. Rasiak, "'The Soviet People': Multiethnic Alternative or Ruse?"—both in Allworth's *Ethnic Russia,* pp. 149–58 and 159–71, respectively.

8.   From chapter 8 of the 1958 Program of the League of Communists of Yugoslavia, in *Manifest Komunističke Partije i Program Saveza komunista Jugoslavije* (Split, n.d.), pp. 256–57.

9.   This argument is developed more fully in my "Yugoslavs into Serbs: Serbian National Identity, 1961–1971," *Nationalities Papers* 25(3) September 1997: 407–426.

10. Roman Szporluk, "Dilemmas of Russian Nationalism," *Problems of Communism* 38(4) 1989: 15–35. Cf. Allworth's somewhat different argument in his editorial introduction: "A Russian Dilemma: Political Equality or Ethnic Neutrality in the RSFSR and USSR," in *Ethnic Russia,* pp. xiii–xxi.

11. Vesna Pešić, "Serbian Nationalism and the Origins of the Yugoslav Crisis," *Peaceworks* 8 (April 1996): 15.

12. For some examples, see Aleksandar Pavković, "The Serb National Idea: A Revival 1986–1992," *Slavonic and East European Review* 72 (July 1994): 440–55.

13. This thesis is convincingly developed in Olivera Milosavljević, "Jugoslavija kao zabluda: Odnos intelektualnih i političkih elita prema zajedničkoj državi," *Republika* 8(135–36) 1–31 March 1996: I–XVI.

14. A compelling brief analysis of the events leading up to Yugoslavia's collapse is Dennison Rusinow's "The Avoidable Catastrophe," in *Beyond Yugoslavia: Politics, Economics, and Culture in a Shattered Community,* ed. Sabrina Petra Ramet and Ljubiša S. Adamovich (Boulder, CO, 1995), pp. 13–38. For an authoritative treatment with more detail, see chapters 6–8 in Lenard J. Cohen, *Broken Bonds: Yugoslavia's Disintegration and Balkan Politics in Transition* (Boulder, CO, 1995).

15. This process is the central theme of my dissertation, "Serb Intellectuals."

16. An excellent discussion of political responses to the crisis is chapter 2 of Cohen, *Broken Bonds.* The best single introduction to Yugoslavia in the early 1980s is the collection of articles in *Yugoslavia in the 1980s,* ed. Pedro Ramet (Boulder, CO, 1985). For the decade as a whole, a very useful analysis with a mainly economic focus is Harold Lydall, *Yugoslavia in Crisis* (Oxford, 1989). For the early use of the term crisis, see Zagorka Golubović, "Od dijagnoze do objašnjenja 'jugoslovenskog slučaja,'" *Sociološki pregled* 27 (1993): 43; and (for LCY President

Mitja Ribičić) Pedro Ramet, "Yugoslavia and the Threat of Internal and External Discontents," *Orbis* 28(1) 1984: 109.

17. See chapter 3 of Lydall, *Yugoslavia in Crisis*; and Susan L. Woodward, *Balkan Tragedy: Chaos and Dissolution after the Cold War* (Washington, DC, 1995), pp. 50–57.

18. Lydall, *Yugoslavia in Crisis*, p. 9.

19. Sabrina Petra Ramet, *Nationalism and Federalism in Yugoslavia, 1962–1991*, rev. ed. (Boulder, CO, 1992), p. 230.

20. Paul Shoup, "Titoism and the National Question in Yugoslavia: A Reassessment," *Yearbook of European Studies* 5 (1992): 70. Elsewhere in the article, in discussing the general process of Yugoslavia's disintegration, Shoup gives great weight to the crisis.

21. George Schöpflin, "The Rise and Fall of Yugoslavia," in *The Politics of Ethnic Conflict Regulation: Case Studies of Protracted Ethnic Conflicts*, ed. John McGarry and Brendan O'Leary (London, 1993), p. 194.

22. Vujačić, "Historical Legacies," p. 774. Vujačić also asserts (p. 763) that "in both cases, the long-term causes of disintegration can be attributed to the unintended consequences of Communist policy on nationalities that contributed to the process of nation building, especially among the peripheral nations with a hitherto weak or not fully developed national consciousness." For the Yugoslav case, this assertion is open to question. The responsibility for Yugoslavia's breakup, after all, lies far more with Serbs, Croats, and Slovenes, who certainly entered the communist era with a "fully developed national consciousness," than with Muslims and Macedonians, the main objects of communist nation building.

23. Shkëlzen Maliqi, "Kosovo kao katalizator jugoslovenske krize," in *Kosovo—Srbija—Jugoslavija*, ed. Slavko Gaber and Tonči Kuzmanić (Ljubljana, 1989), pp. 69–76.

24. See, for example, Lenard Cohen's treatment of "Nationalism as an Elite Resource," in his sophisticated analysis of the Milošević movement. Even while emphasizing that Milošević's mass support depended in part on his promise to resolve the crisis, Cohen attributes his appeal to nationally minded Serb intellectuals simply to his "bold assertion of Serbian interests and his radical departure from Titoist strategies for managing the 'national question'" (Cohen, *Broken Bonds*, pp. 53–54).

25. It is striking that authors who focus on the emergence of Serbian national ideologies tend to give little emphasis to the Yugoslav crisis, while authors who give the crisis center stage give short shrift to ideologies. Examples of the first approach include Ivo Banac, "The Fearful Asymmetry of War: The Causes and Consequences of Yugoslavia's Demise," *Daedalus* 121 (Spring 1992): 141–74; Jasna Dragović, "Les intellectuels

serbes et la question nationale," *L'autre Europe* 30–31 (1995): 98–130 (although Dragović gives more weight to the crisis in her "Les intellectuels serbes dans les années 1980," in *Histoire comparée des intellectuels* [Paris, 1997], pp. 129–41); Nicholas Miller, "Reconstituting Serbia, 1945–1991," in *State-Society Relations in Yugoslavia, 1945–1992*, ed. Melissa Bokovoy et al. (London, 1997), pp. 291–314; Aleksandar Pavković, "Intellectual Dissidence and the Serb National Question," in *Nationalism and Postcommunism: A Collection of Essays*, ed. Aleksandar Pavković et al. (Aldershot, 1995), pp. 121–40, and his "The Serb National Idea." Examples of the second approach include Bogdan Denitch, *Ethnic Nationalism: The Tragic Death of Yugoslavia* (Minneapolis, 1994) and Woodward's *Balkan Tragedy.*

26.   Thus, Olivera Milosavljević, while emphasizing that national ideologies were put forward in politics in response to the Yugoslav crisis, denies that the crisis shaped their content. She maintains that "the basic points of dissatisfaction with the Yugoslav state, the ideologies, the demands and the means of achieving them were identical, whether they were defined in the 1930s or the 1980s ... " (Milosavljević, "Jugoslavija kao zabluda," p. II).

27.   Most of the material in this section has been adapted from "Turning-Point: The 'Memorandum of the Serbian Academy,'" ch. 6 of my dissertation, "Serb Intellectuals." The reader may refer to that chapter for more detail.

In English, there is a brief discussion of the Memorandum and its political context in Laura Silber and Allan Little, *Yugoslavia: Death of a Nation* (New York, 1995), pp. 31–33. Another good source (with more on the Memorandum's content) is Pavković, "Intellectual Dissidence."

Useful discussions from ex-Yugoslavia include Slavoljub Đukić, *Kako se dogodio vođa* (Belgrade, 1992), pp. 111–21, and the same author's slightly different discussion in *Između slave i anateme: politička biografija Slobodana Miloševića* (Belgrade, 1994), pp. 43–48. Đukić, a journalist, concentrates on the political events surrounding the Memorandum. Two in-depth (and highly critical) analytic discussions are Olivera Milosavljević's "Upotreba autoriteta nauke: Javna politička delatnost Srpske akademije nauka i umetnosti (1986–1992)," *Republika* 7(119–20) 1–31 July 1995: II–VI, and the same author's "Jugoslavija kao zabluda," pp. III–VII. See also Miloš Mišović, "Od Memoranduma do rata," *Vreme* (24 August 1992): I–VIII. An interesting discussion of the Memorandum's economic argument is Ljubomir Madžar, "Ko koga eksploatiše," *Republika* 7(123) 1–15 September 1995: I–XVI.

The full text of the Memorandum, which was first published in Yugoslavia in 1989 in the Zagreb journal *Naše teme* 33(1–2), appears in Kosta Mihailović and Vasilije Krestić, *"Memorandum SANU" Odgovori na kritike* (Belgrade, 1995), pp. 101–147. This work by two of the Memorandum's authors is a defense of the Memorandum against its many critics. It also includes a brief account of the work of the Memorandum Commission. It has been published in English as *Memorandum of the Serbian Academy of Sciences and Arts: Answers to Criticisms* (Belgrade, 1995).

28.   For instance, Sabrina Petra Ramet has asserted that the Memorandum "did more than any other tract or pamphlet written up to then to mobilize Serbian resentment of non-Serbs and legitimate Serbian hatred of all non-Serbs, whether inside or outside Yugoslavia." Sabrina P. Ramet, *Balkan Babel: Politics, Culture and Religion in Yugoslavia* (Boulder, CO, 1996), p. 200. Branka Magaš calls the Memorandum "a document that provided the blueprint not only for Serbia's onslaught upon the entire Federal order, but also for the 1991–1992 war." Branka Magaš, *The Destruction of Yugoslavia: Tracking the Break-Up 1980–92* (London, 1993), p. 4.

29.   Maksimović, SANU *Godišnjak* 92 (1986): 97.

30.   A list of commission members, along with a brief account of the commission's work, appears in the proceedings for the December 1986 SANU Convention. *Vanredna skupština Srpske akademije nauka i umetnosti, održana 18. decembra 1986. godine* (Belgrade, 1989), p. 12.

31.   I interviewed Isaković, Krestić, and Mihailović, among others, in the spring of 1994, but found no one willing to assign or claim responsibility for specific parts of the Memorandum text. Krestić stated that no one person had a decisive role: each individual worked on his own section of the text, and any member of the commission could offer ideas or objections.

Isaković headed both the Commission and the Working Group (Krestić and Mihailović, *"Memorandum SANU,"* pp. 14–15). Krestić described himself in a 1991 interview as "one of the authors of the Memorandum, and precisely of that part which deals with national problems." Miloš Jevtić, *Istoričari: Radovan Samardžić, Sima Ćirković, Vasilije Krestić, Čedomir Popov* (Belgrade, 1992), p. 160. Kosta Mihailović's biographical entry in the SANU Yearbook describes him as "one of the authors of the Memorandum" (SANU *Godišnjak* 100 [1994]: 365). Moreover, a pair of usually well-informed journalists have written that Mihailović "is widely believed to be the Memorandum's main author." Silber and Little, *Yugoslavia*, p. 36n1. Finally, Krestić and Mihailović coauthored the defense of the Memorandum (*"Memorandum SANU" Odgovori na kritike*) published by SANU in 1995. Internal evidence for Marković's role is discussed below.

A number of observers have claimed that novelist Dobrica Ćosić was one of the Memorandum's authors, or even its principal author. (See, e.g., Ramet, *Balkan Babel*, p. 200.) Both Ćosić himself and the Memorandum's acknowledged authors have repeatedly denied that he wrote any part of the Memorandum. Ćosić *has* said, however, that he received the draft of the Memorandum in September, and offered the Commission 38 pages of comments just before its work was interrupted. I have found no reason to believe that Ćosić wrote any part of the Memorandum. Its heavily economic emphasis is quite foreign to Ćosić, who has never shown much interest in the specifics of economic policy. And much of what is common to both the Memorandum and Ćosić— such as the interpretation of events in Kosovo—is too general, and was too pervasive among Serb intellectuals in the mid-1980s, to be proof of either authorship or influence. Nevertheless, some parallels between the Memorandum and Ćosić are close enough to suggest his influence, whether exerted directly during the Memorandum's preparation, or indirectly through prior influence on its authors. It is difficult to distinguish between the two, because Ćosić's ideas were so well known among nationally minded Belgrade intellectuals by the time the Memorandum was written.

For more on the question of the Memorandum's sources, see Budding, "Serb Intellectuals," pp. 331–45.

32. See Mihailović and Krestić, *"Memorandum SANU,"* pp. 14–17. Except for the composition of the Working Group, it adds relatively little information to the report that SANU General Secretary and Commission member Dejan Medaković delivered to the SANU Extraordinary Convention held in December 1986 (*Vanredna skupština*, pp. 11–16). See also the convention speeches of Ivan Maksimović (*Vanredna skupština*, pp. 65–69) and Kosta Mihailović (*Vanredna skupština*, pp. 112–13).

33. See *Vanredna skupština*, passim.

34. All citations are taken from the text of the Memorandum published in Krestić and Mihailović, *"Memorandum SANU,"* pp. 101–147. The translations are mine.

35. *"Memorandum SANU,"* p. 101.

36. Ibid., pp. 101–106.

37. Ibid., pp. 110–18.

38. Ibid., p. 111.

39. Ibid., p. 114.

40. Ibid., p. 115.

41. Ibid., pp. 118–20.

42. Ibid., p. 120.

43. A useful monograph on the Praxis group's philosophy and history is Gerson S. Sher, *Praxis: Marxist Criticism and Dissent in Socialist Yugoslavia* (Bloomington, 1977). See also Leszek Kolakowski's pithy discussion in his *Main Currents of Marxism*, trans. P. S. Falla, 3 vols. (Oxford, 1978), vol. 3, pp. 474–78. Miloje Petrović's *Savremena jugoslovenska filozofija: filozofske teme i filozofska situacija 1945–1970* (Subotica, 1979) is a useful study with more detail on the Yugoslav context.

    For specific parallels with Marković's earlier critique, see, for instance, his "Nacionalizam i osnovna ljudska prava, Zimski filosofski susreti, Tara, 5–7 February 1972," *Filosofija* 16(1) 1972: 6.

44. *"Memorandum SANU,"* pp. 121–25.

45. Ibid., p. 126.

46. Ibid., p. 128.

47. Ibid., p. 129.

48. Ibid., pp. 134 and 136 (for Kosovo), and p. 139 (for Croatia).

49. Ibid., p. 146.

50. Ibid., p. 144.

51. Ibid., p. 145.

52. Ibid., p. 146.

53. Belgrade Party chief Dragiša Pavlović, cited in *Borba* 16 October 1986.

54. It is striking, for instance, that Dennison Rusinow includes only the Memorandum's second section in a collection of documents intended to illustrate the rise of nationalism in Yugoslavia, dismissing the first section with the statement that it "discusses 'the crisis of the Yugoslav economy and society' in terms widely accepted throughout Yugoslavia by 1986." Rusinow, "The Yugoslav Peoples," in *Eastern European Nationalism in the Twentieth Century,* ed. Peter F. Sugar (Washington, DC, 1995), p. 332n5. Olivera Milosavljević focuses both her analyses of the Memorandum on the second part, dismissing the first part as completely contradictory to the second: "Begun as an analysis of the crisis of Yugoslav society in general, and finished as a model for a Serbian national program, the Memorandum fell into contradictory interpretations . . . " Milosavljević, "Upotreba," p. III.

55. See Gorbachev's speech of 25 February 1986, in his *Izbrannye rechi i stat'i,* 7 vols. (Moscow, 1987–), vol. 3, p. 181.

56. Mihailo Marković, "Jugoslovenska kriza i nacionalno pitanje," *Gledišta* 29 (March–April 1988): 129–60. (The author's note on the first page indicates that the piece was written in August 1986.)

57. See especially Marković, "Jugoslovenska kriza," pp. 135–40.

58.   Ibid., pp. 158–60.

59.   Ibid., pp. 129–35.

60.   *Književne novine* forum "Jugoslavija—prekjuče, juče, danas. Sutra?"
      held 8 November 1988, reprinted in *Književne novine* 1 December 1988
      and 15 December 1988–1 January 1989. For a more developed version of
      this argument, see the critique of Marković's article by his Praxis col-
      league Zagorka Golubović, "Diskusija o saopštenju Mihaila Markovića
      'Jugoslovenska kriza i nacionalno pitanje,'" *Gledišta* 29 (May–June
      1988): 215–26.

61.   *NIN*, 20 July 1990.

62.   For Marković and Isaković, see Aleksandar Pavković, "Intellectuals into
      Politicians—Serbia 1990–1992," *Meanjin* 52(1) 1993: 107–116. For
      Mihailović, see Silber and Little, *Yugoslavia*, p. 36n1. Also, see the post-
      1987 functions listed in Mihailović's biography in SANU *Godišnjak* 100
      (1994): 365–71.

63.   See, for example, *Borba* 11 May 1990.Useful analyses of the strategies
      pursued by Milošević and others in the 1990 elections include Vladimir
      Goati et al., eds., *Izborne borbe u Jugoslaviji 1990–1992* (Belgrade,
      1993) and Dubravka Stojanović, "Traumatični krug srpske opozicije,"
      Republika 7 (1–31 October 1995): I–XVI.

64.   The most eloquent exponent of this view is undoubtedly Ivo Banac, who
      calls the failures of both Yugoslav states "structurally unavoidable,"
      attributing them to the clash of irreconcilable national ideologies (above
      all, those of Serbs and Croats). See Banac's "Preface to the Second
      Paperback Printing" of his *The National Question in Yugoslavia: Ori-
      gins, History, Politics* (Ithaca, 1991), p. 15, and his "The Origins and
      Development of the Concept of Yugoslavia (to 1945)," *Yearbook of
      European Studies* 5 (1992): 22. Banac and similarly minded scholars do
      not, of course, subscribe to the primordialist view of Yugoslavia's na-
      tional conflicts often summarized as "ancient ethnic hatreds." Rather,
      they share a conviction that by 1918 (or by 1945 at the latest), two or
      more of Yugoslavia's peoples had acquired cultural, ideological, or his-
      torical freight that made their coexistence in a Yugoslav state impos-
      sible.

      This author's view is closer to that put forward by John Lampe in his
      Yugoslavia as History. Lampe argues that "state-building rationales"
      competed with national ideologies throughout the existence of both
      Yugoslavias, and that the eventual victory of the ideologies depended on
      external as well as internal factors. See the broader argument in George
      Schöpflin, "Nationhood, Communism, and State Legitimation," *Nations
      and Nationalism* 1(1) 1995: 81–91.

65. In this connection, it is worth noting that the late 1960s, which saw
     nationalist movements emerge in several parts of Yugoslavia, were also a
     time of perceived systemic crisis. See Budding, "Yugoslavs into Serbs,"
     pp. 417–18.

Europe West and East:
Thoughts on History, Culture, and Kosovo

WALTER D. CONNOR

On 21 June 1999, when President Clinton evoked the prospect of a peaceful and prosperous Balkan future in words aimed primarily at Serbs and Kosovar Albanians, he was speaking in Slovenia. The distance between Ljubljana and Belgrade (or Priština) on the map is not great; the distance in ways more consequential could not be greater. A star performer among postcommunist states, Slovenia had chalked up a record of smooth democratic transition and impressive economic performance since its break from the collapsing Yugoslavia. Prosperous and orderly, Slovenia was fast-tracked for entrance into the European Union along with post-Soviet Estonia and recent NATO entrants Poland, Hungary, and the Czech Republic.

With the NATO bombing halted, but peace still a distant prospect, Serbia and Kosovo were not on any exclusive club's short list. Slovenia had been prosperous and relatively liberal back in the days of Tito's socialist Yugoslavia, but southern Serbia—and especially underdeveloped Kosovo with its high birth rate—had been an economic and political backwater. In the 1970s and 1980s, when people observed that it was possible to go from "Central Europe to Central Asia" without leaving the Socialist Federal Republic of Yugoslavia (SFRY), it was the contrast between Slovenia and Kosovo that they had in mind. (The gaps were prodigious. In 1968, with 20 years of Albanian birth rates well in excess of the ability of the economy to provide jobs still to come, per-capita income in Slovenia was 183 percent of the all-Yugoslav average, while in Kosovo it was only 33 percent of the average.[1] Slovenes were thus nearly six times "richer," and this gap would only grow wider into the late 1980s.)

To Serbs, then—frustrated, smarting, and alarmed at the prospect of losing the territory just subjected to ethnic cleansing in their name—Clinton's admonitions must have rung hollow indeed, for all the distinction he drew between Milošević and the Serb people. And they were, no doubt, all the more unwelcome in view of the venue in which they were delivered. In the President's implicit contrast of Slovenia to Serbia were enfolded many elements of a conception of an East-West cultural/historical divide within Europe itself. For some time, this concept or image has been a part of most historians'—and statesmen's—intellectual equipment. It has come under attack in more recent times, mainly in an academia where "critical theory" and postmodern language have their home, and has been pushed in some cases toward the edge of political incorrectness. From time to time during the eighty-day Kosovo war, the world of journalistic commentary and the op-ed pages had approached the issue of this divide, without on the whole doing much more than deploring the failure of the Balkan world, and especially violence-wracked Bosnia and Kosovo, to move into postcommunism with the ease that had characterized the success stories to the west.

Still, there were those who dealt with it head-on. In a *New York Times* op-ed piece appearing on 7 April 1999, Robert Kaplan wrote of the "new division" that began forming with the collapse of East European communism in 1989: "Even before the outbreak of fighting in Yugoslavia in 1991, the Central European states of Poland, Hungary, and Czechoslovakia were pulling dramatically ahead of Balkan countries like Romania and Bulgaria in terms of progress toward stable democratic rule." Kaplan went on to specify the advantages of the former ("the traditions of the Habsburg Empire . . . sizable middle classes prior to . . . communist rule") and the disadvantages of the Balkans ("burdened by centuries of Byzantine and Turkish absolutism . . . their middle classes . . . mere specks amid vast seas of peasantries"). He warned that the enlargement of NATO had "formalized this dangerous historical and religious redivision of Europe: between a Roman Catholic and Protestant West and an Orthodox Christian and Muslim East."

Kaplan was not opposed to NATO intervention, however—neither as a traditional realist might be, nor as a critic who might see the conflict between Orthodox Christian Serbs and overwhelmingly Muslim Albanians as requiring more nuance than an intervening NATO might possess. He instead called for "complete NATO military victory," sketching out a gloomy picture of the consequences of failure:

> Thus, if the bombing campaign fails and NATO gives up at the negotiating table, it would seal Europe off according to medieval lines, with the newly expanded NATO a mere variation of the old Holy Roman Empire—the old Christian West, that is—and with the Near East beginning where the old Ottoman Turkish Empire once did, roughly on the border between Croatia and Serbia and somewhere in Transylvania where ethnic Hungarians meet Romanians.[2]

A few days earlier, on 4 April, the *Times'* former Moscow correspondent, Serge Schmemann, had explored other aspects of the cultural divide. NATO member Greece was obviously not among the most enthusiastic for a move against Serbia. The synod of the Greek Orthodox Church, as Schmemann reported, had vented its "pain at the military attacks against a heroic and glorious Christian people, such as the Serbs." Looking north at the situation from Athens was obviously a different matter, even for a European Union and NATO member, than looking southeast from London or Bonn; as Schmemann put it, Greece has "always felt itself a junior member of the Western club, included for geographical, not cultural, reasons." *Geo-strategic* might have been a better term than *geographical* in that context, but Schmemann was well onto something, referring to an Eastern sense of "difference and exclusion":

> The recent expansion of NATO to include Poland, Hungary and the Czech Republic—all Catholic or Protestant countries—while excluding the Orthodox states of Bulgaria and Romania affirmed a sense that the West was promoting its own into its exclusive club. The Poles, for example, have always insisted that their Catholicism is their true membership card in the West, even if they are ethnic cousins of the Russians.[3]

Poles themselves would probably observe that they are *distant* cousins—and Russians would generally agree. Russian "Slavophile" thinking was anti-Western, a brand of Slavic solidarity that made room from time to time for the (Orthodox) South Slavs of the Balkans, but hardly for the Poles. This East-West dimension, anything but new, *had* been highlighted by Samuel Huntington earlier in the 1990s as one of the foci of his "clash of civilizations" thesis on the post-Cold War world. In his interview with Schmemann, he underlined his view of the divide as it existed in late twentieth-century minds—or at least, in the minds of those not given to American-style projections of similarity or of aspirations to similar outcomes onto peoples about whom they know little. But in Europe and elsewhere people certainly recognize the idea of "dividing lines . . . West Europeans know what West Europe is; people in Orthodox countries know that however much they want to be in the European Union, they are in a different world."[4]

One need not agree with the major substance of Huntington's "clash" thesis—the implication that *civilizations* will in some sense become actors in a way in which they are not today, and that the role of *states* may thus change—in order to appreciate that this East-West European divide *is* consequential. At the risk of rehearsing what will surely be familiar material to most readers, it may be useful to retreat for a few pages from the journalism and commentary of spring 1999, to review more systematically what this divide has meant.

Europe: The Old Divide

The basic notion of the East-West divide is historic and cultural: in the West, Latin alphabet and culture; in the East, the Greek/Cyrillic alphabet (Romania excepted) and "Byzantine" culture. These are markers of religious identity and heritage. The West received, and is defined by having received, its Christianity from Rome. Latin Catholicism split later in the Protestant Reformation, partly over various clerical abuses and partly over disagreement on the individual's need for a clerical mediator between self and God, and the Reformation called forth a Catholic Counter-Reformation. With these, and the Peace of Westphalia in 1648, the religious map of the West was fixed for centuries to come.

In the East, the Christianity received from Byzantium by Serbs, Bulgars, and the East Slavs who were to develop into modern Ukrainians, Russians, and

Belarusians, had diverged further and further in content and context from the Western version. What had begun not long after Constantine and the dividing of the Roman Empire culminated in the schism of 1054, from which the Orthodox-Catholic divide is dated. The most critical challenges facing Orthodoxy would not be internally generated, as in the West, but would come from the militant Islam that rolled over the Greeks, Serbs, Bulgars, and Romanians with the Ottoman Empire's Balkan conquests in the thirteenth through fifteenth centuries. Farther north and east, beyond the Turks' reach, Russia's Orthodoxy would be protected, but also thoroughly dominated as the official religion of a prematurely centralized (relative to the Western postfeudal experience) autocratic state.

Thus, in neither the Balkans nor Russia would Orthodox clerics have occasion to sharpen their theological/disputational skills in the way that Catholics and Protestants did in the West's more competitive environment. In what was to become Orthodox Christianity, what may have been a bias toward mysticism/symbolism and ritual in the beginning became more pronounced over the years, as did a sort of spiritual collectivism distant from the Western preoccupation with the individual's conscience and moral performance. In the framework of this general understanding, it was quite unexceptionable for a historian of Hungary to note several years ago that with the "choice of Rome over Byzantium" had come not only "particular forms of liturgy and church organization," but also principles that tended to emphasize "individual rather than collective responsibility before God, and a concept of salvation that hinged upon the fulfillment of specific obligations." Thus a legalism was built into the Western version "that spilled over into many areas of private and public life and . . . provided models and sanctions for diverse forms of *secular* behavior" (emphasis added); moreover, it promoted the view that "the relationship between superiors and subordinates—between king and vassal, lord and peasant—should rest on a system of well-defined and reciprocal obligations regulated by contract." Further, given the realities of the many and weak state structures of the West in these centuries, Rome and the Church were stronger, able to maintain an autonomy unknown in the East, so that "the position of the Church and its relation to the secular state provided a model for the autonomy of other political and social entities . . . "[5]

Given this description, it followed that as Greek "Orthodoxy" was "shaped by Near Eastern philosophies and, under their influence, eschewed the philosophical foundations of Western Christianity" it would elaborate in its various national forms different canonic principles which

> came down strongly on the side of community and affect, and inspired a far more diffuse set of social and political relationships . . . The ruler is a stern father, not a supreme judge or legislator. He requires the love of his subjects, but also retains the prerogative to define and redefine their duties, and to expect total filial devotion from them rather than mere compliance with specific commands.[6]

Such observations are no doubt familiar to the reader. The point to make here is simply that the religious/cultural "tilts" of Western and Eastern Christianity are different, and thus we may expect—if not assume—that their distinct political/ organizational implications will be reflected in some way in divergent political realities across *today's* East-West divide among postcommunist states.

There are yet other ways of locating the divide: at the boundary (roughly) between the old Western and Eastern Roman Empires, or at the line south and east of which the Ottoman conquest lasted from the fourteenth or fifteenth century into the nineteenth, placing the Balkan Christians under Muslim rule. Both "work" for the Balkan boundaries, but do not include those lands of "barbarians" in Roman times that would later become the states of northwestern Europe.

One could also argue that this European "West" is where certain things happened—Renaissance, Reformation, Counter-Reformation, Enlightenment—which did *not* happen in the East. These pegs on which Western history is hung, these chapter headings in a "Western Civ" textbook, are not the common property of all Europeans. For those who (as some put it) "privilege" the Western experience, they are stages in the development of the political-economic West which rose to dominance in the nineteenth century, nearly destroyed itself in 1914–1918, and after a century of progress and turmoil, brutal wars and massive technological advances, stands more than ever at the pinnacle of power. The West sets standards in its wealth and stability which other peoples and states may accept or reject, but against which they must measure themselves.

Belonging to the West, then, has its attractions—above all for those peoples and states who arguably fit the definition of "Western" laid out above, but have been located at the margins, not quite sure that the rich, confident "farther-west" West recognizes them. The post-World War II communist states arising from the successor states of the Habsburg and Romanov Empires have all been stuck, along with the Balkans, in an "East" that signified Soviet domination and opposition to the West of the Marshall Plan, NATO, and, later, the EU. It has been those most directly involved who have tried hardest to make the distinctions. Historians have insisted on the difference between *Eastern* and *Central* Europe, careful to stake out the latter turf as theirs, or to use the term *East* Central Europe—sometimes without real specification of what *West* Central Europe might be, sometimes simply identifying it with Germany—but in all cases firmly anchoring themselves outside the East, outside the lands of East Slavdom, and outside the Balkans.[7] Political dissidents of the 1980s made the same point, and none more emphatically than Milan Kundera in "The Tragedy of Central Europe"; with Western audiences in mind, he evoked the notion of a West "kidnapped" Eastward.[8]

On today's map of Europe, the line distinguishing West from East in the manner described here runs (starting in the north) along the eastern border of Finland and heads southward along the eastern borders of Estonia, Latvia,

Lithuania, and Poland. Further on, it curves with Slovakia's and Hungary's eastern/southern borders, drops south from central Hungary to encompass Yugoslavia's Vojvodina, runs west toward the Adriatic, and then turns sharply southeastward to include Croatia (both inland Slavonia and littoral Dalmatia). The line ends on the coast as Croatia runs out. Our line has thus run in such a manner as to exclude from the "West" the non-Baltic peoples of the former USSR, notably the East Slav Belarusians, Ukrainians, and Russians who border the Baltics, Poland, Slovakia, and Hungary to the east. Further south, it excludes Romania, Bulgaria, Macedonia, and Montenegro; it excludes both the Serbs *and* the Albanians, the Turks *and* the Greeks. On its western/northern side, and therefore "included," are the (Protestant) Estonians and Latvians, the (Catholic) Lithuanians, the West Slavs—Poles, Czechs, Slovaks—and the Hungarians; and in the former Yugoslavia, Croats, Slovenes, and (some peoples of) the Vojvodina.

Everyone familiar with the region will understand the historic/cultural/ linguistic rationales for drawing the line *approximately* this way, though nearly everyone would have (competing) proposals for some of the gray areas. Thus, in a historical sense the line might have been drawn further eastward around Poland to encompass some of its prewar eastern territories—the *Kresy*—later taken by Stalin and attached to Belarus and Ukraine. Historically, the majority populations were Ukrainian and Belarusian, but the cities and "high culture," the monuments and official architecture, were largely Polish. Indeed, the southern reaches around Lviv (Lwów) had never been part of the Russian Empire, but were part of the Habsburg domains before the reestablishment of Poland in 1918—as Poles are wont to point out. Should the line through Croatia not take account of the Krajina and other areas in which, for centuries, *Serb* majorities existed—as they did up to the collapse of Yugoslavia a decade ago—as a result of Habsburg recruitments of tough outlanders to guard the military frontier against the Turk? What about the Vojvodina, where Serbs now constitute a majority and Hungarians are no longer so numerous as they were when Tito recognized them in the land's semi-federal status as an autonomous province within Serbia? Is there a way to draw the sort of line Kaplan suggested, somewhere in Transylvania, that would divide most ethnic Hungarians from the Romanians whose *state* has encompassed Transylvania since Versailles and Trianon? And how, in this kind of cartography, to accommodate Bosnia? We need to recognize these questions, but we need not answer them (assuming we could) in order to proceed.

Realities, Perceptions, Effects

This is not, obviously, merely an intellectual/cultural exercise—though, again, there is nothing "mere" about issues whose resolutions may later frame the views of decision makers, as well as commentators, more than they may realize.[9] Judgments about what is East and what is West in Europe, and the whole preceding discussion, may be subject to attack from postmodernist perspectives and derided as "politically incorrect" distinctions typically made by Westerners used to hegemony of all sorts—especially that of "privileging" their own perspectives. Such Western judgments, implying the superiority of Western-style democracy and Western-style capitalist markets, and assuming that these work better for most people than the alternatives (which are not, therefore, *really* alternatives), are also open to attack by those who reject them on grounds anything but "postmodern," including romantic nationalisms of all sorts, Islam, and Russian Slavophilism in its older and newer variants. Westerners, then, set the bar as they see fit for admission to their exclusive clubs.

(Actually, of course, the "club" label/concept does not really capture as much as it might: relevant to some problems of Western coordination during the Kosovo conflict, but to much more besides, is the fact that NATO contains the "non-Western" states of Turkey and Greece, and the EU contains Greece, with Turkey eagerly asserting its qualifications for admission. But these *are* Western clubs, and Greece and Turkey are hardly—leaving aside their own historic enmity—the happiest or most secure members. Greece had no heart for NATO's move in Kosovo, and barely went along. As the *Times*'s Kaplan again put it, the rest of NATO "demands that Greece behave like they do because it is middle class and a member of NATO." But hapless Greece "can't, because it is in the Balkans and . . . fated to live next door to the Serbs long after any NATO troops leave."[10] Turkey, its size and military scale on a level well above Greece's, is legendarily a "staunch NATO member," yet its real contribution to NATO military efforts is by many measures not huge. It is axiomatic also that as a "Western club," NATO insists on civilian control of the military. But it is equally obvious, at least to some, that the NATO of Brussels, Washington, and London is quite happy, in fact, with military veto power over *civilian* politics in Turkey, given the alternatives it perceives.)[11]

As the commentator William Pfaff put it in a discussion of the Russians and the Kosovo crisis, the old Russian Slavophile thinking claimed

> that it was better to be poor and backward but close to nature than to be rich and civilized like the French and English, whose advanced development proved only that they were on the brink of decadence. Serbia is also a victim of such ideas, causing Serbs to think they are inherently superior to their neighbors . . . When others strike back, Serbs complain that they are the innocent victims of conspiracies by enemies of the Slavs.[12]

But the point is that other judgments being made today are about winners and losers, and successes and failures, among the postcommunist states and peoples. They are judgments about politics and economics, and about the negotiation of the rough waters of democratic and market transitions. These judgments favor the Western postcommunist states on the whole, and, at least for now, they run against the Eastern ones. They are based not on prejudice or projection, but on performance and results, as these are observed by a variety of ("Western-dominated") institutions like the IMF, the Organisation for Economic Co-operation and Development, and the European Union itself—all of which should warn us against assuming the irrelevance of Europe's *pre*communist East-West divide in the era of *post*communism.

Politics Good and Bad

The year 1989 saw first Poland, then Hungary, then Czechoslovakia end their communist regimes peacefully in the new international context created primarily by Gorbachev's readiness to abandon the USSR's old external empire. The first two went by way of "pacted" transitions, though of somewhat different sorts; Czechoslovakia's "velvet revolution" and, soon after, the end of East Germany with the breaching of the Wall, were reactions to regimes so repressive that they *had* no organized opposition with which to pact their exits. Before year's end, Bulgaria's old communist government fell in a palace coup, to be replaced by avowedly reform communists committed to free elections, and who, after some time, honored their promise. Romania's strange, brutal regime fell in December 1989, in bloodshed, with "reform" communists again speaking for the new forces of democracy. But the actual scenario, from the heavy involvement of the Romanian security forces in what looked to many like an anti-Ceauşescu move, through the firing-squad executions of the Ceauşescus, to the composition of the leadership that emerged, is still murky.

The post-Hoxha Alia regime in Albania would last a bit longer, and in 1989 what would soon become "the former Yugoslavia" was entering into some of the conflicts and power plays that would lead to its dissolution. However, these would assume their real significance less as parts of the story of Yugoslavia's collapse than as elements of the stories of the emergence of the post-Yugoslav successor states. By late 1991, as the USSR itself headed for dissolution, that emergence was well along.

At 10 years' remove from 1989, a fairly clear and, in a sense, stable picture of the varieties of postcommunist European politics has emerged. Four—perhaps five—star political performers outshine the rest: Poland, Hungary, and the Czech Republic all live comfortably with the new political systems that have been established since 1989–1990. Poland's system, a mix of presidentialism and parliamentarism somewhat on the French model, and the more standard parliamentary structures in Budapest and Prague, have all undergone those peaceful transfers of power which are the tests of new democracies; all have seen new democratic-left parties, descended from the old ruling parties, accept and play by the rules of democracies within market systems. Post-Yugoslav Slovenia and post-Soviet Estonia—both small, both "exceptional" in their old contexts and to a degree in their new ones—complete the list.

All five are "Western." They are the five short-listed for EU admission, and they include the three new members of NATO. All this is familiar ground: those who talk of a NATO/EU bias toward, let us say, "peoples who look like us" might not be completely off the mark in connecting such a bias to the dynamics of club expansion. But in fairness, they would have to note that it is not simply a matter of "looks." Politically, these states behave more and more in the manner of those who have invited them aboard, and this behavior, though motivated to some degree by the promise of acceptance and validation by NATO, the EU, and other such organizations, is a product not of aid packages but of these polities and societies themselves.

Not all Western states fit in this category. Estonia has outshone Baltic neighbors Latvia and Lithuania, but economics rather than politics per se may have something to do with this. Tougher cases altogether are Slovakia and Croatia. As of summer 1999, signs were hopeful in the former. The thuggish forces around Mečiar, which had dominated political life since the "velvet divorce" that sundered the Czech and Slovak republics, gave way to the "cleaner" people around Dzurinda who seemed eager to make up for lost time and prove that they, too, could soon fit EU and NATO templates.

Croatia, it could at least be said, was in no sense as badly off as Serbia. But under Franjo Tudjman, who could hardly be called a democrat—and who was still too invested in both the Croatian territory only recently "cleansed" of Serbs who had lived there for generations and the Croat-Muslim condominium in part of Bosnia—there seemed to be little progress toward building a stable politics of group-formation and interest-representation rather than national expression. Converting Habsburg style, Roman Catholicism, and other Western attributes into a package that will attract the interest from the West that the Croats seek may take longer than reconverting the Adriatic coast to profitable tourist use.

(At the onset of postcommunism, Croatia and Slovakia shared a legacy that complicated their politics: for each of these junior partners in a by now failed federal state, the "golden" period of national independence was, unfortunately, the period from the late 1930s to the end of World War II, wherein they functioned, effectively, as Nazi puppet states. Even in the rare instance where communist civics bore some relation to fact, they had not succeeded in convincing Slovaks and Croats of much. Many were surprised to find that the world, and more importantly "Europe," actually took negative views of Monsignor Tiso's Slovak government and the Ustasha regime in Croatia. They *are* learning—faster in Slovakia perhaps than in Croatia—and everything about the West whose acceptance they seek will encourage them to "revise" their own historical perspective.)

Further east and south—whether one wants to talk of "problem-ridden political transitions," "the weight of history," or "the absence of civic traditions of democracy and/or individualism," the reality is that politics and political life are bleaker. We need not do a country-by-country inventory to make a point already confrmed by too many sources and too many modes of analysis, from high journalism to public opinion polling and from constitutional theory to studies of political party formation and voting behavior. On the whole, politics in the "East" is not working so well as it is in the West—and in the absence of any clearly articulated and accepted alternative "Eastern" criteria beyond variants of exclusivist nationalism, the West *is* the standard here.

This is not just a matter of parliamentarism versus presidentialism, of the new structures of government and how good or bad their initial post-1989 (or pre-1939?) design may be, or of how many times, and how, they have been changed since 1989. It also has to do with the quality of the media and of public discourse (related to but not quite the same as freedom thereof), and perhaps ultimately, with the sorts of questions politics addresses in the parliament and on the streets. Happy are the states and societies that managed long ago to settle —or avoid—the "great questions," the nagging national pride-and-identity issues so affect-laden and in the end often so disastrously unresolvable, and to create a broad consensus, at least among the emergent political elites, that rules whole classes of questions off the table. Here too, the West has done better—or has been more fortunate—than the East. Poles, Czechs, and Hungarians today contest politically over, *inter alia*, domestic socioeconomic issues of welfare and employment policy—though many would say prematurely—much as do their richer neighbors to the West.[13] They can vote for or against postcommunist parties of the left without thereby delivering verdicts of guilt or innocence before society and history on the years of the Soviet model.

Russians, Serbs, and others are bedeviled by questions of this sort, however, as well as by the problem of seeing themselves as "done to," wronged by history and uniquely denied the right to express *their* nature, while other ethnic groups linked to them in the now-defunct federal structures of the past look upon them as hegemonic and imperialist. Belarusians, Ukrainians, Bulgarians, and Romanians are all likewise burdened, for some combination of specific political reasons of long duration and/or the broader but real matter of "heritages" with little to no democratic/civic content. (To be fair, Bulgaria's turn to hard-minded but successful economic policy in recent times suggests some light at the end of one Balkan tunnel.)

To all indications, then, it will be a long time before there is any reasonable prospect of a general levelling-up of the standards of political principle and performance in the East to match what has occurred in the West. Economics has something to do with this, and solving some of the problems of the East-West lag will help here (see below), but politics retains a large degree of autonomy.

Follow the Money

Money managers are notoriously unsentimental. The historical/cultural regionalisms discussed here will mean little to them if they have no economic effect. (New York and London, after all, put a lot of money into Japan—and vice versa.) Politics is a different matter; investors and businessmen must pay attention to how politics affects the economic environment. But politics need not be civil or squeaky clean in order to promote the sort of environment in which money can be made in predictable fashion. Democratic or authoritarian, most varieties of politics past a certain point of basic development will do—in that a market economy *will* emerge. Basically, the market will emerge—though not always gracefully or free of corruption—wherever the polity and its coercive resources are not employed to crush and prevent it. Under the Soviet model, of course, they *were* so employed, making for a unique legacy.

By and large, following the money leads us toward that same postcommunist West and away from the East, regardless of whether it is foreign money or the domestic variety. Success in the hard business of transition out of the Soviet-model economies of the past and toward the market has not come easily anywhere, but the states that have thus far made the best of their postcommunist politics have, by and large, done as well with their economics.

A decade ago, for a whole set of reasons—ranging from the persistence of historical zones of deepening underdevelopment as one moved eastward[14] to the political and economic histories of postwar communist regimes themselves—most observers would have bet that in the process of market transition, the Western states of the Soviet external empire (Poland, Hungary, and [then] Czechoslovakia) would have the easiest going. These would have been the places to put one's money, literally and figuratively. Less attractive by far were Romania and Bulgaria, two countries where no real challenges to Soviet economic structures (via partial, "in-system" attempts at reform) or to the suppression of political and civil life had really arisen. Such challenges had arisen in the West, in 1956, 1968, 1970, 1976, and 1980–1981. Further east yet, as the USSR dissolved, the prospects of Russia, Ukraine, Belarus, and other states were quite unclear, though the Baltic states were given economic and political "points" for their evident resolve to do whatever had to be done.

That bet made in 1989–1990 would have been quite a good one. A decade later, in a survey published on 30 June 1999, *Financial Times* drew a distinction between the successful states and those "caught in the transition trap," and titled a graph indexing average transition indicator scores for 25 postcommunist states: "It helps to be close to Berlin." In the northeast winner's corner of the graph were Hungary, Poland, and the Czech Republic (and near them Slovakia, Slovenia, and Croatia); at the other extreme were the five states of ex-Soviet Central Asia.[15]

Was it belief in the "Western-ness" of the winner states that determined the flow of funds—a self-fulfilling prophecy articulated in deutschmarks and dollars? Such beliefs could not hurt, but there is much more to it than this. It helps if there is something attractive at the outset. Poland, Czechoslovakia, and Hungary *had* histories of market reforms within socialism, even if they had not, in the end, been successful. (Hungary's record in this regard was the most consistent. The 1968 New Economic Mechanism, modified over the years, sometimes stalled but never abandoned, had cumulated effects over 20 years that proved far from trivial. Hungary got the lion's share of early Western direct investment after 1989.)

Russia, Ukraine, Romania, and other states lacked these things and what they seemed to imply, which led to relatively lower levels of investment and engagement there. What did attract investment to Russia was its abundance of natural resources—something that Eastern Europe lacked. But over time, since 1989–1991, those natural riches have lost a good deal of their pull as Russia has failed to sort itself out or to provide the legal, financial, and cultural conditions to facilitate normal business and investment. Russia's rough conditions have not prevented some individuals and cabals from amassing fantastic wealth, as the existence of the "oligarchs" attests. But the conditions that in fact facilitated the acquisition of these fortunes are of the sort that mark a country "high-risk" and deter normal foreign investment. This is not, then, a matter of a "constructed" Russia, an *image of* Russia that deters investment; nor is it a matter of using Russia as a constituting "other" whose riskiness and uncivilized economy make Central Europe look so benign by contrast. There is something very concrete indeed about the movement of money and the decisions that lie behind it.

The broad world of "emerging markets" divides roughly into two categories: weak, or formerly weak, mainly third-world, traditionally market economies with varying performance problems, and transition economies making their way out from under the legacy of Soviet-type centrally planned structures. The latter have become more differentiated over the last decade. The common institutional heritage and broadly similar problems of transition—as they were perceived earlier—have lost some of their salience. In place of the tendency to see similarities foremost, more nuanced, discriminating judgments among countries are now being made, based on nearly a decade of observation of what has been done, and not done, and where. Earlier in the transition period, a crisis in one transition economy was likely to prompt investors to run for the exits in *all* of them—but this is no longer the case.

Governments do many things: one of the things they do regularly is borrow money. Bonds and similar government instruments are, essentially, a sovereign debtor's promises to repay the lender with interest. How much is that promise worth? How trustworthy the sovereign? The more doubts there are about these matters, the higher the rate of interest required to attract lenders. Poland, the Czech Republic, and Hungary today need not offer extraordinary rates of return to move their paper. The investing public (actually a public made up of institutions) has made judgments about these economies and the near-certainty of payback that make them tolerant of rates of return not much above normal.

Not so with Russia and some other cases. To attract investors, the less successful transition economies must look first and foremost to the strong-stomached, the courters of risk—for who else would head to the "wild East"? To engage them, the Russias of the world must offer whopping interest rates as a hedge against greater possibilities of default due to a huge drop in the value of the borrower state's currency. Interest rates in the 70 percent range on ruble-denominated securities attracted investors (bettors) when the ruble was relatively stable versus the dollar, but in the summer of 1998, things fell apart as the Russian central bank left the ruble to fall. The wise had removed their gains from the table earlier; those who stayed got burnt. Russia, to put it mildly, constitutes an investment environment of a different type than East Central Europe. (And such an environment, under the "right" circumstances, reattracts its previously burnt investors, also of a different type. The Russian equity market—which also collapsed in the summer of 1998—was, in the first half of 1999, the best-performing in the world.[16] The strong-stomached are going back in.)

Most importantly, the Russian financial meltdown of August 1998, unlike earlier in the 1990s, did not affect investor attitudes toward the East Central European transition states in any major, long-term way. These states were not forced to use extraordinary rate increases to sell their bonds to warier investors, or indeed to induce people to hold *złotys*, korunas, or forints at home. Over time, these states had graduated to a level at which the rich investing countries of the world accorded them the ultimate mark of confidence—putting money in without any special provisions. Russia, never really part of the club to begin with, had slid backwards. That Russia and similar states had a harder selling job was made clear in investment language in a May 1999 bulletin on Eurobond issues:

> By and large, money managers have identified Eurobonds as *the fault line that divides Europe* [emphasis added]. One fund manager calls emerging market Eurobonds "as good a measure of investment confidence as you can get in these volatile places." Looking at the spreads, an investor can quickly spot the risk leaders: Russia, Romania and Ukraine. Currently, these three countries' Eurobonds are trading between 2,000 and 4,000 basis points above US treasuries . . . Despite the financial crisis that shook Russia and Romania . . . Slovenia recently launched a Eurobond at 86 basis points over German Bunds, a sign that investors view its debt as investment grade. Croatia's recent Eurobond, meanwhile, debuted at 375 basis points over Bunds.[17]

A quick review of some numbers should add an element of concreteness to these assertions. In midsummer 1999, the prevailing short-term interest rates underlined how the Central European states and Russia inhabited quite distinct neighborhoods. Russia's 55 percent rate put it in the same category as some very troubled emerging markets: of 25 of these tracked by *The Economist*, only Turkey's was higher at 80 percent. Poland at 13.31 percent, Hungary at 15.06, and the Czech Republic at a very modest 7.01 percent all fell into a more comfortable and confidence-inspiring range.

The "cost of money" depends on numerous factors beyond the general health of economies, of course, and we need not pursue the subtleties here. But it *is* worth looking at the value of the respective currencies—or more correctly, at changes in their values—versus the U.S. dollar from June 1998 to June 1999. The Russian crash of August–September 1998 was a real crash of the ruble, from 6.0 to the dollar to 24.5 a year later. The Central European currencies slipped versus the dollar as well, but in a way that marks the generally orderly dynamic of paced devaluation versus a *very* strong dollar; thus Poland's *złoty* went from 3.47 to 3.93 to the dollar, Hungary's forint from 217 to 241, and the Czech koruna from 33.4 to 35.9.

Lastly, another way of "following the money" is to look at the figures on direct foreign investment per capita. The figures arrayed below represent average annual investment, 1996–1998, in $US per capita, thus ironing out to some degree what in some cases are large year-to-year swings. For the purposes of comparison, "Eastern" countries are in the left column, "Western" countries in the middle, and the three post-USSR Baltics on the right.

Average Annual Investment Per Capita 1996–1998 ($US)[18]

Bulgaria	$34.86	Croatia	$75.45	Estonia	$183.76
Romania	$35.18	Czech R.	$132.80	Latvia	$147.23
Russia	$14.84	Hungary	$171.06	Lithuania	$130.59
Ukraine	$11.79	Poland	$114.82		
		Slovakia	$37.10		
		Slovenia	$136.71		

The figures make the point yet again: the money goes "West" to countries both large (Poland) and tiny (Slovenia). A range of total direct foreign investment in 1998 that runs from a *high* of less than $36.00 per soul in Romania to a derisory $11.79 in Ukraine demonstrates the lack of interest in these states among investors. Given the conditions that account for this lack of interest there is no reason to think that, in the absence of measures that these countries can take on their own to increase their attractiveness, foreign investment will jump-start these laggards into some kind of growth. Slovakia will probably improve its laggard performance as its politics change, and Croatia may follow after Tudjman's exit. For the rest, including the Baltics, the world is a very different and more open-handed place.

Conclusion

The point of this brief essay, then, is simply that *real*, not "projected," "imagined," or "constructed" differences in politics and economics distinguish postcommunist states on either side of Europe's East-West divide. These are differences in fact. Though they are not unalterable, they must be reckoned with by the (farther, richer) West.

The practice and patterns of the less successful transition states will not be easy to alter. The lag of the "East" in the business of political and economic transition is understandable, since it seems consistent with long history, but also particularly problematic in the present context for several reasons.

First, the failures are thrown into sharper relief by the success stories. Poland, the Czech Republic, Hungary, Estonia, and Slovenia all demonstrate that having had a single-party Marxist-Leninist polity and a Soviet-type economy is not fatal; that transition is *not* impossible. Since it is not, something is "wrong" with the countries that have not made it, and that "wrongness" may have to do with deep elements of politics and culture beyond the "merely" economic and public policy realms. Though a relative failure thus far, Russia may be in a special category in the West's eyes: "too big" (or as some put it, probably more accurately, "too nuclear") to fail. In the absence of this sort of basis for special consideration, there is little reason for the "rich West" to be particularly solicitous about the laggard states—it is they who have to prove themselves.

Second, failure in the business of market/democratic transition for these states is a failure to begin the process of catching up, not with states *somewhat* more "advanced" than they, but with the triumphant West as it exists in the here and now at the century's turn. Effectively, the seventy-odd years of Soviet history were a detour down the dead-end street of a colossally misconceived economic design. Eastern Europe's time under the Soviet model, imposed from above and abroad, was essentially a forty-year loss in a century of unprecedented economic and technological dynamism. Today the members of the Group of Seven, the leading economic powers and players in the world market, exist virtually on another planet, so great is their remove from Russia, Romania, and similar cases. But that "East" which has made so little progress—or has yet to get started—is paying a very high price for its failure. For most practical purposes, those states that have not yet learned how to fit themselves into the global market, and have not yet found either something to sell in it or some useful place in the international division of labor, find themselves *irrelevant*. The developed world does not depend upon, and could without much difficulty find alternatives to, the little that the 250-plus million people in these states supply to it. To be dependent on charity to a significant degree is a heavy judgment indeed.

Finally, though, it may be the very dramatization of the gap between East and West by the Kosovo conflict that prompts the West, for the first time, to do (or talk about doing) something about it—to try to breach the gap. The Yugoslav breakup, the consequent Bosnian horrors, and now Kosovo are being seen by some as "wake-up calls," warnings to the rich West of brutally destabilizing consequences if it retreats from and tries to isolate that troubled Orthodox/Muslim, Balkan/East Slav, poor and unstable other Europe. In this view, rather than setting the West's economic and political barriers for club admission high, it is time for the West to reach out and gather in the East, lest the clubhouse go up in flames.

Hence, there arises a new argument—beyond France's earlier failed one—that Romania *should*, blemishes aside, be admitted to NATO; and another argument, perhaps, that Macedonia's plea for NATO admission, made most loudly when it was being inundated with Kosovar refugees and trying to "collect" from the West, might not be so far-fetched; or that Bulgaria deserves very serious consideration by the EU, not so much because of a solid recent monetary-policy performance with a currency control board, but because of its economic deficiencies through so much of the 1990s.

These, and any similar moves, would "stretch" the NATO and EU rationales to be sure—which is precisely the point, as the advocates of this approach would argue. New measures are required for new times, for a new Europe wherein the West and East of this essay would ultimately lose a great deal of their significance. Such a massive project of "inclusion" would be hugely expensive, in monetary and other terms. The East cannot compel it; it would have to be offered by the West. Without leaning toward undue pessimism, it is difficult to see the West of 1999, with its own continuing preoccupations and expensive domestic practices, opening a new century and a new millennium with any "grand bargain" or Marshall Plan-scale exercise in vision, hope—and risk.

NOTES

1. Bogdan Denitch, *The Legitimation of a Revolution: The Yugoslav Case* (New Haven, 1976), p. 143.

2. Robert Kaplan, "In the Balkans, No Wars are Local," *The New York Times* 7 April 1999: A21.

3. Serge Schmemann, "Storm Front: A New Collision of East and West," *The New York Times* 4 April 1999: 1.

4. Samuel Huntington quoted in Schmemann, "Storm Front."

5. Andrew C. Janos, *The Politics of Backwardness in Hungary, 1825–1945* (Princeton, 1982), p. 12.

6. Ibid., p. 13.

7. See, e.g., Oscar Halecki, *The Limits and Divisions of European History* (Notre Dame, 1962), esp. pp. 105–41.

8. Milan Kundera, "The Tragedy of Central Europe," *New York Review of Books* 26 April 1984: 33–38. Since its original publication, this piece has been reprinted in many collections. For a discussion of the "divide" and its intellectual and political roots and consequences, see George Schöpflin and Nancy Wood, eds., *In Search of Central Europe* (Cambridge and Oxford, 1989).

9. The point here is the interpretation of what were taken to be *real* differences (between peoples, civilizations, cultures, etc.) as "socially constructed," and in some sense less "real," or less deserving of treatment *as* real. There is an ever growing literature written from this viewpoint, and it is well beyond my purposes here to offer an overall critique—one in any case unlikely to convince those not ready to be convinced. To take an earlier "model" of this sort of work, Edward Said's *Orientalism* (New York, 1979), deals with the West's "construction" of a distinct world of Araby: very well received and interesting in its own right, it nonetheless seems to me to underplay the degree to which differences between that West and the Arab world simply *are*. They exist, they are obvious, they may be interpreted, but they need not be "constructed."

 With respect to East and West in Europe, the literature that asks how much of the divide is thus "constructed" is likewise interesting, though I entertain the same sorts of reservations about it. See, e.g., Iver B. Neumann, "Russia as Central Europe's Constituting Other," *East European Politics and Societies* 7(2) Spring 1993: 349–69; and on the Balkans, Maria Todorova, "The Balkans: From Discovery to Invention," *Slavic Review* 53(2) Summer 1994: 453–82; idem, *Imagining the Balkans* (New York, 1997).

10. Kaplan, "In the Balkans, No Wars are Local."

11. The point of these observations is simply that NATO, as a military alliance, could not exclude realpolitik from its composition. Neither Greece nor Turkey had any pedigree as model democracies when they were enlisted early in the Cold War. They were a "flank" abutting the Soviet world, but "NATO's troubled southern flank" became a catch-phrase mainly because of the enmities between *them*. On the whole, each was no happier with the other in the same "camp" than were Romania and Hungary as allies of the Third Reich. Greek and Turkish "discomfort" in the Western clubs to which they belong is not a matter of their own hypersensitivity. Greece is still a net "receiver" in the EU, and obviously no enthusiastic NATO operative. Turkey suspects—rightly, I think—that it will not be accepted into the EU in any policy-relevant time frame, and that this is because it is seen, because of its religion and geography, as not European at all. In this, I suspect the Turks again are correct. They are, perhaps, asking too much of Brussels. Indeed, there are those within the U.S. and Western military who, with the end of the Cold War, have expressed the view that NATO could do quite well with Greece and Turkey *out*—territorial disputes as well as "culture" are relevant here—though they have not typically expressed this view for attribution.

12. William Pfaff, "Russia's Foolish Gesture," *The Boston Globe* 21 June 1999: A23.

13. Indeed, the focus of a recent volume on postcommunist social policy formulation and implementation is very much on the three "leaders," to the effective exclusion of all the other states save Russia. See Ethan B. Kapstein and Michael Mandelbaum, eds., *Sustaining the Transition: The Social Safety Net in Postcommunist Europe* (New York, 1997).

14. This is familiar ground, but very well covered on the basis of a good deal of late communist-period research in *The Origins of Backwardness in Eastern Europe: Economics and Politics from the Middle Ages until the Early Twentieth Century,* ed. Daniel Chirot (Berkeley and Los Angeles, 1989).

15. Martin Wolf, "Caught in the Transition Trap," *Financial Times* 30 June 1999: 11.

16. John Thornhill, "Short Memories, Long Odds," *Financial Times* 9 July 1999: 13.

17. Margaret Coker, "Eurobonds Mark New Iron Curtain: Eastern Europe Divided by Access to Credit," *CBS MarketWatch* 7 May 1999, via Internet.

18. Figures calculated from *The Economist*'s Internet service, *Business Central Europe* <http://www.bcemag.com>.

Progressive Judaism in Poland:
Dilemmas of Modernity and Identity

STEPHEN D. CORRSIN

The purpose of this essay is to outline and comment upon the development of "progressive"—or "liberal," or "reform"—Judaism up to the Second World War in the partitioned Polish lands from the mid-nineteenth century until 1918 and in the independent Second Republic (1918–1939).[1] The focus here is on religious reform rather than on secular developments (acculturation, secularization, assimilation, etc.). The present contribution represents an initial attempt to frame the key issues in this topic. In addition to basic questions of the movement's historical development, a critical question to ask—and keep asking—of the material, is whether there was a "Polish road" to Jewish religious reform, or merely certain "Polish variations" on larger Central and East European Jewish religious themes.[2]

Jewish religious reform in Poland has never been examined comprehensively or in significant depth. A modest number of articles and monographs have surveyed the history of particular synagogues or of reform efforts in individual cities, but in general, the subject has been briefly and unsatisfactorily subsumed under discussions of the movement toward Jewish social, cultural, and political acculturation and assimilation in Poland. This is in part because East European Jewish historiography has tended to be much stronger on political and social developments than on religious topics. It is noteworthy that the ongoing conflicts within modern Judaism worldwide have turned serious study of religious history into something of a minefield. These conflicts approach the level of "culture wars" among the main movements, ranging from Reform and Reconstructionism on the left of the conventional spectrum, through Conservatism and neo-Orthodoxy in the middle, to various more extreme Orthodox elements, including Hasidism, on the right. Jewish Orthodoxy tends to claim that it is the sole branch of Judaism which continues authentic Jewish tradition, and it condemns other movements as having fallen away from or broken with tradition. And even though more liberal elements have intentionally moved away from the demands of traditional law and custom, Reform and Conservative Jews continue to spend a great deal of energy debating which elements of the enormous range of Jewish traditions they are willing or obliged to perpetuate.

Regardless of claims of authenticity and adherence to tradition, all Jewish elements have been changed profoundly over the past 200 years by the general movement in the Western world toward dynamic religious change and, in particular, by the weakening of organized religion's hold on behavior and belief. Much of the extreme nature of contemporary fundamentalism, paradoxically, results from fear of modernity and its effects and temptations.

In the 1980s, Michael Meyer of Hebrew Union College-Jewish Institute of Religion (Reform Judaism's seminary) rewrote the history of the reform movement in Judaism. It seems most sensible to use Meyer's work as a starting point for any further study. In his most important work, *Response to Modernity: A History of the Reform Movement in Judaism*, he does not concern himself with Eastern Europe—either Poland or Russia—to any significant degree.[3] For the study of the progressive movement in Eastern Europe, his 1985 article titled "The German Model of Religious Reform in Russian Jewry" (published in a collection of essays about Gdańsk/Danzig) is of considerable importance. He covers some territory in it that he does not cover in his book.[4]

In the prologue to *Response to Modernity,* Meyer acknowledges the difficulties of defining "the Reform movement" in Judaism. From its earliest stages at the beginning of the nineteenth century in Western Europe, the movement was defined by its "unity of purpose" rather than by its "institutional identity." Therefore, "it is not possible to isolate a doctrinal essence of the Reform movement." Meyer continues:

> Given the impossibility of fixing upon any one self-designation or religious idea in order to decide definitively what falls within and what outside the Reform movement, its boundaries must necessarily remain indistinct . . . Most broadly conceived, the Reform movement might be understood to embrace efforts to establish any Judaism that differs from inherited forms and beliefs as a result of encounter with the modern non-Jewish world . . . The conceptualization which thus emerges for our study may be summed up in this way: the Reform movement came into being gradually out of a coalescence of elements; it was subject to a complex dynamic of external and internal interactions and was renewed by recurrent generational breaks with tradition. It varied in relative salience among its adherents both at any one time and over time, extended from radical rejections of tradition to very mild ones, and eventually touched virtually all of Western Jewry. It coheres as a historical entity more on account of a perceptible center of gravity created by the overlap and abundance of significant elements than on account of fixed definitions or boundaries.[5]

The doctrinal vagueness and lack of organized structure that characterize the reform movement, including progressive or reforming synagogues in Poland, leave scholars in some difficulty. A key first point is that all branches of Judaism have changed radically due to this "encounter with the modern non-Jewish world"; it is characteristic of the reformers that they set about actively and consciously "adapting Judaism to the modern world"—to quote the title of the first chapter of Meyer's book. Further, certain specific markers are needed for a productive discussion of the history of progressive Judaism, in the areas of practice as well as doctrine. A number of particularly important markers stand out. Meyer mentions several doctrinal points that have typically appeared: acceptance of Judaism's historical nature (that is, recognition of Judaism's change over time, as opposed to the view that its essence and main characteristics are unchanging), progressive revelation (as opposed to the notion of the written and oral Torah and other teachings as having been fixed in their entirety at Sinai), universalized rather than solely Jewish messianism, and opposition, in its early decades, to Jewish national or ethnic claims. Certain other, nondoctrinal points can serve as key markers as well. The following are among the most important for the examination of the topic of Jewish religious reform, whether in Poland, Russia, Germany, the United States, or elsewhere. It is not possible to cover these topics in any depth at this point: this can only serve as an outline of critical areas for future research.

1. Reforming synagogues (or other "houses of prayer"): which ones exist, and what is their genealogy? What term is applied to them (e.g., "German" or "Polish" synagogue)?

2. The architecture of the synagogue: in what style is it built?

3. The interior design or layout of the sanctuary: where is the ark with the Torah located? Where is the reading desk? How are the cantor and rabbi, or other prayer leaders or sermon givers, placed? Where are congregants placed, and how are they separated by gender?

4. The style and ambience of the service: is "decorum" called for?

5. The order of the service: which prayers and prayerbooks are used? Are the prayers entirely in Hebrew, or is a vernacular (e.g., German or Polish—although the services were never entirely in the vernacular) used in some cases? Is there a sermon, and if so, what kind—a homily or a more traditional *d'rash* (short explication of a Torah text)? In which language is it given?

6. The rabbis: how are they trained? What are they expected to do, both in religious services and in any pastoral or legal roles?

7. The cantors and the music: how are the cantors trained? What is the style of music? Is there a chorus? An organ?

Accepting that these rank among the most important markers, we can move ahead to other critical questions in Jewish religious reform in the Polish lands. But another basic, nonreligious point must be discussed before going further, particularly for the pre-1918 period: What is meant by "Poland"? Or, as Brian Porter put it in the title of his 1992 article on the rhetoric of Polish nationalism: "Who is a Pole and Where is Poland?" Of course, these questions should be asked, primarily for the postpartition era but also for the interwar period, with reference to an "imagined Poland" that might be accepted by most branches of Polish nationalism. It must also be recognized that there were profound disagreements among these branches. As Porter observes, "at the turn of the twentieth century most Polish political activists dreamed of recreating the Polish state, although they disagreed about where the new Poland should be located and whom it should include."[6]

Answers to the question, "Where is Poland?" for the post-Napoleonic era (1815–1918) normally included not only Congress Poland, the Kingdom of Poland and the central Polish lands under Russian rule, and the southern and southeastern areas of Galicia under Austrian rule (even though the population of eastern Galicia was heavily Ukrainian). The Prussian, Baltic coastal, and Silesian areas which were under Prussian and then German imperial rule would also presumably be included in this "Polish Poland," as would large parts of the Polish "eastern borderlands," or the "western region" in the Russian imperial view—essentially, today's Lithuania, Belarus, and central Ukraine, though the exact boundaries would be disputed even among Poles.

Thus, the following might profitably be asked as well: "Who is a Polish Jew, and where is his or her Poland?" Or should that be, "Who is a Jewish Pole?" What about *Polak wyznania mojżeszowego*, or *Polak pochodzenia żydowskiego*, or even *Polak-Żyd* or *Żyd-Polak*. The latter two in particular are turn-of-the-century terms that seem bitterly quaint nowadays, but they were significant in their day—even down to questions of which word came first (*Żyd* or *Polak*) and whether one or both were capitalized. Moreover, what about Jews who were immigrants to traditionally Polish lands from other parts of the Russian or Austrian Empires—for example, the Russian Jews in Warsaw or Łódź?

Congress Poland and Galicia presumably would be included in most Jewish answers to the question, "Where is Poland?" through most of the period after the partitions. Territories *not* usually included would be those under German rule, because the Jewish populations of these regions quickly assimilated to German Jewry. Located in these territories were the cities of Poznań/Posen, Gdańsk/Danzig, and Wrocław/Breslau, the last an especially significant center for Jewish religious reform. Neither would the Polish "eastern borderlands," where the Jewish populations soon assimilated to what might be termed the Russian "Pale mainstream," be included. By the latter part of the nineteenth century, the major cities of these territories, Warsaw, Łódź, Lublin, and Cracow, would be considered part of Poland in most Jewish world views; Lviv/Lwów/Lemberg was also probably included; but Wrocław, Gdańsk, Poznań, and Vilnius/Wilno/Vilna almost certainly were not. Thus, the geography of "Jewish Poland," at least before 1918, was significantly different from that of "Polish Poland," and, indeed, "Jewish Poland" was much smaller in size.

The interwar period (1918–1939) provides a different picture. As Ezra Mendelsohn has written, the Second Polish Republic had several separate Jewries, their distinctiveness developed after the partitions. In his *Zionism in Poland: The Formative Years, 1915–1926*, he states: "In fact, strictly speaking, there was no such thing as one Polish Jewry, but at least three Polish Jewries, which were united only because of the accidents of war that determined the borders of the new Polish state." Looking in even greater depth at the Jewish population of the Second Republic, it is possible to distinguish four Polish Jewries. There were not only the Jewish communities of Galicia, Congress Poland, and the territories that had been part of Germany; there were also the Jews of the Russian-Polish borderlands. Mendelsohn writes that these border-lands were "a truly multinational area, where no single nationality dominated and which served as a kind of buffer between ethnic Russia and ethnic Poland. The Jews here were little affected by Polish culture, and to the extent that they were acculturated they adopted the Russian orientation which dominated the local secular educational institutions. But there was little real assimilation . . ."[7]

To return to the question raised at the beginning—whether there was a "Polish road" to Jewish religious reform—it is most probable that the answer would be in the negative, in part because of the existence of three or even four Polish Jewries. The "Polish variations" are worthy of note, though they tend to be no more than attempts to graft pieces of modern, secular Polish language and culture onto Jewish practice. The primary reason for the existence of several Polish Jewries is, of course, the fact of the partitions and the widely differing policies and attitudes of the partitioning powers toward their Jewish populations.

Jewish religious reform was very weak in Eastern Europe, including the territories that now make up Poland and the successor states of the Soviet Union. Following Meyer, we see that attempts at reform were relatively stronger in Austria, today's Czech Republic (historic Bohemia and Moravia), and parts of Hungary—though rarely as strong as in parts of Germany proper. Further, it was quite weak in Hungary, including the Slovak territories under Hungarian rule, outside of the major cities. In Congress Poland as well as in the larger Russian Empire, meanwhile, significant attempts at religious reform could be found almost exclusively in the largest cities, Warsaw and Łódź.

Compared to Germany, religious reformers in the "East" faced a much greater mass of traditional Jewry, profoundly rooted in the energetic Orthodox movements of the Hasidim and their anti-Hasidic opponents in the Orthodox rabbinate, the *Mitnagdim*. Further, state policies had enormous impact. It is especially important to take into consideration the degree of authoritarianism and the depth of official antisemitism, as well as the often quite complex government attitudes toward Jewish religious reform. Both the Orthodox and the reformers repeatedly tried to use the power of the state against each other. This was also true in the German states in the nineteenth century, and, indeed, everywhere where such maneuvers were possible.

Religious reform, with all of its related developments, needs to be studied as a separate case in each of the partitioned Polish territories. Galician Jews were strongly influenced by developments in the Habsburg Empire as a whole, and somewhat more open to the Haskalah or "Jewish Enlightenment" movement coming from Germany. From the 1860s on, the process of religious reform, like that of acculturation as a whole, made some progress due to the declining authoritarianism of the Habsburg Empire and the government's relatively positive attitude toward its Jews. This is relative, of course, to the situation in the Russian Empire. Jews in Congress Poland, for example, had to deal with the much more authoritarian and antisemitic Russian state, which moreover enacted policies profoundly hostile to its ethnically Polish population as well. Religious reform here was particularly weak before World War I, largely limited to the establishment of a few "German" synagogues in the second half of the nineteenth century.

The social, cultural, and religious distinctions between Galicia's and Congress Poland's Jews should not, however, be overstated. The Jews of Congress Poland and Galicia shared many characteristics, and particularly the power of the conflicting religious heritages of Hasidism, its *Mitnagdic* rivals, and the Haskalah. The actual boundaries between the empires, and between each of the empires and Germany, were crossed all the time; it might be of particular interest to track the peregrinations of rabbis. Moreover, concrete steps toward religious reform, in terms of doctrines and practices, were in fact not much stronger in Galicia than in Congress Poland: in both regions it was very limited in scope and extent compared not only to Germany, but even to the Czech lands or the metropolises of Budapest and Vienna. Still, reform went somewhat farther in Galicia than in Russian Poland, in part because the Habsburg Empire was more open than the Russian Empire to reforming tendencies emanating from Germany, and because official, institutionalized antisemitism went into decline after the mid-nineteenth century in the Habsburg lands. The Russian imperial government's deep antisemitism combined with its strong opposition to western liberalizing influences in many areas. Although this constituted an important factor in the weakness of the movement to reform Judaism in the Russian Empire, one must not underestimate the ability of Orthodox elements to resist reform, due to the continued energy and hold of Hasidism and other orthodoxies over the greater part of the population.

With regard to interwar Poland, the historiography of religious reform is significantly weaker than for the pre-1914 period. It is clear that acculturation went very far in the 1920s and 1930s within the Jewish populations, in part because of new educational opportunities, and also as part of a general push toward secularization. But the drive toward acculturation and secularization had little in common with the drive toward religious reform. Rather, in their hopes for redemption, Jews turned to secular movements: Zionism, Jewish socialism, etc.

Neither in his *Response to Modernity* nor in his article on Russian Jewry does Meyer attempt to treat Polish developments in any depth, or even to address any unified "Polish" entity. Nor does he use the existing Polish-language literature on the topic. While this literature is very limited, it does provide greater context and texture, as well as a number of interesting details. It is almost entirely locally based, focusing on how it was done in Warsaw, or in Lviv, or in Cracow. In fact, the main monuments of organized Judaism were often linked to religious reform efforts of the nineteenth century, including, for example, the Great Synagogue in Warsaw, the Progressive Synagogue in Lviv, and the Tempel in Cracow. However, there is very little material on any other place, except for the Prussian and Silesian cities of Gdańsk, Poznań, and Wrocław—where, again, developments were closely tied to those elsewhere in Germany. There is, in fact, little question that Jewish religious reform in Poland was concentrated in the major cities, but it is unfortunate, if perhaps inevitable, that so little has been done to examine reform efforts elsewhere. Of course, an enormous amount of archival material was destroyed during World War II, when the synagogues themselves and other Jewish institutions were destroyed by the Nazis—who made no distinction between reformers and Orthodox in their campaign to destroy the Jews.

The literature on Warsaw consists of studies, chiefly article- or chapter-length, which focus on the "German" or "Polish" synagogues, as they were variously called, from the earliest days of the movement up to 1878, when the Great Synagogue on Tłomackie Street was opened. The local Jewish press, particularly the weekly *Izraelita* in the pre-1914 period, also discussed related matters. For the nineteenth century, pleas and polemics by such reformers as Hilary Nussbaum are available.[8] Lviv is the subject of the most significant book-length monograph in the field, Majer Bałaban's *Historia Lwowskiej Synagogi Postępowej*.[9] The great historian, who died during the Second World War, wrote this work on commission from the Synagogue and drawing on its since-lost archives. For Cracow, the most useful study seems also to have been written by the prolific Bałaban; here again the subject is treated briefly and within the context of his two-volume history of the Jews in Cracow and its largely Jewish suburb, Kazimierz.[10]

Studies on the larger topic of acculturation and assimilation often provide interesting material, but they rarely have much to say about religion beyond general comments about the establishment of progressive synagogues. Memoirs by members of assimilationist or acculturated families chiefly document the lack of religious practice within their families, or the younger generation's move away from the faith and practices of their parents.

A particular problem with the older literature is the fact that history seems to come to an end when the local "progressive synagogue" or "temple" opens—in Warsaw, Cracow, and Lviv in the mid-nineteenth century. Thanks to Bałaban's book, this is less the case for Lviv than for the other cities. But even his monograph focuses on the "heroic age" of the 1840s to 1870s, with relatively little of moment happening in the half-century before the Second World War. Perhaps this reflects the persistent sensitivity of the topic of Judaism and Jewish religious practice in Poland in the interwar period (as opposed to Jewish politics and society, for example), which has made historians reluctant to take on the topic. Or, since many historians were associated with Zionist, socialist, or folkist orientations, they may have felt this story of religious change to be of secondary importance. Their reticence may also reflect the fact that the energy of the religious reformers themselves failed once the synagogue's opening ceremonies were complete, and the congregations settled down into a long and quiet twilight of lukewarm reform. Further, it reflects the fact that the historiography of the larger topic of Jewish acculturation and assimilation in Poland is much stronger for the pre–World War I period than for the interwar decades. A final but most critical point: it is only in the 1980s and 1990s that the field of Polish-Jewish historiography in general has begun to recover from the terrible losses of the Second World War.

In his 1985 article on Russian Jewry, Meyer again notes that "the religious reform movement in modern Jewry . . . is scarcely visible at all in Russia except in those instances where German-speaking Jews ventured eastwards." Since the greater part of Polish Jewry fell under Russian rule as a result of the partitions, it should be noted that "Russia" in this instance includes most of historic Poland as well. Meyer thus begins his article from German Jewry as the point of departure for studying religious reform in the Russian Empire. He continues:

> Synagogue reform in Eastern Europe was not modeled on the German Reform movement; it was associated with German Jewry as a whole . . . What became exemplary of modern religious expression . . . was the formal ambience of the synagogue service which, with variations, had become standard in the central synagogues of many German communities by the middle of the nineteenth century. Reformers in Eastern Europe drew on those elements which had become the common reform of German Judaism . . . Little wonder that the East European congregations which introduced reforms were not thought of as reforming but simply as recreating a German synagogue in the Russian Empire.
>
> Toward the middle of the nineteenth century, "German" prayer services were established in a number of Russian cities: in Odessa, Warsaw, Riga, and Vilna. The distinguishing elements common to these congregations were principally aesthetic. The service was conducted in an orderly, decorous manner. A cantor and a choir of boys presented the musical portions of the service, introducing uniformity of cadence . . . The Western-style sermon represented the greatest innovation. On the German model, it was a moral discourse intended to edify, inspire and instruct. It differed both from the learned Talmudic discourses delivered upon occasion by East European rabbis and from the entertaining, often ingenious biblical interpretations of the popular Magidim. This new type of sermon, borrowed by German Jewish preachers both from the Christian counterparts and adapted to Jewish values and symbols, was usually delivered in the German tongue . . . though there were also Hebrew examples, and during the second half of the century Russian and Polish began to take the place of German.[11]

To conclude, the topic of Jewish religious reform in Poland has never ranked high on most agendas for historical research. The assimilationist movement in Poland with which it was associated was often interpreted as somehow spiritually and intellectually bankrupt, even before the destruction of Polish Jewry by the Nazis. Of course, the notion of bankruptcy is precisely the sort of value judgment which historians should avoid.

It is unquestionably the case that Polish Jewish religious reform was neither strong nor widespread. Further, the reforms introduced were tepid at best, and lacked doctrinal or organizational originality. Their proponents were few in both absolute and relative terms, particularly as compared to those in the German Jewish community or even in communities elsewhere in East Central Europe, in the cities of Austria and Hungary. The larger Jewish middle and lower classes in Poland were, by the twentieth century, more inclined to move toward secularist positions (often with politically messianic goals, whether Zionist or socialist, replacing religious goals as objects of fervent belief and desire), rather than toward some position similar to that of the moderately religious American "center" which has kept the Reform movement strong in Judaism. The model of moderate "civic religion," which is strong in America, has never taken hold in Europe. Many of the children and grandchildren of the nineteenth-century Jewish reformers, in Poland as elsewhere in Europe, moved far from their Jewish roots, and some converted to Christianity.

Nonetheless, there are several important reasons for studying Jewish religious reform in the Polish lands. First, it is of interest for its own sake. Second, the reformers were strong enough in the nineteenth century to build synagogues which were regarded—by friends and enemies alike—as symbols of the larger Jewish communities. Finally, developments in the Polish lands were part of the overall Jewish and European "response to modernity" in the nineteenth and twentieth centuries, and the success or failure (or rather, the mixture of the two) of Jewish religious reform in Poland is significant for what it can tell us about the nature of the larger "response." The transformation of religious identification in modern times is of critical importance for understanding other aspects of the transformation of modern identities as well.

NOTES

An earlier version of this article was presented at the 1996 Annual Conference of the American Association for the Advancement of Slavic Studies.

1. It must be understood that no *organized* movement for Jewish reform, or "Reform with a capital 'R,'" existed in Poland. The formally organized reforming movements within Judaism, particularly those now known as Reform, Conservative, and Reconstructionist Judaism, are essentially American movements, albeit descended from nineteenth-century German undertakings. I have chosen to use "Progressive" as the preferred term in this essay to differentiate efforts in Poland from the organized movements in the United States, and because the synagogues concerned (for example in Lviv) sometimes used the Polish term "synagoga postępowa," which can best be translated as "Progressive Synagogue." Meyer (see below) typically refers to "Reform," but that term, capitalized, is not appropriate for Eastern Europe.

2. There is a large and extremely uneven literature on Jewish acculturation and assimilation in Poland, reflecting the still controversial nature of that movement. Scholarly studies focusing on the topic before the First World War include Alina Cała, *Asymilacja Żydów w Królestwie Polskim (1864–1897): Postawy, konflikty, stereotypy* (Warsaw, 1989) (summarized as "The Question of the Assimilation of Jews in the Polish Kingdom [1864–1897]: An Interpretative Essay," *Polin* 1 [1986]: 130–50); and Jerzy Holzer, "Zur Frage der Akkulturation der Jüden in Galizien im 19. und 20. Jahrhundert," *Jahrbücher für Geschichte Osteuropas*, n.s., 37 (1989): 217–27.

3. Michael A. Meyer, *Response to Modernity: A History of the Reform Movement in Judaism* (Detroit, 1995).

4. Michael A. Meyer, "The German Model of Religious Reform and Russian Jewry," in *Danzig Between East and West: Aspects of Modern Jewish History*, ed. Isadore Twersky (Cambridge, MA, 1985), pp. 67–91.

5. Meyer, *Response*, pp. ix–xii.

6. Brian A. Porter, "Who is a Pole and Where is Poland? Territory and Nation in the Rhetoric of Polish National Democracy before 1905," *Slavic Review* 51 (1992): 639.

7. Ezra Mendelsohn, *Zionism in Poland: The Formative Years, 1915–1926* (New Haven, 1981), pp. 17, 21.

8. Hilary Nussbaum, *Z teki weterana warszawskiej gminy starozakonnych* (Warsaw, 1880); idem, *Szkice historyczne z życia Żydów w Warszawie* (Warsaw, 1881); and idem, *Przewodnik judaistyczny obejmujący kurs*

literatury i religii (Warsaw, 1893). Nussbaum also wrote didactic novels on the theme of Jewish enlightenment. The literature on the history of Warsaw's Great Synagogue tends to the anecdotal. Earlier research is summarized in Jacob Shatzky's *Geshikhte fun Yidn in Varshe* (New York, 1947–1953).

Among the recent scholarly studies are Alexander Guterman, "The Origins of the Great Synagogue in Warsaw on Tłomackie Street," in *The Jews in Warsaw: A History*, ed. Władysław T. Bartoszewski and Antony Polonsky (Oxford, 1991), pp. 181–211; and idem, "The Congregation of the Great Synagogue in Warsaw: Its Changing Social Composition and Ideological Affiliations," *Polin* 11 (1998): 112–26. On earlier efforts, see Sara Zilbersztejn, "Postępowa synagoga na Daniłowiczowskiej w Warszawie," *Biuletyn Żydowskiego Instytutu Historycznego w Polsce* 74 (1970): 31–57, which is an abbreviated version of a 1934 thesis directed by Majer Bałaban. On Łódź, the second largest city of the Kingdom of Poland, see articles by Krzysztof Stefański: "The Synagogues of Łódź," *Polin* 11 (1998): 154–67; idem, "Budownictwo synagogalne Łodzi," *Biuletyn Żydowskiego Instytutu Historycznego w Polsce* 169–71(1–3) 1994: 9–19; and idem, "Architektura sakralna Łodzi w latach 1860–1914," *Kwartalnik Architektury i Urbanistyki* 33(2) 1988: 141–71.

9. Majer Bałaban, *Historia Lwowskiej Synagogi Postępowej* (Lviv, 1937). Julian J. Bussgang, "The Progressive Synagogue in Lwów," *Polin* 11 (1998): 127–53. Bussgang draws on Bałaban.

10. Majer Bałaban, *Historia Żydów w Krakowie i na Kazimierzu, 1304–1868,* 2nd ed. (Cracow, 1931–1936).

11. Meyer, "The German Model," pp. 69–70.

The Slavic Saint Jerome: An Entertainment

JOHN V. A. FINE

Despite the cantankerous character of the original, the Saint Jerome that emerged in Dalmatia and then spread to Slavic communities in Rome and eventually to the papal establishment was a much loved figure, a Slav who made huge contributions to Slavic Catholic culture. His alleged contributions included the creation of the Slavic written language and the alphabet in which it was written (namely, Glagolitic), and then producing the text of the Slavic Mass.[1] In fact, Jerome, a fourth-century figure—and the century he lived in was recognized by many of the South Slavs advancing the myth—lived prior to the Slavic migrations which began in the sixth century. Moreover, as is well known, the Old Church Slavonic written language was codified in the ninth century by Constantine/Cyril and Methodius and taken in the Glagolitic alphabet to Great Moravia. In the 880s, in trouble with political authorities, the mission was run out of Great Moravia, and large numbers of its members showed up in Bulgaria. There Glagolitic letters soon were replaced by Cyrillic ones. However, other disciples of the two saints arrived in Croatia and Dalmatia, where under different Church jurisdiction, they and their heirs kept the Glagolitic alphabet and, despite attempts by the educated Dalmatian hierarchy to force Latin on them, succeeded in certain places—like the diocese of Senj, the region around Zadar, the island of Krk, and the other Gulf of Kvarner islands—in keeping Slavic (with Glagolitic texts) into the nineteenth century. The number of Catholics attending Slavic-rite churches was huge. For example, Bishop Martin Brajković of Senj and Modruš in 1701 stated that in his bishopric he had no priests who knew Latin; they all served in "Illyrian," the term commonly used for Slavic at that time. In 1725 the Archbishop of Zadar, Vicko Zmajević, noted that there were 70 parishes of his diocese which used only "Illyrian." At the time, outside of the town of Zadar itself, his diocese had 70 parishes. This meant that every parish in his archdiocese, except the town itself, used Slavic exclusively.[2]

Attacks upon Slavic in Dalmatia, and in neighboring parts of Croatia, began in the tenth century and were taken up at least once in every succeeding century by the Latin-speaking hierarchy in Dalmatia. All sorts of edicts against Slavic came out of councils and from bishops, but exceptions were usually attached to these decrees since in large parts of this region priests simply did not know Latin.

The first of these councils was held in Split in 925 for the purposes of straightening out jurisdictional issues and creating a metropolitan for Dalmatia. Split achieved that status, and the council then turned to the issue of Slavonic in the services. The Italianate bishops in the major sees, strongly supported by the pope, who had expressed his opinions in a letter to the council, unanimously called for Latin; holding the Mass in what the pope called barbarian languages—Slavonic, in this case—was condemned. But an escape clause remained, namely Slavonic could be used in the event that priests of an area knew no Latin.[3] This clearly was the case in most of Dalmatia and Croatia proper, outside the major cities. So, the choice was to retain Slavonic services or shut down the Catholic Church in most of Dalmatia. Slavonic thus continued to thrive.

The issue of Slavonic in services arose again in the third quarter of the eleventh century, and Pope Nicholas II issued an edict, surviving in Pope Alexander II's confirmation from the 1060s, which threatened with excommunication anyone who ordained as a priest a Slav who did not know Latin. The Archdeacon Thomas of Split, writing in the thirteenth century and very much opposed to Slavonic being used liturgically, writes (and I paraphrase): In the time of Archbishop Lovre (1060–1099), who was greatly honored by the kings and rulers of Slavonia (i.e., the Slavic lands), there arose in the Kingdom of Dalmatia and Croatia a crisis. All the prelates of Dalmatia and Croatia condemned the Mass in the Slavonic language. And no one utilizing that language might enter holy orders. There had been, they say, a heretic (!) named Methodius who wrote in this very Slavonic language many lies about the Roman Catholic Church. When these regulations against Slavonic were proclaimed all the Slavophone priests were very unhappy: all their churches were closed and they could no longer carry out their accustomed services. But it then happened in the Croatian regions that a priest named Ulfus (Vulfo or Vuk), bringing gifts from the Croatians, went to Rome to appeal the injunction and convince the pope to restore the former position of the churches and priests in the Slavic kingdom. Ulfus told the pope that he was from the Dalmatian regions. After his visit, Ulfus returned to the Goths (!). [Thomas consistently equated the Slavs with the Goths.] The pope eventually decided against the Slavists and sent an envoy, Cardinal John, to extinguish the flames of godless schism in the Slavic regions.[4]

Despite the papal decision, Slavonic (written in the Glagolitic alphabet) continued to be used in large areas of what we now think of as Croatia, in particular in the regions of Istria and Vinodol, the area in and around Senj, and the islands of the Gulf of Kvarner. Nada Klaić has shown that political divisions greatly facilitated the deep roots that Slavonic grew and which were to guarantee its survival in certain places. First, there was the rivalry for the papal throne between the reform Pope Alexander II (whose reforms included opposition to Slavonic) and the anti-pope Honorius II, to whom Ulfus had turned and who, needing support, accepted Church Slavonic and the hierarchs who favored and used it. Secondly, the political territorial divisions at various times contributed to the absence of any uniform enforcement of papal Latinizing policies: for example, between Byzantine areas (where the administration tolerated Church Slavonic), the Croatian state (often lined up with the reform papacy), and various short-lived entities like the March of Croatia and Dalmatia in the second half of the eleventh century, which included much of Istria, Senj and its hinterland, and some of the Kvarner islands. Since the March was under a German noble family that supported Henry IV against the reform papacy in the Investiture Controversy, it is not surprising that Church Slavonic was not opposed at the time in the March.[5] So, in much of Dalmatia and Croatia proper, outside the major cities, Church Slavonic continued to thrive.

In the mid-thirteenth century, in response to one of these attacks, an appeal from Philip, the bishop of Senj, won papal exception for his whole diocese. We do not possess his letter, only the papal reply. I think it safe to assume that the justification given by the pope had in fact been provided by the bishop of Senj. In any case, the pope, Innocent IV, in a rescript in 1248 declared that since the Slavic language (understood here as the written version) and also the Slavic service/Mass had been created by Saint Jerome—and thus was an ancient heritage—he approved its use in that diocese.[6] Four years later the Benedictines of the monastery of St. Nicholas in Omišalj on Krk sent a similar appeal to the pope. The island had been conquered by the Venetians in 1244, and Venice had imposed a ban on Slavic in the island's churches. The Benedictines in their appeal to the pope stated that as Slavs they used Slavic letters and simply were unable to learn Latin. The Benedictines were successful and received a papal decree in their favor in January 1252.[7] By the end of the century, three orders in the region of Senj, Zadar, and the Kvarner islands—the Benedictines, the Third Order Franciscans, and the order of St. Paul—were all using Slavic almost exclusively.

Once accepted, the Jerome myth spread rapidly throughout the Catholic Balkans and beyond. The Church Slavonic language was usually called Slavic (or some variant of that), and sometimes Illyrian—a term that emerged for the South Slavs in the fifteenth century—but also occasionally "Jerome's language." With some frequency the Glagolitic alphabet came to be called "Jerome's characters" or "letters." A good example of how the myth penetrated into the thinking of even highly educated churchmen can be seen in the case of George (Georgius) of Slavonia (ca. 1355–1416). George grew up in what is now Slovenia, spent time in Krbava in Croatia, and then went to France. He received his Master's from the Sorbonne and ended his career as a cathedral canon in Tours, where he died. George made some marginal notes on a manuscript of St. Jerome's letters. In one letter to a colleague Jerome had referred to translating the Psalms. The saint did not specify the languages involved, but clearly it was a matter of translating from Greek and/or Hebrew into Latin. However, George's marginal comment stated that Jerome was translating the

Psalter into Slavic, and later on George notes that this was "into my language."
Elsewhere in margins of the text George refers to Jerome's (Glagolitic) alphabet as being Croatian.[8] Thus the myth of the fourth-century saint's creation of
Slavic letters had taken deep hold, and the believer here was not some backwoods rustic but a magister from the Sorbonne. Moreover, because Slavs in
and around Dalmatia were not well informed about their origins, some at that
time (and in increasing numbers in the years to follow) expressed the view that
the Slavs (or certain particular subgroups among them) were indigenous to the
region. The obvious anachronism between Jerome's dates and those of the
Slavic migrations was therefore not apparent to them.

The Jerome myth came to be used as justification for Slavic services and
texts each time the Latinists were to launch an attack against them. These
attacks came frequently, in spite of papal approval. But, interestingly, there is
no evidence that any opponent, even as late as the eighteenth century, ever
challenged this myth. An interesting question is why they did not, which I
cannot yet answer. In any case, the development of the legend is a fascinating
story in its own right.

The making of the early Illyrians into Slavs was easily done, since by this
time South Slavs were frequently being called, and calling themselves,
"Illyrians." In the late fifteenth century, under the influence of humanism and
its classical focus, the term "Illyria/Illyrian" emerged to refer to the South Slav
lands and their population. The Illyrians, a pre-Slavic population, were not
Slavs at all, but intellectuals from Dalmatia were not clear on this point. In any
case, in 1470 Antonio Marcello from Cres wrote a description of the "Illyrian
coast." Shortly thereafter, in 1487, the most famous "Illyrianist" from this
period, Juraj Šižgorić, published his work on the region of Illyria and city of
Šibenik. Koriolan Cipiko (Cippico: 1425–1493) in his writings used the term
"Illyrian" for all the Slavic peoples, particularly those from Dalmatia.[9] The
Dubrovnik native Ilija Crijević, on the occasion of the death of the poet Ivan
Gučetić (1451–1502), referred to the deceased as an Illyrian poet and spoke of
his "Illyrian nectar."

The term "Illyrian" was to spread rapidly, especially in Church circles and
in Rome. It became common by the century's end. Nicholas, bishop of Modruš,
was an active papal legate, working in Bosnia and Hungary to try to bring about
common action against the Turks. He regularly used the term "Illyria" for the
Slavic area he covered; for example, in one text he spoke of the difficult
situation the various peoples were then facing from the Turks, especially the
"Illyrian people."[10]

The myth of St. Jerome, who was believed to be an Illyrian—and therefore
also a Slav—surely contributed to this new "Illyrian" nomenclature. In any
case, Jerome certainly gave substance to and reinforced this terminology. In the
process, Jerome became a major patron saint for the Catholic South Slavs
(often referred to as the "patron of the Illyrian nation"), for whom numerous
churches and Dalmatian infants were named. Furthermore, the Slavic guest

house for "Illyrian" pilgrims in Rome, founded in 1453, and its church were named for Jerome. Those who attended its church (be they visitors or expatriates) made up the Congregation of St. Jerome of the Illyrians. Its emblem, designed in the seventeenth century, consisted of a portrait of St. Jerome with the legend "The Society of St. Jerome of the Nations of Illyricum," and also the coats of arms of Croatia, Dalmatia, Slavonia, and Bosnia. A document from 1667, written by one of the directors of this guest house, Jerome Pastrić, states that the Illyrian priests and brothers of its church recited the Mass in the Illyrian language.[11] Since this church functioned in Rome under the watchful eye of a Cardinal protector, "Illyrian" language here refers to Church Slavonic, for the Vatican strongly opposed the Mass being conducted in any vernacular language.

The great poet Marko Marulić (1450–1520) from Split reacted strongly to the claim of an Italian, Jacob Philip from Bergamo, that St. Jerome was an Italian, insisting that he was an Illyrian.[12] Marulić also was most likely the compiler of a life of St. Jerome that exists in two Latin manuscripts and several Slavic ones. A sixteenth-century Slavic version, though full of errors, surprisingly, does not have Jerome translating into Slavic, although it does call him a Slav. In a very confused passage on Jerome and languages, Marulić (or whoever composed the text) states, " . . . all of his life, day and night, he [Jerome] labored for fifty years and six months, translating the Old Testament from Chaldean and Jewish (*židovski*) into Latin, and the New Testament from Croatian (! *hrvaskoga*) into Latin, that means the whole Bible. Jerome is our Dalmatian; he is glorious, honored, and famed, and the holy crown of the Croatian language." Shortly thereafter in the text, the anonymous author credits Jerome with creating a papally accepted Divine Office. But, interestingly enough, he does not make it a Slavic one, even though the tradition was already widespread among the Catholic South Slavs that Jerome had created the Slavic letters (Glagolitic) and the Slavic Mass. The "Life" (at least this text) makes his service a normal Latin one: "The pope, knowing that Jerome was wise in languages, [knowing] Greek, Latin, and Jewish, begged him to make up an office . . . And after he had created the office, he sent it from Bethlehem to Rome to the Holy Father, the pope, and the pope with all the cardinals (!) confirmed it and commanded that the Office of the Christian Faith be said in the way that the blessed Jerome had drawn it up; and from that day to this the [Sacred] Office is said as the blessed Jerome drew it up."[13]

The distinguished Slavicist Vjekoslav Štefanić believes that Marulić was also the likely author of a handwritten gloss (written in what Štefanić sees as an early sixteenth-century hand) in a text of another life of St. Jerome printed in 1485 in Senj. This gloss states that Jerome was from Stridon which lay in the region between Dalmatia (clearly used in a broad sense), namely, that part now vulgarly called Curetia or Croatia, and Pannonia that is now called Slavonia and not Schiavonia (a name the glosser evidently disliked for its link with the word "slave"). The author of the gloss also points out that the term *Slavonia* means "glorious land" (from *slava*, "glory"), and the language is called *Slovine* derived from the River Slava. This conflation of the River Sava with *slava* is unique, but this river, running through Slavonia, might not have been well known by the Dalmatian glosser. The author of the gloss then goes on to say that Jerome was from an Illyrian family, which means that he was a Dalmatian or a Croat—a glorious man produced by a glorious land.[14]

Vinko Pribojević, a Dominican from Hvar, delivered an address there in 1520. Looking to nearby Istria and wanting to show its essence to be Slavic and not Latin, he insisted that the inhabitants of Trieste and Gorica and elsewhere in the region used among themselves only Slavic speech. St. Jerome, who was from Istria, was not an Italian but a Slav. We [the Dominican and his audience] should all learn from that Dalmatian [Jerome]. How can one put the Thracians, Mysians, and Illyrians among the Greeks and Epirotes, from whom they differ in language and customs? Illyrians, Thracians, and [ancient] Macedonians then (!) as now are of the same Slavic family/people (*natio*) and language. And the orator goes on to associate the name Slav with the word "glory."[15] Pribojević's text, when it was printed in 1532, was also important because it introduced the South Slavs to the text of Alexander the Great's donation charter. [16]

This same general Slavic or South Slavic vision—as opposed to a focus on any particular people within that group—underlay the work of the much better-known author Mavro Orbini, who published his famous history of the [South] Slavs in 1601. Orbini nicely, but incorrectly, solves the Illyrian-Slav problem. He keeps the Illyrians as Slavs, but aware of the Slavic invasions (which he describes), he presents a mixing of old Slavic inhabitants (Illyrians) and the Slavic newcomers. Unlike many of his humanist-influenced contemporaries, however, Orbini preferred the term "Slav" to "Illyrian." Thus Orbini spoke consistently of the Slavs, the Slav nation (*la natione Slava*), and the Slavic language. The language received particular emphasis, for, as he stated, the unity of speech generally demonstrates the unity of a people. And throughout his work Orbini emphasizes the common speech among the different Slavic peoples.

Orbini lays out his views in the first two chapters of his *Kingdom of the Slavs* (*Il regno degli Slavi*). According to him, the Slavs were descended from Japhet, Noah's son, whose progeny migrated to Scandinavia. From there they spread out and conquered many lands and peoples. One of the first places many settled was Sarmatia, their second homeland; from there they moved out in several different directions. The ones in Sarmatia were the Russians, and back in Roman times some of them settled Illyricum. The indigenous peoples of the Balkans, the Thracians, Dacians, and Illyrians all spoke the same Slavic language, as did the Goths. Though it is clear that the Goths were from Scandinavia, it is not clear when they appeared in the Balkans. But, in any case, in the seventh century, those labeled the Slavs arrived there. These Slavs laid waste to Illyricum in company with the [Slavic] Goths. Many say that before this seventh-century migration the people in Dalmatia spoke Latin and Greek, but this is not true. The people in Illyricum always spoke Slavic. The [Slavic-speaking] Illyrians were overrun by the Goths and Slavs and this may have affected their original Slavic speech. But, for all practical purposes, the language spoken in Illyricum remained the same after the Slavic invasions of the seventh century. The only Latin speakers on the east side of the Adriatic were the Romans who had occupied certain Dalmatian cities. This can be seen by the fact that St. Jerome, who lived 200 years before the [later] Slavic invasions, spoke Slavic and created the Slavic liturgy. He could not have done this had he not been a Slavic speaker. Thus Jerome's "Slavicness" had become a major established fact, able to be used to prove other things, i.e., the "Slavicness" of the Illyrians.

Orbini then repeats much material emphasizing the relationships among various peoples. In Scandinavia all the Slavs had been called Goths. Particularly important in this Slavic-Goth confederation were the Vandals, who moved south toward the Mediterranean. To the Vandals belonged the Muscovites, Russians, Poles, Bohemians, Circassians, Dalmatians, Istrians, Croatians, Bosnians, Bulgarians, and Rasciani (Serbs). Moreover, the Scandinavian origins of the Slavs allowed Orbini to make the original Normans into Slavs as well. The Avars, too, were Slavs. And so were the Macedonians of Alexander of Macedon and even the Amazons.

Orbini also solved a dilemma that arose after more had been learned about Cyril and Methodius, and certain contradictions had emerged between what they allegedly had done and what had been done by Jerome. Orbini's solution would be repeated thereafter by those few others who became aware of this contradiction. To clarify the apparent confusion between the two great "Slavic" saints, Jerome and Cyril, Orbini explicitly explains that the first Slavic letters (literally letters, i.e., Glagolitic) had been worked out long ago by St. Jerome, whereas St. Cyril had later created a second alphabet, Cyrillic.[17]

*   *

*

Sadly, this attractive figure was entirely myth, undeserving of the love and credit attached to his name. The real Jerome showed himself to be an intolerant pit-bull, who never let go of anyone who disagreed with him, endeavoring to bring about that individual's destruction, including his own former close friend Rufinus of Aquileia.[18] But his image was instrumental in preserving a living written Slavic language in notarial and clerical circles in parts of Dalmatia and Croatia into the nineteenth century. So, whereas the dominant peoples of Europe, like the French and Germans, had to forego their languages in churches or else become Protestants, the South Slavs of northern Dalmatia and northwest Croatia could remain Catholic and worship in their own language or a near variant of it.

When, after the collapse of Venice in 1797 and the Austrian takeover of Venetian Dalmatia, the Church hierarchy (excluding the bishop of Senj) used the opportunity to go after Slavic services again, this time on the Kvarner island of Lošinj, the people of Lošinj appealed to Rome and Vienna still referring to the controversial service as the Mass of St. Jerome, venerated by the Dalmatian nation. The hierarchical dissident, the bishop of Senj, himself also threatened, rallied to the islanders' defense and, in learned appeals, brought out the whole history of the service's approved use by Rome, going back to the privileges of 1248 from Pope Innocent IV and noting that from that time on Catholics of this region had retained the privilege of using the Slavonic language printed in the characters of St. Jerome.[19] The Austrians had little sympathy for such antiquarianism, and Napoleon's French—in their brief Illyrian interlude—had even less. The Church hierarchs, therefore, were free to take what measures they wanted, and in the course of the nineteenth century, one by one the Glagolitic-Slavic clerics were replaced by shiny new educated clerics performing Latin Masses unintelligible to everyone but themselves. But, even though the Mass of Jerome disappeared in the nineteenth century, it still had held sway in much of northern Dalmatia for nearly six centuries. Thus, one may argue that, if we were to exclude the real Jerome's truly monumental biblical translations, the positive contributions of pseudo-Jerome would greatly outweigh those of the actual fourth-century Church Father.

NOTES

1. A distinction might be made between Old Church Slavonic (the language codified by Cyril and Methodius and used in Slavic Orthodox churches well into this century) and Slavic (the general family of languages to which Russian, Serbo-Croatian, etc. belong). Of course, Old Church Slavonic constitutes a Slavic language. When the Roman Catholic Church did grant permission for "Slavic" in services for certain particular areas, it had Old Church Slavonic and its later recensions in mind. The Catholic Church opposed vernaculars for the Mass, though it allowed them for sermons and pastoral work. However, few texts (whether by locals, travelers, or the Church) distinguished between Church Slavonic and local Slavic dialects, and simply referred to the language in church and on the street as Slavic. And, in fact, there often was no difference, for, despite regulations, many local priests did not know Church Slavonic and conducted the whole service (including the Mass) in their local dialects. Service books, called Šćavets, also existed that provided in everyday language the services the priests were to conduct during a calendar year. The local bishops (mostly foreigners) were not able—and probably few even tried—to enforce Slavonic over vernaculars. As foreigners, they probably could not tell the difference between different recensions of Slavic and, in any case, the Church could serve the congregations better in a language the populace understood. When the term "Illyrian" came into use to mean "Slavic" or "South Slavic," it too did double duty and was used both for spoken dialects and the proper Church language. The term "Glagolitic" strictly should be used only for an alphabet. However, it was also used for the language (both Church and spoken) of those who employed it, and Slavic-language priests were very frequently called "glagoljaši." In this article, I make no attempt to employ the Church Slavonic/Slavic distinction rigorously, since most of the sources I used did not make it.

2. The two examples cited by Jerko Fućak, *Šest stoljeća hrvatskoga lekcionara u sklopu jedanaest stoljeća hrvatskoga glagoljaštva* (Zagreb, 1975), p. 117.

3. On the Council of 925, see John V. A. Fine, *The Early Medieval Balkans* (Ann Arbor, 1983), pp. 266–73.

4. For Thomas's text (which I have presented in an abridged paraphrase), see Thomas Archidiaconus, *Historia Salonitana*, ed. Franjo Rački (Zagreb, 1894), pp. 49–55. [=Jugoslavenska Akademija Znanosti i Umjetnosti (henceforth JAZU), Monumenta spectantia historiam Slavorum meridionalium, 26.]

5. On these struggles between popes and anti-popes, the different policies of the different political administrations, and on the short-lived so-called

March of Croatia and Dalmatia, see Nada Klaić, "Historijska podloga hrvatskoga glagoljaštva u X i XI stoljeću," *Slovo* 15–16 (1965): 225–79, esp. pp. 258–79.

6.   Tadija Smičiklas, ed., *Codex diplomaticus regni Croatiae, Dalmatiae et Slavoniae*, vol. 4 (Zagreb [JAZU], 1906), p. 343.

7.   Ibid., p. 479.

8.   On George of Slavonia, see Franjo Šanjek and Josip Tandarić, "Juraj iz Slavonije (oko 1355/60–1416): Profesor Sorbonne i pisac, kanonik i penitencijar stolne crkve u Toursu," *Croatica Christiana periodica* 8, no. 13 (1984): 1–23, esp. pp. 2–3, 6–7.

9.   On Marcello and Cipiko, see Miroslav Kurelac, "Paladije Fusko— Palladius Fuscus: Život i djelo," Kurelac's introduction to Paladije Fusko, *Opis obale Ilirika (De situ orae Illyrici)*, Latin text and Serbo-Croatian translation, ed. and trans. Bruna Kuntić-Makvić (Zagreb, 1990), pp. 28, 49. On Šižgorić, see Juraj Šižgorić (Šibenčanin), *O smještaju Ilirije i o gradu Šibeniku (De situ Illyriae et civitate Sibenici)*, Latin text and Serbo-Croatian translation, ed. and trans. Veljko Gortan (Šibenik, 1981).

10. On Nicholas of Modruš and Ilija Crijević, see Marin Franičević, *Povijest hrvatske renesansne književnosti* (Zagreb, 1983), pp. 25, 174, 298.

11. On the St. Jerome guest house in Rome, see Ivan Crnčić, "Imena Slovjenin i Ilir u našem gostinjcu u Rimu poslije 1453 godine," *Rad* (JAZU) 79 (1886): 1–70.

12. Franičević, *Povijest hrvatske renesansne književnosti*, pp. 114, 222.

13. On these anonymous texts (and the likelihood of Marulić being involved in them), see Vjekoslav Štefanić, in his introduction to *Hrvatskog književnost srednjega vijeka* (Zagreb, 1969), pp. 43–44; and Vjekoslav Štefanić, "Glagoljski Transit svetoga Jeronima u starijem prijevodu," *Radovi Staroslavenskog Instituta* 5 (1964): 149. For the Slavic text, see "Život svetoga Jeronima," in Vatroslav Jagić, "Ogledi stare hrvatske proze," *Starine* (JAZU) 1 (1869): 226–36.

     The most amusing expression of languages in translation at this time comes from a chronicler, Priest Andrija of Istria. Writing around 1520 in Glagolitic, he stated that "this book [his chronicle] was translated from grammar into the Croatian language." His "grammar" presumably refers to a formal and non-spoken language, probably Latin, but conceivably Church Slavonic.

14. Vjekoslav Štefanić, "Glagoljski Transit," pp. 144–52; for the text itself, p. 145.

15. Vinko Pribojević (Vincentius Priboevius), *O podrijetlu i zgodama Slavena (De origine successibusque Slavorum)* ed., intro., notes Grga Novak, Serbo-Croatian trans. Veljko Gortan (Zagreb [JAZU], 1951), pp. 169–75.

16. Vinko Pribojević published a Latin version of Alexander's donation to the Slavs in 1532 along with his speech's original Latin text. Pribojević claimed that the document had been discovered in Constantinople and translated from the Ancient Greek. According to the document, Alexander, Lord of the World (*dominus mundi*), in the twelfth year of his reign, pleased with the faithful service his Slavic troops had given him in his campaigns, issued to the Slavs from his court in Alexandria a donation charter awarding them more or less all of Eastern Europe from the Danube to the North Sea. The territory is worth noting, since it more or less excludes the South Slav lands; but the reason for this is not hard to find, since the earliest version of the text appears in a thirteenth-century Polish chronicle from which it found its way seemingly into a fourteenth-century Czech one. Thus, the territorial assignment was expressed to suit the needs of these West Slavs. Many others would make use of this text, including Orbini (whom we turn to next), who published an Italian translation of the donation in his major work on the Slavs. Moreover, Pribojević, in depicting the ancient Macedonians as Slavs, implied Alexander was one. And this belief about Alexander's ethnicity was to be explicitly stated by various Renaissance writers including Hanibal Lucić, Dinko Ranjina, Dominico Zlatarić, and Ivan Gundulić. (Hrvoje Morović, "Legenda o povelji Aleksandra Velikoga u korist Slavena," in Hrvoje Morović, *Sa stranica starih knjiga* [Split, 1968], pp. 109–124.)

   Though scholars have accepted the northern (or West Slav) origin of the Alexandrian donation, Morović, on the basis of circumstantial evidence, advances good reasons to suggest a so-far-undocumented South Slavic provenance for it. After all, Macedonia lay in what became South Slavic territory; classical sources on Alexander known at the time reported that he had Illyrians as allies; and already in the thirteenth century, the Illyrians were being depicted as Slavs by Catholic South Slavs (the whole St. Jerome complex). Though the earliest reference to the donation was in a thirteenth-century Polish text, Morović argues that it would be plausible to postulate a slightly earlier origin for it among the actual people who perceived themselves as descendants of those who were the recipients of Alexander's donation; for the grant has that ruler honoring those Slavs who had been his faithful military supporters. Moreover, the thirteenth century was the time when the bishop of Senj had persuaded the pope to recognize the Slavonic liturgy in his diocese, because it had been created by the Illyrian-Slav St. Jerome. And finally, Morović notes that the earliest Czech reference to the donation is in a document found in the Slavonic monastery of Na Slovanech in Prague, which was resurrected in that period and had close association with Glagolitic monks from what is now Croatia. These monks, Morović suggests, thus could easily have been the source for the Czech tradition. Should Morović's speculation be correct, one could postulate that the earliest version of the donation would have had a more southernly territorial assignment, but that that section had been altered in local interests by the Polish chronicler. However, despite plausibility, no early South Slavic text has been uncovered.

17. Mavro Orbini, *Kraljevstvo Slovena*, ed. Sima Ćirković (Belgrade, 1968). See also front material in this volume, Miroslav Pantić, "Mavro Orbini— Život i rad"; and Franje Barišić, "Kratak sadržaj prvog i drugog poglavlja Orbinova dela," pp. CXXXIX–CLII.

18. On the real Jerome (seen with more sympathy than I can muster) and Rufinus, see J. N. D. Kelly, *Jerome: His Life, Writings, and Controversies* (New York, 1975); Ellen Poteet, "In a Parting Sea: The Apostolic Tracks of Christian Controversy in the Lives of Athanasius, Jerome, and Rufinus, 325–411 A.D.," Ph.D. dissertation, University of Michigan, Ann Arbor, 1998.

19. On the Lošinj events, see Šime Ljubić, "Borba za glagoljicu na Lošinju," *Rad* (JAZU) 57 (1881): 150–87.

Surzhyk: The Rules of Engagement

MICHAEL S. FLIER

On 23 August 1994, Ukrainian state radio altered its hourly time announcement, reverting to the Soviet model: у Києві вісім годин 'The time in Kyiv is
eight o'clock'.[1] The change elicited passionate responses from readers of
Literaturna Ukraïna, among others. One of them, an academician from Lviv,
went so far as to contact the appropriate authorities to complain and reported
the results in a letter to the newspaper readership:

> As the board of radio broadcasting informed me, it was forced to do it on the
> basis of an administrative decision in the presidium of the Ukraine State TV-
> Radio Broadcasting Company, allegedly made in connection with numerous
> letters from radio listeners who can't understand [«не понімают»] the Ukrai-
> nian «восьма година».

Perceiving this change as an attempt by state radio broadcasting to further
President Kuchma's original Russian-language initiatives (later rescinded) in
Ukraine's official language controversy, the writer concluded with a mordant
response of his own:

> If that is how it is, you might as well switch immediately to «восемь часов»,
> and skip the Uke-ified hodge-podge «вісім годин» altogether.[2]

This vignette conveys a larger truth about language reality in modern
Ukraine, a nation in which "the medium is the message" has special resonance.

No question has been more central to the notion of Ukrainian nationality
than the choice of Ukraine's official language.[3] The Ukrainian SSR Language
Law of 1989[4] and the Ukrainian Constitution of 1996 assign to Ukrainian the
status of state language (державна мова) or official language (офіційна
мова), but Russian (as well as other "minority" languages) may also be used
alongside Ukrainian in an official capacity in clearly defined situations.[5] As
contentious as the battle for language supremacy has been, the choice has
generally been framed as one between standard languages, Ukrainian or Russian. What has tended to be ignored officially is another linguistic struggle, this
for the very integrity of the Ukrainian language itself. In this confrontation, the
choice is not Ukrainian *or* Russian, but Ukrainian *and* Russian, in the form of a
hybrid—*surzhyk*—a nonstandard language that incorporates elements of both.[6]

Disregarded by officials and despised by purists, Ukrainian-Russian
surzhyk, which I shall represent henceforth as Surzhyk with a capital "S,"
remains a poorly understood phenomenon in contemporary Ukrainian society.

There are no statistics about it because it is not recognized as a valid alternative in government questionnaires. Furthermore, its substandard status often results in linguistic stigmatization,[7] which in turn affects speaker response. Apparently significant numbers of speakers, for whom Surzhyk is a first language, live in and around urban centers outside western Ukraine, where the southwestern literary norm predominates. Without reliable statistics, however, it is impossible to determine their fluent command of either Ukrainian or Russian as distinct languages.[8]

As Ukrainian and Russian have competed with each other to fulfill the role of high language in Ukraine, Surzhyk has performed the function of low language.[9] In so doing, Surzhyk has gained a certain cachet in the past five years as the language of the alienated and the rebellious, of those who press against the norms of social convention, whether members of the youth culture, the underworld, the military, or the socially conscious hip crowd. During this same period, a number of modern authors have written works of prose—mostly short stories in urban settings—that make effective stylistic use of Surzhyk in presenting characters from these various segments of Ukrainian society.

Surzhyk is commonly attacked in newspaper articles, letters to the editor, and style manuals as an insidious phenomenon in modern Ukraine. Perhaps the most ardent brief against it is *Antysurzhyk,* a style manual cum etiquette book published in 1994 under the auspices of the Ministry of Education.[10] The editor, Oleksandra Serbens'ka, has described the Russian component of Surzhyk as a virus slowly infecting a helpless Ukrainian organism, the result of an original Soviet plan to carry out "systematic linguicide," the conscious destruction of the Ukrainian language. In her understanding of Surzhyk, the mixing of Ukrainian and Russian components is done arbitrarily [довільно].[11]

One might well question, however, the extent to which a plan for linguicide is systematic, if the means for implementing the resultant hybrid are so arbitrary. Can any Ukrainian words be mixed with Russian words in Surzhyk, as Serbens'ka claims—a kind of macaronic speech writ large—or are there constraints on their juxtaposition? Are *all* Ukrainian nouns, pronouns, adjectives, and verbs capable of inflecting according to Russian models, or only some? Are the phonological norms of Ukrainian violated at will in Surzhyk or are there limitations? In this linguistic contest between Ukrainian and Russian, what are the rules of engagement, if any? The present report investigates in a preliminary way the questions raised above in order to establish a typological basis for an extended analysis and objective discussion of Surzhyk in the future.

Since there are sources of substandard Ukrainian other than those generated by Russian contact, it is useful to limit reference of the term Surzhyk in this study to that hybrid in which the *entire* grammar of Ukrainian—phonology, morphology, syntax, lexicon—contains Russian-influenced elements or distribution not otherwise represented in an identical function in Contemporary Standard Ukrainian.[12] It is this *total* grammatical criterion that may be used to distinguish Russian-induced forms of Surzhyk from Ukrainian dialectal forms or substandard speech found in the grammars of some Ukrainian speakers (or speakers of Surzhyk, for that matter), but not prompted by any direct connection to Russian.

It is useful to begin with the etymology of *surzhyk* itself to provide a clearer sense of its nature and status. The word *surzhyk* or related forms is found in many East and West Slavic languages, cf. Ukr. *су́ржик*; Russ. *су́ржанка, су́ржанец*; Pol. *sążyca, sążyca*; Cz. *souržice, sourež*. All are derived from the Late Common Slavic prefix *sǫ-* 'with' plus the nominal root *rъž* 'rye' and a variety of nominal suffixes. The original meaning, as posited by Vasmer [Fasmer],[13] is 'impure wheat with an admixture of rye'. According to Hrinchenko's dictionary,[14] *surzhyk* refers to mixed bread grains or flour made from them, e.g., wheat and rye, rye and barley, barley and oats. The root 'rye' presupposes that the originally narrow reference of *surzhyk* was eventually broadened to include various mixtures of grain. Metaphorically *surzhyk* was eventually extended beyond the agricultural sphere to human reproduction. The second meaning of *surzhyk* in Hrinchenko's dictionary denotes a person of mixed stock (человек смешанной расы)—in his example, Ukrainian and Gypsy.

The Academy dictionary[15] essentially reproduces Hrinchenko's first meaning, omits the second, but then adds a new abstract, colloquial meaning, one remarked only in the Soviet period:

> Elements of two or more languages, joined artificially [штучно], without adhering to the norms of the literary language; impure language.[16]

A closer look at the course of the etymology and its subsequent development reveals a structural asymmetry present in all usages of the word, direct and metaphorical, that requires clarification. In the original sense of *surzhyk* as a blend of grains, wheat and rye, the ingredients were not equivalent in value. *Surzhyk,* glossed roughly as 'with rye mixture', was not so much mixture as admixture, with wheat as the basic, unmarked and thus unstated, component together with smaller amounts of rye.[17] The development of secondary meanings such as 'mixed breed', 'hybrid', 'non-normative impure language' manifests an evaluative dimension that derives from the original asymmetry. This is no neutral blend of ingredients but rather an impure, sullied product of contamination. The reference to a mix of breeds, for example, assumes the pure, positive, unmarked "us" as basic with an admixture of the impure, negative, marked, polluting "them."

It is thus reasonable to assume that Ukrainian-Russian Surzhyk is also based on asymmetry: it implies a Ukrainian base with an admixture of Russian, or more properly speaking, ukrainianized Russian, which can be represented symbolically as $S = U/r^U$.[18] Because the word *surzhyk* technically can refer to a hybrid of any two (or more) languages, it would be possible in future studies to analyze Ukrainian-Polish surzhyk (U/P^U) in western Ukraine or Russian-Ukrainian surzhyk (R/u^R) in eastern Ukraine, this latter, a hybrid consisting of a Russian base with an admixture of russianized Ukrainian. Ostensibly each of these hybrids has its own rules of combinability, a consequence of distinct rules of engagement between different grammars in different positions of dominance (base or admixture). The complications of this variety of possibilities demonstrate the inadequacy of descriptive terms such as "arbitrarily" and "artificially" used to describe Surzhyk (U/R^U) in the present study.

In attempting to discern a rule-governed basis for Surzhyk, we leave aside obviously important pragmatic, sociolinguistic, psycholinguistic, and political dimensions that deserve separate study, especially the status and function of Surzhyk in contemporary Ukrainian society.[19]

An analysis of Surzhyk depends on access to reliable data, preferably whole texts of connected discourse that present the hybrid as a functional form of communication in a variety of contexts, a database rich enough to support far-reaching generalization. Unfortunately no such database exists. What we have instead are scattered words, phrases, single sentences, and occasional paragraphs found in journalistic writings, prescriptive manuals, and political and social analyses. These sources either document the phenomenon or, more likely, condemn its ill effects.[20]

Because Surzhyk at this point is largely an oral rather than written language, there is a pressing need to record a large corpus of conversations containing it. In such a project, speakers would be characterized according to such sociolinguistic criteria as place of birth, age, gender, education, and profession to enable researchers to plot the development of Surzhyk across various parameters, including generation and social class. Lacking that, we must rely on the few sources available for a preliminary evaluation.

In the second chapter of *Antysurzhyk* Serbens'ka presents paired columns of examples of Surzhyk juxtaposed with correct Ukrainian usage. Virtually all the examples provided represent primary types of lexical or syntactic substitution, and show effects of morphological and phonological influence.

(1) *Lexical transfers*

Surzhyk	Ukrainian	Gloss
a. **Прихожа** в нас велика.	**Передпокій** у нас великий.	Our foyer is large.
b. Візьми **гвозді**!	Візьми **цвяхи**!	Take the nails!
c. Діти, **завтракать**!	Діти, **снідати**!	Children, breakfast is ready!
d. Вчора я був на **стражі**.	Вчора я був на **сторожі**.	Yesterday I was on guard duty.

A lexical transfer (borrowing) in Surzhyk is a Russian-based form not otherwise found in Ukrainian. Examples of Russian transfers are given in (1) along with the suggested Ukrainian versions provided by Serbens'ka. We can represent in italics the phonemic spellout of the Russian model and its Surzhyk product with a linear sequence of morpheme boundaries, the actual derivation of the underlying stem simplified for presentation.[21]

The russified transfer has replaced its Ukrainian counterpart, but not without modification where required. In (1a) the substantivized R adjective *pr'i-xož-aja* conforms to the U adjectival paradigm as *prÿ-xož-a* with nom.sg.fem. ending {a}, and is subject to U morphophonemics through the replacement of the R prefix {pr'i} with U {prÿ}. In (1b) R *gvozd'-i* substitutes for U *c'vjax-ÿ*, but with the regular morphophonemic substitution of *h* for *g*.[22] In (1c) Russian *zavtrak-a-t'* serves as the infinitive for 'to breakfast', with an adjustment of the frequency of the infinitival suffix allomorph *tÿ* in favor of *t'*.[23] The S phrase *на стражі* 'on guard' in (1d) shows the preference for the Russian Church Slavonic layer of the Russian lexicon as opposed to the native East Slavic representation of U *на сторожі*.[24]

(2) *Lexical extensions*

Surzhyk	*Ukrainian*	*Gloss*
a. **Столова**—на право.	**Їдальня**—направо.	The dining room is on the right.
b. Ми **переписуємося**.	Ми **листуємося**!	We correspond.
c. Ви шиєте **юбки**?	Ви шиєте **спідниці**?	Do you make (sew) skirts?

A Ukrainian lexeme with a set of meanings that has been extended to match those of its Russian counterpart is a lexical *extension* in Surzhyk, symbolized $^{+n}$ to represent the *n* number of extended meanings accorded the erstwhile Ukrainian form. In (2a) the Ukrainian adjective *столова* 'table' is extended to express both meanings of Russian *столовая*, 'table' (adj.) and 'dining room' (substantivized adj.), hence S *столова*$^{+n}$. The Surzhyk verb *переписувати(ся)*$^{+n}$ 'copy, transcribe; rewrite'; *and* 'correspond' in (2b) is used in conformity with Russian *переписывать(ся)*. The Ukrainian noun *юбка*, normally limited to meaning 'skirt' in a technical sense, is extended in S *юбка*$^{+n}$ (2c) to refer to an article of clothing, as in the Russian usage.

(3) *Lexical calques*

Surzhyk	*Ukrainian*	*Gloss*
a. **розположення** статей	**розміщення** статей	the placement of the articles
b. **накінець**	**нарешті**	finally
c. **покупателі**	**покупці**	shoppers

Calques may be lexical or syntactic. In either case, the collocation of elements in the embedded language (Russian) provides the model of concatenation for the analogous elements in the matrix language (Ukrainian).[25] In (3a) R stem *roz-po-lož-en'ij-* provides the model for S *roz-po-lož-en'n'j-*, which preserves U morphophonemic consonant gemination {en'j ⇒ en'n'j}.[26] Another option permits the substitution of the Russian suffix {en'ij}, thus S *roz-po-lož'-en'ij-*. The S adverbial calque *na-kin-ec'* is patterned after R *na-kon-ec* in (3b), but retains the Ukrainian nominal root {kin} and the suffix {e$^{\emptyset}$c'} with the uniquely Ukrainian *c'*.[27] In (3c) R *po-kup-a-tel'-i* provides the model for the Surzhyk form, but Ukrainian phonotactics in this instance may render the t of the suffix {tel'} with hard [t°] instead of the soft [t'] used in Russian, although the latter is reported as well.

There are few immediately obvious constraints on lexical transfers, extensions, and calques for nouns, verbs, and adjectives.[28] Future study will reveal the extent to which syntactic relations (especially specifier-head and head-complement relations), stylistics, pragmatics, and other discourse factors constrain choice. In modern fiction, for example, the introduction of Surzhyk into an otherwise Ukrainian text produces an abrupt transition that signals a change in atmosphere, a shift in topic, a deepening of character development, etc. Even so, the proportion of Russian-based forms to Ukrainian forms and forms appropriate to Ukrainian and Russian is roughly 1 out of every 4, that is, around 25 percent (see below).

(4) *Syntactic calques*

a.	S	нарада по проблемам	'a conference on issues (problems)'
b.	S	три конкурсних екзамена	'three competitive examinations'
c.	S	в десять годин	'at ten o'clock'
d.	S	самий дорожчий	'the most expensive'
e.	S	більше мого	'bigger than mine'
f.	S	пробач мене	'excuse me'

Since the majority of case marking patterns of verbal, nominal, and adjectival government in Ukrainian and Russian are identical, most of the syntactic calques result from the incorporation into Surzhyk of localized Russian constructions, e.g., prepositional phrases, numeral phrases, or phrase heads with distinctive government.[29] In (4a), for example, case is marked for dative with the preposition *no* in the delimitative sense of 'on', 'concerning', 'as regards', as seen in R *совещание по проблемам,* as opposed to U *нарада з проблем,* with preposition *з* + genitive. The U preposition *no* does not otherwise select the dative. Russian syntax is invoked as well in (4b), in which the numeral *три* marks the noun as gen.sg. but the adjectival modifier as gen.pl., in contrast to the Ukrainian pattern with the noun and adjective modifier marked for nom.pl., e.g., U *три конкурсні екзамени.* The time expression 'at ten o'clock' in (4c) is rendered with the preposition *в* plus the accusative of the cardinal numeral 10, which itself governs the genitive plural of the noun, all according to the Russian syntactic pattern, as compared with the Ukrainian *о десятій годині,* with the preposition *о* plus the locative singular of the ordinal numeral and the noun. In (4d) the analytic Russian-based superlative construction *самый дорогой* provides part of the model for S *самий дорожчий,* the other part derivable from the synthetic Ukrainian counterpart *найдорожчий.* In this instance Surzhyk has produced a third alternative, with Russian-induced *самий* juxtaposed to the U comparative degree of the adjective *дорогий,* a construction absent in Russian and Ukrainian. The comparative *більше мого* in (4e) governs the genitive as in Russian, unlike the analytic U constructions *більше від мого* or *більше ніж мій.* The Russian-induced accusative case in (4f) displaces the Ukrainian dative after the verb *пробач,* thus S *пробач мене* (cf. R *извини меня*) instead of U *пробач мені.*

In principle, syntactic calquing appears to be open-ended within the relatively narrow range of actual Ukrainian-Russian difference, subject only to the kinds of syntactic, stylistic, pragmatic, and discourse constraints that may be operative in the case of lexical transfer and extension.

(5) *Morphemes subject to russification in Surzhyk*

	prefix	suffix	ending	root
pronoun	NA	NA	–	–
adjective	–	–	–	+
verb	–	(+)	(+)	+
noun	–	+	+	+

+	=	occurs	–	=	does not occur
(+)	=	occurs rarely	NA	=	not applicable

The chart in (5) presents a gradient hierarchy of morphemes subject to russification in Surzhyk. The morphological component, which governs the phonemic shape of morphemes, appears to be the most conservative in the grammar of Surzhyk, a result predicted by sociolinguistic experience.[30] It is noteworthy that in all the examples of Surzhyk cited in Serbens'ka's manual, the Ukrainian inflectional endings of pronouns, adjectives, and (with few exceptions) verbs are preserved intact; and nominal and numeral desinences are minimally altered. The closed classes of morphemes, such as pronouns, prepositions, prefixes, and suffixes tend to preserve their Ukrainian formal properties most consistently.

Pronouns. The personal pronouns retain their Ukrainian shape in all of Serbens′ka's examples, thus third-person singular *він* (nom.sg.masc.), *йому* (dat.sg.masc.-neut.), *ним* (inst.sg.masc.-neut.), not **он, *їму,*[31] **ім*; and second-person singular *тебе* (gen.-acc.), *тобі* (dat.-loc.), *тобою* (inst.), not **тебя, *тебе, *тобой,* respectively. Likewise determiners and quantifiers such as *цей, той, весь, всякий*; interrogative-relative pronouns such as *хто, що, котрий,* and qualitative pronouns such as *такий, який* retain their Ukrainian form in her manual.

Adjectives. The Surzhyk variant of U *рекомендований лист* 'registered letter' is *заказний лист,* not **заказной лист,* which would have introduced not only the lexical transfer stem *zakazn-*, but the stressed R allomorph *-ój.*

Verbs. The third person marker $\{t'^{\varnothing}\}$ in the non-past forms of verbs is *never* replaced by its hard Russian counterpart in the Surzhyk represented in Serbens′ka, thus *він носить, вони носять* 'he/they carries/carry', never **носит, *носят.* The zero allomorph of $\{t'^{\varnothing}\}$, assigned to first-conjugation non-past third singular forms without the reflexive particle, is not replaced by *t'* in imitation of the overt Russian allomorph, thus, *вона знає, читає, називає,* not **знаєть, *читаєть, *називаєть.* The masculine singular past tense suffix $\{v\}$ is never replaced by its Russian counterpart $\{l\}$, thus, *виложив, ощущав, убєжав,* never **виложил, *ощущал, *убєжал.* The verb suffix $\{ÿ\}$ in second-conjugation verbs such as *ходити, носити, просити* is never replaced by its counterpart, R $\{i\}$, **ходіти, *носіти, *просіти.*

The Russian use of N-P/1pl. forms in an imperative function is transferred to Surzhyk, thus standard U imperative *сходім(о)* in alternation with *сходим,* with an apparent preference for the full 1pl. morpheme $\{mo\}$. The allomorphy of the R infinitival suffix $\{t'i^{\varnothing}\} \Rightarrow t'i \sim t'$ (R *nes-t'í, plák-a-t'*) may be extended to Surzhyk, as noted above, thus $\{t'ÿ^{\varnothing}\} \Rightarrow t'ÿ \sim t'$ (S *nes-t'ÿ́ →* [nestÿ́], *závtrak-a-t'*).

Nouns. Surzhyk nominal inflection follows the Ukrainian pattern for the most part. There are four cases, however, in which Surzhyk inflection regularly reflects the Russian pattern in the manual: the vocative, the gen.sg.masc. in $\{u\}$ for inanimates, the dat.-loc.sg.masc. in $\{ovi\}$, and the nom.pl. in $\{a\}$ of certain masculine nouns.

Surzhyk does not typically employ the separate vocative forms of Ukrainian, but uses the Russian pattern instead, namely, the nominative case in most situations,[32] and the limited first-declension Russian vocative forms of endearment with a $\{\varnothing\}$ desinence as an option distinct from the nominative, e.g., *Іван, Гриць, Оксана, Наталія* instead of U *Іване, Грицю, Оксано, Наталіє*; and *Ваня ~ Вань, Саша ~ Саш, мама ~ мам, Наташка ~ Наташк.*

The second-declension gen.sg.masc. desinences {a} and {u} have complementary markedness values in Russian and Ukrainian. In Russian {u} is marked as the so-called second genitive, typically associated with quantification, e.g., R *сахару* 'some sugar', *чаю* 'some tea'. The unmarked ending {a} occurs in other, nonquantitative contexts. In Ukrainian, it is {a} that is marked, limited to masculine animates, a small set of masculine inanimates, and neuters. The unmarked ending {u} occurs elsewhere. Surzhyk tends to follow the Russian pattern; cf. S *завтрака* 'breakfast', *екзамена* 'examination' and U *сніданку, екзамену*.

The dat.sg.masc. second-declension desinence {ovi}, especially favored for animate nouns in Ukrainian, is commonly replaced by {u} in Surzhyk, e.g., *офіцеру* 'officer' instead of *офіцерові*. Analogously, the Ukrainian loc.sg.masc. desinence alternation {ovi} ~ {i} or {u} is constrained to {i} or {u} in Surzhyk, e.g., *офіцері* instead of *офіцерові, батьку* instead of *батькові*. In these cases, the Russian pattern with dative {u} and locative {i} simply affects the frequency of choice; the distribution in both cases favors options other than {ovi}.

Surzhyk tends to prefer the Russian nom.pl. desinence {á} to the Ukrainian {ý} in the small set of masculine second-declension nouns with that selection pattern in Russian; cf. S *доктора́* 'doctor', *професора́* 'professor', *учителя́* 'teacher', *корма́* 'fodder' and U *доктори́, професори́, учителі́, корми́*.

Russian-influenced lexical specification can have inflectional consequences for Surzhyk stem morphology as well. The borrowing *бельйо* or *більйо* 'linen, underwear' (cf. U *білизна*) continues to be specified as indeclinable, and thus not an exception to the regular U morphophonemic rule that replaces nominal desinence-initial {o} with {e} after soft consonants; cf. {pól'+o} ⇒ *pól'+e* → [póle] (U *поле* 'field', nom.-acc.sg.neut.). Had the transfer been construed as declinable, one would have expected the Surzhyk form to be *бельє* or *білье*. Another russianism is the specification of Ukrainian names in -*nko* as indeclinable, cf. S *площа Івана Франко* 'Ivan Franko Square' and U *площа Івана Франка*. In some cases, gender, declension class, and stress pattern distinguish the Ukrainian forms from their russified Surzhyk counterparts (Russian transfers); cf. U *адре́са* '(street) address' (fem.1st decl.), *я́рмарок* 'market, fair' (masc. 2nd decl.) and S *а́дрес* (masc. 2nd decl.), *я́рмарка* (fem. 1st decl.).

Surzhyk also displays Russian-based lexical specification in the morphosyntactic treatment of a small set of semantically inanimate nouns treated as inanimate in Surzhyk as compared to their specification as animate in Ukrainian, e.g., *лист* 'letter'; cf. S *я написав лист* 'I wrote the letter' and U *я написав листа*. Collective nouns such as *листя* 'leaves' (coll.) are lexicalized as syntactic plurals rather than neuter singulars under Russian influence, thus S *сухі листя* 'dry leaves' but U *сухе листя*.

Morphophonemics. In Serbens'ka's sampling, Surzhyk displays definite tendencies in morphophonemic patterning, occasionally favoring the Ukrainian model, but most often the Russian. Morphophonemic attraction is especially apparent in correlations, sets of etymologically correlated forms.

We have already had occasion to mention the resolution between Ukrainian *h* and Russian *g* in favor of the former,[33] e.g., R *grúz-čik-Ø* 'loader', S *hrúz-čўk-Ø*. Likewise, the characteristic velar-dental alternations in nominal declensions before the dat.-loc.sg. ending {i} in first-declension nouns, and loc.sg. in second-declension nouns, are preserved, irrespective of whether the stem is a native Ukrainian one or a Russian-based transfer, e.g., S *рука, руці* 'hand, arm' > *Бог, Бозі* 'God' > *остановка, на остановці* 'stop' (bus or tram). In correlations that contrast Russian *C'i* and Ukrainian *C°ÿ*, Surzhyk tends to preserve the Ukrainian sequence, unless specific morpheme boundaries intervene, in which case R *T'-i* may replace U *T°-ÿ*, cf. R and S *rót'-ik-Ø*, U *rót-ÿk-Ø* (diminutive nominal suffix); but R *xod'-í-t'* 'to walk, go', U and S *xod-ÿ́-tÿ* (verbal class suffix).

The vast majority of Surzhyk forms in Serbens´ka favor Russian morphophonemic attraction. The Russian mid-vowels *e* and *o* are among the strongest targets for Surzhyk correlations, regardless of the corresponding Ukrainian morphophonemic behavior. Thus, the high front vowel *i*, the characteristically U reflex of Rusian *ě*, often yields to the R reflex *e*, e.g., U *díl-o* 'business, matter', *smíx-Ø* 'laughter', S *dél-o*, *sméx-Ø*. Likewise, there are a number of roots or suffixes that differ primarily in the shape of the mid-vowel, *e* in Ukrainian and *o* in Russian, e.g., U *téšč-a* 'mother-in-law' (wife's mother), *sél-a* 'village' (nom.-acc.pl.), *klén-Ø* 'maple', *id-é-š* 'go, walk' (N-P/2sg.), *kontrol-ér-Ø* 'controller, ticket-taker' *versus* R *t'óšč-a, s'ól-a, kl'ón-Ø, id'-ó-š, kontrol'-ór-Ø* . Surzhyk typically follows the Russian pattern with *o* in these cases, according to the frequency hierarchy roots ≥ suffixes ≥ endings.[34] The vowel substitution is accompanied by the softening of a preceding dental consonant, thus U *Te* ⇒ S *T'o*.

Patterns of mid-vowel alternation (R *e°, o°*; U *e°, o°, ei, oi*) are typically modeled after the Russian in Surzhyk, e.g., U *rémin'-Ø, rémen'-a* 'belt, strap'; *rót-Ø, rót-a* 'mouth'; *holív-k-a* 'head' (dim.) and *holov-á* 'head' *versus* S *remen'-Ǿ, remn'-á; rót-Ø, rt-á; holóv-k-a* and *holov-á*.

Apart from the two cases of U attraction noted above, Russian consonantism serves as the target for Surzhyk consonantism, and thus one finds voiced fricatives *z, ž* replacing affricates *ʒ, ǯ* respectively, and no gemination of dentals[35] and palatal obstruents before *j*, e.g., U *ʒérkal-o* 'mirror', *horǯ-ú-s'a* 'be proud of' (N-P/1sg.), *níčč-ju* 'night' (inst.sg.) *versus* S *zérkal-o, horž-ú-s'a, nóč-ju*.

A hard-soft consonant alternation in Russian triggered by the presence of a specific class of grammatical suffixes is preserved in Surzhyk, if permitted phonologically. In practical terms, such alternations are limited to the dentals, e.g., S *rót-Ø* 'mouth' and *rót'-ik-Ø* (dim.) *versus* U *rót-Ø, rót-ÿk-Ø*. Compare R *kúb-Ø* 'cube' and *kúb'-ik-Ø* '(children's) block' (dim.) *versus* S *kúb-Ø, kúb-ÿk-Ø*.

Phonology. On the phonological level, Surzhyk in Serbens'ka rests on a gradient continuum between Ukrainian and Russian, but it is not always possible to discern the actual state of affairs from the data at hand. It is difficult to assess, for example, the influence of Russian stress patterns on Surzhyk since stress is not indicated. Indirect evidence suggests that if and when Russian stress patterns are used, the Ukrainian base of Surzhyk makes necessary adjustments. Thus, the Surzhyk 2pl. imperative *приходíть* is formed according to the regular pattern for suffix-stressed forms in Ukrainian, as compared with U *прихóдьте,* which represents the regular morphological pattern for stem-stressed forms.

Unfortunately, Serbens'ka provides no information on Russian-induced vowel reduction phenomena in Surzhyk. Similarly, it is unclear whether Surzhyk tends to favor Russian or Ukrainian patterns in voicing and compactness neutralization.[36]

. Like Ukrainian, Surzhyk resists *phonemically* soft labials, palatals, and velars in prevocalic environments; they are categorically excluded in all others, as shown in (6).

(6) *Sharping (palatalization, softness):*

a. Russian: P° P' T° T' Č K° K'
   Ukrainian: P   T° T' Č K

b. Surzhyk resistance to R *phonemically distinct P'* before back vowels

   R   *kov'or-Ø* 'rug'   *sv'ókl-a* 'beet'
   S   *kovjor-Ø*   [s'v·ókla] ← *svjókl-a*

The Russian transfer *ковёр* 'rug' is rendered as Surzhyk *ковйор* (*kovjor+Ø*). Russian *свёкла* 'beet' elicits Surzhyk *свьокла,* which looks at first blush to contain a phonemically soft *v'* before back vowel. In fact, the *phonetic* softness of the labiodental in this case is the product of the regular absorption of *j* after two or more consonants, thus *svjókl+a* → [s'v·ókla].[37]

By contrast, the phonemically paired hard and soft dentals permit the direct realization of the latter before back vowels, in case the Russian model dictates that sequence. Examples in Surzhyk include *ступеньок* 'little step' (gen.pl.fem.), *тьоща* 'mother-in-law' (wife's mother), *посьолка* 'settlement' (gen.sg.neut.), and *вперьод* 'forward'.

Much more complex is the Surzhyk treatment of consonants before front vowels, a traditional environment in Ukrainian for the neutralization or predictable variation of hardness and softness. Unless specified morphological boundaries intervene, the hardness or softness of all Ukrainian consonants is predictable.[38] The Ukrainian distribution is represented in (7):

(7) *Ukrainian hardening/softening of C before front vowels*

		{lis} 'forest'	{babus'} 'grandma'
a)	C → [C°] / __ ÿ, e	[l'isÿ]$_{nom.pl.}$	[babúsÿn]$_{poss. adj.}$
		[l'íse]$_{voc.sg.}$	[babúseju]$_{inst.sg.}$
b)	C → [C'] / __ i	[l'is'ív]$_{gen.pl.}$	[babús'i]$_{gen.-dat.-loc.sg.}$

The forms in (7) show that whether the underlying stem-final consonant is hard like *s* in {lis} or soft like *s'* in {babus'}, the phonetic realization of the consonant depends on the shape of the front vowel. Rule (7a) determines that a consonant (C) is realized phonetically as hard (→ [C°]) before [ÿ] or [e], whereas (7b) determines that a consonant is realized phonetically as soft (→ [C']) before [i].

The Russian neutralization of *phonemically* hard consonants as soft is limited to the environment before [e], as shown in (8):

(8) *Russian softening of C° before* [e]

	{bes} 'demon'	{les} 'forest'	{ruk} 'hand, arm'
C° → [C'] / __ e	[b'és]$_{nom.sg.}$	[l'és]$_{nom.sg.}$	[ruk'é]$_{dat.-loc.sg.}$

The Russian transfer *ленты* 'ribbon' (nom.-acc.pl.), phonetically [l'énty], represents an immediate problem for Ukrainian Surzhyk. The likely morphophonemic representation would be *lent+ÿ*, which would be rendered by Ukrainian phonology as [léntÿ]. But the more common Surzhyk form [l'éntÿ], transcribed *ленти*, seems to indicate that the Ukrainian neutralization of consonants before *e* (C → C°) is overridden by the Russian neutralization of phonemically hard labials (P°), dentals (T°), and velars (K°) before [e] (C° → C'), according to which all are rendered soft, thus *lént+ÿ* → [l'éntÿ]. Since palatals are not affected by the Russian rule (C° → C'), the only model for Surzhyk would be one in which labials, dentals, and velars are softened before [e]. Because Surzhyk lacks *phonemically* hard labials and velars, the Russian rule is modified to suit Ukrainian phonology as (C → C'), so that *any* basically hard consonant—not only phonemically hard—is susceptible to softening before [e], construed for nondentals as variation rather than neutralization. The invocation of Surzhyk rule (C → C') accounts for the instances of phonetically soft labials appearing before *e* in Russian transfers, e.g., Surzhyk *свет* 'light', *примерочну* 'fitting room' (acc.sg.fem.), *убежала* 'she ran away'.

On closer analysis, however, the notion of one phonological rule simply overriding the other cannot account for the Surzhyk forms with mixed Ukrainian-Russian realizations in Serbens'ka, e.g., Surzhyk *клевер* 'clover' (soft dental, hard labial), *Петєнька* 'Petey!' (hard labial, soft dental) as compared with U *клевер, Петрику! (Петрусю!).*

The application of the Surzhyk rule (C → C') is apparently constrained by factors that make it more or less likely to occur. In the case of *клевер,* for example, softening has affected the *l* but not the *v,* a result that in part must reflect the relative strength of softness in Ukrainian consonantism. The dental is more likely than a labial to be softened before *e* in Surzhyk because dentals are paired for softness, whereas all the other consonants, including labials, are not: *j* is redundantly soft, the others are basically (nonphonemically) hard. Thus, the Surzhyk rule (C → C') is constrained by the contextual softness hierarchy T ≥ P K Č. Softness would be more likely if the affected segment were a dental than if it were a labial, velar, or palatal.[39] Additionally, the Surzhyk rule (C → C') would apply only if the Ukrainian rule (C → C°) were suppressed, as symbolized in (9c).[40]

(9) *Surzhyk softening of C before [e]*

$$(C \rightarrow C')^R \quad / \quad \begin{array}{ll} a) & \{ \_e \}^R \\ b) & [T \geq P, K, Č] \\ c) & +(C \rightarrow C')^R \supset -(C \rightarrow C°)^U \end{array}$$

The softness hierarchy in (9b) favors the softness of the dental before that of the labial and thus predicts Surzhyk *Петєнька*. The hierarchy would permit *Петєнька* (labial and dental softened), but would disallow **Петєнька* (labial softened, dental not).

To sum up our findings based on the material in Serbens'ka, the syntax and lexicon of Surzhyk seem most open to russification, whereas the inflectional morphology is the most resistant. The phonology makes some accommodation to the Russian pattern, but utilizes Ukrainian-based hierarchies of constraint in its implementation. It will be useful to compare these impressions with Surzhyk as presented in current fiction.

We must be clear at the outset that the authors of fiction-based Surzhyk are not trained linguists; they attempt to reproduce certain details of Surzhyk speech they deem characteristic or particularly striking to create a desired tone or effect, but they are not always consistent. "Literary" Surzhyk is obviously no substitute for a large recorded and transcribed database of connected Surzhyk speech that remains a research desideratum. Nonetheless, there are typological features of literary Surzhyk that occur with sufficient frequency among different authors to convince me that they are reasonable candidates for inclusion in the ultimate grammar (or grammars) of Surzhyk.

For my sample, I have chosen texts by Bohdan Zholdak ("Mania or Tania"),[41] Oleksandr Irvanets' ("Our Scoutmaster Freddy Krueger: A Thriller" and "Holian's Demise"),[42] Oksana Zabuzhko (*Fieldwork on Ukrainian Sex*),[43] Mykola Zakusylo ("A Vampire Ate Dad"),[44] and Volodymyr Danylenko ("The Kiev Dude").[45]

A comparison of morphological russification in literary Surzhyk and in Surzhyk presented by Serbens'ka reveals the slight conservatism of the latter. As the chart in (10) indicates, the russification represented in literary Surzhyk has made marginal inroads in pronominal roots, adjectival endings, and pronominal endings, as well as in those morpheme categories noted by Serbens'ka.

(10) *Russification of Surzhyk morphemes: Serbens'ka + vs. others ✚*

	prefix	*suffix*	*ending*	*root*
pronoun	NA	NA	– (✚)	– (✚)
adjective	–	–	– (✚)	+ ✚
verb	–	(+) (✚)	(+) (✚)	+ ✚
noun	–	+ ✚	+ ✚	+ ✚

In all cases, these rare roots and endings were included within the context of whole phrases, the ideal environment for extensive russification, e.g., the noun phrase *етот негодяй* 'this lowlife' (VD), verb phrase *начинай свойо дело* 'do your thing' (BZh), and prepositional phrases *вместо нийо* 'instead of her' (BZh), *во сне* 'in a dream' ~ *уві сні* (BZh), *ко мне* 'towards me' (BZh). In each instance the construction contained a russified head or specifier, thus *негодяй, начинай, дело, вместо, во, ко* instead of U *негідник, починай, діло, замість, у, до.* The softness of the nasal *n* in the negative particle *ne* is apparently dependent on whether the negative phrase dominates a Russian complement or not, e.g., *не могу* (BZh) but *не можу* (BZh); cf. the syntactically independent *не* 'no' (OI-94).

In several examples, however, the Ukrainian preposition *з* permits russification, e.g., a substantivized adjective with a russified stem and gen.sg.fem. ending {oj}—*з проходной* 'from the hall' (OI-94) *versus* U *з прохідної*—or a Russian transfer with nominal complement—*з самого начала сезона* 'from the beginning of the season' (OI-94) *versus* U *з самого початку сезону.* In general, the evidence from literary Surzhyk suggests that phrase markers may play a role in constraining russification, so that those marked with Ukrainian specifiers and heads will be less likely to permit russification than those not so marked, or marked Russian. For example, the S phrases *цілу смену* (OI-94) or *вечірній туалет* (OI-96) demonstrate that the marking of a noun phrase as R does not entail the marking of the dominating adjective phrase as R. The converse, a noun phrase marked U with dominating adjectival and prepositional phrases in R, although theoretically possible, is much rarer, at least in literary Surzhyk. Clearly, such tendencies can only be confirmed by examining a statistically significant database, but if true, they would predict that collocations of the sort *етот негідник, починай свойо дело, замість нийо,* and *у сне* would be less likely, if not impossible. Apart from such exceptional cases, the results from literary Surzhyk are consistent with the morphological typology based on Serbens'ka.

Literary Surzhyk provides new evidence on morphophonemic and phonological data. The velar-dental alternation before the desinence {i} in first-
declension (dat.-loc.sg.) and second-declension (loc.sg.) nouns is lost when the
desinence is replaced by the Russian-induced {e}, e.g., S *на гражданки* 'in
civilian life' (BZh, cf. R *на гражда́нке*); S *на кушетки* 'on the couch' (BZh,
cf. R *на куше́тке*). Ukrainian tends to neutralize unstressed *e* and *ÿ* as [eʸ] or
[ÿᵉ], which may account for Zholdak's rendering of underlying *na hraždank-e*
and *na kušetk-e* with hard [kÿ].

The Surzhyk softening rule in (9) predicts the sort of softness variation
found in literary Surzhyk, e.g., S *діскотека* 'discotheque' ~ U *дискотека*
(OI-96), S *лагерь* 'camp' ~ *лагерь* (OI-94, OI-96); S *особенно* (OI-94) 'especially' ~ *особино* (BZh). From these few cases, we note immediately that
particular authors prefer to render specific features of Surzhyk in distinctive
ways. Scant evidence suggests that Russian geminate consonants, whether
morpheme-internal or across boundaries, may be reduced to a single consonant
according to the Ukrainian pattern, e.g., *особенно* and *особино* above,
условленому (BZh). Irvanets' renders the labial *b* soft before the [e] in
особенно, whereas Zholdak leaves it hard and reproduces the aforementioned
Ukrainian phonetic merger of unstressed *e* and *ÿ*. Impressionistic evidence
from literary Surzhyk generally indicates that consonant softening before [e] in
Surzhyk is more likely before stressed [é] than unstressed [e]. If so, the hierarchical ranking must be included in a modified Surzhyk rule (C → C') as shown
in (11):

(11) *Surzhyk softening of C before [e]*

$$(C \rightarrow C')^R \quad / \quad \text{a)} \quad \{ \_é \geq \_e \}^R$$
$$\text{b)} \quad [T \geq P, K, Č]$$
$$\text{c)} \quad +(C \rightarrow C')^R \supset -(C \rightarrow C°)^U$$

There are occasional indications of Russian-influenced vowel neutralization
(akan'e, ikan'e) in literary Surzhyk, e.g., *харашо* 'all right' (BZh, cf.
R *хорошо* [хərʌšó]), *ні достіг* '(I) didn't achieve' (BZh, cf. R *не достиг*
[n'iᵉdʌs't'ík]), *красавіц* 'good-looker' (BZh, cf. R *красавец* [krʌsáv'ıc]),
канешно 'of course' (VD, cf. R *конечно* [kʌn'éšnə]). Such examples are
rendered so inconsistently, however, that it is impossible to tell whether the
neutralization itself is typical and frequent.

Our preliminary review indicates a set of apparent hierarchies of
russification in Surzhyk as shown in (12) below. Only a detailed investigation
of an extensive Surzhyk database will permit us to refine these categories and
gain a deeper understanding of the mechanisms that control the engagement
between the Russian and Ukrainian grammatical systems in Surzhyk.

(12) *Hierarchies of russification in Surzhyk*

   a.   transfer ≥ correlation ≥ calque ≥ native
   b.   marked-Russian ≥ unmarked ≥ marked-Ukrainian
   c.   noun ≥ verb ≥ adjective ≥ pronoun
   d.   root ≥ suffix ≥ ending ≥ prefix
   e.   morphophonemic R attraction ≥ morphophonemic U attraction
   f. $(C \rightarrow C' \: / \: \_\_e)^R \geq (C \rightarrow C° \: / \: \_\_e)^U$

Despite the many possibilities for russification, a random sample of paragraphs of Surzhyk text (140–240 words each) from Zholdak and Irvanets', for example, shows that roughly 25 percent of the words in Surzhyk are Russian-based; 25 percent are shared by Ukrainian and Russian; and the rest are Ukrainian (50 percent). Even such gross measurement is suggestive of a Ukrainian base in Surzhyk capable of constraining russification, through probability scales that vary according to the functional role of each element in the sentence, and through hierarchies of implicational relationships that tend to favor or disfavor the appropriation of Russian features. Some russianisms may be incorporated into Surzhyk under specific circumstances, whereas others are impossible. The selection from "Holian's Demise" is representative in this regard.

At the beginning, the protagonist Izelina speaks to a taxi driver in pure Ukrainian as she alights at the entrance to her workers' dormitory. Her telephone conversation inside (russianisms underscored) provides the immediate context for using Surzhyk with her friend Natashka, whom she meets later to continue the discussion:

—Ало! Ало! <u>Наташка</u>? <u>Наташка</u>, <u>прівєт</u>,[46] щось погано чути. Ти давно вже приїхала? <u>Да</u>? Ну, от я <u>наконєц</u> до тебе <u>звоню</u>. Звідки? З <u>проходной</u>, з <u>общежитія</u>. Ало, щось погано чути! Ало! Чуєш мене? Я же у <u>лагєрі</u> була, цілу <u>смєну</u>. Ой, там такий <u>случай</u> був! Один <u>мальчик</u>.... <u>Ладно</u>, <u>потом</u> розкажу. Давай через <u>півчаса</u> на <u>остановці</u>! Добре?..

—Ой, <u>Наташк</u>, які <u>кра-асовки</u>....Фірма...<u>Родітєлі</u> купили? <u>По-дарив</u>?...<u>Ні</u> <u>фіга</u>...А в мене...<u>Он</u>, <u>ідьом</u> на лавочку, поки нічого не їде, сядемо, розкажу. <u>Да</u>. Так от. Був там, у <u>лагєрі</u>, один <u>мальчик</u> — ну, чудо. Чорненький, високий, <u>глаза</u> голубі....Весь у фірмі, аж до <u>трусіків</u>. <u>Представ</u> собі, бачила. А <u>шо</u>[47] тут такого? <u>Сєрьожа</u> звали. <u>Да</u>, саме звали. Не перебивай, дай по порядку розкажу. <u>Хотя</u> <u>нє</u>, по порядку не вийде. Я приїхала, він там вже <u>работав</u>, з самого <u>начала</u> сезона. <u>Фізруком</u> <u>работав</u>. Рано встане, зарядку проведе, і до обіду спить.[48]

This example of authentic Surzhyk (code-mixing) may be profitably compared with literary representations of code-switching, in which a character or narrator inserts Russian words or whole sentences into a Ukrainian or Surzhyk text. Thus, a Russian statement reported by a narrator otherwise using Ukrainian and occasional Surzhyk should not itself be confused as Surzhyk, e.g., "«Мальчікі, —кресонула навідлі голосом, аж забриніло, —да што ж ви ето, в самом дєлє, а?!» і вирвала хлопця . . . "[49] (OZ). In this example, we note the distinction between *мальчікі,* which is simply a direct rendering of the Russian form, and *мальчик,* the Surzhyk form used by Danylenko, with the underlying suffix {čÿk}, its Ukrainian form preserved with *ÿ*. The Surzhyk nominative plural would be *мальчики.*[50] Likewise, the language of Danylenko's Kiev Dude is essentially Russian, whereas the narrator shifts between Ukrainian and Surzhyk, e.g., —Пєрєсєчьомся? —запропонував Мальчик. —Как у тєб'я нащот врємєні?[51] (VD). Zakusylo's prose in contrast contains Surzhyk mixed with a great many substandard Ukrainian forms, including dialectisms, e.g., *з кров'ею* 'with blood', *конхіскація* 'confiscation', *і п'ють ее* [*кров*] 'and they drink it [blood]'.

Quite apart from the numerous combinations of standard languages, substandard speech, and dialect forms that are no doubt encountered in everyday parlance in Ukraine, it is important to distinguish the characteristics of specific hybrids from one another for the purposes of research. On this view, it is possible to separate out Surzhyk, the Ukrainian-Russian hybrid, from all the other possible generic surzhyks that no doubt exist in Ukraine, to study it in its own right, and to determine the patterns that underlie this particular engagement of the two major East Slavic languages.

Even the quite preliminary typology of interaction at the levels of lexicon, syntax, morphology, and phonology examined here shows that the process of russification within Surzhyk is by no means random or illogical, but is governed by specific hierarchies and implicatures that are as valid in prescriptive materials as they are in literary Surzhyk. The future study of an extensive Surzhyk database will no doubt correct and refine the typology, the hierarchies of russification, and the rules of engagement outlined in this study, but it will not alter the reality of their existence: the essence of Surzhyk is neither arbitrary nor artificial.

NOTES

I wish to express my gratitude to Taras Koznarsky, a doctoral candidate in Slavic Languages and Literatures at Harvard, for his assistance in assembling a representative sample of texts containing Surzhyk and for his insights into its literary function. I also extend thanks to Volodymyr Dibrova, a popular contemporary Ukrainian author currently teaching advanced Ukrainian at Harvard, for his useful discussions on Surzhyk in modern Ukraine.

Phonetic representations are enclosed in square brackets [ ], phonemic representations are given in italics or enclosed in braces { } when discussed in a morphological context. Morphophonemic processes are represented by the directional double-line arrow ⇒, phonological processes by the directional single-line arrow →, e.g., {nj} ⇒ *n'n', babús'-e* → [babúse]. Individual underlying morphemes not yet subject to morphological and morphophonemic rules that replace, add, delete, or permute elements are cited within braces { }. Individual allomorphs, contextually determined alternative shapes for underlying morphemes, will be cited in their phonemic spell-out shape. Morphemes concatenated in phonological words are connected with the general morpheme boundary symbolized with a hyphen (-), but where needed, a plus sign (+) will indicate a desinence boundary.

In phonological transcription, the Ukrainian front high-mid vowel phoneme is transcribed *ÿ* and the corresponding allophone, [ÿ]. The Russian central high allophone of the phoneme *i* that occurs in the environment after hard consonants is transcribed [y]. Hardness of consonants is indicated by a raised degree mark (°), full softness by an apostrophe (') in the case of dentals, and moderate softness by a raised dot (˙) elsewhere

The following abbreviations will be used for grammatical categories: nom. (nominative), acc. (accusative), gen. (genitive), dat. (dative), loc. (locative), inst. (instrumental), voc. (vocative); masc. (masculine), fem. (feminine), neut. (neuter); sg. (singular), pl. (plural); 1, 2, 3 (first, second, third person); N-P (nonpast).

1. This date is reported in a letter from reader Mykola Leshchenko in *Literaturna Ukraïna* 15 September 1994: 2. The Ukrainian model was eventually reinstated.

2. "Тоді доречніше відразу перейти на «восемь часов», оминаючи хохляцький суржик «вісім годин»." Letter from academician M. Holubets′ in *Literaturna Ukraïna* 15 September 1994: 2.

3. On language and nationalism, see Roman Szporluk, *Communism and Nationalism: Karl Marx Versus Friedrich List* (New York and Oxford,

1988), pp. 82–89, 156; and Benedict Anderson, *Imagined Communities,* rev. ed. (London and New York, 1991), esp. chs. 5 and 8.

4. The Law on the Ukrainian Language in the Ukrainian SSR is reproduced in *Ukraïns'ka mova i literatura v shkoli* 1990 (5) 399: 3–10.

5. See article 10 of the Constitution, approved 11 March 1996, and published in *Holos Ukraïny* 23 May 1996: 3.

6. I will transcribe Ukr. суржик as surzhyk, using the Library of Congress system, since the word has come to the attention of the scholarly community in this form, primarily in the press and in scholarly publications in the social sciences, especially history, sociology, and anthropology. Otherwise I will use standard linguistic transliteration with diacritics for Cyrillic.

7. Laada M. Bilaniuk, "The Politics of Language and Identity in Post-Soviet Ukraine," Ph.D. dissertation, University of Michigan, 1998 (Ann Arbor: UMI, text-fiche), pp. 84–88.

8. I have personally encountered speakers who claim to be bilingual in Russian and Ukrainian, when, in fact, they speak standard or substandard Russian and Surzhyk. It is doubtful that such cases are exceptional.

9. Bilaniuk, p. 88.

10. Oleksandra Serbens'ka, ed., *Antysurzhyk* (Lviv, 1994).

11. Ibid., pp. 5–6.

12. This caveat is specifically intended to reject as Surzhyk cases of standard Ukrainian spoken with an obvious Russian accent. In her 1998 doctoral dissertation, Laada Bilaniuk subjected native speakers of Ukrainian to a so-called Matched Guise Test, in which the informants listened to politically neutral texts recorded in standard Ukrainian and in a standard Russian translation of the former. The speakers reading the texts were native speakers of Ukrainian and/or Russian. Bilaniuk was interested in informant reaction to the speakers themselves in terms of such sociological parameters as pleasantness, intelligence, diligence, trustworthiness, etc. The primary *linguistic* difference among speakers was the presence or absence of Ukrainian or Russian phonological distinctions, including segmental pronunciation, place of stress, and intonation. Bilaniuk (pp. 115–16) purposely excluded from the Test "combinations of lexical and syntactic forms that may be called *surzhyk,*" but then notes, "a few of the readings use Ukrainian pronunciation in the Russian text, or vice versa, resulting in speech that some people would call *surzhyk.*" Speaking fluent, grammatical Ukrainian or Russian with a complementary Russian or Ukrainian "foreign" accent does not imply the deeper morphological, syntactic, and lexical alterations associated with Ukrainian Surzhyk. For that reason, it should be treated as a separate phenomenon.

Russian-accented Ukrainian is not Surzhyk. But Surzhyk typically implies Russian-induced alterations of the entire grammar, including phonology.

13. Maks Fasmer [Max Vasmer], *Etimologicheskii slovar' russkogo iazyka,* trans. and exp. O. N. Trubachev, ed. and pref. B. A. Larina, 4 vols. (Moscow, 1964), s.v.; and Max Vasmer, *Russisches Etymologisches Wörterbuch,* 3 vols. (Heidelberg, 1955–58), s.v.

14. B. D. Hrinchenko, *Slovar' ukrainskogo iazyka,* 4 vols. (Kyiv, 1907–1909).

15. *Slovnyk ukraïns'koï movy,* 11 vols. (Kyiv, 1970–80).

16. Use of the word *artificially* (штучно) is decidedly odd in reference to Surzhyk, given the relatively common occurrence of code-switching and hybridization found in communities with two or more competing languages.

17. It is interesting to note that Classical Greek ἄρτος 'bread' referred specifically to unmarked bread, that is, bread made from pure wheat (cf. *A Greek-English Lexicon,* ed. Henry George Liddell and Robert Scott, 9th ed., rev. and exp. [Oxford: Clarendon Press. 1940]; *Oxford Dictionary of Byzantium,* ed. Alexander P. Kazhdan et al., 3 vols. [New York: Oxford University Press, 1991], s.v.), as compared with μάζα, made from barley. It is ἄρτος that is used at the Last Supper (Mt 26:26, Mk 14:22, Lk 22:19).

18. By considering Surzhyk a Ukrainian-based hybrid, I do not deny the fact of numberless varieties of same, of idiolectal and regional variations. Analogous varieties of the standard language across Ukraine, for example, do not prevent us from speaking about Contemporary Standard Ukrainian, a normative ideal against which variants may be compared and classified.

19. Cf. Dominique Arel, "Language and the Politics of Ethnicity: The Case of Ukraine," Ph.D. dissertation, University of Illinois, Urbana-Champaign, 1994 (Ann Arbor: UMI, text-fiche); Bilaniuk, "The Politics of Language and Identity in Post-Soviet Ukraine"; Andrew Wilson, *Ukrainian Nationalism in the 1990s: A Minority Faith* (Cambridge, 1994).

20. E.g., Sviatoslav Karavans'kyi, *Sekrety ukraïns'koï movy* (Kyiv, 1994); Roman Malovs'kyi, "Stan ukraïns'koï movy v suchasnykh zasobakh masovoï informatsiï," in *Pro ukraïns'kyi pravopys i problemy movy,* ed. Larysa M. L. Z. Onyshkevych et al. (New York and Lviv, 1997), pp. 184–90; Nataliia Pazuniak, "Problemy, pov'iazani z movnymy standartamy v Ukraïni," in ibid., pp. 96–102.

21. Many approaches to inflectional and derivational morphology assume that stems are constructed by additive processes that build up the underlying structure in layers, more elementary sequences nested within more complex ones. This level of detail is unnecessary for our purposes here.

22. The morphophonemic rule $g \Rightarrow h$ is based on the standard pronunciation of a voiced velar stop g in Contemporary Standard Russian. If the Surzhyk speaker speaks with a South Russian accent, the analogous velar will be the fricative γ, in which case, the morphophonemic rule will be $\gamma \Rightarrow h$, assuming that the speaker adopts a Ukrainian pronunciation of the fricative in Surzhyk (see note 33).

23. The U infinitive suffix $\{t'\ddot{y}^{\emptyset}\}$ is realized as $t'\ddot{y} \rightarrow$ [tÿ] in CSU, but among many speakers, especially those in eastern Ukraine, the vowel $\ddot{y}$, if unstressed, is typically replaced by $\emptyset$ (the superscript $^{\emptyset}$ indicates an alternation with the preceding segment), thus revealing and preserving in actual expression the underlying softness of the consonant, e.g., CSU xod-$\ddot{y}$-$t'\ddot{y}$ $\rightarrow$ [xodýtÿ] ~ xod-$\ddot{y}$-t' $\rightarrow$ [xodýt']. The metaphorical terms "soft"/"hard" will be used here to refer to palatalized/nonpalatalized or sharp/nonsharp consonants. A phonological rule (see 7a above, p. 124) hardens all consonants (except j) before [ÿ], hence $t'\ddot{y} \rightarrow$ [tÿ]. In the case of Surzhyk, the infinitival allomorph t' would clearly be favored among U speakers who themselves prefer it in Ukrainian, but the Russian influence in allomorph choice among all speakers of Surzhyk is patent as well.

24. In this case, the Late Common Slavic root *$star\check{z}$- is realized in South Slavic (and thus South Slavic-based Church Slavonic) with the metathesis of the liquid r and the concomitantly lengthened vowel as *$str\bar{a}\check{z}$-, (OCS стража), and in East Slavic with the replication of the short vowel after the liquid, so-called pleophony (U повноголосся) as *$stara\check{z}$- (U сторожа).

25. See Carol Myers-Scotton, "Code-switching" in *The Handbook of Sociolinguistics,* ed. Florian Coulmas (Oxford, 1997), pp. 217–37 (esp., pp. 220ff) for a succinct description of the Matrix Frame Model with terminology and remarks on code-switching and code-mixing.

26. With few exceptions, sequences of *CCj* are realized phonetically without [j]; see Michael S. Flier, "Now You See It, Now You Don't: The Ukrainian Phoneme *j* in Context" in *Mir Curad. Studies in Honor of Calvert Watkins*, ed. Jay Jasanoff, H. Craig Melchert, and Lisi Oliver (Innsbruck, 1998), pp. 101–114.

27. Morphophonemic $\{e^{\emptyset}\}$ indicates the midvowel e in alternation with $\emptyset$ in inflection, the latter appearing if the following morpheme begins with a vowel, the former elsewhere; cf. the correlated noun кінця (*kin-$\emptyset$c'-á*, gen.sg.), кінець (*kin-ec'-$\emptyset$*, nom.-acc.sg.), 'end, finish'.

28. There are apparently certain basic Ukrainian lexemes or morphological groups that are never replaced by their Russian-based counterparts, e.g., forms of бути 'be', verbs of the крити 'cover' group. Only a statistically representative sample of Surzhyk will permit a more authoritative statement on such cases.

29. See Pazuniak, "Problemy, pov'iazani z movnymy standartamy," pp. 96–102.

30. R. A. Hudson, *Sociolinguistics*, 2nd ed. (Cambridge,1996), pp. 54–55.

31. The written form of Surzhyk here attempts to reproduce Russian vowel reduction where possible. The underlying representation is {j-omu} in Surzhyk, as it is in Russian and Ukrainian. The broad phonetic transcription, however, would be similar to the Russian [jimú] rather than the Ukrainian [jomú], hence the Surzhyk spelling with *i*.

32. The use of the nominative in such situations is common for speakers of western Ukraine as well. Because the speakers of Surzhyk are concentrated in the central and eastern Ukraine, it is likely that Russian has been a greater influence in eliminating the vocative.

33. The phonetic realization of *h* among Surzhyk speakers—as a U laryngeal, voiced [ɦ] or voiceless [h], or a South Russian voiced velar [ɣ]—remains to be clarified.

34. The symbol ≥ is to be read as 'at least as or more likely than'.

35. Ukrainian dentals except *r, r'* are geminated in the environment before *j*.

36. With a few, well-defined exceptions, Ukrainian typically restricts voicing neutralization to that of voiceless obstruents before voiced obstruents, e.g., молотьба [d'b] 'threshing', просьба [z'b] 'request'. Voicing is not neutralized before voiceless obstruents or in word-final position, e.g., душка [šk] 'little soul' and дужка [žk] 'little bow', пліт [t] 'raft' and плід [d] 'fruit'. In Russian, voicing is neutralized not only before voiced obstruents, as in Ukrainian, but also before voiceless obstruents and in word-final position, thus, R дужка [šk] and плод [t]. In Ukrainian obstruent clusters, compactness assimilation, involving palatals and dentals, is reciprocal. Thus the dental assimilates to the compact palatal in без шуму [žš], whereas the palatal assimilates to the noncompact dental in у книжці [z'c']. See *Suchasna ukraïns'ka literaturna mova,* ed. I. K. Bilodid, 5 vols. (Kyiv, 1969–73), vol. 1, pp. 385–92, 396–401. In Russian, only the first neutralization is valid, e.g., R без шума [šš], самодержца [šc].

37. See Flier "Now You See It . . . ."

38. Labials, palatals, and velars, which are not paired according to the hard-soft opposition, are moderately soft before *i*. The consonant *j* is redun-

dantly soft in all environments. Dentals, which are distinguished as phonemically hard and soft, appear in the environment before *i* as fully soft in the Kyivan variant of CSU.

39. There is insufficient evidence thus far to make further discriminations in the context hierarchy, that is, to determine whether labials are more likely to be softened before *e* than velars or palatals. There are very few examples for velars and even fewer for palatals, principally *č* (always soft in Russian).

40. Rule 9 states that a consonant C will be realized phonetically as soft [C'] with the following conditions met: (a)—in the environment before [e] in a form marked Russian (R), (b)—according to a hierarchy of likelihood in which dentals (T) are at least as or more likely to soften than labials (P), velars (K), or palatals (Č), and (c)—with the implication (⊃ = implies) that the Ukrainian rule (C → C°), according to which consonants harden before [e] and [ÿ], will not operate.

41. Bohdan Zholdak, "Mania chy Tania," *Ialovychyna (Makabreska)* (Kyiv, 1991), pp. 18–22. Henceforth *BZh*.

42. Oleksandr Irvanets', "Zahybel' Holiana," *Suchasnist'* 1994 (5): 19–25. Henceforth *OI-94*. Also, "Nash Fredi Kriuger. Triller," *Vizantiiskii angel* 1996 (2): 21–3. Henceforth *OI-96*.

43. Oksana Zabuzhko, *Pol'ovi doslidzhennia z ukraïns'koho seksu* (Kyiv, 1996). Henceforth *OZ*.

44. Mykola Zakusylo, "Vupyriaka Bat'ka z'ïv," *Desiat' ukraïns'kykh prozaïkiv,* ed. V'iacheslav Medvid' (Kyiv, 1995), pp. 41–47. Henceforth *MZ*.

45. Volodymyr Danylenko, "Kievskii mal'chyk," *Kvity v temnii kimnati. Suchasna ukraïns'ka novela* (Kyiv, 1997), pp. 92–104. Henceforth *VD*.

46. Note the appropriation of the single-morpheme Russian greeting with soft *r'* (*pr'ivét*) without the perception of a prefix, as opposed to the actual instances of the prefix, without exception rendered with hard *r°* as {prÿ}.

47. The pronunciation of U *що* as [šo] rather than literary [ščo] is a dialectal variant recorded in manuscripts as early as the fourteenth–fifteenth centuries. See S. P. Bevzenko et al., *Istoriia ukraïns'koï movy. Morfolohiia* (Kyiv, 1978), p. 136. It has nothing to do with Russian influence.

48. —Hello! Hello! Natashka? Hi, Natashka! For some reason, it's really hard to hear. Have you been here a long time? Yeah? Well, I'm finally calling you. Where from? From the hall, from my dormitory. Hello? For some reason, it's really hard to hear. Hello! Can you hear me? I was at the camp, a whole shift. And, oh, what happened there . . . There was this

one guy . . . Ok, I'll tell you later. Let's meet in a half-hour at the stop. All right? . . .

—Oh, Natashka, what neat sneakers! Designer! Your parents bought them? He gave them to you? No shit! And me . . . ? Well, let's go over to the bench as long as nothing's coming; we'll sit down, I'll tell you the whole story. Yeah, so . . . There was one guy there, at the camp . . . a dream. Tall, dark, blue eyes . . . Dressed completely in designer stuff, even his shorts. Imagine! I saw him in them. And what's someone like that doing here? His name is Seryozha. Yeah, that's really his name. Don't interrupt me, let me tell everything as it happened. Maybe not, it can't be done. When I arrived, he had already been working there from the start of the season. He was the exercise leader. He would get up early, lead the exercises, and then sleep until lunch.

49. "Boys," the sparks generated by her voice resounded in a blast, "what the hell did you do this for? Are you nuts?" and she yanked the boy out.

50. The distinction between Russian and Surzhyk here is significant. Note that the listeners who cannot understand (*не понімают*) the Ukrainian pattern for telling time (see p. 113) are speakers of Russian, not Surzhyk, which would otherwise be indicated by the presence of the 3rd person marker {t'}, thus *не понімають*.

51. "Wanna get together?" the Dude suggested. "How're ya fixed for time?"

Native Land, Promised Land, Golden Land:
Jewish Emigration from Russia and Ukraine

ZVI GITELMAN

From their very inception, mythic or not, Jews have been a migrating people. Their tribal religion was launched in a rather unusual way. In the Biblical account, the first recorded words that God spoke to the first Jew, Abraham, were not some majestic declaration of God's presence, power, or oneness, but rather a pithy command to migrate: "Go forth from your land, your birthplace and your father's house."[1] Jews have migrated to several continents and are most prominent in modern European migrations. Of 65 million people who migrated from Europe to the Americas between 1840 and 1946, four million, or 6 percent, were Jews, though they constituted only 2 percent of the European population in this period. Thus, the intensity of Jewish migration was three to four times that of general European migration. More Jews migrated in these years than existed in the entire world at the end of the eighteenth century.[2] The migration and dispersal of Jews has influenced their culture and economy.

Dispersal led Jews to acquire many languages and positioned them very well for international commerce. Jews also have tended to have a more global perspective than many other ethnic groups. Because of their roots in other countries and the presence of fellow Jews around the world, Jews are generally more concerned with international affairs than others of similar education and social status.

Migration is so closely associated with Jews that they and others have constructed myths in which migration plays a central role. For Jews, wanderings in the diaspora became God's punishment, mitigated by an ultimate redemption and a final return migration to the Land of Israel; for Christians, Jewish dispersal was the punishment for deicide, with its precedent in Cain's punishment for fratricide. Jews and Christians could agree with Leo Pinsker's observation in the Russian Empire that the Jews "are everywhere as guests and are nowhere at home."[3]

Russian and Soviet Jewish Migration

Since the 1880s, no group of Jews has migrated as often, in such great numbers, and with such important consequences as the Jews of the Russian Empire and the former Soviet Union (FSU). The mass immigration of Russian/Soviet Jews played a great role in shaping the character of the two largest Jewish communities in the world, those of the United States and Israel. American Jewish and

Israeli politics, religion, culture, and economics have been, and are still, profoundly influenced by those who came and are coming from the former Soviet Union.

From 1881 to 1912, almost 1.9 million Jews emigrated from the Russian Empire, 84 percent of them to the United States, 8.5 percent to England, 2.2 percent to Canada, and 2.1 percent to Palestine.[4] Jews from the Russian Empire made up more than 70 percent of the Jewish immigrants to America in that period. In 1881 to 1910, Jews made up 48.3 percent of all immigrants coming from the Russian Empire to America.[5] From 1989 through 1998, more than one million Jews and their non-Jewish first-degree relatives emigrated from the FSU. Assuming that about 30 percent of the emigres are non-Jews attached to Jewish families, we can conclude that about 737,000 Jews have emigrated in the past decade. Astonishingly, this represents slightly more than half of the Jews enumerated in the 1989 census.[6] Of the emigres, 759,652 have gone to Israel. If one assumes that 30 percent of these are not Jewish, this means that about 531,000 Jews have come to Israel from the FSU in the decade 1989–1998. Thus, 70 percent of those who left the USSR immigrated to Israel where, together with the 170,000 Soviet Jews who arrived between the late 1960s and the late 1980s, they constitute the single largest "ethnic group" in the Jewish population. By the mid-1990s, more Jews had immigrated to Israel from the former Soviet Union than from any other country in the world. The great irony is that they came from a country which had militantly opposed Zionism throughout its history, condemning it as racism; allowed no Zionist emissaries, publications, or films; banned the study of Hebrew, the only language to be so treated; severely curbed the practice of Judaism; had no diplomatic relations with Israel for over two decades; and supported politically, militarily, and economically groups and states committed to the destruction of Israel. A further irony is that over 300,000 Jews have immigrated from the Soviet Union to the United States, the USSR's cold war enemy. This is by far the largest Jewish immigration to the United States since the early 1920s.

The Politics of Emigration

There have been large variations in the volume and destination of this emigration. The volume has fluctuated wildly: 914 people emigrated in 1986, but over 200,000 did so in 1990. This was due not to radical shifts in the desire to leave the USSR, but to the vagaries of Soviet policy. The volume of applications for invitations to leave (*vyzovy*) remained quite steadily high, though when emigration was severely depressed, quite naturally fewer people applied to leave, because such application could bring them only grief, not an exit visa. Recently revealed Soviet documents confirm this supposition. In January 1988, the Ukrainian deputy minister of the interior, Vasyl' Durdynets', reported a fourfold increase in 1987 over the previous year in the number of applications to emigrate. He attributed the rise to the government decision that by 1 January

1988, exit permits would be given to people "without taking account of the degree of family connections the applicant has, whether close or distant relatives, if there are no security [*rezhimnykh*] constraints or unfulfilled obligations [on the part of the applicant]."[7]

Why did mass emigration of Soviet Jews, which had ceased in the early 1920s, become an issue on the international political agenda? In the broadest sense, the issue was legitimized by a sea change in the international system. As James Rosenau points out, there are today a larger number of actors in world politics than ever before, many of them entities other than states. Interest groups, multinational corporations, ethnic and religious groups, and international organizations play larger and more effective roles in the international arena, breaking the monopoly once enjoyed by sovereign states. Education and mass media have involved ordinary people increasingly in world affairs; as a result people have a stronger sense of political efficacy and have become more willing to question authority.[8] Technology has made the transmission of political messages more rapid and effective; the Iron Curtain was increasingly penetrated by messages the regime did not want to hear. The high levels of education and urbanity of both Western and Soviet Jews made them likely candidates for political involvement. Western Jews felt guilty, rightly or wrongly, for not having saved more of European Jewry during the Holocaust, and shame at their political impotence in the 1930s. The inspiration of the American Black civil rights movement, the origins of so many Western and Israeli Jews in the Russian Empire, and traditions of cross-boundary solidarity played a role in mobilizing world Jewry on behalf of Soviet Jews and their emigration. Moreover, Soviet Jewry emerged as the single most consensual issue among diaspora and Israeli Jews when support for Israel, the great mobilizing force among diaspora Jews until the late 1970s, had begun to dissipate over disagreements about Israeli policies. Of course, Soviet Jewish activists took the lead and, like other national and cultural dissidents, defied a sclerotic Soviet regime, using the new international audience and the new technology to protect themselves to the extent possible.

Western governments responded to the calls for action for several reasons. Like the Jews themselves, some felt guilt over the Holocaust and the immigration policies of the time which effectively condemned hundreds of thousands to death. Conservatives rejoiced in the campaign, for it was directed against the "Evil Empire." Liberals could join in what was a genuine human rights issue. American President Jimmy Carter had successfully struggled to make human rights a legitimate concern not only of international bodies but also of individual governments. Just about all American Jewish organizations were advocating on the issue, so elected officials felt they could only gain by supporting it.

The USSR was under pressure to change its traditional policy—pressure that was coming also from the Federal Republic of Germany in regard to Soviet Germans. But Soviet responses were inconsistent, at times accommodating and at times rejecting. What explains the shifts in Soviet policy? Most observers see them mainly as a function of East-West relations: when the USSR wished to ingratiate itself with the West, particularly the United States, it opened the faucet of emigration. To show its displeasure, it closed it. If one draws a curve representing the state of Soviet-American relations and graphs the flow of emigrants, the two lines are roughly parallel. No doubt, there were some domestic considerations influencing Soviet policy, though those who argue that they were dominant and determining fail, in my view, to produce convincing evidence. Laurie Salitan argues that 1976–1979 was a period of tension in U.S.-Soviet relations, and yet there was a high volume of emigration. I would view tensions over Angola, the Horn of Africa, stalled SALT negotiations, and Sino-American detente as irritants, not major conflicts. By contrast, the Soviet invasion of Afghanistan, which was followed by a steep drop in emigration, was a major downturn in the superpower relationship. Renewed emigration under Gorbachev, Salitan argues, was the outcome of his commitment to the rule of law.[9] I am less impressed by Gorbachev's commitment to the rule of law than by his strong desire to win Western support for his political and, especially, economic policies.

Robert Brym's attempt at a statistical analysis showing that there is no correlation between U.S.-Soviet relations and emigration is also flawed, in my view, because he takes the volume of trade between the two countries as the sole measure of their relations. Many factors affect the volume of trade, not least of which are economic calculations. Trade was not simply a function of political relations and it is far too crude a measure of them. Brym argues that U.S.-China and U.S.-Soviet trade, as well as the American consumer price index and the net increase in the size of the Soviet labor force, do not correlate with emigration. I am not surprised, since I do not see these as sufficient, and in some cases, even relevant, measures of Soviet-American relations. Brym argues further that in the 1970s, the Soviets permitted Jewish emigration because they were worried by an oversupply of highly educated personnel; by the 1980s there were labor shortages, so emigration was curtailed. This is more plausible, but the evidence cited is somewhat sparse.[10]

Newly published documents from archives in the FSU appear to support my contention as to what actually determined Soviet emigration policy. In a Politburo meeting on 20 March 1973, Leonid Brezhnev urged his colleagues not to enforce the "education tax" which compelled emigrants to "repay" the Soviet state for the cost of their higher education and reprimanded Yuri Andropov, at the time head of the KGB, for delaying implementation of a decision to suspend collection of the tax. Brezhnev told his colleagues:

> The Zionists are screaming, [Senator Henry] Jackson bases himself on this, and [Henry] Kissinger goes to Dobrynin and says, "We understand, this is an internal matter, we cannot interfere, we also have laws." At the same time he says: "Help us somehow, Nixon can't pass a bill [on his own], he has to work with senators." Who needs this million?[11] . . . There is a group of Republicans who aim to stop the improvement of relations between the USSR and U.S.A.

Nixon is for it, the administration is for it, but many senators are opposed [just] because we extract payment from the Jews.[12]

Brezhnev then went on to raise the possibilities—"I'm not raising my hand in favor of what I'm saying. I'm keeping my arms at my sides and am turning it over in my mind"—of opening a Jewish school and a Jewish theater in Moscow. He then told his colleagues that once, in the 1930s, he and a non-Jewish friend had stumbled into a concert of Jewish music in Dnipropetrovsk, where the crowd—"100 percent Jews except for me, my friend and our spouses"—clapped enthusiastically for "some Aunt Sonia" who was singing. If a Jewish theater opened in Moscow, Jews would flock to hear their Aunt Sonias and "this will bring income to our budget." Alexei Kosygin replied, apparently without humor, "I will put it down as income." Brezhnev commented, "You can count on a million, they'll give you a million, even though they don't earn that much."[13]

Aside from the volume of emigration, the second fluctuating dimension has been the destination of the emigres. Roughly speaking, there have been three waves of emigration since 1970, as defined by both volume and destination. The first wave came in 1971–1974, consisted of 100,000 people, and headed almost exclusively to Israel. This has been called a "Zionist" emigration, motivated by ideology, but it was only partly that. Religion and tradition, and not Zionism alone, motivated Georgian Jews and others from the Western territories of the USSR who were statistically overrepresented in this wave. Thus, between 1968 and 1976, a quarter of the immigrants to Israel came from Georgia, where in 1970 only 2.5 percent of the Soviet Jewish population resided. They were not fleeing the Soviet Union, where they suffered little discrimination, but were expressing their traditional values, which included both a religious-based yearning for Zion as well as a commitment to close-knit, hierarchical families. Thus, when the head of a family decided to emigrate, many would follow. The *Zapadniki*, or Westerners, i.e., those who had become Soviet citizens as a result of the annexation in 1939–1940 of the Baltic republics, eastern Poland, and Bessarabia-Bukovyna, were far less acculturated than those living under Soviet rule since 1917 or 1921. The *Zapadniki* had stronger memories of and commitments to Hebrew, Yiddish, and Zionism. About one-third of the *aliyah* (immigration to Israel) of the 1970s came from these areas, whereas they were probably no more than 10 percent of the Jewish population in 1970. By contrast, only about 40 percent of the immigrants came from Russia, Belarus, and Ukraine, which together contained 81 percent of the 1970 Soviet Jewish population.

The second wave came largely from the three Slavic republics and headed for America. From 1975 to 1989 (inclusive), 68.6 percent of the emigres chose not to settle in Israel. The trend away from Israel sharpened in 1978. By 1988, a total of 89 percent resettled in the United States. After 1976, about 85 percent of those coming to America came from Russia and Ukraine. About 90 percent of those leaving Moscow, Leningrad, Kyiv, and Odesa, where Jews were most acculturated, chose the United States, not Israel, as their destination. On the other hand, those from cities incorporated late into the USSR were less likely to go to America. For example, in 1974, of those leaving Moscow and Leningrad, 55 percent went to the U.S., but only a third of those leaving Lviv (Lvov), formerly in Poland, and 3 percent of those departing Chernivtsi (Chernovtsy), formerly in Romania, did the same. Fewer than 10 percent of those who left Vilnius and Kaunas (Lithuania) went to America in 1974, but 51 percent of Kyivans and 58 percent of Kharkovites did so.[14]

Thus, there was a direct relationship between involvement in Jewish culture and the propensity to immigrate to Israel. The Jews of the Slavic republics, many of them third-generation Soviet citizens, cut off from Jewish culture for decades, had little reason to go to Israel and sought political and cultural freedom, economic opportunity, and social equality in the West. Since they left on Israeli visas, but "dropped out" in Vienna and transferred to Rome, where American Jewish organizations facilitated their entry to the U.S., they became a bone of contention between the Israeli government and the Jewish Agency, on the one hand, and the American Jewish community on the other. Frustrated by the general lack of *aliyah* and embarrassed by the fact that tens of thousands of Soviet Jews chose not to go to Israel, Israelis charged that American Jewish organizations were seducing the immigrants in order to justify their staffs and budgets. In turn, most of the American Jewish community declared their support for freedom of choice for the emigres and rejected the kind of Zionism-by-coercion that Israelis seemed to them to be advocating. American Jews were fascinated, energized, and mobilized by the immigration of tens of thousands of people from the territories from which most of their ancestors had come within the past century. The debate between Israelis and Americans ignored the backgrounds of the emigres and the fact that Israel's economic and political difficulties in the post-Yom Kippur war period could predictably result in a preference for the United States, quite apart from myths of seduction. The myth of America as the *goldeneh medineh* (Golden Land), which had fired the imagination of the immigrants of an earlier era, still had the power to move large numbers of people.

The direction of emigration was abruptly reversed in October 1989 when the United States, perhaps under Israeli pressure, announced a change in policy. In 1989 alone, 59,024 Soviet immigrants settled in countries other than Israel—almost all in the U.S. The new American policy limited Soviet immigration to 50,000 people per year, of whom presumably 40,000 would be Jews. The effect of this change was immediate. In 1990, fully 97 percent of the largest single emigration in Russian Jewish history went to Israel. Not just the destination, but the nature of the immigration, had changed again. These were not "born again" Zionists, but panicky refugees who viewed with dismay the economic deterioration of the USSR, the growing ethnic strife, and the emergence of a public, virulent, grass-roots antisemitism.[15] This was clearly a case of "push" rather than "pull" driving the emigration. In recent years, most of those admitted to the United States have first-degree relatives there. There has been another change in the mid- and late 1990s. Except for immigrants from strife-torn regions such as Tajikistan and Georgia, most are leaving the FSU today not so much because of fear of imminent chaos but because of the prolonged political and economic crisis in most of the former Soviet republics, because the steady departure of Jews leaves them more lonely and insecure, and, probably most of all, because they have close family and friends abroad. Thus, it is likely that chain migration alone will sustain a steady outflow of Jews both to Israel and to the United States.

Emigration from Russia and Ukraine: Comparisons and Conundrums

Russia and Ukraine had the two largest concentrations of Jews in the Soviet Union. When Jews were confined to the Pale of Settlement before 1915, few were permitted to live in Russia. After the Revolution, they migrated en masse from the *shtetlekh* (hamlets) of Belarus and Ukraine to the larger cities and to the cities of the Russian republic. In 1926, when the first Soviet census was taken, Jews in Russia and Ukraine made up 78.5 percent of the total Jewish population of the USSR, and in the last census (1989), they made up 70.5 percent.

Table 1. Jewish Population of Russia, Ukraine, and the Soviet Union[16] (percent of total Soviet Jewish population)

	Russia	*Ukraine*	*USSR*
1897	316,500 (6%)	2,155,800 (41%)	5,215,800
1926	525,000 (20%)	1,574,000 (59%)	2,672,499
1939	956,599 (32%)	1,532,776 (51%)	3,028,538
1959	875,307 (39%)	840,311 (37%)	2,267,814
1970	807,915 (38%)	777,126 (36%)	2,150,707
1979	700,126 (39%)	634,154 (35%)	1,810,876
1989	536,848 (37%)	486,326 (34%)	1,450,500

As indicated in Table 1, the proportion of the Jewish population living in Ukraine declined over time, while that in Russia increased. In the post–World War II period, the proportion living in each republic has remained approximately the same, with 2 to 4 percent more living in Russia. Yet, more Jews have left Ukraine than have emigrated from Russia. From 1970 through 1997, more than 308,500 Jews emigrated from Russia, but more than 422,000 did so from Ukraine.[17] Secondly, a far larger proportion of Ukrainian Jews has immigrated to the United States, while a larger proportion of Russian Jews has gone to Israel.

Two questions arise: why have more Ukrainian than Russian Jews emigrated; and why have Ukrainian Jews been more inclined to immigrate to the United States than their co-ethnics from Russia?

The proportion of Ukrainian Jews who have emigrated is almost the same as their proportion in the Soviet Jewish population: in 1970–1993, Ukrainian Jews constituted 37.5 percent of the total Jewish emigration from the USSR, and in 1970, the base year for emigration, they were 36 percent of the Soviet Jewish population. By contrast, whereas Russian Jews constituted 38 percent of the 1970 population, they were only 26.2 percent of the emigration. Ukrainian and Russian Jews have emigrated in far lower proportions than have Jews from Georgia, Lithuania, and Tajikstan, whose departure has resulted in the rapid decline of their communities.

The greater tendency of Ukrainian Jews to emigrate, as compared to Russian Jews, is consistent throughout the quarter-century of large-scale emigration. As the following table shows, Ukrainian Jews emigrated at a higher rate than Russian Jews in each of the intercensal periods.

Table 2. Number and Percentage of Jewish Emigrants from Russia and Ukraine by Intercensal Period[18]

	1970–1979	1980–1988	1989–1997
Russia	23,006 (2.8%)	15,081 (2.2%)	271,901 (50.6%)
Ukraine	62,807 (8.1%)	18,361 (2.9%)	318,804 (65.6%)

In the first and third periods, both the absolute number and the proportion of emigrants from Ukraine are significantly higher than the figures for Russia. If one takes the period of highest emigration, 1989–1992, one finds that 24.2 percent of Russia's Jews emigrated—the lowest proportion of any Soviet republic—and that 37.2 percent of Ukraine's Jews left, which puts Ukraine about in the middle of the ranking of republics by proportion of emigrants. In 1989, more Jews left Ukraine than any other republic, and even as a proportion of the republic's Jewish population, Ukraine ranked near the top (6.7 percent of Ukrainian Jews emigrated in that year alone).[19] Without a doubt, much of this is accounted for by flight from the effects of the Chornobyl nuclear accident. Probably for the same reason, more than 11,000 Jews left Kyiv in 1989—a peak in the number leaving one locality in any single year.

Is the reason for lower emigration by Russian Jews the fact that they were better off materially and better placed in Russian society, and therefore less inclined to leave? We do not have sufficient information about comparative social status, income, and education to support this hypothesis fully. It is true that in 1970, when 82.4 percent of Russian Jews had seven or more years of schooling, the parallel proportion in Ukraine was 75 percent. Moreover, in the 1960s, Jews may have found it harder to obtain higher education in Ukraine than in Russia. There is some evidence that the Jews of Moscow and St. Petersburg (Leningrad) enjoyed higher income levels than Jews anywhere else, but this may not be true of the Russian republic as a whole.[20] Perhaps Russian

Jews were marginally better off, but in the recent past Ukrainian Jews have been as urbanized as Russian Jews, though somewhat less well represented in the intelligentsia. In any case, available data are insufficient to support the conclusion that educational and income differences explain the large disparity in emigration.

Perhaps the larger emigration from Ukraine could have been due to more permissive policies in that republic than in Russia. There does not appear to be any evidence that this was the case, though. Thirty-four percent of the invitations sent to Russia in 1968–1977 resulted in exit permits, and 40 percent of those sent to Ukraine yielded permits.[21] However, in 1968–1978, nearly three times as many Israeli visas were issued to Jews in Ukraine as were issued to Jews in Russia, so the demand for emigration was far greater than the disparity between the proportions of invitations yielding exit permits.[22]

Another possibility is that Ukrainian Jews have emigrated in higher proportions than Russian Jews either because they have been less attached to their land, people, and culture, or because they have been more fearful of their position than Russian Jews. Of course, weaker attachment to their native country may be the result of persecution or fear of it. There is a considerable history of Jewish suffering in Ukraine and there may be a "collective memory" among Ukrainian Jews—facts, images, stereotypes, and family lore—passed on within families. After the Bolshevik Revolution, knowledge of Ukrainian-Jewish hostility could not be perpetuated in publications and schools, but it may have been part of the socialization of successive generations of Jews and Ukrainians alike.

In this regard, the roots of Jewish distance from Ukraine, its culture, and its people, go deep. The uprising of Ukrainian peasants led by Bohdan Khmel'nyts'kyi against Polish landlords in 1648 resulted in the massacre of perhaps 100,000 Jews. More recently, the pogroms of the 1880s and 1903–1905 and the massive pogroms of the civil war period (1918–1921), when about 50,000 Jews were murdered and 100,000 left homeless, all took place on Ukrainian territory.[23] In 1939–1941 there were more pogroms against Jews in west Ukraine.[24] During World War II, Ukrainian nationalists collaborated with the Nazis against the Soviet regime and participated as individuals and in organized groups in the murder of local Jews. The motivations, extent, and nature of collaboration by some Ukrainians with the Nazis in the mass murder of Jews is still a contentious and highly sensitive issue for both Jews and Ukrainians, and only in recent years has it begun to be aired, though mostly outside Ukraine.[25] Even after the war the Soviet government had to acknowledge, albeit only within government and Communist Party circles, that antisemitism was significant in Ukraine.[26] Thus, especially in the turbulent years of perestroika, the collapse of the Soviet Union, and the infancy of an independent Ukrainian state, Ukrainian Jews might well have felt even more insecure than Russian Jews.

Ukrainian hostility to Jews, which came to be reciprocated, was based on some of the same sources which fed anti-Jewish animus in the rest of Europe: the teachings of Christian churches about Jewish responsibility for the killing of Christ and the popular view of Jews as heretics and sinners, disrespectful of Christianity; the economic position of Jews as middlemen between landowners and peasants, perceived by the latter as exploitative agents of the former; and later, direct economic competition between Jews and Ukrainians.[27] Jews were a "mobilized diaspora," multilingual, highly achievement oriented, and skilled in trade and communication. On interethnic economic competition, John A. Armstrong notes that "as the society becomes more fully modernized, members of other ethnic groups seek to obtain these [white collar] positions, frequently before their skills make them competitively equal to mobilized diaspora members."[28]

Finally, and perhaps most fundamentally, in a culture in which difference and diversity were seen as disruptive rather than enriching—and this is still the case throughout most of the world—Jews were the "most different" of the peoples in Ukraine. Difference bred, in many cases, suspicion and hostility. Jews differed not only in religion, one of the most important social markers, but in speech, area of residence, occupation, language, styles of life, dress, and food. Though Jewish music, dance, food, and even language were strongly influenced by Ukrainian equivalents, Jews and Ukrainians saw themselves as radically different from each other.

A second reason why a Ukrainian Jewish identity did not emerge until recently is that, as Roman Szporluk suggests, what exactly constituted Ukraine was by no means clear. Novorossiia (south-central/southeastern Ukraine) was not included in Ukrainians' mental map until quite late. In 1897, less than 10 percent of the population of Odesa was Ukrainian.[29] It was only at the end of the nineteenth century that Ukrainians began calling themselves by that appellation; before that, they were called "Ruthenians" in the Austrian part of the Hapsburg Empire, "Rusnaks" in the Hungarian part, and "Little Russians" or "Cossacks" in the Russian Empire.[30]

Jews apparently felt no strong affinity for Ukrainians, a people who defined themselves rather late in history. Ukraine is absent from Yiddish rhetoric and the Jewish geographical imagination until after the 1917 Revolution. My impression from reading Sholem Aleichem, the great Yiddish writer born in Ukraine (Poltava Gubernia) in 1859, is that he uses a good deal of Ukrainian in his works and portrays clearly Ukrainian characters, but does not refer explicitly to "Ukraine" or "Ukrainians."[31] The "Jewish map" of Eastern Europe includes Poland, *Liteh* (roughly, Lithuania and present-day Belarus), and Galicia, but not "Ukraine." Prayerbooks refer to "the ritual of *Poilin* [Poland], *Reisin* [roughly, Belarus], and *Zamut* [Zmudz area of Lithuania]" or that of *Liteh*, but never to the "ritual of Ukraine." Even "Ukrainian Jewish history" began to be written as such only recently, though Jews have lived on the territory of present-day Ukraine for at least a millennium. As Philip Friedman noted, "The history of Jews in Ukraine has been treated until now . . . largely as an incidental aspect of the history of Polish or Russian Jews."[32] Since Ukraine was never independent, but was part of Polish-Lithuanian, Austro-Hungarian, Russian, Polish, or Soviet states, Jews treated Ukraine as a vague entity with no defined borders. Therefore, it is not surprising that "a specifically Ukrainian Jewish identity . . . failed to develop in Ukraine, even though the history of the Jews in the region stretches back some two millennia [*sic*] and the population reached roughly two million at the beginning of this century."[33] Jews who lived in Ukraine called themselves, and were called by others, "*Rusishe Yidn*," not "*Ukrainishe Yidn*." When Jews immigrated from Ukraine to the United States before 1918, they were officially classified as "Russian." Consciously or unconsciously adopting the view of imperial Russian officialdom, Jews and others thought of Ukraine as "Little Russia."

Moreover, Ukrainian hostility to Jews as radically different was complemented by Jewish assumptions about the inferiority—indeed, perhaps the absence—of Ukrainian culture. Russians and Poles, though largely peasants like Ukrainians, at least also had urban populations and high, literary cultures. Ukrainians were seen as peasants exclusively—quite an accurate perception until after the First World War. Of course, most Jews were not concerned with whether Ukrainians had their Tolstoys and Pushkins, Mickiewiczes and Słowackis, though this might have been important to the *maskilim* ("enlightened" Jews), but all could appreciate the fact that Russians and Poles owned the land and wielded political power, whereas Ukrainians (and Jews!) did not. As more Jews gained general education from the mid-nineteenth century on, the perceived cultural disparity between Ukrainians and the other peoples may have become more important. In Lviv in May 1993, I was struck by the pride with which an elderly Jew told me that he had "graduated from a *Polish* gymnasium" when the city was still Lwów. Further conversation elicited the clear feeling that Polish education was classical, deeply rooted in a "real" culture, whereas Ukrainian education was somehow ersatz, the latter-day, politically motivated invention of a people who just recently were stomping about in peasant clogs.

One should be cautious in attributing the contemporary Jewish emigration from Ukraine to these historical and cultural factors. After all, it seems that more Jews immigrated to the United States from the northwest part of the Russian Empire (*Liteh*) in the 1880s and 1890s than from Ukraine, though the size of the population in each area was about the same and the pogroms had hit Ukraine much harder than the northwest. Some suggest that the economic boom in Ukraine at the time kept people there, despite the hardships, whereas poverty drove the others to America. So one should not place too much of an explanatory burden on the historical factor, but it might play a role in the contemporary exodus from Ukraine.

Whatever the reason, Jews in Ukraine (and elsewhere) see themselves as rather distant from Ukrainians and their culture. In independent Ukraine, Jews are Russophone and are doubly alien: to Ukrainians, 88 percent of whom listed Ukrainian as their mother tongue in the 1989 census, they are part of the Russian-speaking (*russkoiazychnoe*) population (only 2 percent listed Ukrainian as their mother tongue in the 1989 census), but to the Russians they are Jews. They are in a different position than Jews in Russia, who are at least linguistically indistinguishable from Russians. Surveys taken both before and after Ukrainian independence demonstrate clearly that Russian Jews are more attached to Russia, Russians, and Russian culture than Ukrainian Jews are attached to Ukraine, Ukrainians, and Ukrainian culture. Ukrainian Jews are therefore more easily moved from their native land to either the Promised Land of Israel or the Golden Land of America.

Moreover, until the crash of 1998 in Russia, Ukrainian Jews viewed the economy and future prospects of Ukraine more pessimistically than Russian Jews saw the economy and future of Russia. However, contrary to what one might expect, Ukrainian Jews are somewhat less fearful and insecure than Russian Jews and they report fewer direct experiences with antisemitism (though this may not uproot deeply held fears that the situation could easily change). In fact, when asked in which country a future holocaust might occur, over half of the 1,300 Russian Jews surveyed in 1997 in Moscow, St. Petersburg, and Ekaterinburg named Russia, whereas only a quarter of the 2,000 Ukrainian Jews questioned in five Ukrainian cities named Ukraine (20 percent named Russia and nearly a quarter named Germany). The combination of distance from the titular nation and its culture with pessimism about its future differentiates Ukrainian from Russian Jews in the post-Soviet period. This distance preceded independence and may help explain the proportionately larger Ukrainian emigration both before and after 1991. In independent Ukraine, additional motivations for emigration are lower confidence in the Ukrainian economy than Russian Jews display in the economy of their country and the presence of many relatives and friends abroad.

In a series of interview projects I conducted with different groups of Soviet Jewish emigres beginning in 1980, it became apparent that Jews had a generally poor opinion of Ukrainian-Jewish relations and of Ukrainians when compared with others. They had much warmer feelings toward Russians and Russian culture. In interviews with nearly 900 Jews who left the USSR in 1977–1980, respondents were asked about relationships between several pairs of nationalities.[34] They ranked Jewish-Ukrainian relations the worst, as can be seen in the following table.

Table 3. Perceived Relations Between Pairs of Nationalities

Best relations	Lithuanians-Latvians
	Russians-Belarusians
	Jews-Moldovans
	Russians-Uzbeks
	Russians-Ukrainians
	Russians-Estonians
	Georgians-Armenians
	Jews-Russians
Worst relations	Jews-Ukrainians

Respondents were also presented with pairs of adjectives ranged on a seven-point scale and asked to locate each of several nationalities on the scale. By combining average scores from each pair of adjectives, I was able to get a mean "rating" of each nationality. The following table shows the mean scores given the nationalities by the total Jewish sample and by Jews from Ukraine alone.

Table 4. Mean Scores of Nationalities, Based on Adjectival Scales

Total Sample		Ukrainian Jews	
Ukrainians	4.9392	Central Asians	5.2857
Moldovans	4.8226	Ukrainians	5.0013
Central Asians	4.7396	Georgian Jews	4.5796
Russians	4.0612	Moldovans	4.3906
Lithuanians	4.0318	Georgians	4.1111
Latvians	3.8706	Russians	4.0191
Georgian Jews	3.6677	Lithuanians	3.9633
Georgians	3.4956	Latvians	3.8498
Jews	3.4262	Jews	3.5014

The higher the score, the more *negative* the evaluation of the nationality. Thus, Jews rank most favorably, as could be expected. Ukrainians rank low among Jews from all republics. Georgian, Central Asian, and Baltic Jews gave Ukrainians the lowest rating, Russian and Ukrainian Jews gave them the second lowest, and Moldovan Jews the third lowest. Ukrainian Jews rated Ukrainians quite a bit less favorably than other groups of Jews had on many of the adjectives (cruel, antisemitic, mean, untrustworthy, dishonest, and prejudiced[!]). However, Ukrainians are also seen as cultured and efficient. Overall, only Moldovan Jews came close to those from Ukraine in their negative attitude toward the titular nationality of their republic. Surely this is connected to the finding that at the time Ukrainian Jews reported more frequent antisemitic encounters than those from five other regions.[35]

In a 1985 study based on interviews with Jews from non-European areas of the USSR, Ukrainians again ranked low on an ethnic distance scale. Twelve ethnic groups (five of them Jewish) ranked higher than Ukrainians, but Kazakhs, Tatars, and Chechens ranked lower.[36] Ukrainians also ranked the lowest of the European nationalities on other measures in the study. These patterns held into the 1990s. In interviews with 808 Jewish immigrants to Israel who arrived in 1989–1992, respondents were asked how close they felt to each of 17 groups. Ukrainians ranked twelfth, though only three non-Jewish groups—Americans, Russians, and Georgians—ranked ahead of them. One Jewish group—Moroccan Jews—ranked below them. The others who ranked lower were Tajiks, Uzbeks, Azerbaijanis, and Arabs, all predominantly Muslim. On another measure, however, they also ranked lower than Ukrainians, as in the table below.

Table 5[37] "Warmth of Feeling" Toward Select Nationalities*

Jews	78.4059
Russian Jews	78.2649
Russians	41.2626
Ukrainians	26.0952
Georgians	20.0790
Bukharan Jews	18.0264
Moroccan Jews	17.4705
Ethiopian Jews	4.4372
Azerbaijanis	7.5433
Tajiks	7.0505
Arabs	4.6114

* The higher the score, the "warmer" or more positive the feelings toward the nationality.

Note how much lower Ukrainians rank than Russians, though they rank ahead of all non-Europeans, including Jews. On adjectival scales, Ukrainians rank lower than Russians and Georgians but higher than Central Asians, Azerbaijanis, Arabs, and Moroccan Jews.

These findings are based on experiences in the Soviet period. Have perceptions changed since the breakup of the USSR and Ukrainian independence? A 1993 survey of 2,000 Jews in five Ukrainian cities (Kyiv, Kharkiv, Lviv, Odesa, Chernivtsi), conducted by Vladimir Shapiro and Valerii Cherviakov of the Russian Academy of Sciences' Institute of Sociology, showed that Jews remained socially distant from Ukrainians and Ukrainian culture. When compared to a parallel survey done in Moscow, St. Petersburg, and Ekaterinburg (Sverdlovsk), it turns out that Russian Jews were much closer to Russian culture and Russians than Ukrainian Jews were to Ukrainians and their culture. Though half the Ukrainian Jewish respondents claimed to be "equally close" to

Jews, Russians, and Ukrainians in their city, less than 1.0 percent said they were closer to Ukrainians than to Jews or Russians. Nearly half the Jews surveyed in the three Russian cities said they felt closer to the Russians in their city than to Jews in Belarus and Ukraine, but only 2.4 percent of Ukrainian Jews felt closer to local Ukrainians than to Jews in Russia.

When asked whether "there is much that is Russian [Ukrainian] about you," the two groups of Jews gave strikingly different answers.

Table 6. "In your view, is there much/little/nothing that is Russian [Ukrainian] about you?" (*percent*)

	Russian Jews	Ukrainian Jews	
	Russian	*Ukrainian*	*Russian*
Much	54.0	7.9	47.3
Little	30.2	41.5	37.1
Nothing	5.5	46.6	12.4
Don't know	10.2	4.0	3.3

Nearly the same results were obtained from this question in 1997–1998. Russian Jews feel there is "something Russian" about them, whereas Ukrainian Jews see little or nothing about themselves that is Ukrainian. On the other hand, when asked in a separate question (combined here in the table for convenience), whether there is something Russian about them, Ukrainian Jews respond almost as affirmatively as Russian Jews. Asked whether they feel closer to Russians/Ukrainians or to Israeli Jews, Ukrainian Jews are far less likely than their co-ethnics in Russia to identify with local people and take the easy option of "both are equally close." A clearer picture emerges when respondents describe the atmosphere and style of life in their households. Less than 2 percent of Ukrainian Jews describe it as "more Ukrainian than Russian or Jewish." The most frequent responses are that their households are "all three equally," or that they are predominantly Russian or Jewish. In Russia, by contrast, the most frequent response in both years is that a Russian atmosphere and lifestyle dominate.

In 1993 only 3 percent of Ukrainian Jews said they have mostly Ukrainian friends, whereas 21 percent of Russian Jews had mostly Russian friends. In Russia and Ukraine, similar proportions of respondents (43–49 percent) said that their friends come equally from the three nationalities. By 1997–1998, when so many Jews had gone and those left in Russia and Ukraine were presumably more assimilated, the proportion of Jewish friends declined, but Russian friends were still more frequently mentioned than Ukrainians.

Having seen that the social distance between Jews and Ukrainians is greater than that between Jews and Russians, we turn to Jewish views of the respective countries. Asked to name the country they considered their motherland (*rodina*), the 3,300 respondents in 1997–1998 gave the following answers:

Table 7. "Which Country Do You Think of as Your Motherland—Motherland in Capital Letters?" (*percent*)

	Russian Jews	Ukrainian Jews
Russia	77.6	3.3
Ukraine	0.5	54.6
USSR	1.5	20.2
Israel	10.3	12.6
Other country	1.1	1.2
Other response	4.5	1.9
No answer	4.4	6.3

While 78 percent of Jews in Russia consider "Russia" their homeland, only 55 percent of Ukrainian Jews name "Ukraine" as their homeland. Moreover, few Russian Jews think of the USSR as their homeland, but one of every five Ukrainian respondents does. Is saying you were born in the USSR a way of avoiding identification with Ukraine as a motherland? Probably not. Most likely, one-fifth of the Ukrainian Jews identify their country of birth as "the USSR" (though 61 percent of those born in Ukraine do identify Ukraine as their "Homeland") because they were born when Ukraine was not a separate entity and they are not emotionally driven to assert their Ukrainian identity. This parallels the finding of the survey analyzed by Yaroslav Hrytsak in this volume that residents of Donetsk, east Ukraine, think of their homeland as the Soviet Union or Russia. Some may also associate the USSR with Russia much more than with Ukraine, and see the Russian Federation as the main successor state to the USSR. It is easier for a Jew in Russia who was born in the USSR to name "Russia" as his or her place of birth than it is for a Ukrainian Jew to do so. Still, it is striking that only slightly more than half the Ukrainian respondents, the large majority of whom were born in Ukraine, name Ukraine as their homeland.

There are other, less ambiguous indicators in the survey of Ukrainian Jews' looser attachment to their native land compared to the Jews of Russia. In both 1992–1993 and 1997–1998 they agreed in a higher proportion than Russian Jews with the proposition that "all Jews must sooner or later return to their historic homeland, Israel." They were also more willing to entertain the prospect of emigrating. In 1992–1993, a total of 61 percent of Russian Jews said they would "never" leave or that they did not intend to leave now, but that changed circumstances could make them leave. At the same time, only 48 percent of Ukrainian Jews responded this way to a question about their intention to emigrate. In 1997–1998, more than three-quarters of the Russian interviewees said they would not leave, while only 59 percent of the Ukrainian Jews gave this response.

The impulse to leave is fueled not only by the presence of relatives and friends abroad and perhaps by distance from Ukraine and its people, but also by skepticism about personal prospects and the future of the country as a whole. In the 1997–1998 survey, 25 percent of the Russian Jews said they could best realize their creative potential and use their professional talents in Russia, and 21 percent they could best do so in Israel (35 percent said it was the same in both countries); only 14 percent of Ukrainian Jews saw their best prospects in Ukraine whereas over 44 percent saw them in Israel. While 38 percent of the Russian Jews thought they could attain material satisfaction and a high standard of living in Israel, and only 13 percent thought they could do so in Russia, in Ukraine 65 percent cited Israel as the place where they could fulfill their material aspirations and only 7 percent cited Ukraine. Ukrainian Jews, to a greater extent than Russian Jews, cite lack of faith in the improvement of the situation in their country as a motivation for *other* Jews' emigration. They also cite the desire for "a civilized life" as a reason for others' leaving more often than do Russian Jews. Since the assessment of the prospects for Jewish national life in their countries is very similar among Ukrainian and Russian Jews in both years, it is clear that it is not the Jewish but the general situation that makes Jews in Ukraine more pessimistic.

This brings us to the surprising finding that Ukrainian Jews are somewhat more secure in their country than Russian Jews are in Russia. Nearly half of both groups say they would feel more secure in Israel and over a third say there is no difference between Israel and Russia or Ukraine in this regard. But a slightly greater percentage (8.6) of Ukrainian Jews see themselves as more secure in Ukraine than the percentage (6.9) of Russian Jews feeling themselves most secure in Russia. However, substantially more Russian than Ukrainian Jews say it is antisemitism that drives the emigration, whereas for Ukrainian Jews pessimism about the future of their country is the driving force behind emigration. Finally, Ukrainian Jews in both years of the survey report antisemitic encounters on the street, in the neighborhood, at work or in government offices only a bit more frequently than Russian Jews. In both years they claim that antisemitic tendencies in their city have weakened rather than strengthened, whereas Russian Jews in 1992 saw antisemitism rising and in 1997 perceived it as weakening to a lesser extent than did Ukrainian Jews.

Table 8. "In the Past Year (12 Months), Antisemitic Tendencies in Your City . . . " (*percent*)

	Russia 1992	Russia 1997	Ukraine 1992	Ukraine 1997
Strengthened	42.1	11.6	19.8	6.0
Weakened	9.6	23.6	25.4	40.4
Stayed same	38.4	53.5	49.3	44.0
Didn't /don't exist	1.2	0.7	2.0	
Don't know/ no answer	9.9	10.1	4.9	7.8

Ukrainian Jews also evaluate more positively than Russian Jews the efforts of their respective governments to combat antisemitism. In sum, though distant and recent history provide ample basis for greater insecurity among Ukrainian Jews—though Russian Jews would also have reason to worry—the former seem less concerned about their security and more disturbed by their general prospects and those of their country. After all, in 1992–1993 nearly twice as many Ukrainian as Russian respondents said that "we live from payday to payday, often have to borrow in order to buy essential goods, and can save nothing." Forty-four percent of the residents of Ukraine said this in 1997–1998, while only 19 percent of the Russian residents placed themselves in this category.

The Ukraine-America Connection

Having tried to discover why Ukrainian Jews have emigrated in greater proportions than Russian Jews, I turn to the second question—why Ukrainian Jews have immigrated to America in significantly larger proportions than Russian Jews. One should remember that more Ukrainian Jews have gone to Israel than to the United States (over 200,000 to Israel and over 145,000 to the U.S.), but while over 250,000 Jews have gone to Israel from Russia, only about 80,000 have come to the United States.[38] It is striking that between 1974 and 1996, the number of immigrants who came from Ukraine to the United States (142,670) was almost twice the number who came from Russia (74,554). Only in 1981 and 1982, years of relatively small emigration, did Russian Jews constitute a larger proportion of the immigration to America than Ukrainian Jews. From 1980–1989, a total of 32,850 Jews came to America from Ukraine, while 20,237 came from Russia.[39] In 1989–1997, a total of 55,845 Jews came to America from Russia, but 96,708 came from Ukraine; in the same period, 216,056 went to Israel from Russia and 222,096 went there from Ukraine. So whereas 1.7 times as many Jews came to the United States from Ukraine as from Russia, only 1.03 times as many came to Israel from Ukraine.

This pattern may be counter-intuitive. After all, Russian Jews seem to be less attached to Jewish culture and even to Jewish people than Ukrainian Jews. In the 1920s, the percentage of intermarriages involving Jews was 3.4 times greater in the European RSFSR than in Ukraine.[40] Even in the 1970s and 1980s, a smaller proportion of Ukrainian Jews married non-Jews than did Russian Jews.[41]

Ukrainian Jews were also closer to Yiddish. In 1959 and 1970, the proportion of Jews declaring Yiddish as their native language was slightly higher than in the RSFSR, though in the following two censuses there is no significant difference between the two republics. However, in southwestern Ukraine (areas formerly in Poland, Romania, and Czechoslovakia) there were substantial pockets of Yiddish speakers as late as the 1970s. Ukraine, not Russia, was the area of the *shtetlekh* and their culture, and in small Ukrainian towns such as

Bershad, Slavuta, and Berdichev, Yiddish was spoken in public as late as the 1960s. By contrast, the proportions of Yiddish speakers in Russia and of Yiddish school students in the 1920s and 1930s were far smaller than in Ukraine. Russian Jews, though they were mostly migrants from Ukraine and Belarus, tended to move away from tradition and Jewish culture even more rapidly than their co-ethnics in the other republics. Thus, one could assume that Ukrainian Jews, more closely tied to Jews and Jewish culture, would be "pulled" to Israel, whereas Russian Jews might be "pushed" from the Soviet Union but not as much attracted to Israel as to the United States.

Obviously, this has not been the case. I can only offer two speculative hypotheses to explain why so many more Jews from Ukraine than from Russia have chosen the United States as a country of immigration. One is based on the observation that from 1974 to 1979, though there were no dramatic differences between Russia and Ukraine in the proportions of the overall emigration going to the United States, the greater *numbers* of Ukrainian emigrants meant that more Jews from Ukraine settled in the U.S. than in Israel. These then served as a larger magnet to those still in the FSU, and the disparity between Ukrainian and Russian Jews grew exponentially. Thus, in 1974–1979, while 30,191 Jews came to America from Ukraine, only 8,741 came from Russia. By 1988, when the ratio of Russian immigrants to the U.S. compared to those going to Israel was about 4:1, the ratio for Ukrainian Jews was about 19:1. Thus, "chain migration" might explain why the disparity between Ukrainian and Russian Jewish emigration grew.

In a sense, this begs the question, why did more Ukrainian Jews go to America already in the early 1970s? Perhaps this is due to the fact that the *aliyah* movement was centered in Moscow and Leningrad, as well as the Baltic states, and Russian Jews may have been more intensely directed to Israel than were Ukrainian Jews. It may be that since the first to go to Israel from the European USSR were ideological Zionists, they attracted others from their place of origin. Another possibility is that the collective memories and experiences of Jews in Ukraine made them skittish about going to Israel. Having suffered the traumas of pogroms and the Holocaust to a greater extent than Russian Jews—all of Ukraine was under Nazi rule during World War II but only part of Russia was—Ukrainian Jews might have been more fearful of war in the Middle East and more sensitive to the dangers they and their children would face. Therefore, they opted for the more tranquil United States. I have not found attitudinal data to support this hypothesis and it remains a hesitant speculation.

A final hypothesis is that *zapadniki*, those from the western and southern peripheries of the USSR who had become Soviets only in 1939–1940, left in disproportionate numbers at the beginning of the emigration. Since the emigration moved largely to the United States after 1974, it served as the first links in the chain of migration that brought relatives and friends. Between 1970 and 1980, some 55 percent of all Jews in Transcarpathian Ukraine, formerly in

Czechoslovakia, and 48 percent of Jews in Chernivtsi oblast, formerly in Romania, emigrated, compared to 11.4 percent of Ukrainian Jewry as a whole.[42] To substantiate this hypothesis, it remains to determine whether these emigres moved disproportionately to the United States.

Conclusion

The irony—perhaps the tragedy—in Ukraine today is that just as a Ukrainian state is reaching out to Jews, abjuring antisemitism and encouraging the rebuilding of Jewish cultural, social, and religious life, Jews are leaving in droves. It has now been over a century that Ukraine has been "exporting" Jews, and though the forces propelling emigration are different from those of a century ago or of the period following the First World War, the results are the same: a decline in the Jewish population in Ukraine, which has been diminishing rapidly owing to internal factors,[43] and a demographic, cultural, and economic enrichment of what have become the two centers of world Jewry, Israel and the United States. As they leave, and as Ukraine confronts the great challenges of economic reconstruction, building a new political system, integrating its regions into a cohesive state, and deciding whether it will be an ethnic or civic state, Jews are probably fading from the consciousness of Ukraine's peoples. The "Russian question" and the "Crimean question" are far more important to Ukraine's peoples and their future.

As for Jews who remain in Ukraine, they will have to define their place in it. Will they continue to identify with Russians and their culture? If Ukraine remains a civic state, as it has been since independence, they should have no problem doing so. If, however, the voices urging "Ukraine for Ukrainians" or "Ukraine above all"[44] prevail, Jews will either have to leave or acculturate into Ukrainian culture, and even that might not suffice if some of the more radical nationalists prevail. In a Ukraine which is a civic state, Jews can develop their own culture or remain part of the Russian cultural community, or even evolve a Russian-Jewish culture, much as Jews in English-speaking countries have developed Anglo-Jewish cultures. The last option is far more likely than a return to a self-contained Yiddish- or Hebrew-speaking community, with its special niche in the economy and its great social distance from both landlord and peasant.

Jews in Ukraine are all citizens, but some see themselves as sojourners, while others regard themselves as an integral part of the indigenous population, despite their difference from the titular nation. Their attachment to Russian culture and Russian people has developed over more than half a century, but it does not mean that it is permanent. Perhaps the example of the Jews in Bohemia and Moravia is instructive. At the end of the nineteenth century, Jews in the Bohemian countryside were bilingual, "employing Czech [goyish?] in daily intercourse with the local population, but educating their children in German and preferring German for use in Jewish institutions."[45] In 1890, of the Jews of Prague, where over a third of Bohemian Jewry lived, 74 percent declared themselves German.[46] A decade later, 55.4 percent declared themselves Czech, and already in 1921, after the formation of independent Czechoslovakia, 20 percent of Prague's Jews listed themselves as Jewish by nationality (while the proportion of "Czechs" remained about the same). The changes recorded in the censuses of 1900 and 1910 indicate "not that the Jews had become committed Czech patriots overnight" but that they were firmly bilingual and were seeking to integrate in a divided society.[47] Ukrainian Jews have returned to the same crossroads at which millions of their co-ethnics have stood ever since emancipation. They must answer the simple question that is the title of a story written a century ago by the Ukrainian-born Hebrew writer Mordechai Zeev Feierberg: *"Le'an?"* (Whither?).

NOTES

1. Genesis 12:1.

2. Jacob Lestschinsky, "Jewish Migrations, 1840–1946," in *The Jews: Their History, Culture, and Religion*, 4 vols., ed. Louis Finkelstein (Philadelphia, 1949), vol. 4, pp. 1198–1200.

3. Leo Pinsker, *Autoemancipation*, quoted in Shlomo Avineri, *The Making of Modern Zionism* (New York, 1981), p. 76.

4. On modern Jewish migration, see Mark Wischnitzer, *To Dwell in Safety* (Philadelphia, 1948); and Ronald Sanders, *Shores of Refuge* (New York, 1988).

5. Daniil S. Pasmanik, *Sud'by evreiskogo naroda* (Moscow, 1917), p. 145. See also Samuel Joseph, *Jewish Immigration to the United States* (New York, 1914), p. 101 [=Columbia University Studies in History, Economics and Public Law 59(4)]. For the period 1881–1910, Joseph counts 1,119,059 Jewish immigrants to America. The discrepancy between his figures and Pasmanik's is due, not only to the two additional years included by Pasmanik, but also to the fact that before 1899 immigrants were classified by country of birth or residence, not nationality or ethnicity, so that figures for the years before that are necessarily estimates.

6. My calculation of the total "Jewish" emigration from the former Soviet Union (FSU) from 1989 to 30 September 1998 as 1,042,793 is based on data from the Jewish Agency for Israel, National Conference on Soviet Jewry, and the Hebrew Immigrant Aid Society (HIAS). I then subtract the 30 percent of the emigres estimated to be non-Jewish but part of families in which there is at least one Jewish member, and arrive at a total of 729,955 Jews, just about half of the 1,450,000 people who identified themselves as Jews in the January 1989 Soviet census. The proportion of non-Jewish emigres was probably lower in the earlier part of the period, especially among those who went to Israel, but there is reason to believe that the proportion of non-Jews in the immigration to Germany and the United States is higher.

7. Vasyl' Durdynets' [Vasilii Durdinets], *"O rabote organov vnutrennykh del po neitralizatsii emigratsionnykh namerenii sredi otdel'nykh sovetskikh grazhdan,"* Ministry of Internal Affairs (MVD) Ukrainian SSR, No. 24/7–24c, Secret. 15 January 1988. This policy superseded the decision by the USSR Council of Ministers of 28 August 1986, to refuse emigration to those who had most of their relatives in the USSR. I am grateful to Matvei Chlenov of Moscow for showing me this document.

8. James Rosenau, *Turbulence in World Politics* (Princeton, 1990).

9. Laurie Salitan, "Domestic Pressures and the Politics of Exit: Trends in Soviet Emigration Policy," *Political Science Quarterly* 104(4) 1989–

1990: 671–87. Salitan elaborates her argument in her monograph, *Politics and Nationality in Contemporary Soviet-Jewish Emigration, 1968–89* (London and New York, 1992). My assessment of her argument may be found in *Political Science Quarterly* 107(4) Winter 1992–1993: 781–82.

10. Robert Brym, "Soviet Jewish Emigration: A Statistical Test of Two Theories," *Soviet Jewish Affairs* 18(3) 1988: 15–23; and his "The Changing Rate of Jewish Emigration from the USSR: Some Lessons from the 1970s," *Soviet Jewish Affairs* 15(2) May 1985: 23–25. Even more speculative—and erroneous—arguments are made by John Scherer who opines that the "Soviets probably decided to issue an approximate number of visas by five-year periods and made annual adjustments depending on the political situation and on the number of visas required to fulfill the Plan." The large number of visas issued in 1979 (before the invasion of Afghanistan) was due to a desire to fulfil the plan. "If emigration does not rise in 1986 [it didn't], it probably will not rise during the decade." It did, and to unparalleled heights. John Scherer, "A Note on Soviet Jewish Emigration, 1971–84," *Soviet Jewish Affairs* 15(2) May 1985: 37–44.

11. A figure of 1,561,375 rubles collected from the "education tax" had been reported to the meeting.

12. Boris Morozov, *Evreiskaia emigratsiia v svete novykh dokumentov* (Tel Aviv, 1988), doc. 45, pp. 164–67.

13. Ibid., p. 167.

14. Calculated from data in Zvi Alexander, "Netunim statistiyim shel ha'yetsia," *Hainteligentsia hayehudit bivrih'm* 4 (June 1990); and Zvi Alexander, "Jewish Emigration from the USSR in 1980," *Soviet Jewish Affairs* 11(2) 1981: 3–21.

15. For an analysis, see Zvi Gitelman, "Glasnost, Perestroika and Antisemitism," *Foreign Affairs* 70(2) Spring 1991: 141–59.

16. Sources: Solomon Schwarz, *The Jews in the Soviet Union* (Syracuse, 1951); Mordechai Altshuler, *Soviet Jewry since the Second World War* (New York, 1987); and Mordechai Altshuler, *Distribution of the Jewish Population of the USSR, 1939* (Jerusalem, 1993). Data from the questionable 1937 census have become available but are not included here since they are only partial results. See Akademiia Nauk SSSR, *Vsesoiuznaia perepis' naseleniia 1937 g.* (Moscow, 1991), pp. 83, 85, 94.

17. I am grateful to Dail Stolow of HIAS for supplying me with data on Soviet Jewish immigration to the United States. In 1990, there were 31,283 immigrants to the United States, but HIAS did not issue a statistical report for that year and so the distribution of the immigrants by republic of origin is not known to me. The emigration and immigration

data in this essay are derived mainly from the following sources: Yoel
Florsheim, "Jewish Emigration to Israel and the United States from the
Former Soviet Union, 1992," *Jews in Eastern Europe* 3(22) Winter 1993:
31–39; idem, "Emigration of Jews from the Soviet Union in 1989," *Jews
and Jewish Topics in the Soviet Union and Eastern Europe* 2(12) Fall
1990; Central Statistical Bureau, Israel, *Monthly Bulletin of Statistics*;
Nunu Magor, *"Haolim miBrih'm vehanoshrim shehigiu leArha'b—skira
demografit hashvaatit (1.1.74–30.6.79)"* (Jerusalem: Ministry of Immigrant Absorption, July 1980) [mimeographed report]; Zvi Alexander,
"Jewish Emigration from the USSR in 1980," *Soviet Jewish Affairs* 11(2)
1981: 3–21; David Prital, ed., *Yehudai Brit ha-Moetsot*, 1–14 (Jerusalem:
Hebrew University, 1984–1991); Zvi Alexander, "Mediniyut ha-aliyah
shel Brit Ha-moetsot (1968–1978)," *Behinot* 8–9 (1977–1978); HIAS,
Statistical Abstracts; Joseph Edelman, "Soviet Jews in the United States:
A Profile," *American Jewish Yearbook* 1977; Steven Gold, "Soviet Jews
in the United States," *American Jewish Yearbook* 1994.

18.   The table shows the absolute number of emigrants from each republic in
      each period. Percentages are the proportion of emigrants in the popula-
      tion as measured by the censuses of 1970, 1979, and 1989, respectively.
      Figures do not include Russian and Ukrainian Jewish immigration to the
      United States in 1990. Somewhat different figures, which do not alter the
      overall pattern, are given in Yoel Florsheim, "Jewish Emigration from
      the Former Soviet Union in 1993," *Jews in Eastern Europe* 1(26) Spring
      1995: 25–33.

19.   Florsheim, "Emigration of Jews from the Soviet Union in 1989," p. 28.

20.   Altshuler, *Soviet Jewry since the Second World War*, pp. 107, 124, 145.

21.   Zvi Alexander, "Immigration to Israel from the USSR," *Israel Yearbook
      on Human Rights* 7 (1977): 328.

22.   Alexander, "Mediniyut haaliya shel Brit Hamoetsot," p. 44. There were
      64,522 visas issued to Jews from Ukraine and 23,557 to those from
      Russia.

23.   On the civil war period, see A. D. Rozental, *Megilat hatevakh* (Jerusalem
      and Tel Aviv, 1927); Elieh Khefetz, *Pogrom geshikhte* (New York,
      1921); L. Khazanovich, *Der idisher khurbn in Ukraine* (Berlin, 1920);
      Bernard Lecache, *Quand Israel Meurt* (Paris, 1927?); Elias Tsherikover,
      Antisemitizm un pogromen in Ukraine 1917–1918 (Berlin, 1923); idem,
      Di ukrainer pogromen in yor 1919 (New York, 1965). An analysis of
      Ukrainian-Jewish relations in the civil war period is provided by Henry
      Abramson, *A Prayer for the Government: Ukrainians and Jews in Revo-
      lutionary Times, 1917–1920* (Cambridge, MA, 1999).

24.   See David Kahane, *Lvov Ghetto Diary* (Amherst, 1990).

25. See, for example, Philip Friedman, "Ukrainian-Jewish Relations During the Nazi Occupation," *YIVO Annual of Jewish Social Science* 12 (1958–1959): 259–96; Yaroslav Bilinsky, "Methodological Problems and Philosophical Issues in the Study of Jewish-Ukrainian Relations During the Second World War," in *Ukrainian-Jewish Relations in Historical Perspective*, ed. Peter Potichnyj and Howard Aster (Edmonton, 1988), pp. 373–407; Aharon Weiss, "Jewish-Ukrainian Relations in Western Ukraine During the Holocaust," in the same collection, pp. 409–420; David Marples, "Wartime Collaboration in Ukraine: Some Preliminary Questions and Responses," ch. 4 in his *Stalinism in Ukraine in the 1940s* (New York, 1992); and John-Paul Himka, "Ukrainian Collaboration in the Extermination of the Jews During the Second World War: Sorting Out the Long-Term and Conjectural Factors," *The Fate of the European Jews, 1939–1945: Continuity or Contingency?* ed. Jonathan Frankel (New York, 1997), pp. 170–89 [=Studies in Contemporary Jewry, 13].

26. Mordechai Altshuler, "Antisemitism in Ukraine toward the End of the Second World War," *Jews in Eastern Europe* 3(22) Winter 1993: 40–81.

27. John-Paul Himka, "Ukrainian-Jewish Antagonism in the Galician Countryside During the Late Nineteenth Century," in Potichnyj and Astor, eds., *Ukrainian-Jewish Relations*, p. 148.

28. John Armstrong, "The Ethnic Scene in the Soviet Union: The View of the Dictatorship," in *Ethnic Minorities in the Soviet Union*, ed. Erich Goldhagen (New York, 1968), p. 4.

29. Personal communication, 9 September 1995. I am grateful to Professor Szporluk for his helpful comments.

30. Roman Szporluk, "Des marches de L'empire à la construction d'une nation," *L'autre Europe* 30–31 (1995): 135. See also David Saunders, "What Makes a Nation a Nation? Ukrainians Since 1600," *Ethnic Studies* 10 (1993): 101–124; Paul Robert Magocsi, "The Ukrainian National Revival: A New Analytical Framework," *Canadian Review of Studies in Nationalism* 16(1–2) 1989: 45–62; Zenon E. Kohut, "The Development of a Little Russian Identity and Ukrainian Nation-Building," *Harvard Ukrainian Studies* 6(3–4) December 1986: 559–76; and Orest Pelech, "The State and the Ukrainian Triumvirate in the Russian Empire, 1831–1847," in *Ukrainian Past, Ukrainian Present*, ed. Bohdan Krawchenko (New York, 1993), pp. 1–17.

31. In his stories of "Tevye *der milkhiker*," the clearly Ukrainian characters, whose village council is the *hromada*, are always referred to as "goyim" [gentiles], never as Ukrainians, or Russians for that matter. See the stories "Khave" and "Lech Lecho" in *Ale verk fun Sholem Aleichem*, 4 vols. (New York, 1925), vol. 1.

32.   Philip Friedman, "Geshikhte fun di Yidn in Ukraine," in *Yidn in Ukraine*, 2 vols. (New York, 1961), vol. 1, p. 1. Jacob Sholem Hertz does not take up the question of the existence of a "Ukrainian Jewry" in his *Di Yidn in Ukraine* (New York, 1949). A contemporary history published in Ukraine simply assumes a "Ukraine" from the earliest times of Jewish settlement. See Iakov Samoilovich Khonigsman and Oleksandr Iakovych Naiman, *Evrei Ukrainy* (Kyiv, 1993).

33.   Abramson, *A Prayer for the Government*, p. 40.

34.   For details of the study, see Wayne DiFranceisco and Zvi Gitelman, "Soviet Political Culture and 'Covert Participation' in Policy Implementation," *American Political Science Review* 78(3) September 1984: 603–621.

35.   For a discussion, see Zvi Gitelman, "Perceptions of Ukrainians by Soviet Jewish Emigrants: Some Empirical Observations," *Soviet Jewish Affairs* 17(3) 1987: 3–24.

36.   Details are in Zvi Gitelman, "Ethnic Identity and Ethnic Relations Among the Jews of the Non-European USSR," *Ethnic and Racial Studies* 14(1) January 1991: 24–54.

37.   Data taken from a study reported in Zvi Gitelman, *Immigration and Identity: The Resettlement and Impact of Soviet Immigrants on Israeli Politics and Society* (Los Angeles, 1995).

38.   This does not include the 1990 immigrants for whom HIAS did not compile figures by republic, or the immigrants of 1983–1986, when there was a total emigration of only 4,264, most of whom probably came to the United States.

39.   Steven Gold, "Soviet Jews in the United States," *American Jewish Year-book* 1994, p. 44.

40.   Altshuler, *Soviet Jewry since the Second World War*, p. 194. See also Zvi Gitelman, ch. 6 in *Jewish Nationality and Soviet Politics* (Princeton, 1972).

41.   In 1978, of Jewish men in the RSFSR who married, 59.3 percent married non-Jews, and 43 percent of the Jewish women marrying that year married non-Jews. In Ukraine, the corresponding figures were 44.7 percent for men and 34.2 percent for women. By 1988, the Russian figures were 73.2 percent for men and 62.8 percent for women, and the Ukrainian figures were 54.1 percent for men and 44.7 percent for women. Mark Tolts, "Trends in Soviet Jewish Demography Since the Second World War," in *Jews and Jewish Life in Russia and the Soviet Union*, ed. Yaacov Ro'i (London, 1995), p. 372. On the demography of Jews in Ukraine, see Mark Kupovetskii, "Osobennosti etnodemograficheskogo razvitiia evreiskogo naseleniia Ukrainy vo vtoroi polovine XX veka," in

Istoricheskie sud'by evreev v Rossii i SSSR: nachalo dialoga, ed. Igor' Il'ich Krupnik and Mark Kupovetskii (Moscow, 1992), pp. 52–70. See also his "Der yidisher yishev af Ukraine inem nochmilchome-period," *Sovetish haymland* 7 (1989): 19–128.

42. USSR Ministry of the Interior, 10 February 1981, no. 1/675, in Morozov, *Evreiskaia emigratsiia*, p. 230.

43. Of Jews marrying in 1988 in Ukraine, over 60 percent married non-Jews. See "Data on Ethnic Intermarriages," *Journal of Soviet Nationalities* 1(2) Summer 1990: 169. The "vital index" (percent ratio of the number of all children born to Jewish mothers to the number of Jewish deaths) of the Ukrainian Jewish population declined from 127 in 1958 to 59 in 1969, to 26 in 1989. See Mark Tolts, "Trends in Soviet Jewish Demography since the Second World War," in *Jews and Jewish Life*, ed. Yaacov Ro'i, p. 367.

44. A slogan that appears on the masthead of *Holos natsiï*, a newspaper published in Lviv.

45. Hillel Kieval, *The Making of Czech Jewry* (New York, 1988), p. 198.

46. Evyatar Friesel, *Atlas of Modern Jewish History* (New York, 1990), p. 39.

47. Kieval, *The Making of Czech Jewry*, p. 199.

Symbolic Autobiography in the Prose of Mykola Khvyl'ovyi (Some Preliminary Observations)

GEORGE G. GRABOWICZ

When I first attempted to define the notion of symbolic autobiography in my early work on Shevchenko, and then in an essay on Shevchenko and Mickiewicz, I was persuaded (and I still hold it to be largely true) that this is a modality that characterizes, or is specifically empowered by, a Romantic poetics. It thus is marked by writing that is attuned to the unconscious and that implicitly opposes the special authenticity of the inner life to the putatively less authentic external and manifest world.[1] My subsequent recourse to this paradigm in connection with Ivan Franko's late long poems, however, suggested to me that the question of a historical poetics is decidedly secondary to the writer's readiness, indeed his need, to address the concealed or repressed levels and forces of his self—specifically of his sense of self and ultimately of his hidden, "shadow" self.[2] This need continually to reveal and conceal clearly is not confined to any one historical poetics, such as the Romantic. It is a more universal drive, especially evident in the modern period, and as such it is responsive to various interpretative strategies, particularly the psychoanalytic, but also the structuralist and the poststructuralist.

Most generally, the sense of symbolic autobiography involves not so much the writer's readiness to reveal key moments of his internal and hidden life— this confessional principle is quite prevalent, if not altogether universal, and can be said to animate whole genres or modes, such as the lyrical—as to endow them with both narrative extension and a certain narrative autonomy, and in particular to thematize them. As such, this becomes part of a broad modern or modernist tendency of self-referentiality or autothematism.[3] One of the recent outer limits of such autothematism—as we see in the witty collection of self-referential and self-dematerializing pieces written in imitation of and homage to Borges's "Borges and I" by contemporary writers from Albee to Updike[4] — is a kind of ultimate dissociation of "the writer" from the "writer-as-real-person": "the writer" becomes radically other and unreachable, even, or especially, to the "writer-as-real-person" in whom he or she resides. Self-reflection and self-consciousness aside, that which defines symbolic autobiography and gives it its peculiar resonance is not the autobiographical moment, or event, or detail as such (for this is contingent even in "straight" or traditional, or avowedly veristic autobiography), but precisely its symbolic component, its encoding. In Shevchenko, who provides a paradigmatic instance of symbolic autobiography, this encoding conforms to the basic structures of his mythopoesis and involves such key moments as the conflation of the fate of the poet-*kobzar* with the fate of the nation, the patterning of his life (the symbolic biography) in terms of the movement between (and thus recapitulation and reinforcement of) communitas and structure, and above all the enabling, reciprocal relationship between the poet as sinner and prophet.[5]

*   *

*

As much as the psychological content—the basic matrix of the encoding—will differ from writer to writer, there also remains the question of narrative articulation, of individual poetics. In this connection, the figure of Mykola Khvyl'ovyi stands out with peculiar intensity. He is arguably the outstanding Ukrainian writer of the early twentieth century, and he is almost certainly the one writer who like a lightning rod attracted, focused, and transmitted the enormous energies of his day—and the energies and powers of interpretation of succeeding generations. For us, Khvyl'ovyi figures primarily as an author of remarkably evocative, yet still only spottily examined prose. The required basic rereading of his work, however, is clearly beyond the scope of this paper. What I propose here is a preliminary sketch of some basic issues—with particular reference to the way in which they flesh out the concept of symbolic autobiography. The specific moment that I will examine is that of the interface of the literary and the psychological in the context of thematized, self-conscious narrative. In a word, the basic issue I will examine is that of intertextuality; in effect, of symbolic autobiography as intertextuality.

For anyone even generally acquainted with the life and work of Khvyl'ovyi, the paradigm of symbolic autobiography would seem particularly apposite. One of the major tasks in the rereading of Khvyl'ovyi that I am calling for is to distinguish between surface (functionally biographical, ideological, and other such) moments and between deeper psychological structures that through the mediation of narrative regulate the interaction between Khvyl'ovyi's life and art, and effectively modulate the one by the other. Surely the most striking and dramatic of these is Khvyl'ovyi's end—his suicide. As various accounts, and the documentary evidence reveal, it was the culmination of a pervasive and deeply held belief in his being fated to play a role, to act out and, even more importantly, to write out a certain calling. The suicide itself, as we see so powerfully from the account of Antonina Kulish, the wife of Mykola Kulish (Khvyl'ovyi's close friend, who was present at the end) was in the best sense of the term "scripted":

> May 13 was a nice sunny day. Suddenly Khvyl'ovyi rang and called Mykola to the phone. He said, "Hurovych, it's a nice day today. Come to my place, my friend, and we'll go for a walk in the park."
> Mykola was quite puzzled as he walked away from the phone. It'd been such a long time since he had seen Khvyl'ovyi. Almost a year since they last

spoke, even though Khvyl'ovyi lived in the same building and only a few steps
from our apartment. Mykola went. Somehow he later described it to me:

At Khvyl'ovyi's place he met Dosvitnyi, Vyshnia, Epik, Dniprovs'kyi,
Iohansen, Arkadii Liubchenko, and one other man. He was surprised that
Khvyl'ovyi had invited such a large company for a walk in the park.
Khvyl'ovyi began serving tea; his mood was agitated, and elevated, and
purposefully gay. Nobody thought this strange. It was obvious to everyone:
the arrest of Ialovyi was a complete blow; most powerful, perhaps, for
Khvyl'ovyi. Everybody seemed depressed. Some were drinking tea and the
host took a guitar and began singing the words of Pushkin's poem "Besy":

> Хоть убей, следа не видно;
> Сбились мы. Что делать нам!
> В поле бес нас водит, видно,
> Да кружит по сторонам . . .

After this he put down the guitar and went into his study. Suddenly
everyone heard a loud shot from the study. When they ran in Khvyl'ovyi was
sitting in his chair, a trickle of blood was flowing from his right temple and
falling drop by drop onto the floor; his hand with the colt in it was drooping,
and the colt fell out of it. My husband ran with horror into the room and
shouted:

Khvyl'ovyi has shot himself![6]

Apart from his sense of the dramatic, and his underlying and pervasive
autothematism, this event points to another essential feature Khvyl'ovyi shares
with other powerful writers: his profound, uncanny ability to program his own
reception. In his case, this higher performance—his playing out both a role and
a fatum—is expanded into his afterlife.

Immediately after his death, Khvyl'ovyi's image and persona begin to assume iconic and cultic and even mythic dimensions. The funeral orations
themselves, despite their (obviously officially inspired) castigations of the
suicidal act, depict him as unquestionably the central player in the literary
process.[7] In short order, in Soviet Ukraine any positive remembrance was
quickly suppressed and for subsequent decades, up to the final collapse of the
Soviet Union, Khvyl'ovyi became the single most vilified Ukrainian writer and
public figure in the scholarly and parascholarly discourse (considerably more
so than Vynnychenko and Hrushevs'kyi, and unquestionably more than the
avowed nationalist enemy, Dontsov). Outside the totalitarian realm, however,
the growth of Khvyl'ovyi's reputation was intense. Initially, it was possible for
a critic like Mykhailo Rudnyts'kyi to maintain a distanced attitude, to see him
as part of a modernist current, but without apologia and even with some irony
and scepticism.[8] But this was the exception. Writing immediately after
Khvyl'ovyi's death, Dmytro Dontsov saw him as the ideal incarnation of the
Ukrainian will to resist or perish in the struggle, indeed implicitly as his own—
Dontsov's—alter ego and emanation.[9] By the tenth anniversary of
Khvyl'ovyi's death, at the height of World War II, his heroization was in full

bloom: as reflected in the memoirs of Arkadii Liubchenko,[10] Khvyl'ovyi was again depicted as a preternatural force of will and emotion, as a moral leader, and virtually as a prescient, self-sacrificing national martyr. Two years earlier, as he began his diary in a Kharkiv that had just been—as he then saw it— liberated by the Germans, Liubchenko turns to Khvyl'ovyi in the very first lines:

> Away from Moscow! Do you hear, Mykola? If you were around now, you'd
> be with us![11]

For Olena Teliha, who also wrote around this time (and undoubtedly under the influence of Dontsov, her erstwhile lover and editor), Khvyl'ovyi had become a moral, and national, and voluntarist standard.[12] Ievhen Malaniuk, writing a few years later (and somewhat less rhapsodically than Teliha, but with no less passion and with characteristic verve) saw Khvyl'ovyi as the examplar not only of will (the Dontsovian formula), but of reason and of a sublime sense of the cause. Characteristically, too, Malaniuk was able to see and articulate the reciprocal scripting that occurs in Khvyl'ovyi's life and art. "Khvyl'ovyi," he wrote, "was sovereign not so much in art—for this was but one of the manifestations of his creative being—as in life. Thus, too, his death carries the same sign of sovereignty as does his life."[13]

In subsequent decades this line evolved into a curious, but hardly unique hybrid of exegesis and scholarship combined with apologia and hero-worship, as in the writings of Hryhorii Kostiuk, Iurii Lavrinenko, Iurii Boiko-Blokhyn, and Yuri Sherekh-Shevelov. Apart from these literary critics, there were also such political activists as Vasyl' Hryshko and Ivan Maistrenko, for whom Khvyl'ovyi was a basic touchstone for their vision of Ukraine and its recent past. The cult of Khvyl'ovyi also begat a counteroffensive among the right-wing nationalists who saw in Khvyl'ovyi's national communism only the com-munism—and behind it the hand of the Cheka. In a classically naive reading, which mirrors—albeit without the introspection—and thus parodies the per-spective of Malaniuk, art and life were again blurred, and Khvyl'ovyi, with all apparent seriousness, was condemned as the Chekist who in his fanaticism killed his own mother; his story "Ia (Romantyka)," after all, was tangible proof of this.[14] This and other such naive readings, however, should not be simply laughed off. Despite their aggressive and largely inarticulate form, they inti-mate a deeper level—even while they are unable to see beyond the mimetic, the overtly biographical, and, of course, the ideological.

In a word, the cult of Khvyl'ovyi and then the polarization of his reception, his posthumous existence as both hero and *bête noir*, attest to a remarkably powerful symbolic legacy or indeed biography. The question that must now be addressed is how this phenomenon is in turn scripted, encoded, and pro-grammed by a deeper symbolic autobiography.

*   *

*

Part of the answer—in effect, its textual basis—inheres in the fact that Khvyl'ovyi's prose, virtually the entire corpus, is highly autothematic and self-referential, from the early stories of *Syni etiudy* such as "Zhyttia" and "Redaktor Kark" (1923), to such late pieces as "Z laboratoriï" (1931). There are various subsets to this. For one, to a greater or lesser degree many of the works are metathematic and appear almost as exercises or fugues on the process of creation—most overtly "Vstupna novelia," "Redaktor Kark," and "Arabesky." In others, such as "Povist' pro sanatoriinu zonu" or "Z laboratoriï" the meta- or autothematic coexists with a developed, coherent plot and story, which in this coexistence, however, is subtly subverted or decentered. As various critics have noticed—even while the term may not have been used and the systematics not always recognized—the entire corpus of Khvyl'ovyi's prose, his essential style, is highly intertextual. Literature, literary allusions, scenes, characters, topoi, devices, and so on are not only continually intro-duced, varied, and parodied, but this very mode is thematized and toyed with. Not infrequently this is done with a satiric purpose: the conventions and expectations of the readership or of a genre are conjured up only to be mocked. Thus, for example, in "Redaktor Kark":

> Мої любі читачі!—простий і зрозумілий лист.—Я боюсь, що ви мою новелю не дочитаєте до кінця. Ви в лабетах просвітянської літератури. І я поважаю. Та кожному свій час. Творити то є творити. Да. (1:135)

Or the unabashedly mocking opening of "Z laboratoriï":

> Письменник вирішив написати роман. Письменник був не зовсім бездарний (так принаймні авторитетна критика заявила) і безперечно близький пролетаріятові.
>
> Але про що писати?—подумав письменник.—Про старі часи? Ні в якому разі! Про буденні, непомітні дрібниці? Ні за що! Треба писати про великі події наших днів.
>
> Хто робить події,—письменникові відомо: їх робить робітничо-селянська маса! Відомо йому і за чиїм проводом: за проводом комуністичної партії. (3:155)

The satiric and parodic effect is augmented by the fact that these obsequious desiderata are not followed at all, and the narrative, like a runaway horse, cannot be controlled by the socialist-realist bridle.

Even on the surface level, however, the intertextuality, Khvyl'ovyi's "literaturshchyna," is not solely determined by a satiric or even ironic thrust.[15] To be sure, the very fact of drawing one's characters, for example, from the existing "classical" repertoire—the male lead, say, from Dostoevsky (Dmytrii Karamazov) and the servant woman from Kotsiubyns'kyi's "Smikh" (in "Val'dshnepy")—having the heroine's father (in "Iz Varynoï biohrafiï") be a stock character from the vaudeville stage who can only repeat one and the same line, cannot but be seen as something ironic and comic. It is also very much in the air at that time. Without having to refer to the catalog-mantra of distant "great masters" ("Joyce, Proust, Gide, Kafka, Mann"),[16] one can find more proximate examples, of, say, a Bulgakov or a Witkacy, or better still among the representatives of the Ukrainian avant-garde. Maik Iohansen in his masterful "Podorozh uchenoho Doktora Leonardo . . . " for example, programmatically reverses the centrality of landscape and characters—not throughout, but often and in various key scenes. The characters, in short, are movable and inter-changeable cardboard figures. According to the author's tongue-in-cheek, ge-neric self-definition ("quoted" as he says in his English-language prefatory note, "for the use of critics only"), his is a "landscape novel," "something that has never been deliberately attempted before."[17] This process of debunking and dematerializing not only conventions, but such seemingly indispensable liter-ary structures or building blocks as character and plot is part of the poetics of both expressionism and surrealism, and in terms of the latter was strongly represented in the Ukrainian avant-garde theater by Les' Kurbas.

In Khvyl'ovyi's prose, intertextuality appears as a profound and ironic sense that the repertoire of literature (implicitly all literature) can be reduced to a kind of cultural shorthand, or, indeed, a detritus of culture. In terms of this implicit "poetics of impermanence and contingency" there seems to be a resonance between Khvyl'ovyi and his near-contemporary, the remarkable Polish prose writer Bruno Schulz.[18] But more than philosophical, or culturological, or even satiric commentary, intertextuality provides for Khvyl'ovyi a narrative drive, a mode of self-assertion. For what must be stressed is that the core of his intertextuality is actualized in terms of his own works. In a word, the individual stories constitute, or at least repeatedly allude to an overarching "master narra-tive." Not only do particular stories link up in almost sequential narrative (the most obvious "continuation," for example, is between "Ia (Romantyka)" and "Povist' pro sanatoriinu zonu") or "recapitulate" one another (for example, the scenes of the communist's retreat in "Ia (Romantyka)" and "Iz Varynoï biohrafiï"), but they also project a powerful sense that they are continually circling around, reflecting and refracting one, basic, even if dimly perceived ur-story. The analogy to fragment-variants of a large, central mythos is inescap-able. A full exposition of this requires a close reading that cannot be provided in the space available here. But one key moment, at once highly cathectic and traumatic, may serve as an example.

As can be seen from both the history of Khvyl'ovyi's reception sketched out above and from even a cursory reading of his major works, one of the most central, most memorable and unnerving scenes in his corpus is the killing of the mother in "Ia (Romantyka)." It is a scene that in purely literary, i.e., artistic, dramatic terms would presumably be entirely self-sufficient and in a sense closed off from further narration. In a word, it should not be repeated. But repeated it is. And more than once. It recurs or is "varied" in a different key in

"Val'dshnepy" when in the very first chapter Dmytrii Karamazov, who is growing more and more estranged from his wife Hanna, has a fleeting thought about doing away with her:

Єсть!—подумав Дмитрій і тут же до болю вкусив свою губу: йому раптом спало на думку покінчити з Ганною.

Але вкусив він губу не тому, що насувається щось трагічне, а тому, що згадав: така трагедія по суті була вже. Хіба це не Ганну він розстріляв колись, у часи громадянської війни, біля якогось провінційного монастиря?

Знаєш що, Ганнусю, раптом кинув Карамазов.—Я зараз думав про тебе і подумав, що ти воскресла. Як це розуміти? (2:289–90)

Irony? Yes. Intertextuality? Of course. But clearly there is more here than just that. In "Arabesky," which presumably Khvyl'ovyi wrote just before "Ia (Romantyka)," but which actually was published a few years later, the narrator muses in one of his constant digressions:

І я, романтик, закоханий у свою наречену, знову бачу її сіроокою гарячою юнкою з багряною полоскою на простріленій скроні. Вона затулила рану жмутом духмяного чебрецю й мчить по ланах часу в безсмертя. (1:403)

What emerges here, as I see it, is that the generating force is not literary or stylistic or ironic, but psychological. Khvyl'ovyi, as one can easily demonstrate, is often obsessed with certain elemental events or scenes—and this strongly suggests the working of, or an opening to the preconscious or unconscious levels.

* *
*

On the most basic level the question of role is the question of self-definition. In "Vstupna novelia," for example, a story specifically designed as an introduction to Khvyl'ovyi's collected works (*Tvory*, 1927) and as such turned into a very paragon of meta- and autothematism, its plot—its digressive and self-referential musings aside—is meant to recount how the writer was obliged by his editors and publishers to write an introductory novella. In effect, it is a drawn-out baring of the device—of the writer entering the role of writer. In "Arabesky" this construction/deconstruction of the persona, the hero of the story, is bared even further. The narrator, Nicolas (the same name that is applied to the author-narrator in "Vstupna novelia"), weaves his hyper-romantic (i.e., basically potboiler) biography, of being Soireil, the illegitimate and abandoned son of some functionary and so on, only to seemingly get bored with it and debunk it all as simple role playing. When the woman he is telling this to asks him to continue with the plot ("Слухай Nicolas! А що ж далі? Як же з твоїм чиновником?") he responds: "Маріє! Ти наївничаєш. Нічого подібного не було. Я тільки приніс тобі запах слова" (1:397).[19] At times, the question of role and role playing is specifically bared, as in the late story "Z laboratoriï":

> Марченко теж нічого не говорив, він тільки зрідка позирав на товариша Хруща, і в його погляді було стільки добродушної іронії, ніби він дивився не на дорослого Колю а на Колю страшенно маленького, що, скажім, з цілком серйозною міною грає якусь ролю, яка йому зовсім не під силу і яка його робить надзвичайно комічним. (3:175)

In fact, virtually all the lead characters in Khvyl'ovyi's prose, i.e., those who carry the cathectic line of the narrative, are in some fashion conscious of playing a part. In the story "Pudel'," the main character, Saihor, is the one who provides the perspective—through a clashing mix of irony, trenchant observation, and overflowing sentiment—on a wandering company of students and actors and on their somewhat comical and somewhat erotic outing. Saihor's inability to engage in the erotic play is ultimately revealed as the inability to see the person behind the stereotyped role and with that the inability to be oneself in the presence of the other, in a word, a paralysis of self-consciousness: "Сайгор подумав: що сказати в цей момент? Що кажуть у цей момент?" (1:359). His uncanny feeling that there is an inner double watching our actions is something to which we shall turn in a moment. The most direct articulation of the paralyzing and yet manic, or hysterical sense of role occurs in the story "Ia (Romantyka)":

> Увійшов дегенерат. Він радить мені одложити діла й розібрати позачергову справу:
>
> Тільки но привели з города нову групу версальців, здається, всі черниці, вони на ринку вели одвертагітацію проти комуни.
>
> Я входив в ролю. Туман стояв перед очима, і я був у тім стані, який можна кваліфікувати, як надзвичайний екстаз.
>
> Я гадаю, що в такім стані фанатики йшли на священну війну. Я підійшов до вікна й сказав:
>
> —Ведіть! (2:43–44)

In the social context, role is what one is cast into—with the resultant all-encompassing feelings of helplessness and indeed infantilization. In "Revizor," a story which arguably examines the very paradigm of typecasting, of the ontology of role, so to say, one of the lead characters, Valentyn Brods'kyi, a reporter for a provincial newspaper, is put in the role of attending to the Very Important Guest from the big city, who is nothing short of the bared intertextual "revizor" (even though his name is Topchenko, not Khlestakov). In the process everything that Valentyn does or tries to do—especially in the eyes of his wife, Lesia, who provides the cathectic core of the story—only confirms his provincial character:

> . . . Валентинові взагалі сьогодні не щастило, це Леся одразу ж помітила. Він весь час намагався бути розв'язним, дотепним і зовсім не

провінціалом, але і його в'юнка чорненька і остаточно не мужня фігурка і його банальні дотепи і, нарешті, його мало приховане бажання "показати себе" перед ревізором—все це красномовно підкреслювало, що він провінціал, що він все таки ніяк не може зрівнятися з Топченком. (3:80)

As in Gombrowicz's notion of *gęba*, which is developed with such accuracy and comical variety in *Ferdydurke*, the "mug" or mask that is pasted on you when you are typecast is so powerful—everything you say or do only confirms it—that only the most radical, and seemingly bizarre, countermeasures may (perhaps) suffice in tearing it off.

In Khvyl'ovyi, the sheer presence and variety of such masks, which are mostly traps upon which role and role playing devolve, is remarkable. Whether in the early "Arabesky," "Ia (Romantyka)" or "Povist' pro sanatoriinu zonu," or such late works as "Revizor," or "Z laboratorii," the sense of playing roles or having them thrust upon you is highly marked. In "Val'dshnepy," a work whose political concerns edge it perilously close to a publicistic treatise rather than a novel, but which, nonetheless, maintains a sparkling artistic integrity, the question of role and the pasted-on "mug" is couched in social, and historical, and cultural terms. Specifically, the opposition between things Russian and things Ukrainian which animates the plot and the discourse of the novel and which, characteristically, is also grounded in sexuality, in a battle of the sexes, serves to reveal the mask/trap of the Ukrainian "national character," its role as a device for ready typization and stereotypization: once Dmytrii Karamazov and Ahlaia enter their respective Ukrainian and Russian roles they seem to become permanently scripted, at least in the narrative of the novel. This also becomes, of course, grist for the mill of an obligatory and invidious urban/rural, center/ provinces dichotomy, which now, in turn, is material for an (all too predictable) postcolonial hermeneutics.

*   *

*

The work in which roles and role playing attain the greatest complexity, and clearly link up with the deeper psychological frame that underlies Khvyl'ovyi's oeuvre is "Povist' pro sanatoriinu zonu." Insofar as it forms a diptych with the somewhat earlier "Ia (Romantyka)" one needs to begin with the latter, however. In effect, in "Ia (Romantyka)" role and role playing are revealed as internal psychic processes, and the whole is indeed recast as a psychodrama. While a closer analysis of this diptych is a task for the future, one can note that in "Ia (Romantyka)" (and in contrast to "Povist' pro sanatoriinu zonu") the prioritization of the symbolic over the mimetic (which is a key to the Romantic mode here) and with it the introduction of "archetypical" moments is a clear indication that the story will unfold in internal, not external space. Thus, the struggle between the Bolsheviks and their opponents is largely cast as a "universal" opposition, i.e., as if in terms of the Paris Commune of 1870, with such designations as "insurgenty," "versal'tsi," "komunary"—although the very specific Cheka, to which the autobiographic narrator belongs, also figures in the story. Most tellingly, the elements of plot and the details, which in realist fiction would occupy center stage—precisely as the means for establishing verisimilitude and the discourse of social relevance—are here programmatically distorted. Thus, on the one hand the stylized ("Romantic") setting and on the other the bared schematism of the non-dialogue of the narrator's interrogation of a couple brought before the revolutionary tribunal:

> . . . Портьєра роздвинулась, і в мій кабінет увійшло двоє: женщина в траурі й мужчина в пенсне. Вони були остаточно налякані обстановкою: аристократична розкіш, княжі портрети і розгардіяш—порожні пляшки, револьвери й синій цигарковий дим.
>   Я:
>   —Ваша фамілія?
>   —Зет!
>   —Ваша фамілія?
>   —Ігрек!
>   Мужчина зібрав тонкі зблідлі губи і впав у безпардонно-плаксивий тон: він просив милости. Женщина втирала платком очі.
>   Я:
>   —Де вас забрали?
>   —Там-то!
>   —За що вас забрали?
>   —За те-то! (2:42)

The bared schematism only reaffirms the fact that the only important moment is the psychodrama itself. The revolutionary tribunal—the sadistic, Lenin-like idealogue Dr. Tahabat, the quintessentially brutal "degenerat," the "humanistically" weak-willed Andriusha—are basically all fragments of the "ia," the ego, who is telling the story. There are numerous hints to this effect, for example, this concerning Dr. Tahabat at the beginning of the story: "Цей доктор із широким лобом і білою лисиною, з холодним розумом і з каменем замість серця, це ж він і мій безвихідний хазяїн, мій звірячий інстинкт" (2:37). At another point he thinks of his mother and that she shares the attitudes of the old order, the "versal'tsi," and then his thought takes this turn:

> І тоді, збентежений, запевняю себе, що це неправда, що ніякої матері нема переді мною, що це не більше, як фантом.
>   —Фантом?—знову здригнув я.
>   Ні, *саме це*—неправда! Тут у тихій кімнаті, моя мати не фантом, а частина мого власного *злочинного* "я", якому я даю волю. Тут, у глухому закутку, на краю города, я ховаю від гільйотини один кінець своєї душі. (2:39–40)

The purpose or teleology of the story—and the very fact that its plot is symbolically coded makes this a story that indeed *has* a core purpose and essence—is to show that here the ego cannot hold its various parts, that its unity is torn between what appears to be revolutionary zeal, fanatical possession by the idea, and an inner world of feeling symbolized by Maria, the mother-lover. As he is goaded by Dr. Tahabat, in effect his "revolutionary" convictions, to pronounce the death sentence on his mother, the narrator sums up his quandary, the ego-split itself:

> Так схопили нарешті й другий кінець моєї душі! Вже не піду я на край города злочинно ховати себе. І тепер я маю одно тільки право:
> —нікому, ніколи й нічого не говорити, як розкололось моє власне "я." (2:45)

In light of this structure, the final killing of the mother, adumbrated as it is by echoes of the killing of Andrii by Taras Bulba, can only be seen as the killing of an innermost presence and value, in effect the anima. For its part, the symbolic meaning of "Ia (Romantyka)" must be seen as a confrontation with the shadow, an encounter with the darkness within—and an implicit concession that that encounter is fatal for the integrity of the ego.

This fatalism is given profound elaboration in "Povist' pro sanatoriinu zonu." If "Ia (Romantyka)" presents but the bared rudiments of the psycho-drama (albeit programmatically), and also presents the killing of the anima-mother as still only an implicit suicide, "Povist' pro sanatoriinu zonu" develops both the psychodrama and the suicide with various nuances of mirroring and fragmentation. Significantly, the narrative is now full of seemingly realist action, dialogue, and detail; at the same time, the underlying symbolic cast of the work is evident, particularly its central feature—the duplication of roles and hypostases, the mirroring, reflection, and refraction of the ego. While seemingly endowed with existential autonomy—in "Ia (Romantyka)," in contrast, the various major characters are shown as but projections of the central "Ia"—the characters here are still fictional creations in the diary of Khora ("the sick one"). And Khora herself is dying of consumption; from the content and style—and the very voice of her entries—she clearly is also a hypostasis of Khvyl'ovyi himself. The general atmosphere of the sanatorium, and of the story itself, appears to be one of interpenetrated reality and illusion, overlayered with a hysterical energy that is most concentrated in the figures of the *anarkh* and of Khlonia—who are clearly parodic projections of the author, the former as the archetypical anarchist (removing the suffix from his name, as the narrator says, reveals his hairy nature even further), the revolutionary sick with his own messianic and reformist zeal, the modern Savonarola (which his lover, Maia, ironically punctures as "Savonarolichka") and the latter as the hopelessly sentimental and weak would-be poet. The dramatic counterforce, Karno, the *metranpazh*—literally the page setter—on the surface, the epitome of malicious scepticism and mockery, is also quite evidently a dramatized incarnation of the author's own critical distance and ubiquitous irony; his role, after all, incarnates the final stage—going even beyond that of editor (viz. the autothematic Redaktor Kark)—of preparing the text before it goes to the reader: the ultimate superego. (Characteristically, in this regard, the concluding authorial *profession de foi* also includes ironic and prescient references to the coming new order where everything will be written with the censor in mind.)

With great psychological acuity, the ambient hysteria of the main authorial projections, the *anarkh* and Khlonia, is shown to be deeply rooted in sexual anxiety, and in the case of the *anarkh* and Maia (whose name, as we are reminded in an anonymous letter to the former, is that of an Indian goddess of illusion) an ongoing, irresolvable, and destructive battle of the sexes. In the spirit of D. H. Lawrence and anticipating such writers as Gombrowicz, Khvyl'ovyi clearly also distrusts all desexualized ideas.

The essential permutation in "Povist' pro sanatoriinu zonu" is that of doubling, not only of the more evident pairs, the *anarkh* and Khlonia, Maia and the nurse Katria, and so on, but also of the *anarkh* and Karno who is described not only as a provincial Mephistopheles but as the *anarkh*'s double.[20] The play of doubles, as of the thematically stressed ego-split in "Ia (Romantyka)," reconfirms both the symbolic and the psychological coding of the work, and with it Khvyl'ovyi's pervasive self-thematization, the ever-present mirror image, where he is both author and critic, inspired creator and ironic commentator. In terms of the dramatic—and symbolic—movement of the story, the culminating moment in this play of duality devolves upon the double suicide of Khlonia and the *anarkh*.

*   *
*

Suicide must surely be seen as a key to Khvyl'ovyi's symbolic self-presentation. Its obsessive presence in his work, and the range of its guises or disguises is striking in and of itself. Its shadow is implied in "Redaktor Kark," where the title character cannot but dwell on the pistol in his desk—with the growing intimation that he will ultimately use it. In "Zavulok," the cental character, the Chekistka Mariana decides to commit suicide by getting infected with syphilis. A peculiarly bizarre twist occurs in "Lehenda" where the woman-warrior, in order to become a legend and a martyr, chooses her own death—by impalement. In "Val'dshnepy" putting a bullet in one's head is mentioned as if casually, in the course of a spat between Dmytrii Karamazov and his wife Hanna. In "Povist' pro sanatoriinu zonu," as just noted, there are two suicides by drowning, but since one is the shadow of the other, it basically relates to one core death fantasy. In "Z laboratorii," the rather hysterical Lida Spyrydonova asks her companion (whom she renames Potop or Potopchyk) to throw her into the river. As already noted, the killing of the mother in "Ia (Romantyka)," to the extent that it is a killing of the anima is also a symbolic suicide. In the late story "Maty" (1930)—a work that echoes *Taras Bulba* and resonates with

Tychyna's, and Ianovs'kyi's, images of fratricidal civil war—the death of the mother at the hands of her son, Andrii, who thinks he is killing his brother, Ostap, is a function of her own desire to die. And this list is hardly complete.

The point here, however, is not so much to mark an obsessive presence—although even more remarkable, perhaps, is the fact of how consistently this key moment has been ignored in the critical literature—as to underline the existence in Khvyl'ovyi's work of a highly unified psychic space which animates his works and gives them their remarkable power. The specific and interrelated components of this psychological force field are several—the role of the writer and his will, his sheer voluntarism, which is linked in his consciousness with his inescapable sense of playing roles (which prominently also includes the roles of both writer and political pamphleteer and activist), with an almost paralyzing self-consciousness. The resultant sense of virtually autonomous subunits of the self, of an ego-split that moves, as is so masterfully shown in "Povist' pro sanatoriinu zonu," into virtually clinically accurate dissociation. And the fear of such dissociation becomes a theme in its own right, viz. "Z laboratorii."

But surely there must be more; surely the suicide fantasy, and the underlying psychic anxieties do not exhaust the picture. The attempt at providing a narrative, a story line that approximates the auto*biography* that we have been alluding to will need to build on a closer analysis of Khvyl'ovyi's work, an analysis that is still a task for the future. One can, however, postulate some functions—and in this fashion perhaps intimate the outlines of the plot into which Khvyl'ovyi feels himself inscripted.

On the articulated, textually given level, suicide for Khvyl'ovyi appears as a moment of acceptance of one's own fatedness, one's need not to hold on to life at any cost, but precisely by letting it go to merge with the higher purpose of things. Near the end of "Povist' pro sanatoriinu zonu," for example, the *anarkh* has a vision of "the other side of reality" and it draws him with inexorable strength:

> За декілька темних годин осінньої темряви перед ним пройшло стільки примар і спогадів, скільки він не бачив за все своє життя. Він остаточно вирішив, що вже не існує, що мешкає "на тому боці" реальности. І він не тільки примирився з цим, йому навіть радісно було, що він уже, нарешті так просто, без усяких перешкод, попав у цей невідомий край. (2:167)

In "Maty," the death wish is put even more directly and simply:

> І раптом прийшла матері думка, що ніякого кошмару нема і що все, що діється зараз, є звичайне й природне явище. І коли вона не може зрозуміти цього, то вона, значить, оджила вже свій час, і, значить, на її земне місце прийшли нові люди, з новими думками й з новими, далекими їй бажаннями. І тоді захотілось матері вмерти. (2:367)

In the larger frame of Khvyl'ovyi's work, suicide, the readiness to take ultimate control and disposition of one's life, functions as an act of radical authenticity, a moment when one finds the self without the masks of the ego, and without imposed roles. As unexpected, unsanctioned, and even "bizarre" as it may appear to others (and the variants of suicide just noted seem precisely to test believability, let alone social decorum), it becomes an ultimate assertion of freedom. Against the background of the totalitarian night, it became—as his reception confirmed—precisely an act of assertion, not negation.

In effect, the suicide that is so marked in Khvyľovyi's fiction establishes the basic teleology of Khvyľovyi's symbolic self-representation, or what we can still, most generally, call symbolic autobiography. It does so not solely because of the undercurrent of morbidity (although this aspect of his shadow also needs to be examined), and perhaps not only because of his sense of an overarching *fatum* looming over him and his generation, but because for all his love of life, and openness to play, his sense of self was finally so uncompromising.

NOTES

1. See George G. Grabowicz, "The Nexus of the Wake," in *Eucharisterion. Essays Presented to Omeljan Pritsak on His Sixtieth Birthday by His Colleagues and Students* (Cambridge, MA, 1980), pp. 320–47 [=*Harvard Ukrainian Studies* 3–4]; and, *The Poet as Mythmaker* (Cambridge, MA, 1982). See also idem, "Z problematyky symvolichnoï avtobiohrafiï u Mitskevycha i Shevchenka," in *V litopys shany i lubovi,* ed. V. S. Borodin et al. (Kyiv, 1989), pp. 51–63.

2. See George G. Grabowicz, "Vozhdivstvo i rozdvoiennia: tema "vallenrodyzmu" v tvorakh Franka," *Suchasnist'* 1997(11): 113–38.

3. See Boguław Bakula, *Oblicza autotematyzmu* (Poznań, 1991).

4. See *Who's Writing This? Notations on the Authorial I, with Self-Portraits,* ed. Daniel Halpern (Hopewell, NJ, 1995).

5. See George G. Grabowicz, "Shevchenko iakoho ne znaiemo," *Suchasnist'* 1992(11): 100–112.

6. See "Spohady pro Mykolu Kulisha," in Mykola Kulish, *Tvory* (New York, 1955), pp. 365–433, esp. pp. 415–20. All of the people mentioned here were prominent writers of the time; virtually all were members of VAPLITE, the literary group Khvyl'ovyi had helped to found in 1925. It was disbanded by the regime in 1928.

7. See, for example, *Literaturna hazeta* 27 May 1933: 2; cf. Mykola Khvyl'ovyi, *Tvory v p'iat'okh tomakh* (New York, 1986) (henceforth: *Tvory*), vol. 5, pp. 137–48.

8. See M. Rudnyts'kyi, *Vid Myrnoho do Khvyl'ovoho* (Lviv, 1936).

9. Cf. "Mykola Khvyl'ovyi," *Literaturno-naukovyi visnyk,* 1933 (cf. *Tvory,* vol. 5, pp. 439ff.). The resonance between Dontsov and Khvyl'ovyi clearly requires a separate inquiry.

10. See Arkadii Liubchenko, "Ioho taiemnytsia" (1943); cf. Khvyl'ovyi, *Tvory,* vol. 5, pp. 87–112.

11. *Shchodennyk Arkadiia Liubchenka,* ed. Iurii Luts'kyi [George S. N. Luckyj] (Lviv and New York, 1999), p. 7.

12. See Olena Teliha, "Partachi zhyttia"; cf. *Tvory,* vol. 5, pp. 472–74.

13. Malaniuk, "13 travnia 1933 r."; cf. *Tvory* vol. 5, pp. 468–69.

14. See, for example, V. Koval, ed., *Na sud ukraïns'koï emihratsiï "natsional-komunizm"-khvyl'ovyzm ta ioho propahatoriv! (Materialy z perevedenoï aktsiï u SShA i v Kanadi)* (New York-Toronto, 1959). Cf. also the bibliography in *Tvory,* vol. 5, pp. 691–786.

15. For irony in Khvyl'ovyi, see M. Shkandrii, "Irony in the Works of

Mykola Khvyl'ovyi," *In Working Order: Essays in Honor of George S. N. Luckyj* (Edmonton, 1990), pp. 90–102.

16. Ibid., p. 100.

17. See Maik Iohansen, *Podorozh uchenoho Doktora Leonarda i ioho maibutn'oï kokhanky prekrasnoï Al'chesty u slobozhans'ku Shvaitsariiu* (Kharkiv, 1930).

18. See Bruno Schulz, *Sklepy cynamonowe / Sanitorium pod klepsydrą,* 4th ed. (Cracow, 1992), particularly the "Traktat o manekinach," pp. 35–39.

19. In a ground-breaking essay on "Khvyl'ovyi without politics" Yuri Sherekh takes this passage as emblematic of Khvyl'ovyi's style and mode in general: "Це один з ключів до творчости Хвильового. Скільки критиків Хвильового осмішили себе, бо не відчували запаху слова, не розрізняли гри від життя чи може краще сказати, гри в житті від життя без гри." ("Khvyl'ovyi bez polityky," in his *Ne dlia ditei* [New York, 1964], p. 54.) What Sherekh is calling "play" here is, as I see it, entirely compatible, if not entirely coterminous, with the notion of role and role playing.

20. See the above-noted anonymous letter, *Tvory,* vol. 2, p. 145.

The Odyssey of the Petliura Library and the Records of the Ukrainian National Republic during World War II

PATRICIA KENNEDY GRIMSTED

The Petliura Library in Paris is now located on the second floor of a building that it shares with the Ukrainian Orthodox Autocephalous Church (6, rue de Palestine, 75019 Paris). At present it has only 57 of the close to 20,000 books that it had gathered between 1929 and 1940. From this small remnant of the original collections that remained when the library reopened after the war in April 1946, the library has grown and surpassed its prewar holdings, with a total of 30,000 volumes and an additional 73 runs of newspapers and periodicals. Gone, however, are the more valuable original collections of books, many with dedicatory autographs and other inscriptions. Many of the prewar records of the library and most of the archival materials that had been collected before the war also are gone. The library's postwar revival and the purchase of the building it occupies today were partially aided by funds received from Germany in 1964 as reparation for the looting and destruction of the library during the occupation.[1]

When Arkady Joukovsky (Arkadii Zhukovs'kyi), a Ukrainian emigre professor in Paris, described the history and collections of the Petliura Library in 1990, he presumed that the prewar library had been definitively destroyed or irretrievably lost, or both, during the war.[2] When a brief Ukrainian adaptation of his article subsequently appeared in Kyiv, the editors were not aware that a small part of the library and some of its prewar records were also in Kyiv.[3] In a historical memoir account of the library, Vasyl' Mykhal'chuk claimed that a fragmentary, second-hand report of a box of books marked "Ukrainian Library—Paris" found in the basement of the former Lenin Library (now the Russian State Library) in the early 1990s, was proof that the library that had been seized by the Nazis ended up in Moscow after the war.[4]

Although the bulk of the prewar book holdings have not yet been located and identified, nor their fate definitively established, some have recently surfaced in Minsk and Kyiv, and others in Moscow. In fact, 260 books with Petliura Library stamps identified in what is now the National Library of Belarus were transferred—or, as reported from Minsk, "returned"—to Kyiv in the late 1980s.[5] They are now held in the National Parliamentary Library of Ukraine, although the fact of their transfer and present location has not been published previously. That same library reports having purchased 10 more books with Petliura Library stamps in the early 1980s at auction in Kyiv.[6] We now know that a large part of the Petliura Library records, many of its prewar catalogues, and some of its unique archival materials have survived their wartime odyssey, although unfortunately they are now dispersed among no less than two archives in Moscow and two in Kyiv.

None of the library catalogues remained in Paris after the war, although those associated with the library had a good idea of the nature and extent of the prewar holdings, particularly thanks to Ivan Rudychiv (1881–1958), who had served as the librarian since its foundation. Rudychiv was summoned to Berlin by the Nazis in June 1941 "to look after the library," after they had transferred the library books and archival collections earlier that year. As it turned out, he never saw the library in Berlin before being allowed to return to Paris in October 1942. After the war and until his retirement, Rudychiv helped rebuild the library collections. He never knew about the migrations of the library, nor could he have suspected that many of the library catalogues would turn up in Moscow, or that his own early wartime accounts of the library, diary, correspondence, and other personal papers would surface half a century later in Kyiv.

The fate of the Petliura Library and its archival holdings from Paris is a small but tragic example of wartime and postwar library and archival displacements. In fact, almost all surviving documentation of the Ukrainian National Republic (UNR) throughout the continent was targeted by the Nazis, seized during the war, and then seized again by Soviet authorities in its aftermath. The present attempt to portray the odyssey of the Petliura Library in that context reflects the broader political and ideological clashes of the war and postwar period that have left the remnants of this small but important center of Ukrainian political and cultural life dispersed in the capitals of four nations—Russia, Belarus, Ukraine, and France.

World War II brought with it the greatest archival dislocations in history. Soviet authorities succeeded in evacuating only their most precious secret files to Siberian havens. Others were hidden or intentionally destroyed to prevent them from falling into enemy hands. Some archives fell victim to the bombs that reduced major European cities to rubble. Others were saved by Nazi evacuations to various salt mines, monasteries, and castles. Many were looted, first by the Nazis for a variety of political, strategic, and propaganda purposes, and then by the Allied victors. Little has been known until recently about the many displaced archives that were captured after the war by Soviet authorities. Because of these archives' use for "operational" purposes, most of them were hidden in secret repositories until the end of the Soviet regime. And even since, it has been difficult to identify them, because integral collections were broken up and dispersed for sundry operational purposes; many were never adequately described, and hence are not now being made available for public research. In Moscow and Kyiv today, there are not even preliminary published lists of the variety and location of "trophy" materials, or how and by what name (and number) they have been assigned to fonds in Soviet archives. In many cases, the archives that hold them today have no information about where they were found after the war.

The Records of the UNR and Origins of the Petliura Library

When Petliura's UNR government was forced into exile in 1920, its leaders tried to salvage various government records and related documentation. Files were fragmented, as the UNR leaders found themselves in exile in different countries. Those UNR records remaining in Ukraine were taken into custody by Soviet authorities, as treasures of the growing secret divisions of the new state archives in the Ukrainian Soviet Socialist Republic. Some were among the most valued files that Soviet authorities evacuated to the east at the outbreak of war in 1941. UNR documentation abroad migrated and became concentrated in several different centers during the interwar period. Personal collections of UNR leaders, augmented by related documentation and miscellaneous papers created in emigration, were scattered all over Europe. There was no real archival home for the records of the regime in exile without a country.

The UNR Directorate chairman Symon Petliura initially settled in Tarnów, Poland, with his wife and daughter. A major part of the UNR records in Poland remained in a basement in a house that the UNR had purchased and used as its headquarters in Tarnów, the last seat of government during the abortive Polish-Ukrainian campaign against the Bolsheviks. Records there included many files of the Ministries of Foreign Affairs and Finance, together with what was left of the currency issued by the UNR regime. Additional documentation was in the UNR headquarters and other places in Warsaw. Other UNR documentation, and especially some of the records relating to the UNR military mission in Poland and to military operations, were scattered throughout Poland. Some of these eventually ended up with the archive of General Tadeusz Rozwadowski, the Polish commandant in Galicia, and are now held in the Józef Piłsudski Institute in New York City, from which several documentary collections have appeared.[7] Most recently, some files of the UNR government in exile from the years 1984–1992 (when it was headed by Ivan Samiilenko, a Ukrainian emigre in the United States), were transferred to Kyiv and deposited in one of the national archives (TsDAVO).[8]

Pursued by Soviet agents, Petliura left Poland in disguise at the end of 1923, and settled briefly in Budapest, Zurich, and then Geneva, before moving to Paris in October 1924. In Petliura's immediate entourage was V'iacheslav Prokopovych, his former prime minister and earlier minister of education, who helped him establish the journal *Tryzub* (Trident) in Paris as an organ of the UNR. During the spring of 1926, Petliura was living with his wife and daughter in a modest Latin Quarter hotel. On 26 May 1926 he was assassinated in broad daylight.

Petliura's hitherto unknown assassin, Samuel (or Sholem) Schwarzbard (Shvartsbard) (1886–1938) was a Jewish emigre from the Russian Empire with anarchist leanings, who had first came to France in 1910. Returning to Odesa after the outbreak of the Revolution of 1917, he was active in the Red Brigades during the civil war. Schwarzbard was back in Paris by 1920, continuing to frequent Bolshevik circles, and had reportedly been preoccupied with Petliura's arrival in the French capital.[9]

Schwarzbard was vindicated in a highly publicized trial. The defense represented Schwarzbard as a Jewish hero, seeking revenge for 14 family members killed in anti-Jewish pogroms in Ukraine, for which he held Petliura responsible—an argument strongly supported by Jewish interests, which bitterly linked Petliura to the pogroms that took many Jewish lives.

Was Schwarzbard a lone player? The prosecution accused the assassin of acting on behalf of the Soviet foreign intelligence service, which considered Petliura's leadership of the Ukrainian nationalist cause abroad a threat to the Soviet regime. Schwarzbard was linked to a recognized Bolshevik secret service (OGPU) agent, Mikhail Volodin; but Volodin had expeditiously returned to Moscow before he could be called to testify at the trial.[10] Although no documentation from Soviet sources has yet been released proving Schwarzbard's link to the Soviet OGPU, Soviet authorities clearly had good reason to pursue Petliura. Mindful of the earlier UNR alliance with Poland and Petliura's close ties to Józef Piłsudski, Soviet authorities became more apprehensive—following Piłsudski's May 1926 coup d'etat—that a new Ukrainian-Polish campaign against the USSR might be imminent. They were also anxious to prevent Petliura's wooing of French support. Furthermore, the issue of Jewish-Ukrainian animosity under Petliura lent itself to exploitation by the Bolsheviks to discredit the Ukrainian national cause. Recently, as another twist, a French historian suggested possible French governmental diplomatic and economic interests vis-à-vis the Soviet Union in the acquittal of Petliura's assassin.[11] Others have speculated that Petliura might have been at least partially a victim of rival factions within the Ukrainian emigre political spectrum (with which Moscow interests were perhaps also cynically involved).

The still unresolved interpretations of Petliura's assassination and the acquittal of his assassin are reflected in the historiographical interpretations of the period and appraisals of his political career and the briefly independent regime he led.[12] Be that as may, Petliura's death in Paris focused international attention on Ukraine and produced a martyr to the cause of Ukrainian independence—a cause that waited over half a century to be realized.

More to the point of the present study, Petliura himself had recommended the foundation of a Ukrainian library in Paris earlier that year, pointing as examples to the Polish Library and the Turgenev Russian Library that were already thriving in the French capital.[13] Soon after Petliura's death, a library was established to perpetuate his memory by Prokopovych and other UNR exiles, including Ilarion Kosenko, Oleksander Shul'hyn, and General Oleksander Udovychenko. Although Paris hardly rivaled Prague as a center of Ukrainian emigre intellectual and political life during the interwar period, the Petliura Library, with the support of the Ukrainian community throughout the world, became a focal point of emigre politics and Ukrainian culture.

The Symon Petliura Ukrainian Library in Paris (Bibliothèque ukrainienne Simon Petlura à Paris) opened to the public in 1929. Continuing to grow during the subsequent decade, by January 1940 it housed 14,458 volumes and 143 periodical titles, not counting the relatively minimal holdings of its several branches elsewhere in France—Chalette, Audun-le-Tiche, Lyon, and Grenoble, as well as Esch in Luxemburg. Never rivaling the much more prominent Polish Library (140,000 volumes) that was well supported by the newly independent Polish Republic, or the larger Russian emigre and staunchly anti-Bolshevik Turgenev Library in Paris (120,000 volumes by 1939), which even received a prominent building from the mayor of Paris, the Petliura Library remained a relatively small operation. Initially housed in rented quarters of three rooms (11, place du Port Royal) in the thirteenth arrondissement, it moved in the 1930s to a five-room apartment (41, rue de La Tour d'Auvergne) in the ninth arrondissement, which also housed the editorial office of *Tryzub*.

Among its archival materials, the library preserved a few files of the Petliura government and some of UNR exiled leaders, including the minister of finance in the Central Rada, Pavlo Chyzhevs'kyi, who was subsequently a Ukrainian trade representative in Paris, Geneva, and other European capitals—together with Symon Petliura's own library and a few of his personal papers. In early 1939, the library received the records of the UNR diplomatic mission in Paris and the Ukrainian press bureau. Those archival materials were intermingled with the *Tryzub* editorial records that were also held in the library and included some correspondence of the Russian and Ukrainian writer, Boris Lazarevskii (1871–1936), and the papers of his brother, Hlib Lazarevs'kyi (1877–1949), a journalist and literary specialist active in the Ukrainian movement.[14] The library had built up a significant collection of official printed documents and brochures from the Petliura government, newspaper clippings, and memoir materials from the Ukrainian emigration. There were records of the Schwarzbard trial and the Association of Combatants of the Army of the Ukrainian National Republic. There were some files of the Union of Ukrainian Emigre Organizations in France and other emigre associations. A bibliographic compendium on Petliura, prepared by Petro Zlenko in 1939, was based on the library holdings.[15] With the support of the Ukrainian community throughout the world, the library remained a strong focus of opposition to the Soviet regime that had foiled Ukrainian efforts to establish independence after 1917.

Nazi Seizure of the Petliura Library

When France was invaded by Nazi Germany and Paris fell to occupying forces in 1940—still during the period of the Nazi-Soviet pact—Hitler was already planning his *Drang nach Osten*. As one phase of the preparations, Nazi specialists had targeted various Slavic emigre libraries in France and other countries in Western Europe as important intelligence sources, and their followers as potential allies in the Nazis' subsequent anti-Soviet campaign. As librarian Ivan

Rudychiv confided in his diary in January 1941, the notion "was circulating among Russian emigre circles [in Paris] that Petliura was the first great nationalist, and that Hitler was a student of Petliura." Furthermore, it was rumored, Hitler was already endorsing Ukrainian independence.[16] For Nazi propagandists, although the UNR was traditionally pro-French and pro-Polish and anti-German, Petliura's antisemitic reputation made him a symbol to be manipulated for the Nazi cause. The Petliura Library had an additional appeal, in that its martyr patron died at the hand of an acquitted assassin who sought revenge for Petliura's alleged role in anti-Jewish pogroms.[17] Speculations that his assassin had been encouraged by Soviet intelligence sources could also increase the usefulness of Petliura's martyrdom to Nazi propagandists anxious to exploit anti-Soviet sentiments abroad and in the soon-to-be occupied Ukrainian lands.

Efforts to evacuate the library were too little, too late.[18] Following the Nazi occupation of Paris, already on 13–15 July, the building of the UNR Mission (24, rue Glacière) was searched and many of its contents confiscated (with some of the archival materials from the library that had been moved there); the building was sealed by the Nazi police (Geheime Feldpolizeigruppe 540). German authorities, who were obviously acquainted with Ukrainian emigre affairs, first visited the main library building (41, rue de La Tour d'Auvergne) on 22 July and interviewed Rudychiv for at least an hour. Soon afterwards Rudychiv was required to hand over "the founding regulation of the library, a picture of Petliura's grave, and the maps from the library." On 22 October 1940, the Petliura Library building was sealed by Nazi secret police. By 13 December, the library was officially declared "under German protection" (*unter deutschem Schutz*). The library and its archival materials were confiscated on 20/21 January 1941, with follow-up seizures on 24 January.[19] Rudychiv's detailed accounts of the Nazi visits and subsequent confiscation, his memoir account entitled "Iak tse bulo," and what would appear to have been his own diary for the period 1940–1942, survived the war and are now open for research in Kyiv.[20]

The Petliura Library shared its wartime fate with the two other Slavic libraries mentioned above, the Turgenev Library and the Polish Library, both of which were seized in Paris at approximately the same time. According to contemporary Nazi reports, over 100,000 books were taken from the Turgenev Library, and 130,000 volumes from the Polish Library.[21] Nazi figures show that they seized "15,000 books, maps, photographs, and museum pieces from the Petliura Library in autumn 1940."[22] Rudychiv's reports set the total above 18,000 volumes in the library alone. After confiscation by the Nazi secret police, the materials were first taken to a Paris collection point (45–47, rue La Bruyère), and then were all shipped to Berlin in early 1941.

The Petliura Library in Berlin

One Nazi report noted that "the Petliura Library in Paris owned by the Ukrainian Emigre Union had been evacuated by the Gestapo under orders from Georg Leibbrandt."[23] Leibbrandt (1899–1982), born in the Odesa region, had been one of Alfred Rosenberg's top aides in Berlin since the early 1930s, and headed the Eastern Section (Amt Osten) of Rosenberg's Nazi Party Foreign Policy Office.[24] After the formation of the Reich Ministry for Occupied Eastern Territories (RMbO) under Alfred Rosenberg, which governed the Soviet lands under Nazi occupation, Leibbrandt headed one of the principal sections of the ministry. Liebbrandt first visited the library in Paris in 1937 and made extensive inquiries, according to Rudychiv. His further involvement with the Petliura library is confirmed by Rudychiv, although as it turned out, Liebbrandt had little time for Rudychiv once he arrived in Berlin. Nevertheless, it was apparently Liebbrandt's office that was paying Rudychiv's monthly stipend during his stay in Berlin.[25] Leibbrandt had long been forming his own special collection of archival materials relating to German settlers and communities in southern Russia; he later acquired more significant archival materials relating to German settlements in southern Ukraine, some of which were seized in Odesa in 1941 and 1942 on his request by the notorious Künzberg brigades.[26] He was considered one of the top ministry specialists on Ukraine.

After the Petliura materials from Paris arrived in Berlin in early 1941, they were examined by Reich security forces, the Foreign Ministry, and representatives on behalf of Leibbrandt. However, as it appears from the treatment of Rudychiv, they decided that the library was of minimal political and strategic interest and turned it over to the Special Command of Reichsleiter Rosenberg, the infamous ERR (*Einsatzstab Reichsleiter Rosenberg*). One of the major ideological research and propaganda arms of the Nazi regime, the ERR was involved in looted cultural treasures of all types, and especially those from "enemies of the Reich," such as Jews and Masons. The ERR had already established a major anti-Bolshevik research center in Berlin, along the lines of its Center for the Study of the Jewish Question in Frankfurt. According to Rudychiv's account, the ERR was already involved with the Petliura Library seizure in Paris, although Rudychiv had been told the library was then under the control of the Foreign Ministry and Leibbrandt in Berlin.

Rudychiv had been promised in Paris that the library would be reestablished in Berlin, where he would serve as librarian under the control of the Nazi foreign ministry functionary Döringer.[27] After Rudychiv was brought to Berlin in June 1941, on the eve of the Nazi invasion of the USSR, he met with Döringer at the Foreign Office (Auswärtiges Amt). He also met with the wealthy Ukrainian emigre political leader Oleksander Sevriuk, who had earlier been associated with the UNR, but who at that point was apparently collaborating with the Nazis. Rudychiv was then informed that there was no room to establish the library in Berlin, and that it remained "in packing sacks." Later, in early July, he was told that it would probably soon be shipped to Kyiv after war began on the Eastern Front. He also met with Ivan Mirchuk (Mirčuk), who was then directing the Ukrainian Scientific Institute (Ukraïns'kyi naukovyi instytut) in Berlin, together with Professor Zenon Kuzelia, both of whom received him "coldly" and showed no interest in the library or in Rudychiv's own fate. In fact, Rudychiv never saw the library in Berlin. He was kept in Berlin during the summer and early fall, and it was suggested that he prepare some reports about the library, which he did. In October 1942, he was permitted to return to Paris.[28]

After his return to Paris, Rudychiv prepared a report for the Petliura Library Council in France in December 1942, a copy of which is retained in the Paris library with the library records.[29] But that short report is of much less interest than the more detailed reports he prepared in Berlin, including his memoir account of the demise and disappearance of the library, "Iak tse bulo." According to his December 1942 report, Rudychiv gave that memoir to his old friend Ievhen (or Jevhen) Vyrovyj from Prague, whom he met in Berlin. He also mentions having given him some other documentation relating to the library for the Museum of the Struggle for Ukrainian Independence before he left Berlin.[30] If, presumably, Vyrovyj succeeded in taking Rudychiv's papers and the other documentation from the Petliura Library to Prague, they probably came to Kyiv with the holdings that Soviet authorities seized from Prague after the war.[31]

According to one Nazi report, there had been an inquiry about the library from Oleksander Platonovych Semenenko, who initially served as mayor of Kharkiv under Nazi occupation, but German authorities in Berlin did not want to give any details to him. Apparently, the Nazis had seriously considered shipping the library to Ukraine, but then decided that the library would not be of much official value in occupied Ukraine anyway, because many of the holdings were French books. At that point they quoted a figure of no more than 10,000 volumes in Berlin. If this figure is not an error (elsewhere they referred to 15,000 volumes), it suggests that either they had not shipped all the books to Berlin or had already weeded out almost one-third of them.[32] In fact, under the ERR in Berlin the Petliura materials were almost immediately allocated to the so-called *Ostbücherei*, the special "Eastern Library" relating to Bolshevism and other East European matters, developed under the Rosenberg command. The same fate befell the Turgenev Library and probably at least part of the Polish Library from Paris.[33] Possibly some of the books had been set aside for the planned Central Library of the Hohe Schule, the ERR's planned party ideological training institute to be established in the Bavarian Alps after the war. Books intended for that library were being shipped to the monastery of Tanzenberg in the Tyrol during the war, where they were found and restituted by British military authorities in 1945.[34] After the war two crates with a complete set of the journal *Tryzub* found in Austria were returned to the Petliura Library in Paris by the French Art Reparation Commission, but further details about where they were found are not available.[35]

Many Nazi agencies—not only Leibbrandt and the ERR—were utilizing the propaganda potential of Ukrainian independence. Such interest was not new in Germany and followed German support for the Ukrainian independence movement as a component of its geopolitical strategy of Mitteleuropa at the end of World War I. It was evident that the Nazis intended to use the lure of Ukrainian independence and even Petliura's alleged antisemitism to win the Ukrainian population to the Nazi cause. During the occupation in Lviv, the Nazis allegedly used Petliura's name in connection with some of their own anti-Jewish atrocities. In eastern Ukraine, special efforts were under way to locate and collect Ukrainian archival materials from the immediate postrevolutionary and civil war period. ERR reports now in Kyiv show the extent to which that agency was preoccupied with library and archival sources relating to that period. Work started immediately after occupation in Ukraine to develop a special collection called the "Revolutionary Archive," formed of documentation from the period of the revolution, civil war, and attempts to establish an independent Ukrainian state. This was hindered by the fact that Soviet archival authorities had previously evacuated many of the most sensitive UNR archival materials with the Secret Division from the state archives that were taken to the east.

The ERR Ratibor Center

After Western Allied bombing started in Berlin, many Nazi units were moved from the capital into more remote areas, most particularly to the east. Starting in the summer of 1943, the headquarters of various Rosenberg command units and major ERR research and library operations were transferred from Berlin to the relatively isolated city of Ratibor (*Pol.* Racibórz), 80 kilometers southwest of Katowice on the Oder (Odra) River in Silesia. Among other operations, the anti-Bolshevik research and propaganda units were centered there. As support for those operations, the special library collections of the *Ostbücherei* were also moved to Ratibor, and its holdings organized in several different buildings in the city. Castles and other sites in the surrounding area became storage and work sites for different ERR units. By February 1944, at least some holdings from the Petliura Library—along with those from the Turgenev Library—were housed in the former Lagerplatz Synagogue in the center of the city, under the direction of the Eastern Command (Sonderstab Osten).[36] A December 1944 report notes at least one crate from the Petliura Library being held in that main ERR library center (Niedertorstrasse 3).[37] The Western section of the *Ostbücherei* held related materials in Western European languages, including some of the materials from the Slavic libraries in Paris.

Details regarding the extent of the Petliura collections in Ratibor have not been found. It is possible that not all of the library was shipped to Ratibor—or that many of the crates were never opened, as a surviving picture of one of the ERR warehouses suggests. Most likely, the Ukrainian archival materials from

Paris, which included the records of the Petliura Library itself, the Ukrainian Press Bureau, the journal *Tryzub*, and files from other Ukrainian organizations in Paris, were held by the ERR there as well, but the extent to which ERR records of their Ratibor operations were later destroyed makes it impossible to establish precise details.

It is also not clear whether any of the Paris materials were being integrated with other Ukrainian materials from the 1917–1923 period that the ERR had collected in Kyiv and shipped to Ratibor. The Nazis brought to Ratibor a major segment of what they called the "Revolutionary Archive" from Kyiv, containing politically sensitive materials regarding the Ukrainian anti-Bolshevik governments and their efforts to establish a separate state (1917–1923).[38] This, for them, was of much greater political significance. By September 1942 in Kyiv, they had recorded 2,000 units with original posters, handbills, and leaflets from the years 1917–ca. 1920, including materials from General Aleksandr Denikin.[39] By the time they shipped the collection to Ratibor in 1943, there were at least 3,000 plundered units relating to the various independent Ukrainian governments during the revolutionary and civil war period.[40] The existence of this archive in the ERR anti-Bolshevik research center in Ratibor is also confirmed by a remaining exhibition poster that highlights it, along with the Communist Party archives from Dnipropetrovsk and Smolensk, together with materials from the Anti-Religious Museum in Kyiv.[41] We have no indication of what research was actually progressing or of any tracts or propaganda pieces that were produced in Ratibor on the basis of these materials. In December 1944 the Dnipropetrovsk Party files were being held in the former Lagerplatz Synagogue with the Russian-language part of the *Ostbücherei* (again Niedertorstrasse 3), which is the same address cited for at least part of the Petliura Library at that time.[42]

Reports from the Ratibor operation as late as January 1945 confirm that the ERR did not have sufficient rolling stock to evacuate many of their Ratibor holdings to the west during their retreat. ERR-targeted evacuation sites in the Bamberg/Staffelstein area of northern Bavaria were later taken over by the U.S. Army.[43] The evacuated ERR materials found in those sites were taken to the Offenbach Archival Depot, the U.S. library restitution center near Frankfurt. We have no indication of any materials from the Petliura Library found there.[44] If evacuation was not possible, a remaining ERR agent "was prepared to destroy the materials there with gasoline and canisters readied for the task." According to the last ERR report from Ratibor, many of the most important materials from Ratibor itself had already been evacuated by the end of January 1945, and the report's authors still hoped "it would be possible to take more on open wagons to Castle Banz." They were preparing other Ratibor office files for destruction, but decided not to destroy the *Ostbücherei* because they still hoped to evacuate it and/or return and resume its use, if the war situation changed. If that was impossible, they assumed the abandoned materials would be "captured by the Bolsheviks."[45]

Apparently, the ERR was able to destroy many of its own potentially incriminating operational records before their final evacuation from Ratibor in January 1945. At least, to this date, only a few office records from Ratibor, such as copies of outgoing reports, and copies of incoming reports from the east have surfaced.[46] Fortunately, the Nazis made a point not to destroy the plundered archives and library materials they had collected.[47] But at the same time, evacuation priorities involved further splitting up and dispersal of integral collections. Indeed it was one of the Nazi principles not to move all of a given collection or group of records together for fear that all would be lost. Rather they separated out according to established priorities, or sometimes according to how much time and space they had for a given evacuation shipment. With the speed of the approaching Red Army during the winter of 1945, some of the materials evacuated from Ratibor had to be abandoned en route back to Germany.

Possible RSHA Involvement in Silesia

It is possible that at least part of the archival materials from the Petliura Library in Paris remained with, or was turned over to, the Nazi Secret Police (SD) and eventually to the Reich Central Security Office—Reichssicherheitshauptamt (RSHA) in Berlin (of which the SD was an arm). Available Nazi reports make no specific mention about the archival materials that were seized with the Petliura materials from Paris. An acquisitions register for the Nazi security services archival depot (Auswertungsstelle Frankreich) in Berlin (Neue Friedrichstrasse 50), which survives in Moscow, nevertheless references receipts from "Ukrainian organizations in France" in 1941 and 1942. Neither quantities nor the precise names of organizations are given.[48] If those references were in fact to archival materials among the Petliura Library collections, then it might mean that some of the archival materials had been split off in Berlin from other parts of the Petliura Library and turned over to the RSHA. If this had been the case (as it was with part of the Rothschild family archives and those of other Jewish and emigre organizations from France), then some of the archival materials from the Petliura Library may have been taken from Berlin by the RSHA to their own archival center under their Seventh Office—Amt VII—for Ideological Research and Analysis (*Weltanschauliche Forschung und Auswertung*). We still have only circumstantial evidence for the "division of spoils" between the ERR and the RSHA.

When they moved out of Berlin in 1943, the major archive and library center of Amt VII, *Ausweilstelle Schlesiersee*, was first established in an elegant castle in a village on the shore of the Schlesiersee (*Pol.* Sława).[49] In April 1944, the RSHA acquired the baroque castle of Count von Althann—Schloss Wölfelsdorf (*Pol.* Wilkanów), further southeast near Habelschwerdt (*Pol.* Bystrzyca-Kłodzko). Although some offices and related materials remained in Schlesiersee, the RSHA moved most of their archival holdings to the

Habelschwerdt area in May 1944.[50] As the end of the war drew near, the RSHA was unable to evacuate most of their loot from that region. Because Soviet authorities found all of the RSHA holdings in the Habelschwerdt and Wölfelsdorf locations in the summer of 1945, and shipped them all to Moscow (some were first shipped to Kyiv), we have more information about the actual materials that the Nazis had sequestered there.

Although no surviving materials from the Petliura Library are specifically mentioned in Soviet reports of their seizures from Wölfelsdorf, there were other rich emigre Russian and a few Ukrainian emigre collections in that RSHA center. The fact that the most detailed reconnaissance report from Habelschwerdt that has surfaced to date was prepared by a Ukrainian Communist Party historian, Ivan Shevchenko, sent from Kyiv by the Communist Party Central Committee specifically to examine the archival holdings, makes it unlikely that he would have overlooked the Petliura materials had they been there. He does, however, mention materials from the Polish Library in Paris. He also notes, "among reference materials," some rare publications about Bukovyna and Ukrainian information bulletins in French, published in Geneva in 1931. He might not have recognized the stamp of the Petliura Library (which was only in French), but certainly some of those publications he mentioned could have come from its holdings.[51] Since he did find materials from the Museum of Revolution in Kyiv (which had earlier been identified as part of the Nazis' "Revolutionary Archive" in Ratibor) and Communist Party records from Kirovohrad seized by the ERR, possibly some of the Ratibor holdings ended up in the Wölfelsdorf area in the process of retreat back to Germany. However, had the Petliura materials been involved with the Habelschwerdt/Wölfelsdorf materials, they would most probably have gone directly to the Special Archive in Moscow, TsGOA (now part of RGVA), rather than first to Minsk—the actual route of the Petliura archival materials now in that archive (as we will see below).

The Heeresarchiv and UNR Records from Poland and Western Ukraine

The ERR was not alone in its interest in UNR materials. Immediately following the Nazi invasion in the east, first in Poland, and later in the USSR, the Heeresarchiv (Reich Military Archive) sent out diligent scouts to comb archives in the occupied lands for military-related archival loot of interest to their extensive research operations. In terms of military history, locating records of military operations during World War I was among their highest priorities. They also were interested in operations involving the struggling Ukrainian National Republic (UNR) under Petliura and other attempts to establish an independent Ukrainian state, and assembled a special collection (with a 54-page inventory) of relevant files relating to the Polish-Ukrainian and Ukrainian involvement in the Polish-Bolshevik War (1918–1920).[52] Headquartered in Potsdam, relevant records from Cracow, Lviv, and Warsaw were shipped principally to their subsidiary branch in Danzig-Oliva (*Pol.* Oliwa), together with other Polish military records. In September 1944, the Nazis were already evacuating Danzig, and moved some of the materials to their main centers for Western European military records in Berlin-Wannsee. At least some of these materials were intentionally destroyed in April 1945, and others had perished during the bombing of Danzig.[53] But the fact that Soviet military forces cleared out the Berlin-Wannsee repository in May 1945 explains why many of the Nazi-captured foreign military records, in addition to the Nazi Heeresarchiv operational files, are now held in Moscow.[54]

UNR Records in Cracow and Tarnów

Other Nazi agencies operating in the east were also interested in the archives of the Petliura regime, especially the Reichsarchiv, which—rather than the ERR—handled preservation and, eventually, seizures of more politically oriented archives in occupied countries during the war. As was already mentioned at the outset, a major part of the UNR records had been stored since their creation in Tarnów, Poland, where the UNR had purchased a building that served as one of their operation centers during their active participation as a Polish ally in the military operations against the new Bolshevik regime. Some of the Ukrainian emigration had stayed on in Tarnów during the interwar period, and the city even boasted a museum of Ukrainian history. In the course of the wartime occupation of Poland, Nazi authorities discovered a significant body of UNR records in Tarnów, which had apparently been held in the same building as the museum. These included the records of the UNR Foreign Ministry and Ministry of Finance, a significant quantity of bank notes, and some printed books and other materials. The museum also boasted the records of the Ukrainian military chief of staff and three divisions, but the migration of these materials has not been established. At least part of the archive reportedly had been purchased by Metropolitan Andrei Sheptytskyi, and accordingly, the Nazi archival administration initially planned to transfer it to Lviv to be consolidated with the Sheptytskyi archive there, as is evidenced in an early report in 1941.[55] This was never carried out, however, and the archive was subsequently transferred from Tarnów to Cracow. Nazi archivist Heinz Göring, who earlier headed the State Archive in Królewiec, and who was subsequently in charge of the State Archive in Cracow during the war, personally supervised the transport of 160 crates of the Petliura UNR materials to Cracow in March 1942. So important did he consider the materials that he personally kept the key to the room where they were held.[56]

In contrast to the Petliura Library materials, the UNR Foreign Ministry materials in Cracow were deemed of such high priority that even during the war, manpower was devoted to careful processing and the production of a full inventory. One of the Polish archival directors, Włodzimierz Budka, who had been retained in Nazi archival service in Cracow during the war, was charged with the arrangement and description of the UNR materials from Tarnów.

Between November 1942 and February 1943, he arranged three groups of the materials, namely the bank notes, publications, and archival documents. Then, with the assistance of a Ukrainian specialist from Lviv, Volodymyr Matsiak, by July 1943 he had arranged the Foreign Ministry files and prepared an inventory covering 258 files and bound volumes.[57] A copy of that German inventory (dated 1943) remains among the records of the Nazi State Archival Administration (*Reichsarchivverwaltung*).[58] These portions of the UNR Foreign Ministry records were evacuated to the Wieliczka salt mine in January 1944, along with other Cracow archives.[59] By 1942 the director of the Archival Administration in Cracow was well aware of major concentrations of UNR materials held elsewhere. In one of his survey reports on the subject, he noted the Petliura Library from Kremenets (*Pol.* Krzemieniec) in Volhynia which had been taken to Paris earlier with some Ukrainian books from the University in Kyiv. He went on to explain that the Paris Petliura Library had already been brought to Berlin for the ERR.[60]

Apparently not all of the UNR records found in Tarnów were immediately brought to Cracow in 1942. Among 70 crates left in Tarnów were bank notes and the printing press for the bank notes (cellar at Parkstrasse 22).[61] Later in 1944, the Ukrainian archivist Volodymyr Matsiak processed the materials from the Ministry of Finance (58 packets).[62] A handwritten copy of a summary inventory of those materials prepared for Nazi archival authorities is now held in Moscow among the scattered records of the Reichsarchiv (Potsdam).[63] Those files from the Ministry of Finance also survived the war. All of the materials taken to Wieliczka were returned safely to the State Archive in Cracow after the liberation of the city in January 1945. According to a marginal note on a report of archival developments in Cracow during the war, Soviet authorities removed the UNR materials (then 93 boxes, including bank notes) from the State Archive storage area (54, ul. Grodska) at the end of March 1945.[64]

It is quite remarkable to what extent during the war the Nazis had pursued a thorough survey of all sources throughout Europe relating to the UNR, Petliura, and related Ukrainian national movements. The search and reconnaissance efforts were, as we have already seen, being carried out by a number of different Nazi agencies. Nazi occupation authorities in Kyiv in charge of the archival and library administration in Ukraine were also kept closely informed of what was found elsewhere, and of developments with respect to the UNR archive and the Petliura Library from Paris. In turn they themselves were expected to keep close track of any materials found in occupied Ukrainian lands. As is apparent from the discussion above, they were also kept informed of ERR activities in this respect and working closely with the ERR commando units in Ukraine. A lengthy background report on the subject of UNR materials, together with related documents that were forwarded to the director of the Provincial Archival Administration in Kyiv, was found among the records of the Nazi Archival Administration under the Reichskommissariat Ukraine, which are now held in the Central State Archive of Higher Organs of State Power and Administration of Ukraine (TsDAVO) in Kyiv.[65]

UNR Records in Prague—RZIA/UIK

Prague, as one of the main homes of the Ukrainian emigration, had been a particularly important gathering point for UNR documentation during the inter-war period. The Russian Foreign Historical Archive (RZIA), founded there in 1923, came under the auspices of the Czech Foreign Ministry in 1928, and a subsidiary Ukrainian Historical Cabinet (UIK) was organized the following year. Thanks to Czech support, augmented by that of the Ukrainian community, UIK was able to acquire and assure the preservation of many previously scattered files. Archival organization in RZIA and UIK reflected the order of acquisition. Miscellaneous documents, fragmentary records, and personal papers were numbered according to the collection with which they were acquired, and usually kept together. Some UNR documents acquired as part of larger Russian emigre collections were never transferred to the Ukrainian Historical Cabinet, but rather remained part of RZIA.

As far as can be determined, all of the UNR files that were accessioned by RZIA and UIK remained in Prague throughout the war. Soon after the Nazi invasion of Czechoslovakia and the proclamation of the Protectorate of Bohemia and Moravia, Nazi authorities transferred the administration of RZIA/UIK from the Foreign Ministry to the Ministry of the Interior, where it remained throughout the war.[66] Archivists working under the Nazi occupation continued to prepare descriptions of their contents. The Nazis moved some of the military related materials to a branch of the Heeresarchiv outside of Prague, as mentioned in their reports, but no evidence has been found of UIK materials moved there, and apparently there was no attempt to unite the fragmentary UNR files in RZIA with UNR records found elsewhere.[67] The Nazis investigated what UNR records were to be found in Prague, but when they determined that there were only scattered UNR files, presumably from personal collections, they made no attempt to unite the fragmentary UNR files in RZIA and UIK with UNR records in Cracow or Ratibor.[68]

UNR Records in Vienna

The Nazis also had carefully surveyed the UNR records located in Vienna. One particularly important group there actually comprised the records of the Western Ukrainian National Republic (ZUNR), including the papers of the ZUNR President Ievhen Petrushevych (Evgen Petrushewitz), which the Nazis found in the custody of the Rev. Myron Hornykevych (Gornykewytsch), who was the parish priest of the Ukrainian Greco-Catholic Church of St. Barbara (Plenerstrasse 18). The Nazis had translated a background survey and relatively precise inventory of the contents of the major 27 sections.[69] In 1942, they arranged for these records to be taken into custody in deposit status by the State

Archive in Vienna, together with the papers of the important Ukrainian political thinker V'iacheslav Lypyns'kyi (Wacław Lipiński) and a major segment of
papers of Metropolitan Sheptyts'kyi.[70]

While the Lypyns'kyi archives had their own odyssey and eventually found
a home in Philadelphia, the much larger bulk of ZUNR documentation remained in Vienna until well after the war. It did not fall prey to postwar Soviet
archival trophy hunters, as was the case with other Ukrainian archives in
Vienna.[71] At some point during the postwar period, the archive was transferred
to Rome, where it remains today in the custody of the Saint Clement Ukrainian
Catholic University. Rev. Hornykevych prepared a German-language finding
aid which was more detailed than the summary list of contents prepared by the
Nazis.[72] The majority of the records deal with the activity of the Western
Ukrainian Government during its period in emigration, starting with late 1919.
They include many interesting files of particular emigre leaders (especially
letters), and a collection of Ukrainian emigre newspapers and serials from the
period. Another important group of materials relating to the UNR held in the
Austrian National Archives also escaped both Nazi and Soviet looters. The
records were not disturbed, and later served as the basis for a major postwar
documentary publication.[73]

Postscript: Soviet Postwar Retrieval

Documentation of the postwar Soviet archival retrieval and "trophy" cultural
seizure operations is still fragmentary and dispersed. Nonetheless, thanks to
recently opened files and the seized records themselves, new facts are emerging about where, when, and why, various Nazi-looted archival collections were
seized by Soviet authorities. Often they have with them the surviving records
of Nazi wartime operations. As it turns out, major portions of the archival
materials confiscated by the Nazis from the Petliura Library in Paris, together
with the looted library books and periodicals, fell into Soviet hands after the
war. Surviving groups of records (Soviet-style fonds) in various archives together with operational documentation—both Soviet reports and Nazi
records—provide new clues, and in some cases hard evidence, of what Ukrainian collections the Nazis had seized from Paris and other European centers,
what materials Nazi authorities succeeded in evacuating from Berlin to Silesia
(and from Silesia to the west), and what materials were in turn seized by Soviet
authorities after the war.

In almost all cases, the original order within integral collections and/or their
existing working order in Nazi hands have been lost: Soviet archival practice
required the strict separation of Nazi records from the captured "trophy" archives, and the division (even if it meant fragmentation) of integral collections
by establishing strict separate "fonds" for each subgroup of files that could be
identified as coming from a specific agency, or the personal papers of an
individual. In the haste and confusion of retrieval and "trophy" operations,

many materials arrived in haphazard fragments, with no apparent order at all. Besides, postwar Soviet archival operations under the NKVD/MVD had as their immediate priority the "operational utilization" of archival files to find Nazi collaborators, anti-Soviet or "bourgeois-nationalist" elements, and other potential enemies of the regime, rather than preparing the materials for eventual research use or restitution to their prewar archival home.

It has not been possible to establish where all the Petliura Library materials and other UNR records were recovered by Soviet authorities. Many were found together with the vast library collections that the Nazis had looted from occupied Soviet lands, and of these many were taken to the Ratibor area in Silesia. They were not all recovered at the same time or from the same place. They are now dispersed in many different fonds in two different archives in Moscow, with additional fragments in two more archives in Kyiv. Those fonds that have been uncovered certainly may not reprensent all those that have survived Soviet purges and library and archival "cleansing" operations. We know with certainty that some of the materials were destroyed, but there might be more libraries and archives in which we should search for possible survivors or clues to their fate. The most sizable archival collections from the Petliura Library in Paris came to Moscow from Minsk in 1955 and more materials were transferred from Minsk to Kyiv in the 1980s. Thus, the wartime odyssey of the Petliura Library requires, in turn, a close examination of its migrations and fate in the postwar period.[74]

*   *
*

A terrible fragmentation and dispersal of archival and library collections was wrought by the Nazi regime during the war and the Soviet regime thereafter. The Petliura Library materials are but a poignant example of this fate. What was done by the totalitarian regimes remains a serious detriment to history and culture, and to scholarship East and West. The dispersal of documentation from the Ukrainian struggle for independence (especially from the Petliura regime) throughout Europe resulted from the larger political expediencies that dispersal served. If today there is a real spirit of Ukrainian political renewal, as one hopes, we should also hope that appropriate archival restitution could reunite the archival collections of the Petliura Library and the UNR regime. However, to promote such restitution, or even if some of the collections can only be brought together in library microforms, we still need a thorough, publicly available inventory of their contents and migration. Indeed, the survival of that documentation, and our knowledge about it, may help promote more open research on the Petliura government, its leader, and the many unresolved issues surrounding them.

ABBREVIATIONS USED IN NOTES

APKr   Archiwum Państwowe w Krakowie (State Archive in Cracow)

BA-K   Bundesarchiv, Koblenz (most of the records cited have since been transferred to the new Bundesarchiv facility in Berlin-Lichterfelde, but archivists recommend retaining the BA-K codes)

CDJC   Centre de Documentation Juive Contemporaine (Center for Contemporary Jewish Documentation), Paris

ERR   Einsatzstab Reichsleiter Rosenberg (Special Command of Reichsleiter Rosenberg)

IISH/IISG   International Institute of Social History (Internationaal Instituut voor Sociale Geschiedenis), Amsterdam (*Dutch* IISG)

NKVD   Narodnyi komissariat vnutrennykh del (People's Commissariat of Internal Affairs) (*after 1946* MVD)

OGPU   Ob″edinennoe gosudarstvennoe politicheskoe upravlenie (Unified State Political Administration) (*1922–1934; before 1922,* Cheka; *1934* merged into NKVD)

RGVA   Rossiiskii gosudarstvennyi voennyi arkhiv (Russian State Military Archive), Moscow (*formerly* TsGASA SSSR), also now includes holdings of the formerly separate TsKhIDK

RSHA   Reichssicherheitshauptamt (Reich Central Security Office)

RZIA   Russkii zagranichnyi istoricheskii arkhiv (Russian Foreign Historical Archive), Prague

TsDAHO   Tsentral′nyi derzhavnyi arkhiv hromads′kykh orhanizatsii (Central State Archive of Community Organizations of Ukraine), Kyiv (*former* Party Archive of the Communist Party of Ukraine)

TsDAVO   Tsentral′nyi derzhavnyi arkhiv vyshchykh orhaniv derzhavnoï vlady i upravlinnia Ukraïny (Central State Archive of Higher Organs of State Power and Administration of Ukraine), Kyiv (*formerly* TsDAZhR URSR)

TsDIAL   Tsentral′nyi derzhavnyi istorychnyi arkhiv Ukraïny, Lviv (Central State Historical Archive of Ukraine, Lviv)

TsGOA SSSR   Tsentral′nyi gosudarstvennyi osobyi arkhiv SSSR (Central State Special Archive of the USSR), Moscow (*1992–1999,* TsKhIDK; *now part of* RGVA)

TsKhIDK   Tsentr khraneniia istoriko-dokumental′nykh kollektsii (Center for the Preservation of Historico-Documentary Collections), Moscow (as of March 1999, now part of the reorganized RGVA; *formerly* TsGOA SSSR)

UIK   Ukraïns'kyi istorychnyi kabinet (pry RZIA) (Ukrainian Historical Cabinet), Prague

UNR   Ukraïns'ka Narodna Respublika (Ukrainian National Republic)

US NA   National Archives, Washington, DC

ZUNR   Zakhidnia Ukraïns'ka Narodna Respublika (Western Ukrainian National Republic)

N.B. The archival term "fond" has been anglicized, since there is no exact translation. The term came to the Soviet Union from the French *fonds*, but not without some change of usage. In Russian a "fond" is an integral group of records or a collection from a single office or source. American archivists might prefer the more technical term "record group," which in British usage would normally be "archive group," but the Russian usage of the term is much more extensive, as a "fond" can designate personal papers and/or collections as well as groups of institutional records.

In citations from former Soviet-area archives, numbers are given sequentially for *fond* (record group, etc.) / *opis'* ([*Ukr.* opys] a series or separate numbered file list or inventory within a fond) / and *delo* ([*Ukr.* sprava] file or unit) numbers.

NOTES

1. The German reparations are described in an article in the library bulletin—*Bibliothèque ukrainienne Symon Petlura à Paris / Ukraïns'ka Biblioteka im. S. Petliury v Paryzhi, Informatsiinyi biuleten'* 8(11) January 1964.

2. Arkady Joukovsky, "The Symon Petliura Ukrainian Library in Paris," *Harvard Ukrainian Studies* 14(1–2) June 1990: 218–35 (henceforth *HUS*).

3. See Arkady Joukovsky, "Ukraïns'ka biblioteka imeni Symona Petliury v Paryzhi," *Ukraïns'kyi arkheohrafichnyi shchorichnyk*, n.s. 1 (1992): 439–41, condensed from the 1990 article in *HUS*. See also the even briefer Ukrainian summary by Pavlo Shumovs'kyi, "Korotkyi narys istoriï i rozvytku Biblioteky im. S. Petliury," *Bibliothèque ukrainienne Symon Petlura à Paris / Ukraïns'ka biblioteka im. S. Petliury v Paryzhi, Informatsiinyi biuleten'* 38: 1–3.

4. Vasyl' Mykhal'chuk, *Ukraïns'ka biblioteka im. Symona Petliury v Paryzhi: Zasnuvannia, rozvytok, diial'nist' (1926–1998)* (Kyiv, 1999), p. 103. Colleagues in the Russian State Library (RGB), as the Lenin Library is now known, deny this possibility since all trophy books had been sorted much earlier.

5. The retrieval of Petliura Library materials from Minsk and their "return to Kyiv" is mentioned in passing (with no details other than the name) by Adam Mal'dzis (Maldis), "The Tragic Fate of Belarusan Museum and Library Collections during the Second World War," in *The Spoils of*

War: The Loss, Reappearance, and Recovery of Cultural Property, ed.
Elizabeth Simpson (New York, 1997), p. 80. Their transfer to Kyiv was
confirmed by Mal'dzis in a letter to the author in May 1999, but again
without any details as to the quantity or nature of the books transferred
(Mal'dzis thought in 1993 or 1994); Mal'dzis suggests the probability that
more books remain in Minsk.

6. The transfer to Kyiv was appreciatively mentioned by the Deputy Direc-
    tor of the National Parliamentary Library of Ukraine, Olena
    Oleksandrova (Elena Aleksandrova), in her report at the 1997 conference
    in Minsk—"Poteri bibliotek Ukrainy: problemy vyiavleniia i poiska," in
    *Restytutsyia kul'turnykh kashtoŭnastsei: prablemy viartannia i
    sumesnaha vykarystannia (iurydychnyia, navukovyia i maral'nyia
    aspekty): Materyialy Mezhnarodnai navukovai kanferentsyi, iakaia
    adbylasia u Minsku pad ehidai UNESCO 19–20 chervenia 1997 h.*, ed.
    Adam Mal'dzis et al. (Minsk, 1997), p. 95 [=*Viartanne*, 4]. During my
    July 1999 visit in Kyiv, Oleksandrova verified that in fact the books are
    held in her library—200 in Ukrainian (mostly imprints from Ukrainian
    lands in the 1920s) and 60 French and German imprints in the Foreign
    Language Division. Other sources in Kyiv, including the National Com-
    mission for Restitution of Ukrainian Cultural Treasures, could not re-
    spond as to the present location of the "returned" books, but, according to
    Oleksandrova, the transfer took place before the Commission was
    formed in 1992.

7. See, for example, *Ukraine and Poland in Documents, 1918–1922*, ed.
    Taras Hunczak, 2 vols. (New York, 1983) and *The Ukrainian Revolu-
    tion: Documents, 1919–1921*, ed. Taras Hunczak (New York, 1984)
    [=Sources of Modern History of the Ukraine, 2].

8. Two separate transfers are noted in the booklets published by the Na-
    tional Commission for the Restitution of Cultural Treasures to Ukraine,
    Povernuto v Ukraïnu, comp. Valentyna Vrublevs'ka and Liudmyla
    Lozenko, ed. Oleksandr Fedoruk et al., no. 1 (Kyiv, 1997), pp. 14, 32 (no.
    32); and no. 2 (Kyiv, 1999), pp. 11, 19. As noted there, the first transfer
    consisted of 24 files.

9. Schwarzbard periodically worked as a watchmaker. During World War I,
    he enlisted in the Foreign Legion in 1914, was wounded and received an
    honorable discharge. He gained French citizenship by 1925. His ties to a
    Bolshevik group in Paris have recently been revealed in documents from
    French police records recently published by Marko Antonovych and
    Roman Serbyn, "Dokumenty pro uchast' Shvartsbarda v komunistychnii
    iacheitsi v Paryzhi," in *Naukovyi zbirnyk (1945–1950–1995)* (Ukraïns'ka
    vil'na akademiia nauk u SShA), vol. 4 (New York, 1999), pp. 334–46.

10. Links to Volodin were established in many studies. Elia Dobkowski, an
    active Zionist from Odesa and former deputy commissioner general of

the Central Jewish Commission in France, through whom Volodin met Schwarzbard, testified to that effect during the trial itself and wrote a pamphlet just before the trial further implicating Volodin. See the link to Volodin established in the recent account of Petliura's assassination and the trial by Vasyl' Mykhal'chuk, "Vbyvstvo ta protses Petliury z perspektyvy 70–richchia," in *U 70-richchia paryz'koï trahediï, 1926– 1996: Zbirnyk pam'iati Symona Petliury,* ed. Vasyl' Mykhal'chuk and Dmytro Stepovyk (Kyiv, 1997), pp. 11–40 (on Volodin, pp. 28–31). See also the recent well-documented account of the assassination and trial by Michael Palij, in which Volodin is also directly implicated (*The Ukrainian-Polish Defensive Alliance, 1919–1921: An Aspect of the Ukrainian Revolution* [Edmonton, 1995], pp. 184–95). None of these authors used the extensive materials on the trial that were collected by Elias Tcherikower and are now held in the Archive of the YIVO Institute of Jewish Research in New York. The defense was led by Henri Torrès (1891–1966), an attorney with leftist leanings, who later joined the Communist Party.

11. See the report of the lecture by Sébastien de Gasquet, "L'Affaire Petlura et la France" (Paris, 18 November 1998), as reported in *Bulletin de l'Association français des études ukrainiennes* 11(1) February 1999: 2–4.

12. There is a vast literature in many languages regarding Petliura and his regime, including several studies devoted specifically to the Jewish question. The recent book by Henry Abramson, *A Prayer for the Government: Ukrainians and Jews in Revolutionary Times, 1917–1920* (Cambridge, MA, 1999), presents an up-to-date analysis of the Petliura regime as well as the effect of his assassination and the subsequent trial on the historiography of the regime itself. The book includes an extensive bibliography of archival and published sources. Palij's *The Ukrainian-Polish Defensive Alliance,* although not based on archival sources, includes many published sources in its extensive bibliography. Some of these are also reviewed in the latest brochure by Taras Hunczak [Hunchak], *Symon Petliura ta ievreï* (Kyiv, 1993). See also the appraisals of different interpretations by Mykhal'chuk, "Vbyvstvo ta protses."

13. As quoted by Joukovsky from *Tryzub* 22 (178) 25 May 1929.

14. Boris Lazarevskii and Hlib Lazarevs'kyi were the sons of the prominent Ukrainian historian Oleksandr Lazarevs'kyi; while Hlib was active in emigre Ukrainian politics, Boris is usually considered a Russian writer, although he occasionally wrote in Ukrainian. Boris died in Paris in 1936; Hlib returned to Ukraine in 1939 and died in Lviv in 1949.

15. Petro Zlenko, *Symon Petliura: Materialy dlia bibliohrafichnoho pokazhchyka* (Paris, 1939).

16. Ivan Rudychiv, diary entry, 24 January 1941, TsDAVO, 4362/1/29, fols. 3v–4.

17. Again, see Abramson, *A Prayer for the Government,* for a balanced assessment of this question. He finds no evidence for Petliura's alleged inherent antisemitism (pp. 136–40).

18. Attempts to find a building in Switzerland proved too expensive, and the Swiss had insisted materials taken there could be "only of a folkloric" character. See Joukovsky, "Petliura Library," p. 226.

19. Rudychiv, "Iak tse bulo," TsDAVO, 4362/1/3, fol 3. Rudychiv's account (prepared in Berlin in July 1941) coincides with German accounts. Most of those details are also recorded by Joukovsky, "Petliura Library," pp. 226–28.

20. They now form part of what was established in Kyiv as the fond of the Petliura Library in Paris, TsDAVO, 4362/1/3, fol. 3. More details about this fond are forthcoming in Grimsted, "The Postwar Fate of the Petliura Library and the Records of the Ukrainian National Republic in the USSR."

21. Regarding the seizure of the Turgenev Library and the Polish Library in Paris, see the Fuchs ERR report to Geheime Feldpolizei, Paris, 15.IX.1940, BA-K, B-323/261. See also the ERR reports, 17 September 1940, CDJC, CXLI–181, and 18 September 1940, CXLIII–275. See more details regarding the fate of the Turgenev Library in a forthcoming separate Grimsted study in collaboration with Hélène Kaplan.

22. In addition to the reports cited in fn. 21, the Nazi seizure is confirmed in a Zipfel memorandum, TsDAVO, 3206/5/26, fol. 22, and an ERR report, BA-K, NS 30/53, fol. 234–234v.

23. BA-K, NS 30/53, fol. 234–234v.

24. Leibbrandt was born in the village of Torosovo (*Ger.* Hoffnungsfeld, now in Odesa Oblast) and emigrated to Germany in 1918. He developed an academic specialty on the history and genealogy of Germans in the southern areas of the USSR, and made several trips to the USSR during the 1920s. He subsequently became associated with the Institute for Germans Abroad (Deutsches Ausland Institut) in Stuttgart, which became a stronghold of German expansionist sentiments and was later taken over by the Nazis, as a research and propaganda organ for a Greater Germany, while at the same time serving as a scholarly research center about Germans in Russia. After the war, Leibbrandt continued his scholarly work on Germans in Russia.

25. This is explained in the report Rudychiv filed with the Petliura Library Council after his return to Paris, "Prymushenyi vyïzd bibliotekaria Ivana Rudycheva i ioho perebuvannia v Berlini (Dopovid' na zasidanniu Rady Biblioteky 3-ho hrudnia 1942 roku)," typescript, copy furnished from the original in the Petliura Library in Paris.

26. The seizure of the Odesa materials, particularly those relating to German settlements in the area, is documented in the Künzberg reports, now held in the German Foreign Ministry Archive. Their transfer to Leibbrandt is confirmed by the markings on the crates that were found after the war by Allied commands. They were later retrieved by Soviet authorities in a salt mine in Saxony and all returned to Ukraine.

27. Rudychiv, "Iak tse bulo," TsDAVO, 4362/1/3, fol. 29. I have been unable so far to find independent confirmation of the existence and role of this Döringer, which leads me to believe that Rudychiv has in mind here not the Reich Foreign Ministry, but rather the "foreign affairs" office of the National Socialist Party. This matter needs further research before this part of the history can be fully documented.

28. Rudychiv, "Iak tse bulo," TsDAVO, 4362/1/3, fol. 32; "Prymushenyi vyïzd bibliotekaria Ivana Rudycheva," pp. 65–66. That he never saw the library in Berlin is apparent from the account of the library takeover he prepared under Nazi request in Berlin, which is dated 19 July 1941, and his separate account of the Petliura Library as it was before Nazi confiscation in Paris (Berlin, 1 October 1941)—TsDAVO, 4362/1/5, fol. 4v. A few of the reports he prepared for the Nazis, together with press clippings from that period, are also in the same fond in Kyiv.

29. Professor Joukovsky kindly furnished me a copy of the report, which is much less detailed and interesting than Rudychiv's diary and the reports he prepared while he was in Berlin, all of which are now located in Kyiv (TsDAVO, fond 4362).

30. "Prymushenyi vyïzd bibliotekaria Ivana Rudycheva," pp. 65–66.

31. Regarding the postwar seizures of Ukrainian emigre archives in Prague, including those from the Museum of the Struggle for Ukrainian Independence, see Grimsted, *Trophies of War and Empire: The Archival Heritage of Ukraine and the International Politics of Restitution* (Cambridge, MA, 2000), ch. 9. The Rudychiv papers and other archival materials from the Petliura Library in TsDAVO in Kyiv came there in January 1946, however, well before other materials from that museum that came much later. Vyrovyj committed suicide in Prague in May 1945 as NKVD agents were coming to arrest him. If Rudychiv's papers had remained with Vyrovyj, they might have been confiscated at that time.

32. The Nazi report quoted is found among the records of the Einsatzstab Reichsleiter Rosenberg now in Berlin, BA-K, NS 30/53, fol. 234–234v. If in fact, they had not yet unpacked the library, it is also possible that they did not have an exact count.

33. Regarding the *Ostbücherei* and ERR anti-Bolshevism research activities, see Grimsted, *The Odyssey of the "Smolensk Archive": Communist*

Records in the Service of Anti-Communism (Pittsburg, 1995) [=Carl Beck Occasional Papers in Russian and East European Studies, 1201].

34. Regarding the ERR Central Library, see Grimsted, *The Odyssey of the "Smolensk Archive,"* pp. 11–16; and *Trophies of War and Empire,* ch. 6.

35. The journal had been confiscated from rue de la Glacière. Since details are not available about where in Austria it was found, we do not know if it had been sent to the Tazenberg depot.

36. ERR report, Ratibor (14 February 1944), BA-K, NS 30/22, fol. 246.

37. Report of Lommatzsch (13 December 1944), BA-K, NS 30/50.

38. A number of other ERR reports refer to the collection. For example, a 1942 quarterly report (when it was still in Kyiv) noted that Dr. Granzin was working on the collection with 3,000 documents, 200 of which he had already worked over. "Vierteljahresbericht" (1 July–30 September 1942) (Berlin, 9 October 1942), CDJC, CXLI-147, fol. 3.

39. See the ERR card inventories, the first prepared by Lange (25 February 1942), and a second by Dr. Granzin (8 September 1942), which also noted that an inventory (finding aid) was in preparation—TsDAVO, 3676/1/56, fols. 1 and 2. Both of them bear the index number 132, but other parts of this card registration file have not been found. Neither of the cards mention shipping data, which corresponds to other reports that in September 1942 they were still working on the collection in Kyiv.

40. The location of this collection in Ratibor (Flurstr. 12) is noted in the Lommatzsch ERR report (13 December 1944), BA-K, NS 30/50.

41. The Dnipropetrovsk files are identified in a poster announcement of ERR Ratibor activities reproduced in de Vries, *Sonderstab Musik,* p. 114, photo 10, from a copy in BA-K; the present author has found another copy in an album held in US NA, Still Picture Division, RG 260–PHOAD-III-6.

42. Lommatzsch report (13 December 1944), BA-K, NS 30/50.

43. The ERR evacuation sites were headquartered in the nearby town of Lichtenfels at Schloss Banz, owned by Baron Kurt von Behr, who had directed ERR operations in Paris; they also included parts of the former Benedictine Abbey (Kloster Banz), near Staffelstein, and another building within Staffelstein itself.

44. A few materials presumed to have been in the Ratibor area did reach Offenbach, as we know that is where U.S. intelligence authorities found and seized the over 500 files from the Smolensk Communist Party Archive that are today still in the U.S. National Archives in Washington. For more details on those operations, see Grimsted, *The Odyssey of the "Smolensk Archive."*

45. ERR Stabsführer Gerhard Utikal to Rosenberg, "Aktenvermerk für den Reichsleiter—Dienstgut in Oberschlesien" (25 January 1945), BA-K, NS 8/261; another copy in NS 30/7 is cited in significant sections by de Vries, *Sonderstab Musik*, pp. 57–58. Regarding U.S. Army recovery of ERR materials there, after the suicide of von Berg and his wife, see Grimsted, *Odyssey of the "Smolensk Archive,"* pp. 52–53.

46. Some files among the ERR records in Kyiv (TsDAVO, fond 3476), especially *opys* 2 of that fond, appear to be of Ratibor provenance. Most of the other parts of that fond are records of various other ERR command units.

47. ERR Stabsführer Gerhard Utikal to Rosenberg, "Aktenvermerk für den Reichsleiter—Dienstgut in Oberschlesien" (25 January 1945), BA-K, NS 8/261. This policy is apparent from Nazi procedures in many areas and by different agencies involved with captured archives.

48. "Tagebuch des Auswertungsstelle Frankreich," TsKhIDK, 500/2/215, 1941, no. 669, fol. 267v, and 1942, no. 314, fol. 346v.

49. See a file about the RSHA evacuation from Schlesiersee in late January and February 1945, BA-K, R 58 (Reichssicherheitshauptamt)/1044. The lake, known during the Nazi regime as Schlesiersee with the town by the same name on its shore, is about 30 km. to the north of Głogów (*Ger.* Glogau). Amt VII also had a facility for their Masonic archives, starting in 1943, in Fürstenstein, near Waldenburg (*Pol.* Wałbrzych), further south, but it is unlikely that the Ukrainian materials would have gone there.

50. See notes about the transfer (13 May 1944), with correspondence and shipping details, in TsKhIDK, 500/1/304, fols. 1–2. The rental contract for the castle (14 April 1944) is found in TsKhIDK, 500/1/304, fol. 3–3v. Left in shambles in 1945, the castle itself burned after 1970, and is now in ruins.

51. The Ukrainian Communist Party (CP) historian and instructor in the CP Agitation and Propaganda Division, Ivan Ivanovych Shevchenko (a leader of one of the Ukrainian trophy brigades), had been sent to Germany both to recover Ukrainian materials looted by the Nazis and prospective "trophy" materials to be transferred to Ukraine. The long series of telegrams he sent back to his supervisors and the subsequent composite report that he prepared are held in the former CP archive in Kyiv, now known as TsDAHO, 1/23/1484. (See, for example, his report [fols. 3–5], and scattered references in the incoming telegrams with his reports in the same folder.) The full text of his report is being prepared for publication by the IISH in Amsterdam as part of my detailed study of the ERR Ratibor Center and the RSHA Amt VII Operations in Silesia.

52. See the German inventory, "Übersicht über den Bestand der Beuteakten zum 'Polnisch-Russischen Feldzug' 1918/20" (52 p.), TsKhIDK, 1387/2/12, fols. 16–70; two supplements follow, fols. 74–84.

53. Heeresarchiv (Danzig-Oliva) to Heeresarchiv (Potsdam) (15 September 1944), TsKhIDK, 1387/3/34, fols. 26–27. A secret archival folder that apparently contained inventories of some of these materials from the Danzig holdings, started in August 1941, remains in Moscow with a handwritten list of six inventories indicating materials that were destroyed 3 April 1945. TsKhIDK, 1256/2/17. The inner folder from the Danzig branch remains as part of the present archival file unit.

54. TsKhIDK, fond 1387—Heeresarchiv, Zweigstelle Danzig, Danzig-Oliva, Zimmererstr. 8. Fond 1256—Chef der Heersarchiv (Potsdam)—contains many incoming reports, although the bulk of its files relate to records from Western Europe.

55. TsDIAL, 55/1/253.

56. Details of these operations are found in the files of the Nazi Archival Administration in Cracow, headed by Dr. Randt, which are held in the same fond in the Cracow archive. A copy of one of Randt's reports to Berlin and his detailed survey of these materials "Archiv der ukrainischen Nationalregierung (Petlura) aus den Jahren 1917–1922" (Cracow, 25 March 1942), also remains in the records of the Nazi Archival Administration in Kyiv, TsDAVO, 3206/5/26, fols. 2–5. The transfer and inventory work on the UNR records in Cracow are summarized in the typewritten report of Włodzimierz Budka, "Archiwum Państwowe w Krakowie podczas okupacji niemieckiej (6 September 1939–17 January 1945)," dated Cracow, 2 March 1946, Archiwum Państwowe w Krakowie, Zespół APKr, 167, fols. 25–26.

57. Ibid., fol. 26.

58. "Verzeichnis des Archivs des Aussen-Ministeriums der Ukrainischen-Volks-Republik, 1918–1926," BA-K, R 146/ 73. When I consulted those files, they were still located in Koblenz, but have since been moved to the Bundesarchiv in Berlin–Lichterfelde.

59. A list of records evacuated to Wieliczka dated 16 January 1944 (Nr 20/44)—APKr, Zespół APKr, 69—includes as no. 43 "Ukrainische Akten—Akten der Ukrainischen Volksrepublik (Direktoriat, Ministeriat, Auswärtiges Amt— 1,47 m.)."

60. Randt, "Archiv der ukrainischen Nationalregierung (Petlura)" (Cracow, 25 March 1942), TsDAVO, 3206/5/26, fol. 4.

61. ERR report (March 1942), TsDAVO, 3206/5/26, fols. 4–5.

62. APKr, Zespół APKr, 167, fols. 25–26.

63. TsKhIDK, 1255/2/13. The first five folios give an administrative history of the Ukrainian government; fols. 6–9 constitute a draft inventory of sections of the records of the Ministry of Finance (1918–1921).

64. See the above-cited Budka report, APKr, Zespół APKr, 167, fol. 26v: "Cały ten zespół, więc także uporządkowane przez dra Budkę i Maciaka akta min. spraw zagranicznych i min. skarbu. . . banknotów i przeważnej części druków, został zapakowany do 93 worków i wywieziony przez władze rosyjskie w dniu 29.3.1945 z magazynu przy ul. Grodzkiej 53." A marginal note in the hand of the Cracow archivist Adam Kamiński on the Budka typescript report records the removal of those records by Soviet authorities in March 1945.

65. These materials now form a separate file in that group of records (Reichskomissariat Ukraine, *opys* 5) in TsDAVO, 3206/ 5/26.

66. Some of the administrative records of RZIA/UIK during the war remain in Prague, as part of the records of the Czechoslovak Ministry of the Interior, Státni ústřední archiv, especially nos. 254 B P 1411–P1413.

67. Some of the German-language inventories of the Prague RZIA holdings remain among the RZIA records in Moscow, GA RF.

68. See the Nazi archival report from Prague (25 April 1942), TsDAVO, 3206/5/26, esp. fol. 8.

69. A copy of a two-page description of those holdings, translated from Ukrainian, together with various papers regarding the official deposit in the Reichsarchiv in Vienna (19 October 1942) are found together with a memorandum by Zipfel, head of the Reichsarchiv and Archivshütz, in a file with other reports on UNR and Petliura archives, among the records of the Archival Administration in Kyiv, TsDAVO, 3206/5/26, fols. 11–26.

70. ERR report (March 1942–March 1943), TsDAVO, 3206/5/26, fols. 4–5.

71. See Eugene Zyblikewycz, "The Odyssey of V. Lypyns'kyj's Archives," *Harvard Ukrainian Studies* 9(3–4) 1985: 357–61, and Iwan Korowytsky, "The Archives of V. Lypyns'kyj," ibid., pp. 362–67. The details re-counted in those essays do not fit well with the facts presented in the Nazi documents, but further research is needed to clarify the matter. The ZUNR archives that were clearly referenced in the Nazi documents are not mentioned in either of these accounts, which concentrate uniquely on the personal archives of Lypyns'kyi; but at least some part of the Lypyns'kyi archives are included in the 1942 Nazi list of archives deposited in Vienna.

72. Università Cattolica Ucraina; via di Boccea, 478; 00166 Rome. I am grateful to Dr. Liliana Hentosh of Lviv University for information about the present location and verification of the present contents. A copy of

the Hornykevych finding aid (now held with the records themselves in Rome) was ordered, but not received in time for consideration here.

73.   Theophil Hornykiewicz, *Ereignisse in der Ukraine 1914–1922, deren Bedeutung und historische Hintergründe,* 4 vols. to date (Philadelphia, 1966–) [=Publikationen des W. K. Lypynsky Ost-Europäischen Forschungs-Instituts, Ser. 1–4; added English title page on vol. 1, *Events in Ukraine, 1914–1922, their importance and historical background*].

74.   See the forthcoming sequel by Grimsted, "The Postwar Fate of the Petliura Library."

Taras Bulba on the Pampas and the Fjords: A Ukrainian Cossack Theme in Western Opera

LUBOMYR A. HAJDA

If a Slavist were inadvertently to peruse the recent *History of Argentinian Opera*, he might well be struck by the following statement:

> In the annals of our early national opera there appears one date that divides the waters into past and present. This date is 20 July 1895, when the Teatro de la Opera presented the first opera by Arturo Berutti to be performed in Buenos Aires . . . the lyric drama in four acts *Tarass Bulba,* on a libretto by Guillermo Godio, based on the novel of the same name by Gogol . . . [1]

Were our Slavist by chance also to pick up the standard *History of Norwegian Opera,* his surprise might well be compounded. Describing the operatic scene in Oslo (then Kristiania) in the late 1890s, with a largely Italian and French repertoire presented by Swedish artists, the author singles out the date of 21 April 1897 for its historical significance. This was the date of the premiere of *Kosakkerne* (The Cossacks) by the Norwegian composer, Catharinus Elling[2]— an opera in four acts derived from none other than Nikolai Gogol's tale *Taras Bulba*. About this opera she then makes the following trenchant observation:

> *Kosakkerne* is our first full-fledged national grand opera.[3]

That operas based on Gogol's novel of Cossack Ukraine should, within the space of two years, mark a watershed in the musical history of Argentina and herald the dawn of native opera in Norway is the most striking illustration of a broader, too little-known fact: for over two centuries, Ukrainian themes and settings enjoyed wide currency and popularity on the operatic stages of Western Europe and even the Americas. It is the purpose of this article to call attention to the specific example of *Taras Bulba*, as well as to the broader theme, as research subjects—and perhaps even as performance pieces—deserving the attention of musicologists and cultural historians, especially as Ukraine begins to rediscover its historical connections with the West—and the West with Ukraine.

Nikolai Gogol and His Archetype of *Taras Bulba:* A Primer

Nikolai Gogol's historical novel *Taras Bulba* is too well known to require a lengthy exposition here.[4] It may be useful, nevertheless, to point out some facts about its composition and subject matter that may elucidate its various adaptations to the musical stage.

Nikolai Gogol (*Ukr.* Mykola Hohol'; *b.* Velyki Sorochyntsi [now in Poltava Oblast, Ukraine], 1 April 1809–*d.* Moscow, 4 March 1852) is generally recognized as one of the greatest writers in the Russian language and a major figure in world literature. Born and raised in the heartland of Ukraine, descended from Cossack military nobility, and the son of a Ukrainian writer, Gogol was inspired in his early efforts by the character types, customs and manners, and historical past of his native land. His collections of Ukrainian tales brought him his earliest fame: *Vechera na khutore bliz Dikan'ki* (Evenings on a Farm near Dykanka; 1831–1832) and *Mirgorod* (1835). *Taras Bulba* appeared in the latter.[5]

In his historical novel, Gogol paints on a broad canvas a fictional account of Ukraine at a time when the country was ruled by Poles and Ukrainian resistance was organized in the Cossack host, centered on the Zaporozhian Sich. The time is not explicitly stated, but from references to persons and events it may be placed in the 1630s. The central figures are the Cossack Taras Bulba and his two sons—the older, manly and heroic Ostap, and the younger, more romantic Andriy. The events take place in the context of bitter enmity between the Catholic Poles and Orthodox Ukrainians, the concurrent struggle with the infidel Tatars, and additional social complexities, illustrated, for instance, by the character of the Jewish merchant Yankel.

It was not the general story, however, but the romantic subplot that fired the imagination of operatic composers, even though it constituted but a fraction of the novel's bulk. This subplot, in summary, runs as follows. In chapter 2, as Taras and his sons are traveling to the Zaporozhian Sich, Andriy reminisces about his student days in Kyiv, where he first saw and fell in love with a beautiful girl—the daughter, it turned out, of a Polish military governor (voivode). Later, in chapter 5, as the Cossacks besiege the town of Dubno, Andriy is found in the military camp by a Tatar servant girl of his beloved, who is on the verge of starvation inside the city; taking provisions of bread he follows the servant through a secret passageway to Dubno. The central scene occurs in chapter 6 as Andriy comes face to face with his inamorata; for love of her, he renounces his father, comrades, and fatherland, and casts his lot with his former enemies, the Poles. Andriy becomes commander of the Polish forces, but when, in chapter 9, he leads a charge against his erstwhile Cossack comrades, he is maneuvered into a confrontation with Taras, who shoots his renegade son, uttering the famous words: "It is I who begot you and it is I who will kill you."

Clearly, present here are all the elements of an operatic plot: a Romeo-and-Juliet story of infatuation between the children of bitter foes; national and religious enmities; conflict of love and duty; patriotism and treason; and the shocking denouement of a father killing a son whom he deeply loves. To this could be added the potential of genre scenes: the Cossack revelries in song and dance; somber religious chants of Western and Eastern church traditions; exotic characters represented by the Tatar girl and Jewish merchant; and, if one chose to include it, the moving episode of a mother's parting from her sons whom she may never see again (chapter 1). The few problems posed by the disjunction of events in time and place are dramaturgically resolved easily enough through compression or, alternately, elaboration of the plot development. Giving names to the female characters—none of whom, interestingly, are endowed with such by Gogol—merely allows the librettist and composer to exercise their imagination.

Cossacks in the Steppes of Ukraine: Incarnations of *Taras Bulba* in Ukrainian and Russian Opera

It was Ukrainian and Russian composers who, quite naturally, first saw the operatic potential of *Taras Bulba*. The first setting by a Ukrainian composer (to a Russian-language text) was *Osada Dubno* (The Siege of Dubno) by Petro Sokal'skyi (1832–1887). The score was finished in 1878, and twice published (in St. Petersburg, in 1884 and in a revised version in 1905), but never staged, despite favorable assessments of the work by musicians. Mykola Lysenko (1842–1912), popularly accepted as Ukraine's greatest and favorite composer, completed his setting (in Ukrainian) of *Taras Bulba* in 1890. Its first stage performance, however, took place only in 1924, in the then capital of Soviet Ukraine, Kharkiv. Lysenko's *Taras Bulba* has since been canonized as *the* Ukrainian national opera, whatever difficulties it may still present to musicologists and producers, especially in its orchestration and occasional dramatical lapses.[6]

Four Russian operas based on *Taras Bulba* are known to have been written. All are works of nineteenth-century composers today virtually forgotten. The operas of Vasilii Kiuner (Kühner) (1840–1911) and Vladimir Kashperov (1826–1894) were staged briefly at the Maryinsky Theater in St. Petersburg (1880) and the Bolshoi in Moscow (1893), respectively; those by Nikolai Afanas'ev (1821–1898) and Konstantin Vil'boa (Villebois) (1817–1882) have never been performed.[7]

Cossacks on the Argentine Pampas: Arturo Berutti's *Tarass Bulba*

The world premiere of the Argentine *Tarass Bulba* took place four months before its first performance in Buenos Aires—on 9 March 1895, at the Teatro Regio in Turin. As reported in the *Gazzetta musicale di Milano*, it was a magnificent occasion, not least as a social event: present in the audience were members of Italy's royal family, including the princesses Isabella and Laetitia, and the duke d'Aosta, the king's nephew. The production was judged "a splendid feast for the eye," the performance deemed exceptional, and the music much applauded. The composer, toward whom the audience demonstrated a "warm affection," received 10 curtain calls.[8] Despite just three performances and the lateness of the season, the opera was pronounced a success, a verdict reiterated in the authoritative modern history of the Turin theater.[9] And if parody of an artistic work may be a form of flattery, *Tarass Bulba* received this accolade in the newspaper caricatures of the popular artist Caramba.[10]

The composer of *Tarass Bulba* was Arturo Berutti (*b*. San Juan, 14 March 1858–*d*. Buenos Aires, 3 January 1938), Argentine-born son of Italian immigrants. In the musical family—his brother Pablo also became a noted composer—Berutti received his early lessons from his father. His formal music study took place at the Leipzig Conservatory (1884–1888), after which he began his professional career in Europe—primarily Italy—producing two operas prior to *Tarass Bulba*. Following the latter's success, Berutti returned to Argentina where he remained until his death. He continued to compose successfully, completing five further operas, four of which were on native Argentinian themes, among them the first opera by an Argentine set to a Spanish libretto. This legacy earned Berutti the reputation of the first Argentinian national composer.[11]

The text for *Tarass Bulba*—in Italian—was the work of Guglielmo (*Span.* Guillermo) Godio (dates uncertain), a minor Turin-born Italian writer best known for his travels in Africa and close association with Latin America.[12] His first literary works were in the realm of poetry, dating to the 1870s, and travelogs from Egypt and Sudan dating to the 1880s. He later wrote on problems of immigration to Argentina and published a valuable description of the province of Misiones—interestingly, and perhaps significantly, at a time when Ukrainians were beginning to settle that territory in large numbers. Apart from *Tarass Bulba,* Godio evidently wrote only one other libretto, an obscure *Osmano in Candia* by a composer variously named in the sources as Corti or Curti.[13]

The plot of *Tarass Bulba* is relatively true to Gogol's original, although Godio turns Andriy's reveries about events in Kyiv into a whole act, changes the venue of his death from the battlefield to a town square, and eliminates such major characters as Taras's wife and heroic second son, Ostap. The libretto may be summarized as follows:[14]

Act 1. A garden of a rich palace in Kyiv. Andrea laments over his love for the Polish maiden Olga—a love that pits his national and religious loyalty against hers. He is encouraged in his passion, however, by the Jewish merchant Yankel, motivated by his hatred for the Cossacks. When Olga enters with her Tatar servant girl, Simska, Andrea declares his love, but Olga resists these advances from an enemy of her people. Tarass Bulba enters and informs Andrea of his mother's death. As Tarass and Andrea leave, Olga sorrowfully embraces Simska.

Act 2. A Cossack encampment outside the walls of Dubno, two years later. Tarass, as the Cossack commander, consults with his officers on strategy for taking Dubno from the resisting Poles. They resolve to attack on the morrow. The Cossack troops spend the evening before the battle in song and dance. As the camp retires for the night, Andrea stands guard. Stealthily, Simska makes her way to him and informs him that Olga is in the besieged city, close to starvation. Andrea prepares sacks of bread and follows Simska to save his beloved.

Act 3. A monastery in Dubno. Olga and the nuns pray for deliverance. Andrea appears with the food provisions. Olga greets him as her hero and urges him to remain. Olga's father, the voivode of Dubno, and a crowd of Poles rush in, threatening the Cossack. When Olga explains Andrea's role as her savior, the voivode relents and offers her to Andrea as his wife. For love of Olga Andrea renounces his father, his faith, and his country. Polish reinforcements enter the city, guided there by the treacherous Yankel. The inhabitants rejoice.

Act 4. A public square in front of the cathedral in Dubno. The Poles are victorious. Tarass and other Cossack prisoners are prepared for burning at the stake. They sing a lament for their native land, with the triple refrain: "Farewell, beloved fatherland, Ukraine, farewell." Yankel scoffs at them. Tarass believes that Andrea has perished. But when the Poles emerge from the cathedral as the Te Deum ends, Tarass espies his son in company with the voivode and Olga—and realizes he has become a renegade. With the words: "Your blood is consecrated to Ukraine," Tarass stabs Andrea to death as the crowd looks on in horror.

Following the successful world premiere of *Tarass Bulba* in Turin, Berutti sailed for Argentina to oversee the first production of his opera in Buenos Aires. The anticipation of this event in the capital was enormous. The press, which followed the preparations avidly, announced that *Tarass Bulba* was expected to be "the great novelty and grand attraction of the season."[15] The premiere on 20 July 1895 assumed the character of a state occasion. The president of Argentina and the cabinet of ministers were among the notables in attendance. It has even been suggested that Tarass Bulba, often called "nostro Duce" in the opera, could be viewed by the public as a symbol for Juan Manuel de Rosas, the dictator of Argentina earlier in the century.[16] Be that as it may, the performance was seen as a national triumph ("triunfo de la primera ópera argentina que va a representarse"). The seemingly unending ovations forced Berutti to take 19 curtain calls.[17]

The reviews of the Turin and Buenos Aires performances provide extensive material for judging the critical reception and popular response.[18] The performances themselves—with the renowned conductor Edoardo Mascheroni (considered a predecessor of Toscanini by music historians) leading the orchestra in both cities, and such luminaries as Antonio Scotti (then at the beginning of his career as the leading baritone of his time) in the cast—received total acclaim. The plot was deemed interesting and dramatic, but the libretto itself was faulted by some as conventional and old-fashioned. Berutti's musicianship received high praise, as did the music overall.[19] Some aspects of the music were criticized: occasional reviewers found the orchestration weak, with the strings too prominent ("in the manner of Puccini's *Manon* [*Lescaut*]") and too little use of brass or winds where they might benefit the drama, etc. Singled out for commendation were, in the first act, Andrea's aria, the Andrea-Olga-Simska-Yankel quartet (which called forth "an explosion of applause"), and the quintet that followed with the entrance of Tarass; the intermezzo and Cossack revelries in act 2; the love duet in the third act; and in the final act—the chorus of lament for Ukraine.

The opera provoked a minor, but interesting, polemic over music and nationalism.[20] A French correspondent for *Le Courrier français*, writing under the pseudonym of Candide, had asserted that "it is a grotesque notion to wish to have an Argentinian opera based on the history of Ukraine." To this an indignant (also pseudonymous) journalist responded in the paper *El Argentino*:

> What, in fact, is Candide trying to say? That the work of Señor Berutti is Argentinian because it exhibits a local Argentinian color, or because it was written by a native of the Republic? In the first case, the idea would be *trop baroque*, and we could easily censure a musician who wished to have the Zaporozhian warriors sing tangos, milongas and vidalitas. Needless to say, however, *Tarass Bulba* does not display such contradictions. In the second case, we see no incompatibility between the composer's nationality and his chosen theme. Are *Carmen* and *The Pearlfishers* perhaps not French operas? And is *La Africana* not a German opera? Or *Aida*—Italian . . . ?[21]

After a month-long run in Buenos Aires, *Tarass Bulba*—and its composer and librettist—crossed the Rio de la Plata to Montevideo, Uruguay. There it was staged, again to great acclaim, at the Teatro Solis on 22 August 1895. Apparently Berutti's *Tarass Bulba* was subsequently also performed in Mexico City, at the Teatro Municipal,[22] though precise data are lacking: the theater later burned down and with it perished its archives.[23] Finally, the opera returned once again to Italy, this time to Trieste, but again, the details have yet to be established.[24] With this, the performance history of Arturo Berutti's Cossack opera seems to have run its course—at least for now. Recently, the Berutti scholar Juan María Veniard has called for its revival, both for its seminal importance in Argentine music history and for its intrinsic merits.[25] It is to be hoped that this unusual example of early Argentine-Ukrainian cultural contact may yet be reexamined.[26]

Cossacks on the Norwegian Fjords: Catharinus Elling's *Kosakkerne*

The composition of the opera *Kosakkerne* should undoubtedly be viewed in the context of Norway's nineteenth-century "national awakening." By the last decades of the century, this awakening was proceeding along two tracks: a movement for political independence from the Swedish Crown (achieved in 1905), and the continuing process of cultural emancipation from the still powerful influence of Denmark (from which Norway was separated in 1814 after a

400-year union). Caught up in this development were the country's leading cultural figures, of whom the greatest were the dramatists Henrik Ibsen (1828–1906) and Bjørnstjerne Bjørnson (1832–1910) and the composer Edvard Grieg (1843–1907). Catharinus Elling (*b.* Kristiania [Oslo], 13 September 1858–*d.* Oslo, 8 January 1942) was their younger contemporary and follower.[27]

Elling began his musical studies in Norway and continued in Germany, first at the Leipzig Conservatory (1877–1878) and later for 10 years at Berlin (1886–1896), thanks in part to Grieg's recommendation. Edvard Grieg, in fact, had recognized Elling's promise early. In 1885 he described in a newspaper article how he had received from the young man a parcel of music manuscripts:

> How great . . . was my surprise and delight when I realized from a glance at a few bars that I was in the company of a highly talented lyricist. However much I read, played or hummed them, I could never grow tired of their intensity, which poured out in a broad melodious stream from an overflowing singer's heart. If his great talents are allowed to develop freely, the day will not be far distant when we shall be proud to have him in our midst.[28]

Grieg later frequently included Elling's works in concert performances that he conducted.

Elling began to compose while still in Germany, but his major works date from his return to Norway in 1896. These include an oratorio, two symphonies, much chamber music, and over 200 songs, many of which attained enormous popularity. *Kosakkerne* remained his only opera and, in the opinion of musicologists, probably his most important work.[29] Today, Elling is remembered chiefly as the teacher of a whole generation of Norwegian musicians, an organizer and conductor of performing (mainly choral) groups and, arguably, as the most important collector and editor of a vast corpus of Norwegian folk and religious songs.

The text set by Elling was the work of Edvard Hagerup Bull (1855–1938). Like Godio for Berutti, Bull was no professional librettist. He was, however, an eminent jurist, financier, and politician, prominent in the movement for separation from Sweden. In the last 15 years under the Swedish Crown, Bull was successively a minister on the State Council and a judge on the Supreme Court. When Norway achieved independence in 1905, Bull served as the country's first minister of justice, and later held other high government positions. His memoirs of 1905, diaries, and reminiscences of his contemporaries are important sources for the history of the period. He was also the nephew of Ole Bull (1810–1880), the renowned and phenomenally gifted violinist. It may be this family connection to music, and their mutual cultural nationalist sympathies, that drew Edvard Bull to Catharinus Elling for their collaboration. Apart from the libretto for *Kosakkerne*, Bull left no other artistic legacy.[30]

The plot of *Kosakkerne* diverges from Gogol in ways somewhat different than does Berutti's opera. Gogol's romantic hero Andriy (Berutti's Andrea) is renamed Rodion, and his Polish love is given the name Marylka. Retained are such characters as Bulba's wife (here called Awdotja) and second son, Ostap. Gone, however, are the more exotic figures of Yankel and the Tatar girl—and with her the central incident of the hero's bringing food to save his starving beloved. The following plot summary underlines the major differences between the two operatic treatments.[31]

Act 1. Outside the house of Taras Bulba. Taras Bulba, his wife Awdotja, and guests are celebrating the homecoming of their sons Rodion and Ostap from their studies in Kyiv. Rodion withdraws from the festivities, and when his mother follows him, he reveals to her his love for Marylka. A Cossack arrives with the news that the Poles have attacked their land. Taras and his men prepare to leave for battle. A prayer closes the act.

Act 2. A Cossack camp outside Dubno. The Cossacks are bored and tired of inaction during the protracted siege. They begin to sing, drink, and dance with the women. Ostap joins the revelries, but Rodion remains in solitude. Taras Bulba appears and angrily drives away the women. The Cossacks elect Bulba as their leader. In preparation for an assault on Dubno, Taras sends the Cossack Schilo and Rodion in disguise into the city on reconnaissance. In a monologue, Rodion expresses his love and longing for Marylka.

Act 3. Outside Marylka's house in Dubno, a church in the background. The Poles pray for victory in the church. Marylka's thoughts are with Rodion. Rodion appears and approaches Marylka. They confess their mutual love. Marylka cautions Rodion about their peoples' enmity and his duty to his father and fatherland. For love of Marylka Rodion renounces both: "What is father or fatherland to me? . . . Ukraine was never my fatherland . . . You are my fatherland." They fall into each other's arms.

Act 4. A public square in Dubno. Rodion and Marylka's wedding is celebrated. During the festivities news comes of Polish victory. Cossack prisoners are brought in, among them Taras. Taras sings an epic song about a Cossack who betrays his country and is killed in revenge. In a confrontation with Rodion Taras condemns his son, but also himself and Rodion's mother as parents of the traitor. The recollection of his mother gives Rodion pause. Taras urges him to redeem himself by rescuing the Cossack prisoners and leading them to safety, but Marylka persuades Rodion to remain. Taras then stabs his renegade son. As Marylka's father rushes at Taras, the dying Rodion intercedes for his life and asks to be remembered to his mother. Rodion dies with Marylka's name on his lips.

The first performance of *Kosakkerne* took place on 21 April 1897 and was repeated two days later. Since Kristiania/Oslo lacked an opera house and a resident opera company, the performance was given in the Eldorado Theater by a Swedish guest troupe. Detailed reviews in the press allow us to reconstruct this pivotal occasion in Norway's music history.[32] The libretto was praised as dramatic and varied, but also criticized as too prolix—especially act 4. The assessment of the music, however, was unreservedly positive, with particular mention made of Elling's solid technical skill, careful attention to detail, deft orchestration and choral writing. Singled out for special praise were Rodion's duet with his mother in act 1; his soliloquy in act 2; the love duets in acts 3 and 4; and Bulba's song in the last act. The dances and ballet music were also well received. The audience expressed its enthusiasm by ovations that called the composer and soloists out for many curtain calls.

The subsequent performance history of *Kosakkerne* remains to be investigated; however, it is clear that it did not enter the standard repertoire, even in Norway. Nevertheless, its qualities are still recognized, and orchestral excerpts have been performed recently in concert. The music historian Grinde writes: "Musically, the opera as a whole creates a pleasing impression. The choral sections are excellent, there are many good parts for the soloists, and the orchestration is interesting and imaginative."[33] *Kosakkerne*, then, may well deserve another look, both as a Norwegian musical monument and as an example of modern Scandinavian-Ukrainian cultural interaction.[34]

Cossacks from the English Channel to the Swiss Alps: *Taras Bulba* as English, French, German, and Dutch-Swiss Operas

The Argentinian and Norwegian works are perhaps the most intriguing of the *Taras Bulba* operas, but they are not the only ones. At least four other Western European operatic treatments of the subject can be identified.

Virtually contemporaneous with the Berutti and Elling works is an opera by an English composer, John David Davis (*b*. Birmingham, 22 October 1867– *d*. Estoril, Portugal, 20 November 1942). Davis studied music in Frankfurt with Hans von Bülow, the great Wagnerian conductor, and subsequently at the Conservatory in Brussels. Upon his return to England, he was offered a libretto derived from *Taras Bulba* by one Edward Lawrence Levy, a Birmingham writer on local history and lore (and international amateur weight-lifting champion in 1891). The result was a one-act opera entitled *The Zaporogues*.[35] It premiered in Birmingham on 7 May 1895 with amateur performers to mixed reviews. In 1903 it was staged professionally in Antwerp, in Flemish translation under the title *De Kozakken*.[36] Reduced to a single act, the story was confusing for audiences, and around 1920 the librettist suggested to the composer that he expand the opera into a three-act work. The composer's response was that "he was not taking on any more Bolshevik productions."[37]

More substantial was a work by the French composer Marcel Samuel-Rousseau (*b*. Paris, 18 August 1882–*d*. Paris, 11 June 1955). César Franck and Gabriel Fauré appear as the dominant influences in his musical formation, but also the impressionists Claude Debussy and Maurice Ravel. Himself the son of a composer and prominent pedagogue, Samuel-Rousseau studied at the Paris Conservatoire, where he won the prestigious Prix de Rome in 1905. His distinguished career included a professorship of harmony at the Conservatoire (1916–1952) and appointment as director of the Paris Opéra (1941–1944). In

1947 he was elected to the Académie des Beaux-Arts. Samuel-Rousseau's *Tarass Boulba,* with a text by the eminent librettist Louis de Gramont (among whose other credits is Jules Massenet's *Esclarmonde),* premiered to an enthusiastic reception in Paris on 22 November 1919 at the Théâtre-Lyrique (Vaudeville). It was revived successfully at the Opéra-Comique in 1933, and was apparently also staged at Bordeaux and possibly elsewhere. Samuel-Rousseau composed three other operas, ballets, and a number of orchestral and chamber works.[38]

Germany's contribution to the *Taras Bulba* repertoire is an opera by Ernst Richter (*b.* Dux, Bohemia [now Duchcov, Czech Republic], 26 May 1903–*d.* ?), to a libretto by Johannes Kempfe (1891–1951), a minor writer who otherwise published under the pseudonym of Hanns Eberhard. Richter had been a student of Paul Graener, one of the leading musical figures of interwar Germany, at the Leipzig Conservatory. He had a successful career as an orchestra conductor at some of Germany's main opera houses—Dresden, Leipzig, and finally Hannover, where he became principal conductor in 1953. *Taras Bulba,* his only opera, premiered in Stettin (*Pol.* Szczecin) on 26 January 1935. Its success was such that by the end of the decade it had been seen in Dresden, Hannover, Wiesbaden, Görlitz, Aussig, Altenburg, Regensburg, and Karlsruhe.[39] The reviews—and they appeared in all the major music periodicals—were almost uniformly positive,[40] and led to expectations that Richter's *Taras Bulba* might become a fixture of the modern German repertory. However, there is no evidence of any further performances following World War II, nor is there a record of any other major compositions by Ernst Richter.

The last *Taras Bulba* opera to be considered here may be characterized as a binational work. Its composer was Willem de Boer (*b.* Amsterdam, 7 May 1885–*d.* Zurich, 25 February 1962), a Dutchman who trained as a violinist at the Amsterdam Conservatory, where he became professor and a Netherlands state prize winner, but who was then professionally engaged from 1908 until his death in Switzerland. De Boer was primarily a performing artist—a violin soloist, member of a string quartet which he founded and led in major concerts, and conductor of the famed Zurich Symphony (Tonhalleorchester). His output as composer was mainly in the smaller forms. He did compose two operas, however, one of which was *Taras Bulba,* to his own bilingual Dutch-German text, on which he worked from 1942–1947. To date, the opera has never been performed.[41]

Conclusion

Nikolai Gogol's *Taras Bulba* is but one, although particularly salient, example of the many Ukrainian themes that served as inspiration for generations of opera composers in the West, largely unbeknownst to the Ukrainians and the scholars who study them. Operas based on the historical and legendary exploits of Hetman Ivan Mazepa, for instance, number at least a dozen, by men (and a woman) of French, Italian, German, Belgian, English, and Spanish (Catalan) nationality. But not only Cossacks stirred the musical imagination. The lyric tragedy *Kassya* (1893) by the eminent French composer Léo Delibes is set in Galicia close upon the 1848 revolution; the Austrian Franz Salmhofer's *Iwan Tarassenko* (1938)—a popular hit at the Vienna Staatsoper, styled by one critic as "more than just a Ukrainian *Cavalleria Rusticana*"—takes place near Poltava during an anti-tsarist uprising in 1870; and Horst Platen's *Der heilige Morgen* (The Holy Dawn) (1918) transpires on the eve of World War I. Comic operas also were popular, from the early singspiel *Die Liebe in der Ukraine* (Love in Ukraine) (1787) of Franz Spindler to *Dunja* (1904) by Iwan Knorr, a composer much admired by Johannes Brahms. And these are but a few examples.

Opera is an art form—and, it should not be forgotten, for many decades one of the most popular forms of mass entertainment—that over time involved and affected multitudes: on the creative side—composers, librettists, costume and set designers, directors, choreographers and other artists; on the interpretive side—singers, conductors, the orchestra and ballet corps, even *repetiteurs* and prompters; and on the consumer side—audiences and critics. All in their different ways had to respond to the subject matter before them. In the case of the operas discussed above, this subject matter necessarily involved Ukraine, its history, people, and traditions.

What was the understanding of Ukraine on the part of the creators and interpreters of these works of artistic imagination? Did they understand it as a distinct country with a unique character, or as an exotic extension of Russia or, perhaps, Poland? What were the sources—literary and historical—that informed this understanding? How was the Ukrainian ambience interpreted in the text, dramaturgy, and production? And how were these attempts received and understood by reviewers and the public? These are some questions worth pursuing by cultural historians of Ukraine.

For musicologists and music historians there are additional considerations. What are the musical qualities of these works, now largely forgotten? What attempts, if any, were made by the composers to infuse their music with a Ukrainian flavor, and with what success? How may these operas now be reassessed in the context of the musical histories of their respective countries of composition? Which of them may conceivably be revived, and which may yield excerpts for the concert hall?

The avenues of inquiry are many. With the involvement of scholars and artists, and the potential for international collaboration, the study and presentation of Western operas on Ukrainian themes may become both an intellectually enlightening and culturally enriching effort.

NOTES

*I wish to express my gratitude to Ksenya Kiebuzinski, Peter Jacyk Bibli-
ographer in Ukrainian Studies at the Ukrainian Research Institute, for
her assistance in locating and obtaining many rare bibliographical items
used in this study as well as for sharing her own admirable expertise in
the area of Ukrainian–West European cultural relations.*

1.   Enzo Valenti Ferro, *Historia de la ópera argentina* (Buenos Aires, 1997),
     p. 17.

2.   The spelling "Kosakkerne" reflects the usage at the time; in present-day
     Norwegian orthography it is written "Kosakkene." I use the original form
     throughout.

3.   Ingeborg Eckhoff Kindem, *Den norske operas historie* (Oslo, 1941),
     p. 65.

4.   *Taras Bulba* has been published in innumerable editions—separately, and
     in Gogol's selected and complete works, in Russian and in translation into
     many languages of the world. References here, therefore, will be not to
     any specific edition or pagination, but to chapters, which may be easily
     accessed in any version of the work. Transliteration of the names follows
     established English-language traditions for translation, rather than the
     modified Library of Congress standard used elsewhere.

5.   The scholarly literature on Gogol is enormous. Of greatest relevance to
     our topic is Gogol's complex attitude to Ukraine and his own ambiguous
     Ukrainian/Russian identity. This is treated in depth in George S. N.
     Luckyj, *Between Gogol' and Ševčenko* (Munich, 1971); on *Taras Bulba,*
     see esp. pp. 113–15.

6.   On the Sokal's'kyi and Lysenko operas, see, for example, Lidiia
     Arkhymovych, *Ukraïns'ka klasychna opera: istorychnyi narys* (Kyiv,
     1957), pp. 149–56 and 202–222, respectively.

7.   On these composers individually, see the relevant entries in *Muzykal'naia
     entsiklopediia*, 6 vols. (Moscow, 1973–1982). For a more synthetic pre-
     sentation, see indexed references in Abram Gozenpud, *Russkii opernyi
     teatr XIX veka*, 3 vols. (Leningrad, 1969–1973).

8.   *La Gazzetta musicale di Milano*, 17 March 1895.

9.   Alberto Basso, ed., *Storia del Teatro Regio di Torino*, 5 vols. (Turin,
     1976–1988), vol. 2, p. 461.

10. *La Luna* (Turin), 15 March 1895.

11. Biographical details and critical assessments of Berutti may be found in
     most major reference works on music. See, for example, *Baker's Bio-
     graphical Dictionary of Musicians* (henceforth *Baker's Dictionary),* 8th
     ed., rev. by Nicolas Slonimsky (New York, 1992), p. 178; *The New Grove*

Dictionary of Opera (henceforth *NGDO*), 4 vols., ed. Stanley Sadie (London, 1992), vol. 1, p. 457; *Dizionario enciclopedico universale della musica e dei musicisti: Le biografie* (henceforth *Dizionario enciclopedico*), 8 vols., ed. Alberto Basso (Turin, 1985–1988), vol. 1, p. 507; Carlo Schmidl, *Dizionario universale dei musicisti*, 2 vols. + supplement (Milan, 1937–1938), vol. 1, p. 173. We are particularly fortunate to possess a comprehensive, book-length monograph on Berutti's life and works: Juan María Veniard, *Arturo Berutti, un argentino en el mundo de la ópera* (Buenos Aires, 1988). The study cites archival sources, presents musical illustrations, photographic material, and is especially rich in documentation from the press; on *Tarass Bulba*, see esp. pp. 138–79.

12. Little published information is available on Godio. See, however, the entry in Vicente Osvaldo Cutolo, *Nuevo diccionario biográfico argentino (1750–1930)*, 7 vols. (Buenos Aires, 1968–1985), vol. 3, p. 317 (which does not mention his authorship of the *Tarass Bulba* libretto).

13. See Franz Stieger, comp., *Opernlexikon*, 4 pts. in 11 vols. (Tutzing, 1975–1983), pt. 3: *Librettisten*, vol. 2, p. 369.

14. The summary is based on the libretto published by G. Ricordi & C., the leading music publisher in Italy: *Tarass Bulba. Dramma lirico in 4 atti, di Guglielmo Godio, musica di Arturo Berutti* (Milan, [1894?]). I keep the names of characters here and elsewhere as they appear in the opera text.

15. *La Prensa* (Buenos Aires), 17 July 1895.

16. Veniard, *Arturo Berutti,* p. 143.

17. For details of the premiere and its reception, see Mario García Acevedo, *La música argentina durante el período de la organización nacional* (Buenos Aires, 1961), pp. 87–89; and Veniard, *Arturo Berutti,* pp. 169–79.

18. The reviews are cited *in extenso* in Veniard, *Arturo Berutti,* pp. 169–79.

19. The vocal score was soon published by Ricordi: *Tarass Bulba. Dramma lirico in quattro atti, di Guglielmo Godio, musica di Arturo Berutti. Opera completa per canto e pianoforte* (Milan, [1895?]).

20. I summarize this polemic here from an exhaustive account in Veniard, *Arturo Berutti,* pp. 174–76.

21. The opera here called *La Africana* is a rather poor choice to be styled a German work. Though its composer, Giacomo Meyerbeer, was German-born, he is identified primarily with French grand opera—indeed, as its founding father—of which *L'Africaine* (to give it its original name) is a quintessential example. This misdesignation, of course, does not negate the writer's basic premise.

22. See Veniard, *Arturo Berutti,* p. 179; and Rodolfo Arizaga, *Enciclopedia de la música argentina* (Buenos Aires, 1971), p. 65.

23. Veniard, *Arturo Berutti*, p. 179.

24. Ibid.

25. Ibid., p. 333.

26. Berutti's *Tarass Bulba* is not the only Argentinian opera on a Ukrainian subject. Eduardo García Mansilla (1870–1930) wrote an opera, to his own French-language text, entitled *Ivan,* which is "based on a traditional Ukrainian legend" (*NGDO,* vol. 2, p. 348). The opera was first performed privately in 1905 for Tsar Nicholas II at the Hermitage in St. Petersburg (where the composer served as a diplomat), and was later staged at La Scala in Milan, Teatro Costanzi in Rome, and Teatro Colón in Buenos Aires. See Juan María Veniard, *Los García, los Mansilla y la música* (Buenos Aires, 1986), esp. ch. 7, "Ivan."

27. There is no book-length biography of Elling or study of his works. For summary coverage, see *Baker's Dictionary,* pp. 490–91; *Dizionario enciclopedico,* vol. 2, p. 648; Schmidl, *Dizionario,* vol. 1, p. 491; and *Die Musik in Geschichte und Gegenwart* (henceforth *MGG*), 17 vols. (Kassel, 1949–1986), vol. 3, col. 1281–84. See also Nils Grinde, *A History of Norwegian Music,* trans. William H. Halverson and Leland B. Sateren (Lincoln, NE, 1991), pp. 257–59.

28. "Lovende ung norsk komponist," *Bergens Tidende,* 14 March 1885; reprinted in *Edvard Grieg: Artikler og taler,* ed. Øystein Gaukstad (Oslo, 1957), pp. 111–12; citation taken from the summary English translation, p. 270.

29. Grinde, *History of Norwegian Music*, p. 259.

30. For a brief overview of his life and accomplishments, see, for example, the entry "Edvard Hagerup Bull" in *Aschehougs Konversasjonsleksikon*, 5th ed., 20 vols. (Oslo, 1968–1973), vol. 3, p. 534.

31. The plot synopsis is based on the published libretto: *Kosakkerne. Operatekst i fire akter frit efter Gogols fortælling "Taras Bulba" ved E. H. B.* [=Edvard Hagerup Bull] (Kristiania [Oslo], 1897). The score has not been published; the autograph manuscript remains in Oslo, in the collection "Norsk Musikksamling" of the Nasjonalbiblioteket. I wish to thank Dr. Ingunn Lunde of the University of Bergen, a visiting scholar at the Ukrainian Research Institute, for her assistance in obtaining a copy of the libretto from Norway and information on the score, and for her patient elucidation of the Norwegian-language material used in this study.

32. My summary is drawn from the review in *Morgenbladet* (Oslo) 24 April 1897, which is based on both performances. Other reviews, including that in the paper *Aftenposten,* were not available to me at this writing.

33. Grinde, *History of Norwegian Music,* p. 259.

34. Another intriguing example of this may be the opera *Stepan* by the noted Danish composer Ebbe Hamerik (1898–1951). The opera, set in Ukraine during the Bolshevik Revolution, had a sensational premiere in 1924 in

Mainz, Germany, and quickly made the rounds of many European the-
aters, including Antwerp, Lübeck, and the Royal Opera in Copenhagen.
For an assessment, see, among others, Bo Wallner, *Vår tids musik i
Norden från 20-tal till 60-tal* (Stockholm, 1968), pp. 41–42.

35.   On John David Davis, see *Baker's Dictionary,* p. 400; Schmidl,
       Dizionario, vol. 1, p. 415; and the older *British Musical Biography,* ed.
       James D. Brown and Stephen S. Stratton (Birmingham, 1897), p. 119.
       The vocal score has been published: *The Zaporogues. Lyric Drama in
       One Act. Libretto by Lawrence Levy. Music by J. D. Davis. Op. 23* (Bir-
       mingham, [1888?]).

36.   See August Monet, *Een halve Eeuw Nederlandsch Lyrisch Tooneel en
       Vlaamsche Opera te Antwerpen* (Antwerp, 1939), p. 150.

37.   E. Lawrence Levy, *Birmingham Theatrical Reminiscences* (Birmingham,
       n.d.), p. 37.

38.   On Marcel Samuel-Rousseau, see *Baker's Dictionary,* p. 1551; *NGDO,*
       vol. 4, p. 161; *Dizionario enciclopedico,* vol. 6, p. 473; and *MGG,* vol. 11,
       col. 1104; and many histories of French music in the twentieth century.
       The music publisher Choudens has put out the libretto: *Tarass Boulba.
       Drame musical en trois actes et cinq tableaux, dont un prologue. Texte de
       Louis de Gramont, d'après Gogol. Musique de Marcel Samuel-Rousseau*
       (Paris, 1919); the vocal score: *Tarass Boulba. Drame musical en cinq
       actes, d'après Gogol, par Louis de Gramont. Musique de Marcel Samuel-
       Rousseau. Partition chant et piano* (Paris, 1933); and the full score:
       Tarass Boulba . . . Partition d'orchestre (Paris, 1919). (Note the different
       disposition of acts in the libretto and the two scores.)

39.   There are no entries on Ernst Richter in any of the major musical lexicons
       or encyclopedias. Some details of his biography may be gleaned from the
       numerous reviews of his opera and the published histories of the theaters
       where he worked. See in particular Heinrich Sievers, *Die Musik in
       Hannover* (Hannover, 1961), pp. 119, 155. The full orchestral score has
       been published: *Taras Bulba. Oper in 3 Akten, frei nach Gogols
       gleichnamigen Roman. Musik von Ernst Richter. Text von Johannes
       Kempfe. Partitur* ([Berlin], 1934); as well as the piano/vocal reduction:
       Taras Bulba . . . Klavierauszug (Dresden, 1934).

40.   An exception was a critical review in *Die Musik* February 1935: 363, by
       Herbert Gerigk. From 1935 to 1945 Gerigk was a leading Nazi official in
       charge of music policy in the Third Reich; on him, see Willem de Vries,
       Sonderstab Musik (Cologne, 1998), pp. 43–48. It is an intriguing question
       whether there were ideological or political, rather than simply musical,
       reasons for his negative attitude to the opera.

41.   Information on Willem de Boer is largely to be found in Swiss publica-
       tions on music. See, for example, *Musiktheater. Zum Schaffen von
       Schweizer Komponisten des 20. Jahrhunderts,* ed. Dorothea Baumann

(Zurich, 1983), p. 285, and *Schweizer Musiker-Lexikon/Dictionnaire des musiciens suisses: 1964* (Zurich, 1964), pp. 56–57. The score of his *Taras Bulba* has not been published; the autograph manuscript remains, presumably, in Zurich.

The Borderlands of Power:
Territory and Great Power Status in Russia at the
Beginning and at the End of the Twentieth Century

FIONA HILL

> It is important to understand how deeply rooted and symbolically strong
> territorial images may be in mass mentalities.[1]
>
> *Valerii Tishkov, 1997*

> The whole of Russia is looking for an anchor . . . The vestiges of the past
> are more important to us than ever before.[2]
>
> *Petr Khlebnikov, 1997*

> We are now suffering a difficult fateful time. We are infected with nostal-
> gia for prerevolutionary Russia. We want to immerse ourselves in the age
> of 1910 as deeply as possible to bring back—at least in part—the atmo-
> sphere and spirit of that era, to transport it to our troubled days. It is
> precisely there, in the past, that we stubbornly seek the answers to the
> burning questions of the day. We are restoring the pillars of that life—the
> nobility, the Cossacks, Orthodoxy, Autocracy. Is it for naught? Are we not
> living with illusions just as before? Are we not idealizing "the Russia we
> lost," failing to see that we have lost it forever? *That* Russia can no longer
> be reborn; it is long gone and exists only in memory.[3]
>
> *Konstantin Azadovskii, 1995*

In this paper I discuss the propensity among Russian political elites in the
1990s to seek inspiration from their counterparts in late imperial Russia in
creating new reference points for the post-Soviet state. In my analysis I consider the fact that in both the late imperial and post-Soviet periods, the Russian
elite became progressively fixated on restoring past glories and maintaining
Russia's geopolitical status as a Great Power, and demonstrate that the
country's sheer size was identified as one of the key factors in ensuring
Russia's position and influence in world affairs. Further, I examine the Russian
elite's belief in an organic connection between Russian state power and the
country's vast territorial extent both before the Revolution and after the collapse of the USSR. This belief is reflected in the Russian center's fraught
relationship with two of its key borderlands: Poland in the early 1900s and
Chechnya in the 1990s.

Introduction: The Century's Bookends

For Russia, the 1990s have been a tumultous decade, marked by debates within Russia's political elite about the country's political identity. These debates have focused on the formation of a new state, the delimitation of power between state and society and center and periphery, and the status and role of Russia in the international arena. These debates are not, however, without their precedent in Russian history; the themes of the elite debates in Moscow over state and power and the relationship of society to both are persistent over several centuries of Russian political thought. Indeed, there are striking parallels between 1991–1996 (the period of the first Yeltsin presidency) and the decade just prior to the First World War, from 1905–1914 (during the reign of the last tsar, Nicholas II) in terms of both political/economic developments and the issues that gripped the political elite of Russia's capital. In many respects, the debate in Moscow in the 1990s about Russia's present and future is the continuation of the debate in St. Petersburg that was interrupted by war and revolution in 1914–1917.[4]

The first and last decades of the twentieth century were both periods of transition for Russia, marked by defeat in war, imperial and economic collapse, and attempts at dramatic transformation in the form of democratization and the marketization of the Russian economy. Both were also periods of nostalgia, of looking to the past to give substance and legitimacy to the present.

In 1913, for example, the Romanov dynasty celebrated 300 years of rule in Russia. On that occasion, Russia's roots in the medieval Muscovite state were glorified in building projects, court balls, and pageants with seventeenth-century themes. In spite of the capital's modern roots, an old Muscovite-style church was built in the heart of St. Petersburg, and some of the city's buildings were rebuilt in the neo-Byzantine manner.[5] Likewise, in the years leading up to the 850th anniversary of Moscow's founding in 1997, teams of archaeologists engaged in an unprecedented excavation of layers of settlement dating back to the city's medieval beginnings;[6] a statue of Russia's greatest ruler, Peter the Great, was erected on the banks of the Moscow River (in spite of his personal animus toward the city and his construction of St. Petersburg as the new capital of his empire); and buildings were redone in the neo-Byzantine manner. The early 1900s and the 1990s are what one might call the century's "bookends" for Russia.

In 1905, defeat in war by Japan and economic collapse provoked unrest among virtually all groups in Russian society. Major reform was necessary in order to prevent the unraveling of the tsarist regime and the empire. In the late 1980s, the defeat in Afghanistan, the economic failure of communism, and the perceived defeat in the Cold War fueled the centrifugal forces that ultimately led to the disintegration of the USSR in 1991. Radical reform was required to prevent the subsequent fragmentation of the Russian Federation. In both periods, democratization and marketization brought executive power—in the person of the autocrat, Tsar Nicholas II, and the president, Boris Yeltsin—into conflict with newly empowered groups in Russian society. The political elite clashed with the tsar and the president in the Russian legislature, on the pages of newspapers and journals, and in political meetings, while the broader population made its opinion felt through protest and public demonstration against government policies.

The beginning and the end of the century were times of social upheaval, executive-legislative-societal confrontation, and above all, public debate over the direction and substance of reform. Furthermore, they are periods of profound crises of identity in Russian political life. In the first period, failure in the Russo-Japanese War seriously damaged Russia's international standing as a European "Great Power" (*velikaia derzhava*) and the so-called revolution of 1905–1906 challenged the certainties of the autocratic tsarist system. In the second, the dual collapse of the USSR and communism marked the end of Russia's status as one of two post–World War II "superpowers" (*sverkhderzhavy*) and removed the underpinnings of Russia's political, economic, and social system. From 1905 to 1914, and again from 1991 to 1996, Russia was in search of a new defining principle to unify the population and guide the state forward in its internal development and external relations.

The parallels between post-Soviet Russia of 1991–1996 and the Russia of the late imperial period 1905–1914 are striking not only to scholars observing Russia from afar, but also to Russians themselves—who have been acutely aware of them and even deliberately searching them out. Since 1991, there has been a conscious emulation of late-imperial political and cultural institutions at the state level to emphasize the continuity with the Russian Empire and to evoke past glories. This emulation has ranged from the revival in name of the late-imperial Russian State Duma and the re-creation of prerevolutionary parties like the "Kadets" (Constitutional Democrats) to the restoration of potent imperial symbols such as the double-headed eagle. It has involved the resurrection of imperial statuary; the rebuilding of the monumental Cathedral of Christ the Savior in the heart of Moscow and other celebrated churches demolished by the Bolsheviks; the replacement of Soviet-era street names in the Russian capital with their prerevolutionary forms; the publication of books previously banned and new surveys such as a history of Nicholas II; and the opening of imperial archives. The first decade of the twentieth century is now seen again in Russia as a "Silver Age,"[7] not simply as the twilight of the empire and the Russian autocracy.[8] It has become a model and reference point for the "new Russia" that has emerged from the debris of the Soviet Union.

Russia as a Great Power

In both the new Russia and the old Russia, one central idea has dominated the elite debates and motivated the attempts to restore and glorify the past: the idea that "Russia was, is, and shall remain a Great Power."[9] Throughout the first decade of the 1900s and the 1990s, in the Duma, in political and academic speeches, and in the press, Russian political elites have decried the state's weakness, potential disintegration, and loss of influence abroad. They have debated how best to revitalize the state internally and restore its Great Power status externally to prevent international marginalization. In writings, pronouncements, and speeches in both periods, the fact that Russia was still "Great" (*Velikaia Rossiia*) and a "Great Power" has been repeated, like a mantra.

At the beginning of the twentieth century, Great Power status was seen by international observers as critical to heading off challenges at home and abroad.[10] In Russia, maintaining the appearance of Great Power status was particularly crucial for the tsarist system. As British historian Dominic Lieven argues in his book on Russia and the origins of the First World War, "it was essential for the survival of the imperial regime both that it be considered invincible and that it be feared by its subjects." Lieven suggests that for the elite,

> which invested so much of its pride and prestige in foreign and defense policy, defeat in these spheres was quite likely to lead to a loss of self-confidence and even to a questioning of fundamental aspects of the existing political system . . . [and should it] seem that the regime was weak and amenable to pressure, then both the number of those willing to actively oppose the state and the radicalism of their programs would increase tremendously . . . Defeat in war or even diplomacy . . . inspired not respect or fear for the regime but rather contempt.[11]

Russia's physical survival as an empire was also seen to be at stake in the preservation of its status as a Great Power. Indeed, as Prince Grigorii Trubetskoi, the noted Russian diplomat and analyst of international affairs remarked in this period, "the main threat of war for Russia is really contained in too clear a revelation of our weakness . . . and countries incapable of defending either themselves or their national dignity . . . become a subject for compensations and possible divisions."[12] As Lieven notes, in pre-1914 international relations, "the feeble were pushed around by other powers."[13]

Similar views on the significance of Great Power status have been expressed in the 1990s. Russia's First Deputy Defense Minister Andrei Kokoshin, for example, noted in 1995 that maintaining a strong army and state was "one of the most important conditions for deterring aggression against [Russia] and its allies."[14] The prominent Russian commentator Aleksandr Panarin, in a piece in *Znamia* in 1994, worried that if Russia demonstrated weakness, the West might be tempted to simply finish off its former enemy in the Cold War by dismembering its territory.[15] Other analysts concluded that "Russia's foreign adversaries [were] showing themselves more and more boldly and openly" with every sign of decline in Russia's military, economic, and political potential.[16] By 1995, the idea of Russia as a Great Power and the importance of ensuring that position in order to prevent the country from being squeezed out of international affairs had become the dominant theme of political debates.[17]

Size and Power

In elite assertions in the early 1900s and late 1990s, there is both an a priori assumption that Russia is a Great Power and an unspoken consensus on the definition of the term. Among scholars of international affairs, however, there is no clear consensus on the definition of state power. Those definitions that do exist are almost exclusively focused on the state's ability to project its influence abroad to achieve certain goals and advantages in relations with other states. A state's basic power capabilities can be measured using indicators such as size (population and territory), wealth (natural resources, degree of economic development and rate of growth, industrial and technological capacity, GNP, magnitude of foreign transactions, etc.), and political factors (political culture, administrative skill, political will, and the mobilization of the population). None of these indicators, however, is sufficient to gauge the actual ability of a state to put its capabilities into action in the international arena.[18]

Of these indicators of Russia's power as a state and weight as an international force in the twentieth century, one in particular consistently stands out in all of the commentaries: the country's sheer physical size in terms of territory and population. At the beginning of the century, the Russian Empire was the world's largest contiguous state, and at its end—even after the collapse of the Soviet Union—the Russian Federation, with an extent of 17,075,000 square kilometers, was still its largest.

As commentators have remarked since Russia's first emergence as a Great Power after its defeat of Sweden under Peter the Great: "For good or for evil Russia must be a powerful state in Europe and in Asia. A country with one hundred millions of inhabitants, increasing, moreover, with extreme rapidity, cannot be a second-rate power, however badly it be administered."[19] Russia's size not only "put it on the map" but allowed it to dominate that map. Its territorial extent across the Eurasian landmass gave it both regional and global influence.

Territory and Great Power Status in the Early 1900s

In the early 1900s, in contemporary Russian and foreign literature, Russia's vast territory and its rapidly increasing population were frequently referred to as the major elements in the perception of the state as a European Great Power. A state with a territory of continental proportions that extended over a sixth of the world's surface from the Baltic to the Pacific, with a population of 175 million, could scarcely be ignored in international relations. As British historian Francis Skrine noted in the introduction to his 1914 history of the expansion of Russia from 1815 to 1900, "The Russian Empire is an organism unique in the world's history. It embraces an area greater than Alexander's conquests, than the solid dominion built up by Rome, than the realms overrun by Chinghiz or Timur; it is surpassed only by Greater Britain [the British Empire]."[20] Russia's size was seen as the source of her strength by outside observers.

In keeping with the imperial and racial sentiments of the era, foreign scholars in the early 1900s saw an inevitability in Russia's seemingly inexorable push across Eurasia and its incorporation of the peoples of the Asiatic steppe into its empire: "a strong and civilized power which is brought into contact with barbarism has no resource but to conquer and annex."[21] One British commentator observed that "whereas countries like France or Germany are more or less ethnographical or geographical fixed quantities, Russia's kinship and boundaries are like the ever increasing circumference of some elastic circle—their only points of resistance or weakness being either where she comes into contact with rivals or where her own overbearing manner has alienated some unit formerly a source of strength, as was the case with Poland."[22] Russia's expansion was depicted almost as a force of nature—a wildfire raging across the grasslands of the Eurasian steppe.

Russians in the first decade of the 1900s most certainly concurred with the opinion of foreign observers that the course of Russian expansion since the sixteenth century was the inevitable product of Muscovy's location—Russia's own "manifest destiny." They were also convinced that Russia's territorial extent was one of the major factors in guaranteeing its position as a Great Power. The loss of even one *verst* would be an invitation to the partition of its borderlands. Members of the Russian elite, too, believed in Russia's strength by virtue of the vastness of its territory, and had an unshaking faith in the importance of territorial size that found its expression in Fedor Tiutchev's 1849 poem, "Russkaia geografiia" (Russian Geography). In the poem, Tiutchev sketched out the frontiers of a Russo-Slavic realm, with Moscow, St. Petersburg, and Constantinople as its capitals, drained by seven great rivers, extending "from the Nile to the Neva, from the Elbe to China, from the Volga to the Euphrates, from the Ganges to the Danube."[23]

However, the Russian elite was also confronted with the paradoxical fragility that came with this size. In the first decade of the 1900s, the huge population of this equally huge territory was only barely "Russian," and concern for the preservation of Russia's borders led the government and the elite—across all of Russia's wide political spectrum—into the heart of the so-called "national question" (*natsional'nyi vopros*). This question posed a formidable challenge to Russia's survival as a Great Power. As the American observer Wolf von Schierbrand remarked in his 1904 volume *Russia: Her Strength and Weakness*, the country's weakness as a Great Power lay precisely in its size—which required vast outlays of manpower and capital to defend and maintain.[24]

On the basis of firsthand observation, von Schierbrand pointed to Russian weakness in the diversity of the multiethnic population flung across the vast distances of the empire and barely governed from the center; in the paucity of its domestic funds and its consequent reliance on foreign capital; in the backwardness of its agricultural methods, with the consequent difficulties of feeding its population and the persistence of famines; in the decline of the nobility and the agrarian crisis; in the decay of the Church and its moral standing in rural areas; in the slow growth of the middle class; in the policy of russification and growing interethnic conflict; and in the burden of a cumbersome bureaucracy at the center. For von Schierbrand, writing in 1904, Russia was not a Great Power but rather a country teetering on the edge of domestic disaster, driven toward "success abroad" by an elite "puffed up with vainglory and a sense of supposed illimitable power and irresponsibility."[25] Elsewhere he noted that "Russia [was] invulnerable only in one narrow, definite sense—in the sense of her unwieldiness."[26]

Trouble in the Imperial Borderlands

In 1897, the imperial census revealed that "Great" or ethnic Russians accounted for only 43.3 percent of the total population of the empire.[27] Only with the inclusion of the so-called "White" and "Little" Russians—the Belarusians and Ukrainians—was this proportion raised to 65.5 percent and a seeming majority. The other 35.5 percent non–East Slavic population of the empire, including Poles, Jews, Germans, Tatars, Balts, and the disparate peoples of the Caucasus, were spread across the marginal areas of the empire annexed by Russia over the course of the eighteenth and nineteenth centuries.[28] In many cases, ethnic Russians were vastly outnumbered by the non-Russian population. In the Caucasus, for example, ethnic Russians accounted for only 4.9 percent of the total population.[29]

The growth of national movements in these regions in the nineteenth century among the non-Russian peoples of the empire was in part the product of modernization and economic development. The movements were radicalized, however, by policies of russification and repression begun by Alexander III in the 1880s and continued by Nicholas II in the 1890s. Given the minority position of the Great Russian population in the empire, the assimilation of these regions and their consolidation with the center was seen as one of the most important tasks of both internal and external Russian governmental policy. There was, however, no uniform policy for carrying out this task and different areas received different treatment over time. The Russian government directed most of its assimilation efforts against those nationalities whose numerical strength or historical tradition and economic conditions gave them a more independent status. The tsarist regime saw these nationalities as harboring separatist ideas and demands for political autonomy that threatened the unity of the empire.

Poland and the northwestern region were subjected to a policy of "denationalization" much earlier than other regions. In the reign of Nicholas I, after the first Polish rebellion of 1830–1831, a whole system of measures was implemented by the government to subordinate the Kingdom of Poland and reduce its status to a mere "institution" of the empire. After the Polish uprising of 1863, the tsarist regime actively pursued a policy of promoting the official use of the Russian language, and ethnic Poles were ousted, as far as possible, from all spheres of public life. Under Alexander III and the principle of "Russia for the Russians" (*Rossiia dlia russkikh*), ethnic Russian bureaucrats were also sent out to staff the administrations of most regions, including Poland, the Baltics, and the Caucasus. Special Russian printing presses were also established in these areas.

The russification policy intensified in the 1890s with the creation of Russian schools in Poland and Armenia; the dispatching of Russian workers to the borderlands to expand railroads and ethnic Russian influence; attempts to reduce national sentiment and discredit local institutions; the confiscation of Church property from denominations other than Russian Orthodox; and actions to displace local landowners from their land—especially the Baltic Germans and the Poles—in the name of freeing the peasants. This policy had the effect of galvanizing the non-Russian elites in the empire's borderlands and encouraging revolt.

By 1905, all of the major national movements in the Russian Empire had created political parties, and 32 of their representatives had gained seats in the First Duma. Non-ethnic Russians accounted for almost half of the deputies of all parties in this Duma. Most of the national movements did not, it should be stressed, demand the dissolution of the Russian Empire; instead, in Duma debates the consensus favored the establishment of regional autonomy and equal rights for all nationalities.[30] Only the Poles, like the Chechens in the 1990s, adopted a more radical stance. In the First Duma, the Polish parties attempted to chart an independent course and to refrain from joining factions on either the Right or the Left in order to stress their commitment to Poland's freedom.

Polish hostility to the regime, terrorist activity by national movements, and fears that autonomy would lead to the unraveling of the empire were major factors in making the national question one of the most pressing issues for Russian government officials, would-be reformers, and revolutionaries from 1905 to 1914. Resolving the national question was crucial to the preservation of the Russian Empire's territorial integrity.

Elite Fears about the Loss of Russia's Borderlands

In 1906, the journal *Okrainy Rossii* (Russia's Borderlands) was established by a small group of St. Petersburg intellectuals espousing Great (ethnic) Russian nationalist ideals with the specific intent of drawing attention to the problems of maintaining both Russia's control over its borderlands and the dominant position of ethnic Russians in these territories. In the six years of its publication, articles in the journal reflected growing anxiety over the potential loss of Russian territory.

In the preamble to the journal, for example, the editorial board noted that separatism in the borderlands was one of the most significant results of the social and political upheavals in Russia after the Russo-Japanese War, and that these separatist tendencies had even received support from Russian political parties in the State Duma. Finland, Poland, and the Caucasus were all trying to pull away from the Russian state, and Russian political power was ceding ground by attempting to respond to the separatist aspirations of the borderlands. The editorial board asserted that those who professed that they were in favor of "a united, undivided, and whole Russia" could not but be frightened for the future of the state. *Okrainy Rossii* had thus been founded "for the unity of Russia, the great history of the Russian state, the future of the Russian Empire with honor and glory."[31]

In an April 1906 editorial, the journal drew a direct link between Russia's Great Power status and its borderlands. In a piece discussing the frequent debates in the Russian Duma over the problems of national separatism, it stressed that the borderlands should be brought administratively and culturally closer to the center in order to prevent the disintegration of Russia.[32] The editorial argued that, while members of the Russian intelligentsia were divided over the form of government that should prevail in Russia, all the parties in the Duma should be united on the position that above all Russia must be "a strong national power."

The journal noted that the history of other European powers in the nineteenth century had demonstrated that empires and great powers were built on the basis of a strong and vigorous nation, and that the Duma should concentrate on pulling together the "Russians" (i.e., ethnic Russians, Ukrainians, and Belarusians) and other peoples scattered around the European and Asian borders of the empire into a unified whole. The editors stressed that the West was poised to seize some of Russia's territory at the first sign of weakness, and the lack of a national self-consciousness was just such a sign. Rather than appease these centrifugal tendencies and in order to keep the West at bay, the Russian government, together with the Duma, would have to clamp down on the borderlands to reduce and destroy the harmful effects of separatism on the state. All of Russia's borderlands were appendages to the organism of the monolithic Russian state and were crucial to its survival.[33]

This concept of the importance of Russia's borderlands to the survival of the state was not limited to the editors of *Okrainy Rossii*. The celebrated Russian politician and writer Petr Struve, for example, made the same points in a lecture at Cambridge University in England in August 1916, noting that the most fertile provinces of Russia were situated in new lands opened up in the late eighteenth and early nineteenth centuries. He also noted that some of its largest population centers were in its borderlands in Ukraine, whose very name—*Ukraina*—implied a border.[34] Even Russia's capital, St. Petersburg, was on new territory on the Baltic coast.

Proceeding from such ideas, *Okrainy Rossii* criticized initial plans by the Kadet Party in the Duma in the fall of 1906 to grant autonomy to some of the distinct territories in the empire—particularly Finland and Poland. One commentator, Arkadii Chernyi, asserted that if autonomy were given to all of Russia's borderlands, and "Russia" was reduced to the position of one of the many units, then "it would be better simply to erase the word Russia from the lexicon. Our unfortunate, deprived center would not even be worth calling the Muscovite state: it would be better to break it up as in the old days into an *appanage* system of principalities, restore the age-old system, and invite the princes in . . . only for military campaigns against neighboring appanages."[35] By virtue of her inexorable expansion over the centuries, Russia as both a state and a Great Power was, therefore, seen as the sum of its disparate territories. If the borderlands went, so too would the center.

Platon Kulakovskii, the editor of *Okrainy Rossii*, argued that Russia's non-Russian peoples and its vast territories had made the state into a world power, opening doors for the realization of global plans.[36] He noted that having united with Georgia, for example, Russia had opened a door not only to Central Asia, but also to the fulfillment of the great mission of protecting the Russian people from invasion from the Asiatic and Muslim East. Having seized the Baltic region and then Poland, Russia had pushed into the heart of Europe, bringing Western and Eastern Europe together and setting for itself the task of leading Slavdom.[37]

Poland, in particular, was seen as crucial to Russia's status as a Great Power. Russia's annexation of parts of the Polish-Lithuanian Commonwealth under Catherine the Great—although uniformly denounced by European observers—had been seen as a testament to Russia's strength and had raised fears about her further expansion. The Polish Partitions were the apogee of eighteenth-century European Great Power politics, with Russia, Prussia, and Austria all taking their share of a weakened Polish state. As the seizure of Poland had confirmed Russia's rise in the eighteenth century, so its loss in the twentieth century would underscore its decline. If Russia lost Poland, members of the Russian elite argued, so, too, would it lose the rest of its borderlands, and its firm and well-protected place in the world. In sum, Russia would be swept from the international stage.[38]

The "Polish Question" and the Borderlands

In 1908, losing Poland became a real possibility for the Russian Empire after Austria-Hungary's annexation of the South Slavic province of Bosnia-Herzegovina. With this annexation, and the incorporation of the province's South Slavic inhabitants into a German-dominated state, the number of Slavs in Austria was increased by 1.8 million to 17 million. This gave added impetus to a movement among Austrian Slavs in favor of reconfiguring the Austro-Hungarian Empire to create a trilateral federation of Austria, Hungary, and a new

Slavic entity, or, alternatively, to grant autonomy to each of the Slavic peoples.[39] Had this happened, it would inevitably have resulted in a degree of autonomy for Austro-Hungary's Polish population, centered around Cracow, and would have increased the separatist demands of Poles within Russia.

In Poland and the "Polish question," the issues of Russia's borderlands and the internal and external position of the state collided. Neo-Slav ideology and the idea of Slavic unity had experienced a revival at the turn of the century.[40] Russia was the largest Slavic power, with two-thirds of "Slavdom's" total population of 150 million. But Slavdom was not complete without Poland. There could be no Slavic cultural or political unity if the Poles stood aside. Poland, however, was seen by the majority of Russian neo-Slav ideologues as individualistic and ethnocentric, rather than focused on Slavdom in general. As a Catholic (rather than Orthodox) Slavic people, Poles offered an alternative view of the future of the Slavs in Europe. Members of the Russian elite, and especially the contributors to *Okrainy Rossii*, believed that Poland therefore entertained fantasies of destroying and dominating Russia and of leading Slavdom itself. Russia thus could not afford to show any signs of weakness toward the Poles, who were attempting to use the revolutionary and liberation movements within Russia to bring about the empire's disintegration.[41]

As a result of the annexation of Bosnia-Herzegovina, Austria had in fact become, to all intents and purposes, a second "Slavic" power in Europe. As such, it could potentially rival Russia as a magnet for the Catholic Slavs—the Czechs, Slovenes, and Croats in addition to the Poles. Beyond the Catholic Slavs, if a trilateral federal arrangement were to be realized in Austria, it might also act as a beacon for the "Little Russians" (Ukrainians). In this period, Ukrainians were already putting forward their demands for autonomy within the Russian Empire. They also had their own co-nationals in the Carpathian borderlands of the Austro-Hungarian Empire and in the region around the city of Lviv (Lwów, Lemberg). This threatened the barely dominant position of Great Russians within the empire, and raised the prospect of the loss of key borderland territories and a significant portion of Russia's population.

Ideas of the organic link between the Russian center, Poland, and the other borderlands were common among Russian officials.[42] For example, in speeches before the Duma in 1907, Prime Minister Petr Stolypin called for the center and the borderlands to pull together in the hour of Russia's weakness to make the state strong again. He urged Poland and other regions to forego demands for autonomy and to serve the goals of the state as a whole.[43] "Decentralization," he argued, could "come only from the fullness of strength." Decentralization and autonomy at a time of weakness would simply pull apart the threads binding the center and the borderlands and result in the disintegration of the empire. Addressing the Duma's Polish deputies, Stolypin asserted that "all citizens of the empire" should realize that "the greatest blessing of all is to be a Russian citizen," and that they should "carry that name as high as the citizens of Rome carried their name in their time"; then they will "call themselves citizens of the 'first category' and receive all the rights that proceed from this." Stolypin noted that all of the reforms he had initiated after the upheavals of 1905–1906 were aimed at elevating Russia's greatness and thus at increasing the benefits flowing to all its citizens. He urged Russians to look to the West, where there were no examples of struggle against the central power, only the utmost efforts to serve its goals.[44]

In sum, in the first part of the 1900s, fears of Russia's territorial disintegration and the consequent loss of its Great Power position were widespread across the Russian political spectrum and among the intelligentsia. There was a consensus that disintegration would be a catastrophe, but no consensus whatsoever on how to bring the recalcitrant borderlands back into the imperial fold. By the beginning of the twentieth century, the national question had become one of the major issues in Russian domestic and international politics and was intrinsically tied to the revolutionary movement.

Territory and the National Question in the 1990s

In the 1990s, Russia was still the largest country in the world in terms of land mass. However, its post-Soviet population of some 148 million—barely half of the 290 million of the USSR—ranked it well behind China, India, the United States, Indonesia, and Brazil. And whereas its population had been growing steadily in the early 1900s, Russia's population in the 1990s was in dramatic decline. From 1992 to 1996, the country experienced its sharpest population decline since World War II. Deaths exceeded births and life expectancy dropped precipitously.[45] In the face of this demographic crisis, Russia's territorial extent assumed even greater importance.

Although the population of the Russian Federation was in serious decline in the 1990s, "Great Russians" actually constituted a majority—Russia after 1991 was a predominantly ethnic Russian state. While ethnic Russians accounted for only around 40 percent and 50 percent of the total population of the Russian Empire and the USSR respectively, in the new Russian Federation, they constituted 82 percent of the total population.[46] However, Russia's vast territory still had a significant non-Russian population—around 27 million people representing approximately 100 different ethnic groups—which raised the same set of questions at the end of the century as it had at its beginning.

As in the first decades of the century, the relationship between the Russian center and the borderlands—the regions of the Russian Federation—was extremely complicated. Under Gorbachev, nationalist groups in the union republics, especially in the Caucasus and the Baltic states, demanded the revision of Soviet internal borders, increased autonomy from the center, and eventually, independence. Following the dissolution of the Soviet Union and the emergence of a de facto independent Russian Federation in December 1991, demands for territorial and political change from both autonomous regions and administrative units within Russia itself were also given a new impetus. Prior to December 1991, following the independence of the adjacent republics of Georgia, Azerbaijan, and Armenia, Russia's North Caucasus republic of Chechnya also declared its independence from the Federation.

At the end of 1991, Chechnya's declaration of independence and signs of dissent in other national republics suggested that the Russian Federation would follow the USSR down the path of disintegration.[47] Fears of disintegration were heightened in February 1992, when a Federal Treaty designed to create a new compact between the federal center and its 89 administrative units was rejected by both Chechnya and Tatarstan, and criticized by republics such as Yakutia and Bashkortostan.[48] Russia's oblasts (the basic non-national administrative units) protested what they saw as special privileges accorded to the Federation's national republics, demanding equal treatment and increased authority over local economic and political issues. Territorial disputes in the Federation grew increasingly tense. In October 1992, in the wake of the creation of a separate republic of Ingushetia, armed conflict broke out between Ossetians and the Ingush in the Prigorodnyi district of North Ossetia over the jurisdiction of the territory. As in the period between 1905 and 1914, the resolution of the "national question" became a major issue in post-1991 Russian politics.

The Russian government's response to the challenge from the regions was both ad hoc and contradictory—vacillating between legislative measures and bilateral treaties, police action, and military intervention and repression. After the Federal Treaty failed in 1992, the 1993 Russian Constitution marked a further attempt at delimiting powers between the center and the regions. The chapters dealing with the respective authorities of the Federation and the administrative units were submitted to the republics and regions for approval in the referendum on the Constitution in December 1993. A number of republics that had initially signed the Federal Treaty, however, now rejected the constitutional provisions on the grounds that they violated the original provisions of the treaty. To prevent its relations with the regions from falling into legal limbo in the wake of these rejections, Moscow began to conclude bilateral treaties with key republics. The first of these Treaties on Delimitation and Delegation of Authority was signed between the Russian Federation and Tatarstan in February 1994.

As far as Chechnya was concerned, after 1991, the Russian government had made a half-hearted effort to negotiate with its leadership in order to bring the republic back into the Federation, and then resorted to the active support of the Chechen opposition and the promotion of coups. In December 1994, after a failed attempt to overthrow the anti-Moscow government the previous summer and the capture of Russian operatives by Chechen forces, the Russian government launched a full-scale military assault on Chechnya. The assault led to the largest military campaign on Russian soil since World War II, with between 40,000 and 100,000 civilian casualties,[49] and Russia's most significant military defeat since Afghanistan. In August 1996, after the collapse of the over-extended Russian military as an effective fighting force, the Russian government was forced to conclude a truce. In a peace agreement signed on 12 May 1997, Moscow agreed to eschew military intervention in its conflict with Chechnya and to conclude a bilateral treaty on future relations. Although Chechnya's independence was not recognized, the republic was de facto beyond the political jurisdiction of the Russian state.

The debacle in Chechnya emboldened other republics and regions to demand the devolution of powers. Between 1994 and 1996, the Russian Federation was forced to negotiate bilateral treaties with key republics and regions including Sakha-Yakutia, the heart of Russia's diamond industry; Bashkortostan, a major oil-producing region; republics neighboring Chechnya in the northern Caucasus; Perm; Irkutsk; Kaliningrad; Ekaterinburg; Nizhny Novgorod; St. Petersburg; and Leningrad Oblast.[50] In the wake of the May 1997 peace agreement with Chechnya, bilateral treaties became the primary mechanism for regulating Moscow's relations with its entire periphery as well as a means Russia's regions could use to force the decentralization of the state.

The Importance of Russian Territory in the 1990s

Post-Soviet Russia's "national questions" were, therefore, how to reform the administrative structure of the Federation given the preexisting Soviet-era hierarchy of national-territorial units, how to deal with the secession of Chechnya and the demands for increased autonomy from other units, and how to unite and mobilize ethnic Russians and non-ethnic Russians for political and economic reform of the state. The majority of the 27 million non-Russians in the Russian Federation were scattered throughout the country, but there were significant territorial concentrations of around 4 million non-ethnic Russians along the Federation's southern border in the North Caucasus, and of approximately 5 million Tatars, Chuvash, Bashkirs, Mordvins, and other related peoples in the Urals and the upper Volga region.

As in the early 1900s, Russians in the 1990s saw these territories and their populations not as alien lands and peoples, but as integral parts of the state. For example, Valerii Tishkov, one of Russia's leading ethnographers, remarked that "Russia in its new borders is a historical fact, not the result of irresponsible political improvisation. It is a generally recognized geographical entity. Its economic, communication, and administrative infrastructures have been set and developed over the course of the seventy years when it existed as a constituent part of the Soviet Union."[51]

Retaining those borders became the major concern of the Russian elite after 1991. Ramazan Abdulatipov, one of the most prominent politicians from the North Caucasus region—and as of July 1997 Russia's Deputy Prime Minister for nationality and regional issues—remarked in July 1996: "The problem of maintaining the state and territorial integrity of the Russian Federation is the key problem in the current stage of the development of the Russian state, especially after the dissolution of the Soviet Union and the possibility of the transfer of this variant to the Russian Federation."[52]

Compounding this problem was the fact that significant populations of ethnic Russians now lived outside the borders of the Russian state. The problem of Russians in the borderlands, identified by the authors of *Okrainy Rossii* in the first decade of the century, had in the 1990s also become the problem of Russians living in the "Near Abroad." According to most estimates, there were around 20 million of them, scattered across all of the former republics of the USSR, with the largest concentrations of 11 million and 6 million in Ukraine and Kazakhstan respectively. For the first time since the "gathering of the Russian lands," the "Russian national entity" was territorially divided and ethnic Russians had become ethnic minorities in the borderlands of other states. In the estimation of Russian nationalists, Russians had become the victims of repression and persecution in the Baltics and elsewhere in the former Soviet Union in the 1990s.

The dynamic of Russian ethnic and territorial politics had changed dramatically between the beginning and the end of the twentieth century. The fate of Russians in the "Near Abroad" was as potent an issue in the 1990s as the fate of the empire's borderlands and that of fellow Slavs in the Balkans had been before World War I. Russian elites still identified strongly with those territories of the former Russian and Soviet Empires now transformed into foreign lands through the creation of international borders.

It was also not just ethnic Russians who had been marooned beyond the borders of the state, but within the state, members of the elite with mixed parentage were disoriented by the sudden contraction of "Russia" and the loss of territories associated with it for centuries. For example, Amangel'dy Tuleev, the communist governor of Russia's Kemerovo Oblast, stated in the winter of 1994: "I cannot live like it is now [*sic*]. There is no place for me to live until I can reintegrate Russia, Kazakhstan, Ukraine, and Belarus. For me as an individual, today's situation is the end of everything. And there are millions, about thirty million people such as myself, who have mixed blood, mixed marriages, and mixed children."[53]

Indeed, surveys taken across Russia in 1993 showed that a good 70 percent of the population viewed the dismemberment of the Soviet state negatively. Russians' psychological attachment to the "natural boundaries" of the state, sketched out by Tiutchev, was as strong at the end of the century as it was at the beginning.

The "Chechen Question" and the Borderlands

In the 1990s, the territorial image of Russia and the preservation of the territorial extent so important to Russia's position as a Great Power were seriously threatened by the secession of Chechnya. Chechnya was to Russia in the 1990s what Poland was to Russia in the early 1900s.

Chechnya and the North Caucasus were the last strategic areas to be incorporated into the Russian Empire in the nineteenth century—long after the Baltic lands, and even after the southern Caucasian territories of Georgia, Armenia, and Azerbaijan. In contrast to other territories of the Russian Empire, no compacts had been made with local elites or bilateral treaties signed. Instead, the northern Caucasus was subjugated and incorporated militarily. In the so-called Caucasian Wars of the mid-nineteenth century, the people of the northern Caucasus held out against the Russian army for almost 40 years, and it was not until 1865 that the region was "pacified." Chechnya was at the heart of this opposition and was never fully assimilated into the empire. Russian and Soviet repression precluded the kind of integration of the region into the rest of the Russian lands that had taken place in Tatarstan, Siberia, and elsewhere through the co-opting of elites. After 1991, Chechnya took the place of Poland, Finland, and other borderlands of the Russian Empire in terms of confrontation with the center over autonomy and, ultimately, independence.

On a fundamental level, the future of Russia and its continued existence as the Russian Federation were seen to be at stake in Moscow's dispute with Chechnya after the republic's secession—as had been the case in the earlier situation involving Poland. In December 1994, the Russian government's initial justification for launching the war was actually that it was necessary in order to protect Russia's territorial integrity. Government officials expressed fears about the so-called "domino effect" of Chechnya's secession—a rash of copycat secessions by other republics in the North Caucasus and elsewhere in the Federation. The feared "domino effect" was, however, certainly unlikely at this juncture. The general trend in the Russian Federation after 1991 was toward decentralization rather than secession. Chechnya was exceptional in its pursuit of independence.

Even without a string of secessions, however, Chechnya did pose a serious threat to the future of Russia. The nature of this threat was simply not well articulated by the Russian political elite. What Chechnya threatened was the continued legitimacy of the Russian Federation in its geographic and administrative configuration. Chechnya challenged an already shaky post-Soviet status quo in the same manner that Polish demands for autonomy in the early 1900s had raised the possibility of the reconfiguration of the Russian Empire. With its secession, Chechnya implied that the Russian Federation's existing borders and administrative structure were illegitimate and open to radical change.

Like Poland after 1905, Chechnya after 1991 seemed to raise questions about Russia's geopolitical position in Eurasia and its Great Power status. Chechen leadership of the Confederation of the Peoples of the Caucasus gave rise to fears about the creation of a Muslim confederation of states extending from the Caspian to the Black Sea, and cutting off Russia from the South. These fears were reminiscent of the earlier Russian nationalists' fears about the formation of an anti-Russian Slavic coalition led by Catholic Poland in the Balkans and East-Central Europe.[54] The Confederation's objective was the restoration of the 1918 Mountain Republic of the North Caucasus, created after the collapse of the Russian Empire, which was under the protection of Turkey and centered in Dagestan. The Chechen-inspired version had its capital in Sukhumi in Abkhazia, and had full control of the Abkhazian Black Sea coastline and ports. Although by 1993 the Confederation had lost its vigor as a political force because of the individual preoccupations of the northern Caucasian republics, politicians in Moscow, including Ramazan Abdulatipov, were still concerned about the possibility of a "plot against Russian interests."[55]

The 1994–1996 war in Chechnya marked the culmination of the alienation between Chechnya and Russia. It also undermined Moscow's position in other republics in the North Caucasus, increasing tension in the region as well as skepticism about the central government's intentions. In polls conducted in 1993, the majority of Chechens had indicated that they identified themselves with their republic, rather than with the Russian Federation.[56] Between 1994 and 1996, Russia's assault on the republic also demonstrated that Chechnya was not considered part of Russia per se, but rather a remnant of the empire in the nineteenth-century sense: something strategic to be conquered, crushed, and subdued. The personal connection between Chechens in the borderlands and Russians in the center was lost.

After Chechnya's secession in 1991, a hostile attitude not only toward Chechens, but toward all indigenous peoples of the North Caucasus emerged among ordinary Russians. This attitude was reflected in the actions of the Moscow city authorities, which in 1992 began to crack down on traders and vendors from the region and from the southern Caucasus, blaming them for the rise of crime since the collapse of the USSR, and expelling them from the capital. The collective term *litsa kavkazskoi natsional'nosti* (people of Caucasian nationality) was coined by the Moscow government and came into official usage—despite the fact that the "Caucasians" were a collection of disparate peoples and not a unified ethnic group. Another incident that illuminated the prevailing attitude toward Chechens and North Caucasians was the seizure of hostages from the Dagestani town of Kizlyar and the standoff with Russian troops in the nearby village of Pervomaiskoe in January 1996. Although the civilian hostages were members of indigenous Dagestani groups and not ethnic Chechens, the official statements on the incident and reports in the Russian media indicated that the hostages were viewed in the same terms as the Chechens. There were repeated references to the Russian troops as *nashi* (ours), as distinct from the hostages, who were technically all Russian citizens.[57]

In addition, after Aleksandr Lebed's announcement in September 1996 that a total of 80,000 to 100,000 civilians had died in the war in Chechnya, there was no appreciable increase in the level of protests at the center—even though until this juncture the highest official casualty figures had been in the region of 35,000. Indeed, throughout the war, the main motivating factor for domestic protest against the war was the high level of *military* casualties; Russian soldiers' mothers consistently led the anti-war movement. The bulk of civilian casualties in the war were ethnic Chechens. Although in fact large numbers of ethnic Russian civilians were killed in full-scale artillery and air attacks on the Chechen capital of Grozny, the majority of these were long-term residents of the republic with few ties to the center. With a few notable exceptions such as Russian human rights activist Sergei Kovalev, those protesting the civilian casualties were, for the most part, leaders of North Caucasian diaspora groups and non-ethnic Russian political leaders like Presidents Shaimiev of Tatarstan and Aushev of Ingushetia, who attempted to mediate the conflict. This was in stark contrast to the consistent protests in the Russian Duma and in the Russian government over the discriminatory treatment of ethnic Russians in the Baltic states, and to the collective horror at a proportionally tiny number of ethnic Russian civilian deaths during a battle with Chechen hostage-takers in Budennovsk.

Chechnya's Challenge to Russia's Territorial Integrity

Ultimately, as a result of the duration of the war, the growing hostility toward Chechens and other North Caucasians, and the repeated reverses and high losses of the Russian military, the very issue of Russia's territorial integrity was brought into question. By 1996, there was an increasing willingness among ethnic Russians in Moscow and elsewhere to contemplate Chechnya's independence. For example, in September 1996, the *St. Petersburg Times* reported that the number of Russians in favor of granting full independence to Chechnya had doubled since the spring of 1996.[58]

This survey and others supported the contention that the Chechens and their territory had become popularly perceived as *ne nashi*—"not ours"—and not Russian. In government circles, too, after the summer of 1996, there was a gradual shift in nomenclature. In place of the initial references to the Chechen republic as a "breakaway region," to the Chechen government of Dzhokhar Dudaev as "terrorists," and to the Chechen fighting forces as "bandits" and "illegal formations,"[59] some Russian politicians began to talk of the Chechens and the republic of Chechnya as a separate political entity.[60]

Until the summer of 1996, Moscow had been extremely careful to delegitimize the Chechen struggle, and to emphasize that Chechnya was a rebellious sub-unit of Russia with no right to demand either concessions from the center or recognition as a "subject of international law."[61] However, the statement of principles in Aleksandr Lebed's preliminary peace accord of 30 August 1996 clearly referred to the Chechen Republic as an equal negotiating partner, with the right to regulate its relations with Russia "in accordance with generally recognized norms of international law." The statement also laid the groundwork for a possible referendum on Chechnya's independence by 31 December 2001.[62]

Although this peace accord was extremely controversial, and was denounced by prominent members of both the government and the parliament, political and popular sentiment did seem to be evolving in the direction of accepting the possibility, and perhaps the inevitability, of Chechnya's eventual separation from Russia.[63] Were it to happen, this separation would mark the partial disintegration of the post-Soviet Russian state.

Territory and Power after Chechnya

Letting Chechnya go, however, would not mean that other territories more closely associated with the Russian state would be easily relinquished, especially as far as the elites were concerned. For example, a poll conducted in early November 1996 indicated that 62 percent of Russians surveyed were opposed to the idea of establishing the regions' right to secede in the constitution. Professionals and members of the educated elite who participated in the survey were more opposed to the right of secession than were members of the working class.[64]

Russia's territory was still equated with its strength as a state and thus its standing in the international arena. The war in Chechnya had tarnished Russia's international image. It had led to a loss of credibility in key institutions such as the Council of Europe, where Russia came under criticism for the flagrant abuse of human rights in the course of the conflict. Furthermore, Russia's failure to bring a small republic with a population of slightly more than one million back under central control cast doubt on the state's ability to project its power. The August 1996 peace accords in Khasavyurt, spearheaded by Lebed, were frequently referred to in the Russian press and Parliament in terms of Great Russia's humiliation by little Chechnya.[65] Russia could not afford to let something like this happen again.

This fact was underscored in 1997–1998, in the wake of the war in Chechnya, by elite reaction to Japanese overtures toward Russia for the return of the southern Kurile Islands, which had been seized and annexed by Stalin at the end of World War II. In spite of the fact that these islands represented a tiny fraction of Russian territory, were located on its very fringes in the farthest Far East, and were sparsely populated and desperately poor, the Russian elite would not consider their transfer to Japan.

As the prominent Russian commentator Aleksei Pushkov noted in an article on the islands in *Nezavisimaia gazeta* in April 1998, the main problem for Russians was psychological. Relinquishing the islands "would confirm the obvious trend toward the 'shrinking' of Russia's territory, which has been going on over a good dozen years now," and was emphasized "by the loss of internationally recognized Russian territories—[beginning] with the separation *de facto* of . . . Chechnya." Pushkov went on to stress that "returning the Southern Kurile Islands today would be tantamount to nothing less than the confirmation of Russia's inability to keep its own territory intact"; and further, that "only a strong country can give up part of its territory in the name of certain aims or considerations. Russia is a weak state today."[66]

Echoing his predecessors who wrote in *Okrainy Rossii* in the late imperial period, Pushkov worried that giving up the Kurile Islands—a mere *verst* of Russian territory—would be a definitive recognition of Russia's weakness and would open up the country to territorial claims from other neighbors: from Finland for Karelia and from Germany for Kaliningrad. It would, in short, lead to the unraveling of the Russian state.

Conclusion

For members of the Russian elite in the 1990s, like Aleksei Pushkov, Russia's existence as a state was as much linked to the size and configuration of its territory as it had been for the elite in the early 1900s. Russian elites in the 1990s were the prisoners of Russia's past and its expansion across the Eurasian landmass from the marches of Poland to the outermost islands in the Pacific Ocean. Their conception of Russia was still shaped by the image of the borders of its geopolitical space sketched out by Tiutchev.

Ironically, in spite of the secession of Chechnya and demands for autonomy in the regions, Russia was in a stronger position as a state internally in the 1990s than it was in the early 1900s when the center was under siege from overtly nationalist and even revolutionary movements in almost all of its borderlands. In the 1990s, with the exception of Chechnya, none of the territories of the Russian Federation sought secession. There was a consensus that political and economic reform had to take place and that the state had to be kept together—although there was no agreement on how exactly this should be done. But Chechnya's resistance in the 1990s, like Poland's around the turn of the century, had badly frightened the elite. By the end of the 1990s, preserving Russia's territory had become more important than improving relations with a potential ally, as in the case of Japan and the Kurile Islands.

As the twentieth century drew to a close, the key question for the elite was the same as it had been at the century's beginning: Could Russia still be great (*velikaia*) in power by being great (*bol'shaia*) in size? The Russian elite thought that the answer was yes; indeed that *only* by being great in size could Russia be great in power. But international observers in America and elsewhere, having witnessed the tragedy of Chechnya, might be tempted to draw the conclusion reached by Wolf von Schierbrand in 1904: namely, that Russia's fundamental *weakness* lay in its size, and that "Russia is invulnerable only in one narrow sense—in the sense of her unwieldiness."

NOTES

1.   Valerii Tishkov, *Ethnicity, Nationalism, and Conflict in and after the Soviet Union: The Mind Aflame* (London, 1997), pp. 254–55.

2.   The Moscow Director of the Society for the Preservation of Russian Monuments and Culture, cited in Nicole Prevost-Logan, "Moscow Reclaims its Past," *Archaeology* 1997 (July/August): 26.

3.   Konstantin Azadovskii, "Russia's Silver Age, Yesterday and Today," in *Remaking Russia: Voices From Within*, ed. Heyward Isham (New York, 1995), p. 89.

4.   This issue is discussed in detail in my dissertation, which was written under the guidance of Akira Iriye, Richard Pipes, and Roman Szporluk. Fiona Hill, "In Search of Great Russia: Elites, Ideas, Power, the State, and the Pre-Revolutionary Past in the New Russia, 1991–1996," Ph.D. dissertation, Harvard University, 1998.

5.   Orlando Figes, *A People's Tragedy: A History of the Russian Revolution* (New York, 1996), pp. 3–34.

6.   See Prevost-Logan, "Moscow Reclaims its Past."

7.   The term "Silver Age" is used to distinguish it from the imperial "Golden Age" of Peter and Catherine the Great, and the cultural "Golden Age" of Alexander Pushkin in the early to mid-nineteenth century. See Azadovskii, "Russia's Silver Age." At the end of the nineteenth century and the beginning of the twentieth century, Russia experienced a cultural renaissance with the flourishing of the literary, visual, material, and musical arts, and new techniques in theater and ballet. For a general discussion of the achievements of this period see also Nicholas Riasanovsky, *A History of Russia*, 3rd ed. (New York, 1977), pp. 483–502.

8.   Note, for example, the title of British historian Dominic Lieven's biography of the last Russian tsar, *Nicholas II: Twilight of the Empire* (New York, 1993).

9.   Russian Foreign Minister Evgenii Primakov, in a speech delivered on 12 January 1996. See Chrystia Freeland, "Russia Aims to Regain Status of a Great Power," *Financial Times* 13–14 January 1996.

10. See Paul Kennedy, *The Rise and Fall of the Great Powers: Economic Change and Military Conflict from 1500–2000* (New York, 1987).

11. Dominic Lieven, *Russia and the Origins of the First World War* (New York, 1983), pp. 19–20.

12. Quoted in ibid., p. 94.

13. Lieven, *Nicholas II*, p. 190.

14. Andrei Kokoshin, "Natsional'naia bezopasnost' i voennaia moshch' Rossii" (final chapter of draft book; Moscow, 1995), p. 248. [Copy of draft obtained from author for review.]

15. Aleksandr Panarin, "Geopoliticheskii pessimizm protiv tsivilizovannogo optimizma," *Znamia* 1994 (6).

16. Valerii Dement'ev and Anton Surikov, "Strategy for Reforming the Military Forces of the Russian Federation," *Nezavisimaia gazeta* 11 April 1996 [=English reprint in *The Estonian Review* (Estonian Ministry of Foreign Affairs) 19 April 1996].

17. See, for example, Nina Petrova, "Russia's Foreign Policy Must Become Presidential: The Reasons for and the Consequences of Defeats for Andrei Kozyrev's Diplomacy," *Nezavisimaia gazeta* (English version) 17 May 1995.

18. See Klaus Knorr, *Power and Wealth: The Political Economy of International Power* (New York, 1973).

19. Stepniak (Sergei Kravchinsky), *The Russian Storm-Cloud; or, Russia in Her Relations to Neighbouring Countries* (London, 1886).

20. Francis Henry Skrine, *The Expansion of Russia* (Cambridge, 1915), p. 1.

21. Ibid., p. 6.

22. Louis G. Redmond-Howard, ed., *The Nations of the War* (London, 1914), pp. 84–85.

23. Fedor Tiutchev, *Polnoe sobranie stikhotvorenii* (Leningrad, 1987).

24. Wolf von Schierbrand, *Russia: Her Strength and Weakness. A Study of the Present Conditions of the Russian Empire, With an Analysis of its Resources and a Forecast of its Future* (New York and London, 1904).

25. Ibid., p. 297.

26. Ibid., p. 48.

27. In fact, the percentage of ethnic Russians was lower than 43 percent, as the 1897 census counted Russian *speakers* rather than ethnic Russians. It was not until the first Soviet-era census in 1926 that the people of the old Russian Empire were asked to state their nationality or ethnicity as separate from their primary language. See Richard Pipes, *Russia Under the Bolshevik Regime* (New York, 1993), pp. 141–42.

28. For a detailed discussion of this see Z. Lenskii, "Natsional'noe dvizhenie," in *Obshchestvennoe dvizhenie v Rossii v nachale XX-ogo veka*, 4 vols., ed. L. Martov (St. Petersburg, 1912), vol. 1.

29. See K. Zalevskii, "Natsional'nye dvizheniia" in *Obshchestvennoe dvizhenie*, ed. L. Martov, vol. 4, p. 222.

30. See K. Zalevskii, "Natsional'nye partii v Rossii" in *Obshchestvennoe dvizhenie*, ed. L. Martov, vol. 3, p. 304.

31. "Vvodnaia stat'ia o zadachakh i tseliakh gazety *Okrainy Rossii*," *Okrainy Rossii* 1 (5 March 1906): 2.

32. "Gosudarstvennaia Duma i vopros ob okrainakh," *Okrainy Rossii* 8 (23 April 1906): 181.

33. Ibid., pp. 180–81.

34. Petr Struve, "Past and Present of Russian Economics," in *Russian Realities and Problems*, ed. James D. Duff (Cambridge, 1917), p. 53.

35. Arkadii Chernii, "K chemu privedet okrainnaia 'avtonomiia' (II)," *Okrainy Rossii* 41 (11 December 1906): 692. [Continuation of "K chemu privedet okrainnaia 'avtonomiia' (I)," *Okrainy Rossii* 38 (19 November 1906).]

36. Platon Kulakovskii, "Vopros ob inorodtsakh i Gosudarstvennaia Duma," *Okrainy Rossii* 33–34 (11–18 August 1906): 483–86.

37. Ibid., p. 483.

38. Platon Kulakovskii, "Nasha vneshniaia politika i okrainy," *Okrainy Rossii* 12 (21 March 1909): 177–78.

39. See P. Lavrov, "Anneksiia Bosnii i Gertsegoviny i otnoshenie k nei Slavianstva," *Vestnik Evropy* 3 (March 1909): 27–52, continued in *Vestnik Evropy* 4 (April 1909): 483–507.

40. Adherents of neo-Slavic thought saw Russia as the leader of Europe's Slavs, who in the early twentieth century were engaged in struggles for national liberation against the non-Slavic powers of Germany, Austria, and the Ottoman Empire. They also saw the future of "Slavdom" in the Balkans, rooted in the Orthodox legacy of the Byzantine Empire. The idea of the cultural unity of Slavdom was viewed as an antidote to the centrifugal pressures of the nascent national-separatist movements in the empire. Neo-Slavs proposed that a shared belief in the importance of Slavdom on the part of state and society and an active policy in the Balkans would provide the basis for Russia's national unification. See Venedikt Miakotin, "Nabroski sovremennosti: 'Neo-Slavism' i vnutrennie voprosy," *Russkoe bogatstvo* 11 (1908): 198–217.

41. Lavrov, "Anneksiia Bosnii i Gertsegoviny," pp. 483–84. See also Platon Kulakovskii, "Vseslavianskii s"ezd i poliaki," *Okrainy Rossii* 20 (May 1908): 298.

42. In February 1908, under the patronage of the journal, a "Russian Borderlands Society" was established to support projects strengthening the Russian state. The membership included representatives from the Slavic Charitable Society, the State Council, the State Duma, and the Russian

Senate, as well as state bureaucrats and private individuals. Some of the members of the society are listed in *Okrainy Rossii* 14 (5 April 1908): 210.

43. "Rech' Predsedatelia Soveta Ministrov P. A. Stolypina, proiznesennaia v Gos. Dume 16 noiabria," *Okrainy Rossii* 47 (24 November 1907): 687–89.

44. Ibid., p. 688.

45. See "In the Mirror of Statistics Demographic Crisis Threatens Russia's National Security," *Meditsinskii kur'er* 1997 (1).

46. See Valerii [Valery] Tishkov, *Nationalities and Conflicting Ethnicity in Post-Communist Russia* (Cambridge, MA, April 1993) [=Conflict Management Group, Ethnic Conflict Management in the Former Soviet Union Working Paper Series]. This percentage, which was based on the 1989 Soviet census, increased slightly after 1991 with the influx of ethnic Russians from other republics of the former USSR.

47. See Fiona Hill, *Russia's Tinderbox: Conflict in the North Caucasus and Its Implications for the Future of the Russian Federation* (Cambridge, MA, 1995), pp. 17–18 [=Strengthening Democratic Institutions Project, John F. Kennedy School of Government, Harvard University].

48. The 89 administrative units or "subjects" of the Russian Federation consist of 21 nominally non-ethnic Russian republics, 1 autonomous oblast (the Jewish Autonomous Oblast), 10 nominally non-ethnic Russian autonomous okrugs, 6 krais or large strategic borderland territories, 49 oblasts, and 2 cities with special status—Moscow and St. Petersburg. The 1992 Federal Treaty consisted of 3 separate agreements: between the Federal government and the republics; between the Federal government and the krais, oblasts and cities; and between the Federal government and the autonomous okrugs and the autonomous oblast.

49. Estimates of casualties in the war in Chechnya are the subject of considerable dispute in Russia. A figure of 80,000 was offered by then Secretary of the Russian Security Council, Aleksandr Lebed, in the summer of 1996; a more accurate figure of 40,000 was presented by Valerii Tishkov, former Minister of Nationalities and Director of the Russian Academy of Sciences' Institute of Ethnology and Anthropology, in a personal interview in Moscow in May 1997. At a meeting of The Hague Initiative on the Russian-Chechen conflict in The Netherlands in May 1997, Chechen Vice President Vakha Arsanov claimed that more than 100,000 people had been killed in the war. (Cited from personal notes, 23 May 1997.)

50. See James Hughes, "Moscow's Bilateral Treaties Add to Confusion," *Transition* 20 September 1996: 39–43.

51. Tishkov, *Ethnicity, Nationalism, and Conflict*, p. 261.

52. Ramazan Abdulatipov, "Tol'ko zakon mozhet ostanovit' bezzakonie," *Nezavisimaia gazeta* 16 July 1996.

53. *Zavtra* 51(56) December 1994, cited in Tishkov, *Ethnicity, Nationalism, and Conflict*, pp. 251–52.

54. For a discussion of the activities of the Confederation of Peoples of the Caucasus (KNK in its Russian acronym), see Hill, *Russia's Tinderbox*, pp. 24–29. Similar fears of such anti-Russian coalitions extending from the Baltic through the Caucasus to Central Asia were also expressed by Andranik Migranian in a March 1997 article on the future of the Commonwealth of Independent States. See Andranik Migranian, "SNG: Nachalo ili konets istorii?" *Nezavisimaia gazeta* 26 March 1997.

55. "Caucasian 'Highlanders' May Act Against Russian Interests," *ITAR-TASS* 14 May 1995.

56. Tishkov, *Ethnicity, Nationalism, and Conflict*, p. 262. Eighty-seven percent of Chechens surveyed on their conception of their identity in November–December 1993 stated that they considered themselves primarily or exclusively as representatives of Chechnya. Only 11 percent expressed an equal identification with Russia.

57. Personal interview with Enver Kisriev, Dagestan's representative in the Conflict Management Group's Ethnic Conflict Monitoring Network, January 1996.

58. See Dmitry Zaks, "Poll Shows 35 Percent of Russians for Chechen Independence," *St. Petersburg Times* 16–22 September 1996.

59. See, for example, Pavel Felgenhauer, "Seven Peace Plans and No Policy," *The Moscow Times* 29 February 1996; and Russian TV reports, April 1996.

60. See Nikolai Fedorov, "Cease-fire a Value in Itself," *Moscow News* 19–25 September 1996.

61. See interview by Petra Prochazkova and Jaromir Stetina with Chechen military leader Aslan Maskhadov, *Týden* (Prague) 30 September 1996; and interview by Valerii Batuev with Chechen Acting President Zelimkhan Iandarbiev in *Argumenty i Fakty* 1 October 1996.

62. See "Printsipy opredeleniia osnov vzaimootnoshenii mezhdu Rossiiskoi Federatsiei i Chechenskoi Respublikoi," *Izvestiia* 3 September 1996.

63. See, for example, the discussion in Georgy Bovt and Dmitry Kamyshev, "Peace in Chechnya: A Bad Peace After a Bad War," *Kommersant-Daily* 3 September 1996. For discussions of the controversial nature of the Lebed peace plan, see, for example, "Upper House Experts Say Chechnya Peace Deal Legally Null" and "Moscow Mayor Blasts

Chechen Accords Signed by Lebed," *Interfax* 8 October 1996; and Paul Goble, "The Chechen War Resumes in Moscow," *RFE/RL Reports* 4 October 1996, and "Moscow's New Hard Line on Chechnya," *RFE/RL Reports* 9 October 1996. Goble mentions reports from Moscow suggesting the construction of new communication routes bypassing Chechnya—further supporting the proposition that Russia was preparing for Chechnya's possible independence—in "New Moves on the Chechen Front," *RFE/RL Reports* 15 October 1996. This report was also carried in "Moscow to Build Railway Circumventing Chechnya," *Interfax* 10 October 1996. A report in *Interfax* on the same day, "Reformist Says Russia May Hold Referendum on Chechnya's Status," quotes Boris Nemtsov, the politically prominent governor of Russia's Nizhny Novgorod region and later Deputy Prime Minister, as asserting that the majority of Russians would probably not vote to keep Chechnya as part of the Federation if there were a nationwide referendum on the issue.

64. Poll cited in *Interfax* 10 November 1996.

65. See, for example, Maksim Sokolov, "My ochishchaem mesto boiu," *Kommersant-Daily* 31 August 1996; Ilia Maksakov, "Politicheskaia bor'ba vokrug khasaviurtovskikh dokumentov," *Nezavisimaia gazeta* 5 September 1996; Denis Babich, "Reaktsiia na mirotvorchestvo Lebedia," *Nezavisimaia gazeta* 4 September 1996; Petr Berezko, "What Did Lebed Learn From Top Secret Documents? The General Made the Sole Correct Decision That Was Possible," *Novaia gazeta* 7–13 October 1996; and "Anti-Lebed'," *Kommersant-Daily* 8 October 1996.

66. Alexei Pushkov, "Kurile Islands: Weak Country May Not Give Up Part of Its Territory," *Nezavisimaia gazeta* 17 April 1998 (printed in English by RIA Novosti).

Krakivs'ki visti: An Overview

JOHN-PAUL HIMKA

Krakivs'ki visti was the most important newspaper to appear in the Ukrainian language under the German occupation during World War II. In spite of its significance, the publication has been studied very little.[1] The aim of this article is to present a brief overview of the history of the paper, largely based on the archives of its chief editor, Mykhailo Khomiak (Michael Chomiak), preserved in the Provincial Archives of Alberta.

Origins

When the Soviets invaded the eastern regions of the Second Polish Republic in September 1939, thousands of Ukrainians fled from Volhynia and especially Galicia into the German-occupied territories of the General Gouvernement. Many took up residence in Cracow, the capital of the General Gouvernement, which quickly became the major center of non-Soviet Ukrainian life. A Ukrainian delegation under the leadership of the geographer Volodymyr Kubiiovych (Kubijovyč) met with the governor general, Hans Frank, on 19 November 1939 to discuss proposals for the organization of Ukrainian affairs in the General Gouvernement. In the course of the meeting, Frank pledged his support for a Ukrainian publishing house and periodical press.

At their own meeting on the topic of publishing two days later, the Ukrainian representatives decided to establish a publishing house as a limited company headed by Kubiiovych. This was the origin of Ukraïns'ke vydavnytstvo, which was to be the publisher of *Krakivs'ki visti*. Normally, the Germans established the limited companies that published for the non-German population of occupied areas, but the Ukrainians were keen to have their own limited company so as to have more control over their paper. Funds were raised among the Ukrainian population of the General Gouvernement to provide the initial capital for the new company.

The first director of Ukraïns'ke vydavnytstvo, Ievhen Iulii Pelens'kyi, met twice with the German press chief in Cracow, Emil Gassner, who promised to support Ukrainian publishing. Gassner gave Pelens'kyi a document that allowed him to take over the Jewish printing press of *Nowy Dziennik* on Orzeszkowa 7, which had been shut down by the Nazis. Pelens'kyi had much to do to make the press operable. He had to raise money (about 25,000–30,000 *złoty*s) to fix and buy equipment, particularly linotype matrices and type. At one point he had a stroke of good luck: an old friend who now represented a manufacturer of linotype happened to come by from Berlin, and he allowed Pelens'kyi to purchase the necessary equipment with no deposit—just Pelens'kyi's signature on an IOU. Pelens'kyi also had to select personnel for the printing press and put together an editorial board. Oleksander Kostyk and Hryhor Andriïv, former directors of Ukrainian printing presses in Lviv, quickly rounded up a team of workers and helped put the printing press in order. V. Diakiv kept the press's books. The company Ukraïns'ke vydavnytstvo was formally established on 27 December 1939 and officially registered on 16 January 1940. A Supervisory Council (*Nadzirna rada*) was formed with Kubiiovych as its head, and matters were in order by the beginning of 1940.[2]

Frequency and Distribution

The first issue of Ukraïns'ke vydavnytstvo's newspaper, *Krakivs'ki visti*, appeared on Christmas Day, 7 January 1940. It originally appeared twice weekly, on Wednesdays and Sundays (soon changed to Wednesdays and Saturdays). As of issue number 33 (4 May 1940), the paper began to come out three times a week, on Mondays, Wednesdays, and Fridays. In the first issue, *Krakivs'ki visti* announced its intention to become a daily paper,[3] and this goal was achieved beginning with issue no. 111 (1 November 1940). The paper would come out daily (except Sundays and holidays) for the rest of its existence. The last issue of the daily appeared on 29 March 1945. There was a brief interruption when the paper transferred its operations to Vienna as the Red Army approached Cracow (the last Cracow issue was number 227 dated 8 October 1944, and the first Vienna issue probably appeared on 16 October 1944).[4]

When *Krakivs'ki visti* became a daily, the publishers established a weekly under the same title for the rural population, which, they felt, would not be interested in a daily newspaper. The last issue of the weekly was dated 15 October 1944.[5]

Both papers had relatively small press runs. The Germans were unwilling to allot the Ukrainian publishers as much paper as they wanted;[6] they also severely restricted the papers' distribution.

Table 1. *Krakivs'ki visti* (The Daily): Press Run

Year	Number of Issues	Total Newspapers	Average per Issue
1940	156[a]	1,118,680	7,171[b]
1941	292	3,040,100	10,411
1942	291	2,980,000	10,241
1943	295	4,442,000	15,058[c]
1944	298	5,008,775	16,808[d]
1945	70	1,569,505	22,422
Total		**18,159,060**	

Table 2. *Krakivs'ki visti* (The Weekly): Press Run

Year	Number of Issues	Total Newspapers	Average per Issue
1940	8	57,000	7,125[e]
1941	50	357,250	7,145
1942	52?	886,000	17,038?
1943	52	976,000	18,769[f]
1944	42	1,135,000	27,024[g]
Total		**3,411,250**	

SOURCES (TABLES 1 AND 2): "Redaktsiia 'Krakivs'ki visti,'" Michael Chomiak Papers, Provincial Archives of Alberta, 85.191/23; issues of *Krakivs'ki visti* (daily 1941–1944, weekly 1944). Cf. Volodymyr Kubiiovych, *Ukraïntsi v Heneral'nii huberniï 1939–1941. Istoriia Ukraïns'koho tsentral'noho komitetu* (Chicago, 1975), p. 280.

NOTES (TABLES 1 AND 2):

a. 32 issues twice weekly, 78 thrice weekly, 46 daily.

b. At a meeting of the Supervisory Council (*Nadzirna rada*) of Ukraïns'ke vydavnytstvo held on 30 December 1940, a press run of 8,000 was reported. Chomiak Papers, Minutes of the Supervisory Council, 85.191/27.

c. At a meeting of the Supervisory Council held 9 July 1943, a press run of 15,000 was reported. Chomiak Papers, Minutes of the Supervisory Council, 85.191/27.

d. At a meeting of the Supervisory Council held 1 January 1944, a press run of 26,500 was reported. Chomiak Papers, Minutes of the Supervisory Council, 85.191/27.

e. At a meeting of the Supervisory Council held 30 December 1940, a press run of 5,600 was reported. Chomiak Papers, Minutes of the Supervisory Council, 85.191/27.

f. At meetings of the Supervisory Council held 9 July and 18 November 1943, press runs of 18,000 and 20,000 respectively were reported. Chomiak Papers, Minutes of the Supervisory Council, 85.191/27.

g. At a meeting of the Supervisory Council held 1 January 1944, a press run of 26,000 was reported. Chomiak Papers, Minutes of the Supervisory Council, 85.191/27.

The readership of *Krakivs'ki visti* was located mainly in the General Gouvernement and in Germany (where many Ukrainians worked as forced laborers), but also in German-occupied Europe and allied countries (Slovakia, Italy). A few issues were sent to neutral countries of Europe and North and South America, and some even to Manchukuo and China.[7] At the end of 1940, of 5,000 subscriptions to the daily, 2,400 were sent to addresses abroad, and of 3,000 subscriptions to the weekly, 600 went abroad.[8]

The paper could not be sent, however, to the Reichskommissariat Ukraine, where the bulk of the potential readership lived. On 9 March 1943, Kubiiovych, the head of the Ukrainian Central Committee, Khomiak, the editor of *Krakivs'ki visti*, and Ostap Tarnavs'kyi, representing Ukraïns'ke vydavnytstvo, met with Press Chief Gassner to try to convince him to lift the ban on circulating the paper in the Reichskommissariat. Gassner said that it was not in his competence to change the policy, that this was a matter for the Ministry of Eastern Territories and the Reichskommissariat to decide.[9] The editors of *Krakivs'ki visti* did send some issues into the Reichskommissariat as a publication exchange with newspapers there, but with mixed results. The editor of *Ukraïns'kyi holos* in Proskuriv (*now* Khmelnytskyi) wrote to chief editor Khomiak on 9 June 1942: "We inform you that you should not send us your periodical anymore, because we can only receive those periodicals that come out on the territory of the Reichskommissariat Ukraine."[10] On the other hand, on 23 July 1943, the editor of *Dzvin voli* in Bila Tserkva sent over a number of issues of his paper, requesting a regular exchange of publications.[11]

When *Krakivs'ki visti* first appeared, its founders had envisioned an audience made up of peasants, workers, and refugees.[12] The division of the paper into a daily and a weekly marked a differentiation between, respectively, the intelligentsia on the one hand and the workers and the rural population on the other. In 1944, Ukraïns'ke vydavnytstvo made a point of sending the Christmas holiday issues to Ukrainian workers in Germany.[13]

Editors

Pelens'kyi had some difficulty finding a suitable chief editor for his planned newspaper. There were a number of talented editors from Lviv in Cracow, but many of them declined to assume the editorship because they feared Soviet reprisals against their families back home in Galicia. It seems that the first person who was tapped for the position of editor in the very earliest stages of the project was Hryhorii Stetsiuk,[14] who had been editor of the Lviv newspaper *Nash prapor* from 1932 to 1939. The sources leave no clue as to why he did not take up his position as editor of *Krakivs'ki visti*. When the paper first appeared in January 1940, its editor was Borys Levyts'kyi (Lewytzkyj), but he did not last long in the job. According to Kubiiovych, Levyts'kyi had to leave the position at German insistence when he published information on the Russo-Finnish war—even though the article was copied directly and without commentary from official German sources.[15]

After Levyts'kyi, Mykhailo Khomiak was appointed chief editor,[16] and he remained chief editor of the daily until the end. Khomiak belonged to neither of the warring factions of the Organization of Ukrainian Nationalists (OUN), and this non-party status made him *persona grata* to the Germans.[17] Kubiiovych assessed Khomiak's contribution as follows: "I cannot pass over the services of editor M. Khomiak as chief editor of *Krakivs'ki visti*. He was able (always in harmonious cooperation with the leadership of the Ukrainian Central Committee and the directors of Ukraïns'ke vydavnytstvo) to bring aboard regular and free-lance contributors to both papers [the daily and the weekly]—correspondents from the General Gouvernement and beyond; he also had the ability to sense what could be written and how in the severe German reality, and he gained some trust among the German officials, without which the work would have been impossible."[18] Kubiiovych's remark about the always harmonious cooperation with the directors of Ukraïns'ke vydavnytstvo was disingenuous. In fact, Khomiak had a number of unpleasant run-ins with one of the most influential of these directors, Ivan Kotsur. Kotsur felt that discipline at Orzeszkowa 7 was lax, and that this was the reason why the paper was coming out late—after 6:00 PM. He demanded a change of routine at the office and monthly reports from the chief editor. Khomiak regarded this as high-handed and petty, and ignored Kotsur's demands. But Kotsur used his influence to undermine Khomiak quite seriously. He had Kubiiovych appoint Vasyl' Mudryi as the real chief editor of the paper, reducing Khomiak to a mere figurehead. Mudryi would determine the content of each issue and the responsibilities of every member of the editorial board, while Khomiak would be, in effect, his secretary, and would continue to run the text of the paper to the German censors. This arrangement lasted only a short time, from 28 April to 21 May 1941. In his memoirs, Kubiiovych skirts around this incident, mentioning only that Mudryi was excluded from the editorial board by the Germans after he wrote a lead editorial "in which mention was made of the inimical attitude of Ukraine's western neighbors to the Ukrainian people."[19]

The deputy editor for almost the entire existence of the paper was the very talented Lev Lepkyi (brother of the famous novelist Bohdan Lepkyi). Lepkyi, in his fifties, was older than the others. Khomiak, like most of the members of the editorial board, was in his thirties. Others who served on the editorial board of the daily included Roman Kupchyns'kyi, Mar'ian Kozak, Iaroslav Zaremba, and Petro Sahaidachnyi. All of these (as well as Khomiak and Lepkyi) were Galicians. There was one editor from Central Ukraine, Fedir Kovshyk (born in the Poltava region), and one from Pidliashshia, Ariiadna Korovyts'ka.[20]

The first editor of the weekly was Vasyl' Kachmar, but he served only a very short time (until 31 December 1940). For most of the weekly's existence the chief editor was Iuliian Tarnovych, a prolific but narrow-minded man (anti-Jewish, anti-Orthodox) with expertise in the history of the Lemko region. On 6 August 1944, Khomiak took over the editorship of the weekly (in addition to his duties as editor of the daily), but only to preside over its liquidation.[21]

Relations with the Ukrainian Central Committee

The Ukrainian Central Committee (UCC) was formally established in June 1940 as the official umbrella organization of all Ukrainians in the General Gouvernement. It was headed by Kubiiovych, who styled himself "Leader" (*Providnyk*) and envisioned a highly centralized Ukrainian leadership. He was the nominal owner of 13 of the 20 shares of Ukraïns'ke vydavnytstvo.[22]

Kubiiovych felt that as the leader of the Ukrainian Central Committee, he was the ultimate authority in all matters concerning *Krakivs'ki visti*. In a letter to the editorial board on 28 April 1941 he clarified his views, making the following points, among others: (1) *Krakivs'ki visti* was the official organ of the Ukrainian Central Committee, therefore its editorial policy must be completely in line with the policy of the Committee; (2) the editorial board was responsible to him (Kubiiovych) as the Leader of the Ukrainian Central Committee, and he would decide all disputed issues with regard to the editing of the paper. In this letter, Kubiiovych appointed Myron Konovalets' as liaison between the Ukrainian Central Committee and *Krakivs'ki visti*.[23]

A less peremptory formulation was later found in the "Norms for the Cooperation of the Press Organs of Ukraïns'ke vydavnytstvo with the Ukrainian Central Committee" of 1 July 1943. Article I stated: "The press organs of Ukraïns'ke vydavnytstvo, in the first place the daily and weekly *Krakivs'ki visti* and the weekly *Kholms'ka zemlia*, champion the direction of activity and political line of the UCC and endeavor with all their influence to contribute to the success of individual actions of the UCC. On the other hand, they enjoy full moral support and representation before the authorities on the part of the UCC."[24]

An undated self-characterization not only defines the relationship of *Krakivs'ki visti* to the Committee, but affords a more general insight into the paper's self-image:

> The Ukrainian daily *Krakivs'ki visti* is an independent periodical (that is, excepting the censorship limitations and regulations of the authorities, to which it must adhere in connection with the general circumstances); it coordinates its ideological-political direction only with the responsible Ukrainian leadership in the General Gouvernement, that is, at the present moment with the Ukrainian Central Committee. *Kra[kivs'ki] visti* is an all-national organ, beyond and above parties and religious confessions; it stands on the platform of Ukrainian nationalism; it champions the view of the need for a united national front; it steers clear of any internal Ukrainian polemics;[25] it propagates constructiveness, political realism, unity of leadership and obedience to authority.[26]

Relations with the German Authorities

When requesting permission to turn *Krakivs'ki visti* into a daily, Kubiiovych characterized the paper as having "a purely informational character." The only political material would come from the German press agency DNB and from "reputable" German periodicals. With regard to foreign affairs, the paper would strictly follow the line of the press office. It would eschew any involvement with internal Ukrainian polemics.[27]

Even with this profession of complete obedience, the paper was constantly running into difficulties with the German censors. "There was hardly a single issue of *Krakivs'ki visti*," wrote Kubiiovych, "in which the German censor did not cross out at least a few sentences or chapters or even whole articles or feuilletons."[28]

At the meeting of Kubiiovych, Khomiak, Tarnavs'kyi, and Gassner, at which the issue of distribution of the paper in the Reichskommissariat was raised (9 March 1943), the Ukrainians also pleaded for some modification of the censorship. In particular they sought two rights: the right to print articles on historical themes, notably on the Ukrainian revolution of 1917–1920, and the right to publish reports by foreign correspondents. In both cases, they argued, the present German policy was playing into the hands of the Bolsheviks. Gassner replied that only Berlin could change the policy, not he.[29]

The restrictions of German censorship did damage to the paper. Mykola Shlemkevych, who worked in Ukraïns'ke vydavnytstvo's office in Lviv, wrote to chief editor Khomiak on 29 April 1942 to call his attention to the "dangerous editorial crisis" that he—and not only he—perceived in the paper. He argued that the editorial board was "simply paralyzed"; that there was no editorial presence in the paper. There was no attempt to interpret life as it was experienced at the time; it was "only *a mosaic of accidental submissions*, with which the editors fill[ed] the pages of the periodical."[30] In response, Khomiak admitted that in spite of the editors' best efforts, the paper was not what they had hoped it would be. He placed the blame squarely on the German censorship, which prohibited treatment of any of the burning issues of the day: "*Krakivs'ki visti* cannot even publish what the German papers publish, and the German papers themselves have become absolutely colorless, as the Germans themselves recognize."[31]

In spite of these difficulties, there can be no doubt that *Krakivs'ki visti* enjoyed more autonomy than any other legal Ukrainian-language publication under the German occupation.

Regional Tensions and Opportunities

Regional differences have played a prominent role in modern Ukrainian history, and this is true also with regard to the history of *Krakivs'ki visti*.

The paper originally was founded for the Ukrainian population of the General Gouvernement outside Soviet Ukraine, that is, primarily for the Chełm (Kholm) region and Pidliashshia (Podlasie) and for the Lemko region. Yet the editorial board was composed almost exclusively of recent emigres from eastern Galicia. This was to be a source of tension, especially between the editors and the Orthodox archbishop of Chełm and Pidliashshia, Ilarion Ohiienko. Archbishop Ilarion expressed his dissatisfaction with the paper directly to the German press chief, Gassner. When Kubiiovych, Khomiak, and Tarnavs'kyi went to talk to him about other issues altogether (the meeting of 9 March 1943), Gassner first made them listen to the archbishop's complaints and demands. The archbishop accused the newspaper of denigrating the Orthodox Church and propagating Greek Catholicism among the Orthodox population of the Chełm region and Pidliashshia. He demanded more Orthodox representation in the Ukrainian Central Committee and 50 percent of the stock of Ukraïns'ke vydavnytstvo. Although Gassner read aloud the archbishop's grievances, he did not take them very seriously.[32] The Orthodox consistory repeated and concretized the archbishop's accusations against the newspaper in a document Ilarion forwarded to Ukraïns'ke vydavnytstvo in August 1943. When *Krakivs'ki visti* was founded, the memorandum stated, its primary purpose was to spread Ukrainian national consciousness in the polonized Chełm region; but already in 1940 the editors had deviated from this path and turned the newspaper to the service of exclusively Galician and Greek Catholic goals. The memorandum listed a number of articles said to have besmirched the Orthodox Church and propagated Uniatism. It objected to the paper's glorification of the Greek Catholic Metropolitan of Halych, Andrei Sheptyts'kyi, and its denigration of Orthodox hierarchs.[33] Although Kubiiovych and Khomiak regarded Archbishop Ilarion's accusations as totally without foundation, from my reading of the paper I do not think that this is the case.

In spite of such tensions, the most striking feature of *Krakivs'ki visti* was its incorporation of contributors from all regions of Ukraine. By the end of 1941 all Ukrainian lands were either occupied by Germany or by Germany's allies. This resulted in the most intense national-cultural interaction between Ukrainian regions that had ever taken place up to that moment (and the like was not to be repeated until the end of the 1980s). Thus, it was in *Krakivs'ki visti* that many Galician readers were first introduced to the cream of the nationally oriented Soviet Ukrainian intelligentsia, including such luminaries as Hryhorii Kostiuk, Oleksander Ohloblyn, and Iurii Shevel'ov. The Transcarpathian Iuliian Revai also contributed to the paper. Of course, these newly heard voices could not speak on the hottest issues of the day, but they did write some remarkable pieces on history and literature and helped to widen the horizons of the Galician readership.[34] It was this intellectual ferment that made *Krakivs'ki visti* such an interesting paper, in spite of the conditions under which it had to function.

NOTES

1. There is a short survey of all the periodicals published by Ukraïns'ke vydavnytstvo in Cracow: O. I. Luts'kyi, "Periodyka 'Ukraïns'koho vydavnytstva' (1939–1945 rr.)," in *Ukraïns'ka periodyka. Istoriia i suchasnist'. Dopovidi ta povidomlennia druhoï Vseukraïns'koï naukovo-teoretychnoï konferentsiï 21–22 hrudnia 1994* (Lviv and Zhytomyr, 1994), pp. 62–66. There is also one specialized study of *Krakivs'ki visti* alone: John-Paul Himka, "*Krakivski visti* and the Jews, 1943: A Contribution to the History of Ukrainian-Jewish Relations during the Second World War," *Journal of Ukrainian Studies* 21(1–2) Summer–Winter 1996: 81–95 (an earlier Ukrainian version appeared in *Filosofs'ka i sotsiolohichna dumka* in 1994). The paper is not mentioned in the standard study of the Polish-language press in the General Gouvernement: Lucjan Dobroszycki, *Reptile Journalism: The Official Polish-Language Press under the Nazis, 1939–1945*, trans. Barbara Harshav (New Haven and London, 1994).

2. Ievhen Iulii Pelens'kyi, "Pered dvoma rokamy," *Krakivs'ki visti* 2 January 1942. Volodymyr Kubiiovych [Kubijovyč], *Ukraïntsi v Heneral'nii huberniï 1939–1941. Istoriia Ukraïns'koho tsentral'noho komitetu* (Chicago, 1975), pp. 249–58.

3. "Vid redaktsiï," *Krakivs'ki visti* 7 January 1940.

4. "Redaktsiia 'Krakivs'ki visti,'" Michael Chomiak Papers, Provincial Archives of Alberta, 85.191/23. Also Chomiak Papers, 85.191/20, Issues of *Krakivs'ki visti* (weekly 1944). The brevity of the interruption is amazing considering the difficulties caused by the move. See "Vyrobnychi mozhlyvosti u Vidni," Chomiak Papers, 85.191/30.

5. "Redaktsiia 'Krakivs'ki visti,'" Chomiak Papers, 85.191/23; Issues of *Krakivs'ki visti* (weekly 1944); Kubiiovych, *Ukraïntsi v Heneral'nii huberniï*, p. 272.

6. Meetings of the Supervisory Council of Ukraïns'ke vydavnytstvo held 18 November and 29 December 1943, Chomiak Papers, 85.191/27.

7. Kubiiovych, *Ukraïntsi v Heneral'nii huberniï*, p. 278.

8. Meeting of the Supervisory Council of Ukraïns'ke vydavnytstvo held 30 December 1940, Chomiak Papers, 85.191/27.

9. "Zvit z narady u shefa presy," Chomiak Papers, 85.191/29.

10. Ibid.

11. "Vyrobnychi mozhlyvosti u Vidni," Chomiak Papers, 85.191/30.

12. "Vid redaktsiï," *Krakivs'ki visti* 7 January 1940.

13. Meeting of the Supervisory Council of Ukraïns'ke vydavnytstvo held 1 January 1944, Chomiak Papers, 85.191/27.

14. Pelens'kyi, "Pered dvoma rokamy."

15. Kubiiovych, *Ukraïntsi v Heneral'nii huberniï*, p. 274.

16. According to "Redaktsiia 'Krakivs'ki visti,'" Levyts'kyi was editor until 30 January, and Khomiak [Chomiak] took over on 6 February 1940. However, there is a letter of 4 January 1940 from Oleksander Gonta-Skrypchenko already addressing Khomiak as *nachal'nyi redaktor.* Chomiak Papers, 85.191/33.

17. Interview with Alexandra Chomiak (widow), 17 August 1999.

18. Kubiiovych, *Ukraïntsi v Heneral'nii huberniï*, p. 277.

19. Ibid., p. 274 (see also p. 276). Letter of Kotsur to Khomiak, 23 November 1940; letter of Khomiak to Kubiiovych, 26 November 1940; letter of Kotsur to Khomiak, 12 April 1941; letter of Khomiak to Kotsur, 14 April 1941; letter of Kubiiovych to *Krakivs'ki visti* editorial board, Chomiak Papers, 85.191/28; also "Redaktsiia 'Krakivs'ki visti,'" Chomiak Papers, 85.191/23.

20. Fairly full information on the composition of the editorial board can be found in "Redaktsiia 'Krakivs'ki visti,'" Chomiak Papers, 85.191/23. Curricula vitae of *Krakivs'ki visti* personnel can be found in the Chomiak Papers, 85.191/32. Editors' dates and places of birth are given in a letter of Kozak to Abteilung Presse in Cracow, 14 December 1942, Chomiak Papers, 85.191/28.

21. "Redaktsiia 'Krakivs'ki visti,'" Chomiak Papers, 85.191/23; Kubiiovych, *Ukraïntsi v Heneral'nii huberniï*, p. 276. The characterization of Tarnovych is my own, not the source's.

22. Kubiiovych, *Ukraïntsi v Heneral'nii huberniï*, pp. 251–52.

23. Chomiak Papers, 85.191/28. This is also the same letter in which Kubiiovych appointed Vasyl' Mudryi as chief editor.

24. "Normy spivpratsi presovykh orhaniv 'Ukraïns'koho Vydavnytstva' z Ukraïns'kym Tsentral'nym Komitetom," Chomiak Papers, 85.191/30.

25. This refers especially to the paper's formal neutrality with respect to the split in the Organization of Ukrainian Nationalists between the followers of Mel'nyk and Bandera.

26. "Pravyl'nyk dlia Redaktsiï shchodennyka 'Krakivs'ki visti,'" Chomiak Papers, 85.191/28.

27. Letter of Kubiiovych to Leiter des Presseamtes in der Abteilung für Volksaufsklärung und Propaganda bei der Regierung des

Generalgouverneurs in Krakau, 29 September 1940, Chomiak Papers, 85.191/28.

28. Kubiiovych, *Ukraïntsi v Heneral'nii hubernïï*, p. 273. For specific examples, see p. 274.

29. "Zvit z narady u shefa presy," Chomiak Papers, 85.191/29.

30. Ibid. Emphasis in original.

31. Letter of Khomiak to Shlemkevych, 20 October 1942, Chomiak Papers, 85.191/29.

32. "Zvit z narady u shefa presy," Chomiak Papers, 85.191/29.

33. Ilarion to Ukraïns'ke vydavnytstvo, 24 August 1943; "Doklad" of 14 August 1943, Chomiak Papers, 85.191/30.

34. Unfortunately, *Krakivs'ki visti* has never been indexed. The best way to gain an overview of who contributed to the paper is to check the lists of honoraria paid: Chomiak Papers, 85.191/32.

National Identities in Post-Soviet Ukraine:
The Case of Lviv and Donetsk

YAROSLAV HRYTSAK

In the last three decades, the study of nationalism has yielded a number of new theories that have profoundly changed our ideas about what constitutes a nation and how national identities are formed. The theoretical breakthroughs have not been matched by an adequate increase in empirical research, however. As Miroslav Hroch has correctly observed, there is currently an overabundance of theories of nationalism and a dearth of concrete studies of the phenomenon.[1]

While this is true for the field as a whole, contemporary studies of identity formation in post-Soviet Ukraine display the opposite tendency: much of what has been written on the subject is rich in empirical findings but lacking in appropriate theoretical perspective.[2] While most theories of nationalism emphasize the complex, multidimensional character of national identities that cannot be reduced to a single element,[3] many researchers tend to determine national identities on the basis of ethnic and language criteria, the premise being that "the private use of language is closer to the issue of [national] identity" than any other group indicator.[4] As a result, the common practice of late has been to distinguish three main national groups in Ukraine: Ukrainian-speaking Ukrainians (40 percent), Russian-speaking Ukrainians (33–34 percent), and Russian-speaking Russians (20–21 percent).[5] Moreover, some of the surveys conducted during the Ukrainian parliamentary and presidential elections in 1994 indicated that these language differences were highly correlated with political and regional differences between nationalist-minded western Ukraine and pro-communist eastern Ukraine.[6] This finding of deep national cleavages seemingly corroborated alarmist scenarios of ethnic turmoil and possibly even the collapse of independent Ukraine.[7]

Other interpretations of the 1994 elections,[8] as well as some surveys that were conducted at about the same time,[9] have suggested that Ukraine is in fact a relatively stable political community, and that its real problems lie beyond ethnic and language cleavages. The purpose of the present study is to test these propositions on the basis of data from a 1994 survey conducted in Lviv and Donetsk, the biggest cities in western and eastern Ukraine,[10] and from follow-up focus groups in 1994 and 1996.[11] The cases were constructed on the basis of the theoretical assumptions that seemed to offer a better explanation of nation-building processes in post-Soviet Ukraine.

Comparisons between Lviv and Donetsk are problematic.[12] Since, as some authors suggest,[13] these two cities represent the opposite poles of political mobilization in Ukraine, such comparison necessarily corroborates the thesis of threatening ethnic and regional cleavages; that is, the very formulation of the problem implies a ready-made answer. While such caveats cannot be disregarded, there is at least one good reason to focus on these two cities in studies of post-Soviet Ukrainian nation building. A comparative analysis of Lviv and Donetsk is very important for exploring the possible limits of the nation's inner cohesion. The underlying hypothesis is that all other Ukrainian cities and regions would fall somewhere between these two extremes.[14] Moreover, the date of the survey—spring 1994—makes the comparison even more dramatic. During this period, support for Ukrainian independence was minimal in eastern Ukraine, and anti-independence sentiment was highest in Donbas.[15]

At the root of these differences, some analysts would claim, are ethnic and language cleavages. It is true that Lviv is the most Ukrainian city in the country in terms of both language and urban culture. In 1989, Ukrainians made up 79.1 percent of the city's population, and 77.6 percent of the population regarded Ukrainian as their native language. Donetsk, on the other hand, is the urban center of Donbas, the most industrialized and russified region in eastern Ukraine. According to the 1989 census, Russians were in the majority here with 53.5 percent of the population, and Ukrainians, with 39.4 percent, were in the minority. If one adds the language criterion, then the Russian character of Donetsk becomes even more explicit: the percentage of Russian-speakers in the population as a whole is 80.5 percent.[16]

The correlation between language data and political attitudes may be significant—and our survey supports this finding—but it does not explain why these allegedly pro-Russian attitudes in Donetsk have not manifested themselves in sustained political action. While Lviv tends to be consistent in its political demands and preferences, Donetsk demonstrates a certain fluidity in this regard. The victory of the Left in Donetsk in 1994 proved to be short-lived, as it suffered losses in local elections that were held later in the year. Many of the votes went to Donbas neoliberals who displayed a pragmatic, pro-Ukrainian independence orientation.[17]

David J. Meyer recently put forward his own theory of why the Donbas Russians have not mobilized along ethnic lines as have the Crimean Russians. Part of the explanation has to do with the dominant presence of russified Ukrainians in the region:

> Russified Ukrainians, who share many of the concerns and demands of the ethnic Russian minority, dominate the Donbass institutions. They have used their resources and institutional/infrastructural power to co-opt the Russian minority in an alliance which makes political and economic demands on Kiev. However, these demands are not particularistic nor parochially ethnic in nature. Rather, the Donbass Russians' demands are regional, economic, cultural, and political (but not ethno-political). Therefore, the Russians of the

Donbass find it not necessary to mobilize as Russians per se, but as part of a larger, multiethnic, political alliance. Indeed, it seems that the Russian minority has found it more effective to pursue their ends by mobilizing around *social* issues, rather than ethnicity.[18]

Meyer's institutional approach is very promising and deserves further elaboration, but our findings suggest that an approach positing a multilayered, dynamic, and constructed character of national identity may yield a different explanation of this phenomenon. This type of approach is most appropriate to the post-Soviet Ukrainian context where, as a result of the peculiar legacy of Soviet nation building and of Russian-Ukrainian encounters, identities have a highly ambiguous character and are in constant flux.

Looking for a Model: How Many National Identities?

In studies like these, it is essential to frame the questions carefully. One important question is how many national identities exist in contemporary Ukraine. The common assumption is that the issue of identity in Ukraine should be perceived as a Russian/Ukrainian dichotomy, but in fact neither group can be said to be homogeneous. Because of their linguistic and cultural proximity to each other, both groups are suffering from crises of identity. Most analysts focus on the Ukrainian part of this story—that is, on differences between Ukrainian-speaking and Russian-speaking Ukrainians—largely ignoring the fact that Russians also face serious dilemmas of national self-identification. Russian society before the Revolution could not resolve the issue of national identity. The efforts required to maintain the Russian Empire entailed the subjection of virtually the whole population, but especially the Russians, to the demands of state service, and thus enfeebled the creation of the kinds of community associations that commonly provide the basis for the service sense of nationhood.[19] After the collapse of the Russian Empire, the Bolsheviks did not create a Russian nation-state, but rather absorbed imperial Russian institutions into imperial Soviet ones, further postponing a resolution of the question: What is Russia? Is Russia a Russian ethnic core, a territory inhabited by Russians, Ukrainians, and Belarusians (or in other words, "Great Russians," "Little Russians," and "White Russians"), or the whole former Russian Empire/Soviet Union?[20]

The Soviet version of Russian/Soviet identity was promulgated during the last decades of Soviet rule,[21] and found many adherents among Russians—especially those living outside the Russian Federation. According to a December 1990 survey, 70–80 percent of the Russians living in the major cities of the non-Russian republics (including Ukraine) identified themselves as "citizens of the USSR" rather than as "Russians."[22] In addition to the Russians, Ukrainians and Belarusians became the prime targets of the policy of molding a single "Soviet people." The aim of the policy was to obliterate their national distinctions from Russians.[23] In the absence of reliable data, it is difficult to determine how successful the policy was. Still, as Roman Szporluk has noted, by the end of the 1980s, in such heavily populated areas as Donbas, at least four identities were competing for popular support: Ukrainian, "Little Russian" (both Ukrainian and Russian), Russian, and Soviet.[24]

Paul S. Pirie suggests that there are four main routes to self-identification: strong identification with one ethnic group only; strong, stable identification with two groups simultaneously (a bicultural, biethnic identification); weak or unstable identification with two or more ethnic groups (a marginal identification); and strong identification with a group which encompasses several ethnic groups (a "pan-ethnic" identification). His empirical findings have convincingly demonstrated the predominance of the "pan-ethnic" identification in post-Soviet southern and eastern Ukraine.[25]

In keeping with this line of argument, in our 1994 study we assumed the existence of a separate pan-ethnic Soviet identity alongside the Ukrainian and Russian identities. Questions about respondents' identities were formulated in two different ways. In both cases respondents were asked to choose the identity that described them best. In one case we presented a list of 28 possible answers, including Ukrainian, Russian, and Soviet. The interviewees were asked to choose as many identities as they wished to describe the way they thought about themselves. In the second case the range of possible answers was limited to only four identities: Ukrainian, Russian, Soviet, and Other. Regardless of the formulation of the question, the percentage choosing Soviet identity in Donetsk was unexpectedly high—in fact, the highest (see Table 1).

Table 1. National Identities in Lviv and Donetsk

	Multiple List*	List of Four
Lviv		
Ukrainian	73.1%	78.5%
Russian	13.6%	8.3%
Soviet	7.4%	4.9%
Other	(from 0.8 to 69.6%)	4.1%
Donetsk		
Ukrainian	39.3%	25.9%
Russian	30.0%	22.9%
Soviet	40.0%	45.4%
Other	(from 0.5 to 55.6%)	4.7%

* Since respondents were allowed to choose more than one identity in this case, the column will add up to more than 100%.

A high correlation between self-identification and primary language was found only in the case of the Ukrainian-speaking ethnic Ukrainians: 92 percent of this group identified themselves as Ukrainians. Other groups were far from homogeneous. The Russian-speaking ethnic Ukrainians in both cities were split evenly into "Russian" and "Soviet" self-identification (44 in each case), with only 7 percent regarding themselves as Ukrainians. In the case of Russian-speaking ethnic Russians, the breakdown was similar, though here more self-identified as Russians (47 percent) than as Soviets (39 percent). In the smallest group, that of Ukrainian-speaking ethnic Russians, "Russian" and "Other" were the preferred identities (31 percent each), with "Ukrainian" and "Soviet" at 19 percent each.

The introduction of the regional factor creates the impression that the ethnic/language differences amount to a Russian/Ukrainian dichotomy only in Lviv, while in Donetsk the breakdown was softened by the presence of numerous "Soviets." Table 2 reinforces the image of Lviv as a "nationality-minded" city. Within the range of multiple identities most people here consider Ukrainian the most important. That is not the case in Donetsk, where regional and gender identities take precedence (surprisingly enough, gender is the most important identity for women, but not for men). Particularly noteworthy is the relatively low ranking of the Russian identity, which helps us explain why it has not been possible to mobilize people here under Russian national slogans.

Table 2. Preferred Identities in Lviv and Donetsk

Ranking	Lviv	Donetsk
1	Ukrainian (73.3%)	Donetskite (55.6%)
2	Lvivite (69.6%)	Woman (48.8%)
3	Woman (46.0%)	Soviet (40.0%)
4	Uniate (38.4%)	Ukrainian (39.3%)
5	Westerner (38.1%)	Worker (36.6%)
6	Man (37.1%)	Man (33.0%)
7	Worker (36.1%)	Orthodox (31.2%)
8	Democrat (32.2%)	Pensioner (30.2%)
9	Orthodox (31.7%)	Russian (30.0%)
10	Young (27.9%)	Old (27.7%)

Still, it would be premature to draw such conclusions without taking into account the nature of each of these national identities. The preeminent Russian ethnographer Valerii Tishkov has noted that "post-Soviet scholarship and culture to this point have not yet been able to accept that there may exist such realities as Russian, Ukrainian, Kazakh, Latvian, and other nations as poly-cultural political communities."[26] He goes on to say,

> If a Russian was born and is living in Kharkiv [a city in eastern Ukraine], and if he has no other historical fatherland, then he is a Ukrainian in the civic sense of this term, because on the basis of the "zero variant" he has Ukrainian citizenship, he votes in Ukraine, he is loyal to this state, and feels at home

here; therefore, there is no need to burden him with the notion of a "Russian" identity.[27]

Tishkov emphasizes that in regard to both Russia and Ukraine, as well as to other states of the world, one should not talk about a "multinational people," but rather about a "polyethnic nation." He refers here to the distinction between so-called "ethnic" and "political" nations. The former stresses the importance of ethnic distinctions and presumes that the individuals who constitute the nation share a common culture and ancestry. The latter is based on civic solidarity, and refers to groups that lack common culture and ancestry or any illusion thereof. The key issue in this case is the growth of solidarity among the people of a particular territory.[28]

In general, the scholarly literature on nationalism has held that the political concept of nation is more widespread in the West (the classic examples are the British, American, and Swiss nations) and the ethnic concept in the East (German, Russian, and other East European nations). Equality of political rights constitutes the core of the Western model, while common language and traditions are at the core of the Eastern model.[29] There are many exceptions to this geographical division, however. The ethnic model applies to some West European nations that have lost their original languages, as in the cases of Ireland and Norway. Even in the case of the United States, which has been considered a classic embodiment of the civic concept, identity and culture are rooted in the Anglo-American Protestant traditions of the original settlements.[30] By the same token, some of the East European nationalisms—for example Czech and Hungarian—had a civic component. It is correct to assume, therefore, that these two concepts of nation rarely exist in pure form. As Anthony D. Smith has noted, there is

> a profound dualism at the heart of every nationalism. In fact, every national-
> ism contains civic and ethnic elements in varying degrees and different forms.
> Sometimes civic and territorial elements predominate; at other times, ethnic
> and vernacular components are emphasized.[31]

In the history of Ukrainian and Russian identity formation, both concepts of nation have applied at different times. Ukrainian and Russian identities may take on different characters depending on historical circumstances and regional differences. Moreover, it is not quite clear that Soviet identity was purely a "political" one, since the authorities placed great emphasis on the alleged linguistic and historical proximity of Russians, Ukrainians, and Belarusians.[32]

To determine whether civic or ethnic elements are dominant in Lviv and Donetsk, it seems reasonable to analyze respondents' attitudes towards: (1) the language issue; (2) their history; (3) the issue of political independence; (4) the region in which they live; and (5) economic issues.[33] Issues of language and common historical ancestry are considered "ethnic" elements of identity, while the others are considered "civic."

To make an efficient comparison along these lines, it is necessary to define the limits of divergence on these issues. A regression analysis of the 1994 survey data on three main indicators—region (Lviv versus Donetsk), self-identification (Ukrainian, Russian, or Soviet), and the mixed identity of spoken language/objective nationality (Ukrainian-speaking Ukrainians, Russian-speaking Ukrainians, and Russian-speaking Russians)—reveals that region is the most important determinant of respondents' attitudes towards the five issues.[34] Subjective (self-)identification is next in importance. In a finding that contradicts the assumptions of some analysts, the mixed language/nationality indicator is the least important (although still significant) determinant of mass attitudes. In other words, the answers one is most likely to hear from any individual will depend first of all on whether the interview is conducted in Lviv or Donetsk, secondly on the individual's self-identification (Ukrainian, Russian, or Soviet), and lastly, on the language in which he or she answers the questions (Ukrainian or Russian). It makes sense, therefore, to place the comparison of national identities within the larger framework of regional differences.

The Language Issue

One of the biggest differences between Lviv and Donetsk is revealed in respondents' attitudes toward the statement: "Those who live in Ukraine must learn to speak Ukrainian and use Ukrainian in public." Most of the respondents in Lviv agreed with the statement, but in Donetsk most disagreed. Our interviews with the focus groups in 1994 and 1996 confirmed this finding. Participants from Donetsk were concerned that the Russian-speaking majority would suffer if Ukrainian were to be introduced as the official state language. They refer to the example of western Ukraine and Lviv, where the Russian-speaking minority has become the target of discrimination on the basis of language. A negative attitude towards Russian speakers was confirmed by participants of the 1996 focus groups in Lviv.

An interesting finding is that when respondents in each of these two categories—those who are in favor of the policy of establishing Ukrainian as the official language and those who are against it—refer to outside models as examples worthy of following, they choose the classic models of ethnic or civic nationhood. Thus in Lviv respondents mentioned Poland and Germany, where virtually everyone speaks Polish or German, while in Donetsk one woman raised the example of the United States, where Spanish is used in official contexts in some states (she erroneously mentioned French).The general impression is that in terms of language, the ethnic concept dominates in Lviv, while the civic concept dominates in Donetsk. This may be too broad a generalization, however. At least two qualifications should be made: first, there is consensus in both cities that it does not matter what language people speak, as long as they support Ukraine. Second, respondents did not seem to be expressing preferences for the ethnic or the civic concept per se. In both cases, it seemed that people were simply defending their right to speak publicly in the language they use at home. In these terms, the discrepancy is indicative of the different historical and political circumstances of the two regions rather than a conscious choice on the part of the population.

In fact, some of the people interviewed in Donetsk were ready to accept the establishment of Ukrainian as the official public language on two conditions: that they be given more time to prepare for the change, and that Ukrainian be the language of a "strong master" who will bring the situation in Ukraine under control. This supports Szporluk's hypothesis that debates about the status of the Ukrainian language have more to do with the social status of Ukrainian versus Russian speakers than with nationalism.[35]

Historical Memory

Historical myths—the way in which members of an existing or potential community imagine their past—play a particularly important role in the mobilization of national movements. Because of their powerful emotional appeal, they are extremely effective in forming collective identity, even where the potential members of a national group are politically passive. In post-Soviet Ukraine, the "Soviet" and the "Ukrainian national" versions of the Ukrainian past (simplifying, of necessity, the differences between historiographical schools within each version) are battling for supremacy. The "Soviet" paradigm, which presented Ukrainian history as a regional version of Russian history, was introduced through the Soviet educational system and was purported to have a powerful grip on the minds of millions of citizens. In contrast, traditional Ukrainian historiography emphasizes the distinctiveness and independence of the Ukrainian historical process and presents Ukraine as the victim of injustices committed by Russia. This version of Ukrainian history is not new, but it was introduced into Ukrainian schools only recently, after the proclamation of Ukrainian independence.[36]

In our survey, we asked respondents in Lviv and Donetsk to evaluate the importance of certain events in the historical development of Ukraine. The events were selected so as to create two sets representing the two versions of Ukrainian history. In both cities, most of the respondents agreed that the starting point of Ukrainian history lay in Kyivan Rus'. However, there was clear disagreement between Lviv and Donetsk regarding the later periods, and the closer the event to the present, the more pronounced the difference (see Table 3).[37]

Table 3. How important, in your opinion, are the following for understanding the origins of Ukraine?

Very important	Lviv	Donetsk
Kyivan Rus'	72.7%	77.2%
Cossackdom	74.1%	45.9%
Pereiaslav Treaty (1654)	33.4%	77.7%
Ukrainian National Republic	67.5%	23.3%
Ukrainian Soviet Socialist Republic	19.8%	59.7%
Proclamation of Ukrainian Independence (1991)	90.4%	28.0%

In short, there is an evident preference for the traditional Ukrainian version of history in Lviv and for the Soviet version in Donetsk. The focus group discussions provided some additional examples of this tendency.

The extent to which the Soviet era is idealized in Donetsk is particularly noteworthy. The Soviet period is perceived as the "good old days" when the Communist Party provided for the needs of the people, the state bureaucracy was uncorrupted and kept its promises, medical care was free and efficient, refrigerators were full of food, and even husbands loved their wives more ardently. In Lviv, on the other hand, the majority of the respondents had a very negative experience of the Soviet period. They blame the backwardness of the Ukrainian economy on the Soviet legacy. Even so, some also miss the social protections they had enjoyed under the Soviet regime, and recognize that some things were better then than they are now.

The Issue of Ukrainian Independence

At first glance, the results of the 1994 survey seem to indicate that the disintegration of Ukraine is a real possibility. The most salient issue is, of course, Ukraine's relationship with Russia. In Lviv, 62 percent chose Ukrainian independence as the most desirable option, while unification with Russia was among the least popular options. In Donetsk, more than half (57 percent) favor a "new unification" with Russia. On a seven-point scale, where "1" meant "Ukraine and Russia should be completely separate" and "7" meant "Russia and Ukraine should be the same country," respondents in Lviv averaged 2.2 as opposed to 5.74 in Donetsk.

Although it might seem that the desire to reunite with Russia could result from the sharp economic decline after Ukraine declared its independence in 1991, the data do not support this explanation. While respondents in both cities evaluated the economic changes in Ukraine since 1991 negatively or very negatively, Lviv respondents nevertheless supported the idea of Ukrainian independence. It should also be noted that the average monthly income is substantially greater in Donetsk than it is in Lviv (about 40 percent greater, according to our survey), which further belies the relevance of the economic factor to the issue of Ukrainian independence.

The key difference between Lviv and Donetsk is of a political rather than an economic nature. While 74.4 percent of the inhabitants of Lviv evaluate the political changes that have taken place since 1991 positively or very positively, 88.2 percent in Donetsk view these changes as negative or very negative. Another telling finding is that in Lviv, the communists are the most disliked group, whereas in Donetsk it is the Ukrainian nationalists who are most disliked.

Cultural differences appear to be of lesser importance. When asked to place themselves on a seven-point scale where "1" meant "Ukraine and Russia are completely different" and "7" meant "Ukraine and Russia are basically the same," the average in Lviv was 3.96 while the average in Donetsk was 6.17. Although, Lviv and Donetsk differed greatly on this question, the averages were located on the same half of the spectrum.

These observations require further qualifications. The focus group discussions in 1994 and in 1996 indicated that many citizens of Donetsk are not categorically against the political independence of Ukraine. They would be willing to accept it on the condition that Ukraine becomes a viable and efficient state. Some even found the idea of Ukrainian independence attractive, although they believed that the potential for success was overestimated in 1991. A few went so far as to declare their wish that Ukraine would belong to the European community rather than to Russia. They believe that in reality, Ukraine will continue to waver between Europe and Russia, remaining closer to the latter.

Territory

This leads us to the finding that despite their great divergence, the inhabitants of Lviv and Donetsk have something in common: their attachment to the territorial unity of Ukraine. Only 1 percent in Lviv and 5 percent in Donetsk favored the division of Ukraine into several separate countries. The majority in both cities want their region to remain part of Ukraine. That is, while the populations of Lviv and Donetsk disagree profoundly in their desires for the future of Ukraine, they agree that their regions share a common destiny with the rest of Ukraine.

The way the two groups envision Ukraine is nevertheless quite different. In our 1996 focus group discussions, we found varying definitions of the territory with which people identify. Residents of Lviv view Ukraine as their homeland and feel an attachment towards it as their country. On the other hand, when residents of Donetsk refer to their homeland, they have in mind their own region, meaning Donbas, or the former Soviet Union or Russia—but rarely Ukraine. When people were asked about their country, some started to answer about both Ukraine and Russia; only when the interviewer asked an additional question did they understand that they were being asked about Ukraine.

To be sure, territorial patriotism can be affected by political events. For example, the war in Chechnya has increased patriotic feelings towards Ukraine at a time when Ukraine appeared politically more stable than Russia. This tendency was especially pronounced among women in both Lviv and Donetsk, who were concerned about the prospect of sending their sons to war. In general, political stability is highly valued and is a top priority in both cities. Some respondents in Donetsk consider Crimea the most dangerous place to live in Ukraine because they believe a "second Chechnya" is ripening there. Ironically, they see western Ukraine as one of the best places to live in all of Ukraine.

The 1994 survey data indicate that residents of both Lviv and Donetsk tended to overemphasize their regional differences. In many cases, members of one group expected members of the other to hold more radical opinions than they actually held. The focus group discussions appear to support this finding. In general, respondents in Lviv and Donetsk dislike each other. Each group felt that their own region had been exploited for the economic benefit of the other. These negative attitudes were most prevalent among those who did not have direct personal contacts with members of the other group. In the few cases where respondents did have such contacts, their statements were much milder, and they even expressed some sympathy for the other group.

Economic Issues

The majority in both Lviv and Donetsk evaluated the economic changes that have taken place since Ukraine was declared independent negatively or very negatively. In both cities economic problems were perceived as the most serious facing Ukraine today. This is hardly surprising given the severe economic crisis that Ukraine has experienced since the breakup of the Soviet Union. The uniformity of opinion on this question cannot be interpreted as evidence of a single "national" identity; one may doubt whether Russian citizens would differ from Ukrainian citizens in this respect. Moreover, the salience of economic issues mutes the problem of nationality. In both Lviv and Donetsk, respondents considered the degradation of the environment, the increasing economic inequality among citizens, rising prices, and unemployment greater threats to the stability of Ukraine than either war with Russia or conflicts between nationalities.

In addition, there were indications of a certain consensus concerning economic interests and the unity of Ukraine. Specifically, the majority of respondents in both Lviv and Donetsk disagreed that their region would be better off if it were not part of Ukraine. The commonality of economic interests was also reflected in the fact that a majority in both cities agreed with the statements that

"Ukrainians expect too much from other countries" and "nobody will help us—we can rely only on ourselves."

However, the conclusions drawn by each group were different. Respondents in Lviv were inclined to think that each person should look after himself, while in Donetsk they preferred to consider the government the guarantor of employment and a high standard of living for everyone. This difference, as our focus groups demonstrated, may have a national dimension. Respondents in Lviv blame the communist regime for suppressing the psychology of private ownership, particularly in central and eastern Ukraine. They view Poland, where this psychology was retained, as an example of what might have been possible in Ukraine. They see the opening of the former Soviet borders since the fall of communism as a very positive change, providing Ukrainians with the opportunity to travel, make comparisons, and develop ideas about improving their own economic situation. Some theorists suggest that this "catch up" mentality may serve as a breeding ground for national sentiment.[38]

Similar attitudes were found in the Donetsk focus group, but the implications were quite different from those in Lviv. One interviewee had her own ideas about how to improve the situation:

> No matter how often we change our government, our lives won't be better for it. It is necessary to understand that if you have chosen to become president, and to be responsible for the people, then you [really] have responsibility for those people. This is the first point. The second point is that for us to live better our government, our president, our deputies, must necessarily, unequivocally, open the enterprises that have been closed—our own enterprises. The third point is that we have to have our own production both in light and heavy industries. I'm not the only one with this opinion. Our own [production]. The fourth point is that the quality of production must be restored. The fifth point is to put an end to the importation of all of this foreign stuff. You need to close all the borders. [To ban all those] so-called *meshochniks*.[39] To restore our own enterprises. To return our own specialists, our own engineers, our own teachers—well, to return all those specialists to a toy factory or a textile factory and so on. To produce our own metals, to teach our own children, to have our own professors. All this has to be restored. If we don't restore it, it means we are worth nothing.

All this, in her opinion, would necessarily lead to the revival of culture—in this case, Russian culture.

Conclusion

In conclusion, I will examine the correlations between the responses to each of the five issues discussed above and the two different definitions of national identity. The assumption here is that criteria are considered efficient when they coincide with regional differences and provide a persuasive explanation of both political cleavages and the relative political stability of Ukraine. In regard to the first criterion (primary language combined with objective nationality or "passport nationality"), it was the Ukrainian-speaking Ukrainians who were significantly different from the other groups on most issues. Only on the question of the unity of Ukraine were they close to the Russian-speaking Ukrainians; both groups place the interests of Ukraine higher than the interests of the various regions.

In general, the Russian-speaking Ukrainians, Russian-speaking Russians, and Ukrainian-speaking Russians were all closer to each other than they were to Ukrainian-speaking Ukrainians. There were some minor exceptions, though. Russian-speaking Ukrainians were slightly different from the two Russian groups on the question of the possible regionalization of Ukraine (and still, they were against it), and significantly different on the question of political independence (which is not to say, though, that they were pro-independence). Ukrainian-speaking Russians were different from Russian-speaking Russians on the language issue. This may sound paradoxical, but considering that they already speak Ukrainian, it seems natural to them to speak Ukrainian in public.

Self-identification appears to be the most efficient criterion. Those who identify themselves as Ukrainian believe that it is important for people living in Ukraine to use the Ukrainian language in public. They perceive Ukrainian history in traditional "national" terms, but they recognize that the Soviet historical legacy is somewhat important to understanding the origins of Ukraine. Ukrainians by self-identification are more likely to agree that Ukrainians and Russians should be separate and that Ukraine should be a completely independent country. They also believe that Ukraine should maintain its unity rather than break up along regional lines. Since the group of Ukrainians by self-identification largely coincides with the group of Ukrainian-speaking Ukrainians, one may safely conclude that, at its core, Ukrainian identity consists mainly of ethnic elements. It also helps us to understand why language differences are so important to the study of national and political cleavages in Ukraine. The underlying difference is between Ukrainians (who are a linguistically homogenous group) and non-Ukrainians.

The opposite is true for Russians and Soviets. These groups were almost identical in their attitudes. The slight differences are that the Soviets expressed somewhat more opposition to speaking Ukrainian in public, were more supportive of the Soviet version of history, were more likely to believe that Ukraine and Russia should be the same country, and favored more government involvement in the economy. The numbers differ only slightly in all cases except on the question of attitudes toward the political future of Ukraine.

In a rather surprising finding, the Soviets tended to locate themselves towards one end of the attitudinal spectrum. That is, if we place the three groups on a spectrum according to their pro-Ukrainian/anti-Ukrainian attitudes, the sequence is Ukrainian-Russian-Soviet. It might have been reasonable to assume that "Soviet" identity generally would be located between Russian and Ukrainian, combining elements of both, but this is not the case. A correlation analysis of the survey data reveals that the Soviets are more alienated from Ukrainians than are the Russians. A self-identified "Soviet" is much more likely to oppose the use of Ukrainian in public and the national version of history, and much less likely to place Ukrainian interests above regional ones. This leads to another conclusion, which is that the Soviet identity is not a purely "political" one, but in fact comprises some ethnic elements. If this is the case, then the prospects for the "ethnonationalization" of Ukraine are alarmingly real, because the Soviet identity may be transformed rather easily into Russian identity.

There are some silver linings to the Ukrainian situation, however. In most cases, the differences between Ukrainians, Soviets, and Russians are not as essential as they may seem at first glance. To be sure, the groups differ significantly, but for the most part they remain on the same side of the barricade. To put it simply, Ukrainians tend to occupy one end of the spectrum, with Russians and Soviets more towards the center. But the Russians and Soviets rarely cross the line to place themselves in out-and-out opposition to the Ukrainians. The explanation for this seems to be the strong territorial identification that serves as the glue keeping the parts of the whole together.

Another facet of the issue is that the Soviet identity appears to be more than simply a national attitude. People who prefer to call themselves "Soviets" seem to have bought into the whole package of Soviet ideology, including the unrealistically high expectations of government support and the lack of private initiative. Part of that package is an inability to organize continuous and efficient pressure on decision makers and power centers "from below." As our 1994 survey indicated, residents of Donetsk were much less politically mobilized than residents of Lviv. The number of people in Donetsk who have on more than one occasion contacted a national newspaper or a government representative, signed a petition, joined a social organization, or participated in a rally or demonstration is one-half to one-third the number in Lviv. The people of Donetsk may be willing to reunite Ukraine with Russia, but as the experience of the last few years has shown, it is unlikely that they can organize any significant national movement—as their compatriots in Lviv were able to do during the last years of Gorbachev's rule.

It must be remembered, of course, that Lviv was one of the least Sovietized cities of the Soviet Union, and that most of its population cherished memories of the national struggle and political traditions that derived from the Austrian, Polish, and early Soviet times.[40] But the fifty-year Soviet legacy has affected people there as well. They may be very anti-Soviet in the political sense, while sharing some Soviet economic values. The differences between Lviv and Donetsk can be significant, but they are more imagined than real. As our survey shows, people tend to overestimate the differences and to ascribe to their counterparts more extreme views than they actually have.

Our findings suggest that it is the "Sovietness" of the Ukrainian population that provides Ukrainian leaders with an opportunity to keep the country together. This conclusion must be considered very tentative, because one crucial factor—the time factor—is still missing from this general picture. It does not seem likely that Soviet identity will persist indefinitely after the breakup of the Soviet Union. In light of the examples of the Ottoman, Czechoslovak, and Yugoslav identities, it seems that Soviet identity is doomed to fade away in the long term. The crucial question is what new identity or identities will replace it as the Soviet legacy becomes history.

NOTES

An earlier version of this paper was presented at the Harriman Institute of Columbia University in New York on 1 May 1997.

1. Miroslav Hroch, "From National Movement to the Fully-Formed Nation: The Nation-Building Process in Europe," *New Left Review* 194 (1993): 304.

2. This point was made recently by Louise Jackson in "Identity, Language, and Transformation in Eastern Ukraine: A Case Study of Zaporizhzhia," in *Contemporary Ukraine: Dynamics of Post-Soviet Transformation*, ed. Taras Kuzio (Armonk, NY, 1998), p. 102.

3. See Anthony D. Smith, *National Identity* (Reno, NV, and London, 1991), p. 14.

4. Dominique Arel, "The Temptation of the Nationalizing State," in *Political Culture and Civil Society in Russia and the New States of Eurasia*, ed. Vladimir Tismaneanu (Armonk, NY, and London, 1995), p. 169.

5. Andrew Wilson, *Ukrainian Nationalism in the 1990s: A Minority Faith* (Cambridge, 1997), pp. 22–23.

6. Valerii Khmel'ko, "Tretii god nezavisimosti: chto pokazali vtorye prezidentskie vybory," *Sovremennoe obshchestvo* 4 (1994): 17–18; Valeri Khmelko and Andrew Wilson, "Nationalism and Ethnic and Linguistic Cleavages in Ukraine," in *Contemporary Ukraine*, ed. Kuzio, pp. 60–80.

7. See "Ukraine: The Birth and Possible Death of a Country," *The Economist* 7 May 1994; D. Williams and R. J. Smith, "U.S. Intelligence Sees Economic Flight Leading to Breakup of Ukraine," *The Washington Post* 25 January 1994: 7.

8. Zenovia A. Sochor, "Political Culture and Foreign Policy: Elections in Ukraine in 1994," in *Political Culture and Civil Society*, ed. Tismaneanu, pp. 208–226; Roman Szporluk, "Reflections on Ukraine after 1994: The Dilemmas of Nationhood," *The Harriman Review* 7(7–9) March–May 1994: 1–9.

9. William Zimmerman, "Is Ukraine a Political Community?" *Communist and Post-Communist Studies* 31 (1998) 1: 43–55.

10. The project was supervised by Oksana Malanchuk (University of Michigan), Natalia Chernysh (Lviv Franko State University), and the author. The project was funded by the International Renaissance foundation (the Ukrainian branch of the Soros Foundation), and was modeled after the Detroit Area Studies. For earlier publications based on the survey data see: Yaroslav Hrytsak, Oksana Malanchuk, and Natalia Chernysh,

"Skhid i zakhid Ukraïny: integratsiia chy dezintegratsiia?" *UNIAN-polityka: ohliady, komentari, prohnozy* 36(37) 1994: 7–9; Yaroslav Hrytsak, "Social and National Identities in Western and Eastern Ukraine," in *Grappling with Democracy: Deliberations on Post-Communist Societies (1990–1995)*, ed. Elżbieta Matynia (Prague, 1996), pp. 266–69.

11. The focus group discussions were part of a larger project comparing new identities in Ukraine, Estonia, and Uzbekistan during the post-Soviet transformation. The project was carried out under the guidance of Professor Michael Kennedy of the University of Michigan, and with the participation of scholars from Estonia, Ukraine, the United States, and Uzbekistan. The project was funded by the Ford Foundation. The Ukrainian part of the project was carried out by, among others, Oksana Malanchuk (University of Michigan) and Yaroslav Hrytsak and Viktor Susak (Lviv Franko State University). Each discussion group consisted of two male and two female middle-aged workers. Audiotapes and transcribed materials from the focus group discussions are preserved in the Oral History Archive, Institute for Historical Research, Lviv State University, Project on "Identity Formation and Social Issues in Estonia, Ukraine, and Uzbekistan," Ukraine: Focus Group Discussions. Conducted, transcribed, and edited by Viktor Susak (Lviv, 1996–1998).

12. Taras Kuzio made this point at a conference held at Yale University, 23–24 April 1999.

13. Dominique Arel and Andrew Wilson, "The Ukrainian Parliamentary Elections," *RFE/RL Research Report* 1 July 1994: 7; Jackson, "Identity, Language, and Transformation," pp. 100–101; Roman Solchanyk, "The Post-Soviet Transition in Ukraine: Prospects for Stability," in *Contemporary Ukraine*, ed. Kuzio, pp. 17–40. Certainly, to make a more dramatic comparison one may focus on western Ukraine and Crimea; still, for many reasons, Crimea is a special case which cannot be discussed here.

14. This hypothesis has been supported by some recent empirical findings. See Jackson, "Identity, Language, and Transformation," pp. 99–103; Zimmerman, "Is Ukraine a Political Community?" passim.

15. Solchanyk, "The Post-Soviet Transition in Ukraine," pp. 30–31; Viktor Nebozhenko and Iryna Bekeshkina, "Politychnyi portret Ukraïny (skhid, pivden')" in *Politychnyi portret Ukraïny* 9 (1994): 44–45.

16. Data of the Lviv and Donetsk city statistical departments compiled by Viktor Susak. According to our survey, the situation was not significantly different in 1994. In Lviv, 77.7 percent of the population claimed Ukrainian as their native language and in Donetsk 73.7 percent claimed Russian as theirs. The usage of Russian language in Lviv and Ukrainian in Donetsk is clearly declining from older to younger generations: 79.4

percent of parents in Lviv spoke Ukrainian with their children, while the figure for Russian-speakers in Donetsk is 89.6 percent.

17. Maryana Chorna, "Donbass: The Neo-Liberals are Beating the Communists on the Latter's Home Field," *Demos: An Analytical and Informational Journal* 1(1) 1994: 15–18.

18. David J. Meyer, "Why Have Donbass Russians Not Ethnically Mobilized Like Crimean Russians Have? An Institutional/Demographic Approach," in *State and Nation Building in East Central Europe: Contemporary Perspectives* (New York, 1996), p. 320.

19. This interpretation has recently been suggested by Geoffrey Hosking in his *Russia: People and Empire* (Cambridge, MA, 1997), passim.

20. Roman Szporluk, "Dilemmas of Russian Nationalism," *Problems of Communism* 38(4) July–August 1989: 15–35.

21. Yaroslav Bilinsky, "The Concept of the Soviet People and Its Implications for Soviet Nationality Policy," *Annals of the Ukrainian Academy of Arts and Sciences in the U.S.* 14(37–38) 1978–1980: 87–133.

22. "Russkie," *Etno-sotsiologicheskie ocherki* (Moscow, 1992), p. 415.

23. Roman Solchanyk, "Molding 'The Soviet People': The Role of Ukraine and Belorussia," *Journal of Ukrainian Studies* 8(1) Summer 1983: 3–18.

24. Szporluk, "Dilemmas of Russian Nationalism," p. 35n86.

25. Paul S. Pirie, "National Identity and Politics in Southern and Eastern Ukraine," *Europe-Asia Studies* 48(7) 1996: 1079–1104.

26. Valerii Tishkov, "Postsovetskii natsionalizm i russkaia antropologiia," in *Kuda idet Rossiia? Sotsial'naia transformatsiia postsovetskogo prostranstva* (Moscow, 1996) vol. 3 (Mezhdunarodnyi simpozium 12–14 ianvaria 1996 g.), pp. 212–13.

27. Ibid., p. 220.

28. Philip White, "What is a Nationality?" *Canadian Review of Studies in Nationalism* 12(1) Spring 1985: 1–24.

29. See Hans Kohn, *Nationalism: Its Meaning and History* (Princeton, 1955); idem, *The Idea of Nationalism*, 2nd ed. (New York, 1967); Liah Greenfeld, *Nationalism: Five Roads to Modernity* (Cambridge, MA, and London 1991), pp. 12–14.

30. Smith, *National Identity*, pp. 12, 80, 149–50.

31. Ibid., p. 13.

32. Solchanyk, "Molding the 'Soviet People,'" passim.

33. This is a paraphrase of Anthony D. Smith's formulation of the key elements of national identity. Smith, *National Identity*, pp. 8–15.

34. I am greatly indebted to Dr. Oksana Malanchuk who carried out the analysis and explained its results to me. The results of our data were summarized in Yaroslav Hrytsak and Oksana Malanchuk, "National Identities in Post-Soviet Ukraine: the Case of Lviv and Donetsk," unpublished paper, University of Michigan, Ann Arbor, 1997.

35. Szporluk, "Reflections on Ukraine after 1994," passim.

36. Zenon E. Kohut, "History as a Battleground: Russian-Ukrainian Relations and Historical Consciousness in Contemporary Ukraine," in *The Legacy of History in Russia and the New States of Eurasia: The International Politics of Eurasia*, ed. S. Frederick Starr (Armonk, NY, and London, 1994), vol. 1, pp. 123–46; Andrew Wilson, "The Donbass between Ukraine and Russia: The Use of History in Political Disputes," *Journal of Contemporary History* 30 (1995): 265–89.

37. For corroboration of this tendency see the results of the 1997 "Lviv and Donetsk" survey conducted by the Geneza Center for Political Science in Lviv: "Rezul'taty mizhrehional'noho sotsiolohichnoho opytuvannia (Lviv-Donetsk) 'Stan ukraïns'koho sotsiumu naperedodni vyboriv 1998–1999 rr.'" *Stavropihion* 1997 [*sic*]: 181–82.

38. Greenfeld, *Nationalism: Five Roads to Modernity*, pp. 14–17.

39. The term *meshochnik* refers to petty traders who cross borders to sell goods which they carry in their *meshki* (sacks).

40. Roman Szporluk, "West Ukraine and West Belorussia: Historical Tradition, Social Communication, and Linguistic Assimilation," *Soviet Studies* 31(1) January 1979: 76–98; idem, "The Soviet West—or Far Eastern Europe?" *East European Politics and Societies* 5(3) Fall 1991: 474–77.

Text and Subtext in Roman Ivanychuk's *Mal'vy*

ASSYA HUMESKY

The goals of the historical novelist are different from those of the historian, who usually tries to describe the course of events with utmost precision, providing dates, names of characters, circumstances, and so on. The author of historical novels always provides his or her own interpretation, or worldview, and consciously or not draws parallels to his or her own times.

The novel *Mal'vy*[1] by Roman Ivanychuk, conceived at the beginning of the 1960s and published late in the decade, is no exception.[2] The novel is set in Crimea and Turkey on the eve of the Khmel'nyts'kyi rebellion, but it is full of reflections that are relevant to our times. In his article "Iak ia shukav svoï 'Mal'vy'" (How I Searched for My 'Mal'vy'), the author indicates that he had consciously chosen this particular period to illustrate his ideas:

> Я задумав узятися за працю, в якій би міг дати волю роздумам над долями імперій, які неминуче приходять до упадку, над неминучістю пробудження молодих народів, над причинами тимчасових перемог, а теж невдач у боротьбі за визволення з-під чужоземного ярма. Бо саме ці процеси становлять суть історії народів протягом багатьох тисячоліть.[3]

As to the specific choice of material, the author was guided by his interest in the processes by which "a leader is molded" and "the apostate regains his faith." Hence the author chose this particular time period:

> Я знайшов в історії українського народу дуже вдячний відтинок часу, який досі не був відображений в історичній романістиці—десятиліття "золотої волі" польської шляхти й безгетьманства на Україні.[4]

*   *
*

The main story line of the novel follows the life of Mariia, Hetman Samiilo's wife, who is taken prisoner by the Tatars along with her son and daughter. Another son is kidnapped by Gypsies and is sold to Tatars in Crimea. In order to save her life, Mariia converts to Islam, which makes it possible for her to earn some money and eventually return to her homeland. Unaware of his background, the son who was sold by Gypsies to the Tatars becomes a guard in the khan's palace. When he learns of his origins, he joins the Cossacks and dies a hero's death fighting the Tatars. The other son becomes a janissary and consciously serves on the enemy side. But treason does not save him and in the end he dies in disgrace. Mariia's daughter Mal′va falls in love with the khan, becomes his favorite wife, and bears him a son. Mal′va believes that she can convince her husband to help the Cossacks, but her naive hope is not fulfilled, and in despair she poisons herself, her husband, and her son. These story lines are intertwined with many others, in which the figures of Turkish sultans, Nur-Ali—the head of the janissaries, and the eunuch Zambul—a cunning diplomat and a greedy egoist—come to life. We see the feeble minded sultan Ibrahim, unable to rule the empire, carried by the course of events to the very height of power, only to be mercilessly hurled into the abyss later on. We see the wise grand vizier, Azzem Pasha, a true patriot of Turkey, who is unable to prevent the collapse of the Sublime Porte, corroded as it is from the inside by the disease of mutual hatreds and intrigues, and above all by a misguided concept of politics. The figure of the wise old man, *Meddah* Omar (*meddah* is Turkish for "poet, singer, storyteller") stands out against the background of other characters. He knows the Koran by heart, which has earned him the honorary title of *hafiz*. Omar seems to stand somewhat apart from the mainstream events of the novel, but he actually is one of its central characters.[5] The author expresses his deepest feelings and thoughts through Omar's character. In addition to representatives of the Ottoman Empire, Khmel′nyts′kyi appears with his Cossacks in the last part of the novel, as do Polish magnates, and Khmel′nyts′kyi's treacherous allies, the Tatars. The novel ends with the defeat of the Ukrainian side, although Turkey barely makes any gain from the Polish victory over the Ukrainian hetman. There is no discussion about the future of Poland—only the letter from Khmel′nyts′kyi to the "Crimean tsar" is quoted as saying: "Козацтво тобі більше не вірить. Що ж до Москви, з якою ми вступили в дружбу, то це бажання війська мого і моє. Православна Русь не зрадить нас."

Behind the text lies an eloquent subtext. For example, in his conversation with Mariia, a dervish tries to prove the superiority of Islam over all other religions, saying:

> Магомет же казав: "Коли всі народи приймуть іслам, тоді появиться божий посланник Махді, який зробить усіх людей рівними." Нині більше ніж половина світу визнала нашу віру, і недалекий той час, коли зрівняються всі…від султана до ремісника.[6]

The allusion to the communist doctrine of the equality of all people and the belief in the future rule of communism throughout the world is clear. Elsewhere the author describes, using Mariia as his mouthpiece, the full meaning that such a victory would have for the world's nations and for Ukraine in particular:

> Та невже мусульманська віра має стати єдиною в світі? І розіллється страшна чума по всіх краях, і всі народи стануть схожими на турків . . . І не буде пісень, не буде казок, не стане купальських вогнів, вертепів під Різдво, волі! Ніхто нічого не матиме свого…[7]

The theme of "the confluence of all nations" sounds even more ominous coming from Omar:

Це велике горе нашого народу, візирю, почалося з фальшивої догми, буцімто не може бути різних народів на лоні ісламу. Скільки крові марно пролилося во ім'я цього догмату, а що вийшло? Татари залишилися татарами, точніше—озлобленими татарами, болгари і греки ісламу не прийняли. Мало того; в боротьбі проти нашої імперії вони зміцніли духовно, і розплата над турками неминуча.[8]

The loss of the native language is another painful problem for the Ukrainian people which remains unresolved even today. Through russification, the communist regime attempted to create a "Soviet man" who would speak a "universal language" and forget the national essence that had been branded "bourgeois nationalism." Ivanychuk raises this theme in his novel as well:

Алімові [Mal'va's brother—AH] потрібні були нова віра і мова, він розумів це. Тому перестав молитися по-материнському. Бо що з них, тих молитов, коли тут інший бог, і від цього бога він залежить?[9]

The imposition of one way of thinking on everyone, dictated from above, is a feature of all totalitarian regimes threatened by "original thinkers"; these individuals are either destroyed or locked away in insane asylums. In Ivanychuk's novel we read about the dervish threatening Mariia:

Коли ж бо посмієш не прийти сюди на кожне ранішнє і вечірнє богослужіння, наречемо тебе безумною, і вік свій скоротаєш у тімархане [i.e., an insane asylum—AH]. Бо безумний той, хто не вірить єдиній правді на землі.[10]

Earlier, on hearing about the future "equalization" of all people under Islam, Mariia revealed her opinion on the essence of such collectivism by saying that "Ніхто нічого не матиме свого." Now she proudly opposes the spiritual and intellectual enslavement that this "only truth on earth" implies, saying: "Я живу так, як велить твій бог, бо виходу іншого не маю...А думати не заборониш. І ніхто не може заборонити думати людям—ні ти, ні мулла, ні твій Магомет."[11]

Much reflection in the novel is devoted to the theme of power and imperial leadership. The first chapter begins with an epigraph taken from the Koran:

Хіба ви не ходили по землі і не бачили, який був їх кінець? Були вони могутньою силою, але аллаха ніщо не може ослабити ні на небі, ні на землі (Koran, 35th Sura, prophetic).

With regard to Soviet power, Ivanychuk's use of this sura appears to have been indeed prophetic. The author's thoughts on this subject are expressed further through the character of Omar. Because of their continued relevance in the present day, I shall quote them in their entirety:

Між бажанням держави і бажанням людей існує вічна суперечність. Але при розумних, добрих і вчених правителях ця прірва така вузька, що її можна завжди переступити. Що ж сталося у нас? До того часу, поки слава завоювання була спільною метою держави і народу, народ не шкодував свого життя для слави. Потім одна людина взяла владу в свої руки, народ потрапив у залежність до єдиновладця. Одна людина за всіх думати не може, вона впадає в помилки, думки мільйонів не можуть збігатися з думкою однієї людини. І звідси починається та криза, про яку ти говорив. Єдиновладець прагне до розкошів, і витрати перевищують прибутки. Він хоче слави для себе і завойовує чужі землі. Кожна чужа земля сповнює люд тривогою, бо тоді життя його в постійній небезпеці. Народ хоче спокою, а не чужих земель, які не дають йому ні радості, ні хліба. Володар примушує підданих воювати, і піддані нерадо проливають кров за те, що їм не потрібне. Володар здирає податки на воєнні витрати, людське майно перебуває під постійною загрозою, люди втрачають бажання для його придбання. А багатство держави залежить від особистого багатства людей. Якщо його в них немає,—звідки візьметься в держави? Коли народ пригнічений,—скарбниця порожня. . . [12]

There are many examples of such subtext in Ivanychuk's novel. Turkey is described as a country of spies, as a police state where behind every door there is an eavesdropping "stool pigeon." In the janissary barracks, every fifth bed is occupied by a eunuch who has been ordered to listen to what the soldiers are mumbling in their sleep. The government makes an interesting exception: although the janissaries are allowed to sing in their native languages in the barracks, people are seized and dragged to jail for telling political jokes. This is how the grand vizier Azzem Pasha comments on this situation:

Отой бідний ремісник і я, найвищий державний сановник, обидва однаково розуміємо все, що діється нині, але ні він, ні я не можемо протестувати. Навпаки, на свої кошти й своїми силами влаштовуємо цей парад, а в душі сміємося . . . [13]

And here is an excerpt from the janissaries' army oath:

Ви гвардія султана. Ви охорона імперії. Будьте гідними звання йени-чері і не забувайте, що найлютіші ваші вороги—болгарські гайдуки, сербські ускоки, грецькі клефти і українські козаки.[14]

It is appropriate to recall here the mark of the "Mazepist" traitors, which for centuries some have seen as a stain on the Ukrainian people. In his article "Iak ia shukav svoï 'Mal'vy,'" the author mentions that he was "interested above all in the psychology of the traitor." He shows how "history takes revenge on the treacherous ally—who in this historical period is Khan Islam Giray III." At the same time, the author admits that he admires the khan for his courage and "most importantly, his audacity in breaking free from the Sublime Porte forever." Ivanychuk reports that he "was facing the danger of developing an

involuntary affection for [his] protagonist." Moreover, because of his fondness
for the character, he found himself "willing to find excuses for his threefold
betrayal of the hetman."[15] Later he realized that the khan had two "hypostases"—a knight and a two-faced traitor—because that was how he had been
raised. Whether or not it is the author's intent, his fondness for the character
comes across to the reader. Moreover, it leads one to wonder whether a parallel
is being drawn here to Mazepa. In the novel, Khan Islam Giray responds to
Khmel'nyts'kyi's request to become his ally in the fight against the Poles by
saying: "Але ж ти підданий короля і зраджуєш його. Звідки я можу
знати, що не зрадиш мене?" Khmel'nyts'kyi replies:

> Не можна називати зрадою, хане, праведну боротьбу. Гетьман
> Дорошенко не вважав Шагін-Гірея зрадником, коли той почав
> справедливу війну проти Кафського паші і Кантеміра-мурзи. Зрадити
> можна батька, та не губителя свого. А на Україні лядське тиранство
> гірше мучительства фараонів.[16]

Among the characters of the novel there are also "contemptible" traitors such as
the janissary Alim, apostates like Selim who eventually regain their faith, and
people like Mal'va who sincerely believe in their ability to cooperate with the
enemy, but who realize over time that it is impossible. As these characters are
developed, so is a certain attitude toward Ukraine, a philosophy of apostasy
that can be narrowed down to the following formulas: first, there is no Ukraine
and never will be (Straton); second, it is more convenient to live with the
enemy and to adopt his faith (Andrii-Alim); third, you may betray for the sake
of your children (Mariia); and fourth, the prideful will die.

Mal'vy is filled with descriptions of human suffering and psychological
distress. In his article describing how he wrote the novel, the author tells us:
"One historical novelist started yelling at me: 'Who needs this dwelling on
human suffering, despair, spiritual plunges, and painful disillusionment on the
eve of the Khmel'nyts'kyi rebellion that turned out to be so gloriously successful?'"[17] To this criticism Ivanychuk responds that a nation must go through
seven circles of hell to achieve such a victory, and that in his novel, "the
hetman or leader was not supposed to be the protagonist." Rather, he wanted to
show "how a hetman is born from a national tragedy." Therefore,
Khmel'nyts'kyi is an "episodic character" who evokes admiration and respect
when he leads his army to triumph, but who ultimately loses both in his
unsuccessful diplomatic game. Ivanychuk condemns the hetman through the
song of a Ukrainian woman who is taken prisoner by the enemy:

> Бодай того Хмельницького
> Та перва куля не минула…[18]

The author reiterates his condemnation with an epigraph from Shevchenko
in one of the novel's final chapters:

Як запродав гетьман
У ярмо християн,
Нас послав поганяти,
По своїй по землі
Свою кров розлили
І зарізали брата...[19]

It is not surprising that the censoring authorities did not like this treatment of
the glorious hetman, which the author did not even attempt to disguise in the
subtext. When we do turn to the subtext, however, we find not only a
dismissal of Khmel'nyts'kyi's policies, but also disillusionment about whether
any "hetman or leader" will become the nation's savior. The author depicted his
ideal individual in the character of the "holy man" Omar, who sacrifices his
own life to set a heroic example for his people. This ideal is also found in the
legend of the powers of wormwood,[20] and in the description of the heroic death
of 300 Cossacks who were trapped in a cave when the Tatars lit a fire in front of
it to asphyxiate and burn them. The theme of sacrificial death for the sake of the
nation is similar to the Christian concept of Christ's sacrifice for all humanity.
It therefore can be viewed as a type of religious theme.

Herein lies the most important subtext of the novel: the idea that the
nation—the Ukrainian nation—will achieve its salvation by returning to the
Christian faith. Thematically, this idea is connected with the figure of Mariia,
whom the author describes as the personification of "the nation's vitality and
immortality." Mariia is deeply troubled by her conversion to Islam. When the
dervish rips the cross from around little Mal'va's neck and makes her stomp on
it, Mariia whispers in dismay: "God forgive me!" In Mariia's memory, Ukraine
is always associated with the sound of church bells ringing. The scene in which
Mariia meets Omar on the street at a time of day when all believing Muslims
kneel to pray is indicative of the religious quality of Mariia's character. Old
Omar does not kneel, but only raises his eyes up to the sky, and at that
moment "здалося Марії, що ця людина бачить Бога. Отого Бога, яким
торгують всі на світі, не знаючи його, того Бога, який є
найсправжнісінькою правдою, вічно зневаженою і безсмертною."[21] And
Omar himself says: "Ні за що не плати своєю вірою і совістю. Бог єдиний
для всіх народів і приймає він молитви з різних храмів і різними мовами,
аби тільки вони були щирими, аби тільки до них не торкнувся бруд
користолюбства."[22] This philosophy of uniting people on religious and
spiritual principles is expressed throughout the novel, and is especially connected with the image of Mariia, whose very name is symbolic. In one scene,
Mariia comes to a Christian church for the first time after many years of
suffering. It is a church of the Dormition of the Blessed Virgin Mary, located
in a cavern. In it hangs an icon of the Virgin said to have been brought by the
Apostle Andrew as he "announced God's grace" over that place:

Це не була звичайна ікона Божої Матері, яку не раз бачила в церквах. Зі
скелі на юрбу знедолених людей дивилася зажурена жінка з дитиною

на руках. Обабіч неї стояли два молодих чоловіки з німбами над головами, і зовсім не були вони схожі на святих, радше на дорослих синів цієї скорбної матері.[23]

Mariia identifies with this "sorrowful woman" and says, sobbing: "Ти вберегла! Ти вберегла!" and at that moment "пролунав ангельський хор, що заповнив усю долину, весь світ, і народ підхопив пісню різними мовами на один мотив: 'Пресвятая Богородице, спаси нас!'" Clearly, the author sees the true revival and redemption of Ukraine in Christianity, with its profound humanism and its ideal of sacrificial love for all people.

Translated from the Ukrainian by Oksana Nagayets and Volodymyr Dibrova

NOTES

1. *Mal'va* is the Ukrainian word for "hollyhock" as well as a female name.

2. The novel was published in Kyiv in unusually rapid succession by two publishing houses: Dnipro (1968) and Radians′kyi pys′mennyk (1969), both in large press runs. Curiously, when the book was announced in 1968 by *Mezhdunarodnaia kniga* prior to its publication, it was titled *Janissaries (Ianychary)*. In explaining how he wrote the novel, Ivanychuk never mentions this title, but spends much time describing his search for the title *Mal'vy*. Roman Ivanychuk, *Chystyi metal liuds'koho slova* (Kyiv, 1991), pp. 195–96; the chapter is entitled "Iak ia shukav svoï 'Mal'vy.'"

3. Ibid., p. 193.

4. Ibid., p. 194.

5. He is somewhat reminiscent of the "holy man"—a *kobzar* (bard)—in Panteleimon Kulish's novel *Chorna rada*.

6. Roman Ivanychuk, *Mal'vy* (Kyiv, 1969), p. 70.

7. Ibid., p. 70.

8. Ibid., p. 139.

9. Ibid., p. 61.

10. Ibid., p. 21.

11. Ibid., p. 71.

12. Ibid., pp. 128–29.

13. Ibid., p. 48.

14. Ibid., p. 63.

15. Ivanychuk, *Chystyi metal*, pp. 198–99.

16. Ivanychuk, *Mal'vy*, p. 186.

17. Ivanychuk, *Chystyi metal*, p. 197. In his foreword to the collection *Chystyi metal liuds'koho slova*, Mykhailo Slaboshpyts′kyi writes about the lashing Ivanychuk took for his *Mal'vy*, citing the following excerpt from a critical review by the Moscow literary critic Valentin Oskotskii:

    The historical concreteness of the narrative is lost in the stream of romantic, symbolic, and allegorical images. The romanticized belletristic writing of history backfires with the shift of social criteria and the misevaluation of the class processes. Focused on the historical past of the Ukrainian nation, in the end the novel offers neither an artistic piece of research, nor an analytical exposure of actual conflicts discovered by the author in the dialectics of socially motivated characters and circumstances. The novel is rather a collection of "variations on a theme" presented as a romantic legend about love for one's homeland, which severely punishes for treason and generously rewards for loyalty. (pp. 5–6)

In his article "Dominanta," dedicated to Ivanychuk on the occasion of his seventieth birthday, Slaboshpytsʹkyi recalls: "The banning of *Mal'vy* made him famous in Ukraine ... After the publication of the novel, Ivanychuk found himself the center of attention of both the censors and the readers." And further: "Ivanychuk in his *Mal'vy* began as a writer whose primary concern was to record the nation's vision of its past, its suppressed pain and tragedies. That is when the janissary motif appeared in his work—a motif which, when applied to more recent times, acquired a wider and quite a contemporary significance ... This proves that we deal here with one of those rare instances in which a piece of literature, delving into the specific context of national culture, has defined or crystallized in it some uniquely significant feature (in this instance, unfortunately, a particularly negative one)." Mykhailo Slaboshpytsʹkyi, "Dominanta," *Literaturna Ukraïna* 10 June 1999: 5.

18. Ivanchuk, *Mal'vy,* p. 226.

19. Ibid., p. 213.

20. In Ukrainian folklore, wormwood is a magical herb having the power to restore the memory of one's homeland.

21. Ivanychuk, *Mal'vy*, p. 72.

22. Ibid., p. 73.

23. Ibid., p. 98. The image of the Theotokos is discussed later, when the head mullah—Shaikh al-Islam Rehel—suddenly notices how in the mosque "крізь золото літер проступив силует Христової матері, замальований ще за часів Магомета Завойовника." The mullah whispers in fear: "Щезни!...Дотепер не вбита її ікона—неживе мальовило на стіні мечеті, то хіба зуміли ми вбити її в серцях народів?" (p. 170).

Losing Faith: The Slovak-Hungarian Constitutional Struggle, 1906–1914

OWEN V. JOHNSON

The Slovak national movement first flourished in the mid-nineteenth century. Its main goal was to win legal guarantees that would ensure Slovak national existence and sovereignty. It seemed to have achieved part of its program in the establishment of Matica slovenská and three Slovak high schools in the 1860s, but those promising developments were interrupted by the Austro-Hungarian Ausgleich of 1867 and the events that followed it. After failing to win a single seat in two successive elections to the Hungarian parliament (1875 and 1878), the Slovak National Party opted for passivity, refusing to participate in the 1881 elections, and withdrawing from Budapest to the backwoods town of Turčiansky Sväty Martin.[1] The party did not return to the political arena until the beginning of the twentieth century.[2] The end of passivity was conditioned by two factors, one internal and one external.

A significant element leading to the change of tactics was the increasing rate of economic change, which resulted in extensive social change and discontent. A series of bad harvests coupled with a decline in agricultural prices produced a rapidly growing agricultural proletariat that blamed Jews—among others—for its difficulties, and became a willing participant in the new Catholic, antisemitic, and apparently pronationality Hungarian People's Party (Néppárt).[3]

Another internal stimulant was the 1894 trial of Romanian nationalists, which helped promote cooperation among the non-Magyar nationalities in Hungary, culminating in the Congress of Non-Hungarian Nations in Budapest in 1895. Not only did the Congress seek national equality, but it also tied that demand to others that were aimed at democratizing and widening the base of the national movements, such as universal and secret suffrage, and the freedoms of press, speech, assembly, and association.

The main external stimulus came from the West, from Prague. During the years of passivity, Tomáš G. Masaryk, a professor at the Czech university in Prague, gathered about him a number of earnest young students among whom he promoted the idea of closer Czech and Slovak cooperation.[4] From these contacts—strengthened by young Slovaks studying in Vienna, Budapest, and elsewhere—grew the liberal-democratic Hlasist movement, which entered the Slovak public sphere in 1898 with the establishment of the journal *Hlas*. The journal was edited by two physicians, Vavro Šrobár and Pavel Blaho. The

Hlasists did not form a separate political party, but from the liberal side of the Slovak National Party stressed that more sustained grass-roots cultural and economic activity was necessary to secure a future for the Slovak nation.[5] Representatives of a new generation of political elites, they argued that the life of the intelligentsia required something more than subscribing to the thrice-weekly *Národnie noviny*, which since 1870 had served as a bible for members of the Slovak National Party (SNS).[6]

The conservative, moderate traditionalists within the SNS, led by longtime party chairman Pavel Mudroň, responded angrily to the Hlasist charges of inactivity—charges that broke several decades of apparent Slovak political and ideological unity. What is significant is that the stagnant waters of Slovak national life were stirred before the onset of the Hungarian constitutional crisis of 1905–1906.[7] Three distinct strands in Slovak national politics and ideology had been formed, with a fourth, Social Democratic, strand, in the process of formation. What united them was the struggle for a democratic solution to the national question. As the young Budapest lawyer and publicist Milan Hodža put it in 1901:

> Our needs tie us to democracy. We must realize that there is the most certain guarantee of both our national and socioeconomic development. Nationalism without the people, believe you me, is nonsense; but democracy, in addition to defending the nation, has this great benefit: that it also brings the people into public life—in fact, mainly the people. Are today's national pillars really more reliable than the people?[8]

Until the approach of World War I would direct attention elsewhere, the rulers of Hungary and the representatives of these small Slovak political movements would struggle for the hearts and minds of the majority of the population inhabiting Slovakia. The success of the Slovak national movements would depend on their ability to build a mass base by attracting the peasantry and to some degree—as industrialization advanced—the working class, and to find allies either in Hungary or abroad.[9] In this article I focus on the struggle as it played out between 1906 and 1914.

Five years of Slovak experience in Parliament (1901–1906)—with careful observation and analysis of questions of domestic political life—along with the stronger organization of Slovak political life both inside and outside of Parliament had prepared the Slovak population for the 1906 election.[10] With the exception of the Social Democrats, the Slovak national movement sallied forth behind a joint election committee that had adopted a platform nearly identical to the nationality program put forth in Parliament in May 1905 and adopted as a joint program by the Parliamentary National Party (PNS) in March 1906.[11] The platform called for universal and secret suffrage, and asserted the principle of the unity and independence of Hungary. At the same time, it stressed the right of the Slovak nation to national, cultural, and political equality, and demanded the enactment of the 1868 nationality law—including the right to use the

Slovak language in public life, especially in elementary and high schools, public administration, and the courts. It asked for annual aid from the budget for Slovak cultural associations and compensation for the damage suffered by the Slovak nation in 1875 when the government confiscated the holdings of Matica slovenská. Its economic planks were expanded to cover industry as a whole, not just the interests of the peasant, small businessman, and artisan.

Since the Slovak People's Party (SL'S—its members were referred to as "L'udaks") was really only an informal grouping, it did not develop an official platform. Instead, its program was defined by *Katolícke noviny*. While basically congruent with that of the Slovak National Party, it also included demands for the reform of Church-state relations, an increased state contribution to church salaries, religious education in the elementary schools, and social regulations for the protection of workers in industry.[12] Throughout the campaign, its candidates emphasized the needs of the peasant, and stressed that the Néppárt was a false defender of the masses.[13]

The Slovak national movement entered 19 candidates, 14 under the colors of the Slovak People's Party and 5 for the SNS. Among the SL'S candidates were 3 Hlasists—Blaho, Šrobár, and Hodža. The SNS scored its greatest success of the pre–World War I period, collecting 13,340 votes. Even so, this represented only 15 percent of the Slovak votes. This showed that if the necessary organizational and agitational work among voters was undertaken in the individual electoral districts, it was possible to win. Six L'udaks were victorious, as was 1 SNS candidate. Four of the victories came in Bratislava County, three of them in head-to-head competition with the Néppárt. The latter, aided by an agreement of the coalition parties on the division of Slovak electoral districts, saw 18 of its 28 candidates in Slovakia win. Elsewhere in Slovakia, the Constitution Party won 33 seats and the Independence Party won 22.[14] This was also the greatest success of a government majority in elections in Slovakia during the prewar period. The success of both sides helps explain the tension and violence between them in the next four years.

Two quite different trends marked the session of the newly elected parliament (1906–1910). One was the ferocious effort to stamp out the Slovak national movement and to incorporate the Slovaks into the Magyar nation through the persecution of the Slovak leaders, the complete magyarization of the schools, and similar measures. This effort brought the unwanted attention of foreign observers, strengthened Czech-Slovak cooperation, and alienated Slovak mass opinion against the Hungarian government. Another trend was the effort to achieve a peaceful resolution of Slovak demands, whether through the legislation of universal suffrage or through some kind of agreement with Prime Minister Sándor Wekerle. This effort brought only disappointment for the Slovak side, particularly for certain of its leaders.

The efforts to derail the Slovak national movement continued a long-established Hungarian policy. What characterized this period was an increase in intensity. The effort took several forms: judicial persecutions of the leadership, legal measures in the elementary schools, and support for newspapers and dialects designed to fracture Slovak unity. Each action was aimed at a particular subsection of the Slovak population, whether by class or by geography. The history of the judicial persecutions is well known.[15] The overarching goal was to discredit the Slovak leaders before their public.[16] Ferdiš Juriga, the driving intellectual force in the SL'S, was imprisoned for two years. Šrobár, Andrej Hlinka, and Milan Ivanka also served time in prison. František Jehlička, a Christian Socialist theoretician, was discredited when he accepted a university chair in return for his support of the government.[17] One of the leading forces in this campaign was the Néppárt, which was anxious for revenge against many of its former Slovak members. The Catholic hierarchy, which normally stood aloof from the party, took an active part in the persecutions out of fear that the Slovak priests under its jurisdiction were taking too much of an interest in social measures.

It was this conflict that culminated in the Černova "massacre." Andrej Hlinka had raised the money for the construction of a church in a village on the outskirts of Ružomberok, but having been convicted of incitement for his role in the 1906 parliamentary campaign, he was unable to attend its consecration.[18] Church officials sent another representative in his place. The consecration took place on 27 October 1907, and gendarmes were present to maintain order. Some two weeks earlier, a campaign for universal suffrage had culminated in a partial general strike, and this may have had the gendarmes still on edge. For one reason or another, the gendarmes fired into the crowd, killing 12 men and 3 women, and wounding several dozen more.[19] The following year, 59 survivors were tried for incitement. The incident brought Hungary immeasurable negative publicity abroad at a particularly inopportune time.[20] It also ended the Czech-Hungarian cooperation in the Monarchy, something that had pained Slovak leaders.[21]

The story of the Apponyi Acts also is well known.[22] The Hungarian Minister of Culture and Education decreed in 1907 that teachers in church schools were henceforth state employees, and they had to be able to read, write, and teach Hungarian, and by the end of the fourth year of school, non-Hungarian pupils had to be able to express themselves in Hungarian, both orally and in writing. Teachers' promotions were made contingent on their pupils' success in mastering the Hungarian language.[23] The Slovak deputies wanted to obstruct or delay passage of the Apponyi laws, but because of tactical errors, all that developed was a more or less successful debate during which the nationality deputies pointed out the negative side of the magyarization of the schools.

The judicial repression and the educational restrictions led many Slovak peasants, with their newly awakened national consciousness, to take a negative position toward the state—in contrast to the generally neutral views they had held earlier due to lack of contact. The consequences were potentially dangerous for Hungary.

Less well known is the Hungarian government's effort to counteract the spread of the Slovak movement to eastern Slovakia, especially in Šariš County, by increasing the pressure to develop a distinct east Slovak dialect. The Hungarian government had supported such a campaign as far back as 1897, not only in Slovakia, but also among Slovak immigrants in the United States. The efforts of two Slovaks to run for Parliament from Šariš spurred the government to new action. It funded the establishment of a newspaper, *Naša zastava*, in the east Slovak dialect, after recognizing that Magyar papers simply were not reaching the population. The government hoped that exposure to the east Slovak dialect in newspapers would make it more difficult for people to read literary Slovak.[24]

It seems strange that while these repressive measures were being enforced, Slovak leaders in Parliament remained somewhat optimistic about a peaceful resolution to the nationality problem either through the legal enactment of universal suffrage, or through some kind of modus vivendi with the state. Their optimism can be explained in part by the fact that the repressive measures "at home" were often enforced by local Hungarian officials who felt the threat of a Slovak national movement more directly than did Budapest, but also by an idealistic faith on the part of Slovaks that the Hungarian rulers would see the error of their ways and come to a fair and rational resolution of the nationality question. The Slovak leaders were also influenced by a sense of their growing strength, reflected in the outcome of the 1906 elections, in which the nationalities had won 25 seats.[25]

Another reason for optimism was the agreement reached in April 1906 by the Hungarian opposition and the emperor, which included an obligation to prepare an electoral reform at least as far-reaching as one that had been put forward by Minister of the Interior József Kristóffy. The initial Slovak optimism was quickly tempered by Franz Josef's speech from the throne in which he talked about an election law "on the principles of democratization and the maintenance of the national character of the state." Hodža declared these principles to be contradictory,[26] and argued that the old, half-feudal constitutional base of the country needed to be converted to a popular one. The first step should be the legalization of the freedom of assembly, which would help prepare the public for a sensible use of universal suffrage—without which no democratic state could be built in Hungary.[27]

It was more than two years before Count Július Andrássy presented his proposal for electoral reform;[28] the delay dulled the edge of the popular campaign for universal suffrage. While Slovak political leaders refused to cooperate with any of the government parties, they did occasionally make positive remarks about this or that political leader.[29] They reacted positively to the new Radical Party and to its dynamic representative, Oszkár Jászi.[30] Two of the Slovak deputies—Blaho and František Skyčák—concentrated on cultural and educational work among their constituents.[31]

In the fall of 1907, the Slovak leadership, in cooperation with the Hungarian Social Democrats, tried to launch a renewed campaign for universal suffrage. A general strike on 10 October was to be combined with 100 mass rallies in favor of the vote, but the strike lost momentum and the authorities did not allow any of the rallies.[32] A series of 20 rallies was held in the fall of 1908 after the general outline of the proposed reform had become known, but before it was formally announced. Some 30,000 people participated.[33]

In December 1908, Andrássy finally brought forth his proposal for electoral reform, an impossibly complicated system with weighted voting based on education and taxes.[34] While it would have doubled the number of eligible voters, most of the new voters would have had only one-tenth of a vote. Andrássy said his reform was designed to create the type of parliament needed by the Magyar nation—one in which the voices of special interest groups, such as the nationalities, would not dominate the larger national interests.[35]

Much of the Slovak reaction was devoted to determining whether or not Emperor Franz Josef had given his approval to the proposed reform. The conservative Martin position, articulated in *Národnie noviny*, acknowledged that universal suffrage should be a part of the SNS program, but laid greater emphasis on the need to concentrate on national demands and on the just and legal conduct of elections without which universal suffrage was meaningless.[36] Contradictions between the electoral programs of the coalition parties ensured that Parliament never dealt with the proposed reform. It was just as a writer in *Národnie noviny* had predicted:

> A plurality voting bill will be filed in order that there be no voting bill. Andrássy files a proposal for electoral reform on the basis of a plurality system. Strong opposition will be created, composed of all the nationalities, the People's Party, and some of the Independents. Andrássy will be the victim or at least he will play the role of the victim. He falls, and with him falls the bill. What then? Nothing. And in reality, nothing is the goal of the government and the majority. And there will be nothing.[37]

As he had been in the previous term, Hodža was the most active politician in the Slovak camp, both inside and outside Parliament. To advance the Slovak cause, he sought tactical alliances with the nationalities, the Croatians, and the Hungarian opposition parties—especially the new Peasant Party. He maintained contact with Czech political and economic circles, too. In addition, he decided that the ascent of the Crown Prince Franz Ferdinand to the throne would be helpful to the Slovak cause because of the prince's known antipathy to Hungarian ruling circles. To that end, he cultivated a friendship with the prince and had earlier adopted a moderate position on the issue of suffrage.[38] While developing this "higher politics," Hodža maintained his public commitment to a mass peasant base for Slovak politics, proposing in September 1908 that peasants be brought into the SNS.[39] Other than Hodža's, there was minimal discussion about any rearrangement of the domestic political constellation during this period. The Slovak Social Democrats continued to complain about the stepmotherly attitude of the Hungarian Party to Slovak workers. With help from the Czechoslovak Social Democrats, they were able to convert *Robotnícke noviny* into a weekly paper.[40]

The increasing difficulties within the coalition government, the split in the Independence Party, and the fall of the government were greeted with pleasure by all ranks of Slovak public opinion—anything would be better than the previous government, it was widely felt. People were particularly pleased that the caretaker government of Count Khuen-Hedervary had promised to stop national oppression, to institute universal suffrage, and to reform electoral practices. Khuen-Hedervary admitted that the reform would take time. The Slovak political press found his remarks encouraging, especially because the alternative suggested by Istvan Tisza's criticism of the government program seemed far less promising.[41]

The new discussion of electoral reform and the election campaign divided the public's interest in 1910. The SNS platform was theoretically the same as it had been four years earlier, but the majority of the campaign rhetoric centered on the need for universal suffrage.[42]

With the knowledge and support of the SNS leadership, Hodža entered into negotiations about electoral cooperation with the government, which was represented by the state secretary in the Ministry of Interior. The SNS agreed to support the government candidates in certain districts in return for the promise of universal suffrage, the institution of the 1868 nationality law, and the government's willingness not to run candidates in 8 selected Slovak districts. As an indication of good will, the Minister of Justice stopped 100 political trials against non-Magyars.[43]

As a consequence, only 8 Slovaks stood for election. However, *Slovenský týždenník* advised Slovaks not to vote for any Magyar candidates unless they had made a written promise to support universal suffrage and the implementation of the 1868 nationality law. Nevertheless, the Slovak pact was an unmitigated practical and moral disaster. Although the 8 candidates drew 12,329 votes, they won only 3 seats (Blaho, Skyčák, and Juriga in western Slovakia and Upper Orava). Even Tisza was victorious in a Slovak district.[44] Tisza's National Party of Work took 61 seats in Slovakia, and won the support of 8 nonparty deputies. The Néppárt won only 5 of 21 races in Slovakia, and was shut out of its former strongholds of Bratislava and Nitra.

The election results had serious consequences for the Slovak national movement, both inside and outside Parliament. The Hungarian government was able to discredit the Slovak leaders, already exhausted from the persecutions of 1906–1910, in the eyes of the public. For the next four years, the Slovak national movement was wracked by internal disagreements that also damaged cooperation.[45] In Parliament, the Slovak national representation was drastically weakened. The Slovak deputies regularly abstained from parliamentary debates; none was present for a budget debate or for the debate on electoral reform. Skyčák and Blaho each spoke only twice during the session. Blaho instead concentrated on cultural and economic cooperation with the Czechs, maintained his medical practice, and made a speaking trip to the United States. Juriga, now the secretary of the nationality party, was the most active, speaking six times on issues ranging from the use of the Slovak language to peasant questions. Although in general he was critical of the government, he was willing to cooperate if the government would fulfill the basic Slovak demands.[46]

In addition to the internal crisis of Slovak politics, the lack of Slovak activity in Parliament indicated a loss of faith in the Hungarian parliamentary system. Continued efforts to seek support in high places, however, support the contention that the Slovak national leaders still saw some hope that their just demands would be met by the Hungarian government. The final loss of faith was brought about by the government's eventually successful efforts to pass an electoral reform bill that fell far short of Slovak demands. It was particularly important because it shattered Milan Hodža's faith in a just resolution of the Slovak cause in Hungary, and brought him into active cooperation with the Czechs.

The long-promised reform was introduced in December 1912. It raised the number of voters by 40 percent and made education the predominant determinant of voting eligibility. There was universal suffrage at age 24 for male graduates of high schools and colleges. For the rest of the male population, suffrage began at age 30 and was based on several combinations of education and taxes paid. Candidates for office had to be at least 30 years old, and able to read and write Hungarian.[47]

Both the Martin conservatives and Hodža's liberals made painstaking critiques of the law, pointing out how each of the articles worked against the nationalities. *Národnie noviny* hoped that the law would be a "stillborn child."[48] Hodža was most disappointed by the emperor's approval of the reform, observing, "We too will have to construct our policy without him."[49] Paraphrasing František Palacký, he said, "Let the people up there improve their policies toward the masses because we can find other ways [to go]. For we know that the Slovak nation already existed before this Empire did. And we will still exist when the Empire has disappeared."[50]

In Parliament itself, the small Slovak delegation did nothing to stop passage of the bill. It refused to sign a counterproposal for universal suffrage introduced in January 1913 by the Romanian and Serb delegations.[51] The Slovak members did not participate in the parliamentary committee that reported on the bill, nor did they speak during the parliamentary debate.[52] Only one rally, held in Martin, accepted a resolution in favor of the Romanian proposal.[53] The Slovak press gave it minimal attention. On 8 March 1913 the bill passed.

The Slovak national movement never again mounted any sustained action in the Hungarian parliament. Instead, the focus during the last two years before World War I was on two subjects: another internal realignment of political groups and external alliances, especially with the Czechs.

In 1914 an effort was launched to reestablish a joint Slovak platform, in part to respond to the apparently more moderate government of Istvan Tisza. The idea for a Slovak National Council (SNR) was first proposed by Šrobár, perhaps to counteract the political prestige of Hodža.[54] Concrete discussions on the council took place in Budapest on 26 May, with representatives from all four Slovak groupings. The representatives accepted a plan to create an eight-member council plus a chairman that would represent the united will of the Slovak nation externally, and internally would seek to maintain order and concord. Such a council was not actually established until the summer of 1918.

An important question in analyzing the nature of Hungarian-Slovak relations in the early twentieth century is the way in which the changing nature of that relationship affected the developing Czech-Slovak connection. Did the temporary resolution of the Dualist crisis in 1906 in favor of the Magyar rulers contribute directly to a substantial strengthening of Czech-Slovak ties? The Serbs and Romanians in Hungary had long been assisted in their internal struggles by their brethren across the border. Did cooperation with the Czechs prove equally beneficial to the Slovaks? After the war, Masaryk told a Budapest newspaper, "If Hungary had been like Switzerland and the Slovaks had been well led in that situation, neither the Slovaks nor we would have arrived at the idea of changing the situation . . . "[55] In regard to the discussion here, the question is when Slovak leaders may have accepted the idea of changing the situation.

A revival of Czech-Slovak ties had begun in the second half of the 1890s. The revival, which preceded the Dualist crisis by almost a decade, proceeded at first along primarily cultural lines. A pleiad of slovakophile Czech teachers, doctors, lawyers, writers, and journalists propagated the idea of Czech-Slovak cultural and later economic mutuality (*vzájomnost'*). Českoslovanská jednota, an organization formed in 1896 to foster Czech ties with other Slavs, had by 1909 voted to focus its attention on Czech-Slovak ties.[56] It supported Slovak students in Czech schools and sent Czech books and journals to Slovakia.[57]

An important manifestation of the strengthening ties were the "Czech-Slovak Conferences," private discussions held annually at the Moravian spa of Luhačovice, beginning in 1908. Only 28 persons attended the first conference, but by 1913, almost 300 national leaders turned up. Beginning in 1911, the same year that economic issues were first discussed, public rallies were added to the programs. Hardly a single Slovak political or cultural figure did not attend.[58]

Almost without exception, Slovak leaders expressed appreciation and support for the Czech assistance, especially during the periods of most violent repression when they felt the existence of the Slovak nation was in jeopardy. Each political camp expressed reservations, however. Milan Hodža, speaking at the Congress of the Friends of Slovakia held in August 1905 in the Moravian town of Hodonín, expressed appreciation for Czech social and cultural help, but declined any political assistance:

We don't beg any more, alms we don't want, because no nation ever freed itself with alms, but only by its own strength. Furthermore, we seek our freedom strictly in the framework of loyalty to the Hungarian state. We are in Hungary and we want to preserve our rights [there].[59]

He declared that the two nations could cooperate in the struggle for universal suffrage. He warned that continued failure of Austria and Hungary to respond to Czech and Slovak demands could push the two nations closer together politically.[60] After the passage of the 1913 electoral reform bill in Hungary, Hodža followed his own advice, and cooperation with the Czechs became the cornerstone of his political program.[61] He saw no other way to achieve his long-sought goal of the democratization of Hungary.

SL'S-oriented Slovak leaders were characterized by conflicting attitudes about Czech-Slovak cooperation. During their increasing estrangement from the liberal wing of Slovak politics, they gradually withdrew from active participation in the Luhačovice meetings. At the same time, they received continuing support and financial help from the Catholic National Party in Moravia and Silesia, suggesting that their disagreements with Czechs at Luhačovice were not national, but religious.[62] On the other hand, L'udak deputy Ferdiš Juriga tried to use the threat of closer Czech-Slovak ties to club the Hungarian government into action favorable to the Slovak cause. In a speech to Parliament late in the winter of 1914, he warned that if the Slovak nation were not recognized and provided with sufficient cultural opportunities in Hungary, it would join the Czechoslav (*českoslavská*) culture in order to preserve itself.[63]

Although opposed to any ideas of Czechoslovak unity, the Martin conservatives, led by Pavel Mudroň and Matuš Dula, participated in the Luhačovice meetings; by then they saw Czech-Slovak cooperation both as a form of ideological defense against magyarization and as a means for stimulating a specifically Slovak national consciousness.[64]

The year 1914 signaled the dawn of much deeper cooperation between the Czechs and Slovaks, a response to the depressing results of the 1910 census, and more importantly, to the inability to reach agreement with the other non-Magyar nationality groups in Hungary.[65] One result was the agreement, mentioned earlier, to found the SNR. The organizational meeting was purposely held in Budapest because of the presence there of representatives of the Czech political parties. The two sides held intensive discussions and agreed that political representatives of both sides would continue to cooperate closely.[66]

For the first time, the possibility was raised of a political union of Czechs and Slovaks in a federalized monarchy. The concept was strongly urged by Rudolf Pilát, the vice-chairman of the Českoslovanská jednota. Among Slovak leaders the idea received a mixed reception. Pavel Blaho, a conservative Hlasist, preferred a proposal for the creation of a Slovak region (*okolie*). Hodža recommended that the Czechs come out in favor of the mid-nineteenth century program of Karel Havlíček, which included Bohemia, Moravia, Silesia, and Slovakia as one organic part of the Empire.[67] Preparations for the 1914

Luhačovice conference included a proposal that Czech political parties raise the question of revising the Dualist system in the Reichsrat in Vienna. A basic position of Czechs and Slovaks on Czechoslovak national unity was also to be considered.[68] The outbreak of war forced cancellation of the conference.

The repeated declarations of Slovak loyalty to the Hungarian state are a consistent feature of the decade preceding World War I. Czech-Slovak cooperation and mutuality was primarily between elites, with the Czechs in the overwhelming majority.[69] Within the Habsburg framework, the cooperation of Czechs and Slovaks provided Slovaks with more alternatives for the resolution of Slovak national goals. Cooperation with the Czechs opened up a broader perspective on the monarchy, thus strengthening an otherwise weak Slovak interest in the conception of a federalized monarchy.[70] The outcome of the war made those contacts more significant. Certainly the breakup of the monarchy and the creation of independent states was not even considered until after the war had started. It could be argued that, had the war not started, a more positive approach that seemed to be developing in the Tisza government might have turned Slovak attention inward and away from the Czechs.

In this regard, it should be recalled that Czech-Slovak relations tended to develop most strongly during intense Hungarian pressure on the Slovak national movement; that is, during the Bánffy (1896–1899) and Wekerle (1906–1910) governments. The Hungarian repression was thus counterproductive. In contrast, with the exception of the Hodonín manifestation, Czech-Slovak relations during the crisis period of January 1905–April 1906 were at a low point. Czech deputies do not appear to have raised the Slovak question in representative bodies between January 1904 and December 1906.[71]

The facts assembled in this article argue that the period of 1906 to 1914 was not a crucial one in all areas of Slovak-Magyar relations. While certain of the Hungarian government's actions had a significant impact on Slovak domestic affairs, they were not particularly different from those in other periods. Stimulated anew perhaps by the 1905–1906 crisis, the persecutions of 1906–1910 in fact paralleled those of Count Dezső Bánffy in 1896–1899, which had followed the Congress of Non-Hungarian Nations. Education laws had been a constant problem for the Slovak national movement since the 1870s and even earlier. While consideration of electoral reform had not been raised before, it had been an element of Slovak policy in the mid-nineteenth century and was revived at the Congress in 1895.

While the greater freedoms of assembly and association accorded to the public in 1905–1906 facilitated the growth of a mass base to the Slovak national movement, that change had already begun under the impact of the Néppárt and the Hlasists. It can also be argued that the social unrest caused by the 1900–1903 depression and the broader European social turmoil were just as important as any Hungarian government action. In addition, the activization caused by the process of emigration and return has not been adequately studied. By 1914, the Slovak populace was again quiet. The tumultuous events of 1918–

1919 suggest that the political training had not sunk very deep roots except in western and north-central Slovakia. The growth of nationalism was minimally stimulated by the inequities in land distribution—although the resultant increasing numbers of workers that were sent into industry provided a more fertile field for nationalist agitation. The economic developments brought about by the Slovak middle class helped foster contacts that strengthened the Slovak national movement. This was a process that Budapest could not see, although the local Hungarian officials in Slovakia were concerned.

It could be argued that even the basic Hungarian demands during the Dualist crisis were not new. The demand for the use of Magyar as a language of command, for instance, first raised during a parliamentary debate in 1889, had led to the downfall of Prime Minister Kálmán Tisza in March 1890. Slovak attitudes toward the Magyars were not suddenly changed by the events of 1905–1906, but reflected continuing doubt and distrust that had started several generations earlier. While the Slovak populace cultivated the Hungarian lifestyle, it could not fully trust the kingdom's leadership.

With the possible exception of Hodža, the Slovak politicians of the pre–World War I era were an unskilled lot. Still under the influence of nineteenth-century romantic nationalism, they were often naive, shortsighted, and unaware of the developing trends of the twentieth century. Although increasingly willing to be martyrs and to sacrifice for a Slovak national cause, most of them saw politics not as a question of power, but as reasonable argument and discussion among intelligent gentlemen. With the exception of a few liberal Slovak politicians, they did not envision a democratic society, but a mass-participation society with which it would be possible to achieve national goals. The record of the 15 Slovaks elected to the Hungarian parliament was generally not distinguished. Even after repeated defeats and persecutions, most Slovak leaders preferred the comfort of passivity in a society they knew rather than the unknown of some new arrangement with the Czechs. The passive approach chosen by Slovak national politicians when World War I broke out was no surprise.

During the period of 1906 to 1914, the Slovak leaders experimented with different policies and different allies. They lacked a consistent goal and constantly searched for ways to achieve an aim that remained unclear. For Hungarian leaders, the Slovak national movement proved to be a small, amorphous, moving target. It was insufficiently formed for any Hungarian action to have a long-lasting impact.[72] Strengthening Czech-Slovak ties had the potential to change that situation. A more moderate, positive Hungarian approach to Slovak national aspirations, even a mere recognition of Slovak nationality, would have paid off handsomely. In light of the national and socioeconomic changes that were taking place in the early twentieth century, however, such a step would have been unlikely, if not impossible.

While the Hungarian rulers saw the growth of minority nationalism as a threat to their national goals, the real threat was the mass-participation society of the twentieth century. As the failure of the repression efforts showed, it was impossible to suppress directly the growth of national identity. The only way to moderate it was to introduce reforms to allow popular participation.[73] The Hungarian rulers could not allow that because it challenged the basis of their own power. What the Hungarian leaders did not recognize was that even had they achieved through suppression of the nationalities the national unity they sought, that unity would have been flawed by splits along other lines. World War I served as the catalyst for the ultimate solution of Hungary's nationality problem.

NOTES

1. František Bokes, *Dejiny Slovenska a Slovákov* (Bratislava, 1946), pp. 275–85, discusses the ongoing magyarization activities and the Slovak response.

2. For detailed treatment of Slovak politics in the second half of the nineteenth century, see Milan Podrimavský, *Slovenská národná strana v druhej polovici XIX. storočia* (Bratislava, 1983); Pavla Vošahlíková, *Slovenské politické směry v období přechodu k imperialismu* (Prague, 1979); and Jozef Butvin, "Slovenské národnopolitické hnutie na prelome 19. a 20. storočia: Problematika vzniku Hlasu, volebného programu, a politické aktivizacie na začiatku 20. storočia," *Československý časopis historický* 31(5) 1983: 684–710.

3. Robert W. Seton-Watson, *A History of the Czechs and Slovaks* (London, 1943; reprint ed., Hamden, CT, 1965), pp. 271–72. The liberal church reforms instituted by the Hungarian government were a major inspiration for the party. Július Popély, "Boj o liberálne cirkevnopolitické reformy v Uhorsku a založenie katolíckej ľudovej strany," *Historický časopis* 29(6) 1981: 857–70. The final point in the new party's 13-point program contained its stand on nationalities, which expressed the need for just, courteous, and tolerant treatment, so long as the unity of the Hungarian state and its national character would allow (Popély, p. 870). The party was the only Magyar party to admit the existence of the nationalities, and to recognize the legitimacy of some of their educational and judicial demands. See also Popély, "Vzťah medzi štátom a cirkvou v poslednej tretine 19. storočia a korene politického klerikalizmu v Uhorsku," *Historické štúdie* 24 (1980): 77–96.

4. H. Gordon Skilling, *T. G. Masaryk: Against the Current, 1882–1914* (University Park, PA, 1994), pp. 64–80, summarizes Masaryk's prewar associations with Slovaks.

5. This is discussed in detail by Zdeněk Urban, *Problémy slovenského národního hnutí na konci 19. století* (Prague, 1972), pp. 21–62; Robert Kvacek et al., *Dějiny Československa II (1648–1918)* (Prague, 1990), pp. 468–70; Edita Bosak, "Slowakische Studentenorganisationen in Wien, Prag und Budapest und ihre Zusammenarbeit," in *Wegenetz europäischen Geistes II-Universitäten und Studenten: Die Bedeutung studentischer Migrationen in Mittel- und Südosteuropa vom 18. bis zum 20. Jahrhundert*, ed. Richard G. Plaschka and Karlheinz Mack (Munich, 1987), pp. 162–82.

6. " . . . [M]embership in [the SNS] was expressed in reality only by subscribing to *Národnie noviny*." Ľudovít Holotík, "Problém národnooslobodzovacieho boja a politika slovenskej buržoázie pred

prvou svetovou vojnou," *Historický časopis* 3(1) 1955: 41. In reality, the basic SNS document was the 1861 Memorandum, and although there was no formal commitment required, all members were assumed to support the demands. Milan Podrimavský, "Program Slovenskej národnej strany v rokoch 1900–1914," *Historický časopis* 25(1) 1977: 3. A detailed study of the Memorandum is Daniel Rapant, *Viedenské memorandum slovenské z r. 1861* (Martin, 1944).

7.   As Stanley Pech points out, liberal historians have overestimated the importance of the Hlasists ("Right, Left, and Centre in Eastern Europe 1860–1940: A Cross-National Profile," *Canadian Journal of History* 16[2] 1981: 246). Over a longer period of time this is true, but they were an important catalyst in the development of Slovak national life at the turn of the century. The Hlasists broke the hegemony of the Martin conservatives and made the presentation of alternative points of view acceptable. Western historians tend to see Slovak history through the eyes of Prague, which explains why they have considered the Hlasists so significant. The importance of the Hlasists as a group was brief. After the turn of the century, they rapidly lost their influence. Július Mésároš, "Na prahu nového storočia," in Ján Tibenský et al., *Slovensko-Dejiny* (Bratislava, 1971), p. 573.

8.   Milan Hodža, *Články, reči, štúdie,* 5 vols. (Prague, 1930), vol. 1, pp. 187–88.

9.   There was a lack of both class and national consciousness among the Slovak proletariat. See Milan Podrimavský, "K problematike výskumu účasti miest v národnom hnutí v rokoch 1848–1918," *Historický časopis* 29(1) 1981: 102.

10. An overview of the elections to the Hungarian parliament can be found in András Gerő, *The Hungarian Parliament (1867–1918): A Mirage of Power,* trans. James Patterson and Enikő Koncz (Boulder, CO and Patterson, NJ, 1997), pp. 57–105. American Slovaks sent $10,000 in campaign support. Jozef Butvin, "Podnety a vzostup slovenskej buržoáznej politiky v rokoch 1905–1907," *Historický časopis* 32(4) 1984: 566.

11. *Národnie noviny* (henceforth *NN*) 7 April 1906; the joint program of the PNS is found as "Ľudu slovenskému, srbskému a rumunskému!" *Slovenský týždennik* (henceforth *ST*), 23 March 1906.

12. *Katolícke noviny* 13 April 1906.

13. Jozef Butvin et al., eds., *K slovenskému národnému vývinu na východnom Slovensku (1848–1918)* (Košice, 1970), p. 101; Michal Potemra, "K vývinu slovenskej politiky v rokoch 1901–1914," *Historický časopis* 27(1) 1979: 90.

14. Potemra, "K vývinu," p. 91.

15. Seton-Watson, *History of the Czechs and Slovaks,* p. 278.

16. Michal Potemra, "Prejavy supremácie maď'arských a vladnúcich kruhov v politickom živote Slovenska v rokoch 1901–1914," *Historický časopis* 28(1) 1980: 44.

17. Levársky (probably Anton Štefánek), "Príspevok ku štatistike nášeho utrpenia," *Slovenský obzor* 1(7–9) 1907: 385–408, with addenda pp. 663–65, and in vol. 2 (1908), pp. 83–88, provides a case-by-case rundown of the trials. They are tabulated in Potemra, "Prejavy supremácie," p. 56.

18. Alena Bartlová, *Andrej Hlinka* (Bratislava, 1991), pp. 23–28. On the date of the Černova incident, Hlinka was actually on a speaking tour in Moravia. Jozef Jablonický, "Príspevok k česko-slovenskym vzt'ahom od konca 19. stor. do roku 1914," *Historické štúdie* 4 (1958): 31.

19. Slovak partisans say the gendarmes fired into an unarmed crowd. The official Hungarian version is that the substitute priest came only to discuss the consecration and that the crowd was throwing stones at the gendarmes. László Katus, "A nemzetiségi kérdés és Horvátország története a 20. század elején," in *Magyarország Története 1890–1918,* ed. Péter Hának and Ferenc Mucsi (Budapest, 1978), p. 1026.

20. Michal Potemra, "Slovenská otázka v europskom kontexte v rokoch 1901–1914," *Historický časopis* 28(2) 1980: 218; Géza Jeszensky, "Scotus Viator and Hungary," in *Hungarians and Their Neighbors in Modern Times,* ed. Ferenc Glatz (Boulder, CO, 1995), pp. 69–75.

21. Jablonický, "Príspevok k česko-slovenskym," p. 31.

22. Seton-Watson, *History of the Czechs and Slovaks,* p. 277.

23. C. A. Macartney, *The Hapsburg Empire 1790–1918* (New York, 1969), p. 763. In both the curriculum and in actual practice, so much time was spent on teaching Hungarian that too little time remained to cover even the basics in other subjects. Michal Potemra, "Školská politika maď'arských vlád na Slovensku na rozhraní 19. a 20. stor.," *Historický časopis* 26(4) 1978: 532, 534. Making teachers in church schools state employees meant raising their salaries, something the churches often could not afford. A summary of education issues is found in Jan Havránek, "The Education of Czechs and Slovaks under Foreign Domination, 1850–1918," in *Schooling, Educational Policy and Ethnic Identity,* ed. Janusz J. Tomiak (New York, 1991), pp. 249–58.

24. The government watched carefully to make sure that the use of dialect would not develop a national consciousness of its own. The effort by Viktor Dvorcsak to create an east Slovak national movement in 1918–

1919 was a later reflection of this dialectal emphasis. In 1913, there was some official effort made to create a specific Goral dialect in Orava and Spiš counties. This interesting development is discussed by Potemra, "Prejavy supremácie," pp. 50–59. The first Slovak candidacy in an even more eastern district—Giraltovce—ended in a court trial. Potemra, "K vývinu," p. 98. According to Ladislav Tajták ("Maďarizačné tendencie na východnom Slovensku v druhej polovici 19. storočia," in Butvin et al., eds., *K slovenskému národnému vývinu*, pp. 58–59), the Hungarian government succeeded in suppressing the national movement in the east, or at least in suppressing its external organized expression. Also see Tajták's discussion of the press in "Prešov v období rokov 1900–1918," in *Dejiny Prešova*, ed. Imrich Sedlák, 2 vols. (Košice, 1965), vol. 2, pp. 81–82.

25. To this could be added 13 Saxon Germans, and when Croatian questions were discussed, 40 Croatian deputies. Potemra, "K vývinu," p. 91.

26. Milan Hodža, "Bolestne sa dotklo nášho srdca," *ST*, 25 May 1906.

27. Milan Hodža, "Na novom sneme," *ST*, 1 June 1906.

28. Michal Potemra, "Boj za všeobecné volebné právo v Uhorsku v politike slovenskej buržoázie v rokoch 1905–1910," *Historické štúdie* 20 (1976): 188.

29. Ibid., p. 186.

30. Milan Podrimavský, "Oszkár Jászi a národná otázka," *Historický časopis* 20(1) 1972: 65–88. This article is interesting both because it discusses Slovak reactions to Jászi's ideas, and because it deals with an earlier, less-studied period of Jászi's career.

31. Blaho was particularly successful in organizing various savings, food, and other cooperatives in western Slovakia, concentrating especially on the development of agriculture. An example of his effective work was the annual agricultural meetings that he organized. See Miloš Jurkovič, "Roľnícke zjazdy skalické, 1906–1920," *Agrikultura* 10 (1971): 155–75.

32. Milan Hodža, "Sto ľudových shromaždení," *ST* 27 September 1907.

33. Potemra, "Boj . . . 1905–1910," p. 199.

34. The proposal is analyzed in detail in ibid., pp. 189–91.

35. *NN* 14 November 1908.

36. *NN* 8 February 1908.

37. "Pešťbudín," *NN* 18 July 1908.

38. Potemra, "K vývinu," p. 92.

39. Milan Podrimavský, "Organizácia Slovenskej národnej strany v rokoch 1900–1914," *Historické štúdie* 22 (1977): 193. For a detailed discussion

see Vladimír Zuberec, "Formovanie slovenského agrárneho hnutia v rokoch 1900–1918," *Historický časopis* 20(2) 1972: 205–246. The multifaceted and changing nature of Hodža's approach to the realization of Slovak national demands has subjected him to extensive criticism by historians "representing" various political points of view. Two recent efforts are Jan Juríček, *Milan Hodža: Kapitola z dejin slovenskej, československej a europskej politiky* (Bratislava, 1994); and Karel Kollár, *Milan Hodža: Moderný teoretik—Pragmatický politik* (Bratislava, 1994). Unfortunately, almost all of Hodža's private papers were lost or destroyed at several points in his career.

40. Butvin et al., *K slovenskému národnému vývinu*, p. 92.

41. Michal Potemra, "Boj za všeobecné volebné právo v Uhorsku v politike slovenskej národnej buržoázie v rokoch 1910–1918," *Historické štúdie* 22 (1977): 142–43.

42. "Važne slovo—važnym ľudom," *Ľudové noviny* 20 May 1910. The SNS leadership in fact insisted only that its candidates have a Slovak national program. Its organs did not formally declare any program; thus, the 1906 platform remained in effect.

43. Potemra, "Prejavy supremácie," p. 60; Zuberec, "Formovanie slovenského agrárneho hnutia," pp. 224–25.

44. Potemra, "K vývinu," p. 101.

45. The Romanian National Party in Transylvania underwent a similar crisis following the 1910 election when only 5 candidates were victorious—compared to 15 in 1906. See Lucian Boia, *Relationships Between Romanians, Czechs and Slovaks 1848–1918* (Bucharest, 1977), pp. 142–43. The subject is investigated in detail by Keith Hitchins, "The Nationality Problem in Hungary: Istvan Tisza and the Rumanian National Party, 1910–1914," *Journal of Modern History* 53(4) December 1981: 619–51.

46. Potemra, "K vývinu," p. 101.

47. A detailed analysis of the reform is found in Potemra, "Boj . . . 1910–1918," pp. 151–59.

48. *NN* 14 January 1913.

49. *ST* 3 January 1913. This was not the first time that Hodža had been frustrated by the emperor's actions. During the crisis of 1905, Franz Jozef consented to the use of Hungarian as a regimental language. Hodža observed, "From this situation it is logical to conclude that we Slovaks . . . cannot rely on His Majesty's fatherly heart. Let's realize that this heart is really only the usual adding machine on which he very skillfully counts in which way it is necessary to play with the nationalities" (*ST* 7 July 1905).

50. *ST* 28 February 1913.

51. Holotík, "Problém národnooslobodzovacieho boja," p. 46.

52. Potemra, "Boj . . . 1910–1918," p. 159.

53. *NN* 11 February 1913.

54. Alena Bartlová, "Programová línia klerikalizmu na Slovensku (1905–1938)," *Historické štúdie* 22 (1977): 73.

55. Tomáš Garrigue Masaryk, *Cesta demokracie*, 4 vols. (Prague, 1934), vol. 1, p. 72.

56. Michal Potemra, "Rozvoj česko-slovenských vzťahov v rokoch 1901–1914," *Historický časopis* 27(3) 1979: 400.

57. Jablonický, "Príspevok k česko-slovenskym vzťahom," p. 12.

58. A useful source of information is Joža Vochala, *Luhačovické směny Československá* (Prague and Luhačovice, 1936). In reality the Luhačovice forum provided the Slovaks with a much more open arena for the exchange of views among themselves than did even the annual August Slovak celebrations in Martin. An interesting subchapter of Czech-Slovak cooperation is discussed in Z. S. Nenaševová, "Slovenský buržoázny politický tábor a neo-slavizmus," *Historický časopis* 26(3) 1978: 395–408. The Slovak Social Democrats, who received extensive financial and other aid from the Czechoslovak Social Democrats, did not participate in the Luhačovice meetings and in the years 1911–1913 criticized them extensively. Potemra, "Rozvoj," p. 404.

59. *ST* 18 August 1905.

60. Hodža wrote extensively about Czech-Slovak relations. See especially vol. 2 of his *Članky, reči, štúdie*, titled *Československé sučinnosť' 1898–1919* (Prague, 1930).

61. Potemra, "Rozvoj," pp. 415–16.

62. Bartlova, "Programová línia klerikalizmu na Slovensku," p. 72.

63. Potemra, "Rozvoj," pp. 420–21.

64. Nenasevova, "Slovenský buržoázny politický," p. 401.

65. Czech demographers now consider the 1910 census the least reliable of Hungarian censuses. Vlastislav Haufler, "The Ethnographic Map of the Czech Lands," *Rozpravy ČSAV*, r. MPV 83(6) 1973: 7–14.

66. Butvin et al., *K slovenskému národnému vývinu*, pp. 109–110.

67. Ibid., p. 111.

68. Potemra, "Rozvoj," p. 405.

69. Jablonicky reports that only 140 of the 2,364 members of Československanska jednota in 1912 were Slovaks ("Príspevok k československym vzt'ahom," p. 12).

70. The consideration of other potential Slovak allies is beyond the scope of this article. There is a rich literature on the subject, including, for example, Milan Krajčovič, "Slovensko-juhoslovanské vzt'ahy za nástupu imperializmu," *Slovánske štúdie* 19 (1978): 125–52; Mikuláš Pisch, "Politický postoj Slovákov k druhej balkánskej vojne," *Slovanské štúdie* 17 (1976): 135–49; Viktor Borodovčák, "Myslenka slovanské vzájemnosti na Slovensku v letech 1900–1914," in *Slovanství v národním živote Čechů a Slováků* (Prague, 1968); Viktor Borodovčák, "Poliaci a právo Slovákov na sebaurčenie pred prvou svetovou vojnou," *Slovanské štúdie* 12 (1971): 63–85; idem, *Poliaci a slovensky národny zapas v rokoch dualizmu* (Bratislava, 1969); idem, "Ruská politika na Balkáne a Slováci v predvečer prvej svetovej vojny," *Slovanské štúdie* 11 *Historia* (1971): 141–55; idem, "Slovenská demokratická verejnost' a srbská národná politika v predvečer prvej svetovej vojny," in *Československo a Juhoslávia: Z dejín československo-juhoslovanských vzt'ahov* (Bratislava, 1968), pp. 225–39.

71. *Slovenské noviny* 18 January 1904; and *ST* 14 December 1906.

72. The most detailed overview of Slovak-Hungarian relations from a Hungarian perspective is offered by László Szarka, *Szlovák nemzeti fejlődés: Magyar Nemzetiségi politika 1867–1918* (Bratislava [Pozsony], 1995).

73. László Szarka, "The Slovak National Question and Hungarian Nationality Policy Before 1918," *The Hungarian Quarterly* 35(136) Winter 1994: 109.

Was Iaroslav of Halych Really Shooting Sultans in 1185?

EDWARD L. KEENAN

Ukrainian scholars have from time to time shown an interest in appropriating the martial narrative commonly known as the "Igor Tale" (henceforth *IT*), or at the least in pointing out that since much of the action takes place in what was to become Ukraine, and since Igor'/Ihor was prince of Chernihiv, modern Ukrainians have at least as valid a claim to the inheritance as do modern Russians.[1] For most of the twentieth century, however, such claims have been stifled by the domination of Russians in Soviet academe, and by the tenacious Russian nationalism that attends any discussion of the poem's origins.

In the end it is just as well that Ukrainian claims have not prevailed, for the text is not authentic: it was composed by the Bohemian Jesuit scholar Josef Dobrovský, no earlier than August 1792.[2] That so many, especially Russians, should have believed so fervently in its authenticity is a matter that lies in the domain of the nineteenth- and twentieth-century ideologies, which have for several decades been very astutely studied by our *Jubilär*. My purpose in this brief communication is to draw attention to some particularly "Austrian" (particularly, Galician and Bukovynian) aspects of the text itself.

But I must first briefly declare my own views in the matter:

1.   There is *no* documentary evidence for the existence of a putative "original copy" of the *IT*, and, consequently, no plausible basis for the reconstruction either of the details of its "discovery" or of its allegedly medieval paleographical characteristics. All statements by "eyewitnesses" concerning these matters are mutually contradictory or demonstrably false, or both, and almost all such accounts are transmitted by a single unreliable intermediary, Konstantin Fedorovich Kalaidovich (1792–1832).[3] No "Chronograph" is missing from the collection of the former Monastery of the Savior in Iaroslavl,[4] and we have no credible evidence of the existence of any text of the *IT*, of any description, before 1792 or 1793.[5]

2.   By contrast, one *can* demonstrate quite convincingly, on the basis of the authentic correspondence of the principal actors[6] in the generation of legends about the "lost manuscript," that no manuscript of such description was lost in 1812—or, more precisely, that for some years after 1812 no one spoke openly of that loss, even, for example, when pressed on the matter by an enthusiastic believer, Kalaidovich. It is, moreover, possible with some confidence to trace the development of the legend of its disappearance, which did not acquire

general currency until some time after Aleksei Ivanovich Musin-Pushkin's death in 1817.[7]

3.   The presence of learned biblical Hebraisms (урим, ортьма) in the text makes it all but a certainty that it was composed after 1524–1525 (the date of the Hebrew Bible printed in Venice) and highly probable, in view of the widespread Christian fascination with *urim* and *thummim* in the late eighteenth century, that it arose after ca. 1775.[8]

4.   The text abounds in bohemianisms, puns, and classicisms—false and genuine. These features demonstrate time and again that its author possessed an extraordinary familiarity with premodern Slavic languages and literatures, especially Old Czech; a knowledge of the biblical languages, including Hebrew; a deep interest in Slavic valor and unity; a fascination with sound and light effects—especially bird and animal sounds; a deist equanimity with regard to paganism, Christianity, *and* a personified nature; considerable familiarity with printed Russian ballads of the late eighteenth century; and, paradoxically, a deficient knowledge of certain specifically East Slavic linguistic and historical realities.

5.   The originator of the text, Josef Dobrovský, was the leading Slavist of his time. His early biography and training, including his extensive Old Testament studies and knowledge of older Slavic texts, prepared him uniquely for that role. His work in the manuscript collections of St. Petersburg and Moscow in 1792–1793 provided him with access to precisely those manuscript copies of all known possible sources that have the most telling similarities to the text.[9] He arrived in Russia at the peak of interest in Ossian and fascination with Tmutorokan. His *Slavofil* (his word) views, his later reactions to the publication of the *IT*, and his response to the forgeries of "medieval Czech" songs by his students Václav Hanka and Josef Linde are all congruent with this conclusion.

6.   Reexamination of the text in light of this hypothesis permits the satisfactory resolution of an unprecedentedly large number of its obscurities (*hapax legomena*, garbled passages, out-of-place "polonisms" and "classicisms," pagan/Christian contradictions). These solutions, in their turn, confirm the hypothesis of Dobrovský's role in the creation of the text.

Even if we accept these findings, however, we have no direct documentary evidence of Dobrovský's authorship. In such a circumstance the question of motive arises with particular force: what combination of influences and impulses could have prompted so renowned a scholar to create the *IT*? Is there any reason to think that, although he doubtlessly was capable of producing such a text, he would have wished to do so?

At this point we necessarily enter into the shadowy terrain of individual psychology. Before proceding further, we must clarify two matters of definition.

First, Dobrovský did not "forge" the most precious textual relic of "Russia's" past; our perception of the *IT* as a great cultural monument is an artifact of subsequent Russian intellectual history. What Dobrovský did do, seen in context, was to write a few harmless passages in imitation of the *Zadonshchina*, which he had recently read, and in the style of other early Slavic heroic narratives that he knew well. It must be stressed that the act or acts of creating a few fragments of "reconstructed" ancient Slavic text did not seem so outrageous, for Dobrovský or any contemporary in 1792–1800, as the idea of "forging the *IT*" does to us today. Forgeries, imitations, staged discoveries of antiquities of all types, now mostly forgotten, were quite commonplace in Dobrovský's time; for all but a few crabbed scholars, what was important was to evoke and exemplify the "spirit" of a nation or of a bygone age.[10]

Second, any discussion of Dobrovský's behavior and intentions must take balanced account of the course and nature of his well-documented mental illness, in all probability bipolar disorder or manic-depressive illness. Here we tread on treacherous ground, for, like his most intimate contemporaries, we must confront acts and utterances that are bizarre and seemingly inexplicable, but, without doubt, Dobrovský's. It is probable that even if we were to succeed in finding inescapable documentary proof of Dobrovský's authorship of our text, and contemporary accounts of the motivation for some of its features, we might never fully know why he undertook it at all, continued to return to it, and wrote it as he did. Given the manner in which the text seems to have evolved, and taking into account the interventions of its first editor, Aleksei Malinovskii, and perhaps others, it is entirely possible that the text we have represents no single intent of Dobrovský's, but is the product of a concatenation of separate acts—some of them irrational—not all of them his, and over which he ultimately had little control. One should, it seems, discuss not motivation, but impulse.[11]

In this connection we must keep four facts in mind: (a) we know from the historical record that the years in question (roughly 1793–1800) were among the worst of his illness; (b) we know that even during psychotic episodes he was capable of creating perfectly correct text in Latin, German, and Czech, and of discussing complex scholarly matters alongside his delusions; (c) we know from the study of others similarly afflicted that it is common for patients experiencing mania to revisit texts or objects created in earlier episodes; and, (d) we know that the themes and preoccupations of such texts are determined by culture, environment, and personality—that is, that they are not chosen at random.[12]

Having introduced these necessary qualifications, we can turn to our "Austrian" themes, confident in the belief that it is the text itself that will in the end provide the best evidence of its origins.

It requires no great powers of imagination to associate many of the main themes and features of the *IT*, long ago identified by skeptics with late eighteenth-century trends and preoccupations,[13] with Dobrovský personally. If, for example, there is a main "message" in the text (aside from items transported from the *Zadonshchina* and the Hypatian chronicle), it appears to be that when Slavic brothers squabble among themselves for treasure or territory ("Се мое, а то мое же"), they invite disastrous invasion by their neighbors. For Dobrovský, the Partitions of Poland, the second of which had just been accomplished, were an ominous development: Russian Slavs, as a consequence of conflict with and among Polish Slavs, were seizing Slavic territory, and permitting Germans (Prussia and Austria) to do likewise. These matters, and the future of the Slavs in general, were very much on Dobrovský's mind in the years just before the appearance of the *editio princeps*.[14]

By the time of his trip to Russia in 1792 Dobrovský was deeply committed to what he was already calling the *Slavofil* cause. He had just delivered his famous appeal to the new emperor, Rudolf II, in the name of the Slavs of the Empire.[15] While his attitude towards Russia and Russians was somewhat ambiguous (he thought them brave but unsophisticated), he clearly (especially in his delirium) favored the expansion of the Russian Empire "*ad limites Persiae et Indiae*," and to the lands that Slavs, in his view, had "originally" occupied.[16] The geo-political orientation of the *IT* has long been characterized as somewhat anachronistic; it is largely concerned with precisely the southern territories that were the main diplomatic and military preoccupation of the Catherinian empire in the latter eighteenth century, most of them not by any stretch of the historical imagination "Russian." It was this observation that led Mazon to ask, quite aptly, whether the text could not be characterized as little more than "a poetical annex to the Treaty of Iaşi [Jassy]."[17]

In the vast literature devoted to the rebuttal of Mazon's intuitively brilliant hypothesis, this geographical aspect of the matter is not really addressed.[18] And, oddly enough, Mazon himself, while noting the *IT*'s "mention obsédante" of Tmutorokan, did not stress another geographical anachronism: the repeated mentions of the Danube.[19] While some of these have been explained away, or changed by editors to "Don," the problem remains: why does this allegedly twelfth-century epic about the campaign of a prince of Chernihiv in the region of the Don have so much to say about the Danube?[20]

We can solve this little puzzle by beginning with an analysis of one passage that is not usually even mentioned in this connection, presumably because the word "Дунай" does not appear. It is verse 99, at the end of the famous passage known as "Sviatoslav's Dream":

у Плѣсньска на болони бѣша дебрь Кисаню, и не сошлю къ синему морю.

This line has puzzled translators and commentators for two centuries.[21] It presents three distinct problems: the localization of Plesensk; the identification of "дебрь Кисаню (Кисаня?)"; and the interpretation of "и не сошлю."

The first editors, with a reference to Tatishchev,[22] were confident that Plesensk was a "town in the Principality of Halych, on the border with Volhynia." The Poltava-born Roman Fedorovich Timkovskii (1785–1820), a more careful man, could not make up his mind. His hesitation was probably caused by the problem that has long occupied historians and archeologists: the Plesensk well documented by the Hypatian Codex and by modern excavations as a significant twelfth-century town is located in the extreme north of the former Principality of Halych, far from both Kyiv, the apparent site of Sviatoslav's dream, and from most of the action of the rest of the *IT*. The inconvenience of this fact has begotten many attempts to identify Plesensk with some otherwise attested places nearer Kyiv whose names have some similarity to "Plesensk"; the received opinion could perhaps best be described as an average of these hypotheses.[23] But in a dream sequence in a text full of fantasy there is no need for geographical precision, and no bar to tolerating a certain amount of historical incongruity.

In fact, we can say much more. The Plesensk of the Hypatian Codex, Tatishchev's *History*, and the *IT* is beyond reasonable doubt the present-day archeological site of Plisnesko in Lviv Oblast, near the source of the Seret River and the Bystrytsia River.[24] Along with a number of other geographical sites that are not mentioned in the chronicle account of Igor's campaign, Plisnesko is located in what was, in Dobrovský's time, Austrian Galicia.[25] Of note is that it was in an area of Austrian Bukovyna, also "between the Siret [. . .] and the Bistriţa," that the Austrian commander, Friedrich Josias, Prince of Sachsen-Coburg-Saalfeld, quartered his troops during the winter of 1788–1789.[26] The northern Seret/Bystrytsia territory was the former principality of Iaroslav "Osmomysl." The southern Siret/Bistriţa territory was an important staging area for the campaigns of the Russo-Turkish War of 1787–1791, especially for Habsburg troops. And it is in the context of this war—which Dobrovský must have followed avidly from Prague just before his trip to Russia—that the link of Iaroslav and Halych (connected to the Seret and Bystrytsia region in the north) to the Danube (vitally connected to the Siret/Bistriţa region in the south), should be understood.[27] Dobrovský's conflation of the two homonymic regions merges perfectly the historical realia of the *IT* with the "Austrian" viewpoint and *Slavofil* concerns of his own day. Whether Dobrovský planted this as a conscious or subconscious key to his enterprise will be left to the reader's judgment.

The remaining two problems ("дебрь Кисаню" and "и не сошлю") are more complex; this is indeed one of the most obscure passages in our text. Jakobson and others resolved the first by emendation, creating a new text, "на болони бѣшя дьбрьскы сани."[28] But a simpler alternative, one that requires no emendation, is far more convincing: "дебрь Кисаню" is one of several hebraisms in our text.[29]

"Дебрь Кисаню" is to be understood as Heb. נחל קישון, "a wadi running northwest through the plain of Megiddo,"[30] which is "famous as the scene of the overthrow of the Canaanite coalition under Sisera."[31] This wadi, on the basis of Judges 5:21 ("The river of Kishon swept them [the kings of Canaan and Taanach] away, that ancient river, the river Kishon") and 1 Kings 18:40

("... and Elijah brought them [the prophets of Baal] down to the brook Kishon, and slew them there") became an Old Testament metaphor for a place of death and massacre, and evidence of God's providence.[32]

In the Old Testament the proper name קישׁון *always* appears in combination with נחל, "ravine, torrent[-bed]," and, like so many Hebrew words that have entered modern Bible texts via Greek, has many forms (KJV: "the River Kishon, the brook of Kison, the brook Kishon"; Vulgate: *in loco torrentis Cison, torrens Cison*; Kralice Bible [1579–1593]: *Císon*; Skaryna Bible [1517–1519]: *впотоце Киссовѣ*; Ostrih Bible [1581]: *впотоцѣ Кищове*, Greek κισσω, Κε[ι]σων).[33] נחל itself is frequent in the Old Testament, being used also as a word to denote burial places, places for the exposure of children, and the like.[34] And дебрь is commonly used in Slavonic as an equivalent of "ravine, stream, torrent."[35]

This identification permits us in addition to hazard an interpretation of the mysterious "и не сошлю къ синему морю": on the basis of Judges 5:21 where the KJV has "swept them away," the Kralice Bible "*Potok Císon smetl je*," and the Ostrih Bible "изгна я водотечь кадимин [for 'ancient']," we follow Jakobson and others in reading "и несоша ѣ къ синему морю," emending additionally, on the basis of Dobrovský's hypothetical original transliteration, "*i unesoša je*" (falsely construed as "iu ne sošlju) to "дебрь Кисонъ, и унесоша ѣ къ синему морю."[36]

It should be said that this elucidation is not entirely satisfying; the reading "there were [pl.] a Brook of Kison at Plesensk in the suburb, and they were carried away into the sea" still seems somewhat out of joint, and in addition it is possible that the reference to the suburb of Plesensk has to do with the preceding crying of the nightbirds. But it does seem clear that the obscure "дебрь Кисанъ . . . къ синему морю" is a biblical allusion. And a rather scholarly one—worthy of a serious Christian hebraist like Josef Dobrovský, and quite totally out of place in twelfth-century Chernihiv.[37]

Much the same can be said of another "Galician/Bukovynian" passage:

[130–32]
Галичкы Осмомыслѣ Ярославе
(ї) высоко сѣдиши на своемъ златокованнѣмъ столѣ.
Подперъ горы Угорскыи своими желѣзными плъки,
заступивъ Королеви путь, затвори въ Дунаю ворота,
меча времены чрезъ облаки, суды рядя до Дуная.
Грозы твоя по землямъ текутъ;
оттворяеши Кїеву врата;
стрѣлявши съ отня злата стола Салтани за землями.
Стрѣляй Господине Кончака, поганого Кощея
за землю Рускую, за раны Игоревы
буего Святславлича.

There is much to puzzle over here: it is the only text where Iaroslav Vladimirovich of Halych (ca. 1130–1187) is called "Осмомыслъ," whatever that means; much of the rest of this section has defied satisfactory interpretation.[38]

"Подперъ горы Угорскыи своими желѣзными плъки, заступивъ Королеви путь, затвори въ Дунаю ворота . . . суды рядя до Дуная." This is one of many indications in our text of the "Austrian" vantage point that we have mentioned above, and here again we encounter the troublesome Danube. Most commentators agree that the Carpathian Mountains and the Danube are referred to here, but it is usually pointed out that Iaroslav Vladimirovich did not control or build towns on the Danube.[39]

Tatishchev, however, says quite explicitly that Iaroslav fortified towns on the Danube, and of course in the context of the Habsburg-Russian-Ottoman diplomacy of the 1790s, Austrian Bukovyna was thought of as the key to the Danube. Tatishchev is also probably the source of information about Iaroslav's wealth (златъ, златокованний столъ).[40]

The question of which "king" is meant here has been even more problematic.[41]

The juxtaposition of суд- and ряд- in the expression суды рядя is unusual and has no parallel in relevant texts.[42] Later in our text this uncommon combination appears again, prosodically emphasized, in a passage that is one of two linked segments that speak of "суд":[43]

> [159] Всеславъ Князь людемъ судяше, княземъ грады рядяше,

In both instances, the use of рядити with an accusative direct object is very unusual.[44] There is nothing unusual, however, about such combinations in Czech, where the corresponding řiditi, with the accusative, is a standard way of expressing control, direction, or administration. And the juxtaposition of these two lexemes in particular does occur as well in Czech, as, for example, in the title of a book Dobrovský reviewed in 1786: *Wšeobecný řád saudní pro Cžechy, Morawu, Slezsko, Rakausy . . .* [45] We come now to the verse we have questioned in our title:

> [131] Стрѣлявши съ отня злата стола Салтани за землями.

The "Sultans" here (for this is how, since the *editio princeps*, "Салтани" has been rendered) are problematic, despite much careless and anachronistic talk in the commentaries about the putative participation of Iaroslav Vladimirovich (d. 1 October 1187) in the Third Crusade (1189–1192), and much learned discussion among orientalists of the history of the title "sultan."[46] Such a reading, in fact, makes little sense in the context, and requires an emendation based upon the assumption of a rather unusual scribal lapse, Cyrillic "a" for "oy" or "y." It seems clear, in light of our previous discussion, that what was intended by the author, and faithfully transcribed but misunderstood by the first editors,[47] was "съ отня злата стола, съ алтаны [s altany] за землями," that is, from an *altán*[a], which in older Czech meant, as in the original Italian, a small tower, covered terrace, portico, deck, belvedere, or pavilion (see illus., next page). Iaroslav is quite obviously described as shooting "from [his] father's golden throne, from an *altana* that is far [many lands] away." Such a reading, like others we have suggested, requires a trivial emendation and no stretch of the imagination. It is, in addition, supported by the previous text ("высоко сѣдиши на своемъ златокованнѣмъ столѣ") and by the etymology of the original Italian (from *alto*).

Now, since the Italian word *altana* originated as an architectural term during the Renaissance, and entered Czech through German (where it is recorded no earlier than 1417), this passage provides rather telling evidence that the *IT* cannot be a medieval Slavic text, and support for our hypothesis concerning its origin.[48] Dobrovský presumably knew the word both in German, where it was widely used beginning in the sixteenth century, and in Czech, but he seems mistakenly to have thought it an early Common Slavic borrowing from Latin.[49]

*   *
*

Let us sum up: among the abundant incongruities of the *Igor Tale* there are several quite mysterious "Galician" (in truth, "Austrian Galician/Bukovynian") passages. The hypothesis that the text was written not by an unknown Chernihiv "bard," but by a learned Bohemian philologist, on the basis of common preoccupations and knowledge of the 1790s, can account for them all. And the unmistakable presence of the Italian Renaissance architectural term *altana* makes it all but impossible that the text arose before that word entered any Slavic language from German, in the late sixteenth century.

From *Enciclopedia Italiana*, vol. 2, "Agro-Ammi" (Milano, 1929), plate CXXI (opposite p. 682).

NOTES

1. For bibliographical details and discussion of such works, see the articles "Perevody/ukrainskii iazyk," "Sharleman' Nikolai Vasil'evich," "Iatsenko Boris Ivanovich," "Rylskii Maksim Fadeevich," "Peretts Vladimir Nikolaevich," and "Franko Ivan Nikolaevich" in the *Entsiklopediia "Slova o polku Igoreve,"* 5 vols. (St. Petersburg, 1995) (henceforth *ESPI*).

2. I discuss these matters in great detail in a forthcoming monograph, *Josef Dobrovský and the Origins of the 'Igor Tale'* (henceforth *JD and Origins*). For support during this project I should like to thank my admirable colleagues in three Harvard institutions—the Davis Center for Russian Studies, the Ukrainian Research Institute, and Dumbarton Oaks.

3. The recent short biography of Kalaidovich found in the *ESPI*, vol. 3, pp. 5–6, while providing a comprehensive bibliography, is misleading in that it fails to mention Kalaidovich's serious mental illness.

4. See Galina Nikolaevna Moiseeva, *Spaso-Iaroslavskii khronograf i "Slovo o polku Igoreve": k istorii sbornika A. I. Musina-Pushkina so "Slovom"* (Leningrad, 1976; 2nd ed., 1984). E. V. Sinitsyna has shown that no such volume has "disappeared" since the 1770s. See her "K istorii otkrytiia rukopisi so 'Slovom o polku Igoreve,'" *Russkaia literatura* 1992 (1): 85–87.

5. The earliest such evidence is found in a manuscript redacted just before his death on 3 October 1793 by Ivan Perfil'evich Elagin. For the literature, see *ESPI*, vol. 2, p. 165.

6. That is, the "publisher," Aleksei Ivanovich Musin-Pushkin (1744–1817), the editor, Aleksei Fedorovich Malinovskii (1762–1840), and Kalaidovich.

7. The legend grew only slowly: Malinovskii spoke of the loss in 1815, but only privately to Count Nikolai Petrovich Rumiantsev, and to obtain a subsidy for the publication of a forged copy; Kalaidovich mentioned the loss publicly in 1818, but dated it "shortly after [1795]"; Pozharskii was still able to say in 1819 that the manuscript "is found in the collection of [Musin-Pushkin]." These matters are explored further in *JD and Origins*.

8. On *urim* and *thummim*: Cornelis van Dam, *The Urim and Thummim: A Means of Revelation in Ancient Israel* (Winona Lake, IN, 1997). "Урим" in verse 121 is usually removed by emendation. See Roman Jakobson, *Selected Writings*, 8 vols. (The Hague, 1962–1988), vol. 4 (1966), pp. 178–79. (Jakobson's numbering here and below, in brackets within the text.) The most plausible *terminus post quem* is established by the appearance in print of the great Renaissance treatise on the subject:

Jonathan Eybeschütz, *Urim ve-tumim: ... beurim al Shulhan arukh Hoshen mishpat (ad siman 152) ... shene halakim* (Karlsruhe: [s.n.], 535–537 [1775–1777]; another edition in Dubno: [s.n.], 560 [1800]). The original work is: Joseph ben Ephraim Caro (1488–1575), *Shulhan arukh. Hoshen mishpat, editio princeps* (Venice, 1565). On Jonathan Eybeschütz (ben Nathan Nata), see the entry in *Encyclopaedia Judaica*, 16 vols. (Jerusalem, 1972), vol. 6, cols. 1074–76, with bibliography.

9. That is, the *Zadonshchina* and the "note" of Diomid in the *Apostol* of 1307.

10. On some Russian forgeries and mystifications, see Vladimir Petrovich Kozlov, *Tainy falsifikatsii: analiz poddelok istoricheskikh istochnikov XVIII–XIX vekov*, 2nd ed. (Moscow, 1996). See also Ihor Ševčenko, "The Date and Author of the So-Called Fragments of Toparcha Gothicus," *Dumbarton Oaks Papers* 25 (1971): 117–88.

11. It is likely, for example, that he had no idea that the text was to be published. On Dobrovský's illness, see especially Zdeněk Mysliveček, "Duševní choroba Josefa Dobrovského," *Bratislava: Časopis učené společnosti Šafaříkovy* 3(3–4) 1929: 825–35.

12. These matters are discussed at length in *JD and Origins*.

13. Most telling—indeed, astonishingly accurate—are the comments of André Mazon (1881–1967) in his pivotal *Le Slovo d'Igor* (Paris, 1940).

14. *Iroicheskaia pesn' o pokhode na Polovtsov Udel'nogo Kniazia Novagoroda-Severskogo Igoria Sviatoslavicha: pisannaia starinnym Russkim iazykom v iskhode XII stoletiia, s perelozheniem na upotrebliaemoe nyne narechie* (Moscow, 1800).

15. *Über die Ergebenheit und Anhänglichkeit der slavischen Völker an das Erzhaus Österreich* (Prague, 1791).

16. *Korrespondence Josefa Dobrovského,* pt. 1, *Vzájemné dopisy Josefa Dobrovského a Fortunata Duricha z let 1778–1800* (Prague, 1895), p. 356 [=Sbírka pramenův ku poznání literárního života v Čechách, na Moravě a v Slezsku, ser. 2, vol. 2].

17. Mazon, *Le Slovo*, p. 77.

18. As it would appear from a perusal of the place-name indexes of Roman Jakobson, *Selected Writings*, vol. 4, and *ESPI. Slovo o polku Igoreve: pamiatnik XII v.*, ed. Dmitrii Likhachev (Moscow, 1962) has no index. *Slovo o polku Igoreve i pamiatniki Kulikovskogo tsikla: k voprosu o vremeni napisaniia "Slova,"* ed. Dmitrii Likhachev and Lev Dmitriev (Leningrad, 1966), has no geographical index. Jakobson does discuss Tmutorokan and the stone of Tmutorokan, but does not deal with Mazon's claim of anachronism.

19. Verses 130, 167, 169, 212. Mazon noted, of course, that the Danube is out of place in the narrative, and in twelfth-century East Slavic history, but he devoted his attention primarily to philological and literary discussion, especially references to eighteenth-century Russian patriotic ballads and the like. Mazon, *Le Slovo*, pp. 117–18, 122.

20. For the unavailing attempts of commentators to deal with this question, see *ESPI*, vol. 2, pp. 149–51.

21. Oleg Viktorovich Tvorogov, in *ESPI*, vol. 1, p. 133, calls it "*odno iz samykh neiasnykh 'temnykh mest'*" of our text, and M. A. Salmina (*ESPI*, vol. 2, p. 93) calls "дебрь Кисаню" a phrase that is unclear both in meaning and in grammatical form.

22. Tatishchev, Vasilii Nikitich, *Istoriia rossiiskaia,* pt. 3 (Moscow, 1964), pp. 146–47.

23. For details, including some wild speculation, see *ESPI*, vol. 4, pp. 116–18.

24. This is the Seret that drains into the Dnister river, not the Seret (*Rom.* Siret) that has its headwaters southwest of Chernivtsi and drains into the Danube. The identification of the town is best presented in Mykhailo Petrovych Kuchera, "Drevnii Plisnesk," *Arkheolohichni pam'iatky URSR* 12 (1962): 3–9. Cf. *ESPI,* vol. 4, pp. 116–18; *Istoriia mist i sil URSR,* (vol.=) *L'vivs'ka oblast'* (Kyiv, 1968), pp. 133–44. It was a pleasure to learn, after the completion of this article, that our honorand had been taken by his mother to visit the (northern) Seret at an early age.

25. For example, one finds in the same region the village of Horodenka, which should be identified with the puzzling "Grodno/Groden," conjectured on the basis of the phrase (verse 148) "городеньскій."

26. Of course, Dobrovský would have known both sets of rivers with the same orthography, not rendered in modern spellings, as I have done here. See C. A. Schweigerd, *Oesterreichs Helden und Heerführer, von Maximilian I. bis auf die neueste Zeit, in Biographien und Charakterskizzen, aus und nach den besten Quellen und Quellenwerken geschildert*, 4 vols. (Leipzig and Vienna, 1852–1855), vol. 3 (1854), pp. 433–34.

27. For the memoir of a Russian participant, see Lev Nikolaevich Engel'gardt, *Zapiski* (Moscow, 1997), esp. pp. 63, 67, 90 (Prince Repnin on the Danube and Seret).

28. Jakobson, *Selected Writings,* vol. 4, p. 176. It would appear that this solution was first suggested by V. Makushev in 1867 (*ESPI*, vol. 2, p. 94).

29. For others, see verses 38, 115 and 121.

30. [Wilhelm Gesenius], *A Hebrew and English Lexicon of the Old Testament, with an Appendix based on the Lexicon of William Gesenius,* trans. Edward Robinson, ed. Francis Brown et al. (Boston, 1906), s.v. קישׁון .

31. Thomas Cheyne and J. Sutherland Black, eds., *Encyclopaedia Biblica,* 4 vols. (London, 1899–1903), vol. 2 (1901), cols. 2683–2684. See also Rev. Uriah Smith, *The Prophecies of Daniel and the Revelation* (Nashville, 1944), p. 695: "The Vale of Kishon and the region of Megiddo were inevitable battlefields . . . there many of the great contests of SW. Asia have been decided."

32. *The Interpreter's Dictionary of the Bible,* 4 vols. (New York, 1962), vol. 3, pp. 38–39.

33. Examples for KJV and Vulgate are from the website of the *Catholic Encyclopedia:* <http://www.knight.org/advent/cathen/03352a.htm>. The Greek, as quoted in *Encyclopaedia Biblica,* cols. 2683–2684 is Κισσω or Κε[ι]σων.

34. Job 30:6, 21:33.

35. "Vallis, torrens," *Etimologicheskii slovar' slavianskikh iazykov: praslavianskii leksicheskii fond,* ed. O. N. Trubachev (Moscow, 1974–), vol. 5 (1978), p. 176; *Slovník jazyka staroslověnského/Lexicon linguae palaeoslovenicae* (Prague, 1958–), fasc. 10 (1965), p. 538. The word is not present in the *Zadonshchina* or the Hypatian chronicle, and usually means something like "overgrown ravines" in Slavonic. Thus (1216): поидите убо чрезъ болонье и чрезъ дебрь сію. Cf. Josef Dobrovský, *Institutiones linguae Slavicae dialecti veteris, quae quum apud Russos, Serbos aliosque ritus Graeci, tum apud Dalmatas glagolitas ritus Latini Slavos in libris sacris obtinet,* ed. 2, *pretio viliori parabilis* (Vindobona [Vienna], 1852), pp. 273, 296: дебрь *vallis.* Tatjana Čiževska, *Glossary of the Igor' Tale* (The Hague, 1966), p. 139 [=Slavistic Printings and Reprintings, 53], following Jakobson, misconstrues the passage.

36. Dobrovský sometimes employed a rather idiosyncratic system for the transliteration of Cyrillic, in which most common or similar letters (а, б, в, ю, д, е, и, etc.) were represented by their Latin equivalents, but ж, ч, ш, щ and occasionally others were written in their original forms. For examples (*potщaniem mnogogrieшnagω,* etc.), see Galina Nikolaevna Moiseeva and Miloslav Krbec, *Iozef Dobrovskii i Rossiia: pamiatniki russkoi kul'tury XI–XVIII vekov v izuchenii cheshskogo slavista* (Leningrad, 1990), p. 32. Václav Hanka used a similar system in his edition of the *IT;* for an example (*меча bremeny чrez oblaky*), see ibid., p. 205.

37. A final word on дебрь: in Belarus (where the action of some portions of the *IT* seems to take place) дебрь seems to have meant, in Dobrovský's time as in the early decades of this century, "suburb, outskirts, edge of

town," that is, it became a near synonym of болонье. See Bogdana Ia. Koprzhiva-Lur'e (pseud. for Iakov Solomonovich Lur'e), *Istoriia odnoi zhizni* (Paris, 1987), pp. 25–26.

38. The futility of efforts undertaken to date can be glimpsed from articles in *ESPI* by N. F. Kotliar (vol. 5, pp. 289–91), and L. A. Dmitriev and G. M. Prokhorov (vol. 3, pp. 376–77).

39. Thus, *ESPI*, vol. 5, p. 291. Few point out, of course, that the Danube is quite out of place in the story of Igor's campaign.

40. Tatishchev, *Istoriia rossiiskaia,* pt. 3, p. 143: "По Дунаю грады укрепил, купцами населил, торгующим чрез море во Греки и ремесла устрояющим от своих имений помогал"; "Земля же его во всем изобиловала, процветала и множилась в людех, зане ученые хитрецы и ремеслинники от всех стран к нему приходили и грады населяли, которыми обогосчалась земля Галицкая во всем." It is also possible that Dobrovský remembered Engel's words about Iaroslav: "Er selbst schänzte die Künste des Friedens, erhob den Glanz seines Hofes, und verfeinerte die Sitten seiner Unterthanen" (Johann Christian von Engel, *Geschichte der Ukraine und der Cosaken* [Halle, 1796], p. 492 [=Fortsetzung der Algemeinen Welthistorie, 48]).

41. V. L. Vinogradova, comp., *Slovar'-spravochnik "Slova o polku Igoreve"* 6 vols. (Moscow and Leningrad, 1965–1984), vol. 6 (1984), pp. 92–93.

42. Čiževska, *Glossary*, p. 303; Varvara Pavlovna Adrianova-Peretts in *Slovo o polku Igoreve i pamiatniki Kulikovskogo tsikla,* ed. Likhachev and Dmitriev, p. 95; *Slovar'-spravochnik "Slova,"* vol. 5 (1978), pp. 71–73. Note that both lexemes are common in relevant texts, in such phrases as ряд рядити or суд судити, and even судити и рядити; what is apparently unparalleled is *рядь судити or our судь рядити, as astute readers like Tikhomirov and Likhachev, quoted by Vinogradova, have realized.

43. See verses 62–63.

44. Рядити is rather uncommon in Russian as well. The original translators chose "простирая власть свою"; modern translators such as Jakobson, inured to the oddities of the text, have no problem with "суды рядя" (*Selected Writings,* vol. 4, p. 181).

45. (Original spelling retained) Miloslav Krbec and Miroslav Laiske, *Josef Dobrovský,* vol. 1, *Bibliographie der Veröffentlichungen von Josef Dobrovský* (Prague, 1970), no. 96, p. 48 [=Series Slavica, 1].

46. The received view is that we have here "the title of a ruler of Oriental peoples." For details and discussion see *ESPI*, vol. 4, p. 263.

47. For other instances, see above (Urim, Kisan, etc.).

48. In modern Italian, *altana* means, among other things, "roof deck." For the German origin of the Czech words *altán*, *altána*, *altánek*, *altáneček*, which are not attested in Jan Gebauer, *Slovník staročeský* (Prague, 1901–), see Josef Jungmann, *Slovník česko-německý* (Prague, 1989), vol. 1, p. 13: "... ploská střecha nebo prostranstwj na střeše kdež se procházeti možno. (Wysoká pod nebem otewřeným besjdka ...)." In modern Czech, Polish, and Ukrainian the corresponding forms apparently designate gazebos, pergolas, garden sheds, and the like. The Polish word appears for the first time in a 1561 Bible translation. See *Słownik Polszczyzny XVI wieku*, 21 vols. (Wrocław, 1966–1992), vol. 1 (1966), p. 146. In seventeenth-century Litvak Yiddish *altana* seems to have meant "balcony." See the quotation from the Pozna Kahal Record Book in Shmuel A. Arthur Cygielman, *Jewish Autonomy in Poland and Lithuania until 1648 (5408)* (Jerusalem, 1997), p. 191. There appears to be no corresponding word in Russian; see *Slovar' sovremennogo russkogo literaturnogo iazyka,* 17 vols. (Moscow, 1950–1964), vol. 1 (1950), pp. 107–108. For the Italian definition of *altana,* including an architectural sketch of an *altana,* consult *Vocabolario della lingua italiana,* 4 vols. (Rome, 1986–1994), vol. 1 (1986), p. 136: "Terrazzo coperto rialzato a guisa di torretta al disopra dei tetti; é elemento architettonico caratteristico dei palazzi barocchi del'Italia centrale e specialmente di Roma, dove si presenta in forma di loggiato, appariscente per sviluppo di dimensioni e soprattutto per eleganza di architettura." (Identical text in *Dizionario enciclopedico italiano,* 12 vols. [Rome, 1955–1961], vol. 1 [1955], p. 316.) On the derivation from *alto,* see Carlo Battisti and Giovanni Alessio, *Dizionario etimologico italiano,* 5 vols. (Florence, 1950–1957), vol. 1 (1950), p. 114; but note that their sixteenth-century dating for Italian is dubious: the word is already well attested in German by 1500; see Robert R. Anderson, Ulrich Goebel, Oskar Reichmann, eds., *Frühneuhochdeutsches Wörterbuch* (New York, 1986), vol. 1, fasc. 3, cols. 867–68.

49. Dobrovský certainly would have encountered it in the works of Friedrich Schiller or even in the numerous sixteenth-century publications of the works of Hans Sachs (1494–1576). See the *Deutsches Wörterbuch von Jacob und Wilhelm Grimm,* vol. 1 (Leipzig, 1845; reprint Munich, 1984), p. 265 (also vol. 33, p. 778); and the references in Rolf Hiersche, *Deutsches etymologisches Wörterbuch,* Buchstabe A, Zweite Lieferung (Heidelberg, 1986), p. 79. We should add that this reading removes another "ghost orientalism." Among others, to be discussed in full in *JD and Origins,* are деремела, ольберъ, ревуга, шальбер.

The Habsburg Empire (Re)Disintegrates:
The Roots of Opposition in Lviv and Ljubljana, 1988

PADRAIC KENNEY

It may seem rather quixotic to attempt to compare the course of events in two cities which appear to have so little in common. Today, Ljubljana and Lviv are in different worlds. The former is now squarely in a Central Europe defined by a soon-to-be common market. Slovenia belongs to what we might call "civil-society Europe"—that part of the former communist world which is almost never discussed in academic circles without invocation of that magical phrase. Evidence of the penetration of capitalism is everywhere; so too civic associations of all kinds are quite apparent to the visitor of more than a few days. Non-profit organizations have street-front offices and publish handsome newsletters.

Though Lviv is about as far from Budapest (surely the epicenter of civil-society Europe) as is Ljubljana, it seems, again, to have little in common with the capital of Slovenia. Though it is twice as large, it bears the stamp of a provincial city. Little seems to distinguish it, or the rest of Ukraine, from the fate of the non-Baltic former republics of the Soviet Union, except that Ukraine has the virtue of being large and not-Russia, and therefore of special interest to American foreign policy. On the street, at least, capitalism is no more evident than it was in Poland or Hungary in the mid-1980s. And as for civil society: the visitor will find plenty of associations and organizations, but they are usually located up the back stairs, past the doorman who checks one's identification. Whether the measure is internet domains per capita or average income, these two cities inhabit, it seems, different Europes.

A serendipitous research trip in June 1998, however, provoked some intriguing questions. In the space of two weeks, I conducted research in both Ljubljana and Lviv. Each city was then commemorating the tenth anniversary of the demonstrations that led to the fall not only of communism, but of their countries as well. Indeed, one could argue that these were the cities whose political awakening precipitated those breakups.[1] Lviv is a city of "strange politics," in Roman Szporluk's phrase;[2] Ljubljana, too, stands out from the rest of the Yugoslav capitals. While the stark differences today argue against pushing this comparison too far, I would like to explore some deeper similarities masked by that coincidence in 1988, and to suggest some hypotheses which might explain such similarities.[3]

This essay is part of a larger research project, which explores the emergence of new social movements in the 1980s in East-Central Europe; other cases in this study are Poland, Czechoslovakia, and Hungary. The aim of this project is to shift the focus of the narrative of 1989 away from economic breakdown, political philosophers, and Gorbachev, toward the role of ordinary people mobilized around new, concrete issues. As logical as this new approach might be for the other countries mentioned, western Ukraine and Slovenia are generally not included in the same category—not least because their revolutions climaxed two years later, with independence in 1991. Linking them by means of the paradigms usually applied to Poland or Hungary should suggest that they are in fact part of a wider phenomenon of social change.

The politics of both Lviv and Ljubljana can and should, I believe, be seen in a new light. The Slovene case has not been fully rescued from exclusive association with the nationalist explosions in the rest of Yugoslavia. Lviv, in turn, is generally imagined to be a variation on the Ukrainian opposition centered in Kyiv, and peripheral to events in Russia itself.[4] Western Ukraine particularly benefits from such a reexamination. It is almost axiomatic that the outburst of new movements was a response to Gorbachev's policies of glasnost and perestroika. There is no doubt that Ukrainian activists—like those across the Soviet Union—used the language of Gorbachev's reforms to advance their cause, and many did in fact place their hopes in the Soviet leader. There should be no similarity, then, with events in Slovenia, a country outside the Soviet orbit entirely. The common denominator between the two cases simply cannot be Gorbachev (or, at least, not primarily), and thus his relevance needs reassessment.

This essay is based upon just a few dozen interviews conducted in the two cities; I am aware that this is an incomplete, and possibly idiosyncratic, view of the growth of opposition. Nevertheless, I hope to offer new ways to think about the revolutionary conjuncture of 1989–1991. Ten years after the events in question, it may be time to reconsider them, and place some hitherto neglected aspects in the foreground.

That Yugoslavia and the Soviet Union crumbled at the same time, and with not entirely dissimilar results (ethnic violence, continued strength of communist/postcommunist parties or leaders), has not surprised many scholars. Both are seen in hindsight as states that tried futilely to thwart nationalism and self-determination by imposing an ideologically based supra-national unity. In both cases, federal unity was backed in part by the legend of the common struggle of World War II; when the last leaders strongly associated with that war died at the beginning of the 1980s, cracks in that unity began to widen. It is risky, however, to assume that repression of nationalism is the most important factor in the disintegration of these two states. Until we know a great deal more, it is not clearly the case that there existed an "absence of explicit allegiance to the idea of the federal state by the citizenry."[5] That is, we will need to know who supported the central state, who opposed it, and why. For starters, one could note that the some of the staunchest supporters of the idea of the Soviet Union or of Yugoslavia were drawn from the urban intellectual elite—roughly the same milieu as its greatest opponents. Secondly, one would want to ask *what kind* of nationalism? Do nationalisms in western Ukraine and Slovenia have more in common with those in, say, Georgia and Serbia (respectively), or with each other?

Moreover, our interest here should be in the experience at the republic (or sub-republic) level, where repression was only part of the story. Ukrainians and Slovenes alike experienced a curious and constantly shifting combination of centralization or repression and greater autonomy in national-cultural affairs. Slovenia's latitude was much greater, of course, particularly after 1974. Ukraine's cultural autonomy was only nominal until Gorbachev came to power; indeed, the 1970s saw an evisceration of Ukrainian national culture. Nevertheless, each state remained in some way federal until the end.[6]

I would like to point to a common, precommunist history which I think is more important to understanding Slovene and (western) Ukrainian opposition in late communism: in both cases, their modern nationalism developed under Habsburg rule in the last decades before World War I. Ljubljana and Lviv were both part of the Austrian half of the Dual Monarchy, in fact. While each would-be nation began the nineteenth century with no appreciable state tradition or even cultural presence, they ended with a well-developed national consciousness.[7]

While tracing the Habsburg legacy is extraordinarily difficult (and often viewed primarily in the negative, as a tale of disintegration and economic chaos), one can, I think, propose that the experiences of national groups (including Ukrainians and Slovenes) in the Austro-Hungarian Empire have continued relevance to those who engaged in opposition to the communist empires.

First, the Habsburg Empire encouraged a strategy of negotiation with elites instead of revolutionary struggle. While there were exceptions (particularly in the Hungarian half of the Dual Monarchy), national elites in the Habsburg Empire learned to seek compromise in the context of institutions (diets) set up by the empire itself.[8] Specific practices within these institutions, such as respect for law and appreciation for the value of rhetoric, may also have had lasting meaning, as a reading of Robert Putnam would suggest.[9] At the least, however, the latter-day successors to these nationalists might be aware that the regime (and its half-hearted ethnic pluralism) could be used to further nationalist aims—just as their colleagues in other republics would be aware of a glorious tradition of armed insurrection.[10]

A second legacy is a focus on language and culture as bases for nation. While this is not exclusive to nationalism in the Habsburg Empire, there is generally a striking contrast between the romantic struggles just beyond the Austrian world—in Poland, Bulgaria, Serbia, or (again, on the other side of the Dual Monarchy) Hungary—and this more concentrated focus on language and its uses. The establishment of schools, the writing of national poetry and national histories—these are hallmarks of the "cultural awakening" in the Austrian Empire, familiar to any student of these nations. Thus, one might expect that western Ukrainian and Slovene nationalists of the 1990s might situate the defense of language and culture as a priority in the national struggle, ahead of national honor or economic privilege, for example. Language is, of course, an obvious issue in national conflict. Nevertheless, language (and culture generally) can either be at the center of the struggle, as in the two cases under consideration or, as in nations that have practiced romantic armed struggle, can simply be another *illustration* of national grievances centered on land, money, or political power.

Is there, then, a Habsburg legacy in Lviv and in Ljubljana? This alone could explain only the nature, and not the timing, of the events of 1988, of course. Once again, the emergence of Mikhail Gorbachev is an obvious factor. Without discounting Gorbachev's role, I will offer two competing explanations which I believe are more important. The first of these is the influence of Poland—more specifically, new social movements organizing in Poland in the 1980s. As will be clear below, this connection is difficult to document, and is more tenuous in these two cases than in Hungary or Czechoslovakia. Nevertheless, the Polish influence is important also because it distinguishes Ljubljana and Lviv from the rest of their respective countries (with the exception of Vilnius, in the case of the Soviet Union).

The second is the role of a new generation, a similarity which these two cases shared with the rest of East-Central Europe: In the mid-1980s, there emerged a new generation of activists, generally born after 1956. Unlike their elders, who were (in turn) schooled in the bitter struggles of the early postwar years, or lured by the promises of "Socialism with a Human face," or enervated by the long futile years of the Brezhnev/late Tito era, this new generation had neither allegiances nor illusions left. They found "Western" influence natural, and had generally less tolerance for abstractions.[11]

In the history of East European anticommunist social movements, cooperation with official institutions is the exception rather than the rule. By the mid-1980s, an active opponent to the communist regime in Poland or Hungary—and even Czechoslovakia (where restrictions were great, but where assistance from the Polish underground and from the West was nearly ubiquitous) would find it relatively easy to organize without making use of the regime's own structures—one could exist, in other words, in the "parallel polis."[12] Not so in Soviet Ukraine: the price of living as if one were free was likely to be a long sentence in a prison camp. This was the experience of many in the post-1956 generation of Ukrainian dissidents; some found they could continue their opposition activities only in exile.[13] Given that the "inner" Iron Curtain at the Soviet border was far more hermetic than the outer one around the entire bloc, a further price of independent opposition was a near-total lack of resources. Where would the printing presses and meeting rooms so important further west come from in Ukraine? Before 1985, then, opposition in Ukraine could be characterized as morally very powerful, but nearly invisible.

Official institutions—the media, regional government, etc.—played a significant role in the early phase of public activism in Ukraine.[14] As Gorbachev's glasnost began to affect official organizations at the regional and sub-regional levels, the Komsomol organization in Lviv was one of those that began to respond. Most students were members, of course, though they did not attach great importance to the Komsomol; it was simply another part of being a student. Yet the Komsomol lurks in the background of many of the initiatives which emerged in 1987 and early 1988. First and most important of these is Tovarystvo Leva (Lion Society, from the name of the city), created in the summer of 1987 (at a meeting in the Lychakiv cemetery) by, among others, Orest Sheika, an activist in the Komsomol. As an early leader of the Society put it, this was a "spontaneous" organization from below which found support from the Komsomol. Each side needed the other: the Komsomol, hoping to avoid the isolation of official organizations such as was already appearing in the Baltic republics; the Tovarystvo, needing an umbrella for the concrete projects on which it was to focus.[15]

One such project (others will be discussed later) was an ecological expedition down the Dnister River in 1988. The idea began outside the Society, but quickly won its support and assistance. At first, the idea was simply to study the river and meet with people along its banks; when some villagers began to talk about their desire for religious freedom, the members of the expedition began to offer lectures and discussions about the history and traditions of the Uniate Church. Though this often landed them in trouble with local officials, the protection of the Komsomol in Lviv allowed them to continue.[16] At the same time, recalls Oleksandr Starovoit, the Komsomol provided support for regular discussions which began among the younger generation but soon included members of the older generation of western Ukrainian opposition, for example from the Ukrainian Helsinki Association. Thus the opposition used, and benefited from, a more pliant officialdom in Lviv.[17]

In Slovenia, meanwhile, opposition enjoyed a much greater latitude—greater, indeed, than anywhere else in the region. Groups independent of the official structures had been appearing since at least the 1970s. One might say that the stakes were rather higher: activists could afford to be more ambitious raising issues—women's and gay rights, for example, or pacifist issues[18]—which existed only on the extreme fringes of Ukrainian opposition, if at all. For purposes of publicity and organization, there was still value in having official support, even in Ljubljana. Slovenia is a difficult place for the student of anticommunist opposition, schooled in the world of *samizdat* and *tamizdat*, to understand: there were no underground journals, or even an "underground" in the sense applicable elsewhere. Even more perplexing, most members of the opposition as of 1985 were members of the League of Communists. Unlike in Ukraine, where membership might be of necessity, these were people who believed what few others in Eastern Europe did by the 1980s: that the innovations in Marxist and leftist thought since 1968 held promise for either the revitalization of Yugoslav socialism or for some form of opposition to the state.[19]

The center for this activity was the weekly magazine *Mladina*, the official organ of the League of Socialist Youth of Slovenia (LSYS). While most Party youth organizations in Eastern Europe—and in the rest of Yugoslavia—were career-makers, a step to positions of power in the Party and the state, this does not seem to have been the case in Slovenia, perhaps in part because by the mid-1980s Slovenes were less interested in making it to Belgrade. Whatever the reason, the LSYS focused instead on supporting youth initiatives and gaining popularity (as the Lviv Komsomol would also do somewhat later).[20] The first step was supporting punk concerts and recordings, as will be discussed below; one avenue for this was the popular station Radio Študent. Around 1983, some of those active at the radio began to move to *Mladina*; they were led by Mile Šetinc, the son of a prominent Slovene communist. Under Šetinc (who was succeeded by Miha Kovacs in 1986), *Mladina* began to move beyond the school-reform and youth issues that had made Radio Študent popular to "neuralgic" issues like military service, army practices, and Slovenian business and exports.[21]

Contact with the Polish opposition was one of the influences on Slovene ideas of opposition. Throughout the 1980s, many Slovene activists made regular trips to Poland, where they found inspiration from Solidarity. One important sign of this influence was the publication in 1985 of a collection of documents from the Polish movement. Because of their unique position between the two halves of Europe, Slovenes were also able to offer help, for example as couriers between the oppositions in Poland and the GDR.[22]

As in Lviv, then, a communist organization helped to foster an opposition which, in turn, was not shy about using its official umbrella to cover for innovative and increasingly daring forms of opposition. Most importantly, this opposition quickly expanded beyond the confines of the youth organizations— even as the youth organization was disavowing any connection to the powers-that-were, as the LSYS did in 1986. By 1987, representatives of this younger generation indifferent to socialism had taken over both *Mladina* and Radio Študent: Franci Zavrl, for example, became the first non-Party-affiliated chief editor of *Mladina* in early 1987.[23] He and others would push the media in directions their predecessors would not have imagined. In Lviv, where ideology meant much less, the radicalization was just as dramatic. As Tovarystvo Leva was initially protected by the Komsomol, so too Bratstvo, a more radical group focused explicitly on Ukraine's independence, emerged with the organizational help of Tovarystvo Leva (meeting rooms, access to its supporters, etc.).[24] As Gregor Tomc put it in the Slovene case, the communist parties had unwittingly helped to create an opposition party.[25]

As surprising as it was to see nationalism return to prominence late in the twentieth century, the return of language conflict is even more unexpected. After all, the languages were well established: far more people were literate in

Ukrainian or Slovene, for example, than 100 or 150 years earlier, when these nations struggled to establish their presence in the Habsburg Empire. Moreover, both the Soviet Union and Yugoslavia permitted publication and education in republic-level languages, though in Ukraine during the Brezhnev years this increasingly became a rather empty asset subject to ever-greater restrictions.[26] Yet precisely because of this literacy, and the contradictions between federalist and centralist policies in the two states, language and national culture remained themes which would play a central role in the opposition of 1988.[27]

In both cases, "culture" meant not only traditional or folk culture, but youth culture as well. This youth culture pluralized the opposition, adding concrete cultural demands to the more generally nationalist political concerns of the older opposition. In Slovenia, the punk movement was for a time the most prominent expression of national culture. Though punk (which emerged in Slovenia in the late 1970s, and benefited from the publicity of both *Mladina* and Radio Študent) is by nature iconoclastic, Slovene punk focused its energy on the sacred images of *Yugoslavia,* not Slovenia.[28] In 1981, Gregor Tomc (a sociologist and member of Ljubljana's pioneering punk band *Pankrti*) argued that "Punk is problematic because out of all the music it is the least foreign." Rock music was already well established in Serbia, Croatia, and Bosnia, so punk emerged as the purely Slovene alternative.[29] Though the authorities tried hard to link punk to an imagined fascist subculture,[30] punk remained (as it generally has everywhere) an expression of local pride—in fact, the repression only enhanced punk's national role.

At the same time, the older opposition took on a more confrontational stance, with, among other things, the publication of an issue of the intellectual journal *Nova revija* in the spring of 1987 devoted entirely to the "national question." In the spring of 1988, the focus on national culture both traditional and newly minted intersected with the political concerns of the opposition to spark public opposition for the first time. On 31 May 1988, security forces arrested a *Mladina* journalist, Janez Janša, for possession of military secrets; they also arrested two other journalists (one of them *Mladina*'s editor-in-chief, Franci Zavrl) and an army officer. A group at the offices of *Mladina* formed the Committee for the Rights of Janez Janša; this quickly changed its name to The Committee for the Defense of Human Rights, and began to meet at the offices of the Slovene Writers' Association. For the first time, the circles around *Nova revija* and *Mladina* began to have regular contact. This eclectic group began to brainstorm any kind of protest.[31]

That four people had been arrested by the military police for spying was not enough, however, to bring thousands into the street before the courthouse that summer. What mattered to the Ljubljana public was that the trial (in a military court) was conducted in Serbo-Croatian on Slovenian soil. As Franci Zavrl notes, the fact that he was not allowed to have a lawyer was a concern only to human rights activists; that he could not speak Slovenian in court was a different story.[32] A nationalist explosion was simply unexpected at that moment; it would be incorrect to say it was inevitable. Rather, it was the perception that Belgrade threatened Slovene culture that triggered the explosion. A high point of the demonstrations that summer was a concert/demonstration of 35,000 in Congress Square on 21 June; it featured, among others, the punk legends *Pankrti*, a group which had broken up the year before.

Alternative youth culture was naturally more hidden in Ukraine. Punk, for example, was not a significant movement. Its place was taken by the hippie movement, which had a peculiar resonance throughout the Soviet Union from 1968 onward.[33] In Lviv, the hippie community coalesced around the rock group Vuiky[34] in the late 1970s; unlike other rock groups in Ukraine, the Vuiky sang in Ukrainian (and English). Most hippies adopted Russian as a *lingua franca*; many spoke English as well. The best-known hippie in Lviv, Oleh Olisevych, made a point, however, of speaking only Ukrainian in the Soviet context.[35] Thus language became one criterion of the alternative (national) culture in Ukraine.

This culture became opposition in August 1987, when Olisevych attended a pacifist demonstration in Riga. He returned home thinking about making the same statement in Lviv; the result was a demonstration of some 30 people holding placards with mostly pacifist slogans. The group made contact with the Moscow East-West Trust Group, and christened itself Dovir'ia (Trust).[36] Here, Poland again played a role; from the BBC and Voice of America, Olisevych had heard about new movements in Poland such as the Orange Alternative and Freedom and Peace; in the fall of 1987, he began corresponding with the latter group.[37] The meaning of Polish contacts changed for the new generation in Dovir'ia and Tovarystvo Leva: when contacts became more frequent in 1989, recalled one Society member, the older generation would talk with their Polish counterparts about common history and the healing of wounds left by conflicts 40 years old; the new generation talked about concrete problems, like how to publish *samizdat* more efficiently.[38]

Music was the key overlap between Dovir'ia and Tovarystvo Leva; Oleksandr Starovoit, an organizer of the music section of the Society, was also one of the original participants in Dovir'ia. The most remarkable aspect of Tovarystvo Leva's nationalism was its precise focus. Rather than bemoaning the loss of Ukrainian national traditions due to Soviet repression, members of the Society sought to make them come alive. Thus the importance of music: could Ukrainian be used for rock music? Were lyrics or poems in Ukrainian any worse than those in Russian? The Society was attempting nothing less than to "create a new Ukrainian culture" to replace the official one which seemed ersatz and distant. One example of this was the revival of unusual pottery-making traditions in the sub-Carpathian region.[39]

In the spring of 1988, Ihor Mel'nyk, an engineer and an occasional participant in activities of Tovarystvo Leva, began collecting signatures on a petition to form a new society, the Taras Shevchenko Native Language Society. It is difficult to imagine this initiative without the precedence of the Tovarystvo

Leva: not only were signatures gathered in part through Society networks (and at its events), but the Shevchenko Society was following upon themes already articulated by the younger generation.

When authorities at the last minute denied the Shevchenko Society's founders permission to hold a meeting on 13 June hundreds of supporters moved to the park in front of the statue of Ivan Franko. There, western Ukrainian opposition moved into the open, speaking about the need to defend the Ukrainian language; about the "blank spots" in the history of resistance to communism, and about their desire for political reform. Three days later, seven thousand supporters showed up in that same park. Over the summer, Shevchenko Society members conducted meetings across Lviv and western Ukraine, drawing ever larger numbers of participants.[40]

Thus, in both western Ukraine and Slovenia, young activists began from language and concrete manifestations of culture, rather than from general concerns about national sovereignty and identity. They did not invent national opposition, but added to it a new currency. This, arguably, was one of the factors leading to the demonstrations in both cities in June 1988. Before June, national activism was confined to three spheres: an older, intellectual elite (the group around *Nova Revija* in Slovenia; the dissidents who formed the Ukrainian Helsinki Association); a young activist core (around *Mladina* and Tovarystvo Leva); and a more radical cultural fringe (including the punks and hippies). These groups appeared to have little in common, yet they were in fact overlapping circles in a relatively small opposition community.

By the end of June, the general populations of both Lviv and Ljubljana were voicing nationalist demands. Moreover, a kind of popular front organization, pluralist in terms of politics but united around broadly national goals, had emerged in each city: the Shevchenko Society in Lviv and the Committee for Human Rights in Ljubljana. The influence of the youth groups began to fade. Though they were at the center of active opposition until the summer of 1988, the place of Tovarystvo Leva and *Mladina* was (re)taken by the older generation of nationalist dissidents. Within a year, the Shevchenko Society's prominent role had yielded to Rukh's republic-wide movement; in Slovenia, the Committee for the Defense of Human Rights was succeeded by the Demos political coalition. The concerns of national or alternative culture gave way to more ordinary politics, as everything was now reduced to one issue: national autonomy. Though this was a goal the younger activists shared, their movements were more pluralist. It was more difficult for them to have the same kind of impact on the stage of mass politics as could politicians who focused on sovereignty.[41] Nevertheless, the new forms of politics had surely been built on the foundations laid before 1988.

In conclusion, one should also consider significant differences between the two cases. The first of these is the role of religion. It is impossible to understand the nationalism of Tovarystvo Leva without thinking of the Ukrainian Greek Catholic (Uniate) Church; the Society's first public demonstration was a revival of the *vertepy*, the singing of carols by masked/costumed figures at Christmas. One of the most important figures in the opposition—for example, at the meeting on 13 June 1988—was Iryna Kalynets', the founder of the Myloserdia Society, a group which organized outdoor prayer meetings in defense of the Ukrainian Greek Catholic Church.[42] Nationalism in western Ukraine is in part the defense of separate religious traditions marking the region off from the rest of Ukraine. Slovenia, on the other hand, is a Catholic country completely surrounded by Catholic countries. Lay Catholics did establish the Commission for Justice and Peace in 1985 to work for human rights. Yet the Church's role was more peripheral than in Ukraine (or in many other cases), as it was simply another option in a more pluralist opposition.

Another important difference was the range of issues represented in the Slovene opposition. There is simply no parallel in pre-1989 Ukraine to the gay and lesbian movement, or the feminist movement, of Slovenia. There are many reasons for this; one is the ease with which Slovene activists could exchange ideas with their Austrian or Italian counterparts.[43]

These differences (which, after all, could be seen also as further manifestations of regional particularity) between anticommunist opposition in Ljubljana and Lviv are hardly surprising; it is remarkable rather that there remain so many similarities. The two cities have shared very little since they were both part of the Habsburg Empire over 80 years ago. That legacy appears to have left its imprint even upon a generation of activists which knows little of that past.

The creation of nation-states was the most significant result of the Habsburg Empire's disintegration. Here, the Ukrainians and Slovenes may be the exceptions that prove the importance of that result. If we take into account the Slovak and Croat World War II puppet regimes, then among Habsburg successors only the Ukrainians and Slovenes enjoyed no national independence whatsoever until 1991. The desire for nation-states was widespread in 1989–1993; no other nations in communist Europe could be said to have been frustrated in this goal for seventy years. The combination of a Habsburg past and a multiethnic communist present, then, is what makes these cases so comparable.[44] However, a new generation of young anticommunist activists had to emerge to allow Slovenia and western Ukraine to join the wave of change spreading across Eastern Europe.

NOTES

I would like to thank Gregor Tomc, Ihor Markiv, and especially Andryi Poritko for their invaluable assistance in Ljubljana and Lviv. Jeffrey Kopstein provided enormously helpful suggestions on an earlier draft.

1. One might nominate instead Vilnius or Yerevan in the Soviet case; however, Ukrainian nationalism was surely the most threatening to the stability of the USSR. Lviv's demonstrations were the most powerful and radical in Ukraine.

2. Roman Szporluk, "The Strange Politics of Lviv: An Essay in Search of an Explanation," in *The Politics of Nationality and the Erosion of the USSR: Selected Papers from the Fourth World Congress for Soviet and East European Studies, Harrogate, 1990*, ed. Zvi Gitelman (New York, 1992), pp. 215–31.

3. The case of Czechoslovakia could also be included here; though it did not begin the process of breakup, Slovakia would make the best comparison, since it, too, witnessed an upsurge in public opposition in the spring of 1988. However, Czechoslovakia lacked the imperial rhetoric of the other two states. Inclusion of Slovakia would therefore complicate this comparison unnecessarily.

4. Key introductions to late Soviet opposition include Geoffrey A. Hosking, Jonathan Aves, and Peter J. S. Duncan, *The Road to Post-Communism: Independent Political Movements in the Soviet Union 1985–1991* (London, 1992); Geoffrey Hosking, *The Awakening of the Soviet Union* (Cambridge, MA, 1990); M. Steven Fish, *Democracy From Scratch: Opposition and Regime in the New Russian Revolution* (Princeton, 1995).

5. Reneo Lukic and Allen Lynch, *Europe from the Balkans to the Urals: The Disintegration of Yugoslavia and the Soviet Union* (Oxford, 1996), p. 9.

6. On Ukraine, see Roman Szporluk, "National Awakening: The Ukraine and Belorussia," in *The Soviet Empire: the Challenge of National and Democratic Movements*, ed. Uri Ra'anan (Lexington, MA, 1990), pp. 76–78. On the Yugoslav case, see Sabrina P. Ramet, *Nationalism and Federalism in Yugoslavia, 1962–1991*, 2nd ed. (Bloomington, 1992). A good introduction to the Soviet case as a whole is Ben Fowkes, *The Disintegration of the Soviet Union: A Study in the Rise and Triumph of Nationalism* (New York, 1997).

7. See Fran Zwitter, "The Slovenes and the Habsburg Monarchy"; and Ivan L. Rudnytsky, "The Ukrainians in Galicia Under Austrian Rule," *Austrian History Yearbook* 3(2) 1967: 159–88 and 394–429. More recent

work includes John-Paul Himka, *Galician Villagers and the Ukrainian National Movement in the Nineteenth Century* (New York, 1988); and Peter Vodopivec, "Slovenes in the Habsburg Empire or Monarchy," *Nationalities Papers* 21(1) 1993: 159–70.

8.   Robert Kann, *The Multinational Empire: Nationalism and National Reform in the Habsburg Monarchy, 1848–1918*, 2 vols. (New York, 1950), is still the best source on this topic.

9.   Robert Putnam, *Making Democracy Work: Civic Traditions in Modern Italy* (Princeton, 1993).

10.   The partisans of western Ukraine after World War II are obviously an exception to this tradition of negotiation; arguably, the imposition of Soviet control constitutes rather extreme circumstances.

11.   A portrait of the older generation in Ukraine is Taras Batenko, *Opozytsiina osobystist': druha polovyna XX st. Politychnyi portret Bohdana Horynia* (Lviv, 1997). For a description of the middle or "lost" generation, I am indebted to Ihor Mel'nyk: interview, Lviv, 19 June 1998.

12.   See Václav Havel, "The Power of the Powerless," in Václav Havel et al., *The Power of the Powerless: Citizens Against the State in Central-Eastern Europe,* ed. John Keane (Armonk, NY, 1985), pp. 78–81; the phrase is originally Václav Benda's.

13.   On pre-1985 Ukrainian dissent, see Jaroslaw Bilocerkowycz, *Soviet Ukrainian Dissent: A Study of Political Alienation* (Boulder, 1988).

14.   Myroslav Prokop, "Mezhi politychnoï dymky i hromads'koï aktyvnosty v Ukraïni," *Suchasnist'* 332 (December 1988): 58–75.

15.   Interview with Lev Zakharchyshyn, Lviv, 18 June 1998. Interview with Ihor Koliushko, Lviv, 20 June 1998. A meeting in the spring of 1988 on environmental issues, organized by Tovarystvo Leva and Dovir'ia (on which see below), was apparently sanctioned by city officials and filmed by local media. *Ukrainian Review* 36(3) Autumn 1988: 68.

16.   Zakharchyshyn interview.

17.   Interview with Oleksandr Starovoit, Lviv, 19 June 1998.

18.   I discuss these movements (and many others) in the forthcoming book from which this essay is drawn ("Carnival: The Grassroots of the East European Revolutions of 1989").

19.   As a result, they did have some intellectual interest in Gorbachev, not unlike that found in some Western leftist circles. On Slovene opposition in general, see Mark Thompson, *A Paper House: The Ending of Yugoslavia* (New York, 1992); Tomaž Mastnak, "From Social Movements to National Sovereignty," in *Independent Slovenia: Origins, Movements, Prospects,* ed. Jill Benderly and Evan Kraft (New York, 1994), pp. 93–111.

20. Interview with Gregor Tomc, Ljubljana, 13 June 1998. See also Jozef Figa, "Socializing the State: Civil Society and Democratization from Below in Slovenia," in *State-Society Relations in Yugoslavia, 1945–1992*, ed. Melissa K. Bokovoy, Jill A. Irvine, and Carol S. Lilly (New York, 1997), p. 164.

21. Interviews with Ali Žerdin, Ljubljana, 10 June 1998; and with Tomaž Mastnak, Ljubljana, 12 June 1998.

22. Interviews with Mastnak; and with Marko Hren, 11 June 1998. The book is Dana Mesner and Stane Andolšek, *Solidarność v poljski krizi 1980–1982* (Ljubljana, 1985).

23. Interview with Franci Zavrl, Ljubljana, 12 June 1998.

24. Interview with Markiian Ivashchyshyn, Lviv, 18 June 1998.

25. Tomc interview. In some countries, such as Hungary or the GDR (Serbia may also serve as an example), there were close contacts between the reform wing of the Communist Party and senior intellectuals. What took place in Slovenia and Ukraine was quite different, first of all because a different generation was involved; second, even where there was some ideological affinity, the relationship between opposition and Party was organizational rather than programmatic.

26. On Ukraine, see Roman Szporluk, "West Ukraine and West Belorussia: Historical Tradition, Social Communication, and Linguistic Assimilation," *Soviet Studies* 31(1) 1979. On Slovenia, see Ramet, *Nationalism and Federalism*, ch. 3.

27. I. S. Koropets´kyi [Koropeckyj] drew attention to the connection between language and power in Ukraine in "Problema ukraïns´koï movy ta upravlinnia ekonomiieiu," *Suchasnist'* 332 (December 1988): 76–84. On Slovenia, see Ervin Dolenc, "Culture, Politics, and Slovene Identity," in *Independent Slovenia*, ed. Benderly and Kraft, pp. 69–89.

28. Interview with Igor Vidmar, Ljubljana, 11 June 1998.

29. Quoted in Figa, "Socializing the State," p. 165.

30. See Gregor Tomc, "The Politics of Punk," in *Independent Slovenia*, ed. Benderly and Kraft, pp. 113–34.

31. The best source in English is Tone Stojko, *Slovenska Pomlad/Slovenian Spring*, text by Ali H. Žerdin (Ljubljana, 1992). Interview with Alenka Puhar, Ljubljana, 12 June 1998.

32. Zavrl interview.

33. See Timothy Ryback, *Rock Around the Bloc: A History of Rock Music in Eastern Europe and the Soviet Union* (New York and Oxford, 1990), pp. 112–13.

34. The name ("Uncles") is a specifically western Ukrainian term. On the group and its milieu, see Alik Olisevych, "Nam khliba ne treba—my 'Vuikamy' syti . . . ," *Nova Khvylia* 1997 (2): 55–57.

35. Interviews with Oleh Olisevych, Lviv, 18 June 1998; and with Oleksandr Starovoit, Lviv, 19 June 1998.

36. Olisevych interview. See also Mykola Khramiv, "Grupa 'Dovir'ia' u L'vovi: Pershi kroky," *Suchasnist'* 333 (January 1989): 94–96.

37. Oleg Olisewicz [Oleh Olisevych], "Listy ze Lwowa," *Czas przyszły* (Warsaw) 3–4 (Autumn 1988–Winter 1989): 5–16; Olisevych interview. In August 1989, Olisevych was finally able to participate in a Freedom and Peace demonstration in Cracow, on the fiftieth anniversary of the Molotov-Ribbentrop pact.

38. Koliushko interview.

39. Starovoit interview. On Tovarystvo Leva, see Nadia Diuk and Adrian Karatnycky, *The Hidden Nations: The People Challenge the Soviet Union* (New York, 1990), p. 96.

40. Mel'nyk interview; Ihor Mel'nyk, "Desiat' rokiv tomu," *Postup* 13 June 1998: 3; D. O. Svidnyk, "Vidrodzhennia 'Prosvity,'" in *Narys istoriï 'Prosvity'* (Lviv, 1993), pp. 86–95. See also *Ukrainian Review* 36(4) Winter 1988: 43–46 and 52–53.

41. Ten years later, however, one can see a coda of sorts in the emergence of liberal parties in both cities. In Lviv, the local chapter of the National-Democratic Party is more liberal than that in Kyiv; prominent figures have a background in Tovarystvo Leva. So too there was some movement from the *Mladina* circle to the Liberal-Democratic Party. As I traveled from Ljubljana to Lviv with a stop in Budapest, the comparison with another liberal-nationalist party characterized by young politicians, Hungary's Fidesz, came to mind.

42. Interview, Iryna Kalynets', Lviv, 20 June 1998; Diuk and Karatnycky, *The Hidden Nations*, pp. 99–100.

43. Interview, Vlasta Jalušič and Tonči Kuzmanič, Ljubljana, 11 June 1998.

44. See Dennison Rusinow, "Ethnic Politics in the Habsburg Monarchy and Successor States: Three Answers to the National Question," in *Nationalism and Empire: The Habsburg Empire and the Soviet Union*, ed. Richard L. Rudolph and David F. Good (New York, 1992), pp. 243–67; Rusinow focuses primarily on issues of nationality policy rather than experience, but does draw the contrast between Austrian and Hungarian policy.

The Image of Jews in Ukraine's Intellectual Tradition: The Role of *Istoriia Rusov*

ZENON E. KOHUT

In 1828, two members of the Starodub district court in Chernihiv province, Stepan Laikevych and Oleksander Hamaliia, while compiling an inventory of the estate of Princess Kleopatra Lobanova-Rostovskaia in the village of Hryniv, discovered a manuscript copy of *Istoriia Rusov* (History of the Rus′ People) by Archbishop Heorhii Konys′kyi. Impressed by their find, the two lawyers showed the historical tract to Stepan Shyrai, the local marshal of the nobility and a known amateur collector of old documents. Shyrai made a copy for himself and returned the original to the library in the Hryniv estate—and this "original" manuscript has not been seen by anyone ever since. Yet Shyrai's "mastercopy" was copied many times and widely circulated among the Ukrainian nobility before Osyp Bodians′kyi first published the work in Moscow in 1846.[1] It has since been shown that the Hryniv find was not the "original" manuscript copy, for *Istoriia Rusov* was already known in 1825—and probably earlier. Nor was Archbishop Konys′kyi (1717–1795) its author, although there is as yet no agreement on the identity of the author or authors. Moreover, scholars still are debating whether *Istoriia Rusov* was written in the late eighteenth or early nineteenth century, or after the Napoleonic wars.[2]

The origin of *Istoriia Rusov* thus remains one of the most challenging puzzles of Ukrainian intellectual history. There is little doubt, though, as to the work's important place in the national tradition of history writing. *Istoriia Rusov*'s underlying thesis was that Ukrainians have a natural, moral, and historical right to their own political development. Moreover, the Rus′ (Ukrainian) nation has existed as a political entity since Kyivan times: "As is well known, once we were what the Muscovites are now: government, seniority, and the very name Rus′ went over to them from us."[3] The Rus′ people were independent under the rule of their princes until the Tatar threat drove them into contractual relations with Lithuania and Poland "as equal to equal, and free with free."[4] The same contract theory is applied to the Pereiaslav agreement of 1654 with the Russian tsar and the existence of an autonomous Little Russia within the Russian Empire.[5] In this scheme, Ukraine was never conquered and entered into all the political unions in its history as a free and equal partner.

Istoriia Rusov had a profound impact on both the development of a Ukrainian national historiography and on Ukrainian nation building. In the face of the prevailing denial of a peculiarly Ukrainian historical experience, this premodern historical work presented Ukraine as an actor in history, whether affiliated with Poland or Russia. It described Ukrainians as endowed with specific "rights and liberties." In this, *Istoriia Rusov* expressed in concentrated form the ideas of previous generations, particularly the Cossack chronicles, but it also incorporated concepts of the Enlightenment and the French Revolution. It profoundly influenced the founders of the Ukrainian Romantic national awakening and was extremely popular not only within the Ukrainian gentry circles in which it originated, but also among the newly emerging Ukrainian intelligentsia. To the latter it supplied a view of Ukrainian national history and many images of Ukrainians and their neighbors.

The attitude of the author of *Istoriia Rusov* toward Poles, Tatars, and Russians has been covered in a number of studies.[6] However, no study has been done on the image of Jews in the work.[7] Yet, on closer examination, much of nineteenth-century Ukrainian anti-Jewish rhetoric can be traced to *Istoriia Rusov*. It established powerful Jewish stereotypes in Ukrainian historical thought and memory that proved difficult to modify. In this article I will trace how and why *Istoriia Rusov* adopted, developed, and reshaped previous interpretations of this question and passed them on to a subsequent literary tradition.[8]

I

As I have shown elsewhere, early modern Ukrainian historiography emerged in the Hetmanate—the territory that became a de facto independent Cossack state after the Khmel′nyts′kyi uprising and remained an autonomous part of the Russian Empire until the end of the eighteenth century. Initially it was developed in two distinct genres.[9] The Orthodox clergy sought to enlist the protection of the Muscovite tsar by producing a historical scheme of dynastic, religious, and territorial continuity between Kyivan Rus′ and contemporary Muscovy. Within that scheme, they advanced the thesis that the Ukrainian lands were the rightful patrimony of the tsar. The *Sinopsis*, attributed to the archimandrite of the Kyivan Caves Monastery, Innokentii Gizel′, was the foremost example of this historiographic tradition. The book, first published in Kyiv between 1670 and 1674, discussed Kyivan Rus′ and the dynastic history of the Rurikids in great detail, but completely ignored the Cossacks and the Khmel′nyts′kyi uprising. Although it was the work of a Ukrainian cleric, the *Sinopsis* came to be adopted as the first official textbook of Russian history, reprinted 30 times by 1836. Its historical scheme became a springboard for imperial Russian historiography.[10]

The ruling elite of the Hetmanate, the Cossack officer class, was interested in a different kind of history. A general scheme of East European history, the mighty medieval Kyivan state, and the relationship between the Muscovite tsars and the grand princes of old Rus′ all did not appeal to them. The Cossack elite produced a new genre of historical writing—the so-called Cossack chronicles—that emphasized Cossack rights and liberties under both Polish kings and Russian tsars. The chronicles concentrated on what was then relatively recent history: the Polish violations of Cossack rights that justified the uprising, the great liberator Hetman Bohdan Khmel'nyts'kyi, and the presumably contractual nature of Ukraine's union with both Poland-Lithuania and Muscovy. This obsession with the recent past led the Cossack chroniclers to deemphasize the "historical" affinity with Russia. The authors insisted on Ukraine's distinctiveness in the political and social order as well as on its autonomous historical development.[11] *Istoriia Rusov* was, in many ways, the culmination of this literary tradition.

Unlike the clerical writings, the Cossack chronicles focused primarily on the Khmel'nyts'kyi uprising—its causes, course, and consequences. Yet Jews and the description of anti-Jewish violence do not figure prominently in the narratives of the Cossack chroniclers. References to them are few, especially as compared to the attention paid to the Tatars, or to tracing Cossack rights under different monarchs, or to the smallest detail of every military engagement with the Poles. Moreover, the discussion of the Jews, their economic role in Ukraine, and their slaughter by the rebels does not constitute a separate subject (narrative line), but is always inserted into the list of Polish misdeeds or the story of revenge against the Polish lords. The treatment of Jews in the Cossack chronicles is structurally subordinated to the Polish problem.

The chronicle authors did, however, pay much more attention to Jews than the clerics had. Not only did they record the slaughter of Jews along with Poles during the uprising, but they also attempted to show that the Jews, again together with the Poles, were guilty of oppressing the Ukrainians. This is already evident in the first example of the genre, the *Eyewitness Chronicle*, which most likely was written by Roman Rakushka-Romanovs'kyi between 1672 and 1702. The author begins his account of the war with a list of the Polish misdeeds and oppression that caused the Cossack rebellion—a compilation opening with a characteristic statement that "the origin and cause of the Khmel'nyts'kyi War is solely the Polish persecution of the Orthodox and oppression of the Cossacks." Only after dwelling on the Polish misdeeds for some time does the author turn to the Jews, beginning with the observation that the town Jews had control over the liquor monopoly, which prevented the Cossacks from keeping any spirits at home. Then the author turns to the oppression of the peasants, blaming it mainly on the local castle chiefs and vicegerents (*starosty* and *namisnyky*), as well as on Jewish leaseholders:

> That was what befell the Cossacks. It did not apply to the peasants, for they were well off with their fields, cattle and apiaries, but new practices, not customary in Ukraine, were devised by the castle chiefs, vicegerents, and Jews. For the lords themselves did not reside in Ukraine, but merely held offices and therefore knew little of the oppression of the peasants, or even if they knew, they were so blinded by gifts from the castle chiefs and the Jewish leaseholders that they could not recognize that their own property was being

used to bribe them; that they were being given what had been taken from their subjects, of which the subjects would not have complained so bitterly if the lord himself had taken it freely. Meanwhile the lazy scoundrel, the lazy Jew grew richer, riding a carriage drawn by several pairs of horses and thinking up new taxes: the ox tax, the handmill tax, the measuring tax, the marriage tax and others, seizing [debtors'] estates—until [the Poles] encountered one man whose apiary they seized, and that apiary was the source of trouble for all of Poland . . . [12]

In describing the course of the war, the author notes that the rebels "killed the noblemen, castle servants, Jews, and town officials wherever they found them, without sparing even their wives and children." All the property of the victims, including specifically mentioned "Jewish estates," was confiscated. Finally, "no Jews remained in Ukraine," while "the greatest number of Jews perished in Nemyriv and Tulchyn—a countless number."[13]

The next Cossack chronicle, Hryhorii Hrabianka's *The Events of the Most Bitter and Most Bloody War since the Origin of the Poles Between Bohdan Khmel'nyts'kyi, the Zaporozhian Hetman, and the Poles . . .* (1710), also began with a long list of Polish misdeeds in Ukraine. Hrabianka probably used the Eyewitness's lengthy enumeration of complaints, but also, as Mykhailo Hrushevs'kyi has shown, relied heavily on the list of wrongdoings in Ukraine compiled by the Polish author Wespazjan Kochowski.[14] One sentence from this five-page list of Polish misdeeds merits special attention, since it marks the first appearance in Ukrainian history writing of Jews as the leaseholders of Orthodox churches: "Also [the Poles] sold the Lord's churches to the Jews, and infants were baptized with the Jews' permission, and various religious customs of the pious [Christians] were at the mercy of Jewish leaseholders."[15]

Parts of Samiilo Velychko's monumental, if too often fictional, *Chronicle* (1720s) have been lost. It cannot, therefore, be ascertained whether Velychko discussed Jewish oppression of Ukrainians in greater detail. The only relevant surviving mention of Jews in such a context comes from an apocryphal speech by Bohdan Khmel'nyts'kyi to the Ukrainian people dated 28 May 1648: "We shall not describe here comprehensively all the insults, oppression, and devastation inflicted upon us Little Russians by the Poles and their leaseholders and beloved factors, the Jews . . . "[16]

As for Hrabianka, in the subsequent narrative he mentions the Jewish invention of new tributes and the appropriation of debtors' estates, as well as the great landowners' "inflicting upon us" the Jewish tribe (in the text of the letter supposedly sent by Khmel'nyts'kyi to Warsaw). He tells the story of the Polish *szlachta* surrendering Jews to the Ukrainian Cossack colonel, Ivan Hanzha, at Nestervar (Tulchyn), and writes that the Jews defended themselves for three days. When Colonel Maksym Kryvonis took Bar, all the Poles there were slaughtered, as were the Jews, "of whom alone more than fifteen thousand were killed in Bar."[17] Velychko describes the massacre of Nestervar (Tulchyn) in terms almost identical to those of Hrabianka (instead of "defended themselves for three days," he writes that the Jews "defended themselves relentlessly"). Velychko does not mention the killing of the Jews of Bar at all; rather, he says that "fourteen thousand German settlers, nobles who sought refuge there with their treasures, their servants, and others" perished.[18] It is quite remarkable that the Ukrainian chroniclers' accounts of the anti-Jewish violence are so similar. As Velychko's translator, Valerii Shevchuk, has shown, their version of events was based on the widely read Polish historical poem *Wojna domowa* by Samuel Twardowski, published in 1681.[19]

Generally, the anti-Jewish pathos of the Cossack chroniclers can be traced to Polish sources. The most sensational story of "the keys to the church" surfaced suspiciously late in the Ukrainian written tradition, but was first cited in Polish literature as early as 1649. In the latter instance, it was employed as an illustration of Polish tolerance of Jewish exploitation, one of the misdeeds that gave rise to the Cossack rebellion.[20] As Polish historians began looking for the causes of the great uprising, which had precipitated a whole series of tragedies for Poland, they first focused on the magnates and particularly on their stewards, the Jews. In a sense this was an attempt, conscious or subconscious, to admit some responsibility for the uprising, while simultaneously minimizing the blame by identifying Jewish profiteering as the primary cause. In Polish writings, the prewar exploitation of Cossacks and peasants by Jews is described in the most strident terms. Among contemporary Polish authors, Samuel Grondski (Grądzki) in his *Historia belli Cosacco-Polonici* (early 1670s) and Wespazjan Kochowski, who wrote in the 1680s, developed the topic of Jewish exploitation of Ukrainians most prominently.[21] Grondski, for instance, lists 17 causes of the uprising, with Jewish leaseholding, judicial powers, and control of Orthodox religious ceremonies (including payments demanded for the baptismal ceremony) prominent among them.[22] Kochowski provides a similar enumeration of wrongdoings, especially by Jews, and his list, as noted earlier, was appropriated by the Ukrainian chronicler Hrabianka.

All these Polish influences notwithstanding, the Jewish motif in the Cossack chronicles was ultimately subordinated to the anti-Polish theme. In discussing the three fundamental grievances against the Poles—violation of the rights and liberties of the Cossack estate, violation of the rights of the Orthodox Church, and general social oppression—the chroniclers considered Jews to have acted as agents of the Polish lords, not as independent exploiters.

II

By the late eighteenth century, the Jewish factor came to occupy a more prominent place in narratives of the Khmel'nyts'kyi uprising (with particular reference to its causes). Significantly, though, anti-Jewish rhetoric developed together with heightened anti-Polish and anti-Uniate fervor. The compilative *Historical Collection* (1770) by Stefan Lukoms'kyi ends its story in the late sixteenth century, long before the Khmel'nyts'kyi uprising, but the author includes a diatribe against Uniates, Poles, and Jews as a postscript. Again, Jewish wrongdoings are placed at the end of the list:

> Here this Historical Collection ends. What follows is [a description of] various developments in Russia, Ukraine, Poland, and Lithuania from 1606 to 1648, of the wars among different peoples, of how the damnable Union with Rome commenced in all the lands held by Poland and in Lithuania (this has already been discussed above), who was responsible for it, and how it was strengthened, of the persecutions experienced by the faithful Ruthenians and Cossacks who did not accept the Union, how the blameless exarch of the patriarch of Constantinople was exiled by the Uniates to Malbork and died there, and how the Orthodox would yet suffer because of the Union. Also, how the Poles included in the Cossack register only 6,000 of the 50,000 Cossacks who fought against the Turks under Hetman Sahaidachnyi, how [the Poles] abolished the hetman's office and cruelly executed many hetmans, and enserfed the remaining 44,000 Cossacks either by force or by deceit, and imposed the heaviest taxes on the Ukrainian peasants. Finally, [the Poles] leased divine churches to the Jews, to the great grief of the Orthodox, so that the Jews kept the keys to the churches, and should there be a need to celebrate a Christian rite, baptism, wedding, or anything else, [the Jews] charged the Orthodox a special tax, and would also curse, insult and beat the priests, tearing out their hair and beards. In other words, the Poles treated the Ruthenians just as they pleased with no fear of God or Judgment Day, and the following stories will expose their crimes in detail.[23]

The triune nature of the "enemy" in this fragment—Uniates, Poles, and Jews—seems to provide a clue to the sources of Lukoms'kyi's historical imagination. (The Cossack chroniclers were not especially concerned with the Uniate question, for example.) While Lukoms'kyi was writing in the autonomous Hetmanate (under Russian authority) on the Left Bank of the Dnipro, another part of his fatherland, Right-Bank Ukraine, remained under Polish control. Through renewed colonization beginning approximately in the 1710s, the Poles had reestablished the institution of large estates owned by Polish magnates, worked by Ukrainian peasants, and run by stewards. The latter were now not necessarily Jewish; many were recruited from the minor Polish nobility instead. Yet Jews returned this time as well in the capacity of tax-farmers and tavern-keepers.[24] At the same time, the Orthodox Church was being liquidated, and most Ukrainians were at least nominally Uniate. While no Uniates were to be found in the Hetmanate and the Jewish presence there was insignificant, the same issues that sparked the Khmel'nyt'skyi uprising simmered again in eighteenth-century Right-Bank Ukraine. Unlike Hrabianka and Velychko, who wrote in the first two decades of the century, Lukoms'kyi witnessed a series of virtually continuous uprisings west of the Dnipro in 1734 and 1750, and most notably in 1768, when Uniate clergymen, Polish nobles, and Jews were slaughtered in Uman. It was likely under the impression of the 1768 *haidamaka* uprising that Lukoms'kyi wrote his diatribe against Uniates, Poles, and Jews.

Istoriia Rusov is colored by the same heightened sense of Orthodoxy and Ukraine under siege, with even more emphasis on the evil Jews (and Uniates). The work was almost certainly written after the second partition of Poland (1793), when the Right Bank became part of the Russian Empire and brought home the Uniate, Polish, and Jewish questions.[25] Initially, the imperial authorities accepted the existing situation on the Right Bank, including the Polish magnate estates, the Jewish leaseholds, and even the hated Uniate Church. Although the forced conversion of the Uniates began in the 1790s, the Church itself continued to exist until 1839. There was an influx of Polish nobles into Kyiv, and Polish culture predominated there well into the nineteenth century.[26] Thus, for the author of *Istoriia Rusov*, even though Poland had been vanquished, the Polish issue remained very much alive within the borders of the Russian Empire. Inexorably linked to the Polish issue was the role of the Jews. Moreover, there was a massive influx of Jews into Left-Bank Ukraine, where previously there had been no significant Jewish presence. The Hetmanate, where *Istoriia Rusov* was written, found itself included in the emerging Pale of Settlement. Active and visible Jewish involvement in commerce and crafts, as well as their leaseholding practices in the Pale of Settlement (which included almost all of Ukraine, i.e., eight out of nine ethnic Ukrainian provinces), quickly triggered the "discovery" of the Jewish question in the Russian Empire. This discovery came complete with economic anxieties and, subsequently, religious animosity.[27]

In *Istoriia Rusov*, the theme of leasing Orthodox churches to Jews precedes any discussion of economic exploitation. It is developed vividly and in great detail, with the Jews characterized as "irreconcilable enemies of Christianity" who are enjoying this opportunity to trample upon the Christian faith.[28] The theme of economic oppression is generally subordinated in *Istoriia Rusov* to the religious motive: the Jews curse the Orthodox faith in their synagogues, which pleases the Poles, who afford the Jews even more economic opportunities to oppress the Ukrainians.[29] The list of complaints goes on to incorporate the "keys to the church" argument:

> The churches of those parishioners who did not accept the Union [with Rome] were leased to the Jews, and for each service a fee of one to five talers was set, and for christenings and funerals a fee of one to four *złotys*. The Jews, relentless enemies of Christianity, universal wanderers and outcasts, eagerly took to this vile source of gain and immediately removed the church keys and bell ropes to their taverns. For every Christian need, the cantor was obliged to go to the Jew, haggle with him, and, depending on the importance of the service, pay for it and beg for the keys. And the Jew, meanwhile, having laughed to his heart's content at the Christian service, and having reviled all that Christians hold dear, calling it pagan, or, in their language, goyish, would order the cantor to return the keys with an oath that no services that were not paid for had been celebrated.[30]

Given its strong presence in *Istoriia Rusov*, and Polish literature in general, as well as the subsequent increasing preoccupation of Ukrainian writers with this topic, one should at least briefly address the factual basis (if any) of the "keys to the church" theme. Mykhailo Hrushevs'kyi considered the question of Jewish church leaseholding in volume 8 of his monumental *History of Ukraine-Rus'*, concluding that no documentary evidence of such a practice had been discovered, and that the accusation itself had appeared rather late in the Ukrainian written tradition.[31] The Russian Jewish historian Il'ia Galant similarly argued that, although the motif of Jewish leaseholding of churches was present in Polish and Ukrainian historical works and in Ukrainian folk tradition, there was no documentary proof of such a practice.[32] Most recently, Judith Kalik of Hebrew University has indicated that although it was a rare phenomenon, there is clear documentary evidence of the leasing of both Catholic and Orthodox churches to Jewish leaseholders.[33] It is not my aim, of course, to resolve the question of whether Jews actually leased Orthodox churches in Ukraine. What interests me here is the dynamic of the Jewish question's appearance in Ukrainian historical tradition.

Istoriia Rusov includes many more references to Jews—mostly negative—that go far beyond the "keys to the church" theme. Jews are described as "Polish advisors and spies who, with their Talmud . . . also were not forgotten [by the Cossacks during the rebellion of 1630–1631] and were fully requited for their collection of taxes"; Jews were killed mercilessly by the thousands.[34] When the Khmel'nyts'kyi uprising broke out, the hetman "drove the Jews out of the part of Little Russia up to Kyiv and Kaniv." Some "good" Jews, however, were able to purchase their survival and escape to Poland: "The Jews recognized by the people as behaving well and being useful rather than harmful to the community bought their freedom with silver and valuables that the army needed, and were allowed to go abroad without hostility."[35]

In the subsequent detailed narration of Khmel'nyts'kyi's war with the Poles, the author occasionally reminds us that one of the aims of the Cossack units was to clear Ukraine of Poles and Jews wherever they were to be found, although no concrete examples are provided.[36] The author of *Istoriia Rusov* reproduces the text of Khmel'nyts'kyi's fictional manifesto from Velychko (the one that mentions oppression at the hands of "the Poles and their leaseholders and beloved factors, the Jews").[37] The story of the Bar massacre is given in much more detail than in the previous chronicles, although most of the new details concern particulars of the siege and military tactics. The author repeats the story of the 15,000 Jews killed in Bar.[38] He also makes a point of stressing rather minor reports of military action that have some remote connection with Jews; in some cases, he appears to rely on contemporary documents or diaries of Cossack staff officers: "On June 13, Khmel'nyts'kyi received a report from the quartermaster-general, Rodak, from the Siversk land, [informing the hetman] that he had cleared Chernihiv and the vicinity, as well as the Starodub region, including the town of Starodub, of Poles and Jews, and that his corps was advancing rapidly to Novhorod-Siverskyi."[39] According to *Istoriia Rusov*, Khmel'nyts'kyi continued to drive Poles and Jews out of the territories that he was taking, although "useful" Poles and Jews "who did not lord it over the Ruthenian people" were supposedly allowed to stay, paying a contribution in kind. This allegedly took place in Brody and Zamość in particular.[40]

The author goes so far as to claim that the absence of Jewish leaseholding in the Ottoman Empire was a factor to be considered in concluding a treaty with that empire rather than with Muscovy in 1654. He claims, moreover, that some "young officials and Cossacks" brought this consideration to the attention of the council at Pereiaslav.[41] The final mention of the Jews in *Istoriia Rusov* is a telling one: certain "anti-patriots" of Polish and Jewish background are supposedly concealing the original texts of the Cossack treaties with Muscovy that provided for a free and equal union between the Hetmanate and the Russian Empire.[42] Thus, not only have Poles and Jews oppressed Ukrainians in the past, but they are also suppressing the truth about that past.

Istoriia Rusov was written at a great watershed in Ukrainian history. The author observed the ultimate defeat of two of the Hetmanate's greatest enemies, Poland and the Crimean Khanate, but he also witnessed the abolition of the autonomy of his beloved Cossack state, which was reduced to a mere three provinces of the Russian Empire. Moreover, on the Right Bank the Polish magnates still ruled, the Jews held a monopoly on taverns and tax collection, and the Uniate Church continued to exist. To complete the humiliation, his Left-Bank homeland was now included in the Pale of Settlement. It was this constellation of developments that likely gave rise to the author's virulently anti-Polish, anti-Uniate, and anti-Jewish views and his almost fanatical devotion to Orthodoxy. At the same time, the author of *Istoriia Rusov* is a child of the Enlightenment and distinguishes between "good" and "bad" Jews, Poles, and even Tatars. Thus, neither all Poles nor all Jews—nor all Tatars, either— are considered perpetual enemies of Ukraine, and there is hope of achieving harmony with the "good" elements of those nations. (The author does not extend similar consideration to Ukrainian Uniates.)

III

A high point of the Cossack tradition of historical and political thought, *Istoriia Rusov* also became a springboard for the Ukrainian national revival of the nineteenth century and held considerable sway over the next generation of Ukrainian historians and writers. Mykola Markevych's five-volume *Istoriia Malorossii* (History of Little Russia, 1842–1843), a patriotic history written under the influence of Romanticism, was particularly known for literally recasting *Istoriia Rusov*.[43] As far as the image of Jews is concerned, Markevych reproduces the stories concerning the Jewish right to levy duties on blessed bread at Easter, the Cossacks mocking their Jewish victims' curses upon the Christians, the "good Jews" being allowed to leave after paying ransom, the capture of Bar, etc.[44] Markevych's book was very popular in its own right; its importance was magnified, moreover, owing to its use by Ukrainian Romantic writers, most notably Taras Shevchenko. Generally, *Istoriia Rusov* influenced the Romantic literary imagination considerably, both directly and through its "scholarly" adaptation in Markevych's *History*. The negative stereotype of the Jew as leaseholder, Polish agent, or simply go-between found its way into Gogol's *Taras Bulba*, Ievhen Hrebinka's novel *Chaikovs'kyi*, Kulish's poetry, Kostomarov's dramas, and Shevchenko's poem *Haidamaky*. Ukrainian literature would only overcome this stereotype in the late nineteenth and early twentieth century.[45]

The leading Ukrainian historian of the mid-nineteenth century, Mykola Kostomarov, paid considerable attention to Jewish exploitation of the Ukrainian people in his folkloristic, historical, and journalistic works. In a study of Ukrainian folk songs, Kostomarov emphasized their reflection of the historical "tyranny of the arrogant Jews."[46] This condemnation of the social role of the Jews of Ukraine is also prominent in his publicistic writings of the early 1860s:

> When the Judeans settled in Poland and Little Russia, they occupied the place of the middle class, becoming willing servants and agents of the mighty nobility; they clung to the stronger side, and they fared well until the people, rising against the lords, brought under their judgment the helpers of the latter. The Judeans, caring only about their own comfort and that of their tribe, began to extract [advantages] from the relationship that then existed between the nobles and the serfs. In this way, the Judeans became the factotums of the lords; the lords entrusted to them their income, their taverns, their mills, their industry, their property, and their serfs, and sometimes even the faith of the latter.[47]

Kostomarov's widely read book *Bogdan Khmel'nitskii* (1857), written in semi-scholarly style, was marked by the strong influence of Velychko and *Istoriia Rusov*. Nevertheless, Kostomarov dropped *Istoriia Rusov* as a source in the second edition, and in later editions also took into consideration other sources—in particular the testimony of the Jewish eyewitness Nathan Hannover, once it became available in Russia (beginning with the fourth edition in 1884).[48]

Generally, modern Ukrainian history writing evolved in the same direction. As Frank E. Sysyn has shown, with the advent of positivism, new liberal and socialist ideals entered Ukrainian populist historiography, gradually dissolving traditional anti-Jewish rhetoric.[49] The younger contemporary of Kostomarov and doyen of late nineteenth-century populist historiography, Volodymyr Antonovych, declined to perpetuate the story of the church lease. For him, "it was neither faith nor nationality that engendered a hostile attitude toward the Jews [during the Khmel'nyts'kyi uprising],"[50] but the latter's exploitation of the "simple folk." In the debate over the projected Khmel'nyts'kyi monument in Kyiv in the 1880s, the aging Kostomarov successfully opposed the depiction of a Jewish corpse under the hooves of Khmel'nyts'kyi's horse.[51] In 1890, a

younger populist historian, Oleksandra Iefymenko, published a long and generally sympathetic assessment of the German Jewish historian Heinrich Graetz in
the leading journal of the Ukrainian intelligentsia, *Kievskaia starina*.[52]

The greatest Ukrainian historian of the early twentieth century, Mykhailo
Hrushevs´kyi, understood the Khmel´nyts´kyi uprising primarily as a social
movement, with national and religious "motifs" present as well. Incidentally,
Hrushevs´kyi shows great appreciation of Nathan Hannover's account of prewar social antagonisms:

> This Jew from Volhynia penetrated more deeply into the foundations from
> which the uprising developed and produced an even broader analysis of its
> social and ethnic causes than our own "Eyewitness," who, without concentrat-
> ing on the general condition of enserfment, merely refers to some of its
> secondary symptoms and manifestations: the arbitrary behavior of the lease-
> holders, Jewish in particular . . . such superficial attention to various details of
> social relations under serfdom, with no thorough analysis of the primary class
> and ethnic antagonisms, is quite typical: we encounter it in other authors as
> well.[53]

Thus, on the Jewish question, the subsequent development of Ukrainian
historical thought tended to undo the initial influence of *Istoriia Rusov*. At the
same time, the general importance of the book for a national narrative of Ukrainian history increased with time. As the general public "rediscovered" Cossack
glory with the advent of glasnost in the late 1980s and early 1990s, *Istoriia
Rusov* became a bestseller in Ukraine. The 1846 edition was reprinted in 1991 in
a press run of 100,000 copies; in the following year, the translation into modern
Ukrainian of *Istoriia Rusov* was printed in a run of 200,000 copies.[54] Significantly, however, the Ukrainian commentators of *Istoriia Rusov* read it primarily
as an anti-tsarist, anti-Russian indigenous narrative of Ukrainian history. The
anti-Polish pathos of the work, with its attendant anti-Uniate and anti-Jewish
rhetoric, appears to be of almost no importance to the readers of the 1990s.[55]
Thus *Istoriia Rusov*'s Jewish stereotypes have ceased to be a source of the
historical imagination, becoming instead subjects for scholarly examination.

NOTES

1. *Istoriia Rusov ili Maloi Rossii* (Moscow, 1846), pp. 1–24 [=*Chteniia v Imperatorskom obshchestve istorii i drevnostei rossiiskikh* 1 (26 January 1846)].

2. For the traditional account of the find, see Oleksandr Lazarevs'kyi [Aleksandr Lazarevskii], "Otryvki iz semeinogo arkhiva Poletik," *Kievskaia starina* 1891 (4): 113n2. The literature on *Istoriia Rusov* is extensive. Monographs include M. Vozniak, *Psevdo-Konys'kyi i Psevdo-Poletyka? ("Istoriia Rusov" u literaturi i nautsi)* (Lviv, 1939); and E. Borschak, *La légende historique de l'Ukraine. Istorija Rusov* (Paris, 1949). The most recent study by a Ukrainian scholar is V. V. Kravchenko, *Narysy z ukraïns'koï istoriohrafiï epokhy natsional'noho vidrodzhennia (druha polovyna XVIII–seredyna XIX st.)* (Kharkiv, 1996), pp. 101–157.

3. *Istoriia Rusov ili Maloi Rossii* (Moscow, 1846), p. 204.

4. Ibid., pp. 6–7, 209.

5. Ibid., pp. 209, 229.

6. The most recent work is by V. V. Kravchenko, *Poema vol'noho narodu ("Istoriia Rusiv" ta ïï mistse v ukraïns'kii istoriohrafiï)* (Kharkiv, 1996). Twentieth-century researchers have focused on the work's anti-Russian elements, largely ignoring the author's even more vehement anti-Polish and anti-Tatar views.

7. Both Joel Raba and George Grabowicz give examples of negative images of Jews in *Istoriia Rusov*, but neither author analyzes the work in any detail. See Joel Raba, *Between Remembrance and Denial: The Fate of the Jews in the Wars of the Polish Commonwealth During the Mid-Seventeenth Century as Shown in Contemporary Writing and Historical Research* (Boulder, CO, 1995), pp. 228–32; and George G. Grabowicz, "The Jewish Theme in Nineteenth- and Early Twentieth-Century Ukrainian Literature," in *Ukrainian-Jewish Relations in Historical Perspective*, ed. Howard Aster and Peter J. Potichnyj (Edmonton, 1988), pp. 330–31.

8. Portions of this article have been adapted from my larger work, "The Khmelnytsky Uprising, the Image of Jews, and the Shaping of Ukrainian Historical Memory," to be published in a special issue of *Jewish History*. I would like to thank Moshe Rosman and Adam Teller, the editors of the collection, for permission to draw on that work.

9. See Zenon Kohut, "The Development of a Ukrainian National Historiography in Imperial Russia," in *Historiography of Imperial Russia: Profession, Practice, and Interpretation*, ed. John T. Sanders (Armonk, NY, 1999), pp. 453–77.

10. See Hans Rothe, ed., *Sinopsis, Kiev 1681: Facsimile mit einer Einleitung* (Cologne, 1983).

11. On the Cossack chronicles, see Frank E. Sysyn, "Concepts of Nationhood in Ukrainian History Writing, 1620–1690," *Harvard Ukrainian Studies* 10(3–4) December 1986: 393–423; idem, "The Cossack Chronicles and the Development of Modern Ukrainian Culture and National Identity," *Harvard Ukrainian Studies* 14(3–4) December 1990: 593–607.

12. *Letopis' Samovidtsa* (Kyiv, 1878; reprinted Munich, 1972), pp. 3–5.

13. Ibid., pp. 12–13.

14. Mykhailo Hrushevs'kyi, *Istoriia Ukraïny-Rusy,* vol. 8, pt. 2 (Kyiv, 1922; reprinted New York, 1956), pp. 124–25.

15. Hryhorii Hrabianka, *Deistviia prezel'noi i ot nachala poliakov krvavshoi nebyvaloi brani Bogdana Khmel'nitskogo, getmana zaporozhskogo, s poliaki* (Kyiv, 1854) [reprinted in *Hryhorij Hrabjanka's "The Great War of Bohdan Xmel'nyc'kyj"* (Cambridge, MA, 1990), p. 30 (314) {=Harvard Library of Early Ukrainian Literature, Texts, 9}].

16. Samiilo Velychko, *Litopys*, trans. with an introduction by Valerii Shevchuk (Kyiv, 1991), vol. 1, p. 80.

17. Hrabianka, *Deistviia prezel'noi*, pp. 32, 48, 51, 52.

18. Velychko, *Litopys*, pp. 84, 89.

19. Ibid., p. 84n150; cf. also p. 10.

20. Frank Sysyn, "A Curse on Both Their Houses: Catholic Attitudes toward the Jews and Eastern Orthodox during the Khmel'nyts'kyi Uprising in Father Pawel Ruszel's *Fawor niebieski*," in *Israel and the Nations: Essays Presented in Honor of Shmuel Ettinger* (Jerusalem, 1987), pp. xvii–xviii, xxiii.

21. Hrushevs'kyi, *Istoriia Ukraïny-Rusy*, vol. 8, pt. 2, pp. 120–21.

22. Joel Raba, *Between Remembrance and Denial,* pp. 111–12, quoting *Historia belli Cosacco-Polonici authore Samuele Grondski de Grondi*, ed. K. Koppi (Pest, 1789), pp. 32–33.

23. Stefan Lukoms'kyi [Lukomskii], "Sobranie istoricheskoe," in *Letopis' Samovidtsa*, pp. 371–72. Orest Levyts'kyi has argued that Lukoms'kyi planned to continue his narrative with his own translation of Twardowski's *Wojna domowa*, the text of which was eventually lost (cf. Levyts'kyi's "Introduction" in ibid., p. xi).

24. M. J. Rosman, *The Lords' Jews: Magnate-Jewish Relations in the Polish-Lithuanian Commonwealth During the Eighteenth Century* (Cambridge, MA, 1990), pp. 109–110.

25.   *Istoriia Rusov* mentions the Tmutorokan stone, which was found in 1792. (This point was originally made in an article by Anatolii Iershov, "Do pytannia pro chas napysannia 'Istorii Rusov,' a pochasty i pro avtora ïï," *Iuvileinyi zbirnyk na poshanu akademika Mykhaila Serhiievycha Hrushevs'koho* (Kyiv, 1928), vol. 1, pp. 288–89.) Since news of the find would have taken considerable time to circulate in the eighteenth century, it is highly likely that the work was written after the second partition of Poland. Many scholars think that *Istoriia Rusov* was written or edited as late as 1815–1825. See O. Ohloblyn, "Istoriia Rusov," *Encyclopedia of Ukraine,* vol. 2 (Toronto, 1988), p. 360.

26.   Michael F. Hamm, *Kiev: A Portrait, 1800–1917* (Princeton, 1993), pp. 55–81.

27.   Cf. John Doyle Klier, *Russia Gathers Her Jews: The Origins of the "Jewish Question" in Russia, 1772–1825* (DeKalb, IL, 1986), chs. 3–4.

28.   *Istoriia Rusov ili Maloi Rossii* (Moscow, 1846), pp. 40–41.

29.   Ibid., pp. 48–49.

30.   Ibid., pp. 40–41. The translation is adapted (with minor changes) from Grabowicz, "The Jewish Theme," p. 331.

31.   "Notwithstanding a certain interest in this matter, no documentary evidence of Jewish leasing of churches or any related conflicts has been uncovered so far. The blaming of Jews for such misdeeds emerges relatively late in [Ukrainian] historical tradition, but this accusation comes to occupy a prominent and permanent place among the arguments of this historical antisemitism." (Hrushevs'kyi, *Istoriia Ukraïny-Rusy,* vol. 8, pt. 2, p. 126).

32.   Il'ia Galant, "Arendovali li evrei pravoslavnye tserkvi na Ukraine?" *Evreiskaia starina* 1 (1909): 71–87.

33.   Judith Kalik made this claim during the discussion of her paper, "The Orthodox Church and the Jews in the Polish-Lithuanian Commonwealth," at the International Conference "Gezeirot Tah-Tat—East European Jewry in 1648–1649: Context and Consequences" at Bar-Ilan University, 18–20 May 1998.

34.   *Istoriia Rusov,* p. 52. The Jews are again referred to as Polish spies on p. 106.

35.   Ibid., p. 65.

36.   Ibid., pp. 67, 74.

37.   Ibid., p. 70.

38.   Ibid., p. 76.

39.   Ibid.

40. Ibid., pp. 80, 82.

41. Ibid., p. 118.

42. Ibid., p. 122. To substantiate his defense of Cossack rights and privileges, the author claimed that Ukraine's treaty of union with Muscovy in 1654, like Lithuania's union with Poland in 1569, contained a clause whereby the Cossack state united with Muscovy "as equal with equal and free with free" (ibid., pp. 6–7, 209).

43. The most recent study of *Istoriia Rusov*'s influence on Markevych is Kravchenko's *Narysy z ukraïns'koï istoriohrafiï epokhy natsional'noho vidrodzhennia*, pp. 232–56.

44. Mykola Markevych [Nikolai Markevich], *Istoriia Malorossii* (Moscow, 1842), vol. 1, pp. 121, 127–28, 171, 191.

45. For a more detailed discussion, see Grabowicz, "The Jewish Theme," pp. 327–43.

46. Mykola [Nikolai] Kostomarov, "Istoricheskoe znachenie iuzhno-russkogo pesennogo tvorchestva," in *Sobranie sochinenii*, 21 vols. in 8 bks. (St. Petersburg, 1903–1906; reprint, The Hague, 1968), vol. 8, p. 809.

47. "Iudeiam," *Osnova* 1 (1862): 43–44. The English translation is adapted, with minor changes, from Roman Serbyn, "The *Sion-Osnova* Controversy of 1861–1862," in *Ukrainian-Jewish Relations*, ed. Aster and Potichnyj, p. 99.

48. Mykola [Nikolai] Kostomarov, *Bogdan Khmel'nitskii* (St. Petersburg, 1904), pp. 638–50.

49. Frank E. Sysyn, "The Jewish Factor in the Khmelnytsky Uprising," in *Ukrainian-Jewish Relations*, ed. Aster and Potichnyj, p. 46.

50. V. B. Antonovych, *Pro chasy kozats'ki na Ukraïni* (Kyiv, 1991), p. 118.

51. Mykola [Nikolai] Kostomarov, "Neskol'ko slov o pamiatnike Khmel'nitskomu," *Ukraïns'kyi istorychnyi zhurnal* 5 (1994): 145–47 [originally published in the newspaper *Novoe vremia* in 1869].

52. H. Graetz, *Geschichte der Juden von den ältesten Zeiten bis auf die Gegenwart*, vol. 10: *Die Geschichte der Juden von der dauernden Ansiedlung der Marranen in Holland (1618) bis zum Beginne der Mendelssohnschen Zeit (1750)*, 3rd ed. (Leipzig, 1896); Oleksandra Iefymenko [Aleksandra Efimenko], "Bedstviia evreev v Iuzhnoi Rusi XVII v. (Po povodu knigi Grettsa 'Istoriia evreev ot epokhi Gollandskogo Ierusalima do padeniia frankistov')," *Kievskaia starina* 6 (1890): 397–408 (Iefymenko used the Russian translation of one of the earlier editions).

53. Hrushevs'kyi, *Istoriia Ukraïny-Rusy*, vol. 8, pt. 2, pp. 119–20.

54. *Istoriia Rusov ili Maloi Rossii* (Moscow, 1846; reprinted Kyiv, 1991);
     Istoriia Rusiv, trans. Ivan Drach, introduction by Valerii Shevchuk
     (Kyiv, 1991).

55. Fedir Shevchenko, "Z liubov'iu do Ukraïny," *Literaturna Ukraïna* 14
     June 1990: 6; Valerii Shevchuk, *Kozats'ka derzhava: etiudy do istoriï
     ukraïns'koho derzhavotvorennia* (Kyiv, 1995), pp. 296–348; Iaroslav
     Dzyra and Mykola Shudria, "Chyia zh naspravdi 'Istoriia Rusiv'?" *Slovo
     Prosvity* 6 (June 1996): 8–9.

Nationalizing the Public

RITA KRUEGER

Many of the phrases historians have inherited to describe the nineteenth century's era of nationalist agitation—awakening, rebirth, renascence, revival—convey an image of mature nations returning to their rightful place, both in the minds of the individuals who comprise them and in the international arena. Regardless of how one might find fault with these phrases, they do legitimately convey the sense that the nineteenth century represented a watershed in terms of the definition of national identity and the expansion of nationalist aspirations. Given the claims made by nationalists and the manifest political impact of nationalism on the region, it is important to examine the social and intellectual climate of the "prenational" period, namely the late eighteenth and early nineteenth centuries. This was a period of transition from early modern to modern society, and the emergence of a public sphere distinct from the state was an important element of this modernization. In this essay, I will examine the relationship between the establishment of new public institutions and the subsequent growth of national sentiment within them, as well as the role that traditional social elites played in new public institutions and in defining national identity. Bohemia, always caught uncomfortably between East and West, is the focus of this study. Bohemia at the turn of the eighteenth century is particularly interesting because it displayed a series of competing characteristics. It had a traditional rural social hierarchy, but a number of influential nobles in Bohemia were disaffected and had begun to reevaluate their use of land, labor, and industry. Bohemia was also influenced by the French Enlightenment, the German Aufklärung, and Romanticism all at nearly the same historical moment. This evoked a host of political, social, and intellectual responses, including the most important for our purposes here: the emergence and nationalization of the public sphere.

The Public Sphere

While problematic for eighteenth-century East Central Europe, the concept of the public sphere does provide an important framework for examining the intersection of status, class, intellectual influences, and nation building in the region. As Friedrich List wrote, "Between the individual and humanity stands the nation."[1] To get at the role of the public, we might paraphrase List by saying, "Between the individual and the nation stands the public." The idea of a new "public sphere" is historically specific to the eighteenth and nineteenth centuries, and intimately connected with the unique development of European civil society. The public sphere, defined as "the public of *private* individuals who join in debate of issues bearing on state authority,"[2] existed at least in part "in every conversation in which private individuals assemble[d] to form a public body."[3] These "public bodies," essentially the new institutions established in Bohemia in the eighteenth century, included masonic lodges, reading clubs, salons, scientific and agrarian societies, and galleries and museums. The success of all of these institutions was contingent upon the regular participation of a group of individuals with a common purpose. These common purposes were variously defined as individual or public enlightenment, scientific progress, economic competition, clubbing (in other words, socializing), or cultural preservation. The world of letters was at the core of the public sphere; publications and printing constituted a critical contribution to public debate. The influence of printing and the increased circulation of journals, literature, and information not only shaped discourse, but also provided the institutional bases for the further development of the public. The salon—a public institution in a private home—joined "a literary public sphere dominated by aristocrats with the emergent bourgeois political public sphere."[4]

The growth of a new public sphere went hand in hand with significant changes in eighteenth-century urban culture. As Hutchinson and Smith note, urban growth and the increase in urban wealth "encouraged new generations to seek secular education, engage in various branches of scientific and humanist learning, and enter the expanding professions."[5] Urban growth increased the sheer number of venues as well as the number of viable, educated participants. Urban life and culture allowed new and old elites to enjoy social interaction, and it is within urban centers that the institutions of the public sphere were created. Even agrarian societies founded with the intention of influencing the nature of rural life and production tended to be located in urban centers. Urban life also contributed to the professionalization of science and intellectual life.

Institutions established in this period shared several characteristics. These were voluntary institutions, wherein men were to "meet on the level," as the masonic phrase described it. This ensured that traditional status was neither the sole arbiter of men's fates, nor the determinant of their ability to speak critically or act positively in the interest of the communities they represented. Secondly, the founders of a number of these institutions were inspired by both French and German Enlightenment thought, and they often structured the institutions according to imperfect readings of the British system. These influences determined both the type of projects undertaken by members of these institutions, and the way in which the institutions were organized. Thus, in the public sphere, relations among members of an organization were characterized not just by a lack of emphasis on status, but also by overt reference to rational argumentation and natural law as the bases for relations between members of the institution and the reading public.

Theoretically, anyone "with access to cultural products—books, plays, journals—had at least a potential claim on the attention of the culture-debating public."[6] The operative word here is "theoretically." The characteristics outlined above represented the ideal expressed in the founding documents and charters of numerous organizations in Bohemia and elsewhere. However, as many have pointed out, the eighteenth-century public sphere was, by its very nature, limited to the educated, reading public—in other words, to those with access to the world of letters. This meant realistically that the public sphere was comprised of a rather narrow segment of the population: specifically educated, propertied men. This was not inherently negative in terms of initial political mobilization. Because the numbers of the educated were small enough to form fairly coherent groups that could associate through a network of salons, coffeehouses, and clubs, "the possibility of concerted political action by radically minded circles of the intelligentsia gave these new ideas about the nation and autonomy a social base that could translate them into political movements."[7]

Status systems based on birth or traditional social hierarchies could temporarily be jettisoned within the confines of individual institutions. For instance, it was standard practice to leave noble titles "at the door" of masonic lodges. But identity was mutable, and if a title could be left at the door, it could also be picked up again afterward at the bearer's convenience. Therefore, it is worth investigating the degree to which this disregard of status was exported from these institutions to the broader Bohemian community. Despite the erosion of strict, traditional hierarchy and the appearance of inclusiveness, there remained an unresolved tension in the public sphere between principled openness and de facto class limitations. Even with this caveat, it can be argued that these public institutions, despite their imperfections, were important to the definition and success of national movements. To elucidate, we can examine the Bohemian case in greater detail. Starting in the middle of the eighteenth century, there was an unprecedented growth of learned societies, clubs, lodges, and patriotic institutions in Bohemia as elsewhere in Europe. These social groups and institutions, including both regular informal gatherings such as salons and formalized associations such as museums and scientific societies, shared the characteristics of the public sphere described above; that is, they blended social classes. Formalized societies and museums generally had administrative structures that relied on a loose reading of parliamentary procedure, and, in terms of their operating protocols, they focused on individuals and their merits rather than on apportioning influence, prestige, and power on the basis of estate or traditional social status. These institutions also exhibited a public commitment to national progress that was explicit even before the 1790s.

Traditional Elites and the Public

Influential members of the Bohemian aristocracy, a group that was essentially non-ethnic, used their wealth, prestige, ability to travel, intellectual energy, and local power to establish and protect new institutions. The Society of Sciences, the Society for the Patriotic Friends of the Arts, the Patriotic-Economic Society, industrial societies, salons, literary clubs, and eventually the National Museum were all elements of the emerging public sphere. In the Bohemian world of scientific societies and soirées, acceptance was based on education and inclination, regardless of whether an individual was noble. In particular, the downward percolation of scientific inquiry contributed to a leveling of the playing field in intellectual discourse. Thus, whether one refers to informal discussions on botany at the spa in Karlovy Vary, profound and lengthy correspondences between intellectuals, or the formal sittings of the Society of Sciences, one can see that social distinctions did not count in institutions that were founded for intellectual endeavors and based on ability and merit. This new mode of social interaction had a powerful consequence: it enabled people in the public sphere to redefine their individual identities across traditional social divisions. Though individuals within public institutions initially had in common a unified outlook and purpose, the ultimately beneficiary of this was the nation. Elite status was not suddenly entirely immaterial, and language was not irrelevant, but the latter was not yet a critical plank of national identity. Language would of course become a more salient issue, and the institutions of the public sphere were implicated in this transition as well. The intellectual discourse that defined the public sphere in eighteenth- and nineteenth-century Bohemia took place primarily in German rather than in Czech. Curiously enough, the activities of the public sphere so happily promoted by Bohemian elites nurtured institutions and nonaristocratic intellectuals who subsequently supported the exclusion of German and noble individuals from the national public of the nineteenth century.

Before we turn to particular institutions, it is worth noting that the Bohemian aristocracy, which included critical proponents of new institutions in the eighteenth and early nineteenth centuries, has an ambiguous historical legacy for a variety of reasons. From the nationalist perspective, the Bohemian aristocracy was both "foreign," as a result of the Battle of White Mountain in 1620, and highly suspect for its voluntary Germanization in the latter half of the seventeenth century. The role of aristocrats in the Bohemian public sphere is also complex. People from noble families appear in the membership lists of virtually every prominent scientific society, museum, and cultural institution. As in France, salons were also heavily attended by nobles, and sometimes hosted by them. Nobles had a whole range of motivations for promoting political and social change. In political terms, their opposition to the government in Vienna was based on two sometimes incongruous ideas: on the one hand a belief in ancient estatist rights deriving from the heritage of the Bohemian Kingdom, and on the other hand, modern conceptions of intellectual freedom and progress. To bolster political arguments, many also relied on loose interpretations of the works of political philosophers that could be used to support a variety of arguments for greater Bohemian political autonomy. Montesquieu was a particular favorite because his works could be interpreted creatively to support the separation of powers not only within but between states.

Obviously, not all aristocrats were equally committed to progress, and many still believed fervently in protecting their lordly position on the land. The defeat of the Czech forces at White Mountain at the beginning of the Thirty Years' War was a watershed in the social development of the aristocracy and the bourgeoisie. Estates were confiscated, individuals were executed or exiled, and Bohemia was for the most part forcibly re-Catholicized. Families loyal to the Habsburgs, in war or otherwise, were settled in Bohemia. The upper aristocracy of Bohemia was still an important force at home and in other parts of the empire, and its members occupied prominent positions at the court in Vienna. This more entrenched group also had a role to play. Long after Bohemia had ceased to be independent, or even autonomous, there remained the idea of a Kingdom of Bohemia that had historical, political, geographical, and cultural dimensions. The aristocracy embraced this heritage; indeed it was the only group in a position to honor and protect it publicly. Within eighteenth-century Bohemia, centralizing policies and retribution against rebellion had shorn the noble elite of some measure of its old-fashioned, institutionalized political power. Though noble power would remain entrenched long into the nineteenth century, the political confrontations of Josephinism, the French Revolution, and the Napoleonic wars represented a significant challenge to the Bohemian elite. The social interaction reflected in the public sphere would also be altered by these experiences. Regardless of where family history fell on the issue of "Czech or not Czech," individuals from both pre- and post-White Mountain families were engaged in patriotic activities.[8]

In some respects, the activities of the aristocracy in the nascent public sphere resembled noble family life. Indeed, it was an extension of the family circle. This resemblance was a consequence of the culture of noble society. One important element was the nature of aristocratic households. Aristocratic support for new cultural institutions and their nonaristocratic proponents began in the household. Aristocratic families were made up of large entourages encompassing among others the nuclear family, the extended family, tutors, servants, friends, accountants, estate managers, archivists, librarians, historians, cooks, and priests. Social connections and the great eighteenth-century pastime of "clubbing" were determined to a large degree by family influence. Many of the most vibrant institutions of the public sphere grew out of these personal relations. In addition, many of the early elements of the public sphere in eighteenth-century Bohemia can be seen in the context of the responsible noble's public performance of his accepted civic duties, namely charity, philanthropy, patronage, and concern for the public weal.

The Institutions of the Public Sphere

The new public sphere in Bohemia was centered in the societies, clubs, and lodges that ultimately set the tone for patriotic activity.[9] One institution critical to the debate on a national and competitive Bohemia was the Bohemian Society of Sciences. The activities of the society's members, and above all their focus on scientific elucidation, were aimed at exploring and promoting the resources, raw materials, attributes, and industrial possibilities of the region. Individuals involved in institutions like the Bohemian Society of Sciences moved along a trajectory from pure scientific interest to concern "especially to be useful to the Fatherland."[10] The Bohemian Society was founded informally in the 1770s as the Learned Private Society. Educational reform and the expulsion of the Jesuits in 1773 breathed new life into the intellectual community in Bohemia, and particularly in Prague. Suddenly intellectual leadership was opened up, and society scholars began meeting regularly to brief each other on the latest findings and to develop scientific learning for the purpose of contributing to the betterment of the Bohemian lands. At first, members of the society met in the home of Franz Antonín Count Nostitz, who with Ignac Born and Franz Josef Count Kinský had initiated the meetings. The list of individuals involved in the society is a roster of the intellectual and social elite of Prague and all Bohemia.[11] In addition to meeting regularly, beginning in 1775 the group published a circular entitled *Discourses of a Private Society in Bohemia for the Development of Mathematics, the Fatherland's History, and Natural History*, with Ignac Born as the original editor.[12] The journal was a reflection of the newfound fascination with Enlightenment ideology and the new experimental sciences, as well as commentary and criticism on the scholarly endeavors of the day. Six volumes of the journal appeared between 1775 and 1784. The Private Society became public as the official Bohemian Society of Sciences in 1784, and it received a royal seal of approval as the Royal Bohemian Society of Sciences in 1790.

Members of the society came together as scientists, philosophers, and mathematicians interested in a vaguely defined "greater good," or at least in scientific progress, but ultimately it was the nation, the people, that became the focus of their concern. The work of the society was manifold and its membership increasingly diverse. It became involved not just in scientific study, but also in other far-reaching projects not initially within its purview. Meetings generally involved the presentation of new material or the results of scientific experiments. Mineralogy, botany, mathematics, discourses on demography, paleontology, and astronomy were just a few of the fields represented by the society's members. There were also presentations on philology, Slavicism, heraldry, and history. In addition to an array of historical and religious discourses, the society actively promoted concrete scientific studies and sought to apply a systematic method of researching the "nature" of Bohemia to the needs of industry, agriculture, and commerce.

As wide ranging as the work of the society was, in the essay contests the society supported and in all its activities, emphasis was placed repeatedly on certain topics. One of the interesting activities of the Society of Sciences and other scientific institutions like it was the ritual of the essay contest. The society would publish a question or topic and solicit responses from the reading public. Generally, some sort of monetary prize was offered and the winning essay was published and distributed. Watershed historical events, heroic figures, the economic and industrial development of the fatherland, and descriptions of provincial areas were customary themes. The topics were chosen to stimulate research and inquiry into the flora, fauna, and natural and cultural wealth of Bohemia. As problematic as the idea of "invention of tradition"[13] can be, there was a perceptible process at work in the public activities of the society and its members. It was not by chance that they focused on unearthing the authentic Slavic nature of Bohemia, determining the unique quality of Bohemia's ancient jurisprudence, and tracing the history of its social structure and religious traditions.[14] By examining the possible innocence of Jan Hus or ferreting out the story of the duke responsible for Bohemia's feudal subjection to the German emperor, for example, the society's members could shape a Bohemian history independent of Bohemia's current status as "merely" a province of the Habsburg Empire. In particular, the emphasis on the medieval period, with its associated development of a strong artisan class (regardless of ethnicity) and its unequivocally Czech rulers bespoke a nostalgia for an era of Bohemian strength: Bohemia as the heart of Europe, a land with an admirable and seemingly more unambiguous past.

It is clear that the work of the Society of Sciences was scientific and cultural; it was not devoted only to a critical discourse on the state per se. The society's primary public concern was the potential for science to define and enlighten the community. However, correspondences of the society with scholars at home and abroad attest to a continuing fixation on the place and position of Bohemia in the wider scientific and cultural world. By nature of their involvement in science in the fatherland, members of the society were de facto patriots, and addressed each other as such. "Progress," the defining term of enlightened, universalist thought, was specifically attached to national aspirations. In fact, enlightenment itself was less a question of individual edification than national rediscovery. Although the trend was more pronounced after the French Revolution and the Napoleonic wars, it is not uncommon to find references to Bohemia's national "place" in earlier documents. Emerging from the Bohemian public sphere as a professional class, scientists referred directly to Bohemia's ability to compete against many nations and to "boast of a glorious victory."[15] Mercantilism had put on the table the notion of a "national" territory and had encouraged the development of an administration and bureaucracy to promote its wealth. In the early nineteenth century, individual economists like Georg Count Buquoy redefined these concerns in terms of national economy and international competition.[16] The ideas of competition and the role of a nation as one among many also set the tenor of the debate in the public sphere, such that concern about the "others" inside and outside the political territory was echoed in criticisms of state (or elite) authority. Competition also extended beyond the economic realm into areas that are the accouterments of mature statehood: art, artifacts, and history. These issues in particular fell to the museum.

The compelling quality of these societies is even more evident in the institutionalization of the public and the nation in the museum. The intent of the founders of the Museum of the Fatherland, the Society of Sciences, and similar institutions was to confer immutable value on Bohemia while simultaneously improving its prospects. The Museum of the Fatherland, established in 1818 without a permanent home, was designed to display the Bohemian land in all its different facets, whether natural, linguistic, literary, historical, artistic, or productive. The purpose of the museum, aided in part by the Linnaean tradition, was to create an institution uniquely concerned with classifying and exhibiting the output of both prehistoric and contemporary Bohemia. In this sense, the Museum of the Fatherland as an institution suffered from a split personality—the result of the inherent tension between preserving the past and influencing the future.

Museums have a history, but their work entails an attempt to conceal it, "to transform . . . History into Nature."[17] This is nowhere more apparent than in a national museum, an institution set up to confer legitimacy on a nation and to provide it with an unswerving and unquestioned national past. Museums base their entire enterprise on a system of classifying objects and positing those objects as representative and valuable. Classification is particularly important for a national museum because of its apparent objectivity. However classification is presented—and it is usually presented as inherent in the classified object itself, "it always takes place . . . within some externally constructed field, such as the 'nation.'"[18]

Museum displays and the paraphernalia associated with them imbue objects—and the national history these objects represent—with value and authenticity. Dominique Poulot and Daniel Sherman have argued that "nation-states, emergent bourgeois elites, and wealthy individuals have used museums to legitimate their hegemony with the aura of culture. In the process these groups have endowed museums with considerable authority to define and to represent the cultural sphere."[19] This is particularly true of national museums. Even natural history museums, ostensibly bastions of objective science and classification, were organized in their earlier development to reflect the museum's attempt to capture the geographic space, in this case Bohemia, and to shape the public's relationship to it.[20] Museums as institutions had the potential to contribute significantly to cultural debate in the public sphere, and an important dimension of this debate was the way society chose to treat its past. In other words, it matters "how the past is sequestered from forgetfulness; exposed, gathered, formulated, and reformulated in discourse; presented and displayed in specially designated areas."[21] "Using" the past is often a dicey prospect, and in the Bohemian case the past was a critical plank of national "awakening." Under the museum's auspices, archaeology and journeys of national discovery could expose a national past that was "there all the time" but merely hidden, buried, or asleep. The wave of fabricated documents in the nineteenth century, some of them created by very respected scholars, was an outgrowth of this phenomenon, and gave new meaning to the notion of "the invention of tradition."

The agenda of the Museum of the Fatherland was threefold: to collect, preserve, and promote. The charter committee sought to unite all the patriotic efforts of past and present, "bringing them together as a looking glass, vividly revealing the natural connection to the fatherland, and guiding the Bohemians at the same time to the essential condition of all enduring progress: self-realization."[22] As the charter document states, "the Museum of the Fatherland should encompass everything in the area of national literature and national production, and unify everything that nature and human diligence have created in the fatherland."[23] The collections of the museum, initially donated almost exclusively by the aristocracy, were to be the possession of the "Bohemian nation."[24] The intent and meaning of collecting and the mission of the museum were complicated and involved different motivations—namely the desire to preserve, fascination for the exotic, and the prevalent interest in scientific inquiry and classification. The museum's purpose was to educate and to form a central, convenient, institutional hub that would unite the greatest minds of the scientific community. By publishing, collecting, and distributing information, supporting intellectual endeavors, and uniting various collections, the museum committee sought to contribute concretely to the public good. Part of the impetus was also to preserve the best and the brightest of the nation's heritage against the ravages of time and indifference. Collecting literary and historical icons was "saving in its strongest sense, not just casual keeping but conscious rescuing from extinction—collection as salvation."[25]

Not only science and industry benefited from new national aspirations. Art collections, once the virtually exclusive possession of noble (and royal) families, had been housed and viewed in private. Noble art collectors viewed private enjoyment, market value, and prestige as sufficient motivations for acquiring art, with little reference to Bohemia and even less to the national community. The nascent public sphere would affect art collection as well. The Patriotic Friends of the Arts, established in 1796, was the prelude to the creation of a national gallery. The purpose of the gallery established by the Patriotic Friends of the Arts was clear: the gallery would lessen the real danger that invaluable art treasures that should rightly belong to the nation might be sold outside Bohemia for the enrichment of short-sighted individuals. The gallery was to function as a public home for these works, some owned by the Patriotic Friends of the Arts and others borrowed, and would contribute to the edification of the population. With the gallery, Count Rudolf Černín and Count

Francis Sternberg sought to provide Bohemia with its "proper" share of artistic possessions. They believed that no mature nation which hoped to develop a center of learning, art, and culture could be complete without objects of internationally recognized value and splendor, and the Patriotic Friends intended to contribute toward this goal.

Czechs followed the Germans in their reliance on the "bequeathed treasures" of the past. Whereas the French drive to express the national agenda and character often involved the tearing down of old institutions and the shedding of an "oppressive" past,[26] the Germans and the Czechs tended to enshrine the legends of their heritages—with the Germans seeking to glorify and the Czechs to awaken. Part of the essence of the urge to collect and classify was the belief that "the collection is the unique bastion against the deluge of time."[27] Collectors of national wealth deplored the apparent withering away of the nation's finest attributes and future possibilities. By the time Bohemian intellectuals had absorbed some measure of Herder's philosophy and German romanticism, it was possible to rephrase the debate in terms of the rebirth rather than the death of the nation. Nations could be seen as inherent and permanent, needing only to be awakened. Whereas collecting had earlier been inspired in part by the latent belief in a nation in its death throes, the commitment evolved into a desire to awaken a nation not dead, but merely asleep. Like the phoenix of legend, the nation would rise from the ashes to live again in competition with the great nations of Europe. National collections enshrined in museums would serve to represent the maturity and worth of the public domain.

Competing Publics

The discourse on competition among nations brought another element into the public debate on identity. As anthropologists have noted, the "clean" presupposes the "dirty."[28] Identity-building thrived when there was an oppositional other against which the proponents of the national "good" could polemicize. The program of patriotic institutions reinforced the desire to define "us"; it also emphasized what was native to the land and people, and above all what was most to be admired and revered in the national history, culture, and community. What grew out of this attempt at a more clear definition of the community and those who could hope for membership in it, however, was a conflict with the reality of a region that was culturally, historically, and politically diverse. In the eighteenth century, the notion of Germany and Germanness was cultural, and German states—particularly Prussia and Austria—coexisted as legitimate German polities. The existence of multiple states, and multinational states, was taken for granted. Political boundaries and cultural ones did not correspond. In Central Europe, Bohemia was defined as a political and cultural territory, although it did not correspond to linguistic or ethnic boundaries. As the links between public institutions grew stronger, the problem of linguistic difference within the reading populace came to the forefront. If Czech was initially seen as incapable of supporting sophisticated scientific and intellectual discourse, it was the project of the nationalist to ensure that Czech be "returned" to its former linguistic glory.

The problem of exclusivity was not just a national or a linguistic one. The description of the public, according to the theory of Jurgen Habermas, depends on the possibility of setting society and the state apart. The "public" is distinct from the publicity of the ruler and the traditional hierarchy, as well as from the common people—who were effectively excluded.[29] In the West, there was opposition between the state and the group of interested private individuals who came to see themselves as representative of the people. In Central and Eastern Europe, by contrast, the relationship of elites—both bourgeois and aristocratic—to the state was more problematic. The Habsburg administration came to be defined by the critical public as another oppositional "other"—in terms of political opposition and in terms of the nation holding out against those who ruled but did not represent. The project of the new public sphere in Bohemia was less the overt criticism of state authority and the questioning of power and representation than the attempt to define the nature of the represented public. Private individuals looking to organize could draw on a heritage of national distinction and a national character that legitimized their opposition to the state.

Conclusion

The turn of the eighteenth century was a time of great political upheaval; in Bohemia, as elsewhere, intellectual societies, national institutions, and cultural interest flourished. To assess the historical significance of this period and to give form to the intellectual, cultural, and social changes, it is necessary to look beneath the larger political changes at the establishment of national institutions and learned societies as well as at the individuals who constituted the emerging elite and played important roles in it. The story of choices made *in* private life and *for* public action is the story of the day-to-day individual development of identity. The private process of determining one's options in an uncertain world brought a profound alteration in public life overall. The enlightened nobility, though aware of its position and imperial role, used its wealth and influence to nurture new cultural institutions. The cumulative effect of using traditional avenues of aristocratic patronage and power for this purpose was the creation of new social bonds and political agendas: that is, the creation of the public sphere. In the nineteenth century the baton was passed to others, who made the leap to a more radical national program with an overt political component.

To conclude, identity was a question of state of mind and of loyalty, whether to universal scientific principles or to Bohemia. Communities or public bodies formed around these shared loyalties, but they were neither static nor rigid. Nation building was not and is not a linear process. It is rather a process of seismic reverberations, of one factor causing a ripple of reaction. The history of the public sphere in Bohemia was one of these significant ripples. The institutions that made up civil society, and the consequent separation of people from the state, meant that the traditional hierarchy of social relations had been breached. Scientific, literary, and artistic endeavors brought together a diverse group of individuals in Bohemia and thus contributed to the growth of cultural institutions establishing links across class lines. Once a swath had been cut through social boundaries, it was possible for members of this new intellectual elite to articulate a novel cultural configuration: the nation.

NOTES

1. Quoted in Roman Szporluk, *Communism and Nationalism* (Oxford, 1988), Introduction.

2. Craig Calhoun, ed., *Habermas and the Public Sphere* (Cambridge, 1993), p. 7. Geoff Eley describes it as "a sphere which mediates between society and state, in which the public organizes itself as the bearer of public opinion." See his "Nations, Publics, and Political Cultures: Placing Habermas in the Nineteenth Century" in *Habermas and the Public Sphere*, ed. Calhoun, p. 290. One should take note of an important caveat in the discussions in the Calhoun volume, namely that the "public sphere" as a concept is simultaneously "a normative ideal, an ideological fiction, and a social form." Keith Michael Baker, "Defining the Public Sphere in Eighteenth-Century France" in *Habermas and the Public Sphere*, ed. Calhoun, p. 188.

3. Jurgen Habermas, *The Structural Transformation of the Public Sphere* (Cambridge, 1989), p. 49, quoted in Eley, "Nations, Publics, and Political Cultures," p. 289.

4. Calhoun, *Habermas*, p. 12.

5. John Hutchinson and Anthony Smith, *Nationalism* (Oxford, 1994), p. 6.

6. Calhoun, *Habermas*, p. 13.

7. Hutchinson and Smith, *Nationalism*, p. 6.

8. For two discussions of the changing fortunes of the aristocratic class, see Hugh Agnew, *"Noble Natio* and Modern Nation: The Czech Case," *Austrian History Yearbook* 23 (1992): 50–71; James van Horn Melton, "The Nobility in the Bohemian and Austrian Lands, 1620–1780," *The European Nobilities*, 2 vols. (London, 1995), vol. 2, pp. 110–43.

9. The importance of freemasonry in particular should not be overlooked. For an excellent treatment of this subject in West European societies, see Margaret C. Jacob, *Living the Enlightenment: Freemasonry and Politics in Eighteenth-Century Europe* (Oxford, 1991).

10. Ústředni archiv Československé Akademie věd/ Králova česká společnost nauk (henceforth ČSAV/KČSN), fond 33/carton 63/inventory 15 (1791).

11. Besides Born, Kinský, and Nostitz, this group included A. Strnad, Gelasius Dobner, Adaukt Voigt, František Pelcl, Joseph Mayer, Jan Mayer, T. Gruber, Josef Dobrovský, Count Bubna, and others.

12. *Abhandlungen einer Privatgesellschaft in Böhmen zur Aufnahme der Mathematik, der vaterländischen Geschichte und der Naturgeschichte*, 6 vols. (Prague, 1775–1784).

13. See Eric Hobsbawm and Terence Ranger, eds., *The Invention of Tradition* (Cambridge–London–New York, 1983).

14. For a discussion on the writing of history in Bohemia, see Hugh Agnew, *The Origins of the Czech Renascence* (Pittsburgh, 1993).

15. ČSAV/KČSN/33/57/18 (1785).

16. See Georg Buquoy, *Das Nationalwirtschaftliche Prinzip oder Was Zuletzt Alle Nationalwirtschaftliche Anstalten Bezwecken Müssen* (Leipzig, 1816).

17. Daniel Sherman and Irit Rogoff, eds., *Museum Culture: Histories, Discourses, Spectacles* (Minneapolis, 1994), p. x.

18. Ibid., p. xi.

19. Ibid., p. xvii.

20. Ibid., p. xvii.

21. Ariella Azoulay, "With Open Doors: Museums and Narrative in Israel's Public Space" in *Museum Culture*, ed. Sherman and Rogoff, p. 88.

22. Jan Nebeský, *Geschichte des Museums* (Prague, 1868), p. 1.

23. Archiv Národního Musea, Registratura Národního Musea, Section A/1.

24. Josef Hanuš, *Národní Museum a Naše Obrození*, 2 vols. (Prague, 1921–1923), vol. 1 (1921), p. 32.

25. John Elsner and Roger Cardinal, eds., *The Cultures of Collecting* (Cambridge, 1994), p. 1.

26. Detlef Hofman, "The German Art Museum and the History of the Nation" in *Museum Culture*, eds. Sherman and Rogoff, pp. 3–21.

27. Elsner and Cardinal, eds., *The Cultures of Collecting*, p. 1.

28. Ibid., p. 5.

29. Calhoun, *Habermas*, p. 8.

Class Interest and the Shaping of a "Non-Historical" Nation: Reassessing the Galician Ruthenian Path to Ukrainian Identity[1]

HUGO LANE

During the late 1970s and early 1980s, scholars began to take a new look at nationalism, a topic that had attracted scant attention for nearly a generation. Since that time, interest in nationalism has snowballed to such a point that it has even been declared a distinct field of study at some universities. This shift can largely be explained by recent events, such as the emergence of nationalist political movements in a number of seemingly stable West European nation-states during the 1970s, and the more dramatic disintegration of the Soviet Union and Yugoslavia. But on a deeper level, such developments reflect a sense that nationalism is a phenomenon intimately connected to modernity and to the experience of living in the modern world which makes twentieth century society so different from the societies that preceded it.

While not an entirely new observation, this division between the world before nationalism and the world after it has become axiomatic for scholars. So, too, has the belief that, despite what a multitude of national histories maintain, the transition to modern society, in which nationalism is so central, has generally been difficult, if not traumatic—particularly for the traditionally dominant political classes. Often the elite extended active membership in the body politic to those who had previously been excluded only with great reluctance, whether peaceably through parliamentary reform, as in Britain, or as the result of more substantial civil unrest. Moreover, as the Polish case illustrates, this process could be problematic even in the absence of statehood, when the support of the common people was necessary to the achievement of the nationalist goal of independent statehood.

The only exception to this pattern that scholars have shown a willingness to accept has been that of the so-called "non-historic" nations—those nations that lacked a landed elite accustomed to playing a role in government by virtue of their class. While this term is not without controversy, its proponents have argued persuasively that precisely because the nations that fit this category—for example, the Slovaks, the Slovenes, and the Ukrainians—were essentially peasant nations, the elevation of the peasantry to citizenship was recognized as essential by their political leadership from the start. Thus, difficult as it has been for such nations to gain full independence, an event that in many cases has been very recent, their political survival did not allow them to succumb to the same kind of class antagonism that made the emergence of modern national identity so problematic for historical nations.[2]

This description fits the Ruthenians living in Austrian-ruled Galicia who would later declare themselves Ukrainians particularly well. Even in the nineteenth century, they were widely characterized as a "nation of priests and peasants" living in the shadow of the Polish landed elite. As for the divisions between the priests and the peasants, these have generally been downplayed, since the difference between the peasants' standard of living and that of priests and other educated Ruthenians was minimal. Recent scholarship, however, has demonstrated that a divide existed between peasants and educated Ruthenians: the peasants were not predisposed to think nationally and had to be encouraged to do so through the efforts of educated Ruthenians.[3] This raises questions about the depth and significance of class divisions between the educated Ruthenian elite and the peasantry, and about how class relations affected the emergence of Ukrainian national consciousness in Galicia.

The primary difficulty in investigating this problem has been the lack of sources that can be regarded as reliable reflections of peasant attitudes.[4] One set of sources that has been long overlooked, however, is the election results for successive Diets and Reichsrats convened beginning in the 1860s, when Austria moved towards constitutional rule. Since the voting of Ruthenian peasants can be separated from that of other groups, thanks to geography and the curia system, it is relatively easy to follow their overall voting patterns, which provide a window onto the role nationality played in their electoral choices. After correlating these results with the Ruthenian elite's political strategy as revealed in pamphlets, published speeches, and parliamentary activity, it becomes clear that class divisions played an important role in the adoption of Ukrainian identity by Galician Ruthenians during the last third of the nineteenth century.

Class, Culture, and Elections:
The Ruthenian National Awakening in Galicia Reconsidered

Galician Ruthenians first appeared on the European political stage during the revolutionary upheaval of 1848. It was an unprecedented event. Whereas the Ukrainians living in the Russian Empire could point to the legacy of Bohdan Khmelnyts'kyi and the establishment of the Hetmanate, Galician Ruthenians had never asserted themselves *en masse* as having political interests that differed from those of the Galician Polish elite. Close contacts between Count Franz Stadion, the senior Austrian official in Lemberg, and the Greek Catholic hierarchy during the first months of unrest in the province lent credence to Polish suspicions that the Ruthenians were encouraged by Stadion to break with the Poles. Still, whatever machinations occurred at high levels, the most striking feature of the months following was the overwhelming support Ruthenian peasants gave to the idea of a distinct Ruthenian nation and constitutional rule after they learned from their parish priests that serfdom had been abolished.

With the collapse of the 1848 revolution and efforts to set the Austrian state permanently on a constitutional footing, the Ruthenians and other nations that had made their voices heard during the "Springtime of Nations" quickly retreated from overt political activity. True, this can be seen as casting doubt on the Ruthenians' commitment to constitutional rule, or on the sincerity of the Galician Ruthenians' claims to national sovereignty, but Ruthenians' actions in 1848 cast a shadow over the Polish elite's belief that they alone should control Galician affairs. As a result, when circumstances led the Austrian imperial leadership to return to the path of constitutionalism in 1860, the Galician Polish elite had reason to be anxious about how strong support for Ruthenian candidates might be in elections to the newly proclaimed Galician Diet.

The results could hardly be comforting for the Polish elite. While the inequities of the four-curia system that gave the landed elite and propertied town dwellers disproportional representation ensured that the Polish elite did well enough to dominate the Diet, the number of Ruthenian candidates elected was remarkably high.[5] Ruthenians won 46 seats, almost two-thirds of the seats set aside for the fourth curia, to which the vast majority of Ruthenians, as peasants, belonged. Thus, seen as a specific group they actually had 4 more seats than the 42 set aside for the first curia made up of large land-owners.[6] Moreover, given the geographical distribution of Ruthenians in Galicia, these 46 seats actually came close to reaching the maximum number of mandates they could expect to win, and significantly, it was an achievement they never came close to matching as long as Galicia was under Austrian rule.[7]

Ruthenian candidates did not repeat this performance in the two subsequent elections to the Diet in 1867 and 1870. The size of the Ruthenian delegation dropped by nearly a third to 31 following 1870, but that still meant that a considerable majority of the electors chosen by Ruthenian communes were continuing to view Ruthenian candidates as the best representatives of their interests.[8] Moreover, despite these losses, when the first semi-direct elections for the Reichsrat were held in 1873, Ruthenian candidates won all 16 fourth-curia constituencies east of the San River, thus rivaling their performance in the 1861 election to the Diet.[9]

Following the declines of the 1867 and 1870 elections, the Ruthenians' victory in the Reichsrat elections suggested that, if anything, peasant support for Ruthenian candidates was rebounding, making those earlier losses seem transitory. Moreover, peasant trust in the elite appeared to be at an all-time high, since 11 of the Reichsrat delegates were Greek Catholic priests; in fact, the opposite proved true.[10] Following the 1877 elections to the Diet, the Ruthenian delegation dropped by over two-thirds to just 13.[11] The performance of Ruthenian candidates in the 1879 Reichsrat elections was even worse, with only 4 Ruthenian deputies sent to Vienna, and one of these soon announcing his decision to join the Polish club.[12]

Admittedly, the succession of election results presented above must be considered a rather crude instrument for judging the extent to which Ruthenian peasants understood their political interest in national terms. Convenient as it would be to attribute Ruthenian candidates' strong showing in 1861 (as well as their relatively consistent performances in elections into the 1870s) to the depth of the Ruthenian peasantry's national consciousness, other factors must also be considered. The most significant of these was the peasants' general distrust of the Polish elite, which at the end of the 1850s was heightened by the large number of unresolved rights disputes left over from the abolition of serfdom in 1848. Thus, both Polish and Ruthenian peasants had good reason to want to elect people they could trust to support their land claims in the first Galician Diet, and this concern clearly had an effect on the election results that year.

Still, if the desire to send someone who would defend peasant interests knew no ethnic bounds, the electoral results point to an important difference in the ways in which Polish and Ruthenian peasants sought to achieve this aim, as well as in their overall ability to assert their political will. Of the 28 delegates in fourth-curia seats not held by Ruthenian delegates (there were a total of 74 seats reserved for the fourth curia), 17 were themselves peasants. Among the remaining 11 delegates was Count Adam Potocki—no friend of the peasantry. More significantly, there were only 4 Roman Catholic priests, who might potentially have helped serve as leaders for the peasantry.[13] Thus, Polish peasants found themselves without any allies outside their own ranks, greatly reducing their effectiveness in the environment of the Diet, where the Polish elite consistently succeeded in using legalistic conceptions of procedure to confound peasant arguments.[14]

By contrast, peasant districts east of the San River, the traditional divide between ethnically Polish and Ruthenian peasant communities, sent a more mixed group of delegates to the Diet in 1861. Like Polish peasant electors, Ruthenian peasant electors often chose one of their own, but 22, or just under half of the deputies elected, were Greek Catholic priests, and a few others were Ruthenian government officials known for siding with the peasantry.[15] Thus, Ruthenian peasants appear to have trusted non-peasant Ruthenians to a much greater degree than Polish peasants trusted non-peasant Poles, suggesting that the spirit of Ruthenian national unity displayed in 1848 was still alive over a decade later. This provided Ruthenians with a ready and experienced leadership, an advantage that was further strengthened by the presence of the Greek Catholic bishops who sat in the Diet ex officio.[16]

Even if the peasants were in the minority and, consequently, victories for them would be few, the Ruthenian delegation had the potential to serve as an effective opposition that could maintain peasants' confidence that their interests were being well represented—particularly if the delegation were to join forces with Polish peasant deputies. Though the delegation was unable to accomplish the latter, Ruthenian peasants' trust in the Ruthenian elite's leadership remained high into the 1870s, as has already been seen, and what losses did occur hardly foreshadowed the collapse of that trust evident in the election results from the end of the 1870s.

Fourth-curia electors' shift away from backing peasant candidates, and even non-peasants earlier trusted by Ruthenian peasants, has long been attributed to the increased and more adept manipulation of the fourth-curia voting process by Polish landlords.[17] Indeed, the fourth-curia electoral process seemed designed to make manipulation of elections possible. Elections took place in two stages, with villages selecting electors, who then gathered to cast their votes in an open-ballot election—where an outsider could influence the proceedings with bribery and threats of retribution. Still, the relative consistency of Ruthenian candidates' performance in elections into the 1870s tends to suggest that Ruthenians' sense of belonging to a national political community helped protect them from landlords' attempts to influence their voting, making the election results of 1877 and 1879 all the more puzzling.

In considering why Ruthenian peasants lost their apparent national solidarity and succumbed to pressure from the landlords, it is first appropriate to note that the success of electoral corruption requires conditions to be such that the electorate finds the corrupt gains being offered more advantageous than those made by voting one's conscience. Of course, where coercion through bribery or threats is endemic, the advantages of voting one's conscience may seem so far removed from reality that they are not an option. However, given their earlier electoral performance, this cannot have been the case with the Ruthenians. Thus, at least in part, their sharp shift away from supporting their own candidates reflected a conscious decision by Ruthenian electors, if not by the peasant communes, that the benefits of cooperating with the landlords had outstripped those to be gained by continuing to support Ruthenian candidates simply because they were Ruthenian.

Changing political circumstances were probably one important factor contributing to Ruthenian electors' break with their previous patterns. Throughout the 1860s, Galicia's status within the new constitutional structure was up in the air, and while the Polish elite's agreement to support the new constitution creating the Dual Monarchy in 1867 opened the way for Poles to take control of the province, the terms for Galician home-rule were not resolved until the early 1870s.[18] Until that time, therefore, Ruthenian peasants had reason to put their faith in the Diet as a means to assert their displeasure with what they perceived as Polish misrule. In fact, even the particularly strong showing by Ruthenian candidates in the 1873 Reichsrat elections may well have reflected a widespread belief among Ruthenian peasants that the Reichsrat might serve as their last bastion against Polish control of Galicia. But by the late 1870s, the Polish elite's hold over Galician affairs was no longer in question, and the Reichsrat had shown little inclination to challenge Polish ambitions—giving Ruthenian electors, if not Ruthenians as a whole, reason to see collaboration with the Poles as more advantageous than continued opposition.

Unfortunately, plausible as such an explanation may be, solid evidence regarding Ruthenian peasants' electoral behavior during this period, let alone their political calculations, is simply too limited to substantiate its accuracy.

Still, it can be said that the Ruthenian political leadership's political strategy had not gone beyond seeking to convince the Austrian central administration to protect the Ruthenians from the Polish elite's growing influence over Galician affairs. In 1864, following the disappointment with the Polish elite's dominance of the Diet, the Ruthenian leadership renewed the request it had made in 1848 that Galicia be partitioned along ethnic lines, but the Austrian central administration ignored it.[19] Moreover, even after the Austrian administration had conceded control of Galicia to the Polish elite, the Ruthenian leadership repeatedly invoked the imperial Constitution of 1867, with only a little more success, against Polish efforts to restrict the recognition of Ruthenians' cultural rights.[20]

It is certainly hard to imagine that these failures did not affect the peasantry's perception of the Ruthenian elite as competent representatives of their own interests. Yet, what is perhaps even more striking is how little attention the Ruthenian elite actually paid to peasant concerns. While the proposal to partition Galicia may have been intended to rescue Ruthenians from Polish domination in general, it lacked any provisions that would have improved the peasants' position vis-à-vis their landlords. Indeed, it included no attempt to alter the electoral system that so favored the landlords in the existing Galician Diet in any substantial way, were the province to be partitioned and a new Diet for eastern Galicia convened.[21] By the same token, important as determining the legal status of the Ruthenian language in autonomous Galicia was in the minds of both the Polish and Ruthenian elites, it was an issue that had little bearing on the socioeconomic issues, such as land redistribution, that most interested peasants.

Seen in this light, the massive declines in the size of Ruthenian delegations to the Diet and Reichsrat following the 1877 and 1879 elections marked a new level of self-confidence among the Ruthenian peasantry in a perverse way. True, by succumbing to bribery, peasants and electors were forfeiting a strong parliamentary faction to defend their rights. Their experience, however, had shown that the existing Ruthenian leadership had not only failed to protect their interests, but had not even tried to do so. By voting for the landlords' men, peasants and electors were maintaining a working relationship with their landlord. At the very least, this might secure the peasants seed grain for the following year; it could also win them access to forests and pasture lands, which the Ruthenian leadership had failed to win for the peasants through legitimate political activities in earlier sessions of the Diet.[22]

Much of the blame for the failure of the Ruthenian elite to sustain peasants' support can be placed on the Greek Catholic hierarchy, which had not shown serious concern for the peasantry, and was in fact hostile to those within the elite who believed that they should reach out to the peasantry. When a small group among the Ruthenian elite decided to found Prosvita (Enlightenment) in 1868 as an organization for peasant education, the hierarchy attempted to sabotage activities related to its inaugural meeting by forbidding any priest to conduct a service commemorating the event.[23] In part, this reflected the hierarchy's displeasure with the tendency of many in Prosvita to support the view that Ruthenians were Ukrainians, but this was clearly not the hierarchy's only concern. When Ivan Naumovych, a prominent supporter of the Russian-oriented views preferred by the Greek Catholic hierarchy, founded the Mykhailo Kachkovs'kyi Literary Society as an alternative organization for encouraging peasant education, those associated with the hierarchy were no more inclined to back it than they had been to back Prosvita.[24] Thus, the Greek Catholic hierarchy appears to have been bothered by the very idea that the elite should do anything more than tell the peasants what to do.

The situation changed in the aftermath of the collapse of Ruthenian peasant support for Ruthenian candidates. With the Ruthenian clerical elite unable to provide a suitable plan to restore peasant confidence in their leadership, the balance of power within the Galician Ruthenian elite shifted towards those who had favored reaching out to the peasantry. To be fair, even as Prosvita and the Kachkovs'kyi Society had actively sought to enhance the moral state of the Ruthenian peasantry during the 1870s, they had not encouraged Ruthenian peasants to be politically active any more than had the Greek Catholic hierarchy.[25]

But Prosvita in particular was quick to respond to the 1879 electoral catastrophe. Within months of the election, its leaders authorized a revision of its statutes to allow it to become involved in politics, and they established two newspapers, *Dilo* and *Bat'kivshchyna*, to spread their views among, respectively, educated audiences and the peasantry.[26] These newspapers were made available in the reading clubs then proliferating throughout the countryside thanks to the efforts of Prosvita and the Kachkovs'kyi Society. The Kachkovs'kyi Society did not take any similar measures, but inasmuch as its publications announced and reported on Prosvita meetings, it became a tacit ally in the latter's newly political mission.[27]

The efforts of Prosvita and the Kachkovs'kyi Society to interest peasants in politics illustrated the new pragmatism that distinguished the new, more secular Ruthenian leadership that came to the fore after 1879 from its religiously oriented predecessors. No less significant was their willingness to look outside the mainstream of the still generally conservative Ruthenian elite, to those who, like themselves, wanted to encourage peasants to see political activity as a solution to their problems. Thus, Ivan Franko and Mykhailo Pavlyk, two socialists who had been largely shut out of the Ruthenian political debate since their arrest for socialist activity in 1877, became contributors to *Bat'kivshchyna*, writing about political and social injustice (although their principal benefactor, the lawyer Iuliian Romanchuk, ruled out a formal alliance with the socialists).[28]

The way in which reading societies and *Bat'kivshchyna* changed peasants' perceptions of community is a central subject of John-Paul Himka's *Galician Villagers and the Ukrainian National Movement in the Nineteenth Century*.

The elections of the 1880s provide some sense of the pace of this transformation. In the 1883 elections to the Diet, the number of Ruthenian candidates elected dropped by 3 to 10, but at the very least the elections did not see the Ruthenian delegation disappear from the Diet.[29] The 1885 elections to the Reichsrat saw Ruthenians gain a seat in a contested election for the first time, when their delegation increased from 3 to 4, but this performance might well have been stronger had not the Greek Catholic Metropolitan Syl'vester Sembratovych nominated a separate list, thereby splitting the Ruthenian vote.[30]

Despite the understandable initial distrust between the party supported by the secular Ruthenian leadership and the Metropolitan, both sides recognized the value of pluralism and cooperation. Consequently, the Ruthenians fielded only one set of candidates in the 1889 election to the Diet. Moreover, thanks to the cooperation with Pavlyk, who was named acting editor for *Bat'kivshchyna* in the runup to the elections, there was more emphasis on the socioeconomic issues that were likely to give peasants reasons to vote on the basis of their interests rather than give in to bribery.[31]

This new show of unity of purpose brought with it encouraging results. The number of Ruthenian candidates elected to the Diet increased from 10 to 17, and of those 2 were peasants, making this the first time Ruthenians had sent peasant delegates to the Diet since 1870.[32] No less important was the election of 4 Polish peasant delegates to the Diet for the first time since 1861, thanks to similar efforts of peasant mobilization by Polish peasant and democratic activists.[33] Thus, on a broader level, the 1889 elections renewed the foundations for cooperation between the Ruthenian Populists and the nascent Polish Peasant Party that could potentially challenge the Polish elite's continued dominance of Galician politics.

In the months that followed, however, a coalition between the Ruthenian Populists and the Polish Peasant movement based on their common economic interests failed to materialize. Instead, several Populist leaders, including Iuliian Romanchuk and Oleksander Barvins'kyi, ended up in negotiations with the leaders of the Polish elite, including the Viceroy Kazimierz Badeni, which were intended to lead to a different sort of cooperation. After a month of intense talks, on 25 November 1890 Romanchuk announced in the Diet that he and his party were willing to accept the Polish offer.[34] The Ruthenian Populists, however, did not approve the Polish proposal unanimously; the following day Mykola Antonevych, a Russian-oriented gymnasium professor, announced his refusal to go along with the deal, and he was joined by 6 like-minded Ruthenian delegates—including one of the two peasant delegates.[35]

The New Era and Culture:
Casting the Die of Ukrainian Identity in Galicia

As the split in the Ruthenian leadership following the announcement of the New Era program of Polish-Ruthenian cooperation demonstrates, the pragmatism that had been the basis of the Ruthenian leadership's new success could not cover up the ongoing sharp philosophical differences within the elite. At the heart of the matter was the question of culture. The publications of the Kachkovs'kyi Society continued to use the historical orthography that emphasized links between Ruthenians and Russians, while Prosvita's publications were much closer to the vernacular-based orthography that resembled the Ukrainian language of Shevchenko and Kulish. Yet, if there has been a tendency to see those who rejected the New Era as spoilers who were unwilling to recognize that the way forward lay in Ukrainian identity, the conflict was brought to a head when the Ukrainian-oriented faction accepted the Polish offer unilaterally.

This is particularly noteworthy given that the New Era has gone down in history as a failure in which the Ruthenians naively believed that the cultural concessions the Poles made to the Ruthenians would be followed by political concessions.[36] This dichotomy between politics and culture, however, simply does not reflect the political thinking current among Austrian elites at the time. Moreover, it tends to downplay the value of the concessions that the Ruthenians did win from the Poles, and their overall significance for the development of Ruthenian society from then on.

Regarding the first point, had culture not been understood as closely linked to political power, the issue of which language or languages would be given official recognition in various crownlands would never have become as important as it did, and Galicia was no exception here. Even before the terms of Galician autonomy had been worked out, the Polish elite had moved swiftly to make Polish the dominant official language in the province, making only minimal concessions to Ruthenian on the basis of the guarantee of national rights in paragraph nineteen of the 1867 Constitution. Moreover, they continued to push successfully for further restrictions of official recognition of Ruthenian rights into the 1880s.[37]

Such tactics led Ruthenians to draw the same connection between culture and politics as the Poles, particularly given the wording of paragraph nineteen. Yet, the political significance of culture also affected the rivalry that had existed between the Russian- and Ukrainian-oriented factions of the Ruthenian elite since the 1870s, as became clear through the New Era. For if the Poles were going to relent in their policy towards Ruthenian culture, they would be forced to choose between supporting one version of Ruthenian identity over the other, and it was virtually inevitable that Poles would come out favoring the Ukrainian faction.

After all, since all concerned believed that culture mattered, encouraging Ruthenians to think of themselves as Russians would have been only one short step from condoning Ruthenian support for the Russian annexation of eastern Galicia. Indeed, it was precisely this kind of thinking that had led the conversion of the Hnylychky parish from Greek Catholicism to Orthodoxy in 1882 to be seen as such a massive threat to stability by the Polish and Austrian administration that several involved were tried for treason, and the sitting Greek Catholic Metropolitan was forced to resign.[38] The alternative, given that the Ruthenian elite continued to be outwardly hostile to the idea of assimilation to Polish culture, was for the Poles to reach an accommodation with the Ukrainian-oriented faction of the Ruthenian elite, as they finally did in 1890.[39]

For their part, the Ruthenian supporters of the New Era had good reasons to accept the Polish offer that were anything but naive. As the refusal of more than one-third of the elected Ruthenian delegates to the Diet to go along with the idea of cooperating with the Poles indicates, the Russian-oriented view was far from dead.[40] Meanwhile, as long as that cultural disagreement existed, essential matters that would lend legitimacy to Ruthenian culture, including the codification of a standard form of Ruthenian and its adoption as a language of scholarship and high culture, could only take place in a piecemeal and haphazard manner. Just how concerned the Ukrainian faction of the Ruthenian elite was with these cultural issues can be seen in what they gained from their agreement to work with the Polish elite.[41]

In the spirit of the New Era, the Polish elite allowed plans for the establishment of a separate Ruthenian gymnasium in Przemyśl to go forward and made further preparations for the creation of another Ruthenian gymnasium in Kolomyia in 1892. These concessions would not, in and of themselves, benefit the Ukrainian faction of the Ruthenian elite over their Russian-oriented rivals. That same year, however, the Galician School Commission under the direction of Michał Bobrzyński announced the standardization of Ruthenian using the vernacular model preferred by the Ukrainian-oriented faction.[42] In addition, organizations controlled by the Ukrainian-oriented faction, like the Shevchenko Scientific Society, were given state support.[43]

A further step in strengthening Ruthenians' ties with the Ukrainians was taken when the Polish elite agreed to fill the new chair for Ruthenian history, another New Era concession, with a Ukrainian. The Poles' first choice was Volodymyr Antonovych, a professor at Kyiv University, who, while a committed Ukrainian, was actually of Polish noble origin. Yet, while playing a role in encouraging the negotiations that led to the New Era, he declined the offer of the new chair. Instead he recommended his student, Mykhailo Hrushevs´kyi, who was duly appointed to the position, and arrived in Lviv in the fall of 1894 to begin work at the university as well as with institutions controlled by the Ukrainian-oriented faction of the Ruthenian elite.[44]

Neither of these victories on the cultural front could completely eradicate the Russian-oriented faction, but the state backing that the Ukrainian-oriented elite had received left the Russian-oriented leaders little room to make their case. While the Russian-oriented faction did manage to force the Church to continue the official use of the etymological orthography that they preferred,[45] in each new school year after 1892, Ruthenian students learned to read a language close to that used by the Ukrainians and lacking the connection with Russian that the etymological orthography conveyed. Meanwhile, Hrushevs'kyi's influence at the university likewise severely reduced the appeal of the Russian orientation, since he did not hesitate to highlight Russian-Ukrainian antagonism.

The End of the New Era and the
Politicization of Ukrainian Nationality in Galicia

Ironically, by the time Mykhailo Hrushevs'kyi arrived in Lviv, the spirit of cooperation between the Ukrainian-oriented Populists and the Polish elite that had made his appointment possible was fading. That spring, the five left-leaning Populists led by Iuliian Romanchuk joined those opposing the New Era.[46] This left Populists like Volodymyr Barvins'kyi and Anatol' Vakhnianyn, who were content to focus on increasing recognition of Ruthenian culture in a way that only served the elite, as the only Ruthenians still willing to work with the Poles.[47]

According to Kost' Levyts'kyi's partisan and pro-Romanchuk account in his history of Ukrainian political thought, this split came when Vakhnianyn had declared, in an exchange in the Reichsrat, that the Ruthenians now preferred to work with the Poles rather than their traditional allies, the Czechs.[48] Yet, the roots of Romanchuk's break with Barvins'kyi's circle and the Poles go back two years to the Russian-oriented faction's last serious challenge to the Ukrainian-oriented leaders' dominance of Ruthenian politics. It was then that Romanchuk and his supporters began to understand that the price of cooperating with the Poles was not just alienating the Russian-oriented faction of the Populists, but also the Ruthenian peasant majority they claimed to represent.

Despite their strong Ukrainian orientation, Romanchuk's socialist collaborators Mykhailo Pavlyk and Ivan Franko had joined Mykola Antonevych in criticizing the New Era agreement. The two men had become disillusioned with the Ukrainian-oriented faction's leaders after Pavlyk had been fired from his editorial duties at *Bat'kivshchyna* following the 1889 elections. They had gone on to start *Narod*, a newspaper through which they hoped to carry on their efforts to mobilize the Ruthenian peasantry politically. It soon became the organ of the newly established Radical Party, and the editors made plain their view that the Populists were reaching out to the Ruthenian peasants' class enemies rather than their most logical allies, the Polish peasants.[49] Moreover, in drawing up their first party platform, the Radicals made the introduction of universal male suffrage in a single curia a primary goal.

That Romanchuk, like other members of the Populist camp, had ignored his former associates' warning should not be surprising. He appears to have suffered from many of the same parochial tendencies as the rest of the Galician Ruthenian elite, and in 1881 had rejected Franko's suggestion that the Ruthenians cooperate with the nascent Polish peasant movement.[50] Moreover, during the 1880s, like other members of the Ruthenian elite, Romanchuk focused his efforts on cultural issues, rather than on those that reflected the needs and concerns of the Ruthenian peasantry.[51] Yet, if Romanchuk's reaction to the Radical Party's critique of the New Era was predictable, that of the Russian-oriented faction of the Ruthenian elite was not.

Since the 1870s, the members of the Russian-oriented elite had generally shown themselves to be more conservative and narrow-minded than those who promoted the Ukrainian idea in Galicia, and they had been some of the most vociferous opponents of socialism. The Russian-oriented journal *Nauka*, founded and edited by Ivan Naumovych, had attacked the young Franko and Pavlyk for promoting communal wives and godlessness.[52] Yet, in a way, the Russian-oriented faction led by Naumovych was more populist than the Ukrainian-oriented leadership. In founding the Mykhailo Kachkovs'kyi Literary Society, Naumovych had made the peasantry the focus of the organization, inviting peasants to its founding festivities and promoting village reading clubs where members of the Ruthenian elite were scarce.[53]

This spirit was apparent among Antonevych's supporters as well. In order to organize themselves, and perhaps to demonstrate their sizable numbers, the Russian-oriented faction held its first general mass meeting in Lviv in February 1892, just as the New Era began to affect political life in Galicia. Aside from pledging themselves to maintain the so-called etymological orthography for Ruthenian, they also considered other issues, and endorsed the Radical Party platform that called for electoral reform.[54] Moreover, Antonevych and his allies demonstrated their seriousness a month later by presenting a bill calling for universal male suffrage in the same terms the Radical Party had used.

Antonevych's bill was doomed from the start, and there was not even enough support for it to win a second reading. Still, in addition to the four Polish peasant delegates, the Ukrainian-oriented faction also decided to support it, despite their agreement to work with the Polish elite.[55] This suggested that the Ukrainian-oriented faction had been caught off guard, which was confirmed when they hastily put forward a bill of their own that they hoped would be looked upon more favorably by the Polish elite. In contrast to Antonevych's bill, their alternative made no attempt to sweep away the inequities of the curia system, but only proposed that the indirect voting system widely perceived as easing the Polish elite's ability to manipulate election results be replaced with direct voting. The Polish elite, however, was unwilling to accept even that much, and this second bill suffered the same ignominious fate as Antonevych's bill.[56]

The Poles' rejection of the more moderate bill surprised Ruthenian supporters of the New Era, and reawakened their sense that there were limits to what could be acheived by working with the Poles—at least in the mind of Romanchuk and his followers. Above all, the electoral reform issue appears to have reawakened Romanchuk's sense of the need to play to the interests of the peasants who had elected him, and he began backing away from the Polish agreement. Yet, in the short run, Romanchuk's arguably astute decision to reject the New Era completely in 1894 was politically costly. In the 1895 elections to the Diet, he and his colleagues lost their seats along with almost all of the Russian-oriented faction, although enough proponents of the New Era like Barvins'kyi and Vakhnianyn were elected in their place so that the Ruthenian delegation only lost three seats.[57]

Of course, one could maintain that support for the faction led by Barvins'kyi was a real reflection of Ruthenian peasants' preferences, but it is more likely that it was due to the efforts of the Polish elite to keep the New Era alive by manipulating the election. Among other things, a campaign against Antonevych forced him to leave the race in favor of Ivan Franko; he too was unable to win the seat.[58] Yet such efforts backfired, and in the wake of the elections, even Barvins'kyi and his clique had to renounce the New Era as a failure.[59]

With that the Ukrainian-oriented Ruthenian elite at last grasped that it could not succeed without combining its agenda with that of the Ruthenian peasantry. This realization, together with the impact of the cultural concessions won by the New Era, permanently weakened the Russian-oriented faction's political clout. In 1899, Ivan Franko, Mykhailo Hrushevs'kyi, and Iuliian Romanchuk and his allies formed the Ukrainian National Democratic Party as a mass-oriented party that recognized the importance of the peasantry as a political force.[60] This was a move that the Russian-oriented faction never truly countered, since despite the support they had shown for the Radical Party, they were unable to bring themselves to abandon their cultural agenda and focus intensively on the socioeconomic issues the Radical Party's leadership was most concerned with. While several of the opponents of the New Era agreement returned to the Diet following the 1901 elections, the decision by most to accept the Ukrainian-oriented faction's leadership showed how much the situation had changed.[61] No less significantly, by that time, mass-oriented Polish parties like the Polskie Stronnictwo Ludowe (Polish Peasants' Party), the Polish National Democrats, and the Polish Socialist Party were already active in Galicia.

Conclusion

It would be satisfyingly elegant to conclude here that the collapse of the New Era was the point of no return for the emergence of Polish and Ukrainian identities in Galicia. But having recognized that electoral reform was necessary, Polish peasant parties and Ruthenians still could have formed an alliance against the Polish elite. The result would have laid the groundwork for a very different conception of the relationship between cultural and political identity in Galicia. But this did not happen, and so the ultimate success of the Ukrainian-oriented faction of the Ruthenian elite illustrates how important elite concerns remained in shaping the framework in which political issues were conceived.

Even if the elites continued to play a dominant role in politics, what is more striking is the extent to which the introduction of elections changed the nature of political power. For if the peasantry did not have a clear idea of the nation as a political community, they did have a de facto political community based in their common socioeconomic grievances. Thus, when the Ruthenian elite appeared to be representing the peasants' interest, as they did in 1848 and again in the 1860s, peasant support proved remarkably solid. When the elite was seen as uninterested in peasant concerns, or at best impotent in the face of the Polish elite's control of Galician affairs, peasants did not feel bound by the notion that national solidarity was more important than their socioeconomic interests.

This was a lesson the Ruthenian elite was slow to grasp, but this should not be surprising. Like the Polish nobles, the members of the Ruthenian elite were products of a society in which hierarchy was important and education was almost as important a basis of that hierarchal order as were noble titles. But whereas the Polish nobles could still exercise considerable political power, thanks to the way the new parliamentary system was structured, under the new system the Ruthenian elite's political power depended almost entirely on peasant support, undercutting the hierarchal order the Ruthenian elite knew and understood.

This made the Ruthenian elite's task of adjusting its understanding of the basis of political power even more important than it was for the Polish elite, but it did not make it any easier for the Ruthenian elite to conceive of the nation as a community of common interests in which cultural ties were only one element. Thus, even here there appears to be little difference between "historical" and "non-historical" nations, so the distinction may have outlasted its usefulness. The Galician Ruthenians, however, are only one such group, and though the distinction no longer seems applicable to them, research may show that their situation was significantly different from that of other "non-historical" nations.

NOTES

1. While those living in Galicia today are quite comfortable with the term Ukrainian, this was a hotly debated issue a century ago. The argument presented here would be impeded by referring to those people discussed as Ukrainians, since some would have vehemently rejected that idea. Therefore, in this article, in which I am bringing together several topics I discussed in my dissertation, "State Culture and National Identity in a Multi-ethnic Context: Lemberg, 1772–1914" (Ph.D. dissertation, University of Michigan, 1999), I shall generally employ the historical term "Ruthenian," except when referring to the present day, to Ukrainians in the Russian Empire, or to historiographical issues.

2. The most persuasive defense of this dichotomy is Ivan L. Rudnytsky's "Observations on the Problem of 'Historical' and 'Non-historical' Nations," originally published in *Harvard Ukrainian Studies* 5(3) September 1981: 358–68. It has been reprinted in Ivan L. Rudnytsky, *Essays in Modern Ukrainian History* (Edmonton, 1987), pp. 37–48.

3. The two scholars most responsible for this shift in direction are John-Paul Himka and Paul R. Magocsi. Himka's book *Galician Villagers and the Ukrainian National Movement* (New York, 1988) in particular illustrates the importance of the Ruthenian elite in developing Ruthenian peasants' national consciousness. Similarly, Magocsi's adaptation of Miroslav Hroch's schema for the development of national movements to the case of Galician Ukrainians also constituted a significant break from the existing historiography by pointing to the crucial role of the Ruthenian elite in that process as well. See Paul R. Magocsi, "The Ukrainian National Revival: A New Analytical Framework," *Canadian Review of Studies in Nationalism* 16(1–2) 1989: 45–62.

4. Just how limited are the sources on peasant political thinking is illustrated by Himka's heavy reliance on peasants' letters published in the Ruthenian newspaper *Bat'kivshchyna*. Effective as Himka's use of them is, he himself acknowledges that the letters he used come to us through the filter of the members of the Ruthenian elites who actually edited *Bat'kivshchyna*. See Himka, *Galician Villagers*, pp. 80–86, and, particularly, pp. 149–51.

5. Representation to the Diet was divided as follows: large landholders elected 44 delegates, each representing 2,288 voters; the chambers of commerce of the 3 largest towns, Lviv, Cracow, and Brody were also allotted a member each; propertied townspeople had 20 representatives or one for every 45,280 people; and rural communes elected 74 deputies, serving 68,536 moderately well-off peasants, while over a million poorer peasants and townsmen went unrepresented. In addition, church leaders,

the university rectors, and the Viceroy held a total of 9 seats ex officio. Jacek Jedruch, *Constitutions, Elections and Legislatures of Poland, 1493–1977* (Washington, DC, 1982), p. 315.

6. There was no formal national division of the fourth curia, so it is important to keep in mind that referring to Polish and Ruthenian delegations is somewhat artificial, although not unjustified given developments discussed below. Kost´ Levyts´kyi, *Istoriia politychnoï dumky Halyts´kykh Ukraïntsiv 1848–1914* (Lviv, 1926). Also Stanisław Grodziski, *Sejm Krajowy Galicyjski 1861–1914*, 2 vols. (Warsaw, 1993), vol. 2, pp. 146–51.

7. For comparison, it is worth noting that in the Galician electoral reform of 1914, which brought to an end the curia system in the Diet, 48 constituencies were assumed to be so overwhelmingly Ruthenian that they did not qualify for the double mandates intended to represent significant minorities. Stanislaus Ritter von Starzyński, "Eine neue Konstruktion der Minoritätenvertretung," *Österreichische Zeitschrift für öffentliches Recht* 3 (1918): 428.

8. Grodziski, *Sejm Krajowy Galicyjski*, vol. 2, pp. 163–67.

9. The total size of the Ruthenian delegation elected to the Reichsrat was actually 17, as the priest Stepan Kachala curiously managed to win a third curia seat representing Tarnów. See *Index zu den stenographische Protokollen des Abgeordnetenhauses des österreichischen Reichsrathes und der Beilagen derselben VIII. Session (vom 4. November 1873 bis 16 Mai 1879)* (Vienna, 1879), passim.

10. Ibid.

11. Grodziski, *Sejm Krajowy Galicyjski*, vol. 2, pp. 171–75.

12. Levyts´kyi, *Istoriia politychnoï dumky*, p. 175.

13. Three priests were elected in the initial vote. The fourth was elected in by-elections in 1863 to replace representatives whose election had been deemed invalid by the election commission. One more priest was elected in such a by-election, but his election was also subsequently declared invalid. Determining the precise number of peasants is more difficult, but can be calculated by subtracting the number of Ruthenian peasant delegates from the total number of peasant delegates sent to the Diet. Grodziski, *Sejm Krajowy Galicyjski*, vol. 2, pp. 146–51.

14. Keely Stauter [Stauter-Halsted], "From Serf to Citizen: Peasant Political Organizations in Galician Poland 1848–1895," Ph.D. dissertation, University of Michigan, 1993, pp. 113–30.

15. Grodziski, *Sejm Krajowy Galicyjski*, vol. 2, pp. 146–51.

16. Jedruch, *Constitutions, Elections and Legislatures*, p. 315.

17. Himka, *Galician Villagers*, p. 152. Nor was this just the case in Ruthenian peasant communes; see Stauter, "From Serf to Citizen," pp. 113–30.

18. See Piotr Wandycz, *The Lands of Partitioned Poland, 1795–1918* (Seattle, 1974), pp. 218–20.

19. *Denkschrift zur Teilung Galiziens* (Lviv, 1865). Lane, "State Culture and National Identity," pp. 263–65.

20. Lane, "State Culture and National Identity," pp. 216–17.

21. *Denkschrift zur Teilung Galiziens*, p. 22.

22. Himka, *Galician Villagers*, p. 152.

23. John-Paul Himka, "Polish and Ukrainian Socialism," 2 vols., Ph.D. dissertation, University of Michigan, 1977, vol. 1, p. 128.

24. Paul R. Magocsi, "The Kachkovs'kyi Society and the National Revival in Nineteenth Century Galicia," *Harvard Ukrainian Studies* 15(1–2) June 1991: 54.

25. Presumably for that reason, among those who lost their seats in the Reichsrat in 1879 were two of the best known advocates of reaching out to the peasantry, Ivan Naumovych and Stepan Kachala. Himka, *Galician Villagers*, p. 70.

26. Ibid. Prosvita's original statutes explicitly declared it to be a non-political organization.

27. Stella Hryniuk, *Peasants with Promise: Ukrainians in Southeastern Galicia, 1880–1900* (Edmonton, 1991), pp. 94–95.

28. Himka, *Galician Villagers*, p. 75.

29. Levyts'kyi, *Istoriia politychnoï dumky*, p. 201.

30. Ibid., pp. 215–17.

31. Himka, *Galician Villagers*, p. 79.

32. Levyts'kyi, *Istoriia politychnoï dumky*, p. 231.

33. Jedruch, *Constitutions, Elections and Legislatures*, p. 319.

34. Levyts'kyi, *Istoriia politychnoï dumky*, p. 238.

35. Ibid., pp. 240–41.

36. Just how strong this tendency has been is best illustrated by Ivan L. Rudnytsky's reiteration of it in "The Ukrainians under Austrian Rule" in *Nationbuilding and the Politics of Nationalism*, ed. Andrei Markovits and Frank Sysyn (Cambridge, MA, 1982), p. 58.

37. Although the Polish elite had succeeded in pushing through considerable restrictions on the official use of Ruthenian in the late 1860s, the position

of Ruthenian at Lviv University was nominally equal. In 1879, the Poles successfully lobbied the Ministry of Education in Vienna to allow them to replace German as the university's administrative language with Polish, enhancing the stature of Polish over Ruthenian. In 1882, following the promotion of Oleksander Ohonovs'kyi to full professor of law, the Poles sought to limit further appointments of Ruthenian professors. The Ministry of Education once more sided with the Poles, stating that while it would not rule out further Ruthenian appointments, it regarded Lviv University to be primarily a Polish institution. See Lane, "State Culture and National Identity," pp. 219–26. Compare with Ludwik Finkel and Stanisław Starzyński, *Historia Uniwersytetu Lwowskiego*, 2 vols. (Lviv, 1894), vol. 2, pp. 53, 63–64.

38.   For a detailed discussion of the Hnylychky affair, see John-Paul Himka, *Religion and Nationality in Western Ukraine: The Greek Catholic Church and the Ukrainian National Movement in Galicia, 1867–1900* (Montreal, 1999), pp. 73–78.

39.   Significantly, there was a large gap between the rhetoric and the behavior of the Ruthenian elite. In fact, the Ruthenian elite generally showed itself amenable to learning and using Polish within the realm of higher education and scholarship into the 1890s. See Lane, "State Culture and National Identity," pp. 312–13.

40.   Given the Populists' broad-based coalition in 1889, one cannot assume that everyone who voted for Mykola Antonevych and his circle shared their cultural ideas, or that everyone who had voted for Ukrainian-oriented candidates preferred the Ukrainian orientation.

41.   In April 1891, Romanchuk reconfirmed his faction's acceptance of the Polish offer of cooperation in the Diet, but soon thereafter the Galician Diet adjourned and did not meet again until early 1892. Levyts'kyi, *Istoriia politychnoï dumky*, p. 253.

42.   Ibid.

43.   Steven Horak, "The Shevchenko Scientific Society (1873–1973): Contributor to the Birth of a Nation," *East European Quarterly* 7(3) Fall 1973: 253.

44.   Thomas Prymak, *Mykhailo Hrushevsky: The Politics of National Culture* (Toronto, 1987), p. 24.

45.   Levyts'kyi, *Istoriia politychnoï dumky*, p. 253.

46.   Ibid., p. 270.

47.   Ihor Chornovol, "Umovy pol's'ko-ukraïns'koï uhody 1890 roku," *Ukraïna Moderna* 2–3 (1997–1998): 373–75.

48.   Levyts'kyi, *Istoriia politychnoï dumky*, p. 270.

49. "V spravi uhody," *Narod* 1(24) 15 December 1890: 388.

50. Himka, *Galician Villagers*, p. 75.

51. Romanchuk's main goal during his first term in the Diet after being elected in 1882 was to increase the number of Ukrainian gymnasia. See Levyts'kyi, *Istoriia politychnoï dumky*, pp. 208–12.

52. John-Paul Himka, *Socialism in Galicia: The Emergence of Polish Social Democracy and Ukrainian Radicalism (1860–1890)* (Cambridge, MA, 1983), p. 68.

53. Magocsi, "The Kachkovs'kyi Society," pp. 53–54.

54. Levyts'kyi, *Istoriia politychnoï dumky*, p. 253. Compare with Magocsi, "The Kachkovs'kyi Society," p. 70.

55. "Spravy Soimovii," *Russkaia Rada* 22(5) 5 March 1892 [Old Style]: 35.

56. Levyts'kyi, *Istoriia politychnoï dumky*, p. 255.

57. See also Grodziski, *Sejm Krajowy Galicyjski 1861–1914*, vol. 2, pp. 196–200; and Levyts'kyi, *Istoriia politychnoï dumky*, p. 279.

58. Ivan Franko, "Die jüngste Galizische Wahl," *Beiträge zur Geschichte und Kultur der Ukraine* (Berlin, 1963), pp. 299–309 [=Quellen und Studien zur Geschichte Osteuropas, 14].

59. Levyts'kyi, *Istoriia politychnoï dumky*, p. 255.

60. Ibid., pp. 327–28.

61. Ibid., p. 351.

The Polish and Ukrainian Languages:
A Mutually Beneficial Relationship

MICHAŁ LESIÓW

One could expect that the ties between two related languages—West Slavic Polish and East Slavic Ukrainian—would be both lengthy and important for their all-round development. One could further expect that their contact and mutual influence would prove to be a source of enrichment for each. These two languages have a common proto-Slavic root. Besides this, they have maintained a longlasting cultural contact—and over the course of several centuries even existed within one common state, the Polish-Lithuanian Commonwealth. This inevitably led to mutual contacts and influences that enriched the two languages.

Despite this, researchers have failed to pay sufficient attention to the contact between these two languages and the results of that contact. The reasons for this have varied and usually have been non-scholarly in nature. So great a mass of various historical truths, half-truths, and old wives' tales has arisen that it is virtually impossible to try to elucidate the issue of Polish-Ukrainian cultural or linguistic ties, as they say, *sine ira et studio* (that is, truthfully, objectively, and without ulterior motives). There have been—and continue to be—Polonists who refuse to admit the possibility that Ukrainian could have influenced Polish. On the other hand, Ukrainianists, especially the former "Soviet" ones, quite happily speak of the "beneficial influence" of Russian on Ukrainian. For them, though, if Polish has exerted an influence on Ukrainian, then that influence has "polluted" the Ukrainian language whenever and wherever it occurred.

Thirty-eight years ago, when I was a postdoctoral fellow at Kyiv State University, the linguists there persuaded me to investigate the Polish influence on the Middle Ukrainian literary language. "We don't get much of a chance to write about that," they said, "and it is one of the least investigated phenomena in the Ukrainian language."

When we speak about Polish-Ukrainian linguistic interrelations, we have in mind, generally, the following types of issues:

1. Vestiges (and evidence) of Polish influences on the general Ukrainian (both written[1] and literary) language from the beginning of its historical development to the present.

2. Vestiges (and evidence) of Ukrainian influences on the general Polish literary (and book) language during this same almost millennium-long period from Kyivan Rus′ and the Polish of the Piast dynasty to the present day. That is, to

the point at which both Poland and Ukraine became politically and culturally independent states and nations.

3. Elements of Polish influences on the western Ukrainian dialects, especially on the Lemko, San, Dnister, Volhynian-Chełm, and Podlasie dialects—i.e., those dialects that directly border on Polish linguistic territory.

4. Elements of Ukrainian influences on the eastern Polish dialects, first and foremost the so-called *Kresy* dialect—i.e., the southern *Kresy* dialect where Polish speakers exist within a territory with a numerical majority of Ukrainian speakers.

Each of these four broad problems has to a certain degree been raised and investigated in many of its details—although not as fully as one would want. From time to time plausible generalizations have also been made. However, none of these points was ever treated exhaustively. Each needs further detailed research that would permit the construction of broad, supportable hypotheses and conclusions. We shall therefore examine these problems more closely.

The Polish Influence on Ukrainian

It is generally accepted that Contemporary Standard (Literary) Ukrainian (CSU) has comparatively many Polish linguistic elements in it, especially in terms of lexicon and phraseology. One can often tell whether or not a word is of Polish origin by its phonetic characteristics: for example, by traces of nasal vowels in such words as *дощенту, плентатися;* by -ло- instead of -оло- in the word *хлопець;* by -ро- instead of -оро- in the word *крок;* by -лу- instead of -ов- in the word *тлумач;* etc.

In a large number of cases the Polish form of a word has been adapted to a corresponding Ukrainian phonetic substitute, as in the cases: *barłóg > барліг, królik > крілик, przedmowa > передмова,* etc.

How many such words of Polish origin are there in CSU? The first broad monograph that treated Polish loanwords in Ukrainian was written in 1957 by Rosemarie Richhardt, which presented approximately 2,500 Ukrainian words (literary, regional, archaic, and dialect forms) that came into Ukrainian directly from Polish or from other sources through the intermediacy of the Polish language.[2]

As Marian Jurkowski remarked in his review of the work, "The author has hardly exhausted even one-half of the material that would have been evident had she dealt fully with texts of Old Ukrainian literature, Ukrainian contemporary literature (especially western), and dialectal evidence."[3] Jurkowski made one further assertion: "If the author had paid attention only to the Ukrainian literary language, then, of course, the quantity of loanwords from the Polish language would be much smaller than I indicate above."[4]

When considering the study of Polish loanwords in CSU, it is worthwhile examining the 11-volume *Slovnyk ukraïns'koï movy* (Dictionary of the Ukrainian Language), which is the first dictionary of the Ukrainian language that actually uses Ukrainian glosses and apparatus. (Previous dictionaries were either bilingual, or monolingual with Ukrainian entries and Russian or Polish glosses.) It also is the fullest Ukrainian language dictionary, with some 140,000 entries.[5] The *Etymolohichnyi slovnyk ukraïns'koï movy* (Etymological Dictionary of the Ukrainian Language) also is (and will be) a significant aid in this respect.[6]

A detailed analysis of the lexical material that is to be found in these two large lexicographic works might give relatively precise information about the characteristics and quantity of Polish loanwords in the Ukrainian literary language of the most recent period. No one has undertaken this yet and it is an important task, since the quantity of Polish loanwords has changed in the course of the history of the two languages.

George Shevelov had written in 1952 about certain common tendencies in the development of the Old Ukrainian (which some call Old Rus' or Old Ruthenian) and Old Polish languages up to the fourteenth century, but it is difficult to speak about concrete examples of Ukrainian borrowings from Polish in that period.[7] He also deals rather hypothetically with common tendencies in the development of the two languages. Moreover, for this early period, it is more appropriate to talk about the influence of the Ukrainian language on Polish, than the other way around.

Antin Hens'ors'kyi noted a series of expressions in the language of the thirteenth-century Galician-Volhynian Chronicle that were not well attested in other Ukrainian texts of the period. In the opinion of the author, these originated in mutual influences of Old Ukrainian and Old Polish literature. He attests some 30 words of this nature and considers them to be an indication of Ukrainian and Polish cultural relations during the thirteenth century.[8] In the majority of cases where parallels occur in Old Polish and Old Ukrainian, one cannot say with certainly what their language of origin is. On the basis of the few historical facts that we have, we can only assume that these words probably spread from the more advanced Ukrainian written language of that time into Polish, than vice-versa. Some examples:

возбити	— *zbić*	'to abandon, throw aside'
сразити	— *zrazić*	'to cast down, remove'
миловати	— *miłować*	'to love'

We find various examples of borrowings from Polish in the Ukrainian *hramoty* (charters, and official documents and correspondence) of the fourteenth and fifteenth centuries. Research on loanwords of the period has been aided by the appearance of the *Slovnyk staroukraïns'koï movy XIV–XV stolit'* (Dictionary of Old Ukrainian of the 14th–15th Centuries) in two volumes. It contains approximately 11,530 words, taken from secular sources, first and foremost from the Ukrainian *hramoty* of the period.[9] This is an admittedly incomplete dictionary inasmuch as it does not take into account church-oriented, religious, or philosophical literature. It does, however, still reflect to a certain degree the written language of the time. A full third of the entries in it are proper nouns. Of the approximately 8,000 headwords, there are perhaps 600 lexemes that can be considered polonisms, or approximately 7.5 percent of the total. These are marked mainly by characteristic phonetic features—and among them are a number of latinisms and germanisms that came into Old Ukrainian through Polish. These loanwords mainly relate to such areas as trade, urban administration, and martial activities. This undoubtedly represents the beginning of active borrowing by Old Ukrainian from Polish and, through Polish, from the Roman Catholic cultural sphere. This was also the period when a portion of the Ukrainian ethnolinguistic territories became part of the Kingdom of Poland.

In subsequent centuries the quantity of Polish linguistic loans into the Ukrainian literary language increased. A dictionary of the Ukrainian literary language of the sixteenth through eighteenth centuries is being prepared by linguists in Lviv.[10] Once this dictionary is completed and published, researchers will be able to examine this area of linguistic exchange in greater detail on the basis of a corpus that has been selected and classified according to an explicitly defined methodology. At present, we have a series of detailed studies of the language of various writers, individual works, and separate lexical groups. All of these works indicated the comparatively large influence of Polish on Ukrainian during the period, especially in secular literature. The linguistic historian Pavlo Pliushch has written of the Ukrainian language of this period that it was "a creole, an artificial language that was an odd cross between Old Church Slavonic and Old East Slavic elements on the one hand, and ukrainianisms and polonisms on the other."[11]

Some of the writers of this period were essentially bilingual, writing both in Polish and in Ukrainian. Meletii Smotryts´kyi, the author of a famed grammar of Church Slavonic, falls into this category, as do the authors and polemicists Syl´vestr Kosov, Lonhin Karpovych, Petro Mohyla, Ioannykii Galiatovs´kyi, Lazar Baranovych, and others.[12] The writers of that period would at times take Polish words that were necessary for a given situation and, having ukrainianized them, would simply insert them into a Ukrainian text. Further testimony on the linguistic situation of the time is provided by Aleksander Małachowski, a deputy to the Sejm, who reported that "in the Dzieduszycki family, as powerful a family as existed in Ukraine in the eighteenth century, Ukrainian was still used in everyday affairs."[13]

Detailed examples of such linguistic borrowings are given in studies on Ukrainian authors of the sixteenth, seventeenth, and even eighteenth centuries. These are generally descriptions of phonetics, morphology, and syntax, but we know significantly less about the lexicon of the Ukrainian literary language of the period. There are a few works dealing with the language of the period that also take into account the role and influence of Polish on shaping the Old

Ukrainian literary language. The most important study in this regard is by Wiesław Witkowski, who examined the language of Ioannykii Galiatovs'kyi in light of the general status of the Ukrainian literary language of the seventeenth century. Aside from Galiatovs'kyi, he also describes the use of language in 16 different works by individual Ukrainian authors of the seventeenth century.[14]

Writing about Polish elements in the Ukrainian literary language during this period, Ivan Franko had earlier observed, "This language took in many Polish words, especially for the designation of concepts and relations in civil and state life, which, especially after the Union of Lublin, were more or less the same for the entire territory [of the Polish-Lithuanian Commonwealth]."[15]

Some scholars have examined this language from the point of view of a chauvinistic Great Russian–Pan-Slavist perspective. Anton Budilovich, for example, wrote that the Ukrainian language of the sixteenth and seventeenth centuries—which intellectuals of Vilnius, Kyiv, and Lviv used to write polemical tracts, school books, religious dramas, and other such works—was half Church Slavonic and half Polish.[16]

Aleksei Sobolevskii called this language "a mixture of the Belarusian and Polish languages, which in the sixteenth century was used to write documents in the Lithuanian-Ruthenian state, and in the seventeenth century was used to write literary works in southern Rus'."[17]

In the works of Soviet Ukrainian linguists the discussion of Polish elements in Old Ukrainian was rather restrained. More attention to these matters has been paid by contemporary Polish linguists. Among them, Wiesław Witkowski wrote, "The first and most important reason for the influence of the Polish language on the Ruthenian [i.e., Ukrainian] language was the fact that the western Ruthenian lands belonged to a state in which a significant portion of Ruthenian society had almost daily opportunities to interact with the language of their fellow citizens to the west. This penetration by the Polish language was facilitated by the bilingualism of the more cultured elite of Ruthenian society, especially in areas with mixed ethnic populations."[18] This situation was also the reason why Ukrainian linguistic elements entered the Polish literary language, about which we shall speak shortly.

Ilarion Svientsits'kyi delineates four major routes by which Polish linguistic elements affected the use of Ukrainian during the sixteenth and seventeenth centuries: first, the influence of the Polish emigration on Ukrainian lands; second, Polish literature; third, Jesuit schools; fourth, the educational activities of the Mohyla Academy.[19] Witkowski, in turn, in his unusually objective and careful monograph documents the "significant and varied mixing of elements of Latino-Polish syntax" in many Ukrainian publications written in the so-called *prosta mova*.[20]

The present author, on the basis of an analysis of Ukrainian dramatic works of the seventeenth and beginning of the eighteenth centuries, has noted words with traces of Polish phonetics as well as examples of grammatical polonisms, which sometimes are marked by southwestern Ukrainian dialectal features.[21]

The general conclusion from these detailed analyses is that some polonisms entered into the Ukrainian literary language through western Ukrainian dialects, which also were influenced by Polish. Indeed, the analyses make clear that Polish played as important a role as Church Slavonic in the formation of the middle Ukrainian literary language.[22]

In 1975, George Shevelov proposed certain interesting methodological innovations with regard to the study of lexical polonisms in the Ukrainian literary language.[23] Nonetheless, there still is no monograph-length study that analyzes lexemes with Polish origins in Old and Middle Ukrainian. Such a work would suggest which older borrowings have come through to the contemporary language. Such a monograph should be a collaborative effort of Ukrainian and Polish linguists, *sine ira et studio*. The present condition of Ukrainian-Polish relations seems propitious for such an undertaking.

Polish influences on Russian came mainly through the Old and Middle Ukrainian literary languages, as demonstrated in the monograph of Petro Cymbalistyj on Ukrainian lexical elements in the Russian language of the seventeenth and eighteenth centuries.[24]

The Ukrainian Influence on Polish

In the very earliest historical period, there were already some contacts between the ancestors of present-day Ukrainians and Poles. These contacts, of course, could conceivably have had some influence on the Polish literary language. George Shevelov believes that such ancient contacts may explain certain aspects of the historical development of Polish grammar that would be difficult to understand otherwise, and also certain common tendencies in the evolution of both languages.[25]

Antin Hens'ors'kyi called attention to Ukrainian-Polish lexical parallels of the thirteenth century.[26] Stanisław Urbańczyk, in turn, wrote on Ukrainian loanwords in Old Polish on the basis of the material collected in the *Słownik staropolski* (Dictionary of Old Polish). He found more than 150 lexemes borrowed from Old Ukrainian in Polish works up to the end of the fifteenth century. These words belong to such semantic groups as: 1) words relating to certain cultural phenomena in Rus'-Ukraine, e.g., *bojar, tywon, czerniec, diak, kniaź, kryłoszanin, praźnik, wataman* and many others; 2) names of objects of Oriental origin, e.g., *bachmat* 'a Tatar horse,' *kaftan, kitajka, basałyk* 'a type of a whip,' etc.; 3) words connected with topology, geography, or physical descriptions, e.g., *krynica, sioło, połonina*, etc. In light of these examples, Urbańczyk proposed that these loans indicate "contacts between the Polish and Ukrainian people, mainly of a quotidian nature."[27]

This situation changed fundamentally when the Ruthenian/Ukrainian szlachta began to be polonized; the consequences of this began to appear only in the second half of the sixteenth century. A new Polish dialect appeared, which was later named the *Kresy* dialect. This dialect appeared under the influence of the Ukrainian language, and it had a measurable impact on the Polish literary language.

Przemysław Zwoliński wrote in 1956 that "spoken Ukrainian began to have an effect on Polish, which neighbored it to the west, from the fifteenth century. In the sixteenth century its elements began to enter into the language of Polish writers."[28] Beginning with Biernat of Lublin and Mikołaj Rej, Ukrainian influences increase with authors who either were born or spent long periods of time in cities and towns of the eastern lands of the Commonwealth. The influx of ukrainianisms into Polish literature reached its zenith in the seventeenth century. It then slowly receded, cresting once again in the first half of the nineteenth century in the writings of the Polish Romantics of the so-called Ukrainian School.[29]

In the sixteenth century the dominant view was that the "Ukrainian (Ruthenian) language is the oldest of all the Slavic languages," about which Łukasz Górnicki wrote in his *Dworzanin polski:* "Acz są drudzy, którzy powiadają, iż naród i język ruski miałby być najstarszy."[30]

Numerous studies of individual Polish writers provide information about the greater or lesser amount of ukrainianisms in the Polish literary language of past centuries. Historical dictionaries like the *Słownik polszczyzny XVI wieku* (Dictionary of Sixteenth-Century Polish) and *Słownik języka Jana Chryzostoma Paska* (Dictionary of the Language of Jan Chrysostom Pasek) provide us with the opportunity to conduct monographic research on ukrainianisms in Old Polish literature, as was done by Teresa Minikowska in her study of ukrainianisms in the Polish language of the sixteenth century (she found some 600 lexical tokens).[31] It would, however, be necessary to create a "meta" study of these numerous individual, detailed works in order to evaluate the influence of the Ukrainian language on Polish throughout the entire history of the Polish language.

With regard to the question of the contemporary Polish literary language, we simply do not know in detail how many Ukrainian elements there are in it. In order to pursue that question, one could profitably analyze the lexical corpus in the most recent *Słownik języka polskiego* (Dictionary of the Polish Language), edited by W. Doroszewski and M. Szymczak.

Elements of Polish Influence on West Ukrainian Dialects

During the long period of Polish-Ukrainian contact, Ukrainian dialects—especially those directly bordering on Polish ethnolinguistic territory—have been subject to Polish influence. Olexa Horbatsch produced a general study on this topic in 1968.[32]

The Lemko dialect, bordered to the north and west by Polish dialects, exhibits the strongest influence of Polish in any Ukrainian dialects. In the Lemko dialect we even see systemic linguistic traits of Polish origin like the following: fixed stress on the penult; pronunciation of /l/ as [w] in all positions, e.g., [howóva] for *голова* (standard Ukrainian [holová]); 1sg verbal forms with the ending –m in forms like *знам, мам* (instead of *знаю, маю*); and a long list of typically Lemko words that are etymologically related to Polish sources (e.g., *пец, припецок, терас, гадати* 'to speak,' *огін* 'tail,' and many others). The Lemko dialect also has traces of Slovak influence from the south. Because of this, Lemko varies more from the contemporary Ukrainian literary standard than any other Ukrainian dialect—which has even led to attempts to call it a distinct Slavic language.

In terms of quantitative influence of Polish on a Ukrainian dialect, the San River dialects would have to come in second place. These dialects are the furthest west of all of the Ukrainian dialects and come into direct contact with the Little Polish dialects. Polish influence is seen here first and foremost in the numerous lexical borrowings, sometimes with Polish phonetic characteristics, e.g., *барзу, брух, цавкум, дзіржава, гемба, фтенчаскі, кстіті,* etc.[33]

Karol Dejna authored the definitive book on the Ukrainian dialects of the Ternopil region. His work was based on materials—collected before World War II—that he could publish only later, in 1957. He notes a series of attributes in these dialects that are the result of Polish influence, making the general observation that:

> Ukrainian dialects of the Ternopil region are to a certain extent akin to creole dialects [. . .] containing at once the attributes of a transitional dialect between Polish and Ukrainian. As we have seen, the Polish contribution to the Ukrainian dialects of the area under study was great, but it is also of note that the Polish population of this area was not an insignificant proportion of the total ethnic makeup of the region.[34]

The Ukrainian dialects of the Chełm area and Podlasie also contain evidence of considerable Polish influence. Depending on a variety of factors, this influence can be lesser or greater in any given area. Those dialects that extended further to the west were subjected more to local Polish dialects; for example, in the Ukrainian dialect of the village of Kolechowice near Lubartów we can ascertain even such typical Polish attributes as the ending *–źva: ходілізьва,* etc.[35] Of interest too are the data collected by Władysław Kuraszkiewicz in the ethnically Ukrainian village of Dratów (near Lublin), which had been fairly strongly polonized by 1947.[36]

There is now a significant number of detailed descriptions of Ukrainian dialects that have been influenced by Polish dialects or by the Polish literary language. These studies discuss the Polish influence on the appearance or suppression of certain linguistic phenomena from a variety of perspectives: some are rather restrained in their characterization of the relationship, while others sometimes wildly exaggerate it. One would need to review these works and hypotheses, to carry out more detailed field studies, and, in particular, examine the Ukrainian dialectal lexicon that we now have—albeit only very minimally—in the recent *Atlas ukraïns'koï movy* (Atlas of the Ukrainian Language). We still await the much needed *Slovnyk ukraïns'kykh hovirok* (Dictionary of Ukrainian Dialects). However, preparations are being made for collecting materials for the *Leksychnyi atlas ukraïns'koï movy* (Lexical Atlas of the Ukrainian Language). A dictionary of pan-Ukrainian dialects would help to determine the quantity, quality, and content of Polish loanwords in Ukrainian dialects.

Ukrainian Influence on the Polish *Kresy* Dialect

Polish dialects have also been influenced by neighboring Ukrainian dialects and the Ukrainian literary language. It is generally known that the southeast *Kresy* dialect arose mainly under the influence of Ukrainian spoken language. This is the language of Poles who still live in what is today western Ukraine or in the current southeastern portion of Poland (from Sanok and Przemyśl along the eastern Polish frontier up through Bielsk Podlaski, Siemiatycze, and Hajnówka in the north, where we find a mixture of Ukrainian, Belarusian, and Polish linguistic elements). This also is the language of Polish expatriates from Galicia, Volhynia, and Polesie (Polissia), who since 1945 have lived in the eastern counties of Poland. Kajetan Stopa wrote about these people in a 1948 issue of the journal *Odra:* " . . . ci, co śpią i śpiewają, a tak szybko pędzą gościńcem języka, że połowę samogłosek pogubią, a drugą rozpędzą po drodze."[37] Stopa is speaking here about one of the most noticeable attributes of western Ukrainian speech: the lengthening of vowels in the tonic position and their narrowing in non-tonic position, e.g., *си̂ло́, су̊сна́,* etc., which penetrated the *Kresy* dialect and came to be called "Lwów singsong."

This dialect has a series of phonetic and morphological features as well as a lexical corpus that linguists identify as being of Ukrainian origin. These words to some extent are adapted to Polish phonetic and grammatical norms. Tadeusz Lehr-Spławiński partially described the characteristics of this language in 1914.[38]

This *Kresy* dialect has played a peculiar role in the development of the general Polish literary language. Historians of the Polish language believe that the so-called "narrow" *a* (tense *a*) in literary usage changed to the "open" *a* (*czåpka* > *czapka*) under the influence of the *Kresy* dialect.[39] This same influence is used to explain the pronunciation of Polish suffixes *-ic, -owic, -ewic* like Ukrainian affricated *-ич, -ович, -евич* as well as the spread of forms of the type *depczę, plączę* instead of the typical Polish *depcę, plącę.*

There are a few descriptions of Polish dialects that have had direct contact with Ukrainian dialects, mainly in Galicia. These studies have documented numerous features that are of Ukrainian origin.[40] Studies of Polish dialects that are surrounded by Ukrainian have so far been fairly rare, but they are increasing.[41] Thanks to the work of Janusz Rieger, it is possible to distinguish those features that unify these dialects, as well as distinctions that sometimes arise from differences among the neighboring Ukrainian dialects. However, for quite some time the political, rather than scholarly, climate was not at all conducive to such studies. Nonetheless, more and more such specialized studies, be it as separate monographs or volumes of series, are now appearing—many published by Rieger himself.[42]

Most recently, we have seen the inception of studies that explore Ukrainian and Polish dialects in parallel on the very same territory. An impetus to such work came, as far back as 1956, from a plan to publish a dialect atlas of the area around Lublin. The atlas itself was not finished, but in the course of its preparation a significant amount of parallel Ukrainian and Polish dialectal material was collected. This in turn has established an extraordinary base for studying the mutual influences of these speech communities on their linguistic borderland.[43]

The question of the interaction of Ukrainian place names and personal names as well as the mutual links between Ukrainian and Polish folklore would require a separate study. However, these are once again major themes in the ongoing discussion concerning Ukrainian-Polish cultural relations.

From what has been discussed above several conclusions can be drawn:

First, the question of Ukrainian-Polish linguistic ties, mutual influences, and mutual enrichment is very important—as much for scholars of the Ukrainian language as for scholars of the Polish language. The objective and scholarly study of both the detailed and the general issues involved can be realized only in an atmosphere of cordial collaboration between the Polish and Ukrainian philological establishments.

Second, a list of works on this topic would be quite lengthy were one to bring together all of the material mentioned above and analyze all of the particular as well as the generalizing—and at times mutually contradictory—opinions of scholars on Ukrainian-Polish linguistic ties and mutual influences. In this regard, it must also be mentioned that Polish philologists have written somewhat more on this than scholars in Ukraine itself. Scholars in the Ukrainian diaspora also have made substantial contributions to the examination of these problems.

Third, the field very much needs a monograph on the subject—one that would collect even more relevant data, discuss what has been heretofore written and published, and then provide an unbiased assessment of these mutual influences. Such a monograph would be extremely important for the development of both Ukrainian and Polish contemporary culture.

Fourth, and finally, research on the mutual interaction of the Ukrainian and Polish languages, as well as their dialects, has not been easy. It has been hampered by various political powers, both on the left and on the extreme right.[44] But such research is necessary, especially now, when we have the prospect and hope of greater tolerance and mutual respect on the part of the powers that be and other decision-making circles.

Translated from the Ukrainian by Robert De Lossa, with Roman Koropeckyj

NOTES

1. By "written language" I mean the medieval and premodern language of religious and secular "bookmen," which cannot be characterized as the language of a literature, per se, but which is posited to be distinct from a contemporaneous vernacular.

2. Rosemarie Richhardt, *Polnische Lehnwörter im Ukrainischen* (Wiesbaden, 1957).

3. Marian Jurkowski, "Pierwsza obszerna praca o polonizmach w języku ukraińskim," *Slavia Orientalis* 8(2–3) 1959: 157.

4. Ibid., p. 158.

5. *Slovnyk ukraïns'koï movy,* 11 vols. (Kyiv, 1970–1980).

6. The etymological dictionary is planned for seven volumes, but, regrettably, only three have appeared to date. *Etymolohichnyi slovnyk ukraïns'koï movy,* vols. 1–3 (Kyiv, 1982–1989).

7. George Shevelov [Yury Šerekh], "The Problem of Ukrainian-Polish Linguistic Relations from the Tenth to the Fourteenth Century," *Word* 8 (1952): 329–49. See also the discussion of the article in Michał Łesiów, "Nowy problem w historii stosunków językowych polsko-ukraińskich," *Język Polski* (Cracow) 41(5) 1961: 378–79.

8. Antin I. Hens'ors'kyi, "Pivdennorus'ki i pol's'ki leksychni vzaiemozv'iazky v XIII st.," *Doslidzhennia i materialy z ukraïns'koï movy* (Kyiv) 4 (1961): 15–25. See also the detailed discussion of this article in M. Łesiów, "O polsko-ukraińskich związkach językowych w średniowieczu," *Język Polski* (Cracow) 42(1) 1962: 70–71.

9. *Slovnyk staroukraïns'koï movy XIV–XV stolit',* 2 vols. (Kyiv, 1977–1978).

10. The dictionary is being issued over time in installments. At present we have only a few issues of the dictionary, which cover the sixteenth and first half of the seventeenth centuries.

11. Pavlo P. Pliushch, *Narysy z istoriï ukraïns'koï movy* (Kyiv, 1958), p. 202.

12. Smotryts'kyi's grammar is entitled *Hrammatyky slavenskiia pravyl'noie syntagma* (1618) and remained the standard in the Slavic world for over a century. On these authors, see Ivan Franko, "Wzajemny stosunek literatury polskiej i ruskiej," *Pamiętnik Zjazdu literatów i dziennikarzy polskich,* vol. 1 (Lviv, 1894).

13. See "Slovo na zustrichi ukraïns'kykh i pol's'kykh parlamentariïv 4–5.V.1990," *Zustriczi* (Warsaw) 1990 (3–4): 42.

14. See Wiesław Witkowski, *Język utworów J. Galatowskiego na tle języka piśmiennictwa ukraińskiego XVII w.* (Cracow, 1969).

15. Ivan Franko, "Charakterystyka literatury ruskiej XVI–XVII wieku," *Kwartalnik Historyczny* (Lviv) 6(4) 1892: 712.

16. Anton Semenovich Budilovich, *K voprosu o literaturnom iazyke iugo-zapadnoi Rusi* (Iur'ev [Tartu], 1900), p. 15.

17. Aleksei Ivanovich Sobolevskii, "Grammatika I. Uzhevicha," *Chteniia v Istoricheskom obshchestve Nestora letopistsa* 19(2) (Kyiv) 1906: 3.

18. Witkowski, *Język utworów J. Galatowskiego,* p. 13.

19. Ilarion S. Svientsits'kyi, "Elementy zhyvoï narodnoï movy v pam'iatkakh ukraïns'koï literaturnoï movy XVI–XVII stolit'," *Pytannia ukraïns'koho movoznavstva* 3 (Lviv) 1958: 123.

20. Witkowski, *Język utworów J. Galatowskiego,* p. 133.

21. M. Łesiów, "Rola cerkiewizmów i polonizmów w ukraińskim języku pisanym XVII w.," *Z polskich studiów sławistycznych,* seria 2, *Językoznawstwo* (Warsaw) 1963: 345–48.

22. Ibid., p. 348.

23. George Y. Shevelov, "On Lexical Polonisms in Literary Ukrainian," *For Wiktor Weintraub* (The Hague, 1975), pp. 449–63.

24. Petro Cymbalistyj, *Ukrainian Linguistic Elements in the Russian Language, 1680–1760* (London, 1991).

25. For a detailed discussion of these matters, see Shevelov [Šerekh], "The Problem of Ukrainian-Polish Linguistic Relations from the Tenth to the Fourteenth Century"; also, Michał Łesiów, "Wzajemne oddziaływanie polsko-ukraińskie w świetle faktów językowych w średniowieczu," *Między wschodem i zachodem,* vol. 1, *Kultura umysłowa* (Warsaw, 1989), pp. 41–44.

26. Hens'ors'kyi, "Pivdennorus'ki i pol's'ki leksychni vzaiemozv'iazky," pp. 15–25.

27. Stanisław Urbańczyk, "Charakterystyka staropolskich zapożyczeń językowych z języka ukraińskiego," *Studia linguistica in honorem Thaddaei Lehr-Spławiński* (Cracow, 1963), pp. 437–44.

28. Przemysław Zwoliński, *Dzieje języka ukraińskiego w zarysie* (Warsaw, 1956), pp. 34–35.

29. Ibid., p. 35.

30. See Stefan Hrabec, *Elementy kresowe w języku niektórych pisarzy polskich XVI i XVII wieku* (Toruń, 1949). The quote translates as, "some people, however, say that the Ruthenian people and language must be the oldest."

31. See her *Wyrazy ukraińskie w polszczyźnie literackiej XVI w.* (Warsaw–Poznań–Toruń, 1980).

32. Olexa Horbatsch, "Polnische Lehnwörter in den ukrainischen Mundarten," *Slavistische Studien zum VI. Internationalen Slavistenkongress in Prag, 1968* (Munich, 1968), pp. 3–34.

33. For a description of the San River dialects and, especially, their most important characteristics, see M. Pshep'iurs'ka [Maria Przepiórska], *Nadsians'kyi hovir* (Warsaw, 1938). A list of the most characteristic words is found there on pp. 70–85.

34. Karol Dejna, "Elementy polskie w gwarach zachodnio-ukraińskich," *Język Polski* (Cracow) 27(3) 1948: 76.

35. M. Łesiów, "Polonizmy ukraińskiej gwary wsi Kolechowice," *Język Polski* (Cracow) 38(5) 1958: 362–69.

36. Władysław Kuraszkiewicz, "Szkic polonizującej się ruskiej gwary archaicznej w Dratowie pod Łęczną," *Slavia Occidentalis* 18 (1947): 139–52.

37. Kajetan Stopa in *Odra* 52–53 (1948). The quote translates as, " . . . those who sing and sleep, and race along their linguistic way so quickly that half of their vowels are lost and the other half are scattered as they hurry onward."

38. Tadeusz Lehr-Spławiński, "O mowie Polaków w Galicji Wschodniej," *Język Polski* 2 (Cracow, 1914); and idem, "Wzajemne wpływy językowe polsko-ruskie w dziedzinie językowej," *Szkice z dziejów rozwoju i kultury języka polskiego* (Lviv, 1938), pp. 107–115.

39. See Zenon Klemensiewicz, Tadeusz Lehr-Spławiński, Stanisław Urbańczyk, *Gramatyka historyczna języka polskiego* (Warsaw, 1955), p. 93.

40. For example, see Władysław Harhala, "Gwara polska okolic Komarna. I. Głosownia, II. Morfologia," *Lud Słowiański* IIA (Cracow, 1931): 55–91, 156–77; Stefan Hrabec, "O polskiej gwarze wsi Duliby w byłym powiecie buczackim," *Rozprawy Komisji Językowej ŁTN* 3 (Łódź, 1955): 31–76; Karol Dejna, "Gwara Milna," *Rozprawy Komisji Językowej ŁTN* 4 (Łódź, 1956): 5–41; M. Łesiów, "System fonetyczny gwary hutniańskiej," *Rozprawy Komisji Językowej ŁTN* 6 (Łódź, 1956); Zofia Kurzowa, *Polszczyzna Lwowa*, 2nd ed. (Wrocław, 1985), etc.

41. Jan Zaleski has attempted to draw some conclusions from such studies. See his "Polszczyzna kresów południowo-wschodnich," *Studia nad polszczyzną kresową* 2: 9–14. See also Maria Karpluk, "Stan badań nad polszczyzną kresową XVI wieku," *Studia nad polszczyzną kresową* 4: 9–35.

42. See, for example, the two-volume work under his editorship, *Język polski dawnych Kresów Wschodnich* (Warsaw, 1996–1999).

43. On this, see, for example, M. Łesiów, "Polsko-ukraińskie oboczności leksykalne w gwarach z pogranicza," *Z polskich studiów sławistycznych*, seria 5, *Językoznawstwo* (Warsaw, 1978): 279–86; Feliks Czyżewski, *Atlas gwar polskich i ukraińskich okolic Włodawy* (Lublin, 1986), with 204 maps.

44. It is worthwhile repeating here the words of the "Petition of the Peasant Party in Małopolska with Regard to the Nationalities Policy of Poland in the Eastern *Kresy* after the End of the War," which was promulgated on 6 September 1943 in Lviv. Several issues are prominent in it, including abolishing the Ukrainian (here called "Ruthenian") alphabet, promoting words of Polish origin in the Ukrainian language, and attempting to draw the Ukrainian language significantly closer to the Polish language:

> A więc należy bezwarunkowo znieść odrębny alfabet i pozostawiając dla Rusinów język ruski, wprowadzić do szkół, urzędów itp. zachodnio-europejski alfabet łaciński. W słownictwie ruskim należy zaprzestać prowadzonej i dotąd przez oficjalne czynniki polskie tolerowanej, masowej i celowej eliminacji wyrazów o brzmieniu i pochodzeniu polskim (akcja wzorowana na Niemczech), a przeciwnie wpływ bezsprzecznie wyższej kultury polskiej powinien przejawić się w coraz większym upodobnianiu się języka ruskiego do polskiego.

> Consequently, we must unconditionally abolish a separate alphabet and, while retaining the Ruthenian language for Ruthenians, introduce into the schools, institutions, etc. the West European Latin alphabet. In terms of vocabulary, we must stop the massive and complete elimination in Ruthenian of phrases that either sound like Polish or are of Polish origin (a policy modeled on Germany)—something that is now under way and is being tolerated by the Polish authorities. On the contrary, the unquestionably higher Polish culture should be allowed to exert its influence in making the Ruthenian language increasingly like Polish.

See Eugeniusz Misiło, "Kwestia ukraińska w polityce polskiego rządu i podziemia w latach 1939–1944. Dokumenty," *Zustriczi* (Warsaw) 1990 (3–4): 165.

Interwar Poland and Romania: The Nationalization of Elites, the Vanishing Middle, and the Problem of Intellectuals

IRINA LIVEZEANU

In *Cultural Politics in Greater Romania,* which was based on the dissertation that I wrote under the direction of Roman Szporluk at the University of Michigan, I argued that Romania's interwar history was not unique.[1] Poland, Yugoslavia, and Czechoslovakia—to mention only the most obvious examples of multinational states created after World War I—all had parallel experiences with the integration of disparate, newly joined populations. The sudden creation or major expansion of multinational, but ideologically unitarist states gave rise to political and social tensions from the beginning of the interwar period. I also suggested that the efforts deployed to nationalize cultural institutions and elites in Romania after World War I had a profound impact on interwar intellectual history and the history of Romanian intellectuals.

In this paper I will build on my analysis in *Cultural Politics.* First, I will explore further the comparative claims that I made there. Was the process of reunifying disparate regions, of integrating or excluding minority populations, and of confronting urban minority elites comparable throughout the area? Was the ideological-intellectual dimension of nationalization similar in East Central European states other than Romania? As East Europeanists, we are used to making comparisons and sweeping statements, since "our" area spreads across societies, empires, states, and cultures; but to engage in this kind of exercise usefully has always been a challenge. Second, I will extend my investigation from the 1920s, when optimism about national consolidation was a dominant motif in much of Eastern Europe, into the 1930s, when ethnic, political, and ideological polarization emerged as a theme of equal if not greater importance. Third, I will draw out the connections between demography, politics, culture, and ideology. In a comparative analysis of Poland and Romania, I will examine how educated elites of different ethnicities were affected by the political pressures posed first by nation-building policies and by the European political transformations of the late 1930s and 1940s. While most of the Romanian material, which appears in greater detail in my book, is largely based on primary sources, the Polish sources I use here are largely secondary. Fortunately, the Polish historiography—even in English—is generally more extensive than the Romanian literature in this field.

*   *
*

In the 1980s and 1990s, Poland and Romania appeared to be polar opposites socially, politically, and in the past decade, even economically. While Poles surged toward a courageous and peaceful revolution with Solidarity, and managed even under martial law to live in and expand some degree of political freedom, Romanians cowered under the tightening grip of a regime that tolerated no dissent whatsoever. While Poland has been welcomed into the ranks of NATO, and may soon join the European Union, Romania is close to the end of the queue of postcommunist countries and can only "hope against hope" to be accepted into these clubs. While Western investors are wisely keeping their distance from the floundering Romanian economy, they have been much more readily betting their dollars, marks, and now euros on thriving Polish enterprises. Nevertheless, in the interwar period, Romania and Poland had a great deal in common. Although certainly for some Poles, as for many Romanians, their respective countries were not "great" enough, both states had emerged from the First World War and the subsequent peace conference overwhelmingly victorious—territorial gainers in the new European arrangement. For Poland, reconstituted from territories that had been annexed by Austria, Russia, and Germany in the partitions, the victory was absolute. In Romania's case, the gains were also great. The Old Kingdom of Romania, barely out from under Ottoman suzerainty in 1878, and recognized by the great European powers as sovereign only in 1881, in 1919 took over the neighboring territories of Transylvania, Bukovyna, and Bessarabia from, respectively, Hungary, Austria and the Russian Empire—roughly doubling its size.

The Demographic Background

For Romania this "embarrassment of riches" was, as I argue in my book, very much a mixed blessing. Romanian nationalists from the *Regat*, or Old Kingdom, appreciated the newly added territories sometimes more than they did their resident populations. Tensions surfaced among Polish citizens and between institutions from different regions as well.[2] Polish and Romanian citizens belonging to ethnic minorities were especially problematic, whether they were compactly settled in particular regions or hinterlands—like the Belarusians, Germans, and Ukrainians in Poland and the Germans, Hungarians, and Ukrainians in Romania—or were one of the more territorially diffuse groups that sometimes do not appear on demographic distribution maps.[3] The classic example of a dispersed group was, of course, the Jews—both in Poland, where they constituted an estimated 10 percent of the population in 1931, and in Romania, where they were significantly less numerous. In Poland, with its population of just over 32 million in 1931, the Jews were the third largest nationality after the Poles, who constituted 65 percent of the total, and the Ukrainians, who constituted 16 percent. In Romania, the Jews constituted only 4.2 percent of the total population, which numbered just over 18 million in 1930. Jews were thus third in number after the Romanians (71.9 percent), and the Hungarians (7.9 percent), and were approximately equal to the Germans (4.1 percent).[4]

In neither country were the Jews easily represented on demographic maps, precisely because they were dispersed, rather than compactly settled in discreet rural areas. As urbanites, living in high concentrations in towns and cities only, their presence was, however problematic for the majority nations, cartographically invisible. The fact that they could lay no demographic claim to a territory of their own may have contributed to their image as illegitimate intruders in the eyes of the majority. Moreover, urbanism represented only a very small proportion of the Polish and Romanian reality. In 1921, of Poland's population of 27.2 million, 63.8 percent made a living in agriculture, and three-quarters lived in the countryside. Ten years later, 60.6 percent of Poland's population was in agriculture and still only about one-quarter of Poland's population was urban.[5] Similarly, in Romania, only 20.2 percent of the population was urban according to the 1930 census.[6] In both Poland and Romania, the Jews were the largest *urban* ethnic minority, second only to the Poles and Romanians respectively. In Poland, 76.4 percent of all Jews lived in urban areas, and Jews made up 27.3 percent of Poland's urban population in 1931. In 1930, 68.2 percent of Romania's Jews lived in urban areas; Jews constituted 13.6 percent of the urban population.[7]

The Native Intelligentsia and the Jews

Many Polish and Romanian intellectuals viewed their countries' Jewish minorities as problematic in the interwar period precisely because of this urban dimension, and because, paradoxically, many of the Jews *were* eminently assimilable, but assimilable only to a secular, pluralist, liberal polity. Whereas Polish and Romanian governmental institutions tried to use schools and churches to integrate some of the predominantly peasant Christian territorial national minorities, they did not, for the most part, attempt to absorb the urban, acculturated Jews.[8] To ethnic Poles and Romanians, and particularly to the upwardly mobile Polish and Romanian youth who aspired to posts in the liberal professions and positions of influence in their countries' elites, the Jews represented professional competition.

Romanian and Polish integral nationalists discriminated against *all* minorities, of course, but not in exactly the same way or for the same reason. To begin with, proportionally far fewer of the territorial minorities—Belarusians, Germans, Hungarians, and Ukrainians—were interested in entry into Polish or Romanian institutions of higher learning. These nationalities were more rural in their geographic disposition, and most university students came from urban families. Moreover, members of these non-Jewish minorities could, if they desired, attend modern national universities of their own culture and language in neighboring countries.[9]

In general, then, it was the Jews alone—meaning, of course, only *some of* the Jews—who were willing, even eager in some cases, to assimilate to the language, culture, and identity of the dominant nationality;[10] and it was the Jews alone who constituted considerable competition for university slots and employment in elite urban positions.[11] Janusz Żarnowski's sociological investigation supports this view: in Poland, the proportion of intellectuals belonging to the Belarusian, Russian, and Ukrainian minorities was just a fraction of these ethnic groups' proportion in the population. Although Jews—like members of the other minorities—were largely kept out of state employment and some sectors of the economy, they alone of the minority groups represented a challenge to the privately employed ethnic Polish intelligentsia. In the liberal professions, the number of Jews was disproportionately high—to the point that Jews outnumbered Poles—and by 1931 they represented almost 50 percent of those working in these professions. Meanwhile, the proportion of ethnic Poles in the liberal professions decreased in the decade between 1921 and 1931. However, ethnic Poles represented the largest number of intellectuals overall. The proportion of both Polish and Jewish intellectuals rose in the 1920s, while the share of non-Polish Slavic intellectuals—already smaller than their proportions in the general population—decreased.[12]

The animus toward the Jews was for this reason, among others, a special one, as Yisrael Gutman has argued with regard to Poland:

> Unquestionably the Ukrainians and the Bielorussians were discriminated against and denied rights in interwar Poland. In my view, however, the situation of the Jews and the treatment they received were unique. In the case of the Ukrainians and the Bielorussians proposals were advanced for various forms of federation and autonomy on the one hand, and for forced assimilation and . . . Polonization on the other. None of these proposals, however, denied these minorities the very right of settling and living on the land their forefathers had occupied for generations. The Jews fared very differently. They were denied the elementary right of residing on Polish land.[13]

The agitation that ultimately aimed to revoke the citizenship of Polish and Romanian Jews began in youth movements with more restricted goals. In each country, the agitators targeted Jewish university students and later also white-collar professionals—mainly those working in the liberal professions and cultural fields (law, medicine, architecture, journalism, poetry, literature, entertainment and the arts). According to Raphael Mahler's analysis of interwar Poland, this focus on the liberal professions—and the training grounds for them—resulted from the fact that Jews were already practically excluded, with few exceptions, from national and municipal government employment.[14] For the reasons already suggested, the nationalist student movements in Poland and Romania largely ignored the non-Jewish minorities whose numbers in these fields, as in urban areas in general, were disproportionately low. The *numerus clausus* campaigns aiming to increase the numbers of "true" Romanians and Poles in the respective elites of the two countries therefore attacked mainly the Jews' demographic, economic, and cultural positions and their concentration in the urban elites and in the universities that trained young people for elite urban professions.[15] Statistics indicate that in Poland in 1922, roughly 24 percent of university students were Jewish. In Romania, 16.4 percent of university students in the period from 1921 to 1933 were Jewish.[16] An article in *Enciclopedia României* (1938–1941) presents the "Jewish challenge" to native educated elites in a representative way. In the section entitled "The Universities' Population by Nationality," the authors comment only on the proportions of ethnic Romanians and Jews, "the latter being the most numerous of the non-Romanians."[17] The data show that from 1921 to 1933, only 1.5 percent of ethnic Romanian primary school students went on to attend universities, in contrast to 7.6 percent of Jewish children in primary schools. From this they conclude that "the Jews participate in higher education at five times the rate of the Romanians."[18] The implication in the article that a program is necessary to redress this imbalance is obvious.

Although the majority of Polish students may well have been silent or apolitical, vocal student leadership in Poland, as in Romania, passed into the hands of radical nationalists in the early 1920s, when they "managed to gain control of the student organizations and impose their views."[19] From the mid-1920s on, therefore, Polish students generally did not support the authoritarian Piłsudski regime with its socialist roots and opposition to the National Democrats (known as the *Endecja* in Polish); rather, they tended to back the more radical Endeks or groups farther to the right.[20] Thus Polish universities, much like their Romanian counterparts, were hotbeds of antisemitism "from the very beginning of independence."[21] The antisemitic campaign increased in intensity once the young nationalists gained control of student organizations, and once the goal of *numerus clausus* was reached, it was replaced by the more extreme one of *numerus nullus*.[22] In response to student demands, Lviv University first instituted quotas in 1921 in the law and medical faculties—but the Ministry of Education overruled these limits as unconstitutional. Quotas were, however, unofficially reintroduced in 1924 in some institutions, the government then claiming that, given university autonomy, it could do little to stop these measures.[23] Militant student organizations were not satisfied with this ambiguous victory, and called for national legislation to enshrine Jewish quotas. Student groups also asked that diplomas received abroad not be recognized in Poland, in order to limit competition from Jews who had studied in France and other Western or Central European countries and then returned to seek jobs "at home." Almost as many Polish Jewish youths went to universities abroad as stayed in Poland, at least in part because of the antisemitism they faced in the lecture halls at home.[24] According to Antony Polonsky:

> The universities were the scene of continuous political upheaval in the early 1930s. In November 1931 student unrest, sparked off by demands for the reduction of the number of Jewish students, led to the closing, for a short period, of the universities of Warsaw and Cracow, and the Warsaw Polytechnic. Student rioting led by the Right took place the following October in Warsaw, Poznań, and Lwów, as a result of the raising of university fees by the Minister of Education. It was followed in November by more incidents of a markedly antisemitic character, and these led again to the closing of the University of Warsaw. On the occasion of the passing of the Government's bill limiting the autonomy of the universities in March 1933, the right-wing students organized a strike in all institutions of higher learning . . . In March 1934 the university was once again closed following antisemitic incidents involving the distinguished historian Marceli Handelsman, who was of Jewish origin.[25]

It seems quite clear that Polish universities, like their Romanian counterparts, were in turmoil through much of the interwar period, with antisemitism as a major component.[26] Moreover, there is a striking similarity in the forms of agitation, down to the timing of the onset and escalation, the list of conditions, and the specific demands (for Jewish medical students to dissect only Jewish cadavers in their studies and for prohibiting Jews from changing their names to Polish or Romanian ones). Both movements, furthermore, claimed that they represented the natural, spontaneous reflex of their respective nations.[27]

Among the similarities between the two countries is the intensification of university and general political antisemitic agitation in the 1930s. In part, after 1933, this may be explained in terms of the Nazi victory in Germany and the prestige it lent internationally to preexisting fascist and antisemitic programs. Furthermore, in Poland, the economics of the liberal professions seems to have had an impact. In Romania as well, a debate about an "intellectual proletariat" began at the end of the 1920s, reflecting the sudden and substantial increase in university enrollments and diplomas and the fear that there would be no corresponding increase in opportunities for employment.[28] The evidence for a true employment crisis among intellectuals is thinner here, however.[29] Besides, by 1937, at the Universities of Bucharest and Cluj and the Timişoara Polytechnic, most faculties were well on their way to achieving a Jewish *numerus clausus*, and in some cases even a *numerus nullus*.[30] The proportion of Jews in Poland's universities dropped from 20.4 percent in 1928–1929 to 13.2 percent in 1935–1936, 11.7 percent in 1936–1937, and 7.5 percent in 1937–1938.[31] Anti-Jewish agitation "on a previously-unheard-of scale," resulting in "Jewless days" and even "Jewless weeks" were enforced by right-wing student militants. Jewish students, in their diminishing numbers, were continually threatened and harassed.[32] Antisemitic disturbances closed down a number of universities. Jewish quotas and "ghetto benches"—segregated seating in university classrooms—were officially introduced in 1937, as university and ministerial authorities caved in to the overwhelming pressure of student radicals. Jews also had to use separate laboratories in some cases.[33] Rather than satisfying nationalist student demands, however, these nationalist victories became a step towards the ultimate goal of a Jewish *numerus nullus*.

The Professions and the Rise of Official Antisemitism

Antisemitism became increasingly institutionalized and official in the mid-1930s in both Romania and Poland. Anti-Jewish demands began to be heard beyond the walls of the universities where they had first been voiced, Polish and Romanian professional organizations of engineers, doctors, and lawyers began to exclude Jews, and increasingly discriminatory legislation was passed in both countries. Although Romania and Poland ultimately ended on opposite sides in World War II—the Poles resisting Nazi Germany as best they could, and the Romanians allying themselves with the Nazis and conducting a brutal war against the Soviet Union and its own Jewish population—prewar domestic developments in the two countries are far more similar than the wartime record might suggest. Romanian fascism began in student circles, and Poland's right-wing radical movement, whatever we might call it, had similar origins.

The Legion of the Archangel Michael, the Romanian fascist organization also known as the Iron Guard, in fact began as a student movement in 1922. The student leaders of the early 1920s initially helped form the League of National Christian Defense (LANC in its Romanian acronym). This antisemitic party campaigned against the passage of the 1923 Constitution that granted equal rights to all, including the Jewish minority; among student activists and LANC members, the document was known as the "Jewish constitution." The Legion split off from LANC and became an independent organization in 1927. Corneliu Zelea Codreanu, Ion Moța, and other Iron Guard luminaries thus had their political apprenticeships in the nationalist student movement of the early twenties. At first these agitators had struggled to gain a foothold against leftist students who dominated the campuses just after World War I, but in 1922 the nationalists had their first major show of force in Romanian universities, sparked by a protest in Cluj. Soon the nationalists gained hegemony in all universities and the "student movement" became synonymous with the struggle against Jews and for the *numerus clausus*. The students' demand that Jews be forbidden to change their names made it clear that for them, Jewish assimilation was not a goal, but an alarming prospect.[34]

What may be called Polish fascism also began in universities, in student circles agitating for a *numerus clausus*.[35] Unlike Romania, which is widely viewed as the textbook case of East European fascism, there is no agreement about whether fascism even existed in Poland. Nevertheless, Henryk Wereszycki and Piotr Wandycz both recognized that a phenomenon much like fascism had an important influence on Polish youth in the 1930s. Others, like Paweł Korzec and Raphael Mahler, simply assume that Poland's regime from the mid-1930s was fascist.[36] According to Wereszycki, a right-wing youth movement led by Roman Dmowski mounted "an open campaign of a distinctly fascist character" around 1934. Reflecting on the post-1935 Polish regime, Jerzy Tomaszewski has written that "there opened the threatening perspective of a Polish version of National Socialism."[37] Wandycz acknowledges that some genuinely fascist—if minor—formations existed in Poland. Among them were the National Radical Camp, a group that broke away from Dmowski's Greater Poland Camp, and a splinter of the former called Falanga.

According to Wandycz, while Polish fascism lacked a mass following, "its membership was almost exclusively composed of very young people belonging to the intelligentsia." Antisemitism in Poland and elsewhere was not by any means exclusively the province of the fascists, but it figured prominently in their program. Wandycz suggests that Polish antisemitism stemmed from economic competition with Jews, namely the fact that Polish "high school and university graduates faced a genuine problem finding jobs"; hence the strength of Polish fascism in universities, where student organizations "became centers of antisemitism" à la national socialism.[38] Polish "intellectual workers"—so defined by the census—did in fact face rising unemployment; the number of unemployed intellectuals increased from 70,000 in 1929 to 142,000 two years later.[39] Raphael Mahler performs a similar economically based analysis in his 1944 article. Since the economic crisis was much more profound and lasting in Poland than elsewhere in Europe, he writes, "a steady deterioration in the economic position of Polish intellectuals undoubtedly also played a role in the outbreak of the violent offensive against Jewish professionals . . . While other European countries achieved a partial economic recovery as early as 1933, Poland had to wait until four years later for some slight alleviation of her plight . . . The burden fell heavily on the shoulders of the 'mental workers.'"[40] While Mahler and Wandycz do not agree about the actual figures for unemployed Polish intellectuals, they concur that this problem was acute. According to Mahler, the results of the 1931 census showed that 78,000 intellectual workers, or 12 percent of this category, were unemployed; but other official sources put the number higher. The Institute of Social Security for Intellectual Workers, for example, listed roughly 82,000 people, or 30 percent of its members, as jobless in 1935.[41] This situation was especially hard on young professionals who would normally have been employed by the state, such as nonlitigating lawyers headed for administrative or notarial positions and judgeships. As these government opportunities dried up, Mahler suggests, ethnic Poles sharpened their attacks on Jews, who were predominant in the professions.

The professional segregation of the Jews had begun in some sense just after the reestablishment of an independent state: Jews were "virtually barred" from state and municipal public employment in the new Poland. This development was most obvious in Galicia, where many Jews had served as public servants under the Habsburg regime, only to lose those jobs after 1919 with the "wholesale discharge of thousands of Jewish officials."[42] In response to the ethnic purging of the state sector, educated Jews flocked to the liberal professions, and Jewish students to those university departments that held the promise of jobs in the private sphere: mainly medicine and law, but also architecture, engineering, teaching, and journalism. In Poland in 1931 to 1934, approximately 40 percent of all independent lawyers and 49 percent of all barristers (trial lawyers) were Jewish. By 1939, the proportion of Jewish barristers had risen to 52 percent. Similarly, in 1931, an estimated 46 percent of physicians were Jewish, and the proportion of Jewish medical doctors in private practice was 55.5 percent.[43]

Jews had always faced discrimination in the public sectors of these professions, but from the mid-1930s, according to Mahler, educated ethnic Poles set about eliminating the Jews from the private economy as well in order to improve their own employment prospects. At the same time, Mahler is adamant that the intensification of this professional antisemitism was not entirely economic. He cites, among other things, the fact that professional associations that "had never included Jewish members" also participated in the drive to oust Jews from professional life. Mahler's ultimate explanation is the government's "virulent antisemitic drive," which in my view somewhat begs the question.[44] In any case, a drive to oust a sizable group of Polish citizens working in private enterprise could follow few avenues, among them legislation to define the group in such a way as to deny them equal rights and thus out of full citizenship, and collusion with professional associations to exclude Jews by withdrawing their license to practice.

The campaign against Jews in the professions, in the Polish cultural leadership, and in the universities utilized both strategies. The shift in the professional organizations came in the mid-1930s. According to Janusz Żarnowski, the legal profession saw fierce and increasing competition between Poles and Jews beginning in 1935. In 1937 the Association of Polish Lawyers demanded that Jews be barred from the profession, and eventually the Ministry of Justice did eliminate Jews from the bar.[45] Other professional groups also adopted aryanization clauses. The Association of Polish Physicians, for example, resolved on 18 October 1937 that only "Christian-born" Polish citizens could belong, and excluded local chapters in Lviv and Cracow that resisted this policy.[46] In May 1937, the Union of Polish Physicians and the Union of Polish Lawyers had jointly adopted a Nazi-inspired "Aryan paragraph" by a vote of 140 to 103, although several local chapters of the physicians' group refused to go along. The Association splintered as a result. A year later the Union of Polish Physicians resolved to halt the admission of Jews to medical schools until the proportionality issue was resolved; to admit all ethnic Poles wishing to study medicine into expanded medical schools; to allow only Poles to have a say in "the composition of medical chambers"; to halt the nostrification of foreign diplomas; to "penalize Jewish physicians who used Slavonic or Christian names"; to segregate the Jewish physicians into separate curias of the medical chambers; and to demand that Jewish physicians identify themselves as such "on their shingles." The Polish Medical Chamber did not meet all of these demands, but registration by nationality became mandatory, which set the stage for the use of this criterion in further discriminatory measures.[47] The escalating series of resolutions, though not all implemented before the beginning of the war and the imposition of the Nazi regime, were indicative of the mood in the medical and legal professions with respect to Nazi-style aryanization. While they could be construed as economically motivated, I would concur with Mahler that economics can hardly have been the whole story. The 1937 decisions of Jagiellonian University Polonists to oust Jews from their profession, and, a month later, not to honor the renowned Polish poet Bolesław Leśmian (who was of Jewish extraction although not much identified with his origins), reflect a deeper cultural or political rejection instead.[48]

Similar developments in the economy and the professions in Romania can be followed in the reports of the *Alliance Israélite Universelle*. The *Alliance* grew alarmed during this period about a triangular Romanian problem: the success of Nazi influence, the related loss of French influence, and the deteriorating situation of the Jews. An *Alliance* communiqué to the French Ministry of Foreign Affairs in the fall of 1937 made a clear connection between these concerns: "The danger Judaism is experiencing in Romania is connected to that which threatens the position of France in Romania."[49] An 1935 report entitled "Hitlerism gains ground in Romania" had advanced the reasonable thesis that Germany was trying to pull Romania out of the French sphere of influence, using antisemitism to further this goal. According to the *Alliance* author, this tactic was succeeding in poisoning Romanian public opinion, and "above all the intellectuals," such that when French representatives held conferences in Bucharest, as they always had, they no longer found "that warm and friendly reception that had once been traditional."[50]

The 1934 law for the protection of Romanian labor stipulated that as of January 1935 industries serving national defense had to employ only ethnic Romanians, while other industries could employ up to 20 percent non-Romanians. All enterprises had to submit lists indicating not only the citizenship, but also the ethnicity of their employees. It may be doubtful that the letter of the new law was always enforced. In the Bessarabian capital, Chișinău, for instance, the town council had concluded that if the new law were applied rigorously, most of the council's members would lose their jobs because they were Romanian subjects (*ressortissants*), not citizens.[51] But even without *strict* application, such laws were there to be applied selectively and increasingly and to indicate a direction. This led the *Alliance* to worry that the Romanian government was making concessions to the antisemitic parties, of which there were several, and whose gains in popularity had been extremely impressive.[52]

As the new labor protection legislation was coming into force, the liberal professions were also becoming less and less accessible to Jews. Medicine and law, which were still fairly open, were exceptions—but this too was about to change.[53] During the mid-1930s, Romanian professional organizations began agitating for ethnic exclusivity. The integral nationalist leaders of these organizations argued that non-Romanians, who formed "dangerous and intolerable" majorities in many places, threatened the Romanian element. They invoked the state's duty to ensure ethnic continuity and defend the idea of a truly Romanian state. Jewish legal professionals, bankers, engineers, accountants, architects, physicians, and journalists all became targets of this campaign of ethnic purification.[54] Romania's General Association of Intellectual Workers lobbied in favor of antiminority measures in 1935, calling for a *numerus proportionalis* in all the liberal professions, for a *numerus nullus* in the army, the courts, and education, and for the rigorous enforcement of the law regarding Romanian employment in private enterprises.[55] In response to a Lawyers' Union circular sent to all the bar associations in Romania in early 1937, all but one of the associations in the Old Kingdom "rose in solidarity against" allowing "foreigners" to practice law.[56] The situation was more complicated for the lawyers' nationalist project in the recently gained provinces, where "foreigners" greatly outnumbered ethnic Romanian lawyers. According to Ioan Gruia, 64 percent of the lawyers in Transylvania, over 60 percent of those in Bessarabia, and over 80 percent of those in Bukovyna were so-called "foreigners." Gruia does not specify the source of these data or their exact date, but other dates in this section of his encyclopedia article indicate that he is probably referring to the period from 1935 to 1937.[57] In Transylvania, ethnic Romanian lawyers faced an uphill battle on romanization, which it seems they lost. A 1935 article in the influential right-wing newspaper *Curentul* suggests the defeat of the nationalist lawyers' program: "the great struggle was fought in the Transylvanian bar associations, where the Romanian attorneys are in a clear minority. Nevertheless, due to their unflagging resolution, a good number declared themselves for romanization, while the rest entered into compromises . . . " Bukovyna and some towns in Bessarabia and Moldova encountered similar problems.[58] Furthermore, many of the bar associations that adopted resolutions for complete Romanization had non-Romanian ethnic majorities, which suggests that the procedure used to obtain votes in favor of nationalization may well have been coercive and undemocratic.[59]

In his 1938 encyclopedia article concerning the institution of the bar, Ioan Gruia wrote that the Romanian bar was "orienting itself toward a deep transformation. There is talk and there is a struggle for its *romanization*, so as to do away with any constitutional equivocation from the start." He reported that 44 of 59 local bar associations had voted "by acclamation" for their nationalization and that an extraordinary meeting of the Romania-wide bar on 9 May 1937 had also voted "by acclamation" for nationalization "according to the follow-

ing principles: (1) The bars shall have a totally indigenous Romanian composition; (2) In order to achieve and ensure the Romanian composition of the bars, a
verification of all registrations will begin immediately, with those who do not
fulfill these essential conditions having their membership revoked."[60]

The newly constituted bar membership arrogated to itself the right not only
"*to discuss and decide . . . on matters of general and professional interest*," but
also "*to struggle*—including by means of changing the legal order—*for the
harmonization of the legal institutions of the corporation* [of lawyers],
with . . . the organic realities of the nation." The rationale for this step was that
the Romanian nation was threatened in its very existence and that these new
and alarming realities demanded "new legal norms." According to Gruia,
himself a university professor on the Bucharest Law Faculty and counsel for
the Ilfov County bar, a true nation-state could only be achieved "by nationalizing the professions." Moreover, he stated that "from an ethical point of view,"
the nation meant "spirituality based on the law of the blood."[61] These arguments pointed to the ousting of non-Romanians from the legal guild on national, professional, and ethical grounds.

Not surprisingly, given this reasoning, some Romanian professional groups
turned to militancy and even took up arms to reach their goals. Their members,
or at least their effective leaders, felt that worthy ends justified almost any
means. This attitude prevailed during the December 1935 Bucharest bar elections, when the Association of Romanian Christian Lawyers used terror tactics
to win against an independent—and professionally highly qualified—list of
candidates. The Palace of Justice, where the balloting was underway, was
occupied and surrounded by students, interns, and thugs, many of whom were
Iron Guard members. This group permitted entry into the interior of the Palace
of Justice only to lawyers whom they trusted to vote for the nationalist list.
Minority lawyers, expected to cast their vote for the rival list, were struck and
bodily prevented from reaching the ballot.[62] In her 1937 account based on
contemporary press articles, Madeleine Coulon makes clear just how political
and illegal—according to the legal norms the nationalists were contesting—the
Bucharest bar elections of 1935 were. The extreme right-wing newspaper
Porunca Vremii, which supported the nationalist slate, had pointed out that the
nationalist conception "made the [legal] profession . . . a subcategory of the
major category of the Nation."[63] The leading nationalist candidate, Istrate
Micescu, encouraged his followers to use any means necessary, including
violence, to achieve victory. The winning list, led by Micescu, later campaigned for the expulsion of Jewish lawyers not just from the Bucharest bar,
but from the legal profession nationwide. Micescu's antisemitism prompted
him to leave the National Liberal Party for Octavian Goga's National Christian
Party, and he was appointed foreign minister in Goga's 1937–1938 cabinet.[64]

The cases of the Polish and Romanian liberal professions echo the account
of Hungary's free professionals recently told by Mária Kovács. She traces the
evolution of the main groups of Hungarian engineers, lawyers, and doctors

toward "illiberalism," an attitude that ultimately led to a disproportionately greater loss of life among liberal professional practitioners in World War II. These tragic losses were related to several facts: a disproportionately large number of Hungarian professionals were Jewish, as in Poland and Romania; non-Jewish colleagues of theirs had prepared detailed lists for their professional exclusion; and the lists were eventually used for their arrest, deportation, and extermination in Nazi camps. In Hungary, of the three professions Kovács examined, doctors were the most vehement antisemites, whereas lawyers constituted the last bulwark of liberalism in the ranks of the free professions.[65] The same cannot be said of Romania's or Poland's attorneys. The Hungarian data so skillfully presented by Kovács are thus both predictable and surprising in light of the Polish and Romanian cases, and the juxtaposition of the three underlines the importance of detailed, empirically based comparative studies.

In Romania, these troubling developments came to a head during the very brief government (December 1937 to February 1938) led by the nationalist poet Octavian Goga in the wake of elections which, uncharacteristically, defeated the ruling National Liberals. The Iron Guard had performed exceedingly well at the ballot box, garnering over 15 percent of the votes.[66] The National Christian Party of Goga and A.C. Cuza, a well-known professor of law and political economy at the University of Iaşi and a notorious antisemitic theoretician, had finished fourth in the December elections, but the king appointed Goga prime minister for tactical reasons.[67] Once in power, Goga kept to his inaugural declaration, which included—for the first time in an official government speech—phrases such as "kike" and "the domination of Judas." His programmatic statements were no less alarming in content than in their abusive tone towards all minorities, and Jews in particular: "We believe in the rebirth of the Romanian nation with its Christian Church. We believe that it is a sacred duty to put the stamp of our ethnic domination on all areas of political life."[68] Almost immediately, and with few exceptions, Jewish-owned newspapers were banned and Jewish journalists lost their press privileges.[69] According to Paul Shapiro:

> Jews on public payrolls were fired, and all state aid to Jewish institutions was withdrawn . . . Jews were declared "unfit" to hold liquor licenses or to employ non-Jewish female servants under forty years of age. Yiddish, long used as a language of public administration in Bessarabia and Northern Moldavia, was now declared unacceptable. Finally . . . by a decree of January 22, 1938, Goga invalidated all citizenship papers granted to Jews after the beginning of World War I.[70]

These measures elicited protests from the *Alliance Israélite Universelle,* the *Sociétés Juives de France,* and the World Jewish Congress. These organizations appealed to the League of Nations to reestablish the full rights of the Jewish population in accordance with the Minorities Protection Treaty, which Romania had signed.[71] The Goga-Cuza government's anti-Jewish moves also elicited concern from the French, British, and American governments, which could see clearly that Romania was moving closer to Germany and "the totalitarian system."[72]

The situation of Romania's Jews improved somewhat after the Goga government fell, less than three months after coming to power. Antisemitic propaganda decreased, but the law on the revision of naturalization, and others aimed at reducing Jewish employment, continued to erode Jewish rights.[73] The dissolution of the Iron Guard in February 1938 after the declaration of a Royal Dictatorship did not stop the rise of antisemitism, but was probably, like the appointment of the Goga government in 1937, an indication of the Guard's strength.[74]

Comparable developments could be seen in Poland after Piłsudski's death. There is substantial agreement among historians about the rightward turn in Polish politics from 1935 on and about the escalation of tactics in the antisemitic camp. This was the result of several converging factors: the 1934 nonaggression pact between Nazi Germany and Poland, the crisis in the Piłsudski camp following the marshal's death, and the evolution of the policies of the Endek opposition that were appealing to the Polish youth to whom Piłsudski's successors now also wished to appeal. With the disbanding of the Nonpartisan Bloc for Cooperation with the Government (BBWR), the old government party, in October 1935 and the founding of the National Unity Camp (OZON) in March 1937, the government "openly wooed the rightist and reactionary groups," by means of a "clear-cut antisemitic program."[75] At the same time, the National Democrats and its splinter parties "changed from ideological and tactical antisemitism to supporting the organized use of physical force against the Jews. These groups [now] openly called for exceptional legislation to eliminate almost all Jewish rights."[76] Jerzy Holzer describes the diminishing resistance to such a program:

> [G]roups which had previously believed in assimilation began to take an antisemitic position, joining the parties already advocating antisemitism in the form of Jewish segregation and an economic boycott. Thus, the entire political wing representing "restrained antisemitism" was prepared to accept exceptional legislation limiting the rights of Jews in certain areas of economic and cultural life. In effect, antisemitism as an element in political life was openly espoused and increasingly radical.[77]

While some university faculty and the members of the Polish Socialist Party (PPS) in general opposed this trend, they were in the minority and their position involved considerable risk. According to Paweł Korzec, "non-Jewish professors who defended their Jewish students were also assailed by the Endek mob." Non-Jewish students who joined the Jews in their seating ghettoes as a symbolic gesture faced the same mistreatment as the Jews.[78]

Antisemitic organizations and youthful student leaders had already advanced exclusionary programs exemplified by the *numerus clausus* campaign at the beginning of the 1920s. After the great depression and the emergence of a strong Germany under the Nazis, the demands became more radical and perva-

sive. In the mid- and late-1930s, both professional associations and government parties such as the *Sanacja* in Poland and the Goga-Cuza National-
Christian cabinet in Romania adopted aryanization clauses. Racist, exclusionary initiatives thus evolved from youthful marginality to maturity in the liberal
professions and implementation by the legislative and executive branches of
governments in power. Piłsudski's heirs and the Camp of National Unity may
not have agreed with the violent methods of the Endeks and other radical
nationalists, but they shared the *Endecja*'s definition of the problem, and
agreed that the preponderance of Jews in certain economic and cultural spheres
of Polish life was problematic and damaging to Polish state and national
interests. They also agreed that this was an issue to be resolved by boycotts,
disenfranchisement, and forced emigration.[79] As Colonel Koc stated in a February 1937 radio address that preceded the founding of the Camp:

> We have too high an idea of our civilization and we respect too strongly the
> order and peace which every state needs to approve brutal antisemitic acts
> which harm the dignity and prestige of a great country. At the same time, it is
> understandable that the country should possess the instinct impelling it to
> defend its culture, and it is natural that Polish society should seek economic
> self-sufficiency.[80]

The stance legitimizing the exclusion of Polish citizens from full civil and
political rights on the basis of ethnicity was reinforced by the appeal to Christian principles. The OZON leadership invoked these even while admitting that
there were exceptional cases of Jews who had fought and shed blood for Polish
independence, and thus deserved special respect—though still not full and
unconditional membership in the Polish nation. The right of Jews to join the
Camp of National Unity on the basis of Polish citizenship alone was out of the
question.[81] Similarly, in Romania the idea that the citizenship of ethnic (and
Christian) Romanians was fundamentally guaranteed in a way that the citizenship of "others" could never be had become widely accepted in public life by
1938. The influential right-wing journalist, theologian, and politician Nichifor
Crainic expressed this view in his article "Spiritul autohton" (The Native
Spirit):

> Romania includes within its borders almost the whole living sea of our ethnic
> blood, which pulses in 15 million faces. But this homogeneous wave is
> interrupted by considerable minority islands and is sprayed from one end to
> the other by the Semitic vitriol. By comparison to us, these peoples, [which
> were] accepted with equal rights in the political family of the state, but which
> keep themselves strongly apart from the autochthonous community, cannot
> nevertheless be equally entitled to the moral and material properties of our
> country. Generous by nature and tolerant by tradition, the political rights that
> we granted these foreigners are concessions we made as authors and masters
> of the state. The legal constitution, however, can be changed according to
> need, because beyond it stands the constitution of the Romanian blood and
> spirit, the only real basis for and guarantee of the life of this state.[82]

Fascism, Communism, and the Intellectuals

That a polarization and radicalization of political, professional, and ultimately intellectual life took place in Romania and Poland between the two world wars is not in question. This was as much the domestic product of the unifications of 1918—followed by accelerated nation building and the nationalist mobilization of elites—as of the subsequent rise of Nazism and its appeal to intellectuals. In my book I argued that Romania's 1918 unification constituted enough of a political and demographic challenge that it provided fertile ground for the rise of aggressive integral nationalism, particularly among young, educated elites. This is not to deny the importance of external factors in encouraging the radicalization of nationalism: foremost among these were the examples of Mussolini and Hitler in leading successful radical right-wing movements to power. With deteriorating economic conditions, Nazi victory in Germany, and the growing popularity of integral nationalists espousing openly antisemitic programs throughout Eastern Europe, the 1930s saw the gradual disappearance of a political middle ground—a space narrow enough to begin with in post–World War I Eastern Europe. In Romania many ranking intellectuals became engaged in fascist politics.

One of the members of the literary intelligentsia of the 1930s who did not follow suit under the pressures of political regimentation was the Romanian/French playwright Eugen Ionescu (Eugène Ionesco). In 1945, in a letter to an older colleague and literary critic in Bucharest, Ionescu decried the waste of his own generation, the circle with which he had come of intellectual and literary age in the 1930s:

> I've grown aware suddenly how alone I've become, of how old we are. The "Criterion" generation, the proud young generation from 15 and 10 years ago, has decomposed, has perished. None of us is 40 yet—and [yet] we are exhausted.[83] Others, so many, are dead. Your generation is much luckier. And more solid besides. We were a bunch of mad and wretched men. As for myself, I cannot reproach myself with having been a fascist. But this can be reproached to almost all the others.[84]

Ionescu went on to "name names," listing a number of talented, even famous Romanians of the "new generation" who had joined the fascists, among them Emil Cioran and Mircea Eliade, both of whom went on to make brilliant careers in France and the United States.

Westernized, prodemocratic, liberal intellectuals did not disappear altogether in Poland and Romania, but their numbers dwindled in the late 1930s. It was into the ranks of such a Westernized liberal stratum that the secular, assimilationist Jewish intellectuals of Poland and Romania might have been able to merge. With that fragile option endangered altogether, intellectuals of the minority nationalities had two main choices: a national solution of their own, and the continuation of the assimilationist project under the guise of socialism. (Zygmunt Bauman has cleverly dubbed socialism "a program of *assimilation by other means.*")[85] From a literary perspective, Magdalena Opalski has examined the "profound effect" of the "shift to the right of Polish politics in the 1930s" on the assimilated Jewish literary intelligentsia grouped around *Wiadomości literackie.*[86] The publication had earlier taken a neutral stance on the Jewish question. Its assimilated Jewish editors and collaborators had "demonstrated . . . 'evenhandedness'" by, among other things, publishing "both pro- and anti-Jewish views" and downplaying "the importance of antisemitism."[87] By the late 1930s, however, the weekly's "focus gradually shifted toward ideological confrontation with fascism, [and] . . . became more articulate in condemning anti-Jewish violence."[88] Some of the "crème de la crème of the Polonized Jewish intelligentsia," as Opalski calls them, became communists or fellow travelers of the Soviet-backed regime.[89]

Similarly, in Romania, noncommunist, non-Zionist Jewish intellectuals became rarer as World War II approached. The writer, playwright, and journalist Mihail Sebastian was virtually alone among intellectuals of the "new generation"—although in the good company of Eugen Ionescu—in maintaining his distance from politics. Never very much attracted to Marxist solutions, the *Realpolitik* of the late 1930s and 1940s confirmed him in his skepticism of both left and right. The Molotov-Ribbentrop pact elicited from Sebastian a comment about the perfect symmetry of the monstrous treaty.[90] As Europe plunged into war he found himself very much alone, not sharing a political vision with either side. After the Soviet invasion of Poland, Sebastian remarked,

> Happy are those with *idées fixes*! . . . For communists . . . things are still in order and "the revolution on the march." Anything the Soviets do [is] well done. For the [Iron Guard] legionnaires . . . German victory is now assured, and in its shadow, life can be perfect. But me? Since I don't believe in either the ones or the others, but I try to judge not from premises but from facts? Doesn't one have to lose one's mind? Doesn't one have to despair? Isn't one obliged to tell oneself that from here on, truly everything . . . is lost?[91]

And yet, after the long years of despair, when, as a Jew, Sebastian felt in constant danger and almost completely abandoned by his non-Jewish friends, the tide of the war brought him around to a new, mildly hopeful stance. On 23 August 1944, the night Romania abandoned the Axis and joined the Allies, Sebastian was with Lucrețiu Pătrăscanu and Belu Zilber writing for the communist *România liberă.*[92] Not long tempted to join the communists in any disciplined sense, Sebastian quit working for *România liberă* before the end of August in protest against the regime of secret committees and the paper's "doctrinaire imbecility."[93] He not only detested the rampant opportunism of those who quickly turned pro-Soviet after years of professing fascist sympathies; he also despised the new ideological formulas the Soviet victors and local communists tried to impose in their propaganda: "The only thing that I had yearned for was freedom, not a new definition of freedom. After so many years

of terror we no longer need to be told what it means to be free. That we know—
and that cannot be replaced by any formula."[94]

Nevertheless, what is striking about Mihail Sebastian in 1944 is that, however briefly, he admired the Soviets who had saved his life and reinstituted his
full civil rights, although these were soon to be curtailed for everyone in
Romania, and although Sebastian had never much liked Marxism before. His
best friends, largely non-Jews of the "new generation," had been apolitical but
later joined the radical right. Sebastian himself was not one for the barricades,
nor for ministries or party posts. Beyond that we know little of his possible
political or intellectual evolution after the war, because his life ended abruptly
in a traffic accident in 1945. But however abbreviated and skeptical,
Sebastian's shift from apolitical clear-headedness to a new identity as communist fellow traveler illustrates just how narrow the options for secular assimilated Jewish intellectuals had become with the military, but also ideological
and intellectual, hegemony of fascism in Eastern Europe. This is surely one key
to the vexed question of Eastern Europe's Jewish communists.

NOTES

1. Irina Livezeanu, *Cultural Politics in Greater Romania: Regionalism, Nation Building, and Ethnic Struggle, 1918–1930* (Ithaca, 1995). The book analyzes the Romanian efforts to establish a unified nation state from fragments of several other states and nations, and the ideological and political consequences of the process.

2. Hans Roos, *A History of Modern Poland from the Foundation of the State in World War I to the Present Day* (New York, 1966), pp. 88–97; Joseph Rothschild, *East Central Europe Between the Two World Wars* (Seattle, 1974), pp. 29–31; and Antony Polonsky, *Politics in Independent Poland, 1921–1939: The Crisis of Constitutional Government* (Oxford, 1972), pp. 2–10.

3. Paul R. Magocsi, *The Historical Atlas of East Central Europe* (Seattle, 1995), pp. 97–99. According to Magocsi, in ca. 1900, there were approximately 7,468,000 Jews in East Central Europe, yet none appear on the colorful Ethnolinguistic Distribution map on p. 99. Similarly, see Map 3, "Nationalities in Poland according to the census of 1921" in Polonsky, *Politics in Independent Poland*, p. 36. This map represents Poles, Ukrainians, Belarusians, Germans, and Lithuanians, but not Jews, although the latter outnumbered three of the nationalities that are shown.

4. Figures taken from Jerzy Tomaszewski, *Ojczyzna nie tylko Polaków: Mniejszości narodowe w Polsce w latach 1918–1939* (Warsaw, 1985), p.10; Livezeanu, *Cultural Politics*, p. 10; and Sabin Manuilă and Wilhelm Filderman, *The Jewish Population in Romania During World War I* (Iaşi, 1994), p. 60.

5. Polonsky, *Politics in Independent Poland*, pp. 10, 25, 37, 38; and Rothschild, *East Central Europe*, p. 39.

6. Based on Livezeanu, *Cultural Politics*, pp. 9–10.

7. Tomaszewski, *Ojczyzna*, pp. 96–97; Szyja Bronsztein, "Polish-Jewish Relations as Reflected in Memoirs of the Interwar Period," in *Jews in Independent Poland, 1918–1939*, ed. Antony Polonsky et al. (London, 1994), p. 66; and D. Şandru, *Populaţia rurală României între cele două Războaie Mondiale* (Iaşi, 1980), pp. 53, 54.

8. Polonsky, *Politics in Independent Poland*, pp. 462–63, and Livezeanu, *Cultural Politics*, pp. 63–65, 139, 179–80.

9. There were, of course, some exceptions: in the city of Lviv, Ukrainian students were apparently also the target of a campaign to limit their numbers in the university. See Szymon Rudnicki, "From 'Numerus Clausus' to 'Numerus Nullus,'" in *From Shtetl to Socialism: Studies from Polin*, ed. Antony Polonsky (London, 1993), p. 360. Unlike the rest of his article, which is documented in detail, this campaign is not.

10. On the concept of identificational assimilation, see Celia Heller, "Poles of Jewish Background—The Case of Assimilation without Integration in Interwar Poland," in *Studies on Polish Jewry 1919–1939*, ed. Joshua Fishman (New York, 1974), pp. 258–61.

11. Polonsky, *Politics*, p. 360.

12. Janusz Żarnowski, *Struktura społeczna inteligencji w Polsce w latach 1918–1939* (Warsaw, 1964), pp. 170–71.

13. Yisrael Gutman, "Polish Antisemitism Between the Wars: An Overview," in *The Jews of Poland Between Two World Wars,* ed. Yisrael Gutman et al. (Hanover, NH, 1989), p. 101. Gutman is responding to certain scholars, among them some contemporary Polish historians, who point to the overall antiminority policies of interwar Polish governments in rejecting the idea of special antisemitic policies.

14. Raphael Mahler, "Jews in Public Service and the Liberal Professions in Poland, 1918–1939," *Jewish Social Studies*, 6(4) October 1944: 297 and passim.

15. Bronsztejn, "Polish-Jewish Relations," pp. 75–76.

16. For the Polish figures see Żarnowski, *Struktura*, p. 172; and Mahler, "Jews in Public Service," p. 341. For the Romanian figures, see Livezeanu, *Cultural Politics*, p. 238.

17. M. Popescu-Spineni, Iulian Peter, and Iosif Gabrea, "Organizaţia învăţământului în România," in *Enciclopedia României*, vol. 1 (Bucharest, 1938), p. 479.

18. Ibid., p. 480.

19. Rudnicki, "From 'Numerus Clausus,'" p. 360.

20. Polonsky, *Politics*, p. 359.

21. Celia Heller, *On the Edge of Destruction: Jews of Poland Between the Two World Wars* (New York, 1977), p. 119.

22. Rudnicki, "From 'Numerus Clausus,'" p. 360.

23. Heller, *On the Edge*, p. 120.

24. Ibid., p. 121; and Simon Segal, *The New Poland and the Jews* (New York, 1938), p. 198.

25. Polonsky, *Politics*, pp. 361–62.

26. Some of this agitation in Poland was primarily anti-*Sanacja*. See Polonsky, *Politics*, pp. 360–61.

27. Paweł Korzec, "Antisemitism in Poland as an Intellectual, Social, and Political Movement," in *Studies on Polish Jewry 1919–1939*, ed. Fishman, p. 81; and Livezeanu, *Cultural Politics*, pp. 268–69.

28. See Livezeanu, *Cultural Politics*, pp. 240–43.

29. See Irina Livezeanu, "Between State and Nation: Romanian Lower-Middle-Class Intellectuals in the Interwar Period," in *Splintered Classes: Politics and the Lower Middle Classes in Interwar Europe*, ed. Rudy Koshar (New York, 1990), pp. 179–80.

30. Yad Vashem Archives (henceforth YV) P–6/30, "The Situation in Roumania," September 1937, p. 122; and Alliance Israélite Universelle archives (henceforth AIU), Roumanie IX C 61, 11 February 1937.

31. Segal, *The New Poland*, p. 199; and Rudnicki, "From 'Numerus Clausus,'" p. 375.

32. Rudnicki, "From 'Numerus Clausus,'" p. 375.

33. Korzec, "Antisemitism in Poland," pp. 94–95; and Rudnicki, "From 'Numerus Clausus,'" pp. 360, 372–74.

34. See Livezeanu, *Cultural Politics*, "Chapter 7: From Student Movement to Iron Guard"; and "Les désordres juifs en Roumanie," *Paix et droit* February 1923.

35. On Polish fascism see Henryk Wereszycki, "Fascism in Poland" and Piotr Wandycz, "Fascism in Poland: 1918–1939" in *Native Fascism in the Successor States, 1918–1945*, ed. Peter Sugar (Santa Barbara, 1971). Wereszycki coins the term "semi-fascism" to describe the "system of government in Poland between 1926 and 1939" (p. 85), while Wandycz writes that Polish fascism existed "on the margins of Poland's political life," as it "went against the long tradition of Polish ideals of freedom, individualism, and toleration" (p. 97).

36. Korzec, "Antisemitism in Poland," pp. 80 ff; and Mahler, "Jews in Public Service," p. 310. Mahler applies the term specifically to the Camp of National Unity.

37. Sugar, *Native Fascism*, p. 90; Jerzy Tomaszewski, ed., *Najnowsze dzieje Żydów w Polsce: w zarysie (do 1950 roku)* (Warsaw, 1993) cited in William Hagen, "Before the 'Final Solution': Toward a Comparative Analysis of Political Anti-Semitism in Interwar Poland," *The Journal of Modern History* 68 (June 1996): 375–76.

38. Sugar, *Native Fascism*, pp. 95–97.

39. Polonsky, *Politics*, p. 281.

40. Mahler, "Jews in Public Service," p. 310.

41. Ibid.

42. Ibid., pp. 297, 301–302.

43. Ibid., pp. 313–25.

44. Ibid., pp. 311–12.

45. Żarnowski, *Struktura społeczna*, pp. 223–24, and Korzec, "Antisemitism in Poland," p. 97.

46. Korzec, "Antisemitism in Poland," p. 96.

47. Mahler, "Jews in Public Service," pp. 329–33.

48. Chone Shmeruk, "Hebrew-Yiddish-Polish: A Trilingual Jewish Culture," in *Jews of Poland*, ed. Gutman et al., p. 311.

49. AIU XI C 61, October 14, 1937.

50. AIU VIII C 58, end of 1935, "L'Hitlerisme gagne du terrain en Roumanie."

51. AIU IX C 59, no date.

52. *Monitorul Oficial*, 23 January 1935, about decision no. 93.179 of 21 January 1935. Cited in AIU IX C 59, no date; AIU IX C 60, February 1936; and AIU IX C 61, 5 July 1937.

53. AIU VIII C 57, 29 September, 1934; Report by Philippe Erlanger after a visit of several weeks to Romania, AIU IX C 59, 1935; and AIU IX C 59, 24 March, 1935.

54. Report on Pamfil Șeicaru's address to the government of 29 January 1935, in AIU IX C 59, no date; and Report from Emil Fagure, former MP and director of the democratic daily newspaper *Lupta*, in AIU IX C 61, July 1937. Șeicaru was the director of the right-wing daily *Curentul*. Z. Ornea, *Anii treizeci: Extrema dreaptă românească* (Bucharest, 1995), p. 158.

55. AIU VIII C 58, end 1935.

56. P. Manolescu, "Avocații și ideea românizării barourilor,"*Curentul* 24 February 1937.

57. Ioan V. Gruia, "Baroul românesc," in *Enciclopedia României*, vol. 1, p. 360.

58. P. Manolescu, "Avocații"; and Ornea, *Anii treizeci,* p. 158.

59. P. Manolescu, "Avocații."

60. Gruia, "Baroul românesc," p. 360.

61. Ibid. (Italics in the original.)

62. Madeleine Coulon, *De graves événements dans le Barreau Roumain* (Paris, 1937), p. 10.

63. Ibid., p. 10.

64. Paul Shapiro, "Prelude to Dictatorship in Romania: The National Christian Party in Power, December 1937–February 1938," *Canadian-American Slavic Studies* 1974 (Spring): 70–71.

65. Mária Kovács, *Liberal Professions and Illiberal Politics: Hungary from the Habsburgs to the Holocaust* (Washington, DC, 1994).

66. Shapiro, "Prelude to Dictatorship" pp. 45–88. Shapiro points out that even Tătărăscu was increasingly antisemitic and pro-German, and that Goga was the Nazis' favorite Romanian politician; they were undoubtedly his financial sponsors.

67. Ibid., pp. 66–69.

68. Mihail Sebastian, *Jurnal 1935–1944* (Bucharest, 1996), p. 137 (29 December 1937); and Shapiro, "Prelude to Dictatorship," p. 72.

69. Sebastian, *Jurnal*, p. 138, 30 December 1937.

70. Shapiro, "Prelude to Dictatorship," pp. 72–73.

71. AIU IX C 62, January 1938.

72. Shapiro, "Prelude to Dictatorship," p. 74.

73. AIU IX C 62, 10 September 1938.

74. Wilhelm Filderman, the president of the Union of Romanian Jews, reported in July 1938 that both school textbooks and books given to honor roll students as end-of-year prizes had antisemitic content. Among the publications distributed to students as prizes was the annual of the Legionnaire magazine *Sfarmă Piatră*; and this after the Legion's dissolution. Ibid., 26 July 1938.

75. Korzec, "Antisemitism in Poland," p. 93; and Roos, *A History*, pp. 146–48.

76. Jerzy Holzer, "Polish Political Parties and Antisemitism," in *Jews in Independent Poland*, ed. Polonsky et al., p. 199.

77. Ibid., p. 199.

78. Korzec, "Antisemitism in Poland," pp. 95, 98–99, and Zygmund Szymanowski, "The Antisemitism of Academic Youth," excerpted in *Stranger in Our Midst: Images of the Jew in Polish Literature*, ed. Harold Segel (Ithaca, 1996), p. 332.

79. Ezra Mendelsohn, *The Jews of East Central Europe Between the World Wars* (Bloomington, 1987), pp. 70–74.

80. Quoted in Polonsky, *Politics*, p. 424.

81. See Col. Kowalewski's statement in *Gazeta Polska*, 22 April 1937, cited in Polonsky, *Politics*, p. 427.

82. Nichifor Crainic, "Spiritul autohton," *Gândirea* 17(4) April 1938: 164.

83. On the Criterion group constituted briefly in 1932 around Mircea Eliade and his associates, see Liviu Antonesei, "Le moment Criterion—un modèle d'action culturelle," in *Culture and Society: Structures, Interfer-*

ences, Analogies in the Modern Romanian History, ed. Al. Zub (Iaşi, 1985), passim.

84. Maria Alexandrescu Vianu and Vlad Alexandrescu, eds., *Scrisori către Tudor Vianu: II (1936–1949)* (Bucharest, 1994), p. 274.

85. Zygmunt Bauman, "Exit Visas and Entry Tickets: Paradoxes of Jewish Assimilation," *Telos* 77 (1988): 75.

86. Magdalena Opalski, *"Wiadomości Literackie*: Polemics on the Jewish Question, 1924–1939," in Gutman et al., *The Jews of Poland,* p. 435 and passim.

87. Ibid., pp. 436–37.

88. Ibid., p. 449.

89. Czesław Miłosz, *The History of Polish Literature,* 2nd ed. (Berkeley, 1983), pp. 389, 393–95, 405–408; and Madeline Levine, "Julian Tuwim: 'We, the Polish Jews. . . ,'" *The Polish Review* 17(4) Autumn 1972.

90. Sebastian, *Jurnal,* p. 224.

91. Ibid., p. 231.

92. Ibid., p. 556.

93. Ibid., p. 558.

94. Ibid., pp. 561, 564, 574.

Private Property Comes to Russia: The Reign of Catherine II [1]

RICHARD PIPES

Private property in land and in other productive assets, along with civil rights for a privileged minority, first made their appearance in Russia in the second half of the eighteenth century.

The earliest measure to sound the death knell of the patrimonial regime was a 1762 manifesto issued by Peter III which exempted the Russian dvorianstvo in perpetuity from obligatory state service.[2] With one stroke of the pen, and apparently in a quite casual manner, the new emperor annulled the work of his predecessors of the preceding 300 years. The ruling did not immediately alter the country's political and social structure because the great majority of dvoriane were too poor to take advantage of it. Most had neither land nor serfs; of those fortunate enough to possess both, 59 percent had fewer than 20 serfs and only 16 percent more than 100, the number considered the minimum to afford the life of a country squire.[3] The majority of dvoriane, therefore, had no choice but to remain in state service and draw a salary. An important principle, however, had been introduced: henceforth, Russia had a class of free subjects, independent of the state.

The Manifesto of 1762 left undefined the status of the land and the serfs working on it. It could have been interpreted to mean that the Crown turned over the dvorianstvo's estates into its outright property, since it did not require nobles who left the service to surrender their estates. For all practical purposes—though not as yet legally—they now held the land unconditionally. In 1752, Elizabeth had ordered a General Land Survey to determine the boundaries of towns, villages, and estates, a measure which would have led to the landlords' being recognized as de facto owners of their land. The undertaking was not realized, however, until 1765. Landlords in possession of estates were recognized as de jure owners without having to present documentary proof of ownership.[4] In 1769 the Senate laid it down, using rather clumsy terminology, in response to one landlord's petition, that "all private (*vladel'cheskie*) lands . . . belong in property (*sobstvenno*) to the possessors."[5] Two edicts issued in 1782 ruled that the "property rights" of the owners of estates were not confined to the surface of the land but extended to the subsoil, bodies of water, and forests.[6] These *ukazy* seemed to take it for granted that the land belonged to the nobles, and provide evidence that in Russia land was being transformed from possession into property.

The property rights of dvoriane to the land were formally confirmed in 1785 by Catherine II in the "Charter of Rights, Freedoms and Prerogatives of the

Noble Russian Dvorianstvo," one of the most consequential legislative acts in Russian history.[7] The Charter recognized that the dvoriane owned outright their landed estates and enjoyed, in addition, guarantees of civil rights. The recognition came some 600 years after the English monarchy had granted similar rights to its subjects. The reason for this drastic change in attitude toward an institution in which until then the Russian monarchy had seen nothing but a threat to its authority was both political and ideological.

Catherine, who had gained the crown in a coup that cost the life of her husband, Peter III, being both an usurper and a foreigner, felt highly insecure. She consciously—and successfully—sought to consolidate her authority by winning the loyalty of the dvorianstvo at the expense of the other social groups. To bolster the throne, she took the landed gentry into something like a partnership. The need for such an alliance became especially urgent after the peasant rebellion of 1773–1775 under the leadership of the Cossack Emelian Pugachev. This uprising made Catherine aware of her government's weak hold on its far-flung realm and persuaded her to rely on the dvorianstvo as an auxiliary administrative staff, with virtually unlimited authority over its peasantry.

As she knew from the *cahiers* which dvoriane had submitted to the Legislative Commission convened in 1767 to give Russia a new code of laws, a major source of their dissatisfaction was the legally precarious status of their estates. The Moscow gentry, for example, requested that "the right of ownership (*sobstvennost'*) for both inherited and purchased estates be clearly defined." Other petitions sought confirmation that dvoriane owned their immovable properties as unconditionally as their personal belongings.[8] A commission was set up to deal with these questions. It proposed that nobles, and they alone, be recognized as having absolute property rights to their estates, while commoners' rights were restricted.[9] These recommendations were incorporated into the 1785 Charter.

Considerations of *raison d'état* and personal self-interest of the Empress received reinforcement from contemporary intellectual currents in the West, familiar to Catherine from her wide reading, which saw in private property the foundation of prosperity. Like Peter I, Catherine was well aware of the importance of the national economy for the country's power and prestige; but unlike Peter, who was a disciple of Mercantilism with its emphasis on the directing role of the state, she fell under the influence of the Physiocrats and their doctrines of economic liberalism. The theories of the Physiocrats, who regarded private property as the most fundamental of the laws of nature and agriculture as the principal source of wealth, played a part in influencing her to introduce to Russia ownership of land.

Sobstvennost', the Russian word for property, entered the vocabulary of official documents during Catherine's reign, being a translation of the German *Eigentum (Egindum)* which had come into usage in Germany as early as 1230.[10] It appeared in the 1767 Instruction (*Nakaz*) to the Procurator-General laying down the principles that were to guide preparations of the new Code of

Laws: here Catherine defined the purpose of Civil Law as "protecting and making secure the property of every citizen."[11] Articles 295 and 296 of the *Nakaz* read as follows:

> Agriculture cannot flourish where neither the cultivator nor laborer has anything of his own. This rests on a very simple principle: "Every man is more concerned with what belongs to him, than with what is another's, and does not take care of that which he fears someone may take away from him.[12]

The key article (no. 22) of the Noble Charter reads:

> The noble who is the first legally to acquire an estate is granted the full power and freedom to make a gift of it, or to bequeath it, or to confer it as a dowry or a living, or to transfer it, or to sell it to whomsoever he chooses. Inherited estates, however, cannot be disposed of otherwise than as provided by law.[13]

An important and innovative clause in the Charter decreed that the inherited estate of a noble convicted of a grave crime was not to be confiscated but turned over to his legitimate heirs (Article 23). Henceforth, noble properties could not be seized without court judgment.[14] Nobles were entitled to found factories and markets in their villages (Articles 28–29) and to acquire urban real estate (Article 30). Their exemption from personal taxes was confirmed (Article 36) and they were freed of the obligation of billeting soldiers in their rural residences (Article 35).

Although Catherine applied the teachings of the Physiocrats only to the upper class, it did not escape her and some of her more thoughtful contemporaries that they were germane to peasants as well. From the middle of the eighteenth century voices were heard arguing that peasants would be more productive and tranquil if given freedom along with title to the land they cultivated.[15] An international contest launched in 1766 by the St. Petersburg Free Economic Society on her initiative for the best response to the question whether the peasant should own the land which he cultivated, awarded the first prize to a Frenchman, Béarde de l'Abbaye, who answered affirmatively on the grounds that 100 peasant-proprietors would outproduce 2,000 serfs.[16] In the Legislative Assembly opponents of peasant land ownership did not deny the advantages of ownership, but maintained that if peasants were given title to their land they would soon lose it and find themselves destitute.[17]

In her Instruction (Article 261) Catherine hinted that it would be beneficial to grant property rights to serfs (whom she called "slaves"—*raby*). In her notes was found a proposal that all Russian subjects born during and after 1785, the year of the Noble Charter, be treated as freemen. She also drafted a proposal—never acted on—that would allow state peasants to acquire as property unpopulated land.[18]

The effect of such debates and proposals was to raise in Russia for the first time the issue of serfdom and, as a corollary, the question of private property for the common people. The initiative in both instances came from the crown. If, despite influential opinion favoring such a course, serfs were neither freed nor given land it was because considerations of state security, which demanded the support of the gentry, outweighed those of economic progress. It was only a century later, when serfdom came to be seen as a threat to state security, that tsarism ventured on emancipation.

With property rights came personal rights.

According to the 1785 Charter, nobles were not to be deprived of life, title, or property except by the judgment of their peers (Articles 2, 5, 8, 10–12). They were exempt from corporal punishment (Article 15) and permitted to travel abroad as well as to enroll in the service of friendly foreign powers (Article 19).[19] The Charter reaffirmed that nobles did not have to serve the state except in times of national emergency (Article 20). The 36 articles of the first part of the Noble Charter were a veritable Bill of Rights which created, for the first time in Russia, a class of persons whose life, personal liberty, and properties were guaranteed.

It was a revolutionary measure in the fullest and most constructive sense of the word that set the direction of Russia's development for the next 130 years. In their totality, its provisions proved far more innovative than the superficial efforts at Westernization of Peter I which copied Western techniques and manners while ignoring the spirit of Western civilization. True, Catherine's Charter bestowed rights and freedoms on a small minority only: but as Western history demonstrates, general freedoms and rights usually originate in minority privileges. It has proven to be the most reliable way of implanting freedom and rights because it gives rise to social groups interested in protecting their advantages. Thus ancient Athens, the home of modern democratic ideas and institutions, granted liberties to a minority of landowners and denied them to slaves and foreign-born freemen, who constituted the bulk of the city-state's professionals, businessmen, and artisans. The Magna Carta, the foundation stone of English liberties, was a feudal charter benefiting England's barons, not the nation at large. It was demonstrably exclusive:

> Liberties were always attached to particular persons or places; there was nothing general or national about them. They were definite concrete privileges, which some people enjoyed, but most did not . . . it was because they were rare privileges and not common rights that the framers of Magna Carta set so much store upon liberties.[20]

The same held true of the burghers of West European cities who extracted for themselves immunities and other rights from kings and lords, rights which in many ways provided the foundation of modern freedoms: but these, too, originated in exclusive privileges.[21] Freedom of speech had its origin in the exclusive rights granted by the English crown around the fifteenth century to members of the House of Commons.[22] The prerogatives of the fortunate few provide a model for the rest of the population. Once the principle of absolute private property had been established in Russia, therefore, it was only a matter of time before it would be extended to the population at large.

This said, it must be noted that the introduction of landed property into Russia was a mixed blessing because it was purchased at the expense of the serfs. Although the 1785 Charter referred only to land and made no reference to serfs, it had the effect of turning the latter—tied as they were to the land—into the private property of their landlords. Proprietary serfs constituted at the time approximately one-half of the country's population. Since the tsarist authorities neither laid down any rules governing the powers of the landlords over their serfs nor intervened on the serfs' behalf, they effectively surrendered sovereignty over one-half of the country's population to private interests: not surprisingly, in conversation with the French philosophe, Denis Diderot, Catherine referred to serfs as the "subjects" of their masters.[23]

Private property in Russia, therefore, spelled, besides freedom and rights for the few, intensified serfdom for the many. For the serfs private property became anything but a liberating force, and this historic fact had a negative effect on property's reception in Russia. In the words of Richard Wortman:

> From its inception, the right of property [in Russia] became associated with the consolidation of the nobility's power over the peasants and the abuses of the serf system . . . The property rights bestowed by the tsarist regime became identified with its despotic authority.[24]

Indeed, the bestowal of property rights on the gentry would prove to be a major obstacle to the abolition of serfdom. For both in practice and in law, the serfs were considered since 1785 to belong to their landlords: Mikhail Speransky, the chief minister of Alexander I in drafting his constitutional project of 1809, thought so;[25] and so did Sergei Lanskoi, the minister of the interior at the beginning of Alexander II's reign when discussions of serf emancipation got seriously underway.[26]

In the eighteenth century, landlords acquired virtually unlimited power over their serfs. They had toward them only one obligation, and that was to feed them in time of crop failures. Their authority over them precluded only three actions: depriving serfs of life, beating them with the knout (a form of punishment often tantamount to execution), and torturing them. Their powers included the following:[27]

1. They had right to exploit serf labor at will. Several attempts were made to persuade landlords to define the labor obligations of their serfs, but these were never formally enacted.

2. They had (somewhat ambiguous) right to sell serfs. Although Peter I criticized the practice of selling serfs without land ("like cattle"), he passed no law forbidding it and in fact encouraged it himself by authorizing dvoriane to sell peasants to other dvoriane to serve as recruits.[28] Thus, until 1843 when the practice was outlawed, serfs were commonly

sold and bought, with their families but sometimes also individually. Landlords also had the right (with government or court permission) to transport serfs from one estate to another, no matter how distant, which the rich ones did by the thousands.

3. They could force serfs to marry against their will.

4. They could punish serfs in any way they saw fit short of depriving them of life. But since no means existed of supervising the many estates scattered throughout the empire, this prohibition was unenforceable.

5. Since 1760, they could exile serfs to Siberia for settlement[29] and from 1765 to 1807 for hard labor (*katorga*).[30] They could also turn them over to the army for lifelong military service.

6. They owned—legally—all the assets of their serfs.

If, nevertheless, Russian serfs even at the nadir of their condition, in the reign of Catherine II, did not sink to the status of black slaves in the Americas, the reason is to be found in the backwardness of the Russian economy and in the constraints of custom.

Unlike the slave plantations of the West Indies and the southern United States, which worked for the market, Russian landed estates were largely self-sufficient household economies which consumed most of what they produced. They were, therefore, managed in a less demanding manner. The Russian landlord did not care to squeeze the utmost from his laborers by rationalizing agriculture and subjecting his serfs to close supervision. If his serfs paid quitrent, he knew that he would profit most by relying on their own enterprise. If they owed him services (*corvée*), then he faced a natural limit on what he could demand, because unless the serf was allowed to tend to his own fields he would have to be fed. There was no particular interest in obtaining a surplus since there was no market for it. As a rule, Russian serf-owners were more interested in securing minimum returns than in maximizing them, for which reason they were quite willing to let the peasants run their own affairs. The serfs' personal belongings and the fruits of their labor were with few exceptions treated as their own.[31] Indeed, some landlords are known to have helped their serfs circumvent the law by allowing them to buy, in their name, land—even land populated by other serfs: the serfs of one of Russia's richest magnates, Count Sheremetev, owned over 600 serfs.[32] Finally, serfs were "liable to taxation and military service: not benefits, to be sure, but not characteristic of slavery either."[33]

The other factor restraining the landlord's authority over his serfs was the peasant commune. It was in the interest of the landlord to maintain the authority of the commune since it ensured, by the device of collective responsibility, the collection of the soul tax, for which the state held him liable, and rents. The commune, for its part, up to a point could protect the peasant household from landlord interference. A certain equilibrium thus came into being between the theoretically boundless authority of the landlord and the de facto restraints imposed on it by economic realities, custom, and the commune, none of which played any part on slave plantations.

Perceived as self-serving license for the few rather than a basic human right, and moreover acquired at the expense of millions of human chattel, private property in tsarist Russia found few champions, even among conservatives and liberals. It was widely viewed as an enemy of both freedom and social justice. Russian liberals and liberal-conservatives throughout the last century of tsarism stressed law as the foundation of liberty, and failed to perceive a connection between law and private property. It is difficult to find among the theorists and publicists of the late imperial era anyone prepared to defend private property as a natural right and basis of political liberty.[34] Nor has any Russian historian seen it worthwhile up to now to investigate the history of private property in his country.

Russian peasants did not acknowledge that the land was anyone's property but the state's, i.e., the tsar's, and for that reason they never reconciled themselves to the provisions of the 1785 Noble Charter which gave dvoriane land while exempting them from compulsory state service.[35] As far as they were concerned, the Charter robbed serfdom of its rationale inasmuch as their ancestors had been bonded in order to enable the nobles to fulfill their obligations to the tsar. Indeed, in their view *tiaglo* "was not a rent they paid the supreme owner of the land [i.e., the tsar] but the means of serving the government which it was their lot to perform."[36] Why should they continue serving, therefore, when their masters were no longer required to do so?

Catherine also introduced private property in urban real estate. In the "Charter of the Rights and Benefits of the Cities of the Russian Empire,"[37] issued concurrently with the Charter of the Nobility, all Russians living in cities were formed into a corporation, subject to the same duties and responsible to the same administrative and judicial authorities. The office of mayor was elective (Article 31). The urban population was divided into two estates, that of *kuptsy* or merchants, and that of *meshchane*, composed of artisans and tradesmen. The status of the latter resembled that of state peasants in that they bore, collectively, the same obligations, but they were able, by accumulating enough money, to move into the ranks of the merchant class. The merchants, whose status was determined by their capital, received various commercial privileges. The Charter established that urban inhabitants of both categories could own and enjoy undisturbed both movable and immovable properties (Article 4). Nobles who owned real estate in the cities were, from the administrative point of view, treated analogously with commoners, but they did not pay taxes or render *tiaglo* services (Article 13). The cities were formally self-governing, but in fact remained under government supervision.[38] The very first article of the City Charter declared that new cities could be built only in accordance with plans approved by Her Majesty.

It soon turned out that one could not create an urban culture by government fiat. Russian cities developed slowly, for trade was meager: as late as the middle of the nineteenth century, of the approximately one thousand localities designated as towns, 878 had fewer than 10,000 inhabitants and only 2 had more than 150,000.[39] In the final decades of the old regime, the majority of Russia's urban residents consisted of peasant peddlers and the unemployed looking for work. Russian cities were swamped by rural migrants who had neither legal urban status nor steady employment: around 1900, in the empire's two largest cities, St. Petersburg and Moscow, nearly two-thirds of the inhabitants were peasants on temporary residence permits.[40]

Private property in assets other than real estate was encouraged by laws passed in the middle of the eighteenth century under the inspiration of Physiocratic theories. They resulted in the abolition of the numerous state monopolies on manufacture and trade in force since Peter I. In 1762, Peter III removed most restrictions on trade, including commerce in cereals which had been a royal prerogative. In 1762 and again in 1775, Catherine II annulled prohibitions on unlicensed manufacture by allowing Russians of all estates to found factories. The main beneficiaries of these measures were dvoriane, who took advantage of their tax-free status and access to serf labor (now their exclusive privilege) to pursue manufacture and commerce. Before long, most of the industries in Russia were located in the countryside, on or near noble estates. Serfs also benefited from the new economic liberties because landlords, hoping for higher rents, encouraged them to branch out to occupations other than agriculture. In the first half of the nineteenth century, certain sectors of Russian industry as well as retail commerce fell into the hands of serfs. Some of them became millionaires. In the eyes of the law, bonded entrepreneurs had no property guarantees: their landlords could, and occasionally did, appropriate their assets.[41] But such actions were exceptional. The net effect of the laws privatizing industry and commerce was to stimulate and enhance private property in Russia, although the main beneficiary was not the middle, urban class as much as the landlord and the peasant.

NOTES

1. This essay is excerpted from my book, *Property & Freedom* (New York, 1999).

2. *Polnoe sobranie zakonov Rossiiskoi Imperii, s 1649 goda* Series I (covering 1649–11 December 1825) (henceforth *PSZ*) 1st ed., 45 vols. (St. Petersburg, 1830–), vol. 15, no. 11,444 (18 February 1762), pp. 912–15.

3. Richard Pipes, *Russia under the Old Regime* (London and New York, 1974), p. 178.

4. A. Omel'chenko, *"Zakonnaia monarkhiia" Ekateriny Vtoroi: prosveshchennyi absoliutizm v Rossii* (Moscow, 1993), pp. 29, 211. According to A. Kizevetter in *Istoricheskie siluety: liudi i sobytiia* (Berlin, 1931), pp. 47–48, Russian landlords were very pleased with these surveys.

5. *PSZ*, vol. 18, no. 13,235 (19 January, 1769), p. 805.

6. *PSZ*, vol. 21, no. 15,447 (June 28, 1782), pp. 613–15, and no. 15,518 (September 22, 1782), p. 676.

7. *PSZ*, vol. 22, no. 16,187 (21 April 1785), pp. 344–58. A partial English translation is in *Imperial Russia: A Source Book, 1700–1917*, ed. Basil Dmytryshyn, 2nd ed. (Hinsdale, IL, 1974), pp. 108–11.

8. V. N. Latkin, *Zakonodatel'nye kommissii v Rossii v XVIII st.*, vol. 1 (St. Petersburg, 1887), pp. 303–304.

9. Omel'chenko, *"Zakonnaia monarkhiia,"* pp. 178–79.

10. Heinrich Altrichter, *Wandlungen des Eigentumsbegriffs und neuere Ausgestaltung des Eigentumsrechts* (Marburg-Lahn, 1930), pp. 1–2.

11. *PSZ*, vol. 18, no. 12,950 (30 July 1767), Art. 10, p. 282.

12. N. D. Chechulin, ed., *Nakaz Imperatritsy Ekateriny II* (St. Petersburg, 1907), p. 86.

13. The last clause makes obeisance to the ancient tradition which accorded the relatives of the owner of hereditary *votchiny* the right over 40 years to repurchase properties sold to outsiders. The limitations mentioned in Article 22 were not legally defined until 1823 (V. N. Latkin, *Uchebnik istorii russkogo prava perioda imperii*, 2nd ed., St. Petersburg, 1909, pp. 538–39). The complicated rules concerning the disposal rights by testament of inherited (or patrimonial) land in the eighteenth and nineteenth centuries and Russian jurists' attempts to revise them in favor of outright individual property are discussed in William G. Wagner, *Marriage, Property, and Law in Late Imperial Russia* (Oxford, 1994), pp. 227–377.

14. And yet, respect for law was so weakly developed in Russia that in the reign of Catherine's grandson, Alexander I, when the government took

over large areas to settle military colonists—soldiers on active duty who in peacetime supported themselves by agriculture—landlords with estates in these areas were summarily evicted and given land elsewhere. See Richard Pipes, *Russia Observed* (Boulder, CO, 1989), p. 88.

15. See V. I. Semevskii, *Krest'ianskii vopros v Rossii v XVIII i pervoi polovine XIX veka,* 2 vols. (St. Petersburg, 1888), vol. 1, pp. 196–222 and passim.

16. P. A. Khromov, *Ekonomicheskoe razvitie Rossii* (Moscow, 1967), p. 77.

17. V. Iakushkin, *Ocherki po istorii russkoi pozemel'noi politiki v XVIII i XIX vv.,* vol. 1 (Moscow, 1890), p. 192.

18. M. F. Vladimirskii-Budanov, *Obzor istorii russkogo prava,* 4th ed. (St. Petersburg–Kyiv, 1905), p. 247; Omel'chenko, *"Zakonnaia monarkhiia,"* pp. 236–38.

19. Catherine's son and successor to the throne, Paul I, suspended during his reign this provision of the Charter by making nobles convicted of crimes subject to corporal punishment. They were divested of their noble status which automatically exempted them from the privileges embodied in the Noble Charter.

20. A. F. Pollard, *The Evolution of Parliament,* 2nd ed. (London, 1926), pp. 169, 171.

21. Robert von Keller, *Freiheitsgarantien für Person und Eigentum im Mittelalter* (Heidelberg, 1933), p. 68.

22. William H. Riker, "Civil Rights and Property Rights," in Ellen Frankel Paul and Howard Dickman, eds., *Liberty, Property, and the Future of Constitutional Development* (Albany, NY, 1990), pp. 51–52.

23. I. K. Luppol, *Deni Didro* (Moscow, 1960), p. 107.

24. In Olga Crisp and Linda Edmondson, eds., *Civil Rights in Imperial Russia* (Oxford, 1989), p. 16.

25. *Plan gosudarstvennogo preobrazovaniia Grafa M. M. Speranskogo* (Moscow, 1905), p. 305.

26. S. S. Tatishchev, *Imperator Aleksandr II: ego zhizn' i tsarstvovanie,* 2 vols. (St. Petersburg, 1903), vol. 1, p. 308.

27. The following information is based on Latkin, *Uchebnik istorii russkogo prava perioda imperii,* pp. 212–32, and Vladimirskii-Budanov, *Obzor,* pp. 245–47.

28. *PSZ,* vol. 6, no. 3,669 (29 October 1720), p. 252.

29. *PSZ,* vol. 15, no. 11,166 (13 December 1760), pp. 582–84, and no. 11,216 (15 March 1761), pp. 665–66.

30. *PSZ*, vol. 17, no. 12,311 (17 January 1765), p. 10.

31. Commenting on Catherine's Instruction in which she spoke of the desirability of the peasants' owning the land they tilled (Article 295) Prince M. M. Shcherbatov, a leader of the conservative nobility, wrote: "Although the Russian peasants are slaves of their masters, although the land they cultivate belongs to their landlords, who also have the right to their personal belongings, no one, inspired by his own interest, would take the personal property and land of the peasants, and the peasants to this day do not feel that these [objects] are not their property. The assertion [*vterzhenie*] of such ideas has been the cause of various rebellions, including the present one of Pugachev, and the killing of many landlords by their peasants . . . " M. M. Shcherbatov, *Neizdannye proizvedeniia* (Moscow, 1935), pp. 55–56.

32. Khromov, *Ekonomicheskoe razvitie*, pp. 69–70.

33. Geoffrey Hosking, *Russia: People and Empire, 1552–1917* (Cambridge, MA, 1997), p. 200.

34. A notable exception was the liberal Boris Chicherin: see his *Sobstvennost' i gosudarstvo*, 2 vols. (Moscow, 1882–1883). But Chicherin, an immensely learned man given to writing turgid prose, had little influence on public opinion, in good measure probably because of this unpopular position. On Russian thinkers' attitude to property, see K. Isupov and I. Savkin, eds., *Russkaia filosofiia sobstvennosti XVIII–XX vv.* (St. Petersburg, 1993).

35. Victor Leontovitsch, *Geschichte des Liberalismus in Russland* (Frankfurt am Main, 1957), p. 165.

36. Iu. Iakhshiian, "Ownership in Russian Peasant Mentality," in V. P. Danilov, L. V. Milov et al., eds., *Mentalitet i agrarnoe razvitie Rossii XIX–XX vv.* (Moscow, 1996), p. 92.

37. *PSZ*, vol. 22, no. 16,188 (21 April 1785), pp. 358–84. (In this, the first edition of the *PSZ*, this edict was mistakenly assigned the number 16,187, the same as the Nobility Charter.)

38. Iu. R. Klokman, V. P. Danilov, L. V. Milov et al., eds., *Sotsial'no-ekonomicheskaia istoriia russkogo goroda* (Moscow, 1967), p. 119.

39. Peter [*sic*] Miljukoff [Petr Miliukov] in *Vierteljahrschrift für Sozial- und Wirtschaftsgeschichte* 14(1) 1916, doc. 135. In the words of Max Weber, "until the abolition of serfdom, a city like Moscow resembled a large Oriental city from approximately the age of Diocletian: spent there were rents of the land and serf owners and incomes from offices." *Grundriss der Sozialökonomik: III. Wirtschaft und Gesellschaft*, vol. 2, pt. 2, 3rd ed. (Tübingen, 1947), p. 585.

40. Joseph Bradley, "Patterns of Peasant Migration to Late Nineteenth-Century Moscow: How Much Should We Read into Literacy Rates?" *Russian History/Histoire Russe* 6(1) 1979: 22.

41. Pipes, *Russia under the Old Regime*, pp. 212–15.

The Revolutionary Crisis of 1846–1849 and Its Place in the Development of Nineteenth-Century Galicia

ANTONY POLONSKY

> Sir noble, you with your high words
> Too ready seem.'Twere best today
> No more of "forty-six" to say.
> 'Twas you yourselves, you Polish lords,
> Who first shot down the serfs, poor folk!
> Yourselves brought down the storm which broke
> Upon your heads, as your just due.
> Yes noble Sir! Had lords like you
> But looked upon your serfs as men,
> They never would have tried to do
> You harm, but would have helped you then.
> You never think of that at all.
> You make their life a constant hell,
> Yet you as constantly rebel
> When your own selfish interests call.
> But let the Tsisar justly try
> To treat both lord and serf, the cry
> Of confiscated rights you raise
> And swear the people him mislead.
>
> *Ivan Franko,* "The Passing of Serfdom"[1]

The importance of the revolution of 1848 cannot be overestimated. According to George Macaulay Trevelyan, the English liberal historian, 1848 was "the turning point at which modern history failed to turn."[2] Sir Lewis Namier, who was himself born in Koshylivtsi in east Galicia on the estate of his father, a Jewish landowner, referred to it as a "seedplot of history" and wrote that the revolution "crystallized ideas and projected the pattern of things to come; it determined the course of the century that followed."[3] Like most historians of 1848 in Central Europe, Trevelyan and Namier were preoccupied with the failure of the German liberals in Frankfurt to reconstruct Germany on liberal and constitutional principles. Certainly the Prussian king was unwilling to put himself at the head of the movement for German unification in 1848 while the Habsburg governing elite was able to exploit the divisions between "historic" and "non-historic" nations, between landlords and peasants, and between urban and rural revolutionaries to preserve its power. Yet, as Namier in particular has pointed out, the revolution in the Habsburg lands, even though it was unsuccessful in the short-run, highlighted many of the problems which were ultimately to lead to the collapse of the monarchy. In the Austrian province of Galicia it constituted a major turning point in the history of all three of the largest national groups to inhabit the area, the Ukrainians, the Poles, and the Jews.

The revolutionary crisis began here, not in 1848, but rather with the failed Polish revolution of 1846 and the violent peasant *jacquerie* that followed it in western Galicia, which led to the incorporation of the Free City of Cracow into the Habsburg monarchy. The years between 1846 and 1849 were characterized by four interrelated developments which I should like to examine in this article. They are the failure of the attempt by the Polish revolutionaries to regain the independence of Poland by armed insurrection, the emergence of the Ukrainians (then usually referred to as Ruthenians) of Galicia as a self-conscious national group, the final abolition in Galicia of the labor tribute, and the increased political mobilization of the Jewish population of the province. These phenomena were not only interrelated but were also affected by developments in the Habsburg monarchy as a whole and in the other parts of the former Polish-Lithuanian Commonwealth, and indeed by the progress and ultimate collapse of the revolutionary wave over most of Europe.

The crushing of the 1830 uprising in the Kingdom of Poland had been followed by the emigration of between 5,000 and 7,000 revolutionaries, most of whom eventually made their way to France. This "Great Emigration" included the poets Mickiewicz and Słowacki, the historian Lelewel, and the pianist and composer Chopin, as well as other prominent political and cultural leaders, statesmen, generals, and journalists. Most of its members were junior officers; regular soldiers in the army of the Kingdom of Poland had for the most part been forced to accept the Russian amnesty. As a consequence, 75 percent of the Emigration was of *szlachta* origin, though mostly without substantial means.

The members of the Emigration did not see themselves as defeated refugees. They were welcomed as heroes as they progressed through Germany and were convinced that they were the harbingers of an imminent international revolution which would destroy despotism and would make possible the resurrection of Poland within its 1772 frontiers, a goal which they all sought. It was in the years after 1831 that the "Polish Question" was to emerge as a major international problem although the Poles, unlike the Italians, the Germans, and even the Hungarians, did not succeed in the following generation in achieving national independence or unification.

The Emigration was deeply divided politically as the rifts which had already become manifest during the November uprising soon became even more apparent in the conditions of exile. The Conservatives were led by the great aristocrat Adam Czartoryski, who had been a key figure at the court of Tsar

Alexander I. He saw the Polish problem as, above all, a diplomatic question. His aim was to preserve the unity of the Poles in emigration in anticipation of a general European war, which would lead the Western powers, in their own interest, to reestablish Poland as a buffer against Russian expansionism. He hoped to create some links with Austria, whose policies in the Balkans seemed to be leading to a clash with Russia. Internally, he favored a constitutional monarchy and the slow emancipation of the peasantry by the granting of freeholds, with compensation for the nobility.

Czartoryski's left-wing opponents within the Emigration were organized in the Polish Democratic Society, founded in March 1832. Initially, its supporters were convinced that the resurrection of Poland was dependent on the European revolution which they thought to be imminent, and as a consequence, they participated in the activities of the Italian *Carbonari* and the French and German revolutionaries. In the words of one of their number, Józef Kajetan Janowski: "When the future of Poland depends upon the progress of humanity, then he who does not uphold the continuous progress of humanity, does not wish the happiness of Poland."[4]

With the collapse of the anticipated revolutions in 1833, there came a change in mood, and the left came increasingly to the view that only activity in Poland could bring about the restoration of a Polish state. As Joachim Lelewel wrote in January 1834: "It is my belief that the Polish nation cannot resurrect itself except at home and by its own forces . . . not counting upon [outside] help."[5]

By December 1836, the process of crystallization had reached the point at which a "Manifesto of the Polish Democratic Society" could be produced, described by Robert Leslie as "the most influential document in the history of Poland in the nineteenth century."[6] In its preamble, it asserted that Poland, long the bulwark of Europe in the East, had fallen on difficult times because the democratic principle "had degenerated into caste privilege depriving the masses of their just place in the constitution." This obsession with "caste privilege" was the main reason for the debacle of the 1830 uprising. If, during the insurrection, the Polish authorities had appealed to the masses,

> the people would have risen as one man, would have braced the gauntlet of war on their vigorous arm and crushed the invaders without foreign aid; Poland, from the Oder and the Carpathian mountains to the Borysthenes and the Dvina—from the Baltic to the Black Sea would have founded her independence upon the general happiness of her sons.

The manifesto continued:

> If our next revolution is not to be a sad repetition of the past, the first battle cry must be the emancipation of the people, their restoration, unconditionally to the ownership of the soil of which they have been plundered, the restitution of their rights, the admission of all, without distinction of birth or creed to the enjoyment of the blessings of independence.

As a consequence, the Democratic Society favored the emancipation of the peasantry without compensation being paid by the peasants, through the abolition of their obligations to their landlords and the granting to them of the freehold of the land which they at present cultivated. No provision was made for the landless, in accordance with the views of Wiktor Heltman, the chief theorist of the Society, who saw history as a struggle between the principles of individualism which tended to anarchy and collectivism which led to despotism. The goal was to create a class of self-sufficient farmers who could find a middle way between the dangers of anarchy and collectivism. Certainly a feature of the manifesto was its idealization of the Polish peasantry, of which its authors had only the scantest knowledge:

> The suffering people with us do not resemble the suffering people of western Europe; ours have not been contaminated by the corruption and selfishness of the privileged classes; they possess still all the simplicity of their ancient virtues, integrity, devotion, religious feelings, manners benign and pure. Upon a soil so fresh and untainted, and tilled by the honest arm of fraternity and liberty, the old national tree of equality will easily shoot up and flourish anew.

Like other conspiratorial organizations, the Democratic Society adopted a rigid and centralized system of organization, with its headquarters first in Poitiers and then, after 1840, in Versailles. Its goal was to send delegates to the Polish lands who could lead the expected revolutionary upsurge there. For the moment, it was clear that the Kingdom of Poland, exhausted by the insurrection of 1830 and subject to severe tsarist repression, was not suitable terrain for its activities. Neither was Prussian Poland, which was undergoing a major agricultural transformation following a Prussian government decree of 1823. This severed the connection between the village and manor through the cession by the former of a percentage of peasant land (between 33 and 50 percent) in return for freedom from labor dues. Although the Prussian legislation had originally been opposed by the more conservative landlords, it actually worked in favor of the landowners, so that most nobles in the province in the 1830s and 1840s were preoccupied with modernizing their estates. In addition, although a large class of impoverished landless laborers emerged as a consequence of the Prussian reform, it also led to the creation of a significant group of prosperous peasants who had nothing to gain from revolution. Under these circumstances, the main focus of revolutionary conspiracy in the 1830s and 1840s was Galicia, to which a significant number of refugees had moved after the failure of the 1830 Insurrection.

Galicia was in some ways fertile soil for this revolutionary activity. The province had been acquired somewhat reluctantly by the Habsburg monarchy as a result of the first partition of Poland in 1772, and the half-hearted measures of reform introduced there had led to considerable social disruption without creating any firm basis for stable rule. The Habsburg officials had seen the area as reminiscent of what their own state had been like before the reforms introduced under Maria Theresa and later under Joseph II. In their view, permeated as it was by the ideas of the Enlightenment, the problems of the area were essentially social, economic, and political, rather than national, although they were aware of the ethnic differences in the province. They saw Galician society in an extremely negative light. In their opinion, the dominance of the Polish nobility had created an economically unbalanced structure, characterized by exploitative relationships marked by extortion, graft, fraud, and the naked use of force. They were concerned with what they perceived as widespread idleness, dissipation, drunkenness, and the lack of genuine piety, and wanted to establish a "well-ordered police state" marked by social discipline and by the reeducation of the inhabitants of the province to improve their "moral character."[7] This was to be achieved by undermining the social and economic monopoly of power enjoyed by the Polish *szlachta,* by improving the position of the unfree peasantry, by encouraging reform in both the Roman and Greek Catholic churches in the province and by elevating the status of the latter, and by breaking up Jewish communal autonomy in order to transform the Jews into "useful subjects."

A whole series of reforms was introduced with these goals in mind, which undermined the position of the previously dominant elites. The local *sejmiki* as well as the elected municipal councils whose privileges had been guaranteed by Magdeburg law, were abolished and replaced by bureaucrats appointed from Vienna. A consultative Assembly of Estates was set up in Lviv, made up of representatives of the magnates, the gentry (referred to in the legislation as "knights"), and the clergy. It was similar to other such bodies in the Austrian provinces and it was solely advisory in character, with the right to send petitions to the emperor.

Real power in the province lay in the hands of the governor, who was appointed by the emperor, and who ruled through deputies heading the 19 districts (*Kreise*) into which the area was now divided. (One of these was Bukovyna, formerly under Turkish rule, which was governed as part of Galicia until 1848.) The previously privileged position of the nobility was undermined. Nobles lost their tax-exempt status and their control of the judicial system, and their control of their serfs was also now regulated by the state.

As elsewhere in the monarchy, the Austrians introduced the principle of religious toleration. This was of enormous significance for the previously oppressed Greek Catholic majority in the province. The Austrians now referred to the confession as "Greek Catholic" rather than as "Uniate," hoping in this way to raise its status. In 1784, they established a university in Lviv and created an Institute (the Studium Ruthenum) to train Greek Catholic priests. It originally used as its language of instruction a combination of Church Slavonic and the Ukrainian vernacular. In 1808, they reestablished the Greek Catholic Metropolitanate of Saint George in Lviv, which was divided into two eparchies based in Lviv and Przemyśl.

Attempts were also made to improve the position of the peasantry. Serfdom was abolished and landless peasants were allowed to leave the village, provided that they left behind a replacement. Landlords were also no longer able to evict peasants. Peasants were now allowed to marry without the permission of their landlord and to apprentice their children to a craft. Peasant land was not to be appropriated to domainal land and the judicial powers of the landlord were considerably reduced, with peasants given the right to make complaints to the local administration. Labor dues were now limited to three days a week in most cases. Joseph's attempt to replace the labor tribute entirely with a form of rent foundered in the face of aristocratic opposition. Nevertheless as a consequence of these changes the Galician peasant became, in the words of Roman Rozdolski, the foremost student of agrarian relations in the province, "at least an object of law, and not, as before, outside any law."[8]

Joseph also hoped to "reform" the Jewish population of Galicia, along the lines of the reforms he was introducing elsewhere in the monarchy. In return for a guarantee of the right to practice their religion and to dwell securely in the Empire, Joseph expected the Jews to diminish their "separateness" and transform their educational system and occupational structure so that they would become "useful and productive" subjects. In 1789, he promulgated a Toleration Edict for the Jews of Galicia similar to those which he had already issued to the Jews in Lower Austria, the Czech Lands, and Hungary. According to its preamble:

> The Monarch has found it necessary and useful to annul the differences which legislation has so far maintained between his Christian and Jewish subjects and to grant the Jews living in Galicia all the rights and liberties which our other subjects enjoy. Galician Jews will therefore from now on be treated like all other subjects as regards their rights and duties.[9]

The Jews were granted restricted civic (municipal) rights and attempts were made to "productivize" them in accordance with Physiocratic principles. In addition, a network of schools for young Jews was set up and Jews were also permitted to attend German or Polish schools. Jews were now obliged to take surnames and to keep their official records in German, while the scope of Jewish communal autonomy was severely restricted. Jews were also now obliged to serve in the army

The reforming drive of Joseph II did not withstand the widespread aristocratic and clerical opposition which it evoked in the Empire, in Hungary, the Czech lands, and the Austrian Netherlands. Fear of the French Revolution also led his successors, Leopold II (1790–1792), Franz II (1792–1835), and Ferdinand II (1835–1848) to abandon any serious attempts to reform the monarchy, although the abolition of serfdom and some of the centralizing policies were retained. Indeed, in the period after 1815 Franz and his principal minister, Metternich, became the main bulwarks of the attempt to restore the prerevolutionary order in Europe.

The half-hearted character of the reforms introduced by the Habsburgs in Galicia had the effect of significantly destabilizing the province. Those members of the *szlachta* whose claim to noble status was now called into question became increasingly disaffected. By the middle of the nineteenth century, only 30,454 people were recognized as having noble status in Galicia out of a total population of nearly five million (slightly more than 0.6 percent), an enormous reduction from the times of the Polish-Lithuanian Commonwealth when between 8 and 10 percent were recognized as noble.[10] Even in the first days of Austrian rule, the authorities had recognized the noble status of around 95,000 people (3.4 percent of the population).[11]

Moreover, in spite of their intentions, the reforms had not led to a significant improvement in the position either of the peasantry or of the Jews, and both groups remained significantly alienated. For the peasantry, the belief that they could count on the support of the state further undermined their willingness to accept the oppression of the manorial system. After Karol Borkowski, a Polish noble revolutionary, was captured in Galicia in the 1830s, he found himself placed under the guard of two Polish-speaking soldiers. When he remonstrated with them that they too were Poles, they replied, "Oh no, we are subjects of His Majesty the Emperor."[12]

Initally, the conspirators had little success. The majority of landlords felt that they had too much to lose, even though they protested their devotion to the Polish cause. There also developed, particularly among the great magnates, a movement analogous to that which had been established in the Grand Duchy of Poznań, which under the name of "organic work" was attempting to make use of the opportunities provided by Austrian rule to introduce reforms, largely of an economic nature, into the province. Its leader, Prince Leon Sapieha, saw his goal as the creation of those institutions which were necessary for the creation of a modern social system—savings banks, credit banks, schools, and railways. However, in Galicia the peasantry in the eastern part of the province was divided from the landlords by the deep religious and ethnic divide. Even in the western, largely Polish part of the province, national consciousness had had little impact as yet on the peasants. Thus the attempt in 1833 by Colonel Józef Zaliwski, who had come from Paris to spark a revolution among the peasantry by establishing small partisan detachments in Galicia and crossing the frontier into the Kingdom of Poland, failed utterly. So too did the attempt to establish small revolutionary groups linked with the *Carbonari* and with Joachim Lelewel's "Young Poland" movement. These groups, of which the most important was the Association of the Polish People (*Stowarzyszenie Ludu Polskiego*), set up in 1835 by an emissary of Young Poland, Szymon Konarski, were able to find support only among the petty intelligentsia in Lviv and the Free City of Cracow and among some estate officials. Symptomatic of the atmosphere which prevailed in this movement was the well-known revolutionary song "Cześć wam Panowie Magnaci," which condemned the upper classes for their half-measures in 1831 and threatened the nobility with the gallows should there be another uprising.

The self-confidence of the revolutionaries was considerably misplaced, as was evident even to some members of the Democratic Society. An emissary sent to Galicia, Seweryn Goszczyński, reported back to France on 27 December 1838 that revolutionary agitation would not succeed among the peasantry, among whom feelings of hostility towards the nobility were dominant, and that students, though enthusiastic, were too rash and inexperienced to be employed in conspiracy (though they would prove useful once the insurrection was under way). The only element among whom agitation was likely to prove successful was the nobility, both among those who owned land and among estate officials. On the basis of this report, the Central Committee instructed local cells to attempt to win over public opinion by the propagation of democratic ideas, particularly among the "enlightened classes." The goal should be the creation of conditions in which a revolutionary organization could be established in the country, to await a more propitious time for an insurrection. In spite of this caution the conspirators were easily detected by the Austrian secret police, and by the early 1840s all revolutionary activity had ceased in Galicia.[13]

Soon, however, conditions became more propitious for the revolutionaries. The economic difficulties of the 1840s increased the grievances of the peasantry both in the Grand Duchy of Poznań and in Galicia. In the former, the accession of the new Prussian king, Frederick William IV, led to the adoption of a more liberal policy. Flottwell's campaign of Germanization was abandoned and the extradition treaty with Russia allowed to lapse. In these conditions, many Poles from the other partitions came to the Grand Duchy, including some three thousand men seeking to avoid conscription in the Kingdom of Poland, and a number of revolutionary movements were established here which sought to advance the Polish cause by enlisting the support of the peasantry. This development of political activity in Poznania encouraged similar phenomena in western Galicia, particularly in the area around Tarnów.

The emergence of what seemed like a significant political movement in Poznania, western Galicia, and the Free City of Cracow had a major impact on the Central Committee of the Polish Democratic Society in Versailles. Its members became convinced that they would be deeply compromised if they did not support the new mood in the country. After some debate, the Central Committee gave in to pressure from its adherents in Poland and agreed in the winter of 1843–1844 to prepare for an insurrection, taking as its program the Manifesto of 1836. Its outbreak was set for 1846.

This revolution proved a disaster. In Poznania, the uprising was betrayed by a half-hearted conspirator, and its leader, Ludwik Mierosławski, and almost all of his collaborators were arrested. Similarly, in the Kingdom of Poland, a feeble attempt at sparking a peasant uprising was suppressed by the very peasants who were to be its main beneficiaries.

It was only in Galicia and in the Free City of Cracow that the revolution had any impact, and this was not of the sort for which the revolutionaries had been hoping. The whole of southern Poland had been very seriously affected by natural catastrophes in the 1840s, and this had led to substantial peasant unrest. Alarmed by this situation, the Polish landlords had put forward various schemes in the Galician Diet for the abolition of the labor tribute. No action was taken by the Viennese authorities, largely because of the paralysis of the central government which had resulted from the mutual hostility of its two principal figures, Metternich and Kolowrat. The situation in western Galicia in fact had much in common with that which had prevailed among the French peasantry during the *grande peur* in 1789. Wild rumors circulated that the nobility intended to slaughter the peasants. Uncertain of the ability of the Austrian government to protect them, peasants began to form themselves into bands for the purpose of self-defense. The tense climate was exacerbated by the incompetence of the governor of Galicia, the Archduke Ferdinand d'Este, and by the willingness of the Austrian authorities to allow a revolt to take place in Cracow, since this would facilitate their plans for the annexation of the Free City.

Thus when the noble revolutionaries in Galicia proclaimed their insurrection, the peasants in the areas of Tarnów, Rzeszów, Wadowice, Nowy Sącz, and Sanok turned on them savagely, killing some and handing others over to the Austrian authorities. Everywhere they proclaimed their intention of acting on behalf of the emperor and that their action was directed solely against the landlords and their agents. There seems to have been very little anti-Jewish activity.

In spite of what was widely believed among the Polish nobility, the Austrians did not initiate this movement. However, in some areas, local officials, notably the *Kreishauptmann* in Tarnów, Joseph Breinl, did try to conciliate the peasantry by promising them rewards if they acted against the nobility. The rising was almost entirely confined to the Polish-speaking western areas of Galicia. Some peasants in mountainous areas, where labor services were not a source of conflict, did in fact support the insurrection. In all, perhaps 1,100 people were killed, 3,000 were arrested, and 430 manor houses were burnt.

The insurrection was able to take power briefly in the Free City of Cracow. Here the Revolutionary Council proclaimed the abolition of the labor tribute in the small rural area which surrounded the Free City and on 23 February 1846 issued an appeal "To Our Israelite Brothers," which promised the abolition of all distinctions between Jews and other citizens, the first such act on the Polish lands. Given the debacle elsewhere on the Polish lands, this uprising was doomed from the start and after a week it was suppressed by the intervention of Austrian troops. The Free City of Cracow was then incorporated into Galicia.

The consequences of the events of early 1846 on Polish political thinking cannot be exaggerated. The insurrection had been based on the assumption that the people, won over by the generosity of the nobility in granting them the freehold of their lands, would rise up spontaneously against foreign rule throughout the area of the former Polish-Lithuanian Commonwealth. In the words of one of the revolutionaries, Bronisław Trentowski, in 1847:

> Hitherto we have counted with certainty upon the people and today we see that the nation is only the *szlachta*. Confidence in our strength has been extinguished, leaving behind only a silent and painful feeling of shame . . . Not long ago everyone believed, everyone was certain that the Fatherland would by itself throw off its yoke and that soon, perhaps tomorrow or the next day. Now we may not yet think of an independent Poland. Before we may work again for this most holy of political objects, we must see to the end of the social war that has flared up between the peasantry and the noble order. There are those who say that there will be a Poland. But when? After 100, 200, 300 years.[14]

Under these circumstances, the majority of the nobility came to believe that revolution could only lead to disaster and that the only way forward was to cooperate with the partitioning powers for limited goals which would lead to the establishment of a more healthy basis to society. Their views in Galicia were well expressed by Count Fredro, who now argued that a contented Galicia would be a source of strength to the Habsburg Monarchy since it would demonstrate that Slavs could live in peace under Austrian rule. In the wider context, a number of people, most notably the later viceroy of the Kingdom of Poland, Count Alexander Wielopolski, now began to argue that only a compromise with the Russians would serve the national interest. In his *Lettre d'un gentilhomme polonais sur les massacres de Galicie addressée au Prince de Metternich*, he accused Metternich of being a "crowned Jacobin," far worse than his Russian counterparts:

> Like you and together with you, the Russians dethroned our king and destroyed our institutions and our liberties: they however leave intact social order; public justice has been exercised by them with an iron hand, but through the agency of the laws; they have never given up to murderers the sovereignty of the Tsar.[15]

Not all the revolutionaries were prepared to abandon their views. The Democratic Society remained convinced that the basic strategy remained correct, only the tactics had been faulty. Ludwik Mierosławski, who had broken down under interrogation, used his trial in Berlin as a political demonstration in favor of the Polish cause and won some German liberal support. But in general, confidence in the ability of the Poles to achieve their objectives by revolution had been drastically undermined.

This had a considerable impact on Polish behavior during the revolution of 1848. In that year, the Poles essentially placed their hopes in the German revolution, looking particularly to the German left, which was convinced that the first stage of any German revolution would involve a war against Russia, in which the Poles hoped to participate. Polish hopes were misplaced on two counts.

In the first place, the king of Prussia had no intention of being forced by the revolutionaries into a war with Russia. This emerges clearly from a conversation recorded in the biography of Max von Gagern, a member of the Nassau diplomatic service, and a delegate to the Frankfurt Assembly.[16] According to von Gagern, one of the most representative figures of the "Third Germany" (the smaller States in contradistinction to Austria and Prussia) and of the German Liberals of 1848, on 23 March 1848, he was received by the king of Prussia in the presence of Baron Heinrich von Arnim, the Prussian minister for foreign affairs. After Gagern had spoken about the situation in Germany, the king, moved to tears, asked his advice, admitting that "Germany is in full dissolution." Gagern continued:

> "Your Majesty will permit me in this solemn hour to touch upon matters completely outside my official instructions. What your Majesty has done and announced in the last few days to save Germany from imminent danger would, *before* 18 March, have united us all and secured us . . . against any movement, from outside or inside . . . now only a newer, and still bolder, decision—to wage foreign war—can save us from anarchy and dissolution. But not as your Majesty has hinted, a war against France, which at present would not be acceptable, but a war against Russia."
>
> The King: "What? Aggression against Russia?"
>
> Me: "Freeing the Poles will entail war against Russia."
>
> The King: "But Poland will never rearise. She is at peace and the strongest measures have been taken."
>
> Me: "Seeing the magic influence which the idea of nationality now exercises, how can we hope to strengthen the unity of our own nation, and to assert our own nationality, if we oppress and flout that of others? Only a liberation of Poland can save your Majesty and us all."
>
> The King: "By God, never, never shall I draw the sword against Russia."
>
> Me: "Then I look upon Germany as lost."[17]

Even more important, the outbreak of revolution in Prussian Poland revealed the gulf between German and Polish aspirations for the province. Although the new government which came to power in Prussia on 29 March pursued a relatively liberal policy towards the Polish majority in Poznania, and even allowed the formation of a Polish army corps, the Prussian army was determined to take steps to prevent the province from being dislodged from the Prussian state. In early April almost all the Polish levies were dissolved and the resistance of those few who refused to obey this order was overcome by early May. When the question of Poland came up before the Frankfurt parliament on 24 July, the German liberals showed themselves barely more sympathetic to Polish aspirations than the Prussian army.

Under these circumstances, the revolutionaries in Galicia lacked any real faith that they could achieve their objectives on their own, and the progress of the revolution there was almost entirely dependent on events elsewhere in the monarchy, above all in Vienna. In March, following Metternich's flight from Vienna, Polish liberals and revolutionaries, including some members of the Democratic Society, met in Lviv and on 14 April set up a Central National Council (*Rada Narodowa Centralna*), which was to be both a representative and an executive body. Its members agreed on a common program, which was notable in that it only called for the autonomy of Galicia and did not mention Polish independence. In addition, they demanded the abolition of labor services.

The relative weakness of the revolutionary upsurge, partly the result of the widespread fear among landowners of a new 1846, left the initiative in the hands of the new Austrian governor Franz von Stadion. He displayed unusual political skill, appealing for support to the now increasingly nationally conscious Ukrainian majority in the eastern part of the province. This policy had been initiated already in February 1847, when the Austrian government proposed to divide Galicia into its eastern and western parts. In February of the following year, Stadion gave permission for the publication of a Ukrainian newspaper. He also attempted to secure Jewish support by calling on the Austrian authorities in April 1848 to abolish all special taxes paid by Jews. In addition, and most importantly, he did what had not been done in the aftermath of the 1846 *jacquerie:* he managed to persuade the imperial government on 23 April to abolish labor dues, which effectively pacified the countryside in the Austrian interest. As a result, he was able to reestablish Austrian control in Cracow in April and in Lviv in November.

The emergence of a self-conscious Ukrainian (still calling itself Ruthenian) nationalism in 1848 came as a great surprise to the Poles, who saw it as above all a result of the Austrian practice of the principle *divide et impera*. In fact, it was the consequence of a much longer-term development in the whole of the area, which has been well described by John-Paul Himka:

> Few historians of Eastern Europe would dispute that the single most important occurrence in that region from the Age of Enlightenment until World War I was the diffusion of national consciousness to the primarily rural masses of the population. It was this process that laid the foundations for the emergence of independent East European states after the Great War and that made the national antagonisms in the region so explosive during the first half of the twentieth century.[18]

The national consciousness of the almost entirely rural Greek Catholics of eastern Galicia developed in stages. In the generation before 1848 a small Ruthenian intelligentsia began to emerge, the product of the educational and religious reforms of Joseph II. By the early 1840s, for instance, approximately 400 Ukrainian students were enrolled at the University of Lviv. It was in these years that its members passed, in the words of the historian Jan Kozik, from being "Galician-Ruthenian patriots" to a form of all-Ukrainian patriotism.[19] This was in spite of the fact that in 1809 the Studium Ruthenum had been abolished, that from 1817 the university had offered instruction solely in German, and that secondary education was only available in German and Polish. In 1812, the compulsory primary education established by Joseph II had been abolished and it was only in a restricted number of elementary schools that instruction was available in a form of Ukrainian. This situation caused a significant degree of polonization among the younger generation. In addition, the Greek Catholic hierarchy, above all the Metropolitan Mykhailo Levyts'kyi, was strongly hostile to the national revival. In these years, two Ukrainian dictionaries and several grammars (one in German)[20] were published and substantial progress was made on creating a literary Ukrainian language, which would use the modern Cyrillic civil alphabet and would reflect the local vernacular rather than Church Slavonic. This was above all the work of the first conscious literary figures in the area, the Ruthenian Triad (*Rus'ka triitsa*), Markiian Shashkevych (1811–1843), Ivan Vahylevych (1814–1888), and Iakiv Holovats'kyi (1811–1866). It was they who in 1837 published the first book in the vernacular, *Rusalka dnistrovaia* (The Nymph of the Dnister), which had to be published in Buda because it was banned by the local censor. It is necessary to emphasize the tiny extent of this nascent intelligentsia. It was not possible in these years to establish a Ukrainian newspaper and the first part of one of the principal literary products of these years, the two-volume anthology *Vinok Rusynam* (1846–1847) had a circulation of barely 140. An important role in the national revival was played by the Czech officials who were sent to the province, who saw the position of the Ukrainians as analagous to that of their nation a generation previously, and who became strong supporters of Austroslavism. Both Vahylevych and Holovats'kyi conducted extensive correspondences with a number of the principal figures in the Czech national revival, above all Josef Dobrovský and Karel Zap. The Greek Catholic hierarchy was for the most part hostile to the national awakening, seeing it as likely to undermine the faith of villagers and threaten its close links with the Habsburg authorities.

By 1846, a degree of political crystallization had begun to develop. The "Ruthenian Triad" was basically hostile to the Polish revolution of 1846, seeing it as noble-dominated and its leaders as unwilling to recognize the national separateness of the Ukrainian people, whom they considered at best as a separate Polish "tribe." Although the conspiratorial Polish groups in Galicia initially had won some support among the nascent Ukrainian intelligentsia, their refusal to accept any degree of national separateness soon led to estrangement. There had been, for instance, strong and successful opposition to changing the name of one of the principal Polish radical groups, *Stowarzyszenie Ludu Polskiego* (the Association of the Polish People) to *Stowarzyszenie Ludu Polskiego i Ruskiego* (the Association of the Polish and Ruthenian People). Holovats'kyi expressed his view after the collapse of the revolution in an extended article written under the pseudonym Havrylo Rusyn, which appeared in the *Jahrbücher für Slawischer Literatur, Kunst und Wissenschaft* published in Leipzig on 25 June 1846.[21] He adopted an Austro-Slav position, proposing that the government support the Ukrainians, since "in essence they are in a position to constitute a powerful bulwark against revolutionary machinations in Galicia, which have many times shattered themselves on the rocks of Ruthenian loyalty." He strongly praised the policies implemented in Galicia by Joseph II and in particular his educational reforms. Were the Austrians to return to such policies, then "Austria would have such loyal Galician subjects in its civil and military service as the loyal Czechs and Croats, loyal as are the Ruthenian priesthood and the simple people." He also attacked the views expressed by Wielopolski in *Lettre d'un gentilhomme polonais*. In his view only the nobility had "much to hope from Russia," in which landlords could oppress their peasants with impunity.[22]

It was during the revolution of 1848 that the Ukrainians of Galicia for the first time entered modern politics. As the Ukrainian publicist Father Vasyl' Podolyns'kyi pointed out in his Polish pamphlet *Słowo przestrogi* (A Word of Warning),[23] four different orientations were struggling for supremacy within the Ukrainian political leadership in Galicia in 1848. The strongest force at this time was Austro-Slavism, which was supported by the Greek Catholic hierarchy, including the Greek Catholic bishop-coadjutor of Lviv, Hryhorii Iakhymovych, and the Metropolitan Mykhailo Levyts'kyi. It was organized in the Supreme Ruthenian Council (Holovna Rus'ka Rada), which was established on 2 May to act as a counterweight to the Polish National Council. Its organization was encouraged by Stadion and it undertook widespread political agitation, collecting thousands of signatures in support of its objectives, the most important of which was the division of Galicia along the San River into two administrative entities. The degree of political mobilization was considerable. Nearly 200,000 people signed a petition advocating such a division. In addition, 25 Ukrainian deputies sat in the lower house of the parliament established on 25 April. In a resolution of 10 May published in *Zoria halyts'ka,* one of the Ukrainian newspapers established in 1848,[24] the Supreme Ruthenian Council asserted:

> We Galician Ruthenians [*rusyny halyts'ki*] belong to the great Ruthenian [*rus'ki*] nation, which speaks the same language and numbers fifteen million, of whom two and a half million live on the land of Galicia [*Halych— halyts'ka*]. This nation was once independent, it had its own literary language, its own laws, its own princes, in a word, it lived in prosperity, was wealthy and powerful.[25]

Its Austro-Slavism led it to support the Habsburg dynasty and oppose the revolutionary challenge to its position. Thus in the summer of 1848 the Greek Catholic hierarchy forbade the priesthood from celebrating masses on the anniversary of the execution of two Polish revolutionaries, Józef Kapuściński and Wiktor Wiśniowski. At the same time, they organized prayers in gratitude for Radetzky's victory in Italy. The Austro-Slav position was clearly articulated by the Ruthenian politician, Kyrylo Blonśkyi in October 1848, when he made clear his opposition to the revolutionary program of 1848, whose initiators were "the Magyars, the Poles, and the German republicans" and whose goal was

> the overthrowing of the monarchy, so that Bohemia, Moravia, Silesia, Austrian Styria, Tyrol, and Illyria could be incorporated into Germany, a Magyar republic created including the lands which were dependent on it, and a Poland with subject Ruthenes. Then these areas would be Germanized, Magyarized, and Polonized.[26]

It was this point of view that led the Supreme Ruthenian Council to issue an appeal on 21 November 1848 calling on the Ukrainians in Hungary to support the Austrian army against the Magyar insurgents. Late in 1848 permission was given by the imperial authorities for the Ukrainians to form military units. A 1,400-strong Ruthenian Rifleman's Batallion was established but was not trained in time to take part in the suppression of the Hungarian revolution, although it did march into Slovakia in September 1849 and was reviewed in Košice by the Russian General Ruediger.[27]

The pro-Polish orientation was much weaker. It was given political form in the Ruthenian Council (Ruśkyi Sobor), set up in May by the Polish National Council as a rival to the Supreme Ruthenian Council, which called for protection for the Ukrainians' language and culture, but supported the establishment of an independent Polish state and opposed the administrative division of Galicia. It had the support of one member of the Ruthenian Triad, Ivan Vahylevych, a number of Polish noblemen of Ruthenian background, such as Leon Sapieha and the Dzieduszycy brothers, and some polonized intellectuals, like Kasper Cięglewicz. Vahylevych himself edited a short-lived weekly newspaper in Ukrainian printed in both Cyrillic and Latin characters, *Dnewnyk Ruskij* (a misnomer), which appeared between August and October.

For his part, Iakiv Holovatśkyi, the other surviving member of the Ruthene Triad, adopted an ambiguous position in 1848. Initially, he opposed the formation of the Supreme Ruthenian Council, writing to his brother that its creation was an intrigue of the government, which sought "to strengthen its bureaucratic rule, using the Ruthenian nationality and language as a screen, under the banner of Red Rus'." He was convinced that Ukrainians would understand what was involved and would not break with the Poles, but, together with them, would seek to achieve a constitutional system.[28] He soon became disillusioned, writing to his brother Iosyf on 13 June that " . . . we cannot trust our Lords and brothers, the Lachs. They want brotherhood, but at a high price—they want to sacrifice (*poświęcić*) our language, our nationality, all our resources to make possible the creation of an independent Poland."[29] He accepted the post of local secretary of the Supreme Ruthenian Council in the town of Chortkiv, but still criticized the policy of the council, which he saw as counterrevolutionary and supportive of the autocratic Austrian government.[30] He seems to have shared the views of his other brother Petro, who was a member of the delegation of the Supreme Ruthenian Council which was granted an audience by the emperor in February 1849. "Shame on us," Petro wrote to him, "and we should be ashamed, when it becomes apparent to the world that in pursuit of our own national goals we have forfeited the sympathy of other nations and have forgotten our honor . . . all our address [to the authorities] has achieved is to strengthen the government. We have not obtained anything in return . . . "[31] Yet, after the crushing of the revolution, Holovats'kyi again reverted to Austro-Slavism, accepting from the Austrian authorites the newly established Chair in Ukrainian Language and Literature which was created late in 1848 at the University of Lviv.

Holovats'kyi's waverings were not untypical of the more radical section of the developing Ukrainian intelligentsia. As Ivan Rudnytsky has pointed out, "the rupture with Polish society was so painful that the generation of Ruthenian intellectuals which effected the break tended to lean far in the other direction."[32] Moreover, there was no real willingness on the Polish part to recognize the existence of a separate Ukrainian nation. On 7 May, the Polish National Council did come out in favor of cultural equality between the two nations. But it also claimed that it alone represented both nationalities (*narodowości*). At the Slav Congress in Prague, where Austrophile tendencies clashed with the hope of some Poles to free themselves from Habsburg rule, the Czechs succeeded on 7 June in brokering a Polish-Ukrainian compromise. Under its terms, the Ukrainians agreed to postpone discussion of the question of the division of Galicia along the San River in return for a Polish commitment to the equality of the two nations in all administrative and educational matters. The dissolution of the conference as a result of the Austrian recapture of Prague made this resolution a dead letter, and the agreement was not followed by any further rapprochement between the two groups. Indeed, both Poles and Ukrainians saw the agreement as little more than a tactical move to which they were compelled to agree in order to avoid alienating the Czechs.

The two other political orientations which emerged in 1848 were the forces that were to dominate Ukrainian politics in Galicia in the second half of the nineteenth century: the view that Ukraine should seek to solve its problems on its own through self-determination, and the Russophile orientation. Both of these movements were still in their infancy in 1848. Russophilism had been rather weak before 1848 and it was only the historian Denys Zubryts'kyi who (at least in private) had advocated the adoption of the Russian language. In 1848 he was supported by Iakiv Holovats'kyi's brother, Iosyf, and Antin Petrushevych. However, in the aftermath of the revolution, with the disillusionment occasioned by the failure of the Austrian authorities to divide Galicia along the San, this group emerged as a significant political force. Those who favored an independent Ukrainian state were even weaker. The only persons to advocate this in 1848 seem to have been Antin Liubych-Mohyl'nyts'kyi and the maverick Podolyns'kyi, who may have been influenced by Bakunin, and even he believed that the liberation of Ukraine was contingent upon national freedom for all Slavic peoples. The efforts of the Ukrainians would only bear fruit, he wrote, "with the resurrection of all, federative and liberal, Slavdom."[33]

The years from 1846 through 1848 also saw a considerable maturing of the political consciousness of the Jewish population of Galicia. The effect of governmental policies aimed at integrating the Jews and transforming them into "useful and productive citizens" had been greatly to exacerbate the already existing divisions in the Jewish world. A minority was strongly committed to the idea of reform from above. They were also greatly attracted to the German language and German culture, which they saw as embodiments of universal, secular, and liberal values. A majority of the Jews in Galicia, where Hasidism was becoming increasingly important, were strongly opposed to these policies. They were seen as merely a more subtle form of Christian evangelization and those who supported them were believed to be motivated by base and material considerations.

It was in the first decades of the nineteenth century that Hasidism came to dominate the religious life of much of Jewish Galicia. Hasidism had begun as a small circle of disciples around the charismatic Israel ben Eliezer (the Baal Shem Tov or Besht) in Medzhybizh in Podolia. After the Besht's death, the center of gravity of the movement moved to Mezhyrich in Volhynia, where the key figure was Dov Ber, the *magid* (preacher) of Mezhyrich. He sent his followers over the whole area of the former Polish-Lithuanian Commonwealth, Rebbe Menahem Mendel to Vitsebsk, Rebbe Shneur Zalman to Liady, and Rebbe Levi Yitshok to Berdychiv.

It was at this time that two major Hasidic dynasties became established in Galicia—that linked with the court of Rebbe Elimelekh (d. 1787), and that of the Ruzhyner tzaddikim[34] founded in Podolia by Rebbe Israel Friedman of Ruzhyn, who moved in the late 1830s to Galicia. Why did Hasidism so quickly become dominant in Galicia? Much of the recent research on the origins of this movement has sought to discredit the older view of people like Hillel Ben-Sasson that the movement should be seen as a form of social protest by the lower Jewish social orders against their worsening general position and the increased stratification of Jewish society. It is certainly the case that the Besht was no social revolutionary and did not seek in any way to overturn the established order of Jewish society. Yet in Galicia in the early nineteenth century, as was also the case in the tsarist empire, Hasidism appealed to those who saw no advantage for themselves in the policies which sought to transform and integrate the Jews. The new government activism, with its increased taxation and involvement in the internal affairs of Jewish life, was clearly a major factor in the popularity of Hasidic religious revivalism. So too was the economic and political backwardness of Galicia. It was above all in the smaller towns and townlets, bypassed by such progress as was occurring towards the emergence of a more market-based economic system, that the movement established its main strongholds.

Given this economic and political backwardness, it is not surprising that the forces which sought to integrate the Jews into the wider society and acquire civil rights for them were much weaker than the forces of religious conservatism. Who were the reformers? We lack a satisfactory modern study of the Jewish enlightenment, the Haskalah, which went through a whole series of transformations, changing as it moved eastwards from Germany and over the three generations in which its influence was dominant within the modernizing minority in the Jewish world.

In Galicia, there were two separate groups of reformers, whose positions should be distinguished, although there was considerable overlap in their views of the world: the *maskilim*, or followers of the Haskalah, and the reformers or integrationists. The *maskilim* took the view that a modernized and purified Hebrew should be the basis for the reform of the Jews. For the most part, they were politically believers in enlightened autocracy, sharing the popular Jewish distrust of the "violent and anti-Jewish" masses. They bitterly opposed the rise of Hasidism, which they saw as obscurantist and backward-looking, its leaders mostly tricksters deriving a good living from exploiting the gullibility of their ignorant followers. Among the principal exponents of the Haskalah in Galicia were the Czech Jew, Herz Homberg, who was placed in charge of the Josephine network of Jewish schools, the writer Josef Perl, author of *Megillei temirim,* a savage critique of Hasidism, the philosopher Nachman Krochmal, who attempted to combine the Hegelian concept of history as a succession of stages, each characterised by a dominant idea, with a modernized version of the Jewish historical mission, Isaac Erter, and Solomon Leib Rappoport.

The reformers were oriented to German political liberalism. They were not as interested in Jewish religious reform as the *maskilim*, although they did favor a modernized and more organized form of synagogue worship, such as had been instituted by Isaac Noah Mannheimer in the Seitenstettengasse synagogue in Vienna. Here, a pulpit had been introduced alongside the ark, to make possible sermons in German, a choir had been created and the liturgy reorganized by the famous cantor Solomon Sulzer. In addition, a women's gallery made it possible for women to take part in the service more fully. The political orientation of the reformers was liberal—they believed that changes in the position of the Jews would be linked with the establishment of a representative and constitutional government, responsible to an electorate, which would initially be somewhat restricted. They also believed strongly in education, primarily in German, as the road to Jewish reform.

Just as the strength of Hasidism lay in small towns and townlets—Rymanów, Nowy Sącz, Belz, Ropchits, Leżajsk—so reformers were stronger in the largest towns of the province, Brody, Ternopil, the capital Lviv, and Cracow. Lviv, the largest town in the province and its capital, was, not surprisingly, a stronghold of both *maskilim* and Jewish integrationists. The conflict between the supporters and opponents of Jewish integration was very bitter here since, alongside a westernized minority, the town also had a large Orthodox and Hasidic population. Conflicts raged primarily over the school system. In 1831, after a number of objections from the provincial authorities, and following Josef Perl's intervention with Metternich, the emperor gave permission for the establishment in the town of a "Society for Spreading Useful Crafts among Israelites." In addition, many Jewish youths also attended German primary and secondary schools, much to the disgust of the Orthodox. In 1844, a modern synagogue, the Tempel, was founded. Its first rabbi, Abraham Kohn, died tragically in 1848 when he was poisoned by an Orthodox fanatic.

The integrationists were also divided among themselves over whether to favor a German or a Polish orientation. Until the 1860s, the German orientation, represented by the organization *Shomer Israel,* was dominant. It was only with the establishment of provincial autonomy under Polish control that the pro-Polish orientation of *Agudas Achim* gained ground. The principal organ for the expression of assimilationist and pro-Polish ideas was now the weekly *Ojczyzna.*

In Cracow, the pro-Polish orientation dominated from the start. In 1839, a "Society for the Spreading of Useful Crafts among the Israelites," was founded, modeled on the similar body in Lviv, and the following year a "Society for Self-Education among Jews" was established. It included among its members a number of the Jewish elite of Cracow's Kazimierz district, among them Dr. Filip Bondy, Dr. Jonatan Warschauer, Dr. Józef Oettinger, Dr. Maurycy Krzepicki, Szachna, Markusfeld and Jozue Funk. In 1830 a Jewish public elementary school had been created in Kazimierz, and five years later a Jewish public *Realschule* was also founded. In 1837 these establishments were merged and made into a craft and commercial school, which by 1849–1850 had 375 pupils.[35] A small number of Jewish students attended the Jagiellonian University. In the academic year 1826–1827, there had been three such students. Their number rose to 12 in 1846–1847, 15 in 1850–1851, and 26 in 1865–1866, when they constituted 7.7 percent of the student body.

An ardent Polish patriot, Dov Ber Meisels, was elected rabbi in 1831, and in 1844 a modern Orthodox synagogue, the Tempel, was opened. This synagogue did not deviate from normative Jewish practice in its ritual, but it did introduce some important changes in the organization of worship. The *bima* (reading dais) was now placed in front of the ark, so that it could make possible the delivery of sermons, first in German and subsequently in Polish. A place for the choir was also built in the eastern wall and women were seated in a gallery rather than behind a curtain.

During the revolutionary crisis of 1846–1848, Jews in the Habsburg Monarchy were, for the most part, strong supporters of the movement in Austria, in Galicia, and in the Free City of Cracow for the establishment of a liberal, constitutional state. As we have seen, the revolutionary council established in Cracow in February 1846 had proclaimed the equality of the Jews of the Free

City. In response, some 500 Jews, including Oettinger, Warschauer, Funk, and Krzepicki of the Self-Education Society joined the insurrectionary army, which was enthusiastically welcomed by Rabbi Meisels. There was widespread enthusiasm in the Jewish community for the uprising. Both Meisels and Krzepicki called on the Jews to support the revolution "as befits the free and brave sons of the motherland."[36] This did not prevent some of the more reactionary Polish emigrés, such as Wiktor Szokalski, a member of Adam Czartoryski's entourage in Paris, from accusing the Galician Jews of responsibility for the *jacquerie* which followed the outbreak of revolution in Cracow and Austrian Poland. Similar views were propagated in the principal newspapers of the Czartoryski group (the Hotel Lambert) in the Emigration. According to *Dziennik Narodowy* and *Trzeci Maj,* the Jews had participated in the democratic movement to advance their own interests. The activities of Jews, as well as Frankists and other converts, were "harmful to the nation."[37] At the same time, there was an increasing acceptance on the part of the Emigration that equality would have to be granted to the Jews. According to *Trzeci Maj* in October 1846, "We concede that the Jews (*Starozakonni*) are entitled to have the same civic rights as we do."

The humiliating collapse of the revolution and the incorporation of Cracow into Austria was followed by Austrian reprisals against those who had supported it. Some Jews were imprisoned and all restrictive anti-Jewish laws reestablished. In addition, a fine of 50,000 florins was levied on the Jewish community.

During the 1848 revolution in Galicia, Jews were divided in their political stance. Some took an active part in the political struggle, aligning themselves with the Poles. Others, however, did not support the national aspirations of the Poles and adopted a pro-Austrian stand, fearing the increasing strength of Polish antisemitism and the outbreak of anti-Jewish violence. In fact, there was much less anti-Jewish violence in Galicia in 1846 and 1848 than in other areas of Europe, including Alsace, western Germany, the Grand Duchy of Poznań, the Czech lands, and Hungary.[38] No anti-Jewish outrages took place during the *jacquerie* of February 1846, and when anti-Jewish violence threatened in the spring of 1848, an appeal from the Polish National Committee in Lviv calmed the situation.[39] It is not clear why this was the case. The main antagonism both in the western and the eastern parts of the province was between landlord and peasant, and it may be that at this stage, the local Jews enjoyed a degree of trust in the villages which was unavailable to the landlords. This may explain the curious appeal to Jews in the countryside issued in Yiddish in Lviv in June 1848. "Your words," it claimed, "are listened to by peasants . . . you should therefore see to it that there is peace between the lords and the peasants." It went on to assert that the Jews should make sure that the peasants understood that they had received their land because of an initiative of the landowners, who did not want to fight the emperor.[40] Artur Eisenbach has argued that this pamphlet owes its origin to the attempts of the Hotel Lambert group to win over the peasantry for the Polish cause in the aftermath of the debacle of 1846.

As we have seen, Stadion himself attempted to secure Jewish support by calling on the Austrian authorities in April 1848 to abolish all special taxes paid by Jews. This did not stop Jews from being among those who participated in the formation of delegations from the towns of Lviv, Cracow, and Tarnów which called in an address of 6 April 1848 for the summoning of a National Assembly. It affirmed:

> [The] main and indispensable foundation [of this Assembly] should be the representation of the nation, irrespective of class and religion . . . The prosperity of states depends on a free and harmonious development of all national forces, on their being used for the common good. A genuine love of the motherland can only exist if the motherland makes no distinction between its children . . . It seems to us therefore that the classes and religions existing in the nation should be granted equal civic and political rights . . . [and] that all taxes connected with religion as well as religion-based exclusions and restrictions should be abolished.[41]

The revolution certainly saw considerable political mobilization among the Jews of Galicia. Jews played an active role in the national councils set up in Lviv and Cracow and joined the National Guards established in many Galician towns. In Lviv and Cracow, separate detachments commanded by Jewish officers were established. A Yiddish weekly, *Lemberger yidishe tsaytung*, was established under the editorship of Abraham Mendel Mohr.[42] Shortly before the opening of the parliament, delegates from the *kehilot* (Jewish communal bodies) all over Galicia assembled in Lviv and drew up a memorandum demanding full equality.[43]

Jews were particularly prominent in the revolution in Cracow. On 3 May 1848 (the anniversary of the adoption of the Polish constitution of 1791) the members of the Cracow Jewish Self-Education Society issued an appeal. At this moment, when the peoples of Europe were freeing themselves from "the oppression by tyrants," when the Jews too were being granted rights for which they had been waiting for such a long time, it was "the duty of an Israelite to evoke in himself love for the motherland, to be permeated by patriotism for the country in which he was born and awake among his co-religionists a holy zeal for the cause of freedom . . . We shall show the world that we have the Maccabees' blood in our veins, that our hearts, like the hearts of our forefathers, respond warmly to everything that is noble and sublime."[44] On 1 October, the Jewish cultural association of Cracow met and prepared a memorandum for submission to Parliament calling for the granting of full legal equality for the Jews.[45]

Three Jews were elected to the Reichsrat in 1848, from Brody (Rabbi Mannheimer), from Stanyslaviv, and from Ternopil. In a subsequent by-election, Rabbi Meisels was elected from Cracow by an electorate made up of both

Christians and Jews. He expressed well the views of those Jews who supported more moderate Polish aspirations and the revolutionary constitution of April 1848:

> [T]he future of our Polish Motherland can only be secured through organic work [work to raise the economic, social and cultural level of the country] not through the dissolution of society . . . Realizing the needs of humanity in its present phase, I am an ardent believer in the principles of freedom, in the development of political rights, in all citizens having a share in these rights . . . I regard these principles as true democracy which far from lowering, raises everything, which does not destroy but constructs and consolidates the new constitution by love.[46]

The Jewish identification with the Polish cause was bitterly resented by the emerging Ukrainian movement. Ruthenian leaders held the Jews responsible for the economic backwardness of the Ukrainian countryside and, because of the Jews' role as agents for the Polish nobility, for the oppression of the Ukrainian peasantry. On 19 June 1848, the Ukrainian political leadership declared itself unequivocally against the emancipation of the Jews.[47] More favorable views on the granting of equal rights to the Jews were expressed by a number of members of the more radical Ukrainian intelligentsia, such as Vasyl' Podolyns'kyi and Ivan Hrab'ianka.

During the revolution, the government conceded the principle of equal rights for the Jews. The extent to which the rhetoric of the revolution had affected Jewish attitudes can be seen in the behavior of a group of Jews in Tysmenytsia and Zhovkva. In August 1848 they approached the Polish liberal, Franciszek Smolka, asking for his support in their aspirations for full Jewish emancipation. They also submitted a petition to the Austrian parliament which had been elected in June. In it they argued that it was the old governments and laws which had isolated the Jews from the Poles, and that the restrictions imposed on the Jews had weakened the Jewish spirit of freedom. The revolutionary ideas of liberty, fraternity, and equality had now crushed superstitions and prejudices and awoken the Jews from their lethargy. The hour of salvation had struck for all people. All people, Christians as well as Jews, were entitled to equal rights—"all the rights of Man," which were "a noble principle of democracy" and the foundations of the European temple of freedom. Only "through an alliance of all religions can freedom stand up to the storms of the century and survive for ever." Their goals, they concluded, were to raise the educational level of the Jews, encourage agricultural settlement, and increase the knowledge of Polish culture.[48]

Smolka must have been rather put out by the fervent democratic and integrationist zeal of the petitioners. He told them he supported their demands, but cautioned them, should they achieve legal equality, to use their new rights "cautiously and with prudence, not to the disadvantage of the Christian population, for this would provoke a reaction and result in another restriction of their rights."[49]

The petition from Tysmenytsia and Zhovkva was not the only one submitted at this time. Petitions were also sent to the revolutionary parliament in Vienna by leaders of many other *kehilot*. They argued that although the government had now proclaimed the principle of equality before the law, the special taxes on Jews had not been abolished and anti-Jewish discrimination had been maintained in a number of areas of economic life. They called for the establishment of full legal equality and religious freedom.

The Jewish parliamentary representatives also spoke against the restrictive legislation affecting the Jewish community. When the question of special Jewish taxes was discussed at the beginning of October 1848, Rabbi Mannheimer argued that their abolition should be enacted not so much because this was in the interests of the Jews as for the sake of

> the dignity of this legislative chamber. You are the parliament, the first constitutional National Assembly. There is no doubt that the question whether you want to sanction this abnormal, inhuman tax must be solved here. Do you want to legalize this injustice?[50]

In the event, on 5 October, the Parliament voted overwhelmingly by 242 votes to 20 to abolish all taxes which were levied on a particular group in society, including those on the Jews. Further discussion of the Jewish issue in Parliament was forestalled by its dissolution by Alfred Windischgrätz. However, the constitution promulgated by the new emperor, Franz Joseph I, on 4 March 1849 confirmed the principle of full equality before the law, admitted Jews to civic rights and granted them the right to settle anywhere in the country and to purchase any sort of property. In practice, however, serious obstacles still remained in Galicia to the admission of the Jews to municipal citizenship or to their settling outside the Jewish quarter in a number of towns. In addition, some—though not all—of the former restrictions were reintroduced after the revolution was crushed.

The revolutionary crisis was finally brought to an end in 1849 with Russian help. In effect, the Austrian government had won by default because of outside intervention and the divisions among the revolutionaries. Austria would never be as powerful after 1848 as it had been in the post-1815 period. Indeed, the revolution was to leave a lasting legacy both in the monarchy as a whole and in Galicia. The violence of the peasant-noble conflict in western Galicia came as a devastating blow to the Polish hopes, dominant from the time of the emigration following the uprising of November 1830 in the Kingdom of Poland, of restoring Polish statehood by insurrectionary conspiracy. It was now clear that a long period would have to be devoted to internal reform before the issue of independence could again be raised. The influence of those who opposed revolution and who sought compromise with the partitioning powers was greatly enhanced.

The revolution in Galicia also saw the emergence of a self-conscious Ukrainian nationalism and of all those groupings which were to dominate Ukrainian politics in Galicia down to the collapse of the Habsburg state. During the revolution, the main Ukrainian organization, the Supreme Ruthenian Council, had emerged as a major political force which was able to collect thousands of signatures in support of its objectives and also succeeded in electing 25 Ukrainian representatives to the parliament set up during the revolution. It was at this time too that the Galician–Rus' Matytsia was established, in imitation of the similarly named Czech institution. It was intended to promote education and popular culture and was one of the most significant factors in the development of a Ukrainian national consciousness in the 1850s and 1860s.

At the same time, the abolition of the labor tribute put an end to the principal source of conflict in the countryside, both Polish and Ukrainian. However, the way that peasant emancipation was introduced meant that most peasant holdings were barely sufficient to provide a subsistence. Disputes also continued over rights to common grazing land and to forests, where the emancipation law mostly favored landlord interests. The land question had thus not been resolved, and would return to plague Galician politics in the second half of the nineteenth century.

For the Jews, the years of the revolution had seen an unprecedented political mobilization. The declaration of the revolutionary Cracow government in favor of Jewish equality, the campaigns for the revolutionary parliament, which were accompanied by expressions of solidarity between Christians and Jews, and the final achievement of equal rights aroused widespread enthusiasm. The disillusionment occasioned by the crushing of the revolution and the return of many of the old restrictions was thus all the more difficult to bear.

Trevelyan's characterization of the revolution is thus less appropriate in Galicia than that of Namier. This was indeed the "seed-plot" of later Galician history. It was an important phase in the establishment of pro-Habsburg sentiment among the Polish elite in the province and paved the way for the autonomy which was to be granted in the 1860s. It marked the Ukrainians' achievement of political maturity and saw the emergence of those political forces which were to dominate Ukrainian politics in Galicia in the second half of the nineteenth century. It also was a significant stage in the transformation of the views of the Jewish elite of the province from an integrationist position to a belief that the Jews were a proto-nation like the other emerging nations of the area. What makes it so fascinating is the way these different movements and aspirations both conflicted with and inspired each other.

NOTES

1. Clarence A. Manning, ed.; Percival Cundy, trans., *Ivan Franko, the Poet of Western Ukraine: Selected Poems* (New York, 1968).

2. Quoted in *1848: A Turning Point,* ed. Melvin Kranzberg (Lexington, MA, 1959), p. xix.

3. Lewis Namier, *Avenues of History* (London, 1952), p. 55; the title of the chapter is "1848: Seed-plot of History."

4. Józef Kajetan Janowski, "Spomnienia przeszłości—widoki na przyszłość," quoted in Robert F. Leslie, *Reform and Insurrection in Russian Poland 1856–1863* (London, 1963), p. 7.

5. Letter of c. 27 January 1834, quoted in Joachim Lelewel, *Listy emigracyjne Joachima Lelewela,* ed. Helena Więckowska, 4 vols. (Cracow, 1948), vol. 1, p. 240.

6. Leslie, *Reform and Insurrection,* p. 12. The document is reprinted in full in *Towarzystwo Demokratyczne Polskie: dokumenty i pisma,* ed. Bronisław Baczko (Warsaw, 1954), pp. 18–26.

7. The Austrian view of the province was well summed up in the report prepared on the province by its first governor, the Czech Count Anton Pergen. See Franz A. J. Szabo, "Austrian First Impressions of Ethnic Relations in Galicia: The Case of Governor Anton von Pergen," *POLIN* 12: 49–60.

8. Roman Rozdolski, *Stosunki poddańcze w dawnej Galicji,* 2 vols. (Warsaw, 1962), vol. 1, p. 261.

9. Majer Bałaban, *Dzieje Żydów w Galicji i Rzeczypospolitej Krakowskiej 1772–1868* (Lviv, 1914; reprinted Cracow, 1988), p. 47.

10. Kazimierz Ostaszewski-Barański, *Rok złudzeń 1848* (Zolochiv, 1899), p. 75. An even lower estimate is given in Franciszek Wiesiołowski, *Pamiętnik z roku 1848* (Lviv, 1868), p. 7. Both are cited by Lewis Namier in *1848: The Revolution of the Intellectuals* (London, 1946), p. 12. Note that in the 1964 edition of the book, the latter citation is given as *Pamiętnik z r. 1845–6,* to which is appended "(Diary 1845–6)."

11. Paul Robert Magosci, *A History of Ukraine* (Seattle, 1996), p. 390.

12. Karol Borkowski, "Pamiętnik historyczny o wyprawie partyzanckiej do Polski w roku 1833," *Biblioteka Pisarzy Polskich* (Leipzig) VII (1863): 49.

13. The report is reprinted in *Rewolucja polska 1846 roku: wybór źródeł,* ed. Stefan Kieniewicz (Wrocław, 1950), pp. 3–8.

14. Bronisław Trentowski, *Wizerunki duszy narodowej z końca ostatniego szesnastolecia* (Paris, 1847), pp. 2–3.

15. *Lettre d'un gentilhomme polonais sur les massacres de Galicie addressée au Prince de Metternich* (Paris, 1846), p. 39.

16. Ludwig von Pastor, *Leben des Freiherrn Max von Gagern 1810–1889* (Munich, 1912), pp. 230–34, quoted in Namier, *1848: The Revolution of the Intellectuals*, p. 55.

17. Ibid., p. 56.

18. John-Paul Himka, *Galician Villagers and the Ukrainian National Movement in the Nineteenth Century* (Edmonton, 1988), p. 3.

19. Jan Kozik, *Ukraiński ruch narodowy w Galicji w latach 1830–1848* (Cracow, 1973), p. 5.

20. Iosyf Levyts'kyi, *Grammatik der ruthenischen oder kleinrussischen Sprache in Galizien* (Przemyśl, 1834). The other two, by Ivan Vahylevych and Iosyf Lozyns'kyi, appeared in 1845 and 1846 respectively.

21. Havrylo Rusin (Iakiv Holovats'kyi), "Zustände der Rusinen in Galizien," *Jahrbücher für slawischer Literatur, Kunst und Wissenschaft* (Leipzig) IV (1846): 361–79. The article is discussed in some detail by Jan Kozik in his *Ukraiński ruch narodowy w Galicji*, pp. 277–85.

22. Ibid., p. 282.

23. This is discussed in Peter Brock's chapter "Ivan Vahylevych (1811–1866) and the Ukrainian National Identity," in *Nationbuilding and the Politics of Nationalism: Essays on Austrian Galicia*, ed. Andrei S. Markovits and Frank E. Sysyn (Cambridge, MA, 1982), p. 136, and in Feodosii Steblii, "Vasyl Podolynsky's *Słowo przestrogi* and Ukrainian-Polish Relations," *Journal of Ukrainian Studies* 23(2) Winter 1998: 45–58. *Słowo przestrogi* was published in Sanok in 1848.

24. The newspaper is described in Jan Kozik, *Między reakcją a rewolucją: studia z dziejów ukraińskiego ruchu narodowego w Galicji w latach 1848–1849* (Warsaw, 1975), pp. 178–79.

25. *Zoria halyts'ka* (Lviv) 1848 (1).

26. Quoted in Kozik, *Między reakcją a rewolucją*, p. 93.

27. Kozik, *Między reakcją a rewolucją*, pp. 146–47.

28. Ibid., p. 200.

29. Ibid.

30. On this see Kozik, *Ukraiński ruch narodowy w Galicji*, pp. 184–85.

31. Kozik, *Między reakcją a rewolucją*, pp. 206–207.

32. Quoted in Kozik, *Ukraiński ruch narodowy w Galicji*, p. 287.

33. Quoted in Steblii, "Vasyl Podolynsky's *Słowo przestrogi*," p. 51.

34. See David Assaf, *Derekh hamalkut: R. Yisrael miruzhin* (Jerusalem, 1997).

35. Majer Bałaban, *Dzieje Żydów w Galicji*, p. 114.

36. Quoted in Artur Eisenbach, *The Emancipation of the Jews in Poland, 1780–1870* (Oxford, 1991), p. 327.

37. Artur Eisenbach, "Hotel Lambert wobec sprawy żydowskiej w przededniu Wiosny Ludów," *Przegląd Historyczny* 3 (1976): 396.

38. On this see Eisenbach, *The Emancipation of the Jews in Poland*, p. 347.

39. Eisenbach, *The Emancipation of the Jews in Poland*, p. 349.

40. Bałaban, *Dzieje Żydów w Galicji*, p. 166.

41. Quoted in Eisenbach, *The Emancipation of the Jews in Poland*, p. 355.

42. Ibid., p. 344.

43. Ibid.

44. Bałaban, *Dzieje Żydów w Galicji*, p. 162.

45. Majer Bałaban, *Historia Żydów w Krakowie i na Kazimierzu*, 2 vols. (Cracow, 1931, 1991), vol. 2, pp. 741–46.

46. Quoted in Eisenbach, *The Emancipation of the Jews in Poland*, p. 355.

47. Kozik, *Ukraiński ruch narodowy w Galicji*, pp. 192–94, 203.

48. Karol Widman, *Franciszek Smolka, jego życie i zawód publiczny* (Lviv, 1886), pp. 279, 870, 876, quoted in Eisenbach, *The Emancipation of the Jews in Poland*, p. 345.

49. Ibid.

50. Philip Friedman, *Die galizischen Juden im Kampfe um ihre Gleichberechtigung 1848–1868* (Frankfurt am Main, 1929), p. 71.

The First Constitution of Ukraine (5 April 1710)

OMELJAN PRITSAK

One may claim that the modern history of a nation begins with its constitution. The eighteenth century was the period in which several nations received their constitutions: the United States in 1787–1789, France and Poland in 1791. Ukraine led in this respect, with a constitution adopted in 1710.

The Ukrainian and Polish constitutions are analogous in some ways. The Polish Constitution of 1791 was promulgated shortly before the second partition (in 1793) and could be applied only to a remnant of historic Polish territory for about four years until the final partition in 1795. The Ukrainian Constitution was accepted in Bendery (now in Moldova), which at that time belonged to the Ottoman Empire, and Hetman Pylyp Orlyk ruled only on the Right Bank of Ukraine for the next four years (to 1714). Nevertheless, both documents are important achievements in their respective constitutional histories.

There is no doubt that a stimulus for the Orlyk Constitution was the *Pacta Conventa,* the agreement which the Polish political elite (the *szlachta*) usually concluded with the successful candidate to the Polish elective throne. But Orlyk's constitution was not addressed specifically to the agreement between himself (the newly elected hetman) and the Ukrainian political establishment of the time; rather, it was meant to be obligatory for all his successors.

The Constitution of 1710 consisted of the following four parts:

1)   The preamble
2)   The text of the Constitution in 16 articles
3)   Orlyk's oath
4)   A confirmation charter by the Swedish protector, King Charles XII

The Constitution was written in two languages: Middle Ukrainian and Latin. Both versions had equal authority. The text of the Constitution dealt with all aspects of Ukrainian life at the beginning of the eighteenth century. The contents of the 16 articles are as follows:

1)   Concerning religion
2)   Concerning the territory and borders
3)   Concerning relations with Crimea
4/5) Concerning specific problems of the Zaporozhian Host
6)   Concerning the administration of the state and its parliamentary
      system (short constitution)
7)   Concerning the judiciary
8)   Concerning military affairs

9)   Concerning fiscal matters
10)   Concerning the protection of the peasantry
11)   Concerning the protection of widows and orphans
12)   Concerning the security and inviolability of municipal self rule
13)   Concerning the capital, Kyiv
14)   Concerning the fiscal conformity of town institutions
15)   Concerning economic problems of the state's fiscal systems
16)   Concerning the limitation of the power of leaseholders and
       tax collectors.

It is important to stress that the Constitution of 1710 was not just a work of
the Ukrainian political elite in emigration. At that time Hetman Orlyk still had
a part of the Ukrainian territory under his control. His statements (see appendix) bear witness to the fact that the project of the Constitution was also
debated in Ukraine, in spite of the fact that most of the country was under the
oppressive rule of Peter I of Russia.

Orlyk's statement finds corroboration in the fact that in 1717–1723, a copy
of the Constitution was in the Chancery of the Ukrainian State in Hlukhiv
(Heneral'na Viis'kova Kantselariia). At that time the Ukrainian politician and
memoirist Mykola Khanenko (1693–1760) was the assistant chancellor. He
copied the Latin version of the Constitution and some other documents of
Hetman Orlyk and kept these documents in his family archives. In 1847, when
the Ukrainian Slavicist and historian Osyp Bodians'kyi began publishing
Ukrainian documents in the *Chteniia v Imperatorskom obshchestve istorii i
drevnostei rossiiskikh pri Moskovskom universitete,* an unnamed member of
the Khanenko family made the copy of the Constitution available to
Bodians'kyi, who subsequently published it. Unfortunately, the manuscript of
the Latin text has not come down to us. Only an abbreviated version of it is
preserved in the Swedish State Archives in Stockholm.

The Middle Ukrainian text was copied by the Ukrainian historian Dmytro
Bantysh-Kamens'kyi from a copy in the Archive of the College of Foreign
Affairs in Moscow (the archive had been reorganized by his father, Mykola
[1737– 1814]). In 1859 Bodians'kyi published it in the *Chteniia,* but, unfortunately, with numerous errors.

The Middle Ukrainian copy is still preserved in the Russian State Archive of
Ancient Documents (RGADA) in Moscow (fond 13, ed. khr. 9). Judging by its
hand, it was copied sometime in the eighteenth century—probably in the first
half—by a professional scribe for the use of the Russian government. Ukrainian words, not familiar to the Russians, are underlined and glossed in
marginalia with Russian equivalents. I was able to obtain a xerox copy of this
important document through the kindness of the Director of the Archives,
Mikhail P. Lukichev and its curator, Svetlana R. Dolozova. I would like to
express my thanks and appreciation to them. It is the RGADA copy that is
being reprinted here.[1]

APPENDIX

In his unpublished second edition of *P. Orlyk's Deduction* (written between ca. 1945–1950), Elie Borschak [Il'ko Borshchak] mentions the Château Dinteville (near Chaumont, France) copy of the Constitution.[2] It was, in his words, a Latin abbreviated version "brevi style" (apparently not unlike the Stockholm "Contenta pactorum"). The specific feature of the Dinteville text was Pylyp Orlyk's addition in Polish. Borschak assumes that Pylyp Orlyk made his remarks originally in Latin, and it was his son, Hryhor, who in the 1740s translated them into French, while copying the Latin text of the Constitution.

In September 1988, I tried to trace and verify several documents known only from Borschak's publications. Accompanied by Professor Arkady Joukovsky [Arkadii Zhukovs'kyi] of Paris, I visited the present owner of the Château Dinteville, the Marquis de La Ville Baugé, both in Dinteville and in his apartment in Paris. I had access to all of their "Orlikiana," but was unable to trace several crucial documents, among them the text of the Constitution with Pylyp Orlyk's remarks.

Joukovsky, who was Borschak's successor at the Institut des Langues Orientales Vivantes in Paris, made available to me those parts of Borschak's unpublished works and materials which dealt with Pylyp and Hryhor Orlyk. Among them was the unpublished typescript of his second edition of Orlyk's *Deduction*.[3] To be found there are Ukrainian translations of four remarks by Pylyp Orlyk and one remark of Hryhor Orlyk as well as the translation of the unfinished Polish-language addition by Pylyp Orlyk. These included the following (in English translation, with my own and Borschak's parenthetical explanations):

A. Pylyp Orlyk's Remarks

1. "I myself composed most of the Treaty [i.e., the Constitution—E.B.] and edited the entire Treaty [Constitution]. I composed it according to a certain plan, following the way such public treaties were being composed by other nations. I was using specimens in the Library of Mr. [Gustav Henrik von] Müllern, to whom I used to show at that time different articles of the Treaty" (p. 30).[4]

2. "Among the persons who deliberated on the articles of this document [Constitution] were Messrs. [Andrii] Voinarovs'kyi, [Kost'] Hordiienko, [Dmytro] Horlenko, [Il'ia] Lomykovs'kyi, [Fedir] Myrovych, [Ivan] Maksymovych, Ivanenko [?—E.B.], Kostenko [?—E.B.]. Some names I cannot remember any more due to the passage of time, but there were in deliberation with me people of both the secular and the religious estates, and many eminent persons, who took with them our decisions to Ukraine" (p. 10).

3. "Several times, when I would like to stress more exactly some point, I was told [by my co-workers] that they are satisfied with the *generalia*, having trust in my dedication" (p. 77).

4. "We worked on this [article 6 of the Constitution] longer than one month. My emissaries traveled twice to and from Ukraine. This inflicted a burden on me, since I had to code the [Constitution] project in ciphers for the distinguished officers of Ukraine. Mr. Voinarovs'kyi helped me in this task" (p. 12).

B. Translation of Hryhor Orlyk's French Remarks

"This charter [Constitution] has a long preamble which I possess in the Cossack language and which describes the fortunes and misfortunes of the Cossack people. This preamble was accepted unanimously, after short discussion. It was my father himself who inserted there a passage saying that the Cossack people was always vocal against the autocracy.

"Concerning the notion that the Cossack people is the immediate successor to the Khazar state, my father learned it from the Old Latin authors, and one churchman [Parthenius—E.B.], an educated person and friend of my father, found the same proofs in the theological [!—E.B.] books. My father also wrote to me that if the Cossack people had preserved their ancient princes, those princes would have a greater right to the patrimony of the Eastern Empire than the present Russian Empress [Elizabeth, 1741–1762]" (pp. 11–12).

C. Translation of the Polish Addition by Pylyp Orlyk

"The fortress of Bendery is elevated along the Dnister. Down near the river itself lies the plain where His Swedish Highness had his camp at the beginning of our peregrination [1710]. To the south and to the southwest of the Swedish camp on the plain my election to the office of Hetman took place. The town itself, which is commanded by a *serasker* [Ottoman commandant], has a garrison of 1,000 men. Here live Greeks, Armenians, and Jews. The latter live in the suburbs, where they even have their synagogue, rather interesting in appearance, which I, however, failed to view in a detailed way" (p. 14).

NOTES

1. The only study dealing with the Constitution of 1710 known to me is by Mykola Vasylenko, published in *Uchenye zapiski Instituta Istorii RANIION* (Moscow 1929) 7: 153–71. It was translated into English in *The Annals of the Ukrainian Arts and Sciences in the U.S.* 6(3–4) 21–22 (1958): 1260–1295.

2. Borschak visited Dinteville in 1922 as a guest of the grandfather of the present owner.

3. It is titled *Pylyp Orlyk: Vyvid prav Ukraïny. Z rukopysu rodynnoho arkhiva Dentevil' u Frantsiï. Zi vstupom i prymitkamy podav Il'ko Borshchak. Vydannia druhe, vypravlene i dopovnene.* It comprises 3 unnumbered and 92 numbered pages.

4. Numbers in parentheses here represent the pagination of the unpublished typescript of the Borschak second edition.

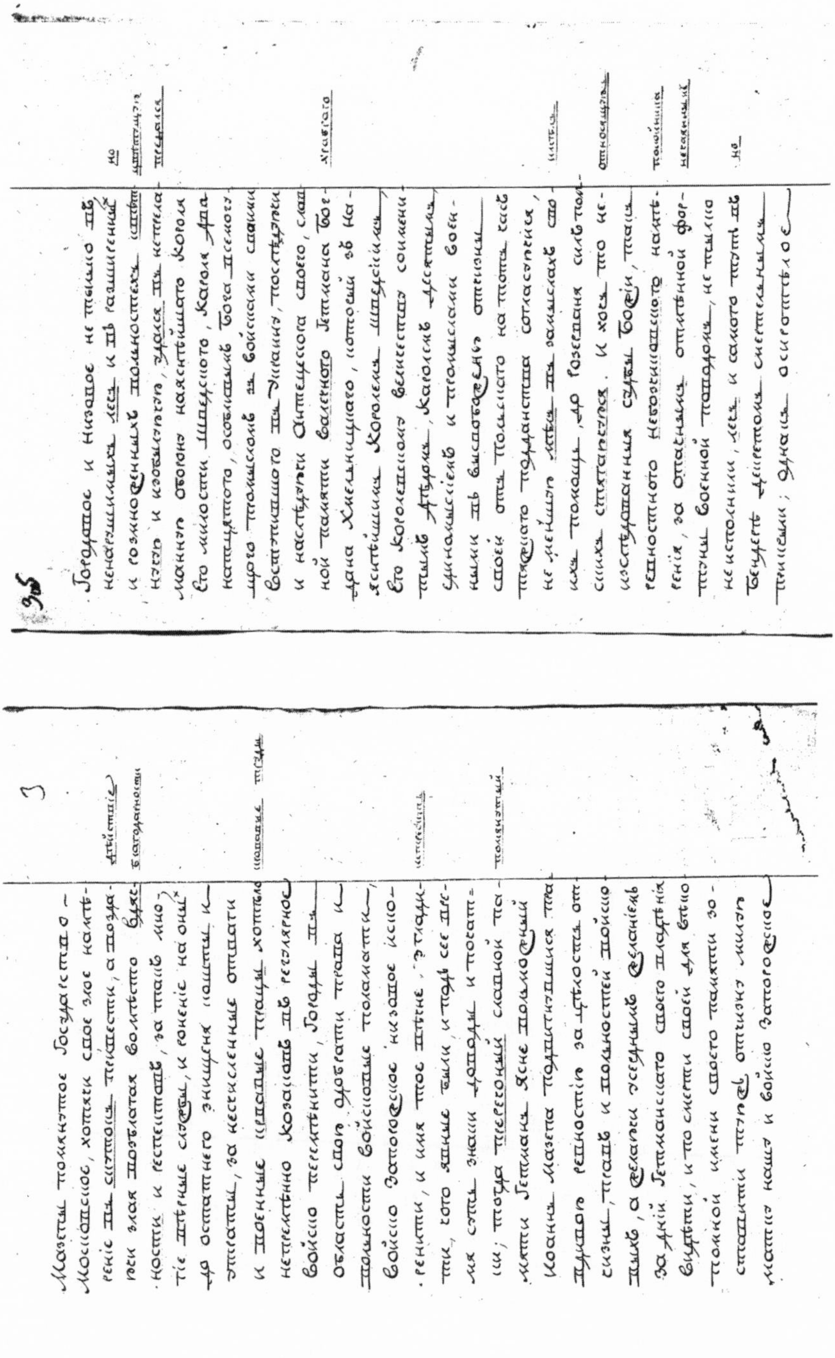

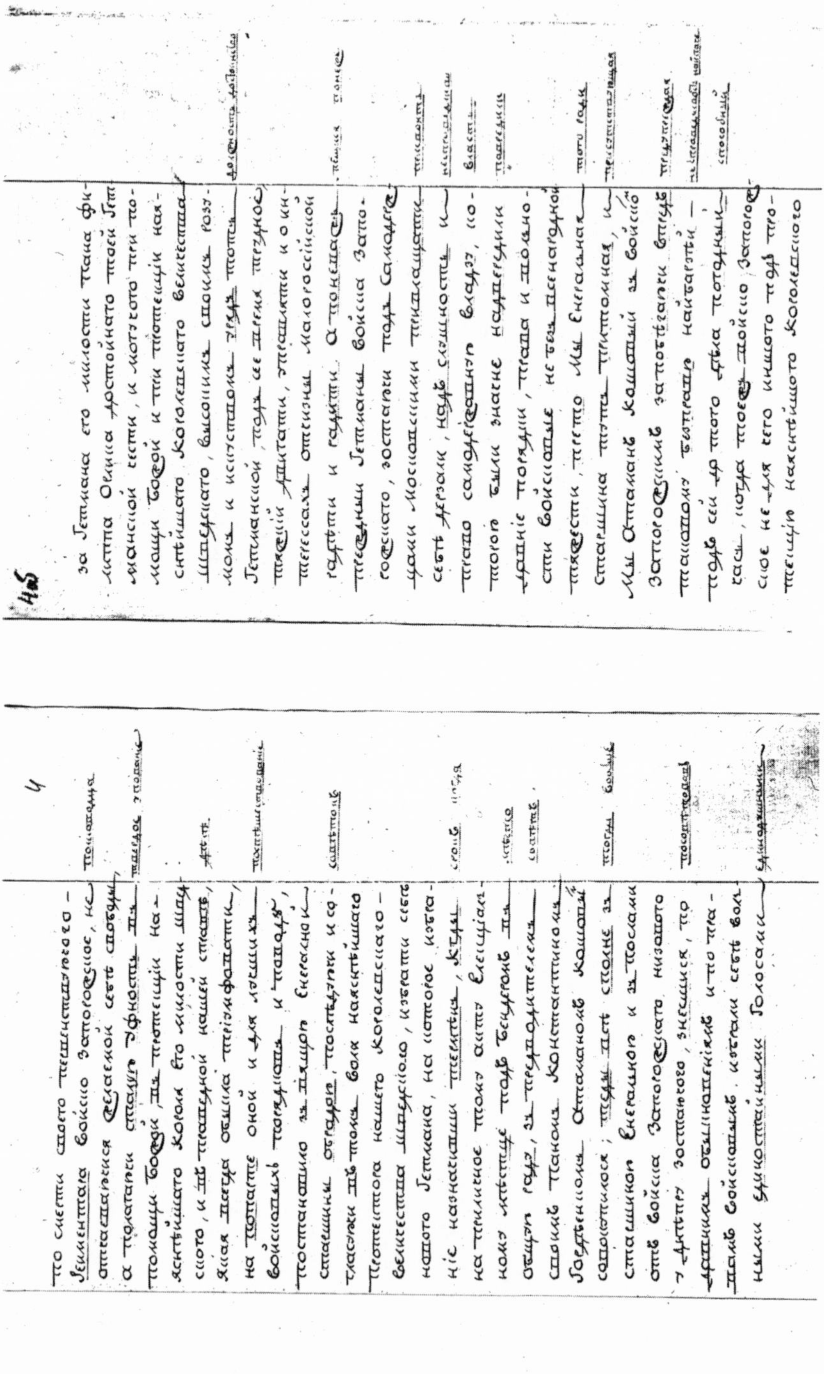
4

по смерти своего пешенствующого —
Гетмана Войско Запорожское, не
отступаючися желаемой себѣ свободы,
а полагаючи статую уфность въ
помощи Божой, въ протекціи Наяснѣйшаго Короля его милости Шведского, и въ теперѣшней нашей смутѣ,
якая всегда обыкла тріумфовати
на упадке оной и для лучшихъ
войсковыхъ порядковъ и поводовъ,
постановило зъ пілною Генеральной
старшины отрадою, посполу и со-
гласуючи въ томъ воли наяснѣйшаго
Протектора нашего Королевского —
Величества Шведского, избрати себѣ
нового Гетмана, на которое избра-
ніе назначивши теперь, [illegible]
на приличное тому акту Елекціал-
ному мѣстце подъ Бендеромъ въ
общую раду, зъ предводителемъ
своимъ Паномъ Константиномъ
Гордѣенкомъ Атаманомъ Кошовымъ
совокупилося; тогды все сполне зъ
старшиною Генеральною и зъ Послами
отъ Войска Запорожского низового
з Днѣпру зосталого, знесшися, по
давнимъ обыкновеніямъ и по пра-
вамъ войсковымъ, избрали себѣ воль-
ными единогласными Голосами

405

за Гетмана его милости Пана Фи-
липпа Орлика достойнаго тоей Гет-
манской чести, и могущого при помощи Божой и при протекціи Наяснѣйшаго Королевского Величества
Шведского, высокимъ своимъ розу-
момъ и искусствомъ уряду того
Гетманского, подъ сее время трудное,
тяжкий двигати, управляти и о ин-
тересахъ отчизны Малороссійской
радѣти и радити. А понеже нѣ-
которыи Гетманы Войска Запорожского, зоставши подъ Самодерж-
цами Московскими, присвояти
себѣ дерзали, надъ слушность и
право самодержавную владзу, ко-
торого были значне надвередили
давніе порядки, права и вольно-
сти войсковые не безъ всенародной
тягости, прето Мы Генеральная
Старшина теперь притомная, и
Мы Атаманъ Кошовый зъ Войскомъ
Запорожскимъ запобѣгаючи впредь
таковому безправію найбарзѣй —
подъ сей до того дѣла потребный
часъ, когда тое Войско Запорожское не для чего иншого подъ про-
текцію Наяснѣйшого Королевского

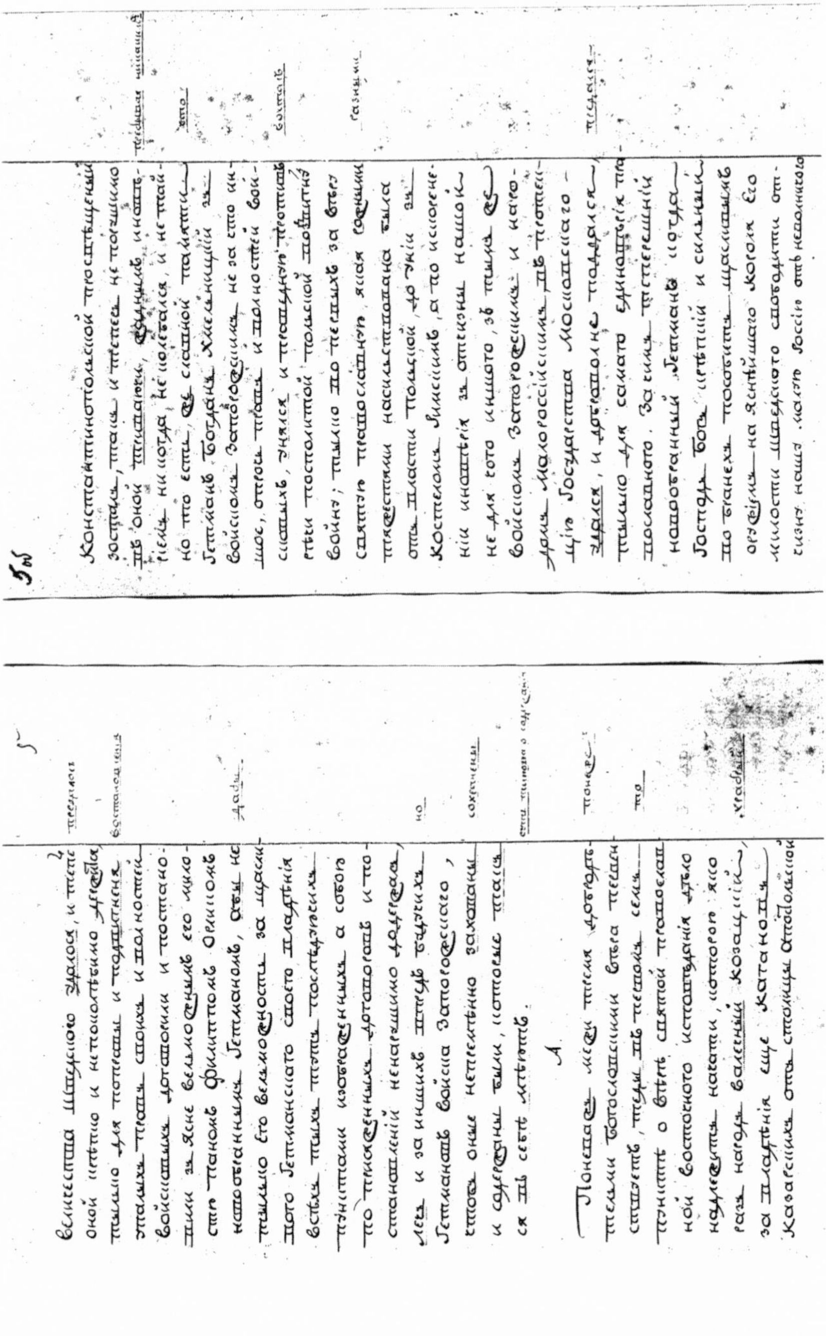

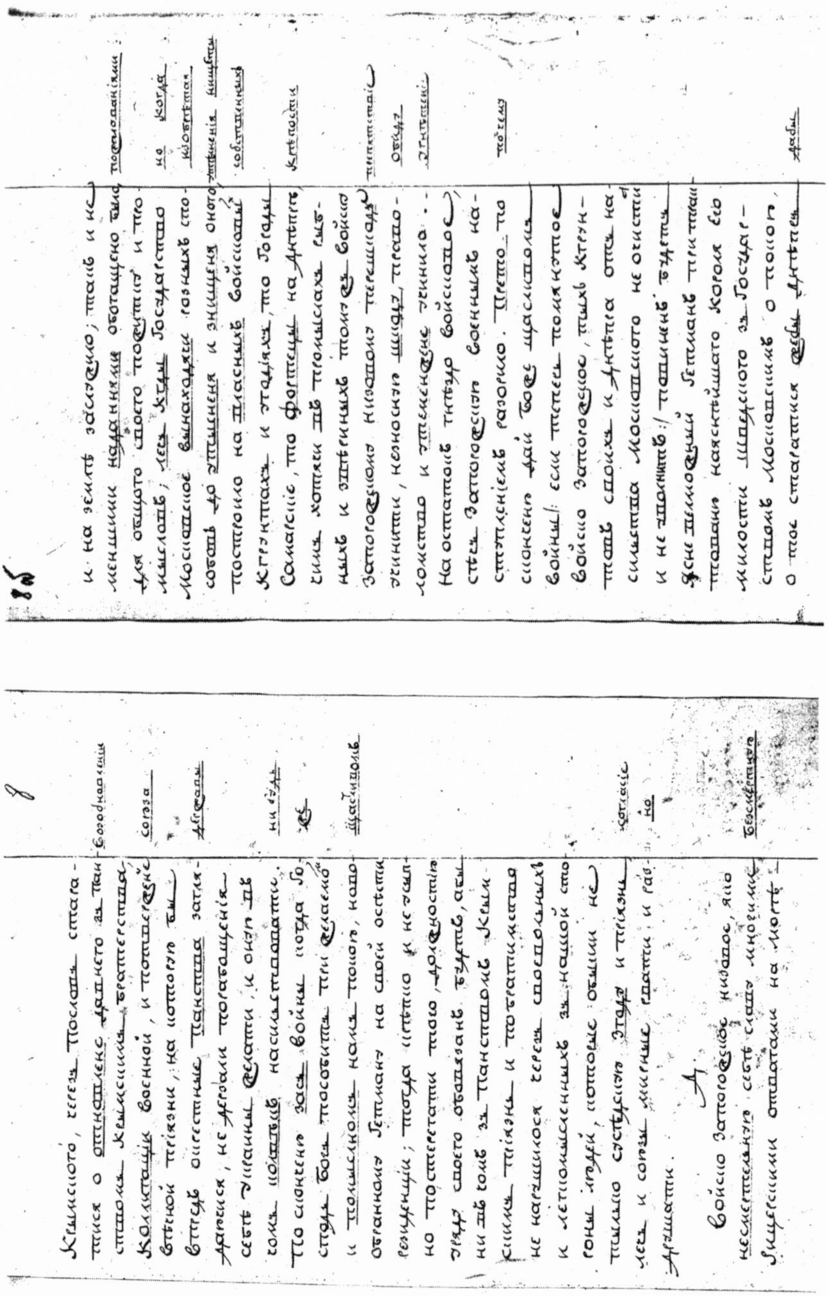

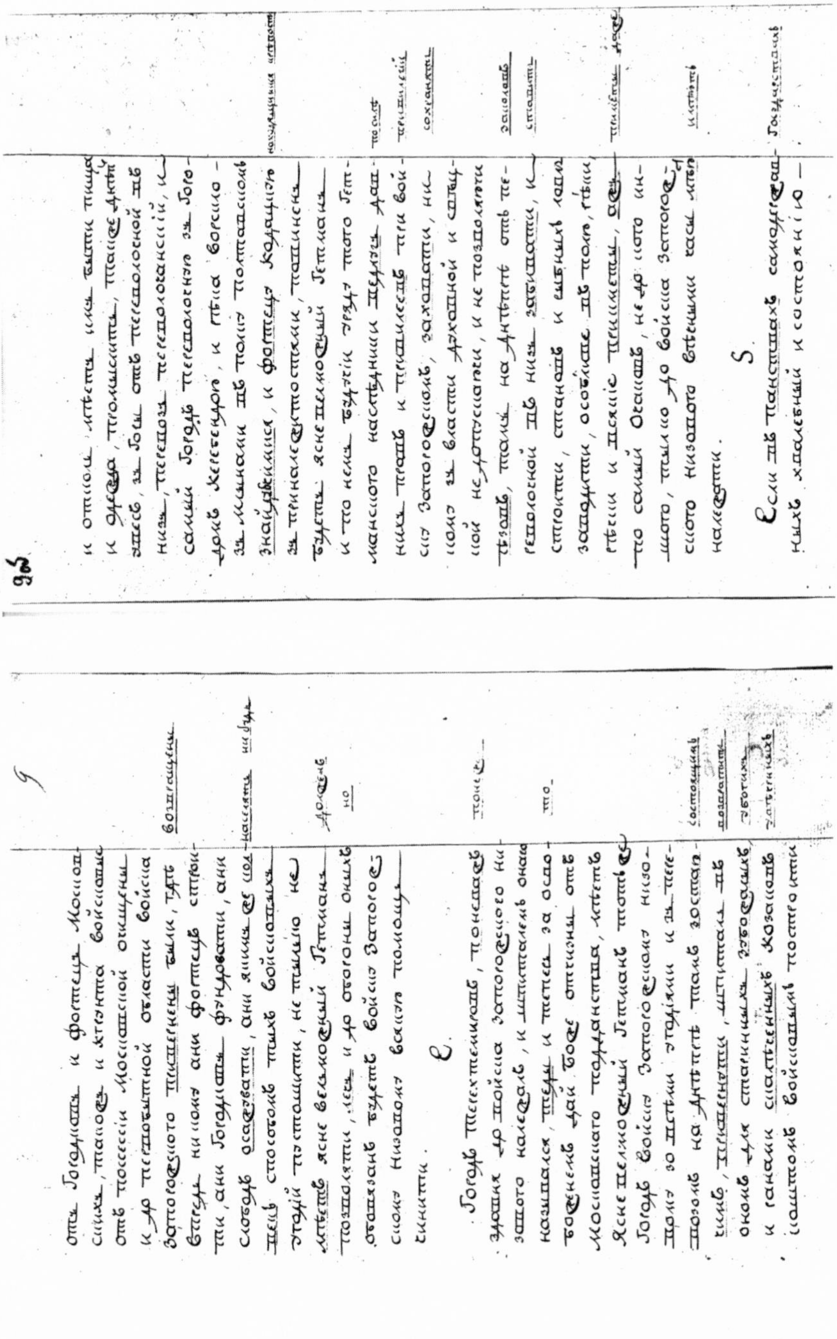

11

будетъ теперешній ясне вельможный	
Гетманъ и его сукцессорове о цѣ-	преемники
лости отчизны, о добрѣ оной поспо-	общественномъ
литомъ и о всякихъ дѣлахъ публич-	
ныхъ радитися, ни чого безъ ихъ со-	совѣтовати
изволенія и совѣту приватного —	
своею владзою не зачинати, не уста-	властію
новляти и въ скутокъ не приводи-	дѣйствіе
ти. Для чого теперь при Елекціи	
Гетманской единогласною всѣхъ	
згодою и ухвалою назначаются	совѣтомъ постановлений
три Генералные, въ кождомъ року	годъ
рады, мѣючіися въ резиденціи Гет-	совѣты имѣющіе
манской отправовати: первая	отправляться
о Рождествѣ Христовомъ, другая	
о Воскресеніи Христовомъ, третяя	
о Покровѣ Пресвятой Богородицы,	
на которые не тылко Панове	только Господа
Полковники зъ старшиною своею	
и сотниками, не тылко зо всѣхъ	
полковъ Генералныи совѣтники,	
лечъ и отъ Войска Запорожского	но
Низового для прислуханя ся и	
совѣтованія Послы мѣютъ и по-	
винны будутъ за присланіемъ къ	
себѣ отъ Гетмана ординансу при-	повелѣнія
бувати, ни чого назначеного терми-	срока
ну не ухиляючи; гдѣ что колвекъ	отлагая ни буд.
будетъ отъ Ясне вельможного —	

и5

Гетмана до общой згоды предло-	совѣта
жено, о томъ всѣмъ благосовѣстно,	
безъ жадныхъ приватного своего	всякихъ
и чужого пожитку респектовъ, безъ	пользы разсужденій
шкодливой зависти, и вражды со-	
вѣтовати обовязаны будутъ такъ	
далеце: жебы ни чого не было на	чтобы
тыхъ радахъ зъ уближеніемъ чести	согласованія уменьшеніе
Гетманской зъ публичною отчизны	
тяжестію, и разореніемъ а не дай	
Боже и погубою. Если бы зась о-	же
проч тыхъ вышреченныхъ до Гене-	
ралной рады назначенныхъ тер-	совѣта сроковъ
миновъ, притрафлялися якіе пуб-	
личные справы, скорого управле-	дѣла
нія, исправленія и отправленя потре-	
буючіе; тогды ясне вельможный	тогда
Гетманъ моценъ и воленъ будетъ	властенъ
зъ згодою Генералной старшины,	совѣтомъ
таковые дѣла поратою своею	властію
Гетманскою управляти и отпра-	
вляти. Такъже если бы якіе пись-	
ма приходилися зъ заграничныхъ	
постороннихъ Панствъ до Ясне-	
вельможного Гетмана одинованные,	
тогды (оные) мѣетъ Его вельможность	тогда имѣетъ
Генералной старшинѣ объявляти	
и отвѣты якіе отписоватимутся	

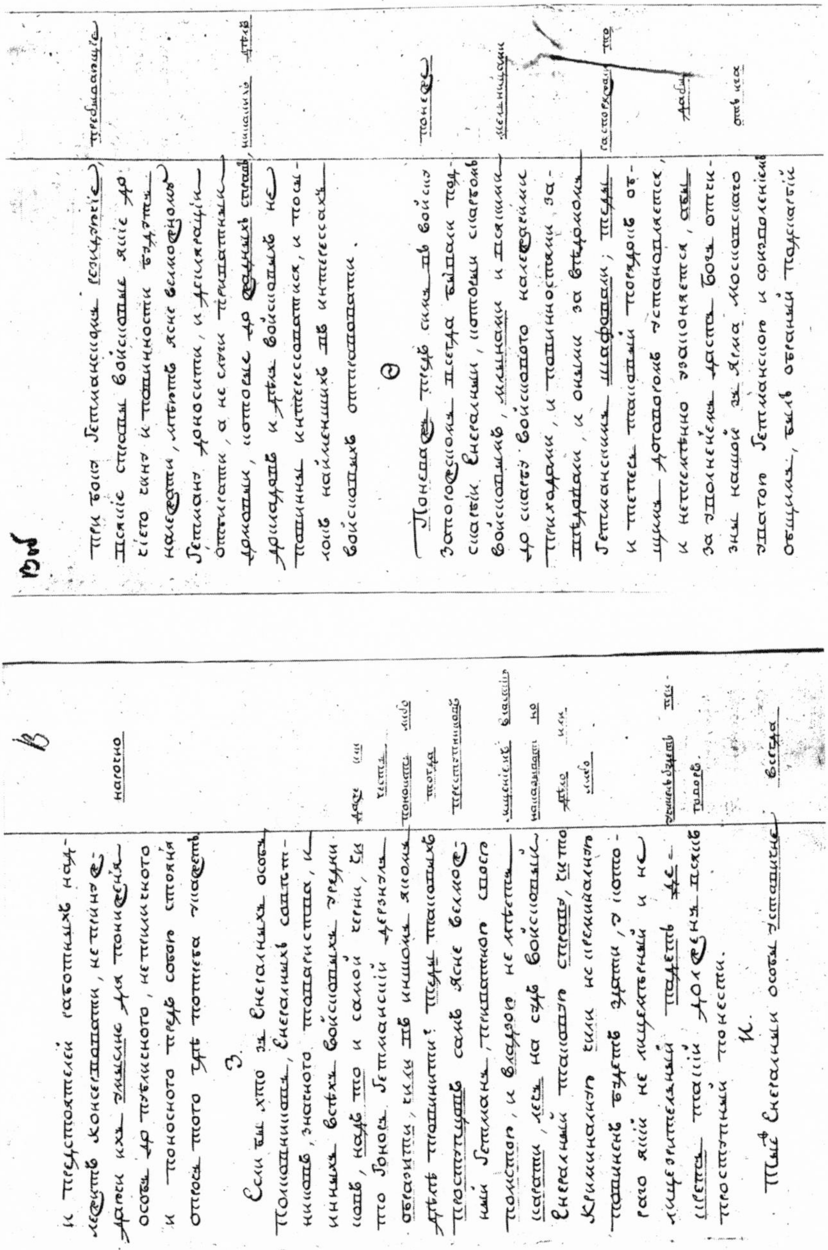

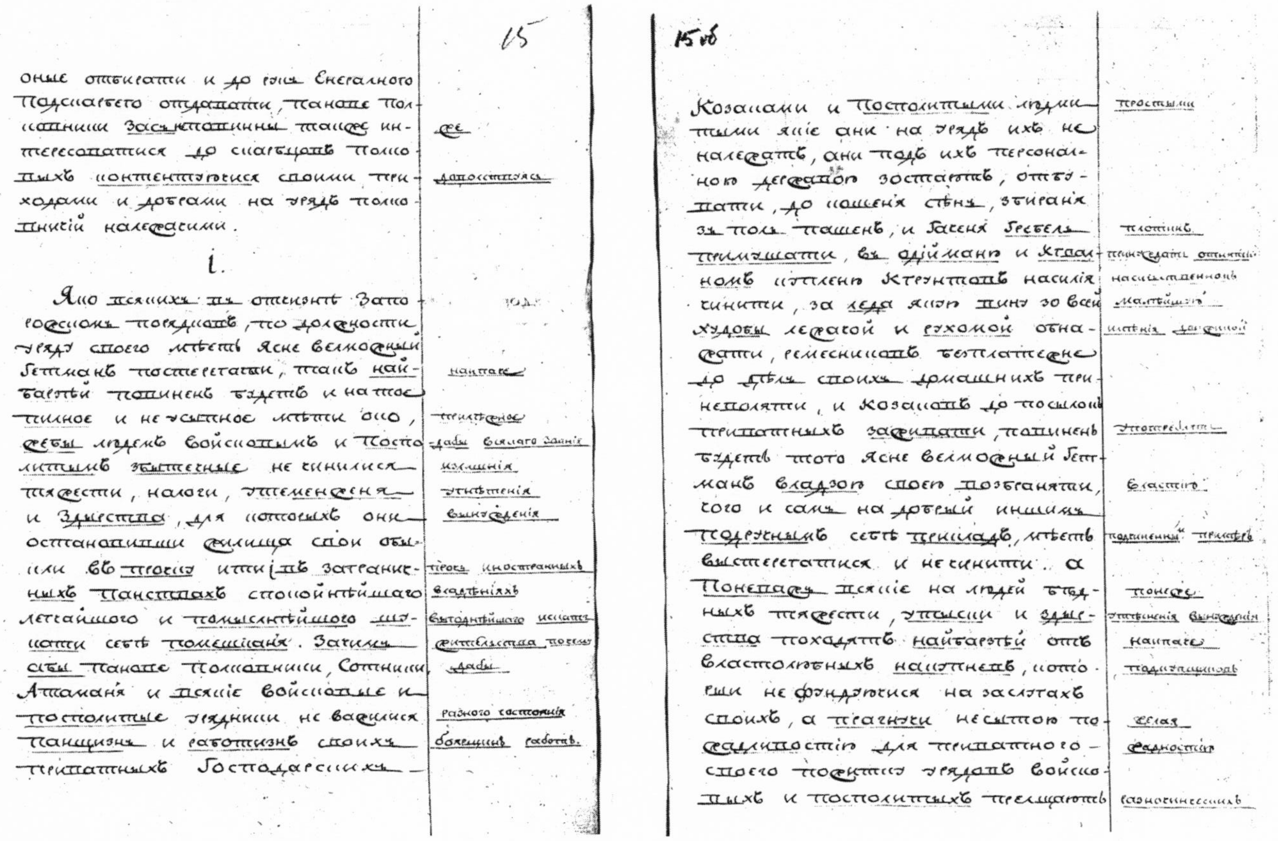

16

серце Гетманское Корупціями,	подкупами
и оными впихаются, безъ пол-	
ного избранія надъ слушностъ	противъ справедливости
и право то на уряды полков-	
ницкіе, то на иншіе власти. Пре-	почему
то всемонесне постановляется,	
абы Ясне Велможный Гетманъ	
жадными хоть бы найболшими	никакими хотя
не уводятися датками и респек-	льститься
тами ни кому за корупція уря-	
довъ Полковницкихъ и иншихъ	
войсковыхъ и посполитыхъ нигдѣ	общественныхъ
не дѣвалъ, и насилно на оные ни-	
кого не настановлялъ, лечъ всегда	но
якъ войсковые такъ и посполитые	
урядники мають быти волными	
Голосами; особливе засъ Полковники	же
обираны, а по избранію владзою	властію
Гетманскою потвержаны; од-	
накъ таковыхъ урядниковъ Елек-	
ціи не безъ воли Гетманской	
отправоватися повинны. Тоежъ	
право должны будутъ и Полковники	
захововати, и не постановляти	сохранять
безъ полного избранія цѣлой Сот-	
ни; Сотниковъ и иншихъ уряд-	
никовъ для корупцій и якихъ же	
колвекъ респектовъ, а для уразъ	ни будь

16об

своихъ приватныхъ не повинны	
такъ же отъ урядовъ отстанов-	
ляти.	
аі.	
Вдовы козацкіе и осиротѣлые	
Козацкіе дѣти, жоны Козацкіе,	
и жоны безъ бытности самыхъ	
козаковъ, когда въ походахъ, албо	или
на якихъ же колвекъ службахъ	
войсковыхъ знайдоватимутся,	
жебы до всякихъ посполитыхъ	дабы
повинностей не были потягаными,	понуждаемы
и вымаганемъ датковъ обтя-	обременяемы
жаны договорено и постановлено.	
ві.	
Не меншая Городамъ Украинскимъ	
и оттоль дѣется тяжесть, же	что
многіе села до нихъ для отбуванья	
всякихъ посполитыхъ повинностей	
належачіе, подъ розныхъ державцовъ	
духовныхъ и свѣцкихъ въ Поссесію	
поотходили, жители засъ ихъ пос-	же простолюдины
политые въ малолюдствіи остав-	
шіеся, мусятъ безъ жадной полег-	принуждены всякой об-
кости тіежъ самые двигати тяжары,	легченія тягости
якіе за помощію оторваныхъ	
и одийшлыхъ селъ на себѣ носили.	
За чимъ за установленіемъ отъ военного	почему

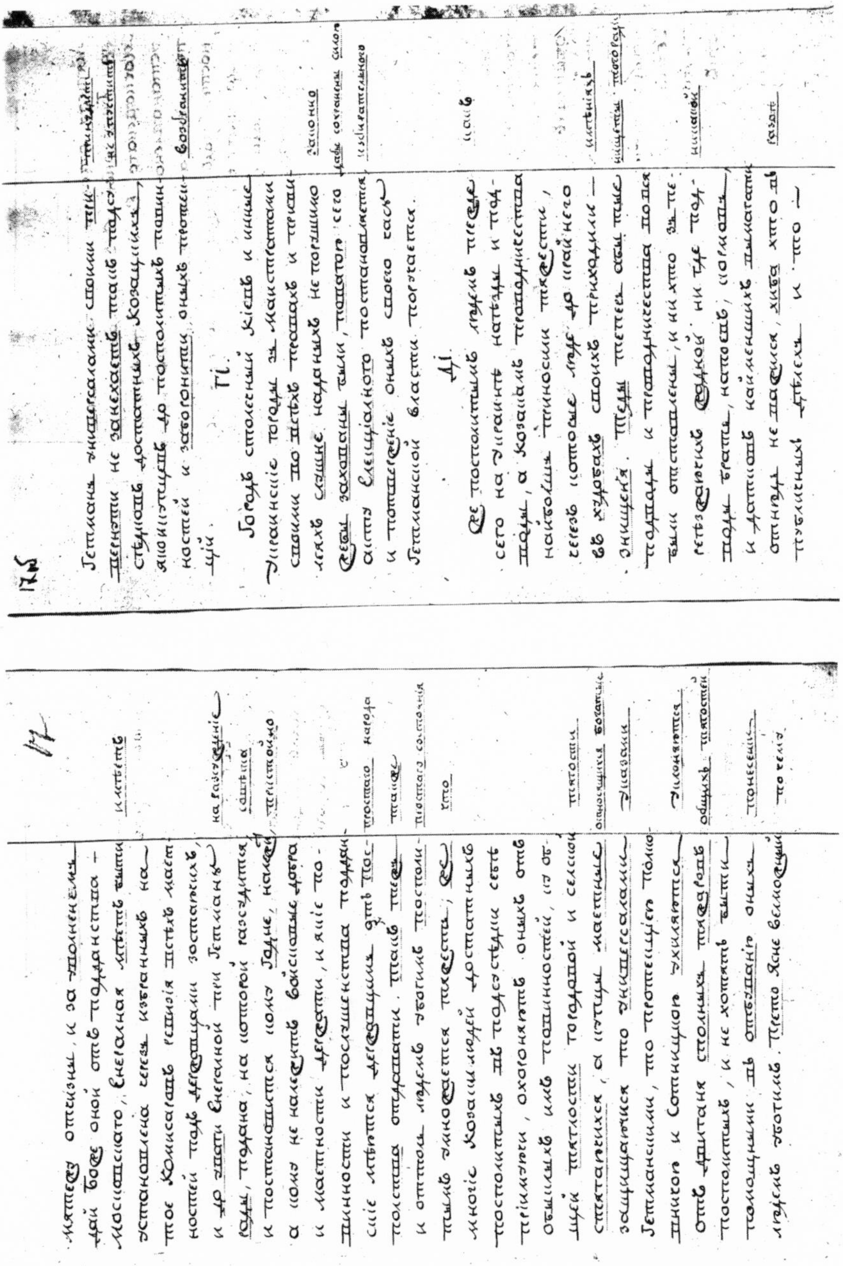

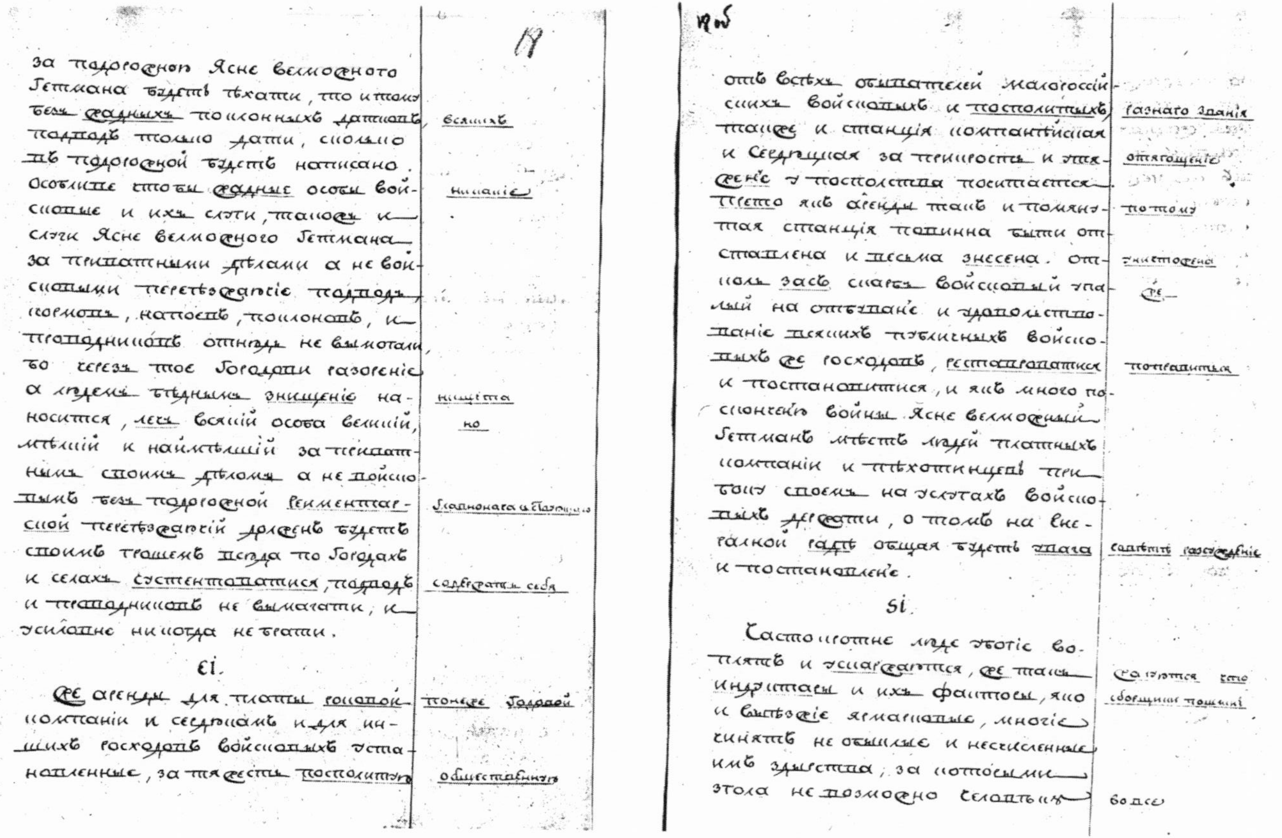

(М.П:)

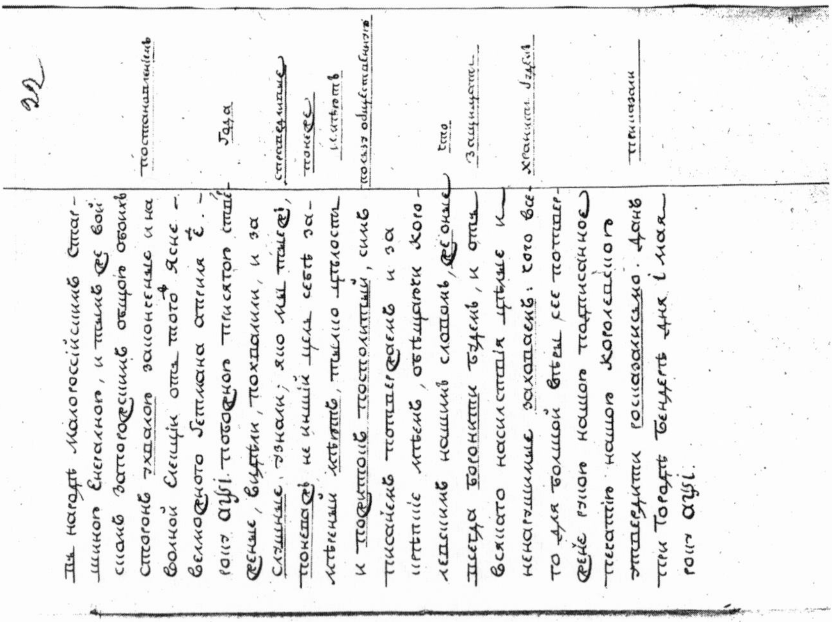

22

тѣ народъ Малороссійскимъ Старшиною Генералною, и тымъ же вой-
скамъ Запорожскимъ общою обоихъ
сторонъ ухвалою законченные и на
волной Елекціи отъ того Ясне-
велможного Гетмана априля є.
року аѱі. поборною присягою ствер-
женые, видѣли, прохвалили, и за
слушные узнали; яко мы тежъ,
понеже не иншій цель себѣ за-
мѣреный мѣтимъ, тылко цѣлости
и покоеви посполитый, симъ
писанїемъ потвержаемъ и за
цѣлые мѣемъ, обѣщаючи Коро-
левскимъ нашимъ словомъ, же оные
всегда боронити будемъ, и отъ
всякого насилствїя цѣлые и
ненарушимые захопаемъ: чого все-
то для болшой вѣры сее потвер-
женїе рукою нашою подписанное
печатїю нашою Королевскою
утвердити росказалисьмо. Данъ
при Городѣ Бендерѣ дня і мая
року аѱі.

- постановленіемъ
- Года
- справедливые
- понеже
- имѣютъ
- покою общественному
- что
- защищати
- хранити будемъ
- приказали

Nationalism and Communist Multiethnic Polities: The Legacies of Ethnicization

TERESA RAKOWSKA-HARMSTONE

The impact of the communist political system and communist policies on the growth of ethnic nationalism within the communist "federations," and the disruptive role of that nationalism, seem to have been largely neglected in the analysis of the breakup of multiethnic communist states. The salience of the communist-generated emphasis on ethnicity in postcommunist nation building has also been largely overlooked, with "primordial" ethnic hatreds and historic conflict usually blamed for ethnic friction, chauvinism, xenophobia, ethnic discrimination, and "ethnic cleansing," all of which have surfaced in the postcommunist political arena.

Yet, the system-specific structural and policy features proved more effective by far in stimulating the ethnic identity and nation-based loyalties of the component nations of the communist federations than in developing the "internationalist" loyalties envisaged by the system's founders. Class loyalties failed to generate political and emotional support, while the salience of ethnic politics for instrumental as well as affective purposes gained strength as the system matured and its various pathologies developed and intensified.[1]

But national loyalties did not aggregate statewide. A common cultural base was too weak, and the development of a new one was doomed *ab initio* by the national ambitions either of the hegemonic nation or of competing major nations. Instead, political legitimacy took root at the level of the constituent national republics that represented the titular ethnic communities. Eventually, as communism collapsed, the republics appropriated the sovereignty that had been vested in the overarching political center, claiming legitimacy on an ethnic basis. The titular ethnicity of the successor states became the framework within which they proceeded to forge their new national identities. In many cases the framework coincided with traditional identity, but sometimes it did not, or else was an entirely new one.

Disintegration

The outcome of disintegration was the same for the three multiethnic communist states and formal federations—the Soviet Union, Yugoslavia, and Czechoslovakia—although objective conditions such as historical, cultural, and demographic factors varied enormously. It can be argued that there were significant variations also in the effect that the systemic features and policies have had on the growth and explosive force of particular nationalisms, depending on the circumstances. The intensity of ethnic fervor appears to have been highest and most disruptive in Yugoslavia and the mildest in Czechoslovakia, with variable intensity observed throughout the Soviet Union.

The Soviet-type system, "national in form and socialist in content," had been adopted by all three federations.[2] Its most important structural feature was that the parallel Party and state structures, common to all communist systems, were established on an ethnic territorial base. In other words, the constituent republics of the federations were based, by and large, on the territorial area of settlement of major ethno-national communities. Thus, the territorial-administrative divisions, shared both by the Party and state bureaucracies, not only conformed to preexisting ethnic boundaries, but were also a formal embodiment of the titular groups' nationhood. The state represented the "national form," while the Party represented the "socialist (class) content" of the Leninist formula and was the decision-making and controlling agent. The republics' parties were merely territorial branches of the central Party apparatus, charged with supervising the state bureaucracies, whose task was to implement Party decisions.[3] The Party program specifically emphasized the centralized character of Party administration in contrast to the formal federal nature of the state. With central control assured, the "national" arrangement was designed to serve purely instrumental purposes, following the Marxist assumption that a superstructure (in this case national identity) takes time to "wither away" after the economic base has been changed. Its instrumental value, moreover, proved useful in the center's pursuit of the "divide and rule" principle.

The formal identity of titular ethnic communities was enhanced further by the cultivation and development in each republic of the titular culture (albeit within "socialist" parameters), including the national language and art forms, and through the political and social preference given to titular cadres. In Soviet practice, the preferential treatment of the titular group was modified by the privileged role reserved for Russian personnel (representing the central authorities), Russian language (as the language of "interethnic communication"), and Russian culture (as a model to be emulated)—a modification that created an additional source of ethnic friction.

Yugoslavia's class-based political loyalties were undercut from the outset by the country's expulsion in 1948 from the Cominform (the post-World War II version of the Communist International), which forced the Yugoslav Party both to revalidate itself in national terms and to find new class legitimacy in the principle of self-management. Both caused a shift of political gravity from the center to the constituent republics. The Yugoslav Party was transformed into a federation of national parties and the primacy of the republics was institutionalized in the 1974 Constitution. The conflicting interests of the republics, combined with the unanimity principle at the federal level, led to the system's paralysis and eventual disintegration after the death of its founder and ultimate arbiter, Josip Broz Tito, in 1980.[4]

The centrally exercised leading role of the Communist Party of the Soviet Union was kept intact in the long years of Stalin's rule. But the process of "nationalization"—the shift from class to nation as the basis of legitimacy— was hastened by World War II, known as the "Great Patriotic War," which was waged in defense of the (primarily Russian) Motherland. Multiple vertical lines of control between the republics and the center served to maximize particular national "solitudes." At the same time, the historical/cultural national identity of the republics' titular communities revived and crystallized on an ethnic basis under the powerful influence of both positive and negative policy stimuli. Cultural policies favoring the titular ethnicity, and modernization—the long-range effects of which brought educational advancement and social and economic development, and created new national elites—belonged in the first category. The second included political subservience to and economic dependence on Moscow, as well as the ubiquitous presence of the Russian "Big Brother."

Centralized control mechanisms were eroded by struggles over political succession and by the system's corruption. There was seepage of political power from Moscow, the all-Union center, to the republican capitals in a quid pro quo of support, privilege, and back scratching rooted in the republic-based informal power networks. The coup de grâce came with the crisis of Gorbachev's reforms, which destroyed the power of the central apparat and empowered the Party-state bureaucracies of the republics—a process in which the Russian Republic (RSFSR) under Boris Yeltsin took the lead. The Baltic republics were the first unequivocally to demand independence. Other republics initially opted for "sovereignty," which effectively preempted the center's power of diktat. Ukraine's declaration of sovereignty was crucial in thwarting Yeltsin's ambition to claim most of the Soviet political space for the new Russia. With the transfer of political power from the supranational to national jurisdiction, the all-Union administrative structures—the Party as well as the state—lost their raison d'être and the USSR ceased to exist.[5]

The system-specific empowerment of the republics was decisive in the disintegration of Yugoslavia and in the opening of a new round of ethnic conflict there. It was of crucial importance also in the breakup of the USSR. In both cases the impact of communism interacted with and enhanced the accumulated historical experience of national identity and ethnic rivalries. Neither the Yugoslav nor the Soviet ethno-national communities had been able to accumulate a body of shared, positive historical experience sufficient to build an overarching political identity. Rather, the cultivation by each republic of its own particular "aquarium"[6] only served to maximize differences. Thus national integration under the common umbrella of a new "Soviet" or "Yugoslav" nation never had a chance.

The same was true in the case of the "Czechoslovak" nation. There the impact of the state on the consolidation of the respective Czech and Slovak national identities both predated and outweighed the relatively short period of communism. For the Czechs, the consolidation of their national identity was the nineteenth-century product of Austrian rule within the Austro-Hungarian Empire. For the Slovaks—subjected to magyarization under Hungarian rule prior to 1918—the decisive period in which their national consciousness had been formed was between the wars, when Czechs and Slovaks were first united in a single political entity. But this common experience did not lead to an effective integration. Interwar democratic Czechoslovakia was unable to grant the Slovaks the desired autonomy because of a German minority more numerous than the Slovaks. Instead, an effort was made to develop a "Czechoslovak" nation, which failed because in Slovak eyes "Czechoslovak" was synonymous with "Czech." Slovak national ambitions were frustrated again after 1945— first, because the Slovak national state had become a Nazi puppet in World War II, and second, because the Czech hegemonic role had been confirmed and enhanced under communist political arrangements. Mutual alienation between the two communities was thus reinforced, and eventually led to the two republics' peaceful separation after the collapse of the communist regime.[7]

In all three cases, demographic realities and the salience of ethnicity in communist politics overshadowed ideological commitment to the class principle. The political momentum of the process of "ethnicization" focused political loyalties on the republics, the national identity of which had been consolidated. In some cases, notably Soviet Central Asia, new identities had actually been created by the "national in form" policy, which elevated local ethnic communities to the status of nations with their titular republics.

An overall assessment begs the question why, given the common political matrix, the Soviet and Czechoslovak breakups were peaceful, while ethnic conflict and armed confrontations have dominated the post-Yugoslav scene. Apart from other factors, the answer in the first two cases can perhaps be found in the consensus of the ruling elites of national republics on the outcome desired: namely, separate statehood. This consensus overshadowed residual conflicts between Soviet republics.[8] In Yugoslavia, on the other hand, the intensity of ethnicization was higher, and national elites were in conflict over three competing dissolution scenarios. The scenarios were: a federation synonymous with "Greater Serbia," promoted by Serbia and Montenegro; a confederation of independent states, advocated by Croatia and Slovenia; and a dual sovereignty in-between model, proposed by Bosnia-Herzegovina and Macedonia, which emphasized autonomy for the minorities. At the time of Yugoslavia's breakup, each republic was in active pursuit of its goals by all available means, including "ethnic cleansing" and military force.[9]

It should be noted, however, that much "ethnic cleansing" took place in the USSR and contiguous East Central Europe under Stalin before, during, and after World War II, and as a result of the Nazi occupation and the Holocaust. In some cases, as in the Polish-Ukrainian historical conflict, the resulting demographic changes in the disputed territories made subsequent accommodation easier. In others—as in Latvia and Estonia, where mass "cleansing" of national elites was followed by a mass influx of Russian immigrants—it had created a new and bitter conflict that has poisoned post-independence politics. In the memory of the nations affected, the cleansing left a legacy of hatred. But in the minds of ambitious politicians, such as Serbia's Slobodan Milošević, it left a perception of routinized legitimacy: the practice was frequently used, and it worked.

Nation Building

Ethnicity and ethnic loyalties have played a crucial role in forging the new national identities of the successor states. Many—as in the case of the Baltic states, Armenia, and Serbia—reverted to their well-defined historical identities, with their frequently attached historical and demographic claims. Some, such as Ukraine or Croatia, were building new nations in centuries-old historical states, or—as in the cases of Slovakia or Moldova—were starting from scratch. All or nearly all have had problems with minorities, of whom some are long-settled and some are more recently arrived. In all cases the communist experience of ethnicization and totalitarian politics has cast a long shadow over the process. The communist past has affected interaction between titular communities and minorities within new polities, as well as their relations with neighbors. Few of the new states are ethnically homogenous. Most have conationals across the border as well as substantial minorities within, and the treatment and status of the latter have been the measure of national integration as well as the touchstone of democracy.

The problem of minorities has been compounded by the fact that the centrifugal forces generated by communist ethnic politics did not stop at the new boundaries. Under the "national in form, socialist in content" formula all ethnic communities in the USSR had the right to have their ethnicity recognized in formally autonomous territorial units such as autonomous republics, districts, or regions, and in the cultivation of their ethnic cultures.[10] In practice, the former were largely reduced in day-to-day administration to name recognition, while the latter frequently amounted to the promotion of folklore. Nevertheless, the momentum of ethnicization survived the breakup. It continued within the successor states and has emerged as a major threat to their nation building and national integration.

The problem has been acute in the Russian Federation, where the minorities are "housed" in 21 ethnic republics, 10 autonomous districts, and one autonomous region.[11] Units with resources, such as Sakha (Yakutia), have pursued de facto independent policies. Most republics stop short of demanding formal independence. Some have claimed sovereignty, as in the case of Tatarstan. Chechnya, on the other hand, has fought two bloody wars to throw off Moscow's control—and that conflict also spread briefly into neighboring Dagestan. The north Caucasian ethno-religious mosaic has been a seething cauldron, with spillover into Georgia and Azerbaijan. Ethno-religious strife has contributed to civil war in Tajikistan and to friction in other Central Asian states.

In former Yugoslavia, only Serbia had two lower-level autonomous ethnic units. Demands for independence in one of these, the predominantly Albanian Kosovo, erupted into a major international conflict.[12]

Special integration problems exist in those post-Soviet states that have large resident Russian populations—not only because of their size, but also their former privileged status, political and economic importance, and, last but not least, their foreign policy relevance in relations with Russia. This group includes seven former Soviet republics.[13] Moscow has taken a fiercely proprietary approach in defending the status of the Russian diaspora there, even using the threat of potential intervention. It has pressed for Russians' right to dual citizenship (Russian in addition to local), and for their civil and cultural (especially language) rights.

The Czech Republic is nearly homogeneous and has had few minority problems, except for discrimination against the Roma (Gypsy) population, and acknowledged xenophobic attitudes. But the treatment of Slovakia's large Hungarian minority—denied cultural rights and deprived, de facto, of civil rights under the government of Prime Minister Mečiar—has been of concern to the international community.

In the states of former Yugoslavia, only Slovenia has been free of minority problems. Elsewhere, the treatment of the minorities and the desire to bring under one flag both the "historical territory" and all ethnic "brethren" have served as a *casus belli,* and in more than one case, an excuse for "ethnic cleansing." The restoration of the peace in Bosnia, with its Muslim, Serb, and Croat communities[14] (the latter two coveted by the respective republics), has required an international occupation aimed at building a viable multiethnic community in the face of seemingly insurmountable odds. Serbs were "cleansed" from Croatia, and in turn engaged in vigorous "cleansing" of Muslims, Croats, and Albanians. The genocide of Albanians in Kosovo was stopped only by a NATO military intervention, which was also followed by an international occupation.

The emphasis on titular ethnicity as the determinant of statehood appears to be the most striking, albeit least expected, legacy of communism. Moreover, it has rarely been identified as such because it fits past historical experience as well as prevalent political paradigms. The legacy builds on the main features of communist-established ethnically defined entities: a political framework that provides the focus for ethnic claims; an "atmosphere" friendly to the titular group but inhospitable to others; and totalitarian methods of repressing troublesome or unwelcome minorities. This legacy has influenced the thinking and attitudes in successor states. But its radical manifestations have been tempered, in most cases, by practical domestic and foreign considerations, and only in exceptional cases were radical politicians able to occupy center stage.

But the trend toward reliance on ethnicity has been unmistakable. Using Gellner's parable of an aquarium, each titular nation has attempted to create its own particular ethnic environment inhospitable to minorities by maintaining barriers, regardless of their communist origins or of their transparency. This is not surprising, given the competing ethnoses and the absence, in most cases, of a civil society that would form a broader social base for political statehood.

The salience of ethnicity to nation building has manifested itself in various ways. A state is generally assumed to "belong" to its hegemonic national community. In the most extreme cases of "constitutional nationalism," exemplified by Croatia and Serbia, the titular group makes an explicit claim in the constitution to the "ownership" of the state, which automatically consigns ethnic minorities to a de facto second-class status.[15] Elsewhere this tendency has appeared in constitutional debates, reflecting a clash between the viewpoints of the titular nation and militant minorities, as in the case of Ukraine or Kazakhstan. Citizenship in most post-Soviet states has followed the "civic" concept, granting the status to all permanent residents of the country at the time of independence. Only Latvia and Estonia attempted to limit the citizenship largely to the titular group, prompted by the fear of the potential political and cultural influence that could be gained by their large immigrant Russian minorities. All but Tajikistan and Turkmenistan (each with relatively few Russians, however) refused to allow their resident Russians double citizenship, despite pressures from Moscow.

Language policy has been an instrument in the titular nations' determined efforts to stamp their ethnic character on the new polity and to keep "nontitular" elements out of the power structure. All successor states have adopted the language of the titular nation as the state language. In the post-Soviet region, the states with large Russian minorities refused, as a rule, to adopt Russian as a coequal official state language. This has been the case in Kazakhstan, as well as in Ukraine, despite the wide de facto use of Russian there in public (and private) life—large segments of the population do not speak the titular language, or speak it badly. Members of titular elites, who are least fluent in their native language, have also been most ardent in promoting it as the sole official language. They see it as a badge of the state's identity, in keeping with the assumption that a state needs to be somebody's homeland, and that this right belongs to the indigenous ethnic community.

Belarus is an exception on the language question. In the April 1995 national referendum, 80 percent of the participants voted to adopt Russian as the second official state language. Belarus had been among the most russified Soviet republics, its sense of national identity having evolved only in the 1980s in the program of a small group of national intelligentsia. Political leadership at independence actually came from the nationalist movement. But its constituency proved too narrow in the contest with the pro-Russian elements that returned to power in 1994. Thus the formation of post-independence national identity has been caught in the conflict between two mutually exclusive versions. One, espoused by the national opposition, favors its own "aquarium," and sees the Belarusian people as a distinct nation of ancient origins. The second, represented by the ruling elite, accepts the long-standing Russian version of a proto-Russian nation composed of three Eastern Slavic branches: Russians, Ukrainians, and Belarusians. The latter concept fits the government's program of reintegration with Russia, but even this group sees such integration as a union of equal partners. Meanwhile, the constituency of "national Belarus" is apparently growing, especially among the younger generation.[16]

Ukraine has decisively rejected the Russian version of a proto-Russian identity in favor of a historical identity stemming from Kyivan Rus', the later Cossack period, and, increasingly, the period of statehood in 1918–1920. A conflict between competing versions of national identity in Moldova (Romanian identity versus the Soviet-developed distinct Moldavian nation) was resolved in favor of a new compromise version which envisions a Moldovan nation with Romanian language and culture. This version has eclipsed the notion of reunification with Romania.

In sum, ethnicity has been an important but dangerous legacy. It has been at the center of both nation building and nation destroying. It has proved to be a superb instrument of political mobilization in support of causes both worthy and nefarious. It has been a detonator of imperial systems, and a glue—as well as a source of friction—in the national consolidation of the successor states. But reliance on ethnicity for nation building carries major caveats. In a replay of earlier historical experience, it promotes the concept of a nation-state defined in monoethnic terms (which hardly ever exists in reality) and precludes a broader civic base. Moreover, the exclusivity and xenophobia highlighted in the communist inheritance have marred even the most successful cases of transition from communism to democracy. Even worse, the emphasis on ethnicity routinized "ethnic cleansing."

A national state defined in ethnic terms relies on group rather than individual rights. It denies equal status to the minorities. This invites discrimination—including, at its most extreme, "ethnic cleansing" and genocide—and creates conflict both within and between states. Finally, by dividing the populace into first- and second-class citizens and subordinating individual to group rights, it is incompatible with democracy.

Reliance on ethnicity has been an important trend and a temptation in the postcommunist world. But, except for the post-Yugoslav turmoil, the advocates of ethnic states have by and large been politically marginalized in competition with the advocates of civic states. The latter support a national state defined in civic terms, which is home to both the titular group and the minorities. It extends citizenship and civil rights to all residents regardless of ethnicity, and guarantees cultural rights to minorities. Such a state develops the national heritage of the titular nation as well as that of the minorities, and protects political freedoms and civic equality. In short, it is compatible with democracy. The civic state concept has emerged as the dominant one in the postcommunist political space, but the legacies of precommunist ethnic quarrels and communist-bred exclusivity and xenophobia continue to survive in political and social attitudes.

NOTES

An early version of the argument presented here will appear in my "Introduction" to a volume entitled "Communist States and Nationalism: Policy and Legacies," Canadian Review of Studies in Nationalism *27(1–2) 2000.*

1. Nationalism proved to be equally effective for the purposes of political mobilization in the nationally homogeneous communist polities where, despite lip service to "internationalism," it became a touchstone of sovereignty and political identity.

2. The federal state structure was adopted formally by Czechoslovakia only in the reform of January 1968, but the federalization did not extend to the Party structure. See H. Gordon Skilling, *Czechoslovakia's Interrupted Revolution* (Princeton, 1976), Appendix C. After the 1948 coup, the Party was structured on the Soviet-type parallel Party-state model, although only the Slovaks had their own branch Communist Party (which was subordinated to the CPCz). (See note 3.)

3. An important anomaly in the Party structure was that the hegemonic nations in the Soviet Union and Czechoslovakia did not have a separate branch of the Party in their titular republics. Both were served by the central Party: the Russians by the Communist Party of the Soviet Union (CPSU) and the Czechs by the Communist Party of Czechoslovakia (CPCz). A partial concession towards equalizing the hegemonic group with the minorities was made in the Soviet Union under Khrushchev with the establishment of a Russian Bureau in the Central Committee of the CPSU, but the Bureau was abolished in 1964. A Czech Bureau was established in the Central Committee of the CPCz in Czechoslovakia in 1968. In Yugoslavia, on the other hand, the Serbs were not strong enough to establish a hegemonic status. Republican branches of the Party gained autonomy vis-a-vis the center as the Yugoslav Party became a federation of republican parties—a process which began in the 1950s and was completed in the 1970s. With decisions based on the principle of unanimity, the power of the center was effectively transferred to the republics.

4. See Dennison Rusinov, ed., *Yugoslavia: A Fractured Federation* (Washington, DC, 1988); and Laslo Sekelj, *Yugoslavia: The Process of Disintegration* (New York, 1993).

5. See Teresa Rakowska-Harmstone, "The Dialectics of Nationalism in the USSR," *Problems of Communism* 23 (May–June) 1974: 1–22; "Chickens Coming Home to Roost: A Perspective on Soviet Ethnic Relations," *Journal of International Affairs* 45 (Winter 1992): 519–49; and "Nationalism and Integration: The Implosion of the Soviet Union," *Canadian Review of Studies in Nationalism* 27(1–2) 2000 (forthcoming).

6. On the concept of "aquarium," see Ernest Gellner, *Nations and Nationalism* (Ithaca, 1983). I am indebted to William Fierman for the reference.

7. See Skilling, *Czechoslovakia's Interrupted Revolution*. Also Igor Lukes, "Czechs and Slovaks: The Failure to Find a Decent Past," *Cultural Survival* 19(2) 1995: 19–24.

8. The Armenian-Azerbaijani conflict over Nagorno-Karabakh, which predated the dissolution of the USSR, was an exception, and internal conflicts such as in the one in Moldova over Transdniester separatism, the Tajik civil war, or the Chechen rebellion in the Russian Federation, did not affect the consensus. Even the republics which did not advocate separation opted for independence as it became available.

9. Dejan Guzina, "The Self-Destruction of Yugoslavia," *Canadian Review of Studies in Nationalism* 27(1–2) 2000 (forthcoming).

10. The principle applied to indigenous groups residing in their traditional territory. It did not apply to migrant communities and it did not apply to the "punished" deported national groups. Soviet censuses enumerated more than 100 distinct national groups. The USSR statistical yearbook for 1989 listed 16 autonomous republics (ASSRs), 5 autonomous regions (oblasts), and 10 autonomous districts (okrugs) in the RSFSR; 1 ASSR in Uzbekistan; 2 ASSRs and 1 autonomous region in Georgia; 1 ASSR and 1 autonomous region in Azerbaijan; and 1 autonomous region in Tajikistan.

11. Under new constitutional arrangements, one ASSR (Chechen-Ingush) was broken into two republics (Chechnya and Ingushetia), and four autonomous regions were upgraded to republics.

12. Vojvodina, the other autonomous province, is multiethnic. Kosovars were refused the status of a republic in the Federal Republic of Yugoslavia—which would have given them independence at the breakup—because of Serbia's historical claims to Kosovo. Instead, Serbia revoked Kosovo's (and Vojvodina's) autonomy and instituted repressive policies.

13. The Russian minority constituted between some 20 and 40 percent of the population in five former republics on the eve of independence: Kazakhstan (38 percent), Latvia (34 percent), Estonia (30 percent), Kyrgyzstan (22 percent) and Ukraine (22 percent). Russians in Belarus and Moldova each constituted 13 percent of the population. All of these republics also have other minorities, making integration all the more difficult.

14. According to the 1991 census, 43 percent Muslim, 31 percent Serb, 17 percent Croat, and 6 percent "Yugoslav." See Guzina, "Self-Destruction."

15. See Robert Hayden, "Constitutional Nationalism in the Formerly Yugoslav Republics," *Slavic Review* 51(4) Winter 1992: 654–73.

16. David Riach, "A History of Belarussian National Thought: The Origins, Emergence and Development of the Belarussian 'National' Idea," Ph.D. dissertation, Carleton University, 2000.

Religious Exclusion and State Building:
The Roman Catholic Church and the Attempted Revival of Greek Catholicism in the Chełm Region, 1918–1924

KONRAD SADKOWSKI

In 1938 the Polish military and local authorities liquidated 127 Eastern Orthodox churches in the eastern Lublin province. The action derived from fears that
Orthodox churches were increasingly becoming centers of Ukrainian nationalist agitation, and was part of a larger campaign to polonize and Catholicize this
Polish-Ukrainian borderland. From the standpoint of the Roman Catholic administrative structure, most of the Orthodox churches were in the Lublin
diocese in the southern half of the province; the others, in the northern half,
were in the Siedlce (Podlasie) diocese. After Poland became independent in
1918, the Catholic clergy in the eastern Lublin diocese (the Chełm region)
strenuously opposed Orthodoxy; the bishop of Lublin, Maryan Leon Fulman,
participated in the work of the government "Coordinating Committee" that
carried out the destruction of the churches. The Lublin Church's anti-
Orthodox activities were one expression of the Polish Church's desire to build
a Catholic Poland after 1918. By the second half of the 1930s, the Lublin
Church's agenda dovetailed with the actions of increasingly nationalistic Polish governments.[1]

Until 1875, however, the Eastern Orthodox Church was virtually absent
from the Chełm (*Ukr.* Kholm) and Podlasie (*Ukr.* Pidliashshia) regions. Instead, the Greek Catholic (Uniate) Church had a strong presence there. While
there were some Polish Uniates, most Uniates were Ruthenian/Ukrainian *(Pol.*
"Rusini")—though they were not nationally conscious. In 1875, the Uniate
Church in the Kingdom of Poland was abolished through a so-called
"dobrovol'noe vossoedinenie" (voluntary unification) with the Russian Orthodox Church.[2] All Uniate properties were "transferred" to the Orthodox Church,
to be used now to russify (or prevent the polonization of) the Ruthenians, or
"Little Russians." After the abolition of the Uniate Church, many Uniates
refused to accept Orthodoxy and became "resisters." Risking fines, jail, or
exile, some Latin-rite priests aided these resistant Uniates, who were more
numerous in the Podlasie than the Chełm region. An important reason for the
different degrees of resistance is that Polish national identity was stronger in
the Podlasie than in the Chełm region.[3]

The situation changed only with the 1905 Russian revolution, when the
Toleration Edict of April 1905 allowed those who had been Uniates in the
territory of the former Polish-Lithuanian Commonwealth to reject Orthodoxy

by converting to another religion—though not to reclaim their Uniate churches and reassert their faith, since it remained officially abolished. As a result of the edict, approximately 175,000 former Uniates converted to Roman Catholicism; after all, the Uniates were loyal members of the Roman Church, though of the Greek rite.[4] However, many other former Uniates and their offspring, especially in the Chełm region, retained their recently acquired Orthodox faith. Though the pre-1875 Uniate churches remained the official property of the Orthodox Church, as a result of the conversions many of these churches were left without congregations.

The conversions themselves were more complex than it might appear. It was natural for the pro-Latin rite resistant Uniates to convert. The bishop of Lublin, Franciszek Jaczewski, however, also embarked on an extensive series of visitations to the Chełm and Podlasie regions in 1905 to convert to the Latin rite as many people of Uniate background as possible—that is, those former Uniates who resisted Orthodoxy but still desired a return of the Uniate Church or those who were not firmly committed to the Orthodox Church. He did this for religious reasons, understanding that the window for conversion provided by the Toleration Edict might quickly close.[5] But he also did it for political reasons. By the turn of the twentieth century, the Catholic Church, as a central institution in Polish society, desired to build a Catholic Polish nation. Thus, from the perspective of nation building, Orthodoxy promoted cultural (and, consequently, national) separatism among the local Ruthenian/Ukrainian populace. Without Orthodox influence, the Lublin Church believed, this overwhelmingly peasant population would be polonized. That conversion as an aid to polonization was an important concern for Bishop Jaczewski is evident when we consider that in 1905, the local Catholic Church no longer desired a return of the Uniate Church to the Chełm and Podlasie regions. This was because the Uniate Church was now a Ukrainian national Church, based in Austrian Galicia. Thus, Bishop Jaczewski understood that if the Uniate Church were reintroduced to the southeastern lands of the former Kingdom of Poland it would promote Ukrainian identity and would detract from the construction of a Polish identity based on the Latin rite.[6] It is not important that the Russian state had no intention of legalizing the Uniate Church on its territory in 1905; what is critical is the real Catholic opposition to the Uniate Church that had emerged on national grounds. By 1905, then, Bishop Jaczewski and other priests saw a strong potential for Ukrainian national consciousness to develop in the Chełm and Podlasie regions. They attributed this especially to the "illegitimate" Orthodox Church, but also recognized that the Uniate Church, if reintroduced, would also promote separatism. The conversions seemingly—and conveniently—prevented the Uniate Church from performing this role, and undermined the position of the Orthodox Church at the same time. Now, the Church had to work to remove what remained of the Orthodox Church and make the Chełm and Podlasie regions firmly Catholic and Polish.

World War I offered the Catholic Church the opportunity to begin to do this. In 1915, the Central Powers expelled the Russians from the Kingdom of Poland. At the same time, Kholm (Chełm) Gubernia was dissolved.[7] It had been created from the Chełm and Podlasie regions in 1912 on the initiative of the Orthodox bishop of Chełm, Evlogii (Georgievskii), in order to "protect" Orthodoxy in the regions after the mass conversions in 1905. In the later stages of the war the Catholic Church repossessed some Catholic and Uniate properties confiscated by the Orthodox Church after 1867.[8] The Church and Polish society, however, were stunned by the February 1918 Brest-Litovsk agreement between Ukrainian and German representatives, which located the Chełm and Podlasie regions in the fragile Ukrainian National Republic.[9] The agreement showed that Ukrainians now also saw this territory as "theirs." The defeat of Germany and fall of the Republic, however, invalidated the agreement. Formal Polish independence in November 1918 finally gave the Church the full freedom it desired to pursue its nation- and state-building goals. With independence, the Church believed even more firmly that if Orthodoxy were eliminated, the Chełm and Podlasie regions would indeed become Polish and Catholic territory. Underpinning this was a strong pro-Catholic and pro-Polish "martyrology" of the regions that developed after 1875.[10] Unfortunately, when Orthodoxy had not disappeared by 1926, specifically from the Chełm region, Catholic priests there began to wage a more resolute campaign to "contain" the Orthodox Church and ultimately eliminate it from the area. In 1938, the liquidation of Orthodox churches was undertaken by the state authorities to further both their nationalist agenda and Catholic hopes in the region.

Both before and after Polish independence the Catholic Church "blamed" the Orthodox Church for "russifying" the Chełm and Podlasie regions, although priests knew that a portion of the regions' population was Ukrainian (if not nationally conscious). Thus, in blaming Orthodoxy for russification, the Catholic Church was really declaring that the Orthodox Church inhibited the polonization of the ethnic Ukrainians. Polonization through Catholicization was already at issue in 1905, as illustrated by the de facto admission that the Church no longer desired a return of the Uniate Church—now a Ukrainian national church—to the Chełm and Podlasie regions. It was an even greater goal after Polish independence—that is, after the Church acquired a new freedom of action, and after the bitter campaign to create Kholm Gubernia (1909–1912) and the shock of the Brest-Litovsk agreement. But was the Orthodox Church the Catholic Church's only concern after 1918? Now that Russian power was gone, did the Uniate Church attempt to return to the Chełm region?[11]

Between November 1918 and 1924 Greek Catholic clerics from former Austrian Galicia, led by their bishops, including the Uniate metropolitan of Lviv, Andrei Sheptyts'kyi, did indeed attempt to revive the Uniate Church in the Chełm region. These attempts, however, were staunchly opposed by the Roman Catholic bishop of Lublin, Maryan Leon Fulman, and Polish authorities. Bishop Fulman opposed the return of the Uniate Church to the Chełm region because he feared that Uniate priests would incite Ukrainian nationalism and weaken the Catholic Church's revival and polonization efforts there. The Polish government feared Ukrainian nationalism as well, and these fears were heightened by the Polish-Ukrainian War of 1918–1919. Generally, the conflict over the reactivation of the Uniate Church in the Chełm region after November 1918 demonstrated how powerful a role religious institutions played in national movements in Eastern Europe in the nineteenth and early twentieth centuries. More specifically, the conflict demonstrated the important interplay at the local level between Catholic and Polish government authorities in the early Polish Second Republic; it also served as a critical transition point in the acceleration of religious-ethnic tensions (i.e., Polish and Catholic versus Ukrainian and Orthodox) in the Chełm region, leading ultimately to the events of 1938.

Before turning to the post-November 1918 period, we must consider Metropolitan Sheptyts'kyi's position toward the Chełm region up to Polish independence. In 1907, Metropolitan Sheptyts'kyi requested and received from Pope Pius X jurisdiction over all the Uniates of the Russian Empire. Between 1908 and 1914 the Vatican reconfirmed this jurisdiction a number of times.[12] The metropolitan's actions were dictated by the deep changes taking place in Russia after the 1905 revolution and by his great ambition to use the Uniate Church to promote the unification of the Eastern and Western Churches. But there was also an important political goal; that is, to prevent Latin-rite priests and bishops from "absorbing" former Uniates into the Latin rite—and polonizing them— because of the lack of proper Uniate jurisdiction in Russia.[13] No doubt, the conversion of 175,000 former Uniates in the Chełm and Podlasie regions to Roman Catholicism in 1905 helped to shape Metropolitan Sheptyts'kyi's thinking, as did the growing nationalist tensions between Uniate and Latin-rite priests and bishops in Austrian Galicia prior to World War I.[14] Thus, in the years prior to Polish independence, Metropolitan Sheptyts'kyi began to position the Uniate Church so that, in the first place, it could work for Church union, but also to fulfill a nation-"preserving" (consequently, nation-building) role among the heavily Orthodox Ukrainian population in Russia—specifically to counter the Polish Catholic clergy. These considerations extended to the Chełm and Podlasie regions and were ultimately evidenced most by Metropolitan Sheptyts'kyi's declaration of ardent support for the provision in the February 1918 Brest-Litovsk agreement to include these regions in the Ukrainian National Republic.[15]

In the months between this very political declaration and Polish independence, Metropolitan Sheptyts'kyi worked to revive the Uniate Church in the Chełm region. As he did so, he continued to present himself, however inadvertently, as a protector of Ukrainian interests. Consequently, he encountered intense religious-national opposition from the Lublin Church, which by this time had far advanced ideas for reconstructing the Chełm region as Catholic and Polish territory.[16] On 2 April 1918, the metropolitan informed the Austro-

Hungarian foreign ministry that he had reestablished the Greek Catholic eparchy of Chełm. On 23 April 1918, however, after it had consulted a number of parties, including the office of the apostolic army curate, the foreign ministry informed Metropolitan Sheptyts'kyi that he or his appointed administrator of the Chełm eparchy, Reverend Iosyf Botsian, should obtain instructions from the Vatican on how to proceed regarding the eparchy. In the meantime, any Greek Catholic faithful in the eparchy would remain under the jurisdiction of the Catholic bishop of Lublin.[17] Awaiting instructions from the Vatican, which never came, on 18 July 1918 Metropolitan Sheptyts'kyi again contacted the foreign ministry, now with a list of five issues pertaining to the Chełm region. Among them were demands by residents of the Chełm region for Uniate priests, who were being prevented from entering the region; the changing of former Uniate churches into Roman Catholic ones; and the mistreatment of Ukrainians and their places of worship in Kosobudy, Lipsk, Szczebrzeszyn and Radecznica (towns and villages in the Zamość district).[18] Ultimately, local authorities in the district carried out an investigation regarding the charges. More significantly for our purposes, the Catholic dean in Zamość, Father Andrzej Wadowski, strenuously denied the charges, writing to his superior in Lublin: "The bringing of such charges against Poles means to agitate, to lie, to provoke—and this the archbishop should not and cannot do."[19]

Given the preexisting interests and tensions between the Latin-rite and Greek-rite Churches, how did priests from Galicia proceed in their attempt to revive Greek Catholicism in the Chełm region after Polish independence in early November 1918? What chances of success did they have? On 18 November 1918 Father Mateusz Chomań, a Uniate priest, wrote to the Ministry of Religious Denominations and Public Education in Warsaw (MWRiOP) asking for a return of the former Uniate churches in Lublin and Chełm to those who were "earlier brutally forced to accept Orthodoxy," but who "today eagerly turn to the Catholic Church according to the Uniate rite," in order to "save this piece of land for the Fatherland and the Catholic Church."[20] Only two days later, on 20 November 1918, another Uniate priest, Father Wasyl Kyryluk, wrote to the Chełm district authorities asking for the return of the former Uniate Basilian cathedral in Chełm ("on the Hill"). "I . . . a former military chaplain with the Austrian army in Chełm," he wrote, "at the request of the Uniate population of Chełm and the surrounding region, have remained [in Chełm] to minister to the religious needs of a large number of people of this region professing the Uniate faith. These people returned to the Uniate faith after the removal of the Russian government. [I have remained because they] would be without any spiritual care because of the departure of all military priests."[21] Not having the authority to decide the matter, the district commissar, Gorowski, sent Father Kyryluk's petition to the MWRiOP. At the same time, he attached a brief note of his own stating that it would be premature to make a "definitive" decision regarding the cathedral. "The [one existing] Uniate church [in Chełm]," he concluded, " . . . is for now even on holidays only half full."[22]

After receiving the requests for the Uniate churches, officials at the MWRiOP indeed did not make any decisions on their status. Rather, on 4 and 6 December they sent the letters they had received to the newly installed bishop of Lublin, Maryan Fulman, for his opinion.[23] Aware now of these requests to the state authorities, and very attuned to the tension between the Catholic and Uniate Churches over the Chełm region, which was being further exacerbated by the ensuing Polish-Ukrainian war, Bishop Fulman took a strong stand on the matter. On 23 December 1918 he wrote to both Father Chomań (residing at the time in Lublin) and Father Kyryluk telling them to present authorization documents for their ministerial activities within one week.[24] The following day Bishop Fulman also wrote to the MWRiOP. He used Church law to convince officials in Warsaw that they should prevent Uniate priests from entering the Chełm region. However, he also made a very strong connection between Catholic belief and Polish state interests:

> In the case of Uniate priests in the Lublin diocese such as Wasyl K[y]ryluk ... and Mateusz Chomań ... I must inform you that until they present the proper Church documents to the bishop of Lublin they cannot perform any priestly functions according to the Code of Canon Law, article 804.
>
> Since the priests mentioned have not yet done this, they have no right to request the return of any churches or to perform public religious services.
>
> There is only one episcopal jurisdiction in this territory and they must submit to it. If they do not, they must be suspected of national goals contrary to the interests of our country.
>
> If Uniates exist [in the Lublin diocese] here and there, they are completely unknown or exist in very small numbers, fulfilling their spiritual needs in the Latin Church, and have never asked for a special priest.
>
> In light of the above, it is in the interest of the Church and Fatherland that similar attempts be obstructed and requests denied.[25]

On 29 December the dean of Chełm, Father Wincenty Hartman, also wrote to Bishop Fulman with his views of Father Kyryluk. "To the extent that Father Kyryluk is very zealous in fulfilling the religious needs of a small group [szczupła garstka] of Greek Catholic believers," Father Hartman wrote,

> he is also a purebred Ukrainian [rasowy ukrainiec] and a fervent propagator of Ukrainian ideas. It is this latter activity—confirmed by those who have known him for some time and in this role—which leads me to say that due to the current situation and chaotic relations [the Polish-Ukrainian War], the presence of Father Kyryluk in Chełm is in no way desirable.[26]

The Father Kyryluk case did not end here; instead, it acquired more significance. Apparently in response to Bishop Fulman's request for authorization from higher Church authorities for his work, on 25 January 1919 Metropolitan Sheptyts'kyi wrote to Bishop Fulman in support of Father Kyryluk. He testified as to his good character and his loyalty to the Catholic faith and the Vatican, and informed Bishop Fulman that Father Kyryluk was instructed not to get involved in the affairs of Roman Catholic believers, but to work only among the Uniates and convert as many Orthodox as possible to Greek Catholicism. More importantly, the metropolitan declared that he had jurisdiction in the Chełm region. He attached copies of his 1907–1908 correspondence with the Vatican on this matter. The metropolitan added that he had 19 more documents confirming jurisdiction—9 signed by Pope Pius X himself, and 5 specifically mentioning the Uniate diocese of Chełm. The last of the documents was issued in March 1914.[27] Metropolitan Sheptyts'kyi's actions are most interesting here. We know that after declaring the reestablishment of the Chełm eparchy in April 1918, the metropolitan sought Vatican approval for the eparchy, which was not forthcoming. The metropolitan was compelled by the Austro-Hungarian authorities to obtain this approval. With the collapse of Austria-Hungary and the inclusion of the Chełm region in the new, independent Polish state in November 1918, the metropolitan, it appears, tried to present the existence of the Uniate Church in the region as a fait accompli, knowing, however, that his request of April 1918 to the Vatican was still pending.

On 8 February 1919 Bishop Fulman responded to Metropolitan Sheptyts'kyi. He disagreed strongly that the metropolitan had jurisdiction in the Chełm region, saying that the documents he sent were insufficient proof of jurisdiction:

> Only a document from the [current] pope would be sufficient. It would have to clearly designate Your Excellency as the apostolic administrator of the orphaned Greek Catholic dioceses in Russia as well as Poland. According to the requirements of [Catholic] legal interpretation, the bestowal and definition of authority must be clear and precise, not incidental without the observance of procedures accepted in administrative documents of the Holy See. The absence of this compels me to tell Your Excellency that, in my opinion, in the Lublin diocese, Catholic episcopal jurisdiction belongs to the bishop of Lublin . . . In light of this, my conscience instructs me to consider all interference from other bishops as unacceptable.
>
> The current situation and unusually difficult political relations are completely inappropriate for priests under Your Excellency's jurisdiction to take up any sort of Uniate-Ruthenian activities in Chełm. Even the conversion of Orthodox [Christians] ostensibly carried out by Father [W.] Kyr[y]luk in Chełm is illusory and practically has no religious value. These same people alternate between the religious services of Father Kyr[y]luk and the Orthodox priest.
>
> In light of the above, I have instructed Father Kyr[y]luk in writing that I forbid him to conduct any manner of Church activities in the Lublin diocese.
>
> As it was after 1875, so today the clergy of the Latin rite in the Lublin diocese will conduct priestly and missionary work among these people [the Orthodox] in order to retain them for the Catholic faith and the Holy See. This work belongs to the bishop of Lublin according to article 1350 of the Canon Law.
>
> In any case, I completely submit to the judgment of the Holy See. Until this comes, I will be guided by my above opinion.[28]

Father Kyryluk indeed departed Chełm after receiving instructions—in the form of a copy of the letter to Metropolitan Sheptyts'kyi—from Bishop Fulman.[29]

As for Father Chomań, it was not until 3 February 1919 that he responded to Bishop Fulman's request for authorization for his ministerial activities. By this time, he had returned to Jarosław (near Przemyśl). His response to Bishop Fulman included a letter of support from his bishop, Josaphat (Kocyłowski), and a justification that the Uniate Church was indeed needed in the Chełm region. He wrote:

> Residents of the . . . region are arriving in Galicia in large numbers [*masowo*] and are asking Uniate priests here for acceptance to the Catholic Church [according to the Greek rite]. This they are doing because Uniate priests are being prevented from going [to the Chełm region] for political reasons and because the Catholic Church is indifferent [to the religious needs of the Uniates].[30]

Father Chomań may have suggested that it was the Polish state and military authorities who were prohibiting the Uniate clergy from entering the Chełm region, but as the Father Kyryluk case showed, the Catholic Church played an important role in shaping the attitudes of state officials toward the Uniate Church.

Another attempt to revive the Uniate Church involved pre-1875 Uniate priests from the Chełm region. While these priests appeared interested in the religious care of their former parishioners, Bishop Fulman once again focused on the political ramifications of Uniate priests reentering the Chełm region. Further, Bishop Fulman denied the existence of any Uniates in the region, a fact he knew was untrue based on his own earlier admission. In July 1919 Father Teofil Harasowski, a pre-1875 Uniate priest in the Chełm region now residing in Galicia, wrote to Bishop Fulman upon hearing the "extraordinary" news that the bishop had consecrated the former Uniate cathedral in Chełm (i.e., the one for which Father Kyryluk had petitioned). Father Harasowski wrote that he and other former Chełm region Uniate priests now wanted to know: "[W]hat goal did this religious ceremony have? . . . While the consecration of the cathedral by a Roman Catholic bishop in itself does not prejudge the matter, we wonder apprehensively whether this is not a coup d'etat against the entire [Uniate] diocese of Chełm by the Polish clergy?" Father Harasowski continued,

> [W]e want to know what your intentions and proposals are regarding the Uniate diocese of Chełm and the remaining Orthodox ex-Uniates. The secular authorities do not want, nor are they thinking, to take a stand on the issue because, though the constitution is not yet written, all preliminary texts and newspaper accounts suggest that religious freedom and respect for national minorities will be observed. And rightly so. Poland always observed [these] principles and never tolerated religious persecution in the full sense of the word . . .

[But] since we have not heard of any negotiations between our [Uniate] Ruthenian bishops our fears seem confirmed. And while the time for negotiations may not be right because this horrible, painful, and fratricidal Ukrainian revolt has aggravated relations between both fraternal nationalities, what fault is this of the poor Chełm region with its abused population! It now looks as if their future will be decided without their knowledge . . .

After we priests were thrown out and dispersed, it was mainly the Polish intelligentsia (in Podlasie, the Łubieńskis), the local Catholic clergy in part, and the Jesuits from Galicia who maintained the spirit of the persecuted. Why now, when the situation has improved for the better, is there such a poor regard for the Union?

I would like to add here what I know from the accounts of travelers who have come here from the villages of Zamch, Obsza and similar others in the neighboring Biłgoraj district. These unfortunate people have said that upon their return from Russia they found their villages burned, and have nothing to eat and must beg. In addition, their [Orthodox] priests are gone. They tell of how their churches have been taken over by Catholic priests, who instructed that their liturgical utensils be burned(?). And now these people do not know what faith they should follow. I am sure there are many similar locales and poor wretches in the districts mentioned above . . .

Would it not be better to take a more positive stand toward the Union and return to the state of affairs that existed [before 1875]?[31]

In his response to Father Harasowski, Bishop Fulman declared that "the revival of the Union in the Lublin diocese is inappropriate because of the military-political situation, and even more so since there are no Uniates here." He asserted further that the local Catholic clergy is carrying out missionary work in the Lublin diocese "with serious results." "Entrusting this work to the Galician [Uniate] clergy is impossible at this time. When the Ukrainian-Polish war ends and peace and order return to Poland, no doubt the Holy See will take a voice in this matter. The former Uniate cathedral will now serve as the seat of the Lublin auxiliary bishop. If the Uniate clergy of Galicia expressed the same spirit as your letter, the revival of the Union would be easier."[32]

Father Harasowski did not quit here, though his efforts could only be fruitless. On 14 May 1922, almost three years after his letter to Bishop Fulman, he wrote to the Lublin province authorities raising the question of the revival of the Uniate Church. His arguments were essentially the same as those in his earlier letter to Bishop Fulman. In this letter, however, he added that Archbishop Józef Teodorowicz, head of the Armenian-rite Catholics in Poland, had written to him in 1919 that the revival of the Union is not simply needed, "but necessary." Blaming the Polish bishops and clergy for the situation of the Uniate Church in the Chełm region, Father Harasowski exclaimed that they "should not impose their patriotism on their faith." He noted that the resolution of the Uniate problem would greatly depend on the sympathetic and just treatment of it by the voivode (provincial head).[33] Following the established pattern of consulting the Latin-rite Church regarding Greek-rite matters, on 4

August 1922 the voivode sent Father Harasowski's letter to Bishop Fulman for his review.[34]

There were at least two more attempts by Uniate priests to take up missionary work in the Chełm region. The first case involved Father Trofim Siemiacki, who apparently received permission from the pope to conduct Latin-rite masses. Subsequently, in October 1922, Bishop Fulman allowed Father Siemiacki to conduct masses in the town of Zawałów (Hrubieszów district) for a three-month trial period. Within three months, however, Father Siemiacki had raised the suspicions of Bishop Fulman, and the bishop instructed a priest in nearby Dub, Father Józef Widawski, to investigate Father Siemiacki's activities. Father Widawski surreptitiously obtained Father Siemiacki's correspondence and ultimately reported to Bishop Fulman: "I suspect that [Father Siemiacki] is an instrument of [Metropolitan] Sheptyts'kyi."[35] It is not known from the documents what eventually happened to Father Siemiacki, though in all likelihood he was forced to leave the Lublin diocese by Bishop Fulman. The second case involved Father Panteleimon Skomorowicz, a Greek Catholic priest in Dyniski in the Rawa Ruska district across the southern border of the Lublin province. On 13 March 1924 Father Skomorowicz requested permission from Bishop Fulman to conduct Uniate masses in the Catholic church in Chodywańcze in the neighboring Tomaszów Lubelski district. According to Father Skomorowicz, a delegation of Orthodox Ruthenians [Ukrainians] from Chodywańcze visited him on 2 March asking for his services, and also declared that "practically everyone [in Chodywańcze] will eagerly and collectively accept the Union."[36] On 10 April 1924 the Lublin curia replied to Father Skomorowicz that "in the current conditions the diocesan authorities cannot fulfill your request."[37]

In both of these cases, as in all previous cases, the Lublin Church adamantly opposed the revival of the Uniate Church in the Chełm region, fearing that such a revival would aid in the growth of Ukrainian nationalism in the region. Influenced in considerable measure by the Catholic Church, as well as, of course, the Polish-Ukrainian war, the state authorities also opposed the expansion of the Uniate Church beyond its Galician borders. At the same time, the state authorities permitted the Lublin Church to claim numerous former Uniate churches and took possession of the remaining Uniate properties of the Lublin province (as Orthodox properties).[38] By 1924 the Vatican itself deemed the Greek Catholic Church too latinized and nationalistic for missionary work among the Christian Orthodox in Poland's eastern *Kresy* (borderlands); it therefore established the Byzantine Slavonic rite, under the control of the Polish Latin-rite bishops, for this activity.[39] This last act constituted a definitive rejection of Metropolitan Sheptyts'kyi's plan to one day unify the Eastern and Western Churches through the Uniate Church.

We should note in closing that while it opposed the reintroduction of the existing "Ukrainian" Uniate Church to the Chełm region, the Lublin Church selectively used the Uniate past of the Chełm region to promote its greater institutional agenda (i.e., the construction of a Catholic Polish society). Thus, the 29 April 1924 conference of Lublin diocese deans noted:

> For the purpose of leaving future generations information about the actions of the Russian government in Church matters, especially as related to the Uniate Church and the Uniates, His Excellency [Bishop Fulman] suggests that those priests who suffered persecution or who were witnesses to persecution write down everything they experienced or saw and convey it to the curia . . . The parishioners who suffered persecution for their faith should also be found and interviewed . . . The same goes for the persecution of the Latin Church. This will be valuable material for the future historian and will also ennoble us before society.[40]

Two things are clear here. First, the Lublin Church refused to acknowledge that had the Uniate Church stayed in the Chełm region after 1875, the latter would, at least in part, have been influenced by the nationally minded Church in Galicia and some Uniate priests would have worked to strengthen Ukrainian identity in the region. In other words, contrary to Catholic thinking, it was not true that had the Uniate Church not been abolished in 1875, all of the Chełm region Uniates would have been polonized.[41] Second, this lack of acknowledgment was further proof that the Lublin Church could not view the existing Orthodox Church in the Chełm region as a "legitimate" Church of the local Ukrainian population, in spite of the way Orthodoxy was introduced to the region in 1875. This failure would contribute to the 1938 events.

To conclude, the Uniate Church's attempt to resume its activities in the Chełm region in the early years of the Polish Second Republic is one part of the much larger history of Polish-Ukrainian relations in the nineteenth and early twentieth centuries. Overall, these relations were further complicated by the fact that both the Greek Catholic and Eastern Orthodox religions were central in Ukrainian identity formation. The Chełm region was a unique microcosm of Polish-Ukrainian relations, reflecting the presence of these religions in the Ukrainian national movement. The Latin-rite Church played an immense role in Polish nation and state building in the nineteenth and early twentieth centuries, as did the Greek Catholic and Eastern Orthodox Churches in the Ukrainian national movement. Concerning the Chełm region after 1918, historians have focused on Catholic-Orthodox relations. But while scholars recognize that these relations cannot be understood without considering the pre-1875/1905 history of the Uniate Church in the region, they have overlooked the role of the Uniate Church in the evolution of the Catholic-Orthodox (i.e., Polish-Ukrainian) relationship in the early Polish Second Republic.

As I have shown, Uniate clerics attempted to revive the Uniate Church in the Chełm region after Polish independence in November 1918. Bishop Fulman and the Catholic clergy, however, categorically opposed these attempts based on the belief that the Uniate Church, if allowed to reenter the region, would incite Ukrainian nationalism. Bishop Fulman did his utmost to convince state authorities not to return any pre-1875 Uniate properties to the Uniate Church.

He effectively used Church law to do so; however, his real motivations were political. By 1918 a strong pro-Catholic martyrology of the Chełm region existed in Polish society. This, coupled with the fact that the Catholic Church was a powerful Polish nation-building institution, meant that the Church would not "share" the Chełm region with the Uniate Church—now indissolubly tied with the Ukrainian nation—even though the Uniate Church was a component of the Catholic Church. For the Polish Catholic Church, convinced that Orthodoxy was illegitimate even though many people in the Chełm region had adopted this religion, opposition to the Uniate Church was a necessary first step to the eventual elimination of Orthodoxy itself from the Chełm region and the final reconstruction of the region as Catholic and Polish territory.

Lest this be construed as a one-sided condemnation of Roman Catholic actions, we must note that in late 1918 conditions, had the Uniate Church in fact been permitted to reestablish itself in the Chełm region it would surely have engaged in Ukrainian nation building, and some Uniate priests would have provoked Ukrainian nationalism. Contrary to Metropolitan Sheptyts′kyi's noble plan and best intentions to work for Church union through the Greek Catholic Church, it is most unlikely that the metropolitan would have been able to fully control the lower clergy. Despite his good intentions, Metropolitan Sheptyts′kyi confronted an Eastern Europe in turmoil where religious elites, because of the absence of national states, not to mention democratic ones, engaged extensively in the politics of nation and state building. And as his actions surrounding the Brest-Litovsk agreement, the Chełm eparchy, and the Father Kyryluk case showed, Metropolitan Sheptyts′kyi himself was not immune from politicizing religious belief.

NOTES

I would like to thank the Fulbright Program of the International Institute of Education and the East European Studies Committee of the American Council of Learned Societies for funding received between 1992 and 1994 for dissertation research and write-up. This paper is based largely on that research. Ukrainian proper names are as I found them in the sources, the only exception being Andrei Sheptyts'kyi (for Andrzej Szeptycki).

1. On the 1938 events, see Konrad Sadkowski, "From Ethnic Borderland to Catholic Fatherland: The Church, Eastern Orthodox, and State Administration in the Chełm Region, 1918–1939," *Slavic Review* 57(4): 813–39.

2. The Uniate Church was abolished in Russia's western provinces in 1839; therefore, the Uniate believers in the Kingdom of Poland formed the final outpost of the Uniate faith in the Russian Empire. On the "dobrovol'noe vossoedinenie," see Luigi Glinka, *Diocesi ucraino-cattolica di Cholm (Liquidazione ed incorporazione alla Chiesa russo-ortodossa) (Sec. XIX)* (Rome, 1975); and Theodore R. Weeks, "The 'End' of the Uniate Church in Russia: The *Vozsoedinenie* of 1875," *Jahrbücher für Geschichte Osteuropas* 44 (1996): 28–40.

3. Transmitted by the predominant lower gentry, a stronger sense of Polish national identity existed in the Podlasie region. Conversely, in the Chełm (broadly, Lublin) region, the estate-dominated social structure with its more entrenched serfdom inhibited the development of Polish national consciousness. See Zygmunt Łupina, "Narodowa Demokracja w lubelskiem, 1919–1926. (Zasięg organizacyjnych i politycznych wpływów na terenie województwa lubelskiego)," Ph.D. dissertation, Uniwersytet im. Marii Curii-Skłodowskiej, 1974, pp. 19–24. A Lublin region priest provides a personal example in his memoirs: "The Uniate from the Lublin [Chełm] region was a terror to [Catholic] priests. Here, it was the rare priest who served a Uniate. Here, the Uniate and priest were easily betrayed by anyone and given over to the Muscovites [*Moskalom*]. Everyone trembled. Here, the Muscovites completely controlled the situation and the battle with them was almost always lost. It was completely different in the Podlasie region. The greater the persecution, the greater the heroism and opposition of the Uniates. For this reason, the work of priests was exciting." See [Przez] X, *Moje wspomnienia* (Lublin, 1934), pp. 8–9. Finally, on the ethnography of the Chełm and Podlasie regions as well as the Ruthenian dialects of the regions, see Oskar Kolberg, *Chełmskie. Obraz etnograficzny,* 2 vols. (Cracow, 1890–1891); Mykhailo Lesiv, "Narodni hovirky Pidliashshia ta Kholmshchyny," in *Nadbuzhanshchyna,* ed. Mykola Martyniuk, 3 vols. (New York,

1986–1994), vol. 1 (1986), pp. 649–70; and Iurii Havryliuk, "Zabutyi region," in *Nadbuzhanshchyna*, vol. 2 (1989), pp. 749–53.

4. This is the figure that Lublin diocese Catholic authorities derived. In 1905 alone, 164,000 converted to Catholicism. See Franciszek Stopniak, *Kościół na Lubelszczyźnie i Podlasiu na przełomie XIX i XX wieku* (Warsaw, 1975), p. 324. A figure of "no less than 168,000" is given in Gosudarstvennaia Duma, *Prilozheniia k stenograficheskim otchetam, 1910–1911 gg.*, vol. 5 (St. Petersburg, 1910–1911), no. 440, pp. 1–21. The research on the conversion of "resistant" Uniates to Roman Catholicism in 1905 is considerable. See, for example, the chapter on the Chełm region in Edward Chmielewski, *The Polish Question in the Russian State Duma* (Knoxville, 1970); and Robert Blobaum, "Toleration and Ethno-Religious Strife: The Struggle Between Catholics and Orthodox Christians in the Chełm Region of Russian Poland, 1904–1906," *Polish Review* 35(2) 1990: 111–24.

5. Stopniak, *Kościół na Lubelszczyźnie i Podlasiu* , pp. 292–300, 315–24.

6. The evidence for Catholic opposition—on national grounds—to the reestablishment of the Uniate Church in the Chełm region in 1905, while circumstantial, is considerable. First, and maybe most important, Catholic priests in the Chełm region were not blind to the nationalist tensions between Catholic and Uniate priests in Galicia. Second, during the mass conversions of 1905, some Catholic priests changed Ruthenian names to Polish names. Finally, in a letter to Bishop Fulman in 1919 inquiring about the bishop's attitude toward the Uniate Church, Father Teofil Harasowski, a former Uniate priest from the Chełm region argued that the fate of the Uniate Church was already decided in 1905. Father Harasowski wrote that in 1905 he had contacted Stefan Wydżga, a local notable in the town of Raciborowice, about the possibility of reactivating the Uniate Church in the Chełm region. Wydżga responded: "The Union has no right to exist here . . . It lies in no one's interest—neither us Catholics nor the government itself. I should add that were the Union revived it would be harmful to our Church. It could serve as a revolutionary instrument, fulfilling religious and political propaganda roles, as is taking place to no good effect there in Galicia among the Ruthenians. [The Ruthenians are simply] pawns in a political game played by clever agitators. Here we want nothing to do with the Union. It would only lead to disaster." Though Wydżga was a layperson, Harasowski wrote in 1922 to the Lublin province voivode (provincial head), "we must believe that the decision [to oppose the return of the Uniate Church to the Chełm region] was taken during Bishop Jaczewski's visitations." See Krzysztof Krasowski, *Episkopat katolicki w II Rzeczypospolitej. Myśl o ustroju państwa—postulaty, realizacja* (Warsaw and Poznań, 1992), pp. 178–80; Stopniak, p. 296; and Archiwum Archidiecezjalne w Lublinie (hence-

forth AAL), Rep. 61.XII.5 (The Propagation of the Union in the Chełm Region, 1915–1936). Letter from Father Teofil Harasowski to Bishop Maryan Fulman, 19 July 1919; and copy of letter from Father Teofil Harasowski to the Lublin province voivode, 14 May 1922. See also Konrad Sadkowski, "Church, Nation and State in Poland: Catholicism and National Identity Formation in the Lublin Region, 1918–1939," Ph.D. dissertation, University of Michigan, 1995, pp. 68–72.

7.   Chmielewski provides a good overview of the creation of the Kholm gubernia.

8.   Wolfdieter Bihl, "Sheptyts′kyi and the Austrian Government," in *Morality and Reality: The Life and Times of Andrei Sheptyts′kyi*, ed. Paul Robert Magocsi (Edmonton, 1989), p. 24; and Sadkowski, "Church, Nation, and State in Poland," p. 143.

9.   Ryszard Torzecki, "Sheptyts′kyi and Polish Society," in *Morality and Reality*, ed. Magocsi, p. 80.

10. See Sadkowski, "From Ethnic Borderland to Catholic Fatherland," pp. 815–18.

11. From this point forward, I separate the Podlasie region from my analysis and focus on the Chełm region. The main reason for this is that I do not possess data on the attempted revival of the Uniate Church in the Siedlce (Podlasie) diocese after Polish independence in November 1918. It was at this time that the diocese was reactivated, after being unilaterally dissolved by the Russian authorities in 1867. Between 1867 and 1918 the Siedlce diocese, for all intents and purposes, was part of the Lublin diocese.

12. AAL, Rep. 61.XII.5. Copy of letter from Metropolitan Andrei Sheptyts′kyi to Rev. Aleksei Zerchaninov, appointing him deputy of the Kamianets eparchy (diocese) and all other Greek Catholic eparchies in Russia, dated 1907; copy of letter from Pope Pius X to Metropolitan Andrei Sheptyts′kyi approving the appointment of Rev. Zerchaninov, 14 February 1908; and letter from Metropolitan Andrei Sheptyts′kyi to Bishop Fulman, 25 January 1919. See also Ivan Muzyczka, "Sheptyts′kyi in the Russian Empire," in *Morality and Reality*, ed. Magocsi, pp. 314–16.

13. Muzyczka, "Sheptyts′kyi in the Russian Empire," p. 315. While making the claim that Metropolitan Sheptyts′kyi sought jurisdiction to avoid the "complete absorption" of Eastern-rite Christians by Latin-rite priests who encountered converts, Muzyczka does not make the claim that the metropolitan attempted to avoid polonization. I believe, however, that this was at issue as well.

14. Krasowski, *Episkopat katolicki w II Rzeczypospolitej*, pp. 178–80.

15. The metropolitan expressed his support for the Brest-Litovsk agreement in the Vienna parliament soon after the agreement was signed. See Bihl, "Sheptyts'kyi and the Austrian Government," pp. 22–25; and Bohdan Budurowycz, "Sheptyts'kyi and the Ukrainian National Movement after 1914," in *Morality and Reality*, ed. Magocsi, p. 50.

16. For example, in May 1919, soon after Polish independence, the Hrubieszów deanery clergy agreed to "reclaim all [unnecessary or abandoned] Orthodox and former Uniate churches so as to return a Polish and Catholic character to the deanery as quickly as possible." See AAL, Rep. 61.I.6 (Deanery Clergy Conference Minutes, 1918–1924), Hrubieszów deanery clergy conferences, 22 May 1919 and 12 May 1921; and Zamość deanery clergy conference, 6 June 1921.

17. Bihl,"Sheptyts'kyi and the Austrian Government," pp. 23–24.

18. Bihl, "Sheptyts'kyi and the Austrian Government," pp. 24–25. See also AAL, Rep. 61.XII.5 for an abbreviated copy of Metropolitan Sheptyts'kyi's complaints to the Austro-Hungarian authorities.

19. See AAL, Rep. 61.XII.5. Copies of protocols taken by local authorities in Kosobudy, Lipsk, Szczebrzeszyn, and Radecznica, 24–28 August 1918; and letter from Father [Andrzej] Wadowski to the "administrator" of the Lublin diocese, 10 September 1918.

20. AAL, Rep. 61.XII.5. Copy of letter from Father Mateusz Chomań to the Department of Religious Denominations and Public Education [MWRiOP], 18 November 1918.

21. AAL, Rep. 61.XII.5. Copy of letter from Father Wasyl Kyryluk to the Chełm district authorities, 20 November 1918.

22. AAL, Rep. 61.XII.5. Copy of letter from the Chełm district People's Commissar, Gorowski, to the MWRiOP, 20 November 1918.

23. AAL, Rep. 61.XII.5. Letter (no. 40210/243) from the MWRiOP—Department of Religious Denominations (signature illegible) to Bishop Fulman, 4 December 1918; and letter (no. 40187/269/151) from the MWRiOP—Department of Religious Denominations (signature illegible) to Bishop Fulman, 6 December 1918.

24. AAL, Rep. 61.XII.5. Draft letter (no. 2811) from Father Władysław Koglarski to Father Mateusz Chomań, 23 December 1918; and draft letter (no. 2812) from Father Władysław Koglarski to Father Wasyl Kyryluk, 23 December 1918. Father Koglarski held the title of Vicar General and represented the bishop. The letter to Father Kyryluk was presented through the Chełm dean, Father Wincenty Hartman.

25. AAL, Rep. 61.XII.5. Draft letter (no. 2920) from Bishop Fulman to the [MWRiOP] Department of Religious Denominations, 24 December 1918.

26. AAL, Rep. 61.XII.5. Draft letter (no. 2850) from Father Władysław Koglarski to the dean of the Chełm deanery, 23 December 1918; and letter (no. 115) from Father Wincenty Hartman to Bishop Fulman, 29 December 1918.

27. AAL, Rep. 61.XII.5. Copy of letter from Metropolitan Andrei Sheptyts'kyi to Rev. Aleksei Zerchaninov, appointing him deputy of the Kamianets eparchy and all other Greek Catholic eparchies in Russia, dated 1907; copy of letter from Pope Pius X to Metropolitan Andrei Sheptyts'kyi approving the appointment of Rev. Zerchaninov, 14 February 1908; and letter from Metropolitan Andrei Sheptyts'kyi to Bishop Fulman, 25 January 1919. See also Muzyczka, "Sheptyts'kyi in the Russian Empire," pp. 314–16.

28. AAL, Rep. 61.XII.5. Draft letter (no. 567) from Bishop Fulman to Metropolitan Andrei Sheptyts'kyi, 8 February 1919.

29. AAL, Rep. 61.XII.5. Draft letter (no. 567) from Bishop Fulman to Father [W]asyl Kyryl[u]k, 8 February 1919; draft letter (No. 568) from Father Władysław Koglarski to the dean of the Chełm deanery, 8 February 1919. As an aside, on 22 February Father Kyryluk wrote to Bishop Fulman informing him that after his departure to eastern Galicia he was interned in the prisoner-of-war camp in Wadowice, near Cracow. "It is now your holy obligation" Father Kyryluk wrote, "to see to it that I am released since it was due to your instruction that I left Chełm." After the Lublin curia appealed for his release to the Minister of Military Affairs in Warsaw, he was in fact released. See AAL, Rep. 61.XII.5. Letter from Father Wasyl Kyryluk to Bishop Fulman, 22 February 1919; letter (no. illegible) from Father Władysław Koglarski to the Minister of Military Affairs, 10 March 1919; letter (no. illegible) from Father Władysław Koglarski to Father Wasyl K[y]ryluk, 10 March 1919; and letter (no. IV/1458) from the Cracow district military commander (signature illegible) to the Lublin diocese curia, 5 April 1919.

30. AAL, Rep. 61.XII.5. Letter from Father Mateusz Chomań to Bishop Fulman, 3 February 1919; and "Lecturis Salutem" on behalf of Father Mateusz Chomań signed by the Greek Catholic Bishop of Przemyśl, Josaphat, 1 February 1919.

31. AAL, Rep. 61.XII.5. Letter from Father Teofil Harasowski to Bishop Fulman, 19 July 1919.

32. AAL, Rep. 61.XII.5. Draft letter (no. 2253) from Bishop Fulman to Father Teofil Harasowski, 26 July 1919.

33. AAL, Rep. 61.XII.5. Copy of letter from Father Teofil Harasowski to the Lublin province voivode, 14 May 1922.

34. AAL, Rep. 61.XII.5. Letter (no. L:6308/Pr.) from the Lublin province voivode, Stanisław Moskalewski, to Bishop Fulman, 4 August 1922.

35. AAL, Rep. 61.XII.5. Curriculum vitae of Father Trofim Siemiacki, undated; draft letter (no. 3040) from Bishop Fulman to Father Jan Żółtowski, 28 October 1922; and letter from Father Józef Widawski to Bishop Fulman, 20 December 1922.

36. AAL, Rep. 61.XII.5. Letter from Father Panteleimon Skomorowicz to Bishop Fulman, 13 March 1924.

37. AAL, Rep. 61.XII.5. Draft letter (no. 764) from Father Władysław Koglarski to Father Pantele[i]mon Skomorowicz, 10 April 1924.

38. See *Dziennik Praw Państwa Polskiego*, 21, position 67, 28 December 1918; *Monitor Polski: Dziennik Urzędowy Rzeczypospolitej Polskiej* 135 (20 June 1919); and *Monitor Polski* 116 (2 August 1922). The third law placed 115 former Orthodox properties in the Lublin province under the jurisdiction of the Lublin voivode. The laws are reprinted in Serafin Kiryłowicz, "Z dziejów prawosławia w II Rzeczypospolitej Polskiej: Niektóre problemy na tle polityki wyznaniowej państwa, 1918–1939," *Posłannictwo* 1–2 (1983): 67–75. See also Sadkowski, "From Ethnic Borderland to Catholic Fatherland," pp. 818–20.

39. On the Byzantine Slavonic rite and the impact of the 1925 Concordat between Poland and the Vatican on the Uniate Church, see Jerzy Wisłocki, *Konkordat polski z 1925 roku. Zagadnienie prawno-polityczne* (Poznań, 1977), pp. 120–42. On the Latin-rite clergy's eventual resistance to the Byzantine Slavonic rite, see Konrad Sadkowski, "The Roman Catholic Clergy, Byzantine Slavonic Rite, and Polish National Identity: The Case of Grabowiec, 1931–1934," *Religion, State and Society* 2 (2000) (forthcoming).

40. AAL, Rep. 61.I.6, Lublin diocese clergy conference, 29 April 1924.

41. On how this thinking continued into the late 1930s, see Sadkowski, "From Ethnic Borderland to Catholic Fatherland," p. 817.

Inscriptions East and West in the First Millennium: The Common Heritage and the Parting of the Ways

IHOR ŠEVČENKO

At some point in their careers most historians of Ukraine have to face the identity question expressed by the formula "East and West." It is in the nature of things that these historians deal mostly with East-Central and Eastern Europe, and with the second millennium of our era. It is worth recalling, however, that in Christian civilization dichotomies and transitions involving East and West occurred on territories extending from Spain to eastern Asia Minor and the Caucasus. These dichotomies and transitions were taking shape in the first millennium. I hope that Professor Roman Szporluk, who is among the prominent historians of modern Ukraine and who, as a practitioner of the comparative method, likes to search for the roots of things, will find the present offering to be of some interest.

I

In this broad outline I will deal with Christian inscriptions in Latin and Greek that for the most part come from the territory of what was, or had been, the Roman Empire, and which, roughly speaking, were produced during the first thousand years of our era.[1] A commonsensical assumption underlies the outline's subtitle: in their form and content, epigraphical documents, like other manifestations of written culture, reflected the evolution of social structures and cultural settings, and the changes within institutions and social groups that produced them.

With respect to early Christian and early medieval epigraphy, one could expect a priori to find numerous common traits, at least initially, irrespective of the geographical location of the evidence and the language in which it has been transmitted. The persistence of these common traits was made possible, in the first place, by the unity of the Empire in the first four centuries of our era—a unity that had as its consequence much administrative and cultural uniformity. Such uniformity on the imperial scale also created preconditions for the free movement of people who carried their cultural, and therefore their epigraphical, habits from one end of the Mediterranean world to the other. This freedom of movement is illustrated by the fourth-century tombstone of a (perhaps Jewish) wine merchant who hailed from Alexandria in Egypt, but died in Tomis, which is Constanța in modern Romania.[2] These common traits were also due to the close ideological bonds that held the producers of Christian inscriptions together. These bonds transcended, if only on a superficial level, the multilingualism of the early Christian culture. In the case of Greek and Latin, this led to graphic and terminological hybrids, reflecting cultural interpenetration, especially among the lower layers of Christian society. An inscription in Latin thus would be written in Greek letters;[3] or a tomb with enough room for two bodies would be called *visomus* in a Latin inscription from fourth-century Rome (from the Latin *bis,* "twice," and the Greek *sōma,* "body"),[4] while on the other hand, dozens of tombs in the late antique Greek East were called *mnēmorion* (cf. the Latin *memoria*).

Between the end of the fourth and the end of the fifth century, the political unity of the Empire was first weakened and then made to collapse altogether, at least in the West. The bond of multilingualism began to yield to divisive monolingualism both East and West, with, on the Western side, a vestigial prestige of the Greek leading to the epigraphical use of the Greek alphabet and distorted Greek words by Latin show-offs ignorant of the Greek language (illustrative examples come from seventh- to eighth-century Milan).[5] This was the reverse of the earlier state of things, when the Greek alphabet was used in inscriptions by commissioners or stonecutters of Greek culture to write in Latin, of which they had only a superficial knowledge.[6]

In time, the cultural bonds within Christianity loosened as well. Newcomers to the Mediterranean civilization, such as the Lombards, while absorbing, with mixed results, the standards of Latin high culture that they found in the conquered territories, brought in values of their own. Again, one would expect a priori that this linguistic, political, and cultural drifting apart would find its reflection in epigraphy.

II

These general considerations are still to be validated by scholars in full detail. In the meantime, some preliminary spot checks, made to a large extent with the help of evidence coming from Italy and the area south of the Danube (more precisely, present-day Romania), will provide material for such validation.

Throughout the Empire, early Christian sarcophagi exhibited traits inherited from pagan times. Tools of trade were displayed on funerary monuments for both pagan and Christian craftsmen. Pagan—and Jewish—formulae lived on in Christian funerary vocabulary. Here are some examples datable to the third to ninth centuries: *hyper euchēs*, "in completion of the vow"; *oudis* [*sic*] *athanatos,* "nobody is immortal"; *non fuimus et fuimus,* "we were not and we came into being"; *cheireete* or *cheireste* [*sic*] *xeny* [*sic*] *kai parodite* [*sic*], "greetings, strangers and passers-by"; *zōmen en theō,* "let us live in God"; *vibas* or *biba*[*t*] [*sic*] *in deo,* "may you (or he) live in God (or the Lord)"; *pax tibi* or *eirēnē soi,* both meaning "peace be to you."[7] Some longer epigraphical formulae employed both East and West were also holdovers from pagan times; these include statements about penalties to be exacted from eventual violators of the grave (the penalties were to go to the treasury or to the Church, depending on the faith of the deceased). Regardless of the place of their provenance, important early inscriptions contain the same covertly Christian—or syncretistic—traits. Such is the case of the queen of all the early Christian inscriptions, the Aberkios poem from Hierapolis in Asia Minor, and the Pektorios inscription from Autun (the ancient Augustodunum) in France, both monuments dating from the third century.[8]

The bilingual milieu of early Christian Rome produced bilingual inscriptions in the city's cemeteries. A distant parallel is offered by a fourth-century epitaph from another imperial capital, Trier in northwest Germany; in it, the deceased "Oriental's" (he is called *anatolikos* in the inscription) approximate age was given twice, once in Greek and once in Latin. In the Greek part of the epitaph, the formula *mikrō plio* [*sic*], "somewhat more," that is, "more or less" was used; this was a "Westernism," corresponding to the frequent *plus minus*, "more or less," on sixth-century Latin inscriptions from Italy (the Greek *plio* [*sic*] *elatton*, "more or less" also occurred in fifth-century Syracuse).[9]

Sometimes it is difficult to say what the stonecutter's or glazier's mother tongue may have been. Consider the *vivas pie zēsēs* formula:[10] is its *pie* the Latin adverb "piously," or the Greek imperative "drink"? Or consider a late third-century inscription from Rome, with its hybrid spelling *ann* (in Latin letters) followed by *ōroum* (in Greek letters), resulting in one word meaning "years" in Latin, followed by the Roman numeral X for "ten" and by the horror *mēsōroum* (in Greek letters) to represent *mensium*, "months" in Latin, followed by the word *septem*, "seven," in the same language.[11]

Even when inscriptions were executed in separate languages, they were cast into the same poetic molds. The hexameter was such a preponderant mold. It was Virgilian in inspiration in the Latin West (and occasionally even in Constantinople, as long as Latin remained one of the official languages there); Homeric and, after the fifth century, Nonnian, in the East. This uniformity in the matter of literary forms gives one the sense of the vastness and cultural unity of the Empire even as late as the year 600 or so. The famous Byzantine general Comentiolus spoke of fortifications and buildings he had erected in the Spanish Cartagena in Virgilian and Ovidian hexameters in an inscription he dated to the reign of the Byzantine emperor Maurice (d. 602); earlier in the sixth century, Solomon, a general who reconquered Africa from the Vandals, spoke in his own, if worse, hexameters of similar fortifications he had erected on that continent.[12]

Several epigraphical formulae continued to be used both East and West up to the eighth century. These include the formula threatening the transgressor with the curse of the 318 Fathers assembled at the First Ecumenical Council of Nicaea. This formula, routine in the East, is also found both in fifth-century Rome and in eighth-century Ravenna. Excerpts from the *Credo* occur on Greek and Latin inscriptions, with examples coming from Corinth (Justinian's time) and Italy respectively.[13] Door lintels, not only from Syria and Palestine, but also from Africa, display similar apotropaic quotations, culled from the Scriptures (especially the Psalms) and from liturgy. Even the Semitic formula *heis theos,* "God is One," may have its counterpart in the Latin epigraphical expression *unum deum crededit* [*sic*], "he believed in One God."

We know from Palestine of the habit of donors—often Jewish—to state in inscriptions how many feet of a mosaic floor had been laid out owing to their generous contributions. The same practice is attested for the fifth- to sixth-century Veneto or Lucca: *fecit pedes XXVII,* "he had twenty-seven [square] feet made," or, in a bilingual inscription, *fecerunt pedes C,* "they had a hundred [square] feet made."[14] The acronym *XMG, Christon Maria gennā* ,"Mary gives birth to Christ," is usually associated with Syria, where it occurs on many inscriptions. It is also, however, attested in other parts of the Empire; not only in Rome (on late fourth-century roof tiles in the Church of Santa Maria Maggiore), but also in the Romanian coastal cities of Histria and Constanţa (on sixth-century amphorae, although these amphorae may have been an import from the East). And Tropaeum Traiani in modern Romania offers a late (fifth–sixth century) example of a bilingual inscription that repeats the same message twice: + *stauros thanatou kai anastaseōs* + *crux mortis et resurrectionis,* "the cross, [symbol] of death and resurrection."[15] We shall close this sample of closely related formulae with three more random examples, coming from West and East respectively. As late as the seventh century, a sarcophagus from Rovigo (Veneto) displayed the liturgical formula for the repose of the deceased's soul, *repausa e(a)m in seno Abraam et Isac et Gacob,* "put her (i.e., the soul) to rest in the bosom of Abraham and Isaac and Jacob." The same liturgical formula enjoyed great popularity on funerary inscriptions both Coptic and Greek, in the Egyptian Coptic realm and in Christian Nubia. The cryptic use of two letters *koppa* and *theta* with the numeric value of 99 (90 + 9) to express the word *amēn,* the combined numeric value of whose letters is 99 as well (a = 1; m = 40; ē = 8; n = 50) was widespread in the Semitic realm, Egypt, and Nubia; but we also find it on a column of the Parthenon in Athens, where it stands at the end of an (eighth- or ninth-century?) inscription.[16] And the ubiquitous *phōs zōē,* "light, life" formula is attested, to quote sixth-century examples alone, in an area extending from Antioch on the Orontes (today's Turkey) to Palestine and to the Romanian Constanţa.[17]

III

When do we begin to notice the parting of the ways of the respective epigraphies of the East and the West? For parts of Italy, the beginnings of this process overlap with the late years of Byzantine domination (roughly speaking, the middle of the eighth century). By that time, the Latin functional counterpart to the Greek formula *enthade katakeitai,* "here lies," is often no longer *hic positus est* or *hic iacet,* "here has been deposited" or "here lies," but the by now familiar *hic requiescit in pace,* "here rests in peace."[18] A good example of this kind of divergence is the floor mosaic of the Church of St. Francis in Ravenna (the building predating the saint), where the traditional Greek *mnēsthēti Kyrie,* "remember, O Lord," located in one part of the mosaic in the fifth to sixth century is paralleled by the Latin *iste locus sancti complectitur [ossa Neonis],* "this place contains the bones of Saint Neon," inserted in the ninth century in another. By the fifth to sixth century, Latin inscriptions from Italy are often dated by the year of a Western consul, not that of the Byzantine emperor.[19]

Clear signs of a drifting apart of East and West, however, date from the eighth century and can be juxtaposed with the effects of two seventh- and eighth-century events, one cataclysmic, one more local: the Arab invasions and the establishment of the Lombards in their kingdom and principalities in Italy.

For the Arabs, two cases will stand for the others. The eighth-century inscription of Bishop Arcadius stated that he had come to Italy (Chiusi) from Spain *veniens ab Hispaniis Ismaelitar(um) clade sublatus,* "swept away by the calamity [brought about by] the Ishmaelites." The melancholy content of Arcadius's inscription is vastly different from the self-assured tone of the inscription in the city walls of Nicaea in Asia Minor that celebrated "putting the enemies' insolence to shame" and the successful defense of that city from the Arab attack in 727.[20] The two societies, facing the same Islamic danger that was coming from the West and from the East respectively, fared differently and turned their backs upon each other.

The Lombard conquerors, their kings and dignitaries, continued to use the hexameter in inscriptions they commissioned, but they introduced a new element—pride in the commissioner's noble origin. In Pavia in about 700 one *dux* Audoald boasted in rhythmical lines that hardly deserve to be called hexameters that he was *claris natalibus ortus,* "issued from famous ancestors," and King Cunincpert let it be known that he was the grandson of a king and the son of a queen.[21] In Byzantium, putting such a premium on genealogy came about two centuries later, and was reflected in epigraphy at an even later date.

As the Byzantine point of chronological reference was no longer obligatory for the Lombards, they dated their inscriptions by their own kings, while dating in Byzantine Ravenna continued to be done by the regnal years of Byzantine emperors. Moreover, a Beneventan inscription of 796 counted the years *ab incarnatione Domini,* "from the incarnation of the Lord,"[22] a formula that was recent at the time, but that subsequently was to acquire the monopoly in the West (a monopoly only briefly interrupted by the French Revolution, Napoleon, and Benito Mussolini), and not by the years of an emperor's reign. True, the latter type of dating fades away in "Eastern" Byzantine inscriptions as well. From about the same time—the eighth century—come the graffiti of the Parthenon in Athens, in which counting from the creation of the world is first epigraphically attested in the form of the "Byzantine era."[23] Both West and East introduced new ways of dating inscriptions, but they replaced the old common system by two divergent ones. (The dating by the Christian era appeared in Byzantium proper only in the last years of its existence, and was the result of Western influence.)

A mosaic floor from Ivrea in Northern Italy, dating from the tenth century, depicts five ladies, *gramatica, philosofia* [*sic*], *dialectica, geometria, aritmetica*; one of them, the *dialectica,* points to an inscription that I read as *tr(i)v(i)u(m)*, that is, the course of instruction in three disciplines. I do not recall any Byzantine inscribed representation of personified subjects of the trivium and quadrivium. Byzantium was aware of this educational system by the ninth century, but it formally discussed it only in the thirteenth.[24] A similar observation can be made about the heirs to the hexameter that in the earlier centuries predominated in poetic inscriptions East and West: by about the year 1000 in Western inscriptions, hexameters were being transformed into rhymed entities, to end up as *versus Leonini*; in Byzantine ones, they were yielding to dodecasyllables which had played a less prominent role in earlier centuries (although, true, they had been used in seventh-century Ravenna).

In short, one senses that by the tenth century the two worlds were dealing with their own inscriptions in their own ways.

IV

In presenting the model of initial unity and subsequent divergence in the world of Eastern and Western inscriptions, I have given short shrift to differences between the two epigraphies that had existed from the early times on. I shall select only one case in point here: it has to do with the differential treatment of vernacular languages, and therefore of vernacular epigraphy, East and West respectively. In the Western part of the European continent at least, where Latin was the only language with a developed written past and where the Latin Church ran a tight *navicula Sancti Petri,* vernacular epigraphy used Latin letters only (if we except the rare Southern Runic inscriptions) and was a late bloomer. French inscriptions begin in about the year 1200, the German ones (if we disregard the *rarissima* of the tenth century), in the thirteenth century.

The situation was different in the Byzantine cultural sphere, with its greater permissiveness, even if the latter existed more in fact than in intention. It is understandable that languages with a tradition, such as Coptic, heir to the Egyptian, and Syriac, heir to the Aramaic, should have created their own epigraphies (with borrowed or indigenous alphabets) at their early Christian beginnings, and even that Semitic speakers of Syria should have developed a particular sequence (from right to left) for writing numbers in their own Greek epigraphy.[25] It is more noteworthy that the Turkic Bulgarians composed inscriptions not only in Greek, but also in their own language (true, in Greek letters) even before 864, the date of their baptism; that a special alphabet for the Slavs (both those baptized and those still to be baptized), the Glagolitic, was developed by the Byzantines as early as the 860s and left epigraphic monuments; and that Southern and Eastern Slavs (the former relative, the latter genuine, newcomers to Mediterranean culture), should have developed their vernacular epigraphies no later than a mere half a century or so after their respective Christianizations. The earliest dated Bulgarian inscription (in Slavic and in the Cyrillic alphabet) thus comes from the second decade of the tenth century, while the earliest securely dated East Slavic graffito in Slavic was written in 1052.[26] Undated, if tantalizing, testimony must be left out of the present broad outline: the one-word Cyrillic graffito on a vessel from Eastern Slavic territory, the earliest Novgorodian documents on birch bark (if they can be called epigraphic), and the two or three surviving Orthodox Christian inscriptions in Alan language and in Greek letters, coming from the North Caucasus (they seem to date from the twelfth century, while the Alans were Christianized in the tenth).

V

A Byzantinist attempting to undertake a comparative study of inscriptions East and West will soon make a melancholy discovery. Information presented about the period beyond that covered by manuals of early Christian epigraphy that he derives from synthetic treatments of Medieval Latin epigraphy by such authors as Rudolf M. Kloos (1980), Robert Favreau (1974 and 1989), Walter Koch, Iiro Kajanto, and Pierre Petitmengin and his team (1989), quickly makes it evident how much farther ahead his Western colleagues have progressed compared to his fellow Byzantinists. This realization seems to be true with respect to teamwork, institutional underpinnings, planning, or publication of corpora. Although they might find some solace in the smaller size of the corpus of their epigraphical evidence compared to the late antique and medieval materials available to their Latinist colleagues, Byzantine epigraphists still have their work cut out for them.

NOTES

The following works will be adduced in an abbreviated form in the body of this article: Kaufmann = Carl Maria Kaufmann, *Handbuch der altchristlichen Epigraphik* (Freiburg in Breisgau, 1917), quoted by page and figure (this remains a reliable workhorse); Diehl = Ernestus Diehl, *Inscriptiones Latinae Christianae veteres,* 3 vols. (Berlin, 1961–1967), quoted by inscription number; Rugo = Pietro Rugo, *Le iscrizioni dei sec. VI–VII–VIII esistenti in Italia,* 5 vols. (Cittadella, 1974–1980), quoted by volume and inscription number; Popescu = Emilian Popescu, *Inscripţiile greceşti şi latine din secolele IV–XIII descoperite în România* (Bucharest, 1976), quoted by inscription number; Guillou = André Guillou, *Recueil des inscriptions grecques médiévales d'Italie* (Rome, 1996), quoted by inscription number.

1. Of central importance to our subject is Guglielmo Cavallo and Cyril Mango, eds., *Epigrafia medievale greca e latina: ideologia e funzione. Atti del Seminario di Erice, 12–18 settembre 1991* (Spoleto, 1995).

2. See Popescu, no. 28; also Anna Avramea, "Mort loin de la patrie . . . " in *Epigrafia,* ed. Cavallo and Mango, p. 17 and Catalogue no. 46 (p. 24). Avramea's Catalogue of 420 early inscriptions commemorating people deceased far from their native places eloquently illustrates our point.

3. For example, Diehl, no. 2300 A, which reads in part: *koiougi benignissime [koue] bixit in pake annis biginti et zex* in Greek letters, but in Latin, meaning "to the most kind wife that lived in peace twenty-six years."

4. For *visomus,* see Kaufmann, p. 127.

5. Rugo 5, no. 20, and Guillou, no. 106, with the words *agēōs [s(anc)]tou[s a]mbrosēous papa aikl(aisi)ai maidē[o]lanensēs* = deformed Greek *hagios,* "saint," repeated in Latin as *s(anc)tu[s a]mbrosius, papa eccl(esi)ae mediolanensis* (Saint, Saint Ambrose, pope of the Church of Milan); Rugo 5, no. 34a, and Guillou, no. 107, *agēous Nazarēus o arnoious o Th(eo)u* = deformed Greek *hagios,* "saint," followed by the name of Nazarius (with a Latin *-us* ending); + *o* = article + the deformed *arnion* = lamb (a calque after the Latin *agnus*) + *o* (article in a wrong case) + the correct Greek abbreviation for "God" (Saint Nazarius, lamb of God); Rugo 5, no. 34b (similar deformed Greek with Latin *-us* endings).

6. See Kaufmann, p. 44 and fig. 37 (a. 269); note *mēsōrōn = mensium,* "months," and *deorōn = dierum,* "days."

7. For "nobody is immortal," see, for example, Kaufmann, pp. 166 and 297. For examples coming from East and West of the formula *non fuimus et fuimus,* "we were not and we came into being," and its Greek Pagan and

Christian counterparts *ouk ēmēn, egenomēn, ouk eimi,* "I was not, I came into being, I am no longer," see Kaufmann, p. 134, and Franz Cumont, "Non fui, fui, non sum," *Musée belge* 32 (1928): 73–85 (20 inscriptions); see also Angelo Brelich, *Aspetti della morte nelle iscrizioni sepolcrali dell' Impero Romano* (Budapest, 1937) [= Dissertationes Pannonicae Musei Nationalis Hungarici, ser. 1, fasc. 7], esp. pp. 58–60. An echo of the formula is heard in the Christianized formulation of the Slavic *Vita* of Cyril-Constantine, Apostle of the Slavs, ch. 18:4, where the Saint says towards the end of his life: "I was not and I came to be and I am for ever, Amen." For *xeny kai parodite,* see, for example, Rugo 2, no. 32 (fig. only, p. 110), and Guillou, no. 60. For *zōmen en theō,* see Kaufmann, p. 141, fig. 138; for *vibas* [*sic*] *in deo* and similar formulae, see Kaufmann, p. 141, fig. 149 (3rd c.); Rugo 4. no. 21 (9th c.? Monte S. Angelo); no. 23 (same date and place); no. 64 (7th c., Lucera). For *pax tibi, eirēne soi, in pace, pax, eirēnē,* see Diehl, nos. 2297 G-L; 2298–2300 A.

8. For the famous Aberkios's inscription in hexameters, see, for example, Kaufmann, p. 171. For Pektorios's poetic inscription, see ibid., p. 179.

9. For the Ursicinus inscription from Trier, see Kaufmann, p. 91; for the one from Syracuse, see ibid., p. 196. For the Latin *plus minus* or *menus,* see, for example, Rugo 1, no. 24 (a. 540, Mantua?), no. 46 (a. 525, Brescia); Rugo 4, nos. 28 (a. 503, Venosa), 61 (7th c., Benevento), 72a (a. 541, Cimitile), 77 (a. 557, Cimitile), 90 (5th c., Cimitile), 91 (a. 535, Cimitile), 96 (a. 527, Capua), 105 (5th c., S. Angelo in Formis); Rugo 5, nos. 22 (a. 523, Milan), 79 (5th c., Como), 105 (a. 539, Pavia), 151 (a. 545, Ivrea), 157 (6th c., Vercelli), 168 (a. 527, La Spezia).

10. For examples, see Diehl, nos. 866 B, 866 D, 872 AB, 873, 873 A, 874, 875 A. Also cf. 2289 with 2290.

11. See Kaufmann, p. 140 and fig. 137 (third century).

12. For Comentiolus, see Diehl, no. 792; for Solomon, see ibid., no. 791.

13. The 318 Fathers of Nicea: for Syria and Rome, see Kaufmann, pp. 157–58; for Ravenna, see Rugo 3, no. 9 (a. 731); for a twelfth-century echo of the 318 Fathers' curse formula, see, for example, Guillou, no. 104. The Credo: for Corinth, see Kaufmann, p. 144; for Capua and Como, see ibid., p. 208.

14. See Rugo 2, nos. 18–19 (Iesolo), 47, 47a-b, 49 (Grado); Rugo 3, no. 79 (Florence).

15. For Syria, see, for example, Kaufmann, pp. 413–15, figs. 239–43, and Henri Seyrig in Georges Tchalenko, *Villages antiques de la Syrie du Nord,* 3 vols. (Paris, 1958) [=Bibliothèque archéologique et historique, 50], no. 39b, p. 37 (fourth–fifth century?). For roof tiles of Santa Maria Maggiore, see Kaufmann, p. 425 and Fig. 246; for amphorae, see

Popescu, nos. 139, 140, 187 and 316–24; for the Tropaeum Traiani inscription, see Popescu, no. 173.

16. Liturgical formula from Rovigo: Rugo 2, no. 37; for Egypt, see, for example, Gustave Lefebvre, *Recueil des inscriptions grecques chrétiennes, d'Égypte* (Cairo, 1907), nos. 647, 652, 659, 660; for the same formula in Christian Nubia, see, for example, Jadwiga Kubińska, *Inscriptions grecques chrétiennes* (Warsaw, 1974) [=Faras 4], no. 3, p. 24 (a. 765), no. 5, p. 32 (a. 923) and a number of other inscriptions in the volume. For *amēn* = 99, see, in general, Kaufmann, pp. 75, 143, and, for example, Lefebvre, *Recueil,* no. 659 (but the provenance may be Nubia); Kubińska, *Inscriptions,* no. 1, p. 15 (a. 707); for 99 in the more "Western" Parthenon, see Anastasios K. Orlandos and Leandros Vranoussis, *Les graffiti du Parthénon* (Athens, 1973), no. 141, pp. 113–14. As to the meaning of 99, while the editors were not sure whether the number 99 stood for the *date* of the graffito, they speculated that it may have referred to the *age* of the deceased mentioned in it.

17. See Kaufmann, p. 415 and Fig. 243 (Syria); Rugo 5, no. 18 (Caesarea maritima in Palestine); Popescu, no. 49 (Constanţa?).

18. For the *hic positus est, hic situs,* etc., see Kaufmann, pp. 108 and 110. For the many fifth- to sixth-century examples of *requiesc. in pace,* see, for example, Rugo 1, no. 18 (Osoppo), no. 46 (Brescia), no. 57 (Bergamo); Rugo 4, no. 92 (Avello); Rugo 5, no. 149 (Tortona); cf. ibid., no. 151, 155, 156 (Ivrea).

19. For the two inscriptions in the Church of St. Francis in Ravenna, see Rugo 3, nos. 20 and 21. For dating by Western consuls, see, for example, Rugo 1, no. 18 (a. 524); 4, no. 109 (a. 541, Benevento); 5, no. 108 (a. 539, Pavia), 151 (a. 545, Ivrea), 168 (a. 527, La Spezia). The situation is quite complicated and excellently presented by Jean Durliat, "Épigraphie et société" in Cavallo and Mango, *Epigrafia,* pp. 172–73 (tables).

20. For Bishop Arcadius, see Rugo 3, no. 95 (where Rugo's text is erroneous); for the inscription in the walls of Nicaea, see, for example, Alfons M. Schneider and Walter Karnapp, *Die Stadtmauer von Iznik (Nicaea)* (Berlin, 1938), p. 49 (inscription no. 29) and Plate 50; see also Clive Foss, *Nicaea: A Byzantine Capital and Its Praises: With the Speeches of Theodore Laskaris in Praise of the Great City of Nicaea, and Theodore Metochites' Nicene Oration* (Brookline, MA, 1996), p. 18. The Greek phrase crucial for us is *to tōn echthrōn kataischynthē [sic] thrasos.*

21. For Audoald, see Rugo 5, no. 107 (ca. 718, Pavia); for Cunincpert, see ibid., no. 113 (a. 700, Pavia).

22. Dating by Lombard kings: for example, Rugo 4, no. 8 (Spoleto, a. 770); Rugo 5, no. 160 (a. 691, Turin). Dating by Byzantine emperors in the Exarchate by Ravenna: Rugo 4, no. 51 (a. 796, Benevento). The *Anno*

Domini date of 814 in the inscription (authentic or not) on the tomb of Charlemagne reported in Eginhard's *Vita* does not belong here, since the Christian era (established in the sixth century) was adopted by Western chroniclers such as Bede (d. 735) soon after its creation.

23. See Orlandos and Vranoussis, *Les graffiti*, nos. 34 (a. 693, doubtful), 80 (a. 704), 82 (a. 779), 126 (a. 793).

24. For the floor mosaic from Ivrea, see Rugo 5, no. 150; for the ninth-century Byzantine awareness of the seven liberal arts (*trivium* and *quadrivium*) system, see, for example, Ignatios the Deacon, *Vita Nicephori,* in *Nicephori archiepiscopi Constantinopolitani opuscula,* ed. Carl De Boor (Leipzig, 1880), p. 149, line 27 to p. 151, line 13; and the Slavic *Vita* of Constantine-Cyril, IV, 1–3. For the full Byzantine discussion of the system ca. 1300, see George Pachymeres, *Quadrivium de Georges Pachymère,* ed. Paul Tannery and E. Stéphanou (Vatican City, 1940) [=Studi e Testi, 94], especially the Preface by V. Laurent, pp. vii–xxxiii.

25. Thus, for example, "*ēta, ny, omega*" year = the year $8 + 50 + 800 = 858$. The Medieval Slavic sequence in writing numerals, for example, $bi = 2 + 10 = 12$, is independent from the Semitic one, and has its parallels in the right-to-left sequence of numerals found in native Greek inscriptions from Macedonia.

26. For the Bulgarian inscription from Krepcha, dated to 921, see, for example, Kazimir Popkonstantinov, "Novootkriti starobъlgarski nadpisi ot X vek," in *Paléographie et diplomatique slaves,* ed. Borjana Velčeva et al. (Sofia, 1980) [=Balcanica, ser. 3, Études et documents, 1], esp. p. 289 and Figs. 1–2. The inscription of the Bulgarian "inner Boyar" Mostič (discovered in 1952) dates from the middle of the tenth century. See, for example, St. Stančev et al., *Nadpisъt na čъrgubilja Mostič* (Sofia, 1955), esp. p. 8. For the graffito of 1052 from Saint Sophia in Kyiv, see, for example, Sergej Vysotskij, *Drevnerusskie nadpisi Sofii Kievskoj, XI–XIV vv.,* fasc. 1 (Kyiv, 1966), no. 3, pp. 16–17; see also idem, *Srednevekovye nadpisi Sofii Kievskoj* (Kyiv, 1976), pp. 198–201, for speculations about a graffito that the author dates to 1031–1032.

Russians in Ukraine: Problems and Prospects

ROMAN SOLCHANYK

Before independence, it would have been difficult to imagine that there could be a "Russian question" in Ukraine. Ukraine and Belarus were probably the two non-Russian Soviet republics where ethnic Russians felt most at home; in some respects, they were perhaps even more comfortable in Kyiv or Minsk than in Omsk or Tomsk. Indeed, as Roman Szporluk pointed out some years ago, as a function of the special political status that Russians enjoyed throughout the Soviet Union and because of the specific nature of the historically conditioned Ukrainian-Russian relationship—which, from the Russian standpoint, translated into the notion that Ukrainians and Russians are essentially the same *narod*—Russians in Soviet Ukraine could hardly be considered a genuine national minority except in a literal, arithmetic sense.[1] A well-known specialist on ethnicity and a prominent spokesman for Russian causes in Ukraine recently made a similar observation, arguing that during the Soviet period Russian culture in Ukraine was understood to be Soviet culture that was conveyed in the Russian language and that the close ties between Ukrainians and Russians served to blur ethnic differences between the two groups even further.[2] Stated differently, although Russians were a presence throughout the Soviet Union, it was largely taken for granted that they "belonged" in Ukraine, which in some sense also made them less "Russian" than Russians in Estonia, Georgia, or Uzbekistan.

Szporluk noted that this situation could change if Ukraine were to become independent—that is, that Russians in Ukraine could become an "ordinary" national minority. There are clear indications that such a transformation may be under way. Organized groups representing the Russian community in Ukraine are now troubled by such issues as the decline in the number of Russian-language schools and the perceived marginalization of the Russian intelligentsia and, more broadly, are critical of government policies that affect their interests. Government leaders in Moscow remind their Ukrainian counterparts at official meetings on the highest levels of their concern about safeguarding the rights of Russians and Russian speakers. Respectable Russian newspapers such as *Nezavisimaia gazeta* publish articles bemoaning the "forced ukrainianization" and "ethnocide" of Russians in Ukraine, particularly in Crimea. Some Western scholars have suggested that Ukraine may become, already is, or, in any case, is perceived by Russians as being a "nationalizing state." In early 1994, a U.S. National Intelligence Estimate was cited as having posited a scenario wherein an internal Ukrainian-Russian ethnic conflict could result in civil war, the fragmentation of Ukraine along overlapping regional, ethnic, and linguistic lines, and Moscow's intervention to restore peace and tranquillity. That same year, a prominent Washington-based public policy center published a curious document that imagined a Ukrainian-Russian confrontation along the lines of the Serbian-Bosnian, Armenian-Azerbaijani, and Georgian-Abkhazian models; recommended to Washington that the United States should make clear to Ukraine that it will not countenance "violent repression of Russian separatists or denial of their political rights"; and argued that U.S. interests would be better served if certain Russian-speaking areas of Ukraine became independent or were affiliated with Russia.[3]

All of this suggests, at varying levels of seriousness, that the demise of the Soviet Union and the establishment of an independent Ukraine have created a new situation for the Russian minority. On the one hand, the specifically Soviet political attributes and functions of Russians in Ukraine (as elsewhere in the former USSR) have been rendered largely superfluous. Such typically Soviet concepts as "the national languages," "the national literatures," and "the national republics," which were never applied to the Russian language, Russian literature, and the RSFSR—and which underscored that things Russian had a different status in the Soviet Union—are now anachronisms.[4] At the same time, it would be unwise to altogether ignore or minimize "vestiges of the Soviet past" and their attraction for both Russians and Ukrainians. A nationwide poll conducted in Ukraine in 1996 showed that more than half of Russian respondents considered their "Fatherland" to be the USSR; the corresponding figure for Ukrainians was almost half as much.[5] On the other hand, the historical baggage that has defined the Ukrainian-Russian relationship continues to make its influence felt in a myriad of ways. President Leonid Kuchma, for example, told an audience of students and academics in Moscow in early 1998 that "our country [Ukraine] not only was, but remains a powerful source of nourishment for all-Russian [*obshcherossiiskaia*] culture." But he also said that support for the development of Ukrainian culture and language is dictated by "the necessity of compensating for losses suffered as a result of unintended or conscious russification."[6] In the meantime, most Russians apparently remain convinced that Ukrainians are actually Russians. A poll conducted in Russia in the fall of 1997 revealed that 56 percent of respondents felt that Russians and Ukrainians are one *narod*.[7] It is against this somewhat ambiguous if not entirely contradictory background that Russians in contemporary Ukraine are attempting to define their post-Soviet role and status.

Before taking a closer look at this process and the issues that it has brought to the surface, it may be useful to recall some basic data about Ukraine's Russian population and to briefly survey official Kyiv's approach to nationality and interethnic matters. The 1989 census recorded 11.4 million Russians in Ukraine, representing 22.1 percent of the overall population. Although the proportion of Russians in Latvia, Estonia, and Kazakhstan is higher, in absolute terms Ukraine has the largest Russian community in the so-called Near or New

Abroad. At the end of the 1980s, about 45 percent of all Russians outside of the RSFSR were in Ukraine. At that juncture, slightly more than 42 percent of Ukraine's Russian population had been born there. In terms of regional distribution, almost 70 percent of Russians live in the eastern oblasts of Donetsk, Luhansk, Kharkiv, Dnipropetrovsk, Zaporizhzhia, and in the Autonomous Republic of Crimea. There are substantial numbers of Russians in the southern oblasts of Mykolaïv, Odesa, and Kherson. Crimea is the only administrative subdivision of the country with a Russian majority, which was 67 percent in 1989. That figure has certainly decreased over the past decade because of the return of the Crimean Tatars from their places of exile in Central Asia. It should be noted that Soviet censuses are thought to have yielded inflated numbers for Russians because of, among other things, the perceived advantages of Russian nationality.[8] Critics of the government's policies now fear that the next census will record the reverse process—namely, Russians choosing to become Ukrainians.[9]

The prevailing view among outside observers, including international monitoring groups, is that, with few exceptions, interethnic harmony has been the rule in Ukraine—something that cannot be said of most of the other former Soviet republics. The two regions that do not entirely fit this description are western Ukraine and Crimea. In the former, Russians and other national minorities complain that ultranationalist Ukrainian groups foster ethnic hatred and that local authorities fail to take appropriate action in such cases; in the latter, Ukrainians and Crimean Tatars claim that they are discriminated against by the local Russians. Overall, however, it would be difficult to find fault with the assessment offered by the chief rabbi of Kyiv and Ukraine—namely, that "Ukraine has the best human rights record in the former Soviet Union."[10] Much of the credit for this state of affairs belongs to the country's leadership, which has been consistent in its perception of the Ukrainian nation as a territorial and political concept rather than an ethnic one. Virtually all of Ukraine's numerous political parties share this view. Ultranationalist political groups are few, small, and have little if any impact on national politics. The marginalization of such groups was illustrated during the 1998 parliamentary elections, when the two parties propagating "Ukraine for Ukrainians!" received 0.2 percent of the national party list vote. Equal rights for all national groups are guaranteed by several documents and laws adopted by the parliament, beginning with the preindependence declaration of state sovereignty (July 1990), the Declaration of the Rights of Nationalities of Ukraine (November 1991), and the Law on National Minorities in Ukraine (June 1992).[11]

Language issues must be examined in somewhat more detail because, among other things, they have been the focus of much controversy and heated debate. The Law on Languages in the Ukrainian SSR, which was adopted in the fall of 1989, gives Ukrainian the exclusive status of the state language, a provision that is also embodied in the 1996 Constitution. The language law, as it is more commonly known, also legalized the concept of "languages of internationality communication," and these were identified as "Ukrainian, Russian, and other languages." This was a modification of long-standing Soviet ideological jargon that was used to characterize the special status and "internationalizing" functions of the Russian language. The lawmakers did not specify what was to be understood by this designation, which, moreover, can also be found in the constitution. More importantly, even a casual reading of the law leads to the conclusion that on a practical level the status of Ukrainian as the sole state language is rendered largely meaningless by the fact that Russian and indeed all other languages used in Ukraine are granted broad prerogatives in the public sector, and especially insofar as "places compactly inhabited by citizens of other [non-Ukrainian] nationalities" are concerned. Public officials are expected to know Ukrainian, Russian, and, if necessary, another language. Laws and other normative acts of "the highest organs of state power" are published in Ukrainian and Russian. At lower levels, including the national ministries, official documents may be issued in other languages. The language of instruction throughout the educational system is Ukrainian, but another language may be substituted in accordance with the national composition of a given locality or region. Parents have the right to freely choose the language of instruction for their children. Ukrainian and Russian are obligatory subjects in all general education schools. The law provided for generous timelines of up to 10 years for the implementation of certain of its provisions, specifically those concerning the educational system. No mechanism was established to enforce the law.[12] It is probably quite true that the law had "relatively little impact" in the years immediately after its passage.[13] More precisely, the 1989 language law is still largely irrelevant. What changed is that Ukraine became independent in December 1991, which raised many questions—including questions about the role, status, and future of the Russian language.

The 1992 Law on National Minorities of Ukraine reiterates some of the key postulates of the language law, guarantees all national minorities national-cultural autonomy, and specifies that native-language instruction, or the study of the native language in state institutions or through national cultural societies, is guaranteed by the state. The constitution also addresses language issues. In addition to state status, the state "guarantees the all around development and functioning of the Ukrainian language in all spheres of social life throughout the entire territory of Ukraine." As for "Russian and other languages of national minorities in Ukraine," their "free development, utilization, and protection" are also guaranteed. Russians, therefore, are clearly understood to be a national minority. The state also "facilitates learning the languages of internationality communication."

The main complaint of Russian rights activists is that the use of the Russian language in the educational system is being circumscribed in violation of the law. The argument can be simple and straightforward: officials at the national and local levels issue instructions and orders and institute practices that are in violation of the language law and the constitution. On a more sophisticated level, critics point out that the legislation, decrees, and other official documents emanating from Kyiv that impinge on language issues are often vague and abstract enough so that officials can basically do or not do whatever moves them at the moment. In the fall of 1992, for example, the Ministry of Education ordered that the language status of schools be brought into optimal accordance with the national composition of every region, specifically in the first grade. This had clear implications for schools in eastern and southern Ukraine, where there were few Ukrainian-language schools but where the majority of the population is Ukrainian. The question arises, therefore, as to the guaranteed right of parents to freely choose the language of instruction. The following year, it was decided that, in principle, entrance examinations to institutions of higher learning would be conducted in Ukrainian; incoming students who had less than five years of Ukrainian-language study in the general education schools were exempted. Ukrainian-language instruction would also be introduced during the first academic year.[14] The language law, however, allowed for instruction in non-Ukrainian languages together with Ukrainian in areas with a non-Ukrainian majority. In June 1999, in the midst of the presidential election campaign, Kuchma sent an instruction to the minister of education proposing changes that would allow entrance examinations to institutions of higher learning to be conducted in Russian as well as Ukrainian. A corresponding letter was sent out by the ministry to administrators of the higher schools that "recommend[ed] introducing a supplement to the regulations governing admissions that would provide for the possibility of taking entrance examinations in the Russian language."[15] In western Ukraine, the recommendation is being ignored. The administration of the Lviv State Institute of Physical Culture, for example, declared that even if 10 such instructions were issued, they would not be implemented because Ukrainian is the state language.[16] Clearly, there is plenty of room here for interpretation and discussion. What the Russians would like to see is a clear delineation of their language rights.[17]

The fact that language issues figure prominently in discussions about the "Russian question," and not only in Ukraine, should come as no surprise. Irrespective of whether the Soviet Union fits the description of a "classic" empire and the related question of whether Russians in the Soviet Union can be described as an imperial nation, the fact remains that the Soviet leadership pursued and implemented policies that promoted the Russian language. For Russians in the non-Russian republics, what this meant was that the language question was essentially a nonissue. Russian was the language of the Communist Party, the language of "progress," and much else. Russian-language schools, Russian-language media, Russian-language movies and theaters, and almost anything else in Russian was easily available and accessible, particularly in Ukraine and even more so in Belarus. That is no longer the case to the extent that it was earlier, particularly in the educational sphere.

In the 1990–1991 school year, the proportion of schoolchildren taught in Russian in Ukraine's general education schools was 51.3 percent; in urban areas the figure was 68 percent.[18] After independence, the overall proportions decreased in every successive year, dropping to 34 percent in 1998–1999,[19] with a corresponding increase in the proportion of schoolchildren taught in Ukrainian (see Table 1). This figure is still greater than both the share of Russians listed in the 1989 census (22.1 percent) and the proportion of the

Table 1. Language of Instruction in General Education Schools (percentage of schoolchildren)

	Russian	Ukrainian
1991/92	50.0	49.3
1992/93	47.8	51.4
1993/94	44.9	54.3
1994/95	43.0	57.0
1995/96	41.0	58.0
1996/97	39.0	60.0
1997/98	36.0	63.0
1998/99	34.0	65.0

Sources: Ministerstvo statystyky Ukraïny, *Narodne hospodarstvo Ukraïny u 1993 rotsi. Statystychnyi shchorichnyk* (Kyiv, 1994), p. 384; Ministerstvo statystyky Ukraïny, *Statystychnyi shchorichnyk Ukraïny za 1995 rik* (Kyiv, 1996), p. 446; Derzhavnyi komitet statystyky Ukraïny, *Statystychnyi shchorichnyk Ukraïny za 1996 rik* (Kyiv, 1997), p. 457; and Derzhavnyi komitet statystyky Ukraïny, *Statystychnyi shchorichnyk Ukraïny za 1998 rik* (Kyiv, 1999), p. 429.

total population that declared Russian as their native language (32.8 percent). Interestingly, the census results for native language largely correspond to the data from opinion polls. In 1994–1998, the proportion of respondents who declared Russian as their native language ranged from 34.7 percent to 36.5 percent. Another way of looking at language affiliation is to gauge its use in the family setting. The polls show that between 32.4 percent and 34.5 percent converse exclusively in Russian; another 26.8 percent to 34.5 percent use both Russian and Ukrainian depending upon circumstances.[20] From this standpoint as well, there would appear to be no grounds for serious concern about the language of instruction in schools. A rather different situation emerges when the "language of convenience"—which is defined as the language that respondents feel more comfortable with during survey interviews—is used to determine language preference. According to one source, Russian is the language of convenience for about 55 percent of the population in Ukraine; another source gives the lower figure of 43 percent.[21] These considerably higher figures—which are said to be the most reliable indicator of what might be termed the "comfort zone" for Russians and Russian speakers and that are obviously out of line with language trends in Ukraine's schools—form much of the basis for discussions about Ukraine as a "nationalizing state." At the same time, there is a rather puzzling aspect of this problem. In a 1994 survey, 43.5 percent of Ukrainians opted for Russian as their language of convenience; in 1999, that figure rose to 50.9 percent.[22] The question that arises is: If the Russian language in Ukraine is under threat, declining in prestige, losing its viability, and the like, why are larger numbers of Ukrainians finding it increasingly more "convenient"?

Thus far, our discussion has focused on developments at the national level. But Ukraine is a country with regional distinctions. There are clear differences in the ethnic composition, language preferences, and political orientations of the eastern, central, and western parts of the country. The language of instruction in schools is no exception. In the eastern oblasts and in Crimea—areas with the largest numbers of Russians and Russian speakers—schoolchildren continue to be taught primarily in Russian. There has been virtually no change in Crimea, and in the Donbas Russian-language enrollments have dropped by nearly 7 percent. There has been a very significant decrease of almost 28 percent in Dnipropetrovsk (see Table 2). Overall, the Russian language continues to prevail in those regions where it has traditionally been dominant.

Table 2. Russian-Language Instruction in General Education Schools in the East and in Crimea (percentage of schoolchildren)

	1991/92	1992/93	1993/94	1994/95	1995/96	1996/97	1997/98	1998/99
Crimea	99.9	99.9	99.7	99.7	99.5	99.4	99.7	98.1
Donetsk	96.7	96.1	95.1	95.0	94.0	93.0	91.0	90.0
Luhansk	93.3	92.7	91.6	91.0	90.8	90.0	89.0	87.0
Zaporizhzhia	77.3	75.1	72.5	70.0	69.0	67.0	64.0	62.0
Dnipropetrovsk	68.9	67.4	63.4	58.0	54.0	50.0	45.0	41.0
Kharkiv	72.0	69.4	66.9	65.0	63.0	61.0	57.0	53.0

Sources: Ibid.

In short, the policy inaugurated by the Ministry of Education in 1992 has fallen short of its intended goals.

The trends that are current in the general education schools are also evident in Ukraine's preschool institutions and in the universities and other institutions of higher learning. In 1991, 48.8 percent of preschoolers were taught in Russian; in 1998, the corresponding figure was 25.3 percent.[23] The most far-reaching changes have occurred at the university level and its equivalents. By the end of the 1980s, higher education in Ukraine was almost entirely in the Russian language. In the 1989–1990 academic year, the proportion of students taught in Russian was 93 percent; the following academic year it was 84 percent.[24] Had it not been for the universities in western Ukraine and to a lesser extent Kyiv State University, instruction in Ukraine's higher schools would have been nearly all in Russian.[25] By the 1998–1999 academic year, however, the proportion of students taught in Russian had dropped to between 28 percent and 34 percent, depending upon the level of accreditation.[26] As with the general education schools, the prevalence of Russian or Ukrainian in the pre-school and higher education establishments differs significantly from region to region. In Crimea, the proportion of university and higher school students taught in Russian in 1998–1999 was 100 percent; in the Donbas it ranged from 77 percent to 89 percent.

In the areas of press, publishing, and radio and television, the Russian language has strengthened its position. Between 1990 and 1998, the proportion of the annual print run of journals in Ukrainian decreased from 90.4 percent to 17.5 percent; the corresponding figures for the single-issue print run of news-papers were 68 percent and 39.6 percent. Obviously, the Russian-language press accounts for virtually all of the balance. Between 1995 and 1997, the number of Russian-language journals increased from 101 to 118 and the num-ber of newspapers from 721 to 796. The data for books and brochures appear at first glance to favor the Ukrainian language. In 1997, Ukrainian-language titles accounted for 49.8 percent of the total and Russian-language titles for 37.5 percent. It turns out, however, that nearly half of the Ukrainian titles were textbooks. In 1998, Russian-language broadcasts accounted for 9 percent and 20.6 percent of state radio and television air time, respectively. But almost two-thirds of total radio and television air time was in Russian.[27] The most popular newscast in Ukraine is the *Vremia* program of ORT (Russian Public Televi-sion), which is available by satellite and cable and is also carried by Inter, a private channel.[28] Inter, which is partly owned by ORT and broadcasts in Russian, has captured the largest share of prime time television viewing (32.9 percent) in Ukraine and can reach 70 percent of viewers countrywide. Studio 1+1, a private company that broadcasts in Ukrainian on the state UT-2 channel and can reach 73 percent of viewers, is a close second with 29.2 percent of prime time.[29] Inter and Studio 1+1 were created in 1996 and 1995, respec-tively, and it will be interesting to see how they fare in the commercial marketplace.

Language issues may be controversial, but apparently not for the over-whelming majority of Ukraine's citizens, irrespective of nationality. In the grand scheme of things, few people are concerned about the status of the Russian language. In November 1998, 4 percent were troubled by this issue; in early 1999, it was 2 percent. When asked what sets people apart in Ukraine, 2 percent said language issues and 4 percent identified nationality.[30] Outside of Crimea, there are no specifically Russian political parties in Ukraine. The few parties that campaign primarily on Russian issues are marginalized to about the same extent as Ukrainian ethnic ultranationalists. In the 1998 parliamentary elections, the SLOn—Social-Liberal Union, whose program categorically re-jected what were described as attempts to legalize "the political division of a single [Russian-Ukrainian] people" and supported official status for the Russian language, received 0.9 percent of the national party list vote. The Union Party, which, among other things, advocated recognizing Russians in Ukraine as a "state-forming" nation and the Russian language as the second state language, garnered 0.7 percent of the vote. Finally, the Party of Regional Revival of Ukraine, whose name reflects its main focus but which also promised "legal priorities" for the Russian language, managed 0.9 percent.

There appears to be a fair amount of consensus that the Russian community continues to remain rather comfortable in Ukraine.[31] Russians do not sense that they are being discriminated against, are not leaving the country, and do not seem to be particularly interested in Moscow's protection. Crimea—which at one time was thought to have the potential for becoming a Ukrainian Nagorno-Karabakh, Abkhazia, or Transdniester—is no exception. There was certainly a Crimean problem in Ukraine, which has since faded, but there was never a Russian problem in Crimea. Nonetheless, the conventional wisdom in Moscow seems to be that the Russian minority in Ukraine requires its attention—specifically, that the Russian language and culture are under siege. For several years, one of the main stumbling blocks in the negotiations on the bilateral friendship treaty was Moscow's insistence that Kyiv agree to dual Russian-Ukrainian citizenship. That issue was eventually removed from the treaty negotiations, but it remains on Russia's wish list.[32] On the eve of his visit to Kyiv in May 1997 to sign the Black Sea Fleet agreements, former Prime Minister Viktor Chernomyrdin publicly expressed his concern about "the line, which is increasingly manifesting itself in Ukraine towards restriction and actually ousting of the Russian language and culture from the state and intellectual life of the society."[33] A top aide to Yeltsin told journalists in Kyiv a few days later that restrictions on the rights of Russian speakers to Russian-language education and information would be on the agenda of the presidential summit that ultimately resulted in the signing of the friendship treaty. The Russian State Duma delayed ratification of the treaty for more than a year; according to one Russian lawmaker, his colleagues objected first and foremost to the "artificial restrictions" on the Russian language, Russian schools, and television broadcasting in Russian, and insisted that these be taken into account by the Ukrainian side.[34] When the treaty was approved by the State Duma in December 1998, it was accompanied by a separate statement addressed to the Ukrainian president, parliament, and government that referred to restrictions on the rights of Russian speakers in Ukraine as an issue that needed to be resolved by Kyiv.[35] Two months earlier, the State Duma had adopted a similar document protesting that the Crimean constitution granted Ukrainian the exclusive status of the state language on the territory of the peninsula.[36] Georgii Tikhonov, who headed the State Duma Committee on CIS Affairs and Ties with Compatriots, has argued that Kyiv's policies amount to a "total pogrom against Russian culture" in Ukraine.[37]

Tikhonov's assertions are quite obviously nonsense. What is important, however, is that his views proceed from a frame of reference for Russian-Ukrainian relations—in the broadest sense of the term—that is shared by most of Russia's political class. It is a frame of reference that does not accommodate the notion of Russians in Ukraine as an "ordinary" national minority. Instead, he and other Russian officials have argued that Russians are a "state-forming" nation, a concept that also has its supporters in Ukraine. It is not entirely clear what that means. Another variation on this theme is that Russians in Ukraine should be recognized as a "partner nation,"[38] the implications of which also are less than obvious. There is every indication that a similar discourse is increasingly informing the agenda of Russian rights activists in Ukraine. The 1998 conference on the "Dialogue of Ukrainian and Russian Cultures in Ukraine" adopted recommendations that, among other things, referred to the "juridically unjustified forced and illegal acceleration of eliminating the Russian language and culture from the educational sphere, official information, and state-political life, and the artificial demolition of the historical affinity of the Ukrainian-Russian linguistic and artistic cultures."[39] The First Congress of Russians of Ukraine, which was convened in May 1999, accused the government of "establishing a policy directed at the massive expulsion of the Russian ethno-cultural factor from all aspects of society."[40]

There is every indication that the language question will continue to stir emotions—both within Ukraine and in relations between Kyiv and Moscow. In mid-December 1999, Ukraine's Constitutional Court issued a ruling stating that Ukrainian is the "obligatory language of instruction in all state educational institutions of the country." The use and study of languages of the national minorities, including Russian, is said to require authorization. The Ukrainian language was also declared obligatory "on the entire territory of Ukraine in implementing the authority of the organs of state power and the organs of local self-administration and in other spheres of public life."[41] The Russian Ministry of Foreign Affairs reacted with a note to the Ukrainian embassy in Moscow at the end of January 2000 expressing the hope that Ukraine would implement its policies with regard to Russian speakers in the spirit of the Ukrainian-Russian friendship treaty. At the same time, it made public a statement criticizing Kyiv's moves as a violation of Ukraine's constitution. Fuel was added to the fire when the Council on Questions of Language Policy attached to Kuchma's office approved a draft decree of the Cabinet of Ministers "On Additional Measures to Broaden the Functioning of Ukrainian as the State Language." The proposed decree foresees screening state officials at all levels with respect to their knowledge and use of Ukrainian in the performance of their duties; completing the process of bringing language instruction in schools in line with the country's national composition; regulating the language status of private radio and television channels; developing a program of derussification of the sport and tourist industries; overseeing the compliance of theaters with their language status; regulating the tours of foreign entertainment groups in

Ukraine; and the introduction of tax levers on outside publications disseminated in the country.[42] This prompted the Ministry of Foreign Affairs in Moscow to issue another statement, which asserted that "certain forces in Ukraine seem determined to create a phenomenon unseen in Europe before—to make the native language of the overwhelming majority of the population [*sic*] an actual outcast, reduce its status to marginal, and possibly even squeeze it out."[43] Russia's Human Rights Commissioner urged international organizations to increase their monitoring of the situation in Ukraine.[44] And in Kyiv, Russian rights activists appealed to the Parliamentary Assembly of the Council of Europe to render assistance in the observation of the rights of all citizens of Ukraine regardless of their origin or language.[45]

In one sense, therefore, the Russian question in Ukraine is not very different from any other national minority question. Russians, like most others, are interested in preserving their identity and defending their rights. On the other hand, what distinguishes them from Poles, Hungarians, or Jews is that their former status in Ukraine dictates how they perceive their current situation.[46] What this suggests is that the process of Russians in Ukraine becoming an "ordinary" national minority is part of the lengthy, complex, and larger process of "normalizing" Russian-Ukrainian relations.

NOTES

I would like to thank Stephen Rapawy, formerly of the U.S. Bureau of the Census, for providing me with the most recent official statistics on language in the educational system and in the media.

1. Roman Szporluk, "Russians in Ukraine and Problems of Ukrainian Identity in the USSR," in *Ukraine in the Seventies: Papers and Proceedings of the McMaster Conference on Contemporary Ukraine, October 1974,* ed. Peter J. Potichnyj (Oakville, ON, 1975), pp. 195–96.

2. Nikolai Shul'ga, "Krizis etnicheskogo samoopredeleniia," *Sodruzhestvo NG* 22 December 1999: 12.

3. Robert B. Cullen, *Ukraine, Ukrainian Minorities and United States Policy,* The Atlantic Council of the United States, Occasional Paper Series (Washington, DC, 1994), pp. ix–xiii.

4. Ihor Losiev, "Ukraïns'ke pytannia i rosiis'ka natsional'na samoidentyfikatsiia," *Suchasnist'* 4 (April 1999): 65.

5. Sergei Savoskul, "Russkie v nezavisimoi Ukraine: status, identichnost', perspektivy," in *Ukraina i Rossiia: obshchestva i gosudarstva,* ed. and comp. D. E. Furman (Moscow, 1997), p. 283.

6. For the text of Kuchma's address, see *Uriadovyi kur'ier* 5 March 1998.

7. Interfax, 27 October 1997.

8. See, for example, Iaroslav Dashkevych, "Ukraïna i natsional'ni menshosti," *Derzhavnist'* 1(3) October 1991: 24.

9. N. A. Shul'ga, "Sostoianie russkoi kul'tury v Ukraine: mify i realii," in *Dialog ukrainskoi i russkoi kul'tur v Ukraine. Materialy III-i mezhdunarodnoi nauchno-prakticheskoi konferentsii (12–13 noiabria 1998 goda, g. Kiev)* (Kyiv, 1999), p. 14.

10. *The Washington Post* 28 March 1995.

11. The texts are published in *Natsional'ni vidnosyny v Ukraïni u XX st. Zbirnyk dokumentiv i materialiv* (Kyiv, 1994), pp. 454ff.

12. For the text, see *Natsional'ni vidnosyny v Ukraïni,* pp. 445–52.

13. Jeff Chinn and Robert Kaiser, *Russians as the New Minority: Ethnicity and Nationalism in the Soviet Successor States* (Boulder, CO, 1996), p. 155. Discussions have been under way since at least the mid-1990s about the need to amend the language law and bring it into line with existing realities, but this has yet to be acted upon by Parliament.

14. See the interviews with Anatolii Pohribnyi, First Deputy Minister of Education, in *Demokratychna Ukraïna* 27 April 1993 and *Literaturna Ukraïna* 29 July 1993. For a detailed analysis, see Dominique Arel, "The Temptation of the Nationalizing State," in *Political Culture and Civil*

Society in Russia and the New States of Eurasia, ed. Vladimir Tismaneanu (Armonk, NY, 1995), pp. 174–77; and his "Language Politics in Independent Ukraine: Towards One or Two State Languages?" *Nationalities Papers* 23(3) September 1995: 603–610. See also Jan G. Janmaat, "Language Politics in Education and the Response of the Russians in Ukraine," *Nationalities Papers* 27(3) September 1999: 475–501.

15. Quoted by Shul'ga, "Krizis etnicheskogo samoopredeleniia."

16. *Postup* 29 July 1999.

17. In addition to the articles by Shul'ga, see E. V. Krasniakov, "Pravo obucheniia na rodnom iazyke i ukrainskoe zakonodatel'stvo," in *Dialog ukrainskoi i russkoi kul'tur v Ukraine,* pp. 84–91; and Vladimir Alekseev, "Khuzhe bezzakoniia. O realizatsii konstitutsionnykh garantii v iazykovoi sfere," *Sodruzhestvo NG* May 1999: 13.

18. Ministerstvo statystyky Ukraïny, *Statystychnyi zbirnyk "Osvita ta kul'tura na Ukraïni"* (Kyiv, 1991), p. 6.

19. In a statement issued on 12 February 2000, the Ukrainian Ministry of Foreign Affairs said that currently 31.7 percent of pupils in state schools are taught in Russian. See <http://www.mfa.gov.ua/info/s2000/0212.html>.

20. N. V. Panina and Ie. I. Holovakha, *Tendentsiï rozvytku ukraïns'koho suspil'stva (1994–1998 rr.). Sotsiolohichni pokaznyky (Tablytsi, iliustratsiï, komentar)* (Kyiv, 1999), p. 78.

21. Dominique Arel and Valeri Khmelko, "The Russian Factor and Territorial Polarization in Ukraine," *The Harriman Review* (special issue entitled *Peoples, Nations, Identities: The Russian-Ukrainian Encounter* 9(1–2) Spring 1996: 86; M. I. Beletskii and A. K. Tolpygo, "Natsional'no-kul'turnye i ideologicheskie orientatsii naseleniia Ukrainy," *Politicheskie issledovaniia* 1998 (4): 76.

22. Cited by Shul'ga, "Krizis etnicheskogo samoopredeleniia."

23. Ministerstvo Ukraïny u spravakh natsional'nostei, mihratsii ta kul'tiv, *Informatsiinyi biuleten'* 1(3) September 1995: 40; *Statystychnyi shchorichnyk Ukraïny za 1998 rik,* p. 424.

24. *Slovo* May 1992.

25. For detailed information on the language status of individual universities and other institutions of higher learning, see Ministerstvo osvity Ukraïny, *Statystychni dani do zasidannia kolehiï Ministerstva za pidsumkamy 1994 roku (Vyshchi navchal'ni zaklady)* (Kyiv, 1995).

26. *Statystychnyi shchorichnyk Ukraïny za 1998 rik,* pp. 434 and 436. Levels III and IV, which incorporate universities, academies, polytechnics, and institutes have the higher level of accreditation; levels I and II incorporate primarily the professional and technical schools.

27. *Statystychnyi shchorichnyk Ukraïny za 1998 rik*, p. 456; *Nezavisimaia gazeta* 11 June 1999; *Den'* 2 March 1999; Ministerstvo Ukraïny u spravakh natsional'nostei, mihratsii ta kul'tiv, *Informatsiinyi biuleten'* 1(1) March 1995: 15; and Andrii Popok and Iurii Lagutov, "Ukraïna-Rosiia: Etnopolitychnyi faktor mizhderzhavnykh vidnosyn," *Universum* 1998 (1–12): 18.

28. U.S. Information Agency, Office of Research and Media Reaction, "*Vremya* Newscast Top Rated in Russia, Ukraine," *Opinion Analysis,* M-21-99, 2 February 1999, p. 1.

29. Foreign Broadcast Information Service, *FBIS Media Guide: Ukraine. Kuchma and the Media*, 6 February 1999, p. 13.

30. *Den'* 22 December 1998, 20 March 1999, and 17 October 1998, respectively.

31. See, for example, Evgenii Golovakha, Natalia Panina, and Nikolai Churilov, "Russians in Ukraine," in *The New Russian Diaspora: Russians in the Former Soviet Republics*, ed. Vladimir Shlapentokh, Munir Sendlich, and Emil Payin (Armonk, NY, and London, 1994), pp. 59–71; Paul Kostoe, *Russians in the Former Soviet Republics* (Bloomington, IN, 1995), pp. 166–99; Chinn and Kaiser, *Russians as the New Minority*, pp. 129–62; Savoskul, "Russkie v nezavisimoi Ukraine," pp 278–329; and S. S. Savoskul, "Migratsionnoe povedenie russkikh nezavisimoi Ukrainy," in *Russkie v novom zarubezh'e: migratsionnaia situatsiia, pereselenie i adaptatsiia v Rossii,* ed. S. S. Savoskul (Moscow, 1997), pp. 110–53.

32. See the report by the *Jamestown Foundation Monitor* 20 July 1999, on Prime Minister Viktor Stepashin's visit to Kyiv.

33. See the interview with Chernomyrdin in Interfax-Ukraine, 27 May 1997.

34. Interfax, 22 January 1998.

35. For the text, see *Sobranie zakonodatel'stva Rossiiskoi Federatsii* 2 (11 January 1999): 316–17.

36. For the text, see *Sobranie zakonodatel'stva Rossiiskoi Federatsii* 44 (2 November 1998): 9933–9935. It should be noted that in October 1997 the Crimean parliament, with a third of the deputies abstaining, adopted a resolution making Russian the "official language" of state and administration in Crimea. See Reuters, 15 October 1997, and *Nezavisimaia gazeta* 26 February 1998.

37. *Kievskie vedomosti* 21 July 1998.

38. This was proposed by Valerii Tishkov, director of the Institute of Ethnology and Anthropology of the Russian Academy of Sciences and formerly the minister of nationalities in the Russian government, at a session of the Government Commission on Compatriot Affairs in early 1999. See *Sodruzhestvo NG* April 1999: 10.

39. *Dialog ukrainskoi i russkoi kul'tur v Ukraine*, p. 244.

40. *Financial Times* 25 May 1999.

41. *Den'* 2 February 2000; *Nezavisimaia gazeta* 4 February 2000; and *Izvestiia* 5 February 2000.

42. Ibid.

43. Quoted by Interfax, 9 February 2000. See also *Jamestown Foundation Monitor* 11 February 2000.

44. *RFE/RL Newsline* 11 February 2000.

45. UNIAN, 21 February 2000.

46. Oleksandr Maiboroda, *Rosiis'kyi natsionalizm v Ukraïni (1991–1998 rr.)* (Kyiv, 1999), p. 25.

Nationalism and the Public Sphere: The Limits of Rational Association in the Nineteenth-Century Polish Countryside[1]

KEELY STAUTER-HALSTED

One of the more intriguing questions in the history of Eastern Europe concerns the coming to political consciousness of the peasantry.[2] Historians of the region have variously treated the political arrival of smallholders from the perspective of institutional, economic, and legal developments.[3] Revolutionary moments, when the peasants insert themselves into the public eye, have also received scholarly attention.[4] Yet the slippery issue of the peasantry's specific contribution (or contributions) to political culture has been the focus of far fewer studies. This lacuna in research has arisen partly due to gaps in the archival recording of village activism, but also because existing documentation tends to reflect only the insights of the literate, activist, peasant elite, shedding little light on the thoughts of the larger rural community as it entered formal political life. An examination of the cultural "baggage" accompanying subalterns into political life is important in a number of respects. First, such an exploration can help us assess the dramatic transition to democratic processes that East European successor states experienced in the aftermath of World War I. Similarly, an evaluation of the clash between popular and elite attitudes in public interactions can inform our understanding of the eventual collapse of these interwar East European democracies and their replacement with authoritarian regimes. Finally, broadening our understanding of East European political culture in this respect may help scholars assess the bumpy road to democracy many states in the region have experienced in the postcommunist period.

As smallholders became active in civic life, they brought with them a set of attitudes that would eventually challenge the standards of conduct established by the upper classes. In ways that were barely perceptible to Eastern Europe's political establishment, the inclusion of rural citizens dramatically transformed public life. This essay represents an effort to assess some of the experiences, beliefs, attitudes, and preconceptions Polish peasants brought to formal political engagements once they became fully enfranchised in 1918. I will contrast the fears, concerns, and priorities for public life of Polish-speaking peasants with those of the social elite with whom they eventually served in representative bodies. Specifically, I will examine the ways in which the peasantry's approach to issues of nation forming, national identity, and the constitution of a national "public" differed from the understanding of these concepts among members of the bourgeoisie and the gentry. The discussion will focus predominantly, though not entirely, on peasant activism and public opinion formation in Austrian Poland.

In contrast to the Polish experience in the Congress Kingdom or Poznania, Poles living in the Austrian province of Galicia enjoyed regional autonomy and the freedom to organize politically once gentry conservatives had declared their loyalty to the empire in 1866. The 1860s and 1870s thus saw a mushrooming of civic institutions throughout the Galician crownland, including remote and impoverished Polish- and Ukrainian-speaking villages.[5] It was through this booming associational life that Galician peasants initially experienced public service and debated issues of general concern to fellow villagers, to the crownland as a whole, and eventually even to the larger nation. Galician villagers also were increasingly able to engage in debates about community issues through the handful of newspapers circulating in the countryside by the 1870s.[6]

Vital though these new rural associations and media were to the politicization of the Galician Polish peasantry, the evolution of institutional life in the countryside does not tell the full story of the coming of political consciousness to Galician villagers. Instead, along with an appreciation of the specific activities in which peasant actors engaged and the formal structures through which they channeled their energies, it is necessary to examine the kinds of cultural norms and assumptions rural activists brought to their work. Once we consider some of the less explicitly articulated notions to which villagers subscribed regarding the forces affecting their world, and the ways in which these conceptions affected peasant public behavior, the smallholders' political engagement takes on new meaning.

The various shades of meaning behind the peasantry's organizational activity can be gleaned by looking at the ways in which villagers employed certain words and concepts both in their public speech and in the less formal—but no less significant—performance of songs, plays, and local legends. Ethnographic material, much of it collected by scholars who traversed the Polish countryside in the waning years of the nineteenth century, offers an important lens into this less formal realm of rural public interactions.[7] Key among the new ideas introduced into the countryside in the last third of the nineteenth century was the concept of the Polish nation. Most of the civic institutions that dotted the Galician landscape by the last quarter of the century and all of the periodicals circulating among small farmers were driven at some level by the goals of nationalist intellectuals. Writers, social agitators, clergy, and landed gentry sought through their own rural activism to promote and channel the peasantry's emerging national consciousness. The idea of the "nation"—a multiclass, culturally based community of Roman Catholic Polish speakers who ostensibly shared a common past and customs—arrived in Galician villages at roughly the same historical moment as institutions of civic and political expression. Nationalism, or at least the peasantry's attempt to locate itself within the body of national ideas received from the social elite, thus informed much of the early public debate within Galician village society. How then did nationalist ideas affect civic life in rural Poland, and what influence did the cultural and intellectual attitudes of this politicized, nationalized peasantry have on public life in a united Poland?

Peasants and the Public Sphere

One way to understand the expansion of associational life that we see in Galicia is to view it in the context of the widening rural "public sphere." Jürgen Habermas, in his *The Structural Transformation of the Public Sphere,* distinguishes the "public sphere" as the sector of human interaction between society and the state where private individuals meet together as a public.[8] When citizens confer about matters of general interest in an unrestricted fashion, they create something like public opinion. In Habermas's view, the consensus opinions arrived at through open debate in public-sphere institutions—ranging from social and cultural organizations to the mass media—permit the political classes to critique and control the ruling structures of the state. One essential, though frequently maligned component of this conception, however, is the assumption that exchanges within public-sphere institutions are conducted on the basis of critical reason.[9] Only through the application of a shared logical system based on rationality can consensus views be achieved and brought to bear on governmental bodies.[10] For Habermas, such a sector of human exchange arose only in the modern period, especially among the urban bourgeoisie. In contrast to developments in Western Europe, however, the preconditions for the formation of a functioning public sphere arose much later in the eastern part of the continent. Restrictions on public assembly continued well into the nineteenth century for most of this region and the economic priorities of the great empires prevented the evolution of a strong and independent bourgeoisie. It was only in the second half of the nineteenth century, when increasingly liberal political regimes permitted greater freedom of association, that the beginnings of what could be called public-sphere activity materialized east of the Elbe.

These first stirrings of associational life in Eastern Europe came packaged in the language and institutional trappings of nationalism. It was nationalist intellectuals who led the introduction of public-sphere institutions into the countryside. This situation led, as Geoff Eley has argued, to the "breaking down of parochial identities and the entry of rural societies into national political cultures—or the nationalization of the peasantry" becoming "one dimension of the creation of local public spheres and their articulation with a national cultural and political arena."[11] In other words, opportunities for the creation of a free and unrestricted sphere of public debate came to East Central Europe at a time when public opinion was focused on issues of nation forming and when discussion of national emancipation was oriented toward the inclusion of national peasantries in political movements. Yet, if we are to expand the notion of public-sphere interactions to encompass the activities of the recently enfranchised peasantry of East Central Europe, it is also necessary to examine closely the terms of debate within these opinion-forming bodies. To what degree were the discussions that took place within rural associations *rational* in their application of modern, scientific notions of causality and to what degree, by contrast, did they retain premodern assumptions of power or influence? Given the compelling evidence that many peasants continued to rely on myth, magic, and the otherworldly to understand the world around them, how do we evaluate the function of a public sphere in the political evolution of Polish smallholders? In sum, what explains the evolution of this "modern" forum functioning at least partially on the basis of "premodern" content?

Associational Life in the Galician Countryside

A potential public sphere was constituted in Austrian Galicia through the operation of a wide range of civic institutions. In both Polish- and Ukrainian-speaking villages, members of the national elite—clergy, teachers, and gentry activists—founded associations with the specific goal of convincing the peasantry of their membership in a "nation" that included all social classes.[12] In the Polish case, much of the impetus for bringing the national message to the village came out of the ideology of Organic Work, with its program of cultural and economic reform at the "base" of society.[13] The intellectuals who supported the doctrine of Organic Work, also known as Warsaw Positivism, disassociated themselves from the tradition of armed insurrection after the failed rising of 1863 and sought instead to regenerate Poland's infrastructure in preparation for eventual independence.

The work of positivist intellectuals in the countryside included the founding of agronomic societies and reading circles, as well as the circulation of newspapers throughout the Galician countryside. These new civic fora were the site of open and informed discussions among smallholders. The Agricultural Circle movement, for example, established individual cells in hundreds of Galician villages. Circle members met regularly to discuss the purchase of new machinery, the distribution of seed, and the implementation of new agronomic techniques (the planting of potatoes, crop rotation, fertilizer use, etc.).[14] Reading clubs subscribed to newspapers and other periodicals, amassed libraries of Polish literary classics and self-help manuals, and held informal discussions on the contents of these works. Both of these networks of rural associations had a semipermanent institutional existence manifested in the erection of buildings devoted to their activities, the collection of annual club dues, the drafting of bylaws, the election of officers, and the keeping of minutes for the organizations' activities. The impact of such local organizations often extended well beyond the lives of their individual members, as when they became active supporters of local schools or helped raise funds for the repair of churches and other community buildings.

These semipermanent associations provided the institutional framework for the shaping of public opinion in the newly enfranchised Galician countryside. In the context of Galician autonomy, rural public opinion could conceivably be channeled to the crownland's administrative decision-making apparatus through any number of routes, including local and district government, elections to the Galician Sejm (diet) and the Viennese Reichsrat, and correspondence with representatives to these larger parliamentary bodies. The system of local self-government implemented in Galicia after 1866 offered residents the opportunity to represent themselves in local commune (*gmina*) councils elected by all property-owning members of the municipality. Participation in the work of self-governing communes provided Galician villagers experience serving in and evaluating the performance of administrative organs. Peasants alone were able to vote for village mayors, vice mayors, secretaries, and council members from among their fellow villagers; those who did not hold land in the village commune, such as local gentry or teachers, were ineligible to vote in these elections.

Within a decade after the introduction of the self-governing system, elections to rural office turned into genuine political campaigns, featuring lively debates in the rural press over the credentials of mayoral candidates. Villagers sent letters and petitions to the three main peasant journals critiquing local rulers for fiscal irresponsibility, mismanagement, and cultural backwardness. Correspondents promoted a "progressive" agenda that included the building of country schools, the elimination of rural taverns, and the repair or construction of community buildings such as churches, libraries, and schools. By the end of the century, mayoral candidates who were literate, sober, and energetic were favored over those whose power base was associated with traditional, retrograde practices. Public debate through the instrument of the rural press clearly brought about an evolution in the type of local leaders elected.

The lively debates among villagers over issues of concern to local residents gradually began spilling over into the wider crownland political arena. Peasants increasingly sat in district councils governing the affairs of each of Galicia's 74 counties. Beginning in 1861, they were elected to the provincial diet in Lviv (Lwów), where they would form the Catholic Peasants' Parliamentary Club in 1889. Active campaigning for seats in the Sejm's rural curia began in the 1880s with the formation of Peasant Election Committees. The level of political engagement and debate in the Galician countryside in this period is reflected in the widespread interest peasants took in imperial and crownland elections, even among those who were not entitled to vote. As one observer noted after the 1891 elections to the Viennese Reichsrat:

> Go stand in front of the church. There is a group of peasants who talk about what happened during the elections . . . Go to town to a fair or a tavern, or to a market and there they are still talking about the elections. Go out to the fields with a plow or a harrow, and you will see how the farmers gather together in a

group in the afternoons and chat about the elections. Bah! Even women at markets argue about the elections![15]

The nascent political-party machines that evolved among the peasants who met the property requirement for voting developed a twofold commitment to wresting control of rural seats from Polish conservatives and to electing progressive peasant delegates free of ties to gentry patrons. Vicious attacks on arrogant gentry candidates uninterested in the peasant's plight appeared in the rural press by the 1890s. Letters and editorials decried campaign corruption in the form of vote buying, gala banquets for supporters, and even the altering of election results. Peasant criticism of these well-entrenched electoral practices targeted both the conservative gentry perpetrating the corruption and the gullible peasant electors who willingly fell victim to it. In all of these ways, villagers applied critical reasoning to political practices both outside and inside the Polish village and established a public agenda based on the "modernizing" goals of free elections and the rule of written law.

The "Premodern" in the Public Space

Such "rational" exchanges among peasants and between villagers and members of the Polish elite in Galicia represent only part of the story of the entry of smallholders into public life. The existence of "gullible" peasant voters who traded away their newly won electoral rights for a pint of vodka or a kilo of *kiełbasa* highlights the presence of another stream of public behavior within the Galician countryside. Alongside the rational, "modern" approaches to rural reform found in the activities of agricultural circles, reading clubs, and election committees, Galician peasants also relied on premodern tropes to guide their behavior in public interactions. The decision to accept food and drink in exchange for votes may have been based on a carefully calculated cost-benefit analysis remaining from the early period of peasant enfranchisement. While it was difficult to imagine a small handful of successful village delegates achieving much of benefit to fellow farmers in a diet monopolized by the conservatives, impoverished electors could immediately calculate the value to their households of an additional allotment of meat. The direct personal gain involved in vote-selling, in combination with the overall attraction of the festival-like atmosphere offered in district capitals on election day to those who voted "correctly," helps explain the reliance of peasant electors on such "traditional" practices well into the period of Galician autonomy.

More difficult to explain but no less prevalent in rural society was a consistent pattern of rhetoric in public discussions that employed premodern causality, belief in otherworldly sources of power, and supernatural explanations for everyday events. Participants in such exchanges do not appear to have been limited to those who were shut out of wider power or influence by the crownland's rigid, property-based voting requirements. Certainly, discussions

and performances involving such folk cultural elements appear to have occurred frequently in less formal assemblies such as evenings in the village
tavern, winter flax-weaving sessions, and the numerous saints' day and holiday
celebrations peppered throughout the nineteenth-century agricultural calendar.
Yet we also have evidence of serious concern about evil spirits and creatures
from the underworld disturbing gatherings of a more formal political nature
organized by "modern" institutions, such as agricultural circles and reading
clubs.

Discussion about and celebration of the Polish nation provided one key
focus for such nonmodern systems of thought in the countryside. References to
national heroes and ethnic distinctions appeared frequently in village discourse.
Moreover, in the last third of the century, peasants played an increasingly
active role in the numerous commemorations of important moments in the
nation's past. Yet these historic figures and patriotic events took on different
meanings in the hands of rural participants. A few examples of the ways in
which peasants chose to commemorate national holidays, to explain Polish
historical events, and to understand ethnic distinctions will suggest the outlines
of this parallel pattern of thought.

Beginning in the 1870s, Galician peasants were full participants in a series
of commemorative events honoring significant moments in the Polish national
past. Free under the relatively liberal Austrian regime to mark the centennials
of the eighteenth-century partitions of the Polish state as well as such occasions
as the reburial of the Polish bard, Adam Mickiewicz, peasant leaders made the
most of these public events to highlight their agenda of rural improvements.[16]
In their presentations at the "official" celebrations marking these historic moments they stressed the need for increased public funds to support projects as
diverse as village schools, rural roads and floodwalls, national fire insurance,
and famine relief. Yet alongside the programmatic agenda that can be culled
from peasant speeches and petitions during these events was a vision of the
Polish nation that was closely linked to the folk culture of agricultural rituals
and other "traditional" village practices. Much of this folk cultural content
appeared in local celebrations held in dozens of Galician villages and small
towns. Unlike the commemorative activities organized by crownland administrators in the province's key cities, these smaller festivals witnessed massive
grassroots input and broad popular access.[17]

Peasants participated in large numbers, for example, in the 1891 celebrations marking the centennial of the May Third Constitution. They flocked to
formal commemorative events honoring the occasion in the crownland's two
key cities, Cracow and Lviv, and staged local celebrations in villages throughout the province. Since the anniversary occurred during spring planting and
two days after May Day (traditionally a time for agricultural fertility rituals),
May Third celebrations were often clumsily grafted onto folk celebrations. In
some cases reference to the Constitution itself was wholly omitted in favor of
the celebration of religious or folk content. One village organizing committee

even struck a scheduling compromise between local cultural forces and national imagery by celebrating both May Day and the Constitution simultaneously on 2 May. Participants in the locally staged events erected May poles,
adorned them with flowers and ribbons, and inscribed them with the religious-
political epithet, "Mary, Queen of Poland."[18] Concern about the workings of
evil spirits guided some festival organizers at other commemorative events, as
in the widespread burning of pitch barrels during rural celebrations of the
centennial of the Kościuszko Rising in 1794. These were said to have "smoked
on all the high peaks [of mountain settlements] on the day of the celebration" in
order to drive malevolent members of the underworld away from the assembly.[19]

Whereas such references to otherworldly forces can sometimes be interpreted as a legacy of time-honored agricultural rituals whose meaning had
largely dissipated, premodern thinking was employed as a direct explanation
for historical events in the Polish national past. Peasant storytellers recalled the
legendary King Krakus, for example, for having rid the kingdom of the dangerous dragon living on Wawel Hill. His son, however, according to peasant lore,
became "bewitched" and was forced to take his own life. Moreover, the fourteenth-century King Kazimierz the Great was recalled less for his consolidation
of Polish territorial holdings and attempts to settle the lands with immigrants
from Germany than for his ability to exorcise witches who took possession of
peasant women. The willingness of these early rulers to tangle with spirits who
disrupted peasant lives clearly added to the respect they were accorded in rural
memory.[20] Christian miracles also played an exaggerated role in peasant explanations of well-known military victories, especially King Jan Sobieski's famous defense of Vienna against the "heathen" Turks in 1683. At least two
musical renditions of this battle drastically de-emphasize the Polish king's
credit in routing the Turks and attribute the victory instead to the aid of seventy
Viennese nuns and the intervention of the Virgin Mary herself.[21] Village
storytellers recounted the miracles that helped give Sobieski the advantage
during the battle, including the opening up of "a corner of the sky" allowing
"the sun to shine as if it were day" while the European army marched at night.
An angel reportedly sat alongside the columns of soldiers, leading Catholic
souls into heaven. (But when "a Turk, a Jew, or some other sort of pagan" was
killed, he was sent directly to hell.)[22]

Not only were military and political events understood and celebrated in
peasant culture through references to the guiding spirits of the underworld and
the pantheon of Christian saints, but belief in such forces also informed the
peasantry's perception of ethnic differences. Folksongs and legends ridiculed
members of non-Polish ethnic groups by associating them with otherworldly
forces. Non-Christians and especially non-Europeans frequently appeared in
peasant folklore in the service of the devil. Jews were cast in peasant plays with
horns, tails, and red coats. Village drama tended to use Ukrainian as the
language of witches and devils because, as peasants argued, "to put the Polish

language in the mouth of an unclean spirit would be profanity."[23] Jingles sung among the peasants of Podlasie characterized Belarusians from "beyond the Bug" as pagans, devil-worshippers, and witches.[24] Village songs referred to the devil using the Polish word for German (*Niemiec*); they dressed him in the urban clothes associated with Germans when he appeared in plays.[25]

Finally, witchcraft accusations, while frequently directed at members of the village community who stepped outside expected cultural mores, were also used to label threatening outsiders—including those belonging to other national communities. My examination of witchcraft beliefs in the late nineteenth-century Polish countryside suggests that belief in witches was widespread but selective. Witches were perceived to be a rarity among the permanent residents of the speaker's home village, yet wandering mendicants, craftsmen with some link to urban centers, and especially rootless gypsies were regularly—and almost casually—assumed to be in league with the devil. The Polish-speaking farmers in the hamlet of Rudawo near Cracow explained that witches only rarely made an appearance in their own village, while neighboring parishes were known to possess "whole nests" of these powerful beings.[26] References to people in districts incrementally farther away from the speaker's native village—whether urban centers or more distant rural areas—linked these outsiders with Black Magic in even starker terms.

Here and elsewhere, assumptions of otherworldliness were tied to budding notions of cultural and ethnic difference in the Polish countryside. National sentiment, as it developed among Polish peasants, blended with traditional beliefs and formed a composite of attitudes that was both modern and "primitive." Village cultural output portrayed those who lived beyond the traditional Polish lands and "foreigners" there as being of "another world." Folksongs and legends that depicted Gypsies, Moravians, and Hungarians as having the "power to cast spells" were a way for Polish-speaking peasants to define themselves against these religious and ethnic "others."[27] In this way, ethnic differences were understood among some segments of the village population as the result of the conflict between good and evil, between the Black Magic of the devil and the "white" miracles of saints and nuns. At a moment when ideas about peasant "Polishness" were first appearing in village debate, references to witches and devils may have provided the language many peasants needed for processing and internalizing the cultural differences being presented to them. The "otherworldly" traits assigned to certain individuals and groups allowed peasants to discuss cultural differences in a language that was familiar to them.

Conclusions

Clearly, belief in witchcraft, devils, evil spirits, Christian miracles, and other premodern forces continued to inform village discussions even at a time when modern institutions of democratic governance had made their appearance in the Polish countryside. How then can we reconcile this seemingly peculiar combination of modern forms with a heavy dose of "traditional" content? How do we judge the relative modernity of either the Polish nation at the turn of the new century or the public sphere in which that nation was represented? Patterns of peasant thinking, remembering, celebrating, and explaining in formal and informal interactions suggest that we need to rethink the neat divisions historians sometimes draw between "modern," premodern, and postmodern stages of development. Systems of thought that might appear to be widely divergent appear to be able to coexist within a single "modern" society and even, perhaps, within a single social group or individual.

Part of the answer may lie in an appreciation of how a belief in "supernatural" phenomena aided villagers in adapting to new institutions, laws, and ways of thinking about their communities while still retaining their local sense of "Us-ness."[28] Popular culture, with its grounding in local tradition, helped ease the transition from the relatively isolated existence of peasant serfs to a world in which peasants were expected to participate in civic institutions alongside their former masters. By filtering "modern" concepts through the prism of folkloric tropes, ideas of the nation and of formal politics were absorbed into peasant culture and internalized by the peasant actors. Beliefs of this kind, then, represented one set of techniques turn-of-the century peasants used to retain their sense of community and identity even as they were slowly becoming absorbed into the "modernizing" world around them.

More importantly, however, the cultural limitations on the application of instrumental reason within nineteenth-century associational life in Poland suggest one way in which Habermas's confidence in the victory of consensus politics through modern rationality may be overblown. The kinds of subjective criteria many villagers brought to public debate clearly were founded on a system of priorities, a set of "validity claims," as Habermas would call them, that at times differed from the value norms shared by the Polish bourgeoisie and gentry. The possibility of arriving at consensus within groups whose members employ both "modern" expressions of normative rightness and concerns arising out of folk culture is difficult at best. The most that can be said about these kinds of public-sphere interactions is that the pretense or appearance of consensus is often achieved only when members tacitly agree on vague concepts that are variously interpreted. The illusion of shared goals can arise out of the interpretive laxity of symbolic language.

The existence of such limitations on public-sphere interactions in any society consisting of diverse population groups need not, however, lead us to despair about the future of East European public life. Rather, the continued reliance on myth, magic, religious faith, and other value-based forms of thinking as guides to behavior within public institutions indicates that by the turn of this century, the population of Poland had yet to experience the "disenchantment" explored by sociologist Max Weber, one of Habermas's mentors. When Weber wrote somewhat nostalgically about the "disenchantment" involved in the coming of rationality to the modern world, about the loss of spirituality, faith, and passion that drove human action in "modern" economic and professional life, he assumed that the developed world was leading inexorably in the direction of passionless reason. Weber clearly believed in, but nevertheless feared, the arrival of a society in which individuals proceeded from one decision to the next in a zombie-like manner, as slaves to instrumental logic. If the entrance of Polish peasants into the public sphere is any indication, however, the "enchantedness" of premodern thinking erodes only very slowly, even after the advent of modern political institutions and capitalist economic processes.

One of the ways in which this latent "spiritualism" of the premodern world made its appearance in modern Poland was through the ideology of nationalism that infused much of Polish society's political life. The "nation" in Poland meant different things to different people. It implied varying pasts and futures. For this reason, it was frequently rendered in symbolic terms that could be variously interpreted and accepted. The peasantry's characterization of national fortunes in terms of devils and angels, witches and miracle workers, can be seen as a variation on the mythology and symbolism that the social elite employed to discuss its own nationalist aspirations. In a society where school children were routinely taught that the Virgin Mary was the Queen of Poland, the leap from "premodern" folk culture to elite national sentiment was rather short.

The passion and sense of mission provided by nationalist thinking had several potentially positive implications. The unifying ideal of the nation helped bring together diverse social classes and interest groups in common cause, offering a motivation to work together for social improvements that did not directly benefit any single group or individual. As Benedict Anderson has recently argued, "there is something of value in all of this [nationalism], strange as it may seem." Anderson concludes his reflections on nationalism with the rhetorical query, "in these straightened millennial times, can such Goodness [of nationalism] be profitably discarded?"[29] Unfortunately for the history of Eastern Europe, however, the passions of nationalism are also capable of wreaking terrible damage. Indeed, the newly enfranchised population of Poland (and later, the population of former Yugoslavia) was as capable of being seduced by the charisma of a strong leader or of a utopian political movement in the name of nation forming as it was of being drawn to the appeal of parliamentary democracy. Only time will tell how East European citizens will choose to orient their public "passions" in the future. What is clear is that the "unreason" of nationalism will be with us for a long time to come. For better or for worse, the rule of reason has not been completely victorious, but the continued existence of popular passions within the public sphere represents both an opportunity and a responsibility.

NOTES

1. I would like to thank Arista Cirtautas and David Halsted for their suggestions in constructing this argument.

2. Roman Szporluk has discussed the entrance of peasants into "society" after their emancipation from serfdom in 1848 as a central component in the transformation of the more elite activities of the intelligentsia into a mass movement for national independence. See Roman Szporluk, *Communism and Nationalism: Karl Marx Versus Friedrick List* (New York, 1988), pp. 156–57.

3. See, for example, John-Paul Himka, *Galician Villagers and the Ukrainian National Movement* (New York, 1988); Stefan Kieniewicz, *The Emancipation of the Polish Peasantry* (Chicago, 1969); Katherine Verdery, *Transylvanian Villagers: Three Centuries of Political, Economic, and Ethnic Change* (Berkeley, 1983). In Polish, see Antoni Gurnicz, *O "równą miarkę" dla chłopów* (Warsaw, 1963); Stefan Inglot, *Historia chłopów* (Warsaw, 1972); Krzysztof Dunin-Wąsowicz, *Dzieje Stronnictwa Ludowego w Galicji* (Warsaw, 1956); and Helena Brodowska, *Chłopi o sobie i Polsce: rozwój świadomości społecznonarodowej* (Warsaw, 1984).

4. For the Polish case, this approach can best be accessed through Robert Blobaum's *Rewolucja: Russian Poland, 1904–1907* (Ithaca, 1995), esp. pp. 115–56.

5. I have written extensively about civic life in the Galician countryside in my forthcoming book, *The Nation in the Village: The Genesis of Rural National Identity in Austrian Poland, 1848–1900.*

6. Newspapers intended to be read by or to peasants first circulated in the Galician countryside during the revolutions of 1848. Only in 1875, however, with the appearance of Father Stanisław Stojałowski's alternating fortnightlies, *Wieniec* and *Pszczółka*, did the press become truly interactive. Letters published in these papers and village meetings held by their editors permitted villagers to exchange ideas about public priorities with one another and with representatives of the Galician elite. Bolesław Wysłouch's more socially radical journal, *Przyjaciel Ludu*, joined Stojałowski's in 1889 and in 1894 Stanisław Potoczek founded *Związek Chłopski* as the organ of his short-lived peasant political party, Związek Stronnictwa Chłopskiego. These three papers, which quickly became the mouthpieces for separate peasant political factions, continued to provide a forum for debate on rural affairs until well into the twentieth century. See Irena Turowska-Bar, *Polskie czasopisma o wsi i dla wsi od XVII do r. 1960* (Warsaw, 1963); Jerzy Myśliński, "Prasa polska w Galicji w dobie autonomicznej (1867–1918)," in *Prasa polska w latach 1864–1918*, ed.

Jerzy Łojek (Warsaw, 1976); and Krzysztof Dunin-Wąsowicz, *Czasopiśmiennictwo ludowe w Galicji* (Wrocław, 1952).

7. For an introduction to Polish folklore studies, see Helena Kapelus and Julian Krzyżanowski, eds., *Dzieje folklorystyki polskiej 1864–1918* (Warsaw, 1982).

8. Jürgen Habermas, *The Structural Transformation of the Public Sphere: An Inquiry into a Category of Bourgeois Society,* trans. Thomas Burger with Frederick Lawrence, intro. by Thomas McCarthy (first published in German, 1962; Cambridge, MA, 1989). See also idem, "The Public Sphere: An Encyclopedia Article (1964)," *New German Critique* 1(3) Fall 1974: 49–50.

9. For an evaluation of Habermas's emphasis on critical reason, see Nancy Fraser, "Rethinking the Public Sphere: A Contribution to the Critique of Actually Existing Democracy," in *Habermas and the Public Sphere,* ed. Craig Calhoun (Cambridge, MA, 1992), pp. 109–142.

10. Regarding Habermas's understanding of modern rationality, see Stephen K. White, "Reason, Modernity, and Democracy," in *The Cambridge Companion to Habermas,* ed. Stephen K. White (Cambridge, 1995), pp. 3–16.

11. Geoff Eley has provided a service to East European studies by expanding Habermas's original notion of the public sphere to include the nationalist movements of East Central Europe and the peasantries which joined these movements in the latter years of the nineteenth century. See Geoff Eley, "Nations, Publics, and Political Cultures: Placing Habermas in the Nineteenth Century," in *Culture/Power/History: A Reader in Contemporary Social Theory,* ed. Nicholas B. Dirks, Geoff Eley, and Sherry B. Ortner (Princeton, 1994), p. 302.

12. On the origins of civil society in the Ukrainian Galician countryside, see Himka, *Galician Villagers.*

13. The classic study of Organic Work, also known as Warsaw Positivism, is Stanislaus Blejwas, *Realism in Polish Politics: Warsaw Positivism and National Survival in Nineteenth Century Poland* (New Haven, 1984).

14. The best work on the agricultural circle movement is Antoni Gurnicz, *Kółka rolnicze w Galicji* (Warsaw, 1967).

15. *Przyjaciel Ludu* 1 May 1891: 131. Property requirements and an elaborate curia system limited the peasantry's voting power until the introduction of universal male suffrage for imperial elections only in 1907. Elections in the crown lands remained restricted—and both excluded women from suffrage—until the end of Galicia's existence within the Habsburg monarchy. See Konstanty Grzybowski, *Galicja, 1848–1914: Historia ustroju politycznego na tle historii ustroju Austrii* (Cracow, 1959).

16. On peasant commemorations, see my "Rural Myth and the Modern Nation: Peasant Commemorations of Polish National Holidays, 1879–1910," in *Staging the Past: The Politics of Commemoration in Habsburg Central Europe*, ed. Maria Bucur and Nancy Wingfield (Purdue University Press) (forthcoming).

17. On nationalist commemorations in Galician villages, see Patrice Dabrowski, "Reinventing Poland: Commemorations and the Shaping of the Modern Nation, 1879–1914," Ph.D. dissertation, Harvard University, 1999.

18. J.S. (Zawadka, near Wadowice), May 1891, letter to *Wieniec* 22 September 1891: 225.

19. Reported in *Przyjaciel ludu* 1 May 1894: 140.

20. Szymon Matusiak, "Historya Polska w opowiadaniu ludu," *Przegląd Polski* 15 (1881): 222–26.

21. Bronisław Grabowski, "Pieśń dziadowska o bitwie pod Wiedniem r. 1683," *Wisła* 2 (1888): 350–57; "Przyczynki do pieśni dziadowskiej o bitwie pod Wiedniem roku 1683," *Wisła* 4 (1890): 426–29.

22. Matusiak, "Historya Polska," pp. 238–40.

23. Mikołaj Jańczuk, "Szopka w Kornicy," *Wisła* 2 (1888): 738–39, 751–53.

24. Ibid., pp. 742–43.

25. Jan Bystroń, *Pieśni ludu polskiego* (Cracow, 1924), pp. 123–25.

26. Stanisław Połączek, "Z podań i wierzeń ludowych, zapisanych we wsi Rudawie pod Krakowem," *Wisła* 5 (1891): 624–35.

27. Jańczuk, "Szopka w Kornicy," p. 743.

28. The example of a popular peasant spokesman, Jan Siwiec, who was elected from the village of his birth to the 1861 provincial Sejm in Lviv, but who owned no land in the community demonstrates this. Villagers respected Siwiec for his university education, his position as a legal clerk in Lviv, and his residence in the city—the very factors that barred him from eligibility as an elector from his native village. The case neatly juxtaposes traditional leadership criteria with written law, though in this instance customary practices were not acknowledged by the crownland government which evicted Siwiec from the Sejm's proceedings. See Stefan Suchonek, "Poseł Jan Siwiec: Karta z dziejów ruchu ludowego w Galicji," in *Studia dziejów kultury*, ed. Henryk Barycz and Jan Hulewicz (Warsaw, 1949).

29. Benedict Anderson, "The Goodness of Nations," in his *The Spectre of Comparison: Nationalism, Southeast Asia, and the World* (London–New York, 1998), pp. 360–68.

History and the Making of Nations[1]

RONALD GRIGOR SUNY

In his intellectual work Roman Szporluk has been concerned with matters dealing both with nationalism and with history. From his early work on Mikhail Pokrovsky to his later research on Thomas Masaryk, Friedrich List and Karl Marx, Russian national identity, and the history of Ukraine, the intersection of history and nationalism has featured in his articles and books. In our association together as colleagues at the University of Michigan our shared interest in socialism and nationalism, as well as our evident differences, enriched my understanding of nation and class. My first exposure to the idea of "imagined communities," now so often invoked in discussions of nationalism, came in a faculty seminar that Geoff Eley and Roman Szporluk conducted on Benedict Anderson's newly published book. When the powerful role played by intellectuals—and in particular historians—in constituting the nation became a general theme in the literature in the 1980s, following the work of Ernest Gellner, Eric Hobsbawm, and Anderson, many of us were intrigued by the new avenues of investigation opened up by the theoretical breakthroughs in nationalism studies. But at the same time those preserving some residue of ethnic loyalty also experienced anxiety about the direction that these explorations might take. This paper attempts to understand the ways in which history as a field of study has played both a fundamental role in making nations but more recently has appeared to work subversively to undermine the nation-state.

What Is History?

History as a discipline contributes both to how we understand what nations and nationalism are and to the intellectual constitution of nations themselves. Historians participate in the active imagination of those political communities that we call nations as they elaborate the narratives that make up national histories. As historians helped generate national consciousness and nationalism, their own discipline acquired the task of "discovering" or "recovering" the "national" past. Thus, history as a discipline helped constitute the nation, even as the nation determined the categories in which history was written and the purposes it was to serve.

As an object of study, history does not exist like objects of the physical world to be checked and verified by simple empirical observation. While documents and monuments supply "facts" from which histories can be written, the act of writing a historical account is always one of human creation out of selected materials. In this sense, like a novel, a painting, or a table, history is a fabrication, and like more material things, it can be made only with available ingredients and according to certain rules—in the case of history, critical examination of the evidence, relative objectivity and neutrality, emplotment in the form of a narrative, etc. The historical past, in distinction from all past occurrences, exists in so far as it can be recreated and imagined. "History," writes Anthony Kemp, "is a literary structure whose literariness must always be denied; its grip on the imagination and on the whole perceived structure of the world is so great that its human origin, its createdness, cannot be acknowledged."[2]

From the Greek word *historia,* meaning research, investigation, information, the word "history" evolved through European languages to come to mean (by the seventeenth century) a collection of data on the historical past. Though that data might be organized into a compelling story, perhaps for political instruction or aesthetic pleasure, the narrative in the hands of historians was supposed to stay as close as possible to the empirically discernible facts and not, as in the freer efforts of dramatists, painters, or historians of the ancient and medieval world, to be allowed to depart far from the knowable and verifiable facts. The line between factual history and fiction was often breached, but as historical practice became professionalized and academized in the nineteenth century, a commitment to a more rigorous and austere prose, free of romantic conjecture and overt subjectivity, became more widespread.

The study of history in the modern period was primarily dedicated to change in the evolution of political and social humanity with an effort to explain causality. Historians usually assumed that human experience was neither on the one hand, purely arbitrary, chaotic, and impossible to explain, nor, on the other, subject to immutable laws that had the regularity and predictability of natural phenomena. Thus, history fell uneasily between social science and art in an ill-defined liminal space called "humanities." At one extreme history was sometimes practiced as if its principal purpose was simply the elucidation of facts, the collection of chronicle or genealogy, rather than some synthetic or analytical interpretation of the past. More frequently, from Antiquity through the Renaissance (and even into the present), history was pressed into the service of politics or morality, rather than left as an "objective" search for truth. History was seen as useful for moral understanding or political legitimation. With the reconfiguration of political communities as "nations" in the eighteenth and nineteenth centuries, intellectuals and statesmen used narratives about the past to provide legitimacy for these new political constructs. As a professional discipline of historical study developed, in many ways allied to the nation-state, history was defended as the practice of combining empirical data synthetically into a narrative that explained some aspect of the nature of the social world. But for the empirically minded, the general or the meaningful was not to be imposed on the data artificially from philosophical conjectures. Rather, as Leopold von Ranke put it, "Particulars carry generalities within them." Historical method was a process of induction from facts to generalizations and, perhaps, theories, rather than deductions from philosophical first principles.

For much of the history of modern Western professional history-writing, historians have been inspired by an ideal of objectivity. The past was real and knowable; there was a historical truth that corresponded to that reality. Historical writing was to be factual and free of value, and this would require a sharp separation of the historian from politics or commitment to moral projects. Historical truth existed before interpretation, and the historian's task was to interpret as closely as possible to the facts. As Peter Novick summed up the objectivist position, "Truth is one, not perspectival. Whatever patterns exist in history are 'found,' not 'made.'"[3] Though this ideal of a neutral, distant, and disinterested history was seldom achieved, a certain balance and fairness, an openness to anomaly and contradiction, was recognized as necessary for the professional historian. Yet the idea of "objective truth" in history seemed to many critics to be an ahistorical conceit, and a more historicist approach claimed that everything in the past and present is shaped by its historical time and place, including the historical observer. Nothing, not even so-called "facts" or "events" can exist outside of history, or, indeed, outside of the interpretations or the discourses that give them meaning. In the words of Jacques Le Goff, "The historian starts from his own present in order to ask questions of the past . . . If in spite of everything, the past exists outside the present, it is vain to believe in a past independent of the one constituted by the historians."[4]

Despite the dedication to critical examination of evidence and objectivity, values and politics could not be excluded from most historical writing. Hayden White has written, "it is possible to view historical consciousness as a specifically Western prejudice by which the presumed superiority of modern industrial society can be retroactively substantiated."[5] For those historians, particularly in the nineteenth and twentieth centuries, who have organized their history as encompassing or partially illuminating the story of a nation, historical writing can be viewed as a specifically national prejudice by which the superiority, naturalness, and indeed unavoidability of the modern nation can be retroactively substantiated. The argument of much national history is, in White's terms, "organicist"; that is, its strategy is "to see individual entities as components of processes which aggregate into wholes that are greater than, or qualitatively different from, the sum of their parts."[6] National historians "tend to structure their narratives in such a way as to depict the consolidation or crystallization, out of a set of apparently dispersed events, of some integrated entity whose importance is greater than that of any of the individual entities analyzed or described in the course of the narrative."[7]

A Short History of History

As insistent as modern Western history-writing is that it emerged in a rupture with past forms of history, the writing of national history in particular has an often unacknowledged debt to earlier forms of history, going back at least to the Bible. As Pierre Gilbert argues, for the collective memory of the past to become history, there must be a sense of continuity, something that already appears in the ancient institution of monarchy with Saul, David, and Solomon: "It is to the institution of monarchy that we must attribute Israel's acquisition of a sense of continuity in the knowledge of its past, for even if it possesses a certain sense of this past through the corpus of its legends, even if it had a certain concern for exactitude, it is only with the monarchy that the sense of a continuity without ruptures appears."[8] Jacques Le Goff continues, "But in the Bible, Jewish history is on the one hand fascinated by its own origins (the creation and then the covenant between Yahweh and his people), and on the other drawn toward an equally sacred future: the advent of the Messiah and of the Heavenly Jerusalem which, in Isaiah, is opened to all nations."[9] Continuity is reflected in genealogy as well as in the movement from past origins through the present moment to a glorious future.

Ancient Greek culture, often taken as the originating point for historiography, also had a sense of historical change, but here the past was valorized as a Golden Age and the present as a decadent departure. In contrast, Le Goff writes, "In the Middle Ages, the present is trapped between the weight of the past and the hope of an eschatological future; in the Renaissance, on the contrary, the primary stress is on the present, while from the seventeenth to the nineteenth centuries, the ideology of progress turns the valorization of time towards the future."[10] Medieval time "tossed back and forth between the past and the future, tried to live the present non-temporally, as an instant that was supposed to be a moment of eternity . . . Nevertheless, at the end of the Middle Ages, the past is increasingly understood in relation to the time of the chronicles, to progress in dating, and to the measuring of time brought about by mechanical clocks."[11] The late Middle Ages distinguished present and past in their historical aspects and as a tragic flight of time, and this duality of historical progress and the tragedy of life and death continued into the Renaissance. Only with Enlightenment optimism was the superiority of the moderns over the ancients fully affirmed. Modernity was seen as a rupture with the medieval, progress beyond the darkness of the past.

"Building upon Hebrew antecedents, Christianity introduced a new linear notion of time into the Greco-Roman world," Joyce Appleby, Lynn Hunt, and Margaret Jacob note; "The Judeo-Christian line of time literally began at one moment and would end at another, and it revealed God's purposes. In the Christian schema, the turning points of sacred history—the Creation, Jesus's life and death, and the prospect of the Last Judgment—set the framework for all historical time."[12] Medieval history looked for the finger of God in human affairs and affirmed the universal relevance of Christianity. Whether in lives of saints or tales of miracles or even the accounts of the secular world in chronicles, divine intervention and explanation were paramount. In many periods, however, chroniclers and historians took units of geography, dynasties, or the state as subjects for study, as in the eighth- and ninth-century histories of the Armenians and Georgians or the twelfth-century chronicle histories of the Britons by Geoffrey of Monmouth. Such located histories were more frequent in the early modern period, as testified to by sixteenth-century studies like Machiavelli's *Istorie Fiorentine*, Chemnitz's history of Sweden, or Pufendorf's work on Brandenburg.

A major innovation in historical thinking, largely ignored in its own time, was by an obscure Neapolitan scholar, Giambattista Vico (1668–1744), who wrote of fusing the empirical and the rational into a new science. In his *Principi di una scienza nuova* (New Science) (1725), Vico proclaimed that "the social world is certainly the work of men, and it follows that one can and should find its principles in the modifications of the human intelligence itself."[13] Vico stressed that the study of human society required different methods from the study of nature. Consciousness and will made history a subject distinct from "the insensible motion of bodies." Vico's turn toward the human as cause in history, his refusal to see history as part of nature, his emphasis on time and place and rejection of presentism stimulated nineteenth-century historians as different as Jules Michelet (1798–1874) and Marx, who each in their own way adopted the implied historicism and humanism.

Though varied in their political and philosophical preferences, the secular intelligentsia that emerged in the Enlightenment was relatively united in its commitment to rationalism, empiricism, science, and secularism. They adopted an idea of progress, faith in the individual, tolerance of difference, opposition to traditional constraints imposed by power and religion, and a notion of a shared human nature. In the cosmopolitan spirit of the age, Diderot (1713–1784) confidently wrote to Hume (1711–1776), "You belong to all nations, and you will never ask an unhappy man for his birth-certificate. I flatter myself that I am, like you, a citizen of the great city of the world." Along with their interest in "natural philosophy," Enlightenment thinkers were also dedicated to the development of a "science of man." The Copernican revolution in cosmology and the retreat from divine to natural explanations seemed to require a redefinition of human nature and a new concentration on human history. Both in England and in France the new secularism accompanied a turn toward investigation of primary sources and the borrowing of hermeneutic methods from biblical studies. Archival documents were read critically by writers influenced by a "heroic model of science" and dedicated to the radical excision of the divine from the human record.[14] At the same time, history was made to serve the state-building projects of Europe's monarchs. Enlightened and not-so-enlightened monarchs commissioned historians to chronicle their achievements and challenge the views of foreigners. In Russia, for example, "Peter the Great appealed for a national history to counteract 'Polish lies'; Empress Elizabeth (1742–1761) summoned historians to refute German scholars who described the early Slavs as 'barbarians, resembling beasts'; Catherine [the Great] urged denunciation of the 'falsehood . . . slander . . . and insolence' of the 'frivolous Frenchmen' who wrote histories of Russia."[15]

"Man" was at the center of Enlightenment social science. Though there was no general agreement on what human nature might be, there was a widely held assumption that some fundamental nature was shared by all humans. The category "human nature" remained largely unquestioned and provided the ahistorical language against which historical change and diversity was understood.[16] It involved the natural essence of humans, their capabilities and capacities, their power to absorb sensations and to reason, their aptitude for moral behavior, and their sociability. Though eighteenth-century scientists were fascinated with the diversity of the human species, their study of past civilizations and primitive peoples repeatedly returned to what was constant in humans. The unity of humankind represented an ideal for the Enlightenment historians, and the purpose of writing history was to foster that ideal in the face of evident schisms, divisions, and differences. The past of various societies gave abundant evidence of irrationality, superstition, credulity, passion, and ignorance. But over time, reason expanded until a small group of rational men was able to analyze society's ills and prescribe reasonable remedies. As White puts it, "The Enlighteners, therefore, wrote history against history itself, or at least against that segment of history which they experienced as 'past.'"[17]

Western historiography "made time universal and evolutionary and arrayed all the peoples, structures, and institutions in every epoch along its line, labeling each people and era in terms of its level of development. Time became real and sequential, and historians became those who could measure development by progress toward modern, Western time . . . When the process of creating modern history was completed, Biblical time lay in ruins and the dreams of the millenarians came to be seen as grand self-delusions."[18] Through observation, classificatory schema, and conceptual histories, the Enlightenment theorists attempted to explain the origins and evolution of society and civilization. The Baron de Montesquieu traced the differences among peoples to climate, contrasting the indolent people of the hot climes to the more self-reliant people of the north. Hume argued in a similar way in his "Essay of National Characters," while Rousseau reversed the valences in his *Essai sur l'origine des langues* (Essay on the Origin of Languages) and placed the origins of liberty in the south and of despotism in the north. Human nature was given and to a certain degree fixed, but nature was distinguished from society in which humans constituted certain aspects of their individual and social selves. In the *Essay on the History of Civil Society* (1767), Adam Ferguson wrote, "Art itself is natural to man" who is "in some measure the artificer" of his own nature.[19]

Though society and nature were now seen as two separate realms, the methodology of studying the latter was applied to study of the former.[20] Eighteenth-century students of society saw history as a laboratory in which moral experiments illuminated the constancy of human nature. Hume, for example, saw "wars, intrigues, factions, and revolutions" as "so many collections of experiments by which the politician or moral philosopher fixes the principles of his science, in the same manner as the physician or natural philosopher becomes acquainted with the nature of plants, minerals, and other external objects."[21] History was useful, in Voltaire's view, precisely because statesmen and citizens could compare foreign laws, morals, and customs with those of their own country—all against the background of a human nature common to all. Human society looked to many Enlightenment thinkers like the Newtonian physical universe. Human actions were predictable, their causality explicable much like physical phenomena: "Dominated by a conception of rationalism derived from the (Newtonian) physical sciences, the *philosophes* approached the historical field as a ground of cause-effect relationships, the causes in question being generally conceived to be the forces of reason and unreason, the effects of which were generally conceived to be enlightened men on the one hand and superstitious or ignorant men on the other."[22]

Enlightenment historical theorists, like Bayle and Voltaire, distinguished among true, satirical, and fabulous histories, and observed that actual histories were most often a mixture of these elements. Reason, however, rather than imagination, was the instrument with which to discover truth. History, which was about real life, was to be discerned through the use of reason; fancy and imagination were to be relegated to the realm of art, not life or history.[23] Yet historical knowledge continued to be used for partisan purposes, even polemics, in the service of what was understood to be truth. In his *Essai sur les moeurs* (1756) Voltaire wrote of the development of civilization as the progressive emergence of humane government, tolerant religion, respect for personal rights, equality before the law, and the protection of property against arbitrary state power. Though Voltaire referred to the fate of nations—"When a nation is acquainted with the arts, when it is not subjugated and bodily removed by foreigners, it emerges with ease from its ruins and is invariably restored"— nations as units of analysis were incidental to his overall story. The nation was seen as a political creation rather than a natural phenomenon, something made by and malleable in the hands of a great ruler, and the ultimate objects of historical study were cultures and civilizations.

The nation emerges as a central subject in history in the eighteenth century most importantly in the universal histories of Johann Gottfried von Herder (1744–1803). Often credited as the founder of what would later be called "historicism" or "the historical sense," Herder saw history not simply as the source of political strategems but as a way to understand human reality distinct from the application of abstract reason. The real nature of things could only be discerned in historical development. Each age contained a heritage from the past that it passed on to the next age, and a people, the *Volk*, rather than humanity as a whole, were the carriers of culture. Providence worked through particular peoples to cause humans and institutions to change. Applying Liebnitz's concept of development to peoples, Herder saw civilizations, like flowers, budding, blossoming, and fading. All human values and understandings were historical and national. In the flow and seeming chaos of history there were constancies, namely nations, dynamic and vital, changing but possessing a constancy of spirit.

In two great works—*Auch eine Philosophie der Geschichte zur Bildung der Menschheit* (Another Philosophy of the History of the Formation of Humanity) (1774) and *Ideen zur Philosophie der Geschichte der Menschheit* (Ideas on the Philosophy of History of Humanity) (1784–1791) Herder elaborated his ideas about historical progress, the diversity of human communities, and the fundamental unity of the historical process. While nations differed in terms of climate, blood mixture, and folk spirit, humanity was one unit in which nations should live harmoniously. Nations were individual and possessed different cultures, expressed in law, religion, and poetry. Their national characters were natural essences created by climate and nature, and he celebrated the uniqueness of each phenomenon, the differences and distinctions among peoples: "Every nation is one people, having its own national form, as well as its own language: the climate, it is true, stamps on each its mark, or spreads over it a sleight veil, but not sufficient to destroy the original national character."[24] Herder emphasized transformation and change through time but always with a sense of an overall order. Everything was part of an indispensable whole, a benevolent process. What history has produced and has grown naturally was good; "Every nation has its center of happiness within it."[25] Providence guided history and gave it purpose and the direction of its progress.

His *Nationalismus*, a word he apparently created, was cultural rather than political. In praise of Homer and Shakespeare, Herder proclaimed: "A poet is the creator of the nation around him, he gives them a world to see and has their souls in his hand to lead them to that world." In search of the soul of the nation, Herder collected his people's folk songs, read Norse poetry and mythology, and analyzed the prose of Martin Luther. Language was for Herder intimately connected to culture and community, the medium through which humans understood and thought, were conscious and able to express their inner selves. "Language expresses the collective experience of the group," he wrote.[26] Through language people understand that they share a culture and historical tradition and therefore form a *Volk*. Rather than biological or racial unity, a people for Herder was a matter of shared awareness of the social milieu into which one is born. This shared culture is, in the words of his translator, the "proper foundation for a sense of collective political identity." [27]

Though Herder contrasted the particularity of the nation and its *Volksgeist* to the universalistic rationality of the French Enlightenment, he was at the same time a creature of the Enlightenment, explaining his own philosophy of history in naturalistic and scientific terms. Nature (or God) created the plurality of languages and cultures, or, as Isaiah Berlin put it, "a nation is made what it is by 'climate,' education, relations with its neighbours, and other changeable and empirical factors, and not by an impalpable inner essence or an unalterable factor such as race or colour."[28] Since every nation has its own unique values,

Herder and subsequent historicists eschewed judgment or ranking of peoples. "Everything has come to bloom upon the earth which could do so, each in its own time, and in its own milieu," he wrote, "and it will bloom again, when *its* time comes."[29] But what seems to be a radical relativism and an anarchy of values in Herder is redeemed by the faith that all history, like all nature, reflects God and his divine plan. Humankind for Herder is one, though multiple in form. Truth, value, and beauty are diverse and found in the national spirit, and true art and poetry were always national and historical.[30] Herder gave a normative potency to observable differences, as well as a principal role in human history to nations. Yet, as Hegel would point out, Herder had no explanation of change, and Kant condemned his attempt to relate everything to everything as metaphysical, not scientific.

In proclaiming the national the source of value, Herder stimulated intellectuals around Europe to follow him in collecting folk poetry, in seeking the sources of national spirit in the folk. At the same time, Herder's love of nations did not extend to the state. He despised government and power, the great absolutist monarchs of his time, and celebrated the cleansing force of the French Revolution. But even as Herder's work appeared, the colossal political upheavals in France and the Napoleonic expansion across Europe radically shifted the thinking of his countrymen about history and the nation. The universalist faith of the Enlightenment in general principles applicable everywhere was shaken by the turn toward the Terror and imperialism, and "German educated opinion now agreed that all values and rights were of historical and national origin and that alien institutions could not be transplanted to German soil. Moreover, they saw in history, rather than in abstract rationality, the key to all truth and value."[31]

Herder's more cosmopolitan approach to the nation, in which each nation as part of the tapestry of humankind enriched others, gave way to a more particularistic view of the superior qualities of one nation over another. In 1806 Johann Gottlieb Fichte (1762–1814) proclaimed that, unlike the French, Germans had not lost touch with the original genius that flowed from their language, and in 1814 Wilhelm von Humboldt (1767–1835) sought a harsh peace for France at the Congress of Vienna by vilifying the French national character as lacking a "striving for the divine which the French lack not only as a nation but virtually without exception also as individuals."[32] Increasingly, people, nation, and state were closely identified, and both Fichte and Humboldt saw the state as the principal protector and moral teacher of the nation. Fichte argued in an essay on Machiavelli that "there is neither law nor right except the right of the stronger," and Humboldt proclaimed,

> Germany must be free and strong, not only to be able to defend herself against this or that neighbor, or for that matter, against any enemy, but because only a nation which is strong toward the outside can preserve the spirit within from which all domestic blessings flow. Germany must be free and strong, even if she is never put to a test, so that she may possess the self-assurance required

for her to pursue her development as a nation unhampered and that she may be able to maintain permanently the position which she occupies in the midst of the European nations, a position which is so beneficial to these nations.[33]

It was in the midst of the emergence of this new form of nationalism and the crisis of state building in Germany that professional history took shape in the early nineteenth century.[34] The first chairs of history in European universities were founded in Berlin in 1810 (with Humboldt playing a key role) and in Paris in 1812. The connection between the postrevolutionary nationalism and state politics of Germany and France and professional historians was intimate, and within a decade historical societies were created to collect and publish historical documents along national lines: the society for the *Monumenta Germaniae* in 1819 and the *École des Chartes* in 1821. Governments soon supported these efforts, while professional historians founded their disciplinary journals, usually with a distinct national focus: the *Archiv für ältere deutsche Geschichtskunde* (1820), the Danish *Historisk tidskrift* (1840), *Archivio storico italiano* (1842), *Archiv für österreichische Geschichte* (1848), the *Historische Zeitschrift* (1859), the *Revue historique* (1876), the *Rivista storica italiana* (1884), the *English Historical Review* (1886), the Swedish *Historisk tidskrift* (1889), and the *American Historical Review* (1895). Graduate programs in history, based on the German model, spread eastward to Russia and westward to the Americas at the end of the century, and history-writing became a distinct, professional, academized intellectual practice.

But as Hayden White has pointed out,

> the theoretical basis of its disciplinization remained unclear. The transformation of historical thinking from an amateur activity into a professional one was not attended by the sort of conceptual revolution that has accompanied such transformations of other fields, such as physics, chemistry, and biology. Instruction in the "historical method" consisted essentially of an injunction to use the most refined philological techniques for the criticism of historical documents, combined with a set of statements about what the historian ought *not* to attempt on the basis of the documents thus criticized.[35]

History was conceived neither as a science in the Newtonian sense nor as "free art" in the Romantics' sense of imaginative creativity. Most historians of the nineteenth century conceived of the "historical method" as

> a willingness to go to the archives without any preconceptions whatsoever, to study the documents found there, and then to write a story about the events attested by the documents in such a way as to make the story itself the explanation of "what had happened" in the past. The idea was to let the explanation emerge naturally from the documents themselves, and then to figure its meaning in story form. The notion that the historian himself emplotted the events found in the documents was only vaguely glimpsed by thinkers sensitive to the poetic element in every effort at narrative description—by a historian like J. G. Droysen, for example, and by philosophers like Hegel and Nietzsche, but by few others. To have suggested that the historian

emplotted his stories would have offended most nineteenth-century historians.[36]

Central to the practice of professional history in the nineteenth century, first
in Germany and later throughout Europe and the Americas, was the historicist
approach, or what Georg G. Iggers calls "the German conception of history."
"The core of the historicist outlook," writes Iggers,

> lies in the assumption that there is a fundamental difference between the
> phenomena of nature and those of history, which requires an approach in the
> social and cultural sciences fundamentally different from those of the natural
> sciences. Nature, it is held, is the scene of the eternally recurring, of phenom-
> ena themselves devoid of conscious purpose; history comprises unique and
> unduplicable human acts, filled with volition and intent. The world of man is
> in a state of incessant flux, although within it there are centers of stability
> (personalities, institutions, nations, epochs), each possessing an inner struc-
> ture, a character, and each in constant metamorphosis in accord with its own
> internal principles of development. History thus becomes the only guide to an
> understanding of things human. There is no constant human nature; rather the
> character of each man reveals itself only in its development.[37]

Without a doubt the exemplar, and greatest European influence, of nineteenth-century historiography was Leopold von Ranke (1795–1886). As a
young man he had read and was greatly influenced by Fichte's *Addresses to the
German Nation*, but as a Saxon rather than a Prussian he was less enthusiastic
than many of his intellectual contemporaries about emerging German nationalism and its project of political unification. His historicism led him to defend the
local and provincial particularities of the various German states. Every people,
Ranke believed, had its own genius, its own politics, and, therefore, there was
no need to import foreign political forms. Like the poet Goethe he remained a
cultural nationalist and felt no overriding obligation to Prussia as a fatherland,
even after he became a teacher in the Kingdom of Prussia. Only in the 1830s
did he become a defender of the Prussian state, but his support of Bismarck was
much delayed.

Following the ideas of Humboldt's important essay "On the Task of the
Historian" (1821), Ranke saw history as a particular way to comprehend reality, distinct from deductive philosophy. Critical study of the sources could
establish facts that would become the material for the historian, using his
intuition, to discern elements of the divine plan. Both Humboldt and Ranke
thought that history was an art form that could represent reality as it actually
appeared in time and space. Both believed that the great varieties in history
were part of a harmonious whole that automatically restored the rightful order
if it was disturbed. Ranke's Christian God and His meaning were always
present in history, to be discovered by examining the facts, which were the
concrete manifestations of metaphysical forces. "God dwells, lives, and can be
known in all of history," he stated. The way to discover the order and divine
process in human affairs was to read critically the sources and stick close to the

empirical facts. He opposed the "principles of representation found in Sir Walter Scott's novels of romance," the philosophizing approach of Hegel, religious dogmatism, as well as the mechanistic and positivist analyses of physical science and the prevailing social theory of his time.[38] Ranke also stood against the enemies of the Church (materialism, rationalism), threats to the state (capitalism, imperialism, racism, liberalism), and opponents of the nation (socialism, communism, ecumenical religion). But, as Iggers points out, "inherent in this type of historicism which Ranke espouses is always the threat that, if Christian faith is shaken, history will lose its meaning and present man with the anarchy of values."[39] Closely behind historicism stalked relativism.

In his first major work, *History of the Latin and Teutonic Nations, 1494–1535* (1824), Ranke introduced his approach: "History has had assigned to it the office of judging the past and of instructing the present for the benefit of future ages. To such high offices the present work does not presume; it seeks only to show what actually happened [*wie es eigentlich gewesen war*]."[40] In this work Ranke saw the interaction of Latins and Teutons as the creative foundation of a civilization that could be distinguished from Europe and Christendom as a whole. Though he acknowledged the contributions of various nationalities (and marginalized some like the Slavs), Ranke emphasized the overall integration of cultures into a single amalgamated civilization.

Ranke ultimately wrote twelve volumes of Prussian history, five on the French monarchy, and six on seventeenth-century England, but he saw the thrust of his work as part of general European and world history. "History," he wrote, "is by its nature universal. True, some do concentrate their efforts completely on their fatherland, narrowly conceived, on their own state, on one small dark corner of the earth. But this is more out of a certain prejudice or piety or a praiseworthy tendency toward careful work than from any intellectual forces deriving from the nature proper to the discipline."[41] History, unlike politics, need not, indeed should not, be concerned with a given state. "Great peoples and states have a double character," he asserted, "one national, and the other belonging to the destinies of the world."[42] Churches and states were institutions created by God to bring order to disorderly humanity. They were the institutions through which a people constitutes itself as a nation. In the Middle Ages, he wrote, the "peaceful progress" of peoples into nations was hindered, but eventually reformers emerged in the Renaissance and Reformation who attacked the idea of the universal church and the universal state (while maintaining the essential unity of European culture and Christianity) and introduced the "national" idea. This constitution of nations led to a new phase of European civilization and historical development. New rules for governing the relations of people, church, and state within the nations developed along with rules among the various nations, namely the balance of power. Ranke, like Michelet, saw the French Revolution as the moment when nations came into the final stage of self-consciousness and the great powers found a common purpose in maintaining each by all the others.[43] By the mid-nineteenth century history had ended, and the shape of future development had been fixed.

Though Ranke would be attacked by fervently nationalistic historians in the second half of the nineteenth century for his tepid patriotism, his history was firmly founded in the story of the emergence of nations and contributed to the conviction that this process was a universal, natural or divinely ordained, inevitable process. For Ranke the nation is the sole possible principle of organizing humans for "peaceful progress."[44] The principle of nationality was the only safeguard against humanity's falling back into barbarism and had to be treasured as an eternal, immutable idea of God, though only knowable when actually realized in a historical form when peoples actually become nations. "In short," White concludes, "Ranke made of the *reality of his own time* the *ideal for all time*. He admitted the possibility of genuine transformation, revolution, convulsion, only for ages prior to his own; but the future for him was merely an indefinite extension of his own present."[45]

Like Hegel and unlike Herder, Ranke saw the state as a positive good. The state in his historical work was conceived in the image of the absolutist states of early modern Europe and operated in their own interests, largely unencumbered by internal divisions and politics. Whereas a British historian in the Whig tradition might trace the evolution of parliamentary institutions, or a French historian, like Michelet, might laud the moment of national effervescence in 1789, a German historian of the nineteenth century was likely to emphasize the distance between government and those governed. The state was guided by its own principles and its own interests, which in Ranke's view were the achievement of the greatest independence and strength in the competitive constellation of states.[46] His history, thus, was largely political and diplomatic, its agents great statesmen, warriors, or thinkers. The social setting or role of ordinary people was hardly sketched in. German historians in this tradition "tended to believe that the Hohenzollern monarchy, with its aristocratic and authoritarian aspects and its unique bureaucratic ethos, guaranteed a better bulwark for the defense of individual liberties and juridical security than a democracy in which policy would be more responsive to the whims of public opinion than to considerations of reasons of state."[47] This idealization of political power as it had been constituted in nineteenth-century Prussia and Germany was part of the legacy Ranke passed on to his more secular successors.

"Ranke's influence," a later historian noted, "can scarcely be overestimated." When in the second half of the century German historiography became politicized and historians took up the cause of unification, "he remained the conscience of German historical science even during periods when it entered with nationalist political vehemence into the struggle over Germany's transformation."[48] Ranke was responsible for making historicism respectable. The view that all human institutions and values originate within history and that the nature of things can only be comprehended within historical processes had Enlightenment origins and extended into the early twentieth century with the social thinkers Wilhelm Dilthey (1833–1911), Wilhelm Windelband (1848–1915), and Heinrich Rickert (1863–1936) in Germany. Its most notable practicing historians, like Friedrich Meinecke (1862–1954) and Ernst Troeltsch (1865–1923), believed historicism to have "liberated modern thought from the two-thousand-year domination of the theory of natural law," and to have replaced "the conception of the universe in terms of 'timeless, absolutely valid truths which correspond to the rational order dominant throughout the universe' . . . with an understanding of the fullness and diversity of man's historical experience."[49] But German historicism was not simply a method, as it declared itself, but also had normative and political content. As Iggers points out, it "viewed the state as the product of historical forces" and abandoned the cultural-centered historiography of Voltaire and Gibbon for a nation-centered narrative that tended to idealize certain political forms. In writing such a history they proposed a certain understanding of the proper nation and its relationship to its past and to the state authorities. Even German moderate liberals of mid-century adopted what Leonard Krieger calls "the German idea of Freedom" and, like Hegel and Ranke, saw the state as ethical, a natural product of historical forces and, rather than the foe, the political ally of liberty. Johann Gustav Droysen (1808–1884), the founder of the "Prussian School" of historians, legitimized the House of Hohenzollern's role in history as part of a "divine order" in which Prussia, more than any other state, moved in the line of historical development.[50] When constitutionalism in 1848 failed to bring about German unification, he and many of his fellow historians backed Prussia as the means to the national end.

The tension between a narrative of an emerging nation, with themes of resurrection, past glories and heroes, and the disciplined empiricism preached by Ranke was resolved in several national historiographies, in England, France, Italy, and Russia, in favor of a more romantic representation of the past. Even historians less directly engaged in nationalist or state-building projects were deeply affected by the emerging discourse of the nation that assumed without serious questioning the natural division of humanity into separate and distinct nations, the generally progressive evolution of peoples into nations, and the claim that nations had a unique right to sovereignty and political representation. Though their method was ostensibly objective and "realist," that is, dedicated to apprehending the world "as it actually is," their observations most often confirmed both the shape and the value of the world as it had evolved by the time of their own writing. "As it actually is" slipped imperceptibly into "as it ought to be."

Yet even as they contributed to the constitution of the nation, national or nationalist historians were never simply or completely servants of the nation-state, but often presented critical perspectives that made politicians and patriots uncomfortable. Governments of ostensibly national states, often supportive of the efforts of national historians, were occasionally intolerant of the independence of professional historians and dismissed and punished those whose views conflicted with official policy or popular views. The historian and states-man François Guizot (1787–1874), holder of the first chair in modern history at the University of Paris and the editor of the 31 volume *Collection des memoires relatifs à l'histoire de France* (Collection of Memoirs Dealing with the History of France), lost his post at the Sorbonne for teaching "ideas" rather than "facts." Radicals like Ludwig Feuerbach (1804–1872) and D. F. Strauss (1804–1874) were barred from the academy in Germany. The romantic nationalist Michelet, the most influential historian of France of the first half of the nine-teenth century, was fired when the revolutionary and democratic ideals he espoused were rejected by the Second Empire. Governments of empires, like Russia and Austria, were even less hospitable to nationalist and liberal ideas. In the reign of Nicholas I of Russia (1825–1855), even a conservative patriot like Mikhail Pogodin (1800–1875), a historian who passionately loved autocracy and empire and held the first chair in Russian history at Moscow University, was periodically reprimanded.

Two different kinds of historical writing developed in non-national imperial states like Russia—a state patriotic historiography and a nationalist literature of the subject peoples. With the emergence of an autonomous intelligentsia in the middle third of the nineteenth century, an intense discussion developed on the nature of Russia, its relations with the West and with Asia, as well as with its internal "others," the non-ethnic Russians within the empire. As with other peoples and states of Europe in the postrevolutionary period, intellectuals, particularly historians, were in a sense thinking nations into existence or at least elaborating and propagating the contours, characteristics, symbols, and signs that would make the nation familiar to a broader public. From *Istoriia gosudarstva rossiiskogo* (History of the Russian State) (1816–1826) by Nikolai Karamzin (1766–1826) through the great synthetic works of Sergei Solov'ev (1820–1879) and Vasilii Kliuchevskii (1841–1911), historians treated Russia as something like a nation-state, in many ways reflected in the West European models but uniquely multiethnic in its composition. Karamzin's contribution was particularly significant, for his work was extremely popular among edu-cated readers, and it provided a colorful, patriotic narrative of Russia's past up to the Time of Troubles in the early seventeenth century. As he also empha-sized in his secret memorandum to Alexander I, *Memoir on Ancient and Modern Russia* (1811), Karamzin believed that autocracy and a powerful state were responsible for Russia's greatness.[51]

Nationalist histories were foundational to the conviction that non-ruling nationalities were distinct nations with historical continuity even though they did not possess states of their own. The *Geschichte von Böhmen* (1844–1867) by the Czech patriot František Palacký (1798–1875) or the efforts of the Ukrainian historian Mykola Kostomarov (1817–1885) provided their people with a claim to nationhood precisely because they possessed a history. Jews and Armenians developed national historiographies both in the principal cities of the empires in which they lived (St. Petersburg, Moscow, Tbilisi [Tiflis],

Istanbul) and far from their lands of settlement (in the case of the Armenians, in Venice). Even as Marx and Engels condemned "historyless peoples" to evolutionary oblivion, or called one of their spokesman "a learned German run mad," nationalist historians shored up their future with elaborated pasts.[52]

The idea of the nation in the eighteenth century and early nineteenth century was far from the concept of an ethnolinguistic community that would become dominant later in the century. In both the American and French Revolutions, nation was understood as a community that came together historically and subscribed to shared principles. The nation was proud of its newness rather than desperately searching for ancient roots, as would become the common practice half a century later.[53] If "nations only exist because of the will of their citizens to accept themselves as a unified body," the principal problem for Americans at the time of independence was how "to create the sentiments of nationhood which other countries took for granted. There was no uniform ethnic stock, no binding rituals from an established church, no common fund of stories, only a shared act of rebellion."[54] Americans had to invent what they thought Europeans had inherited: "The fighting of the War for Independence had not turned Americans into a united people. Rather it had created the . . . imperative to form a more perfect union once the practical tasks of fighting a common enemy and securing a peace treaty no longer exerted centripetal pressure . . . The commonalities that did exist among them—those of language, law, and institutional history—all pointed in the wrong direction, backward to the past, toward an association with England, whose utility as a contemptible oppressor could not easily be done without."[55] A distinctly American national identity began to be forged in the 1790s, when the French Revolution validated an interpretation that 1776 had been "the initial act in a historic drama of liberation, now sweeping Europe."[56] A new history claimed that the Declaration of Independence was the end of a long development in colonial times and that American values and behaviors were distinct from those of Europe. God was present in this history, and in the work of the first important American historian, George Bancroft (1800–1891) (a student of Ranke), America's national destiny and God's plan neatly coincided. Not only was the United States unique, not only was it a model for other nations, but its destiny included the conquest of much of a continent.[57]

The early professional American historians have been characterized ideologically as "conservative evolutionists" by John Higham. They viewed American history as the story of "freedom realized and stabilized through the achievement of national solidarity" and were concerned about the need for national unity and reconciliation, particularly after the Civil War and in the face of massive immigration.[58] Moreover, "as Ranke's faith in history as the unfolding of God's grand design protected him from doubts about the objectivity of his labors, so the secular faith of the American professionals . . . guaranteed that their message, for all the austerity of its prose, was a profoundly moral one. There was no tension between disinterested scholarship on the one hand, and patriotic duty or moral engagement on the other: the former, through the self-evident ethical and political truths it revealed, satisfied the latter."[59] Like the national histories of ruling European nations, American historians worked to legitimize the particular form of polity and national community in which they lived.

The German historical method became the model of historical practice for European academic historians in the late nineteenth century, pushing aside the romantic and more flamboyant narratives of earlier French and Italian writers. German historical norms conquered North American historians in the last decades of the century, but, as Peter Novick has shown, when the Americans borrowed the notion of *wissenschaftliche Objektivität* (scholarly objectivity) and Ranke's realism, they left out his search for the divine or "essential" and interpreted his work as the purest empiricism, facts without generalization or interpretation. In America, Ranke was the prophet of secularism, unphilosophical empiricism, and a turn away from speculation and philosophizing. "German *Wissenschaft*," writes Novick, "became Anglo-American 'science.'"[60] Starting with the "blank slate" epistemology of John Locke (1632–1704), American historians added their idea of the inductivism of the scientific method of Francis Bacon (1561–1626)—observation without preconceptions—and a faith in scholarly neutrality. "This, then," Novick sums up, "was the model of scientific method which, in principle, the historians embraced. Science must be rigidly factual and empirical, shunning hypothesis; the scientific venture was scrupulously neutral on larger questions of end and meaning; and, if systematically pursued, it might ultimately produce a comprehensive, 'definitive' history. It is in the light of this conception of *wissenschaftliche Objectivität* that they regarded themselves as loyal followers of Ranke."[61]

In the last third of the nineteenth century historicism was attacked by the new social sciences not only for its naive inductionism, but also "for its presupposition that the nation was the sole possible unit of social organization (and the sole desirable one) and its conviction that, *therefore*, national groups constituted the sole viable units of historical imagination."[62] Social science turned toward more generic human problems of a transnational character and articulated other units of analysis, like society and culture. But the essential historicism of professional history and its focus on and location in the nation remained powerful frames for the practice of history-writing through most of the twentieth century.

NOTES

1. Parts of this essay will appear in a longer article that will be published as a disciplinary study of history and nationalism in *The Encyclopedia of Nationalism*, edited by Alexander J. Motyl.

2. Anthony Kemp, *The Estrangement of the Past: A Study in the Origins of Modern Historical Consciousness* (New York and Oxford, 1991), p. 106.

3. Peter Novick, *That Noble Dream: The "Objectivity Question" and the American Historical Profession* (Cambridge, 1988), p. 2.

4. Jacques Le Goff, *History and Memory*, trans. Steven Rendall and Elizabeth Claman (New York, 1992), p. 107.

5. Hayden White, *Metahistory: The Historical Imagination in Nineteenth-Century Europe* (Baltimore and London, 1973), p. 2.

6. White, *Metahistory*, p. 15.

7. Ibid.

8. Pierre Gilbert, *La Bible à la naissance de l'histoire* (Paris, 1979), p. 391, cited in Le Goff, *History and Memory*, p. 12.

9. Le Goff, *History and Memory*, p. 12.

10. Ibid., p. 11.

11. Ibid., pp. 12–13.

12. Joyce Appleby, Lynn Hunt, and Margaret Jacob, *Telling the Truth about History* (New York, 1994), p. 57.

13. This translation of the famous phrase comes from Edmund Wilson, *To the Finland Station: A Study in the Writing and Acting of History* (New York, 1972), p. 5.

14. Appleby, Hunt, and Jacob, *Telling the Truth about History*, pp. 15–43.

15. Cynthia Hyla Whittaker, "The Idea of Autocracy among Eighteenth-Century Russian Historians," in *Imperial Russia: New Histories for the Empire*, ed. Jane Burbank and David Ransel (Bloomington and Indianapolis, 1998), p. 34.

16. Robert Wokler, "Anthropology and Conjectural History in the Enlightenment," in *Inventing Human Science: Eighteenth-Century Domains*, ed. Christopher Fox, Roy Porter, and Robert Wokler (Berkeley, Los Angeles, and London, 1995), pp. 31–52; and Roger Smith, "The Language of Human Nature," ibid., pp. 88–111.

17. White, *Metahistory*, p. 64.

18. Appleby, Hunt, and Jacob, *Telling the Truth About History*, p. 53.

19. Wokler, "Anthropology and Conjectural History," p. 41.

20. David Carrithers, "The Enlightenment Science of Society," in *Inventing Human Science*, p. 235.

21. Ibid., p. 241.

22. White, *Metahistory*, p. 65.

23. Ibid., pp. 51–53.

24. *Outlines of a Philosophy of the History of Man*, trans. T. O. Churchill, 2 vols. (London, 1800–1803), vol. 1, p. 166.

25. Cited in Georg G. Iggers, *The German Conception of History: The National Tradition of Historical Thought from Herder to the Present* (Middletown, CT, 1968; revised edition, 1983), p. 26.

26. Herder, as cited by Isaiah Berlin, *Vico and Herder: Two Studies in the History of Ideas* (New York, 1976), p. 169.

27. F. M. Barnard, ed., trans., and intro., *J. G. Herder on Social and Political Culture* (Cambridge, 1969), p. 7.

28. Berlin, *Vico and Herder*, p. 163.

29. Cited in White, *Metahistory*, p. 7.

30. Iggers, *The German Conception of History*, p. 37.

31. Ibid., p. 41.

32. Ibid., p. 55.

33. Cited in ibid., p. 54.

34. This essay concentrates primarily on German historiography in the nineteenth century because the German tradition became the dominant model of European and American professional historical writing by the end of the century.

35. White, *Metahistory*, p. 136.

36. Ibid., pp. 141–42.

37. Iggers, *The German Conception of History*, p. 5.

38. White, *Metahistory*, pp. 162, 164.

39. Iggers, *The German Conception of History*, p. 69.

40. Leopold von Ranke, *The Secret of World History: Selected Writings on the Art and Science of History,* ed. and trans. Roger Wines (New York, 1981), pp. 7, 58. Novick notes that Iggers writes that *eigentlich* in the nineteenth century could mean "essentially." Novick, *That Noble Dream*, p. 28.

40. Von Ranke, *The Secret of World History*, p. 115.

42. Ibid., p. 247.

43. White, *Metahistory*, p. 171.

44. Ibid., p. 172.

45. Ibid., p. 173.

46. Iggers, *The German Conception of History*, p. 9.

47. Ibid., p. 15.

48. Walter Goetz, "History and Historiography," *Encyclopedia of the Social Sciences*, 15 vols. (New York, 1935–), vol. 7 (1937), p. 377.

49. Iggers, p. 5.

50. Iggers, p. 106.

51. Nikolai Karamzin, *Memoir on Ancient and Modern Russia*, ed., trans., and intro. Richard Pipes (Cambridge, MA, 1959).

52. Roman Szporluk, *Communism and Nationalism: Karl Marx Versus Friedrich List* (New York and Oxford, 1988), p. 152.

53. William H. Sewell, Jr., "The French Revolution and the Emergence of the Nation Form," unpublished paper presented at the Purdue University conference on the Trans-Atlantic revolutionary tradition; also at the Nations and Nationalism Workshop, University of Chicago, 14 January 1998.

54. Appleby, Hunt, and Jacoby, *Telling the Truth about History*, p. 91.

55. Ibid., p. 95.

56. Ibid., p. 97.

57. That sentiment was neatly captured by the future president and renowned Indian fighter William Henry Harrison, when he queried the representatives of the Indiana territory, "Is one of the fairest portions of the globe to remain in a state of nature, the haunt of a few wretched savages, when it seems destined by the Creator to give support to a large population, and to be the seat of civilization, of science and true religion?" (cited in Appleby, Hunt, and Jacoby, *Telling the Truth about History*, p. 114).

58. John Higham et al., *History: The Development of Historical Studies in the United States* (Princeton, 1965), pp. 158–60.

59. Novick, *That Noble Dream*, p. 85.

60. Ibid., p. 31.

61. Ibid., p. 37.

62. White, *Metahistory*, p. 175.

Grappling with the Hero: Hrushevs'kyi Confronts Khmel'nyts'kyi

FRANK E. SYSYN

In the aftershock of Ukrainian independence, numerous Sovietologists began to reexamine their statements about Ukrainian affairs. This endeavor took place on the crest of a general reevaluation of the national question in Eastern Europe, and in particular its importance in bringing down the communist order and the Soviet Union. Nations were triumphing over states on their way to building nation-states in a way that disquieted Western commentators, who wished to see the state and the nation as identical. They advocated a civic nation and insisted that a population's nationality, culture, or ethnicity should not influence its political loyalties and concept of political legitimacy. To many such commentators, the ethnic nation was a throwback to nineteenth-century Romanticism and twentieth-century blood chauvinism.[1]

These specialists were soon to find ample reason for their forebodings in the violent disintegration of Yugoslavia. Yet at the same time, the breakup of Czechoslovakia occurred as an almost friendly parting of two nations whose elites understood that the identity of the smaller could not be accommodated in a Czechoslovak (or even Czecho-Slovak) state. The small Baltic peoples proceeded toward establishing Estonian, Latvian, and Lithuanian nation-states, while accepting European norms for minorities, including those inherited from the Soviet occupation. Finally, Belarus demonstrated that when a folk overwhelmingly lacked national consciousness, it could not be mobilized either for state building or for overturning the communist order.

Ukraine has remained the major question mark. While the percentage of Ukrainians in the population exceeds the proportions of Latvians and Estonians in their states, the low level of Ukrainian language use and of national cohesiveness and consciousness in Ukraine have impeded the process of state building.[2] In 1991–1992, many of the Western commentators focused their attention on the potential dangers of Ukrainian nationalism, including mistreatment of minorities, and criticized the steps taken towards rectifying Soviet and Russian imperial discrimination against and persecution of Ukrainian language and culture. They did not see that without a certain level of Ukrainian national consciousness, a rebirth of Ukrainian culture and language, and the institutionalization of Ukrainian symbols, the reasons for embarking on the construction of a Ukrainian state were hardly convincing and the chances that it would endure were minimal.[3]

It was in this atmosphere that Abraham Brumberg wrote his controversial piece "Not so Free at Last," in *The New York Review of Books* in the autumn of 1992.[4] For many well-wishers of the new Ukrainian state, the article seemed an unbalanced attempt to find negative nationalist excesses in a state and society that, compared to most in Eastern Europe, had relatively few of them. This historian found questionable Brumberg's portrayal of Bohdan Khmel'nyts'kyi in his effort to demonstrate the baneful influence of the "Ukrainian national myth" in the new state. My letter on the article asserted that it was not modern Ukrainian nationalists, but the Cossack historians of the early eighteenth century who had created the Khmel'nyts'kyi cult, and that a Mazepa cult might well replace the Khmel'nyts'kyi cult in post-Soviet Ukraine.[5] Mr. Brumberg's reply to the letter in the same issue was intended to deride both hetmans in their role as national heroes, citing some of the usual Soviet clichés on Mazepa's wealth. But to buttress his argument on Khmel'nyts'kyi, Brumberg also called upon the assessment of Mykhailo Hrushevs'kyi.[6] In so doing, he drew on the authority of the author of one of the works of the canon of the Ukrainian national movement (or as he would have it, national myth) to support his critique of that very construct.[7]

For most historians, Hrushevs'kyi's view of Khmel'nyts'kyi is the one propounded in his magnum opus, *Istoriia Ukraïny-Rusy* (The History of Ukraine-Rus').[8] From volume 1, first published in 1898, to volume 10, completed before his death in 1934, Hrushevs'kyi used thousands of primary sources and secondary works in his examination of the history of the Ukrainian land and people from prehistory to the 1660s. The reprinting of the 10 volumes (11 books) of Hrushevs'kyi's *Istoriia Ukraïny-Rusy* has been the greatest project in the process of restoring historical memory in Ukraine.[9] Planned in response to the demands that arose during glasnost in the late 1980s, the reprinting was initiated when the Ukrainian revival was at its height in 1991; people waited in long lines to snap up the first volume's massive press run. The project has been completed despite the subsequent economic crisis in Ukraine and curtailment of funding for scholarship, in part because of private support, but more fundamentally because of the significance that Hrushevs'kyi—Ukraine's greatest historian and the leader of the independent state that was declared in 1918— had assumed for the state and society of contemporary Ukraine.

The publication of the reprint of volume 9, part 2, in 1997 has given the Ukrainian public its first opportunity since 1931 to read Hrushevs'kyi's devastating criticism of Khmel'nyts'kyi. Indeed, it might be more proper to say that for inhabitants of pre-1939 Soviet Ukraine, this is really the first opportunity, since by 1931 the Soviet campaign against Hrushevs'kyi and his *Istoriia* had begun; the very purchase of the volume was a dangerous act.[10] The readers who now encounter Hrushevs'kyi's views for the first time may find them troubling, in particular if they have internalized the new national iconostasis, which includes both the hetman and the historian. In this they will be joining scholars who have long found chapter 13 of volume 9 intemperate. Within a year of the volume's original publication, one of Hrushevs'kyi's best students and a major specialist of the Khmel'nyts'kyi period in the next generation, Myron Korduba—despite his great sympathy for his beleaguered teacher— negatively evaluated his appraisal of the hetman in a review written outside Soviet Ukraine.[11]

In volume 9, Hrushevs'kyi pointed out to his readers that he had offered many general evaluations of the Khmel'nyts'kyi uprising in the past and provided a list of scholarly, popular, and literary works.[12] It is through them that one can best trace the evolution of the historian's views on Khmel'nyts'kyi in order to place his appraisal in the *Istoriia* in context. Only through an examination of the occasions when and reasons why Hrushevs'kyi chose to evaluate the hetman can a fuller understanding of the historian's grappling with the image of the hetman emerge.

Hrushevs'kyi's earliest appraisal dates to 1897 and the short story "Iasnomozhnyi svat" (His Grace, the Matchmaker).[13] But the young professor's major scholarly statement on Khmel'nyts'kyi came in the special issue of the *Zapysky Naukovoho tovarystva im. Shevchenka*, published in 1898 to mark the 250th anniversary of the 1648 uprising. By then Hrushevs'kyi, a student of the great Ukrainian populist historian Volodymyr Antonovych of Kyiv, had spent four years raising the level of academic life among the Ukrainians of Galicia—a land where Polish-Ukrainian antagonism shaped all discussions of Khmel'nyts'kyi and the uprising. The excellent source and literary studies by Stepan Tomashivs'kyi and Ivan Franko in the issue demonstrated the high quality of research being undertaken in Lviv. It fell to Hrushevs'kyi to give the general evaluation of the man and the event in his lead article, entitled "Khmel'nyts'kyi i Khmel'nychchyna" (Khmel'nyts'kyi and the Khmel'nyts'kyi Uprising).[14]

On the whole, one finds in this early article many of the assertions that were to dominate Hrushevs'kyi's assessment until 1931. He concentrated on the event rather than the man, insisting that the Khmel'nyts'kyi uprising was as significant for the Ukrainians as the Reformation had been for the Germans and the French Revolution for Western Europe. He maintained that the uprising was epochal because it represented the interests of the masses at least until the Zboriv Agreement of 1649, and that the masses continued to struggle for their interests long after. Yet Hrushevs'kyi described the Khmel'nyts'kyi uprising as a "complete fiasco" in the long run in terms of its social and political outcomes (p. 27): there was no lasting social change benefiting the masses, and the alliance with Muscovy, which had been planned as temporary, determined Ukraine's political fate. Nevertheless, he saw the emergence of ideas of social emancipation, and the masses' adherence to these ideals for a period of more than a century after the revolt, as being of great significance. He viewed the flowering of Ukrainian culture (an evaluation he later abandoned), the awakening of national consciousness, and the attempt to form a Ukrainian polity as positive developments. Indeed, he even referred to the real relation of Ukraine to Muscovy after the Pereiaslav Agreement of 1654 as of a state in a personal union (p. 23). He saw the political culture of the Hetmanate, formed by the Khmel'nyts'kyi uprising, as engendering the concepts of autonomism and constitutionalism that underlay modern Ukrainian nationalism (*natsionalizm*).

Hrushevs'kyi pointed out how controversial Khmel'nyts'kyi had been and remained, referring to Mykhailo Maksymovych's enthusiasm for the hetman and Panteleimon Kulish's hatred of him. Hrushevs'kyi was far from either extreme. He presented his view of the individual in history and underlined the relationship of great men to the masses. He maintained that if, with the development of culture, a person does not become capable of being objective—the true sign of culture—he remains a deeply subjective being. Only rarely do people act solely from theoretical motives not associated with their persons. But one's own deeply held perceptions can give one a key to understanding, a feeling for others, an ability to connect one's own grief and wrong with that of the masses, to act as their spokesman. In this way, subjective reasons are transformed in such a heart into a pain through which great souls develop empathy for the whole world. He said that it was possible not to count Khmel'nyts'kyi among such "great souls," but that one must recognize that he was a person of the highest capabilities and remarkable character.[15]

Hrushevs'kyi then proceeded to make a balance sheet of Khmel'nytskyi's failures and successes. In outlining the hetman's shortcomings, he argued that Khmel'nyts'kyi had begun with no plan other than representing Cossack interests, and that the hetman wasted time after his earlier victories instead of pressing on against the Commonwealth.[16] He accused him of having taken a rash step in his relations with Muscovy. He believed that this misstep occurred because, as an experienced and accomplished diplomat (but not a politician) the hetman did not give any importance to words and forms. (This rather unusual distinction between "diplomat" and "politician" appeared frequently in Hrushevs'kyi's writings.)

On the positive side, Hrushevs'kyi saw Khmel'nyts'kyi's statements on the unity and political freedom of the "Ukrainian-Ruthenian nation" (*narod*)[17] after Christmas 1648 as of great significance. Even though they were not fully crystallized and were not carried out in the hetman's actions, the statements had emerged after centuries during which no such thought had been expressed (p. 8). Hrushevs'kyi asserted that the hetman had quickly understood his mistake in entering into relations with Muscovy: he had acted as the head of a state in his acceptance of the oath of the Pinsk nobility in 1657, and he had revealed his plans for a Ukrainian state in his negotiations with Sweden. Hrushevs'kyi argued that taking into account the circumstances in which Khmel'nyts'kyi operated, one can only marvel at the hetman's great ability in administration and organization. Above all, Hrushevs'kyi maintained that none of Khmel'nyts'kyi's successors came close to equalling him. While he took the hetman to task for his indifference to the masses and his failure to turn to them as his base of support, Hrushevs'kyi saw these failings as reflecting the level of the "Ukrainian intelligentsia" of that age. He declared that while one could regret that Khmel′nyts′kyi did not rise above the wisdom of his age, one could hardly expect that he would do so. He asserted that Khmel′nyts′kyi had to be seen as "one of the most able and talented people of our nation (*narod*)."

The marking of the 250th anniversary of the uprising was only the first of numerous commemorations of the momentous events of the mid-seventeenth century. Hrushevs′kyi took up his pen again to give his views on the 250th anniversary of the Pereiaslav Agreement in 1904. Although the article appeared in a Ukrainian version in *Literaturno-naukovyi visnyk*, it had been written for *Ruthenische Revue*.[18] Hence, unlike the earlier piece intended for internal Ukrainian consumption, this article was originally meant to present the Ukrainian case to the outside world. Hrushevs′kyi depicted the Pereiaslav Agreement as a poorly thought-out series of arrangements from the Ukrainian side, designed to secure Russian military support. He maintained that Khmel′nyts′kyi had considered it a temporary measure, but soon had become convinced that the agreement was a mistake and had sought to overturn it. While maintaining that Khmel′nyts′kyi had reckoned wrongly in thinking of negotiations with Moscow as similar to those with "the powerless government of anarchic Poland" (p. 4), Hrushevs′kyi was in general complimentary to the hetman. He called Khmel′nyts′kyi a great politician as well as an organizer of genius. He maintained that he was a "skillful diplomat" educated in "the highest school of diplomacy—the Oriental," thereby explaining that he had no scruples in making the promises needed to gain allies. This image of the Oriental or Asian hetman was to be expanded in a more negative light in Hrushevs′kyi's later works, but in 1904 it was merely mentioned. In this piece, Hrushevs′kyi repeated his earlier criticism of Khmel′nyts′kyi for his attitude toward the masses. At the same time he informed his Western readers and repeated for his Ukrainian readers that the mistakes of the leaders of the seventeenth-century "revolution" in fulfilling the social aspirations of the masses were not being repeated by the current leaders of the Ukrainian movement. He maintained that the contemporary leaders were seeking to undo the consequences of the failed Pereiaslav experiment.[19]

While the Pereiaslav anniversary dealt with a fateful decision of Khmel′nyts′kyi's hetmancy, the 250th anniversary of Khmel′nyts′kyi's death, marked in 1907, focused attention on the hetman himself. In 1857, Mykhailo Maksymovych's piece on the 200th anniversary of Khmel′nyts′kyi's death had initiated a major debate on the role of the hetman, above all as to whether he deserved a monument and what form that monument should take.[20] One of the harshest critics of the monument proposal and of Khmel′nyts′kyi himself had been the conservative Polish intellectual Michał Grabowski.[21] In 1907, however, the discussion of the character of the hetman had already been preempted by a Polish attack on Khmel′nyts′kyi. This view emerged during the celebrations in 1905 of the 250th anniversary of the lifting of the second siege of Lviv. Central to these celebrations were the writings of Franciszek Rawita-

Gawroński, who in publications such as *1655–1905. Krwawy gość we Lwowie* (The Bloody Guest in Lviv) sought to deride the hetman and through him the Ukrainian population of Galicia.[22] These celebrations of the "All-Poles" (*Wszechpolacy*), which Hrushevs'kyi mentioned in *Literaturno-naukovyi visnyk*, seemed to have influenced the dean of Ukrainian historians to take a more sympathetic view of the hetman when writing his piece on the anniversary of Khmel'nyts'kyi's death.

In "Bohdanovi rokovyny" (The Bohdan Anniversaries), Hrushevs'kyi argued that the very magnitude of the events in which Khmel'nyts'kyi had been involved controlled him more than he controlled them, and therefore they overshadowed him.[23] He maintained that the epochal nature of the events had determined his own contemporaries' and subsequent generations' evaluation of the hetman. Thus, while the Ukrainian masses of his generation had often cursed Khmel'nyts'kyi, subsequent generations had come to see him positively as the representative of free autonomous administration and the struggle for political, economic, and national freedom. Nevertheless, the false praise of the propagators of "Orthodoxy, Autocracy, and Nationality" and the erection of the Khmel'nyts'kyi monument to "One and Indivisible [Russia]" by the Iuzefovychites[24] had besmirched the hetman's reputation for the modern Ukrainian national movement. Hrushevs'kyi went on to call for understanding for this man who had been cursed by the masses, who had been laid low by failures before his death, whose body had been burned and ashes scattered by his enemies. Hrushevs'kyi maintained that those who saw the problems of national renewal in their own time as analogous to those of the seventeenth century might better understand Khmel'nyts'kyi. Could Ukraine under the negative influences of aristocratic Polish rule have produced a more aware or talented leader? Hrushevs'kyi waxed poetic on how Khmel'nyts'kyi was consumed in the great conflagration in which he expended all his energies to fulfill his responsibilities. Turning from the leader to the people in his exposition, Hrushevs'kyi called for the fulfillment of the seventeenth-century great popular movement under a new flag for a free autonomous Ukraine without lord and peasant.

Two years later, Hrushevs'kyi presented Khmel'nyts'kyi to the broad masses in his popular booklet *Pro bat'ka kozats'koho Bohdana Khmel'nyts'koho* (On the Cossack Father Bohdan Khmel'nyts'kyi).[25] Finally, the Ukrainian national movement in the Russian Empire had the opportunity to reach beyond the narrow circles of the intelligentsia and to do so using the Ukrainian language.[26] That Hrushevs'kyi hoped to form the consciousness of broader masses was apparent in his use of the Cossack dumas, a popular poetic form accessible to Ukrainian speakers who still lived in an age of oral literature, throughout the work.

Hrushevs'kyi crafted a sophisticated account couched in simple language. Numerous sources are used and quoted without citations. Negative aspects of the era, such as the violence, the slaughter, and the Tatar raids are mentioned, but the positive outweighs the negative. Hrushevs'kyi begins his account with the image of the Khmel'nyts'kyi monument in the St. Sophia Square. He asserts that no figure has been so loved and so condemned as Khmel'nyts'kyi. Reflecting on the centuries of controversy over the hetman, he maintains: " . . . only for great people is there great love or great hate. And at times the hate brings them more glory than praise. The whole importance lies in who praises and for what reason, just as in who derides and why" (p. 3).

Hrushevs'kyi presented a Khmel'nyts'kyi in accordance with his earlier views, including that the hetman had not begun with a plan to free Ukraine and to improve the lot of the peasantry. Khmel'nyts'kyi is seen as coming to these goals during the uprising. This booklet, focusing solely on the hetman and meant for a mass audience, presents Khmel'nyts'kyi quite heroically. It ends with the conclusion:

> But the memory of Bohdan remained eternally living and dear in the Cossack Host and the Ukrainian people. The Ukrainian people did not forget Bohdan for the good that the glorious hetman wished for Ukraine. It sang praises of Bohdan's deeds in songs and dumas as it did for no other hetman. The people retained these songs and dumas to our times, in a way it did not retain the memory of anything or anyone else in Ukrainian history! (p. 54)

The heroic image as portrayed in the popular biography was less clearly drawn in the illustrated history of Ukraine that Hrushevs'kyi first published in 1911, and reworked in 1912 when the 7,000 run was sold out.[27] He described the work as intended to be accessible, but he also provided a table of contents to his multivolume academic history for readers who wished to delve more deeply into problems. In the one-volume history, he went far beyond the year 1625 that he had reached in the recently published volume 7 of the *Istoriia Ukraïny-Rusy*, bringing Ukrainian history up to the present. Recounting the events of the Khmel'nyts'kyi uprising, Hrushevs'kyi traced the hetman's actions with relatively little discussion of his person. He did describe him as having great political skill and talent as a statesman, and as loving Ukraine and being dedicated to its interests. In the same passage, however, he took Khmel'nyts'kyi to task for seeking foreign help instead of awakening his own people and depending on them. Hrushevs'kyi saw the hetman as too attached to Cossack interests even after his vow in early 1649 to bring about the liberation of the entire Ukrainian people and all Ukraine, though Hrushevs'kyi admitted that the development and fruition of such concepts required time (p. 309). In describing the Hetmanate, Hrushevs'kyi saw Khmel'nyts'kyi as greatly augmenting the hetman's authority and becoming the ruler of the country. He maintained that many political, social, and ideological tensions existed in the newly forming Hetmanate, but they might have been held in check and resolved had it not been for Khmel'nyts'kyi's premature demise (or if Ukraine had enjoyed a decade or more of peace after his death) (p. 324).

In the first years after the revolution of 1905, Hrushevs'kyi was optimistic about the future of Ukrainian society and the Ukrainian movement in the Russian Empire. By 1912 when he wrote "Na ukraïns'ki temy: 'Mazepynstvo' i 'Bohdanivstvo'" (On Ukrainian topics: "Mazepism" and "Bohdanism"), he had seen the full course of the reaction.[28] Responding to the attempts of Russian nationalists to use the image of Hetman Khmel'nyts'kyi against the Ukrainian movement, he turned again to a characterization of Khmel'nyts'kyi, this time in a comparison with Mazepa, whose image he had recently discussed during the 200th anniversary of the Battle of Poltava.[29] This article was Hrushevs'kyi's only characterization of Khmel'nyts'kyi in which there is no criticism of the hetman or mention of the social issue. Answering the Russian nationalist Right and the tsarist bureaucrats who had renewed their persecution of the Ukrainian movement as treasonous, Hrushevs'kyi concentrated on national issues in the present and the past. He called Ivan Mazepa an unlikely symbol for the Ukrainian cause since he had not shown the lifelong dedication to Ukrainian independence that Petro Doroshenko and Pylyp Orlyk had. But he admitted that the statements and anathemas of Peter I and the accusations of Mazepism against the Ukrainian movement in the nineteenth century had associated Mazepa with the Ukrainian cause. He was incensed that there were those who were now trying falsely to use Khmel'nyts'kyi as a symbol of loyalty to Russia in opposition to Mazepa. Calling him "the great hetman," he asserted that Khmel'nyts'kyi had viewed the ties with Russia after 1654 negatively, that many tensions existed between the Russians and Khmel'nyts'kyi after the Pereiaslav Agreement, and that Khmel'nyts'kyi resolutely sought to break with Russia through the Swedish alliance. He called Khmel'nyts'kyi not only a clear autonomist, but a relatively conscious bearer of the Ukrainian state idea (p. 98). He pointed out that the elite of Mazepa's time had seen the alliance with Charles XII as a continuation of Khmel'nyts'kyi's policies.

In the years just before the First World War, Hrushevs'kyi was writing volume 8 and collecting material for volume 9 of the *Istoriia*, the tomes of his work that covered the Khmel'nyts'kyi period. Yet just as he was embarking on this project, new evaluations and interpretations were emerging among Polish and Ukrainian historians. While the major Polish biography of Khmel'nyts'kyi that appeared from the pen of Rawita-Gawroński in 1906–1909 was a virulent diatribe against the hetman and Ukrainians, the distinguished Polish scholar of the seventeenth century, Ludwik Kubala, wrote an evaluation of Khmel'nyts'kyi in 1910 that was the most positive made by a modern historian to that time.[30] Describing Khmel'nyts'kyi as a greater statesman and leader than Cromwell, Kubala called on his fellow Poles to understand that denigrating a man who had brought their state to its knees did them no service.

While the elderly Polish historian's comments did not have an immediate impact on Polish historiography, they contributed to the reevaluation of the hetman and the uprising among the younger generation of Ukrainian historians who were evolving into the "statist" (*derzhavnyts'ka*) school. These historians were already influenced by the return of attention to the role of the great man in history that was occurring in German and Polish historiography. Influenced by the rise of Ukrainian political movements advocating statehood, they were dissatisfied with the Ukrainian populist tradition that almost revelled in the statelessness of the Ukrainians and condemned elites. V'iacheslav Lypyns'kyi, a Polish nobleman turned Ukrainian patriot, headed this movement, and the appearance of his monograph on Mykhailo Krychevs'kyi in the massive volume of materials he edited, *Z dziejów Ukrainy*, revolutionized studies of the Khmel'nyts'kyi period.[31] Lypyns'kyi demonstrated the mass participation of the Ukrainian nobility in the revolt and devoted great attention to its state-building elements. Above all, he considered Khmel'nyts'kyi a brilliant leader and a conscious state builder. The conservative political thinker Lypyns'kyi was working in parallel with a number of Hrushevs'kyi's students such as Stepan Tomashivs'kyi, Myron Korduba, and Ivan Kryp'iakevych, who also saw Khmel'nyts'kyi in a positive light for his state- and nation-building activities. After the First World War and the attempt to set up a Ukrainian state, the statist school became dominant in western Ukraine and the Ukrainian emigration and influenced historians in Soviet Ukraine.[32]

In the 1890s and early 1900s, Hrushevs'kyi was the unchallenged doyen of Ukrainian historians who swept all along with him by his phenomenal erudition and range of expertise from archaeology to medieval diplomatics. When he later undertook his writing on the Khmel'nyts'kyi period, however, he was no longer in such a position, in part because of his own success in training a younger generation of scholars who worked on the period. One can see his reaction to this situation in the historiographical survey on the Khmel'nyts'kyi period in volume 8, part 2, written just before the First World War and first published in 1916. While his description of Lypyns'kyi's contribution was cautiously factual, when he went on to discuss Tomashivs'kyi's recent work he described it as "also having an apologetic and even enthusiastic characterization of the Khmel'nyts'kyi uprising and especially Khmel'nyts'kyi himself."[33]

In introducing the person of Khmel'nyts'kyi in volume 8, Hrushevs'kyi gave one more assessment of the hetman. The short biography of Khmel'nyts'kyi up to the beginning of the uprising sought to separate fact from fiction in the many legends of the hetman's life. Regrettably, the excursuses that Hrushevs'kyi wrote on these complex questions were not published in volume 8, part 2, and his plan to publish them separately was thwarted when they were burnt along with his library during the Bolshevik bombardment of his house in 1918. In depicting Khmel'nyts'kyi's decision to rebel as a result of personal persecution, Hrushevs'kyi believed a turning point occurred in the life of the cautious and levelheaded Cossack captain so great that one might speak of two different people. Hrushevs'kyi characterized Khmel'nyts'kyi as accustomed to hide his intentions and to appear humble. He described him as talkative and witty, and desirous of surprising his listeners. He saw him as an actor who combined sincere directness with Oriental cunning, a mixture of both petty noble obsequiousness and prideful consciousness of his great power and providential election. Hrushevs'kyi believed that the tribulations that Khmel'nyts'kyi suffered drove him to seek solace in drink but at the same time called forth from him extraordinary talents, energy, organizational skill, a remarkable dexterity, and an unprecedented power to influence people, all of which place him in the ranks of the most prominent heroes of history.[34]

Hrushevs'kyi completed the final chapter of part 3 of volume 8, that brought the account of the revolt to early 1650, in 1917, but the first printing was destroyed. He published the three parts together in Vienna in 1922, introducing no changes so as not to allow the momentous events he had just lived through to affect his account. He wrote in the preface to part 3, "Let it be as it was written then, when present-day politics did not yet divide Ukrainians." His next volume, however, was to reflect these divisions.

*   *
*

Hrushevs'kyi resumed his research on the *Istoriia* after his controversial return to Soviet Ukraine in 1924.[35] Since he was partially retracing work that he had completed before the war and the destruction of his archive and papers, this resumption of work on volume 9 must have been stressful. With his customary energy, he carried on new archival searches and organized a network of colleagues in Kyiv, Lviv, Moscow, Cracow, Warsaw, and Vienna to assemble new materials. In his introduction he thanks Myron Korduba, Vasyl' Herasymchuk, A. Vytoshyns'kyi, Volodymyr Iefymovs'kyi, Viktor Iurkevych, Anatol' Iershov, D. Kravtsiv, Mykola Petrovs'kyi and S. Porfyr'ev for their assistance, a group that included both his prewar colleagues and his new colleagues in Soviet Ukraine. Writing the volume between 1926 and 1928, he published the first part in the latter year, and the second part in 1931.

The introduction revealed the historian's leftward drift since 1917 and reflected the new Marxist-influenced climate in which he worked. His insistence that he had sought to illuminate the actions and thought of the popular masses rather than the elites was not a great departure from his traditional populist approach. His terminology on social-economic struggle, class interests, and his ordering of his social-economic discussion before his discussion of changes in consciousness did fit the ethos of Soviet Ukraine. So did his use of terminology and periodization in asserting that the sixteenth-century movement of rebirth had continued its development in the Khmel'nyts'kyi period and had shaped that which in time would be the Ukrainian nation (*natsiia*). The degree to which Marxist-like terminology or Hrushevs'kyi's espoused view of himself as a historian-sociologist shaped the volume has yet to be explored.[36]

More significant for his vision of Khmel'nyts'kyi was the degree to which Hrushevs'kyi viewed his magisterial work as an answer to the statist school and to V'iacheslav Lypyns'kyi in particular. This aim underlay his characterization of Khmel'nyts'kyi and the Khmel'nyts'kyi uprising in chapter 13 of part 2.[37] In discussing his own writings on Khmel'nyts'kyi, Hrushevs'kyi openly admitted that the context in which he had written his works had affected his evaluations, calling his 1898 piece a defense of Khmel'nyts'kyi against attempts (presumably by Panteleimon Kulish and Polish historians) to represent the hetman as "a wild destroyer, a morally flawed nobody" (p. 1496). He asserted that he had since changed some of his opinions, in particular as to whether Khmel'nyts'kyi had stood out above his contemporaries. Indeed there were other changes in his opinions that he did not explicitly point out, such as about the cultural life of Ukraine in the age of Khmel'nyts'kyi, which he now viewed negatively.

Hrushevs'kyi began his chapter with the question to what degree the Khmel'nyts'kyi uprising had been coherent, planned, and constructive. In practice, as he outlined the historiography on the question he also dealt with the evaluation of Khmel'nyts'kyi. He presented the traditional eighteenth-century image of Khmel'nyts'kyi as an all-national (*vsenarodnii*) liberator and the Khmel'nyts'kyi uprising as an all-national struggle for liberation, only differing in emphasis as to whether the interests of the clergy or the Cossack officers dominated. Mentioning Hryhorii Skovoroda's characterization of Khmel'nyts'kyi as "father of liberty, the hero Bohdan," Hrushevs'kyi saw this tradition as one that viewed the hetman as "the finest son of the Ukrainian people and the finest representative of this all-national (*vsenarodnii*) character of Cossackdom, the all-national hero, the liberator of Ukraine, who gave his life to this task and in some way succeeded in it . . . " (p. 1480).

In exploring the questions he posed, Hrushevs'kyi went on to demonstrate how subsequent historical writing had diverged from the traditional view, including the harsh evaluations of Khmel'nyts'kyi by Petr Butsinskii and Panteleimon Kulish. He took into account the opinions of his teacher Volodymyr Antonovych and his own students. His analysis of the changing view of the nature of the Khmel'nyts'kyi uprising then turned to the generally accepted opinion that there had been no equal to Khmel'nyts'kyi among the Cossack elite, a view he himself had earlier espoused. Next, after posing the question to what degree Khmel'nyts'kyi and the Cossack elite had represented general national (*zahal'no-natsional'ni*) and general state interests, Hrushevs'kyi focused on an evaluation of Khmel'nyts'kyi. He maintained that despite the universal opinion of the hetman's great significance, no really scholarly critical analysis existed. Given the considerable attention to Khmel'nyts'kyi in the 1910s and 1920s, above all by V'iacheslav Lypyns'kyi, Hrushevs'kyi was thus denigrating the most recent writing, which he asserted was still under the influence of traditional historiography in emphasizing the fundamental significance of Khmel'nyts'kyi.[38]

Hrushevs'kyi quickly made clear that, in his new view, Khmel'nyts'kyi did not particularly stand out among his contemporaries in his capabilities and influence. He declared that he had wished to use as the epigraph to the volume a statement by Hetman Mikołaj Potocki—"Do they only have one Khmel'nyts'kyi? One could count thousands of them. If they lose one today, in his place they select another still more talented and effective." He maintained, however, that he had wished to do this to illustrate a high evaluation of the revolutionary Ukrainian masses, but had not done so because he feared that it would have been seen as an attempt to denigrate the reputation of Khmel'nyts'kyi. He insisted that this was not his wish (p. 1486). Later, he maintained, "I do not wish to belittle the person of Khmel'nyts'kyi in the least" (p. 1496), and, still later, "I repeat, with this I do not wish to denigrate Khmel'nyts'kyi" (p. 1507). The more he protested the clearer it became that this was exactly what he was doing.

Hrushevs'kyi began the discussion of his views with a presentation of the recent opinions in historical circles. He concentrated on the most striking praise of the hetman by Ludwik Kubala, whom he called Khmel'nyts'kyi's panegyrist. Hrushevs'kyi translated a four-page excerpt from Kubala, which contained his views that Khmel'nyts'kyi had succeeded in the fields of war, finances, state economy, administration, and relations with surroundings states on a territory open to enemies and without the benefit of an established state and an experienced intelligentsia. After citing Kubala's effusive praise of Khmel'nyts'kyi, Hrushevs'kyi called it perceptive. He agreed with certain elements of the characterization of Khmel'nyts'kyi's character: uneven temperament, extraordinary energy, dynamism, sensibility, a deeply developed sense of fantasy, quick-wittedness, a tendency to hyperbole, a talent to use psychological influence, a tendency to theatricality, poor discrimination, ruthlessness, freedom from any moral boundaries, and an extraordinary attachment to rule as a dogma of life. In sum, he selected what might be called the less attractive qualities that Kubala saw in Khmel'nyts'kyi rather than those associated with statesmanship. Still, Hrushevs'kyi concluded this discussion with an assertion that "Bohdan was a truly born leader-ruler and politician-diplomat. He easily captured and aroused the masses, knew how to rule over their moods—with bloody force as well as with a kind word, a humble gesture, in his nature there was something disarmingly charming that drew people to him." But then he queried, "But was he also a politician in the higher meaning—a builder of society and state, an organizer of society and culture? In the long-term perspective?" (p. 1490).

Before dealing with that question, Hrushevs'kyi discussed the views of Lypyns'kyi. He mentioned *Ukraïna na perelomi* (Ukraine at the Turning-Point), which had been published in Vienna in 1920 and was in reality the work his conclusion answered directly.[39] He summarized Lypyns'kyi's view of Khmel'nyts'kyi as a statesman of genius who sought to create a hereditary monarchy and a European society of estates in Ukraine. He also presented Lypyns'kyi's opinion that Khmel'nyts'kyi had engaged in a successful process of first breaking with Poland through an alliance with Muscovy and then limiting Muscovite Asiatic influence in Ukraine, a process that ended with the hetman's untimely death. Hrushevs'kyi ostensibly eschewed a critique of Lypyns'kyi's political concept of a "Tillers' Monarchy," which he saw Lypyns'kyi reading back into the Khmel'nyts'kyi period. However, one cannot divorce Hrushevs'kyi's critique of both Khmel'nyts'kyi and Lypyns'kyi's historical views from Hrushevs'kyi's rejection of Lypyns'kyi's politics.

From then on, Hrushevs'kyi mentioned Lypyns'kyi six times by name and on other occasions in references such as the "adorers" of Khmel'nyts'kyi. His depiction of Khmel'nyts'kyi became an attempt to smash the idol that he saw Lypyns'kyi and the statist school fashioning. It was this new Khmel'nyts'kyi cult, not the traditional Cossack cult, that Hrushevs'kyi saw both as historically incorrect and politically dangerous. The anger that Hrushevs'kyi spewed forth against Khmel'nyts'kyi, the "Great Scythian" who devastated his land, was directed against the Ukrainian conservative statists and their attempt to dethrone the people as the hero of Ukrainian history and enthrone in their place "great men." Therefore, Hrushevs'kyi sharpened his early argument that Khmel'nyts'kyi had begun the revolt without a plan, had not properly taken account of the potential and interests of the Ukrainian masses, and had entered the Pereiaslav Agreement without proper care and attention to the nature of Muscovy. He maintained that although the Ukrainian people were European and strove to be a European society, Khmel'nyts'kyi had too much of the steppe and Asia in him to lead them to this goal. He selected one of the central tenets of Lypyns'kyi's ideology, the importance of territory in defining the Ukrainian society and polity, and argued that Khmel'nyts'kyi had little loyalty to territory, allowing wars to be fought on the Ukrainian land and creating conditions in which much of the population fled eastward. He insisted that not only were the colleagues of Khmel'nyts'kyi equal to him in talent, but that much of the policy during Khmel'nyts'kyi's hetmancy was formulated by the chancellor Ivan Vyhovs'kyi, who was the real proponent of European society. Finally, he maintained that contrary to Lypyns'kyi's assertion, Khmel'nyts'kyi's policies were already in ruins before his death and only his timely demise had saved his reputation.

Hrushevs'kyi's final characterization of Khmel'nyts'kyi was written after he had experienced the failure of the revolutionary upsurge in 1917 and the attempt to establish a Ukrainian state. In his 1907 article, he had pointed out to his contemporaries that having seen the recent difficulties in organizing the masses to rise above their current cultural level (after the 1905 revolution), they could be more sympathetic to Bohdan for what he had achieved in more difficult circumstances. In the late 1920s, he did not find that the revolutionary events of 1917–1921 should make his contemporaries treat the hetman with greater understanding.

Without documentary evidence it is risky to second-guess Hrushevs'kyi's motives and psychological state in 1928 and their influence on his characterization. Yet it is hard to separate his writing from the impact of the revolution and failed attempt to establish a Ukrainian state. While most Ukrainian historians saw these events as proof that populism and leftist thought had lost the struggle and that what was needed was greater discipline, respect for authority, and attention to national above social issues, Hrushevs'kyi took the side of the masses and saw the Ukrainian leadership as failing their interests. He returned to Ukraine and rebuilt Ukrainian culture because he wanted to be with the Ukrainian masses, who, he believed, would be able to regenerate the Ukrainian cause even under Moscow Bolshevik rule. He wanted the Ukrainian movement to have respect for the masses, not leaders. With the tide already running against the non-Marxists in 1928, and the full attack on Hrushevs'kyi and the destruction of his work well advanced in 1931, Hrushevs'kyi may have reacted by placing all hope in the masses. He could not know that by 1932–1933, the Ukrainian village, which he saw as the bearer of the nation, would die.[40]

We are on safer ground when we speculate that part of the emotional tone of Hrushevs'kyi's depiction came from the frustration of the grand old man of Ukrainian historians seeing that by the 1920s not only his political but also his historical views were rejected by his colleagues and students. Concurrently, he was coming under attack by the Marxist historians, who at that time also negatively evaluated Khmel'nyts'kyi, but who already were beginning their transformation of Hrushevs'kyi into the demon of Ukrainian bourgeois nationalism. Writing in the midst of this struggle of historical schools and political groups, Hrushevs'kyi produced a work that reflected the various terminologies and views of these rising forces. He thus dwelt on issues of the state and state building as a positive element much more than he had in his earlier writings, though he hardly could satisfy the statists in his denying Khmel'nyts'kyi's success in this process. At the same time, he cloaked the Khmel'nyts'kyi period with many of the terms current among the Marxists—above all the concept of revolution, which he had used earlier but which was *de rigeur* in Soviet Ukrainian writings, while his description of social conflict also took on the terminology of Marxist class struggle.[41] Still, the Marxists could hardly be satisfied with Hrushevs'kyi's evaluation of the Khmel'nyts'kyi uprising as the "most important epoch in the history of our people—the greatest revolution it has experienced" (p. 1507).[42]

Hrushevs'kyi concluded his discussion by arguing against the unhealthy idealization of the period and person of Khmel'nyts'kyi and the depiction of the age as a lost paradise in which the Ukrainian land flourished, a Ukrainian state was being built, social harmony reigned, and the hetman was loved. He insisted that "the Ukrainian people did not experience its paradise in the time of Bohdan—or in any period of its past. Our social, political, and cultural ideals lie before us, and not behind us." But he still insisted that the Khmel'nyts'kyi movement had been an important stage in the Ukrainian people's journey toward social, political, cultural, and national ideals. He praised it as an age when "simple people" had been able to feel themselves "fully human." It was for bringing about this great upheaval that Hrushevs'kyi was willing to call him the "hero of Ukrainian history" (pp. 1507–1508).

Hrushevs'kyi's final characterization came after the magnificent achievement of his writing the history of Khmel'nyts'kyi's age, which he dedicated to the "creative sufferings of the Ukrainian masses." In many ways his concentration on the masses and his resistance to heroic figures had permeated his entire oeuvre. He himself had pointed out that the situation and genre of his work had influenced his evaluations of Khmel'nyts'kyi throughout his career. What may seem jarring is that his final sharp polemic came not in a political piece or a review article, but in his magnum opus. In some ways, it showed the importance that he attached to the statement that he was making, but it also may reflect the declining level of historical discourse and the more fractious nature of Ukrainian scholarly and political life in the late 1920s. It would be foolish to underestimate the importance of his examination of thousands of sources in forming his evaluation of the hetman. Still, it is likely that the political environment of his time and his own feeling of political and scholarly isolation explain the intemperate nature of Hrushevs'kyi's remarks in comparison to his many earlier evaluations.

Hrushevs'kyi's final characterization of Kheml'nyts'kyi had little impact in undermining the hetman's position as the archetypical Ukrainian hero. He failed to vanquish the statist school, which remained dominant among Ukrainian historians in western Ukraine and abroad. Beginning in the 1930s, Soviet historiography revived the praise of leaders, and the increasing influence of Russian traditional thought turned Khmel'nyts'kyi into the icon of the "Reunification of Ukraine with Russia" by the 1950s. Indeed, Khmel'nyts'kyi was virtually the only Ukrainian political leader after the princely period depicted in a positive light in Soviet Ukraine from the 1930s to the 1980s. The cults of the Cossack-age writings (republished widely in the late 1980s and early 1990s),[43] the statist school, and Soviet historiography combined to make of Khmel'nyts'kyi a national hero in 1991 without any special effort by the new Ukrainian state. Certainly the variety of cults of Khmel'nyts'kyi made him acceptable to very different constituencies in Ukraine. In historical writing, however, it is clearly the statist image that dominates.[44] Whether the reissuing of volume 9 will change either popular attitudes or historical writing remains to be seen. The reprinting of other works by Hrushevs'kyi ensures that not one, but a number of Hrushevs'kyi's confrontations with the hetman will contend in shaping the new image.

NOTES

1. For a theoretical work presenting this argument, see Liah Greenfeld, *Nationalism: Five Roads to Modernity* (Cambridge, MA, 1982). For an influential popular discussion that deals with Ukraine, see Michael Ignatieff, *Blood and Belonging: Journeys into the New Nationalism* (New York, 1995).

2. On the extremely controversial topic of the need for an ethno-national core for new states, see Timothy Garton Ash, "Cry, the Dismembered Country," *The New York Review of Books* 46(1) 14 January 1999: 29–33. His comment that "History suggests that a contemporary European state with less than 80 percent ethnic majority is inherently unstable" (p. 33) states a viewpoint that many Western social scientists and politicians have been loath to accept. Obviously, it does not augur well for Latvia, Estonia, and Ukraine.

3. For an example of such views, see Andrew Wilson, *Ukrainian Nationalism: A Minority Faith* (Cambridge, 1997), and my review article, "Ukrainian 'Nationalism': A Minority Faith?" *The Harriman Review* 10(2) Summer 1997: 12–20.

4. *The New York Review of Books* 39(17) 22 October 1992: 56–63. The title on the cover is the more provocative: "A Nasty New Ukraine?"

5. *The New York Review of Books* 40(3) 28 January 1993: 45–46. On the evolution of views on Khmel'nyts'kyi, see my "The Changing Image of the Hetman: On the 350th Anniversary of the Khmel'nyts'kyi Uprising," *Jahrbücher für Geschichte Osteuropas* 46(4) 1998: 531–45. The decline of the Ukrainian national revival, the deceleration of the movement away from Russia, and the greater influence of the country's east in Ukrainian politics have meant that Mazepa did not replace Khmel'nyts'kyi. Mazepa's name still remains anathema in many circles in Ukraine, although the presence of his likeness on the 10-hryvnia note places him officially on the national iconostasis.

6. In his article, the only work by Hrushevs'kyi that Brumberg cites is the English translation of the *Iliustrovana istoriia Ukraïny*, *History of Ukraine* (New Haven, 1941), though only for a quotation from the introduction by George Vernadsky.

7. On the importance of Hrushevs'kyi's work, see John Armstrong, "Myth and History in the Evolution of Ukrainian Consciousness," in *Ukraine and Russia in Their Historical Encounter,* ed. Peter Potichnyj et al. (Edmonton, 1992), pp. 125–39.

8. The major discussion is in John Basarab, *Pereiaslav 1654: A Historiographical Study* (Edmonton, 1982), pp. 129–33, based only on the *Istoriia Ukraïny-Rusy,* as is the report of a paper by Mykhailo Pasichnyk,

"Het'man B. Khmel'nyts'kyi u M. Hrushevs'koho," *Mykhailo Hrushevs'kyi i Zakhidna Ukraïna,* ed A. Karas' et al. (Lviv, 1995), pp. 116–18.

9. On *Istoriia Ukraïny-Rusy,* see my "Introduction to the *History of Ukraine-Rus',*" in Mykhailo Hrushevs'kyi, *History of Ukraine-Rus',* vol. 1: *From Prehistory to the Eleventh Century,* trans. Marta Skorupsky (Edmonton and Toronto, 1997), pp. xxii–lvii.

10. The possibility of banning *Istoriia Ukraïny-Rusy* was discussed by the government and secret police in Moscow as early as 1925, and a decision was made to gather information on those who were interested in the work or disseminated it. *Mykhailo Hrushevs'kyi: Mizh istoriieiu ta politykoiu (1920–1930-ti roky). Zbirnyk dokumentiv i materialiv* (Kyiv, 1997), doc. 41, p. 64.

11. Myron [Miron] Korduba, "Der Ukraine Niedergang und Aufschwung," *Zeitschrift für Osteuropäische Geschichte* 6 (1932): 30–60, 192–230, 358–85, especially pp. 377–81 (a review of Hrushevs'kyi's vols. 7–9). In a short review of both parts of volume 9 in *Literaturno-naukovyi visnyk* 106 (1931): 1029–1031, Symon Narizhnyi called chapter 13 valuable, but said that it was if not polemical, then very debatable. He maintained that the assertions and conclusions of the author were of great interest, though they called forth significant objections.

12. In addition to the works cited here, Hrushevs'kyi mentions *Pereiaslavs'ka umova* (1917); the belletristic works, "Khmel'nyts'kyi v Pereiaslavi" (1915), "Stricha z Kryvonosom" (1914), "Vykhrest Oleksandr" (1914); and his general works *Pro stari chasy na Ukraïni* (1907), *Ocherk istoriia ukrainskogo naroda* (1904, 1906, 1911; reprint: Kyiv, 1990, 1991), *Illiustrovannaia istoriia ukrainskogo naroda* (1913; reprint: Kyiv, 1996), "Istoriia ukrainskogo naroda," in *Ukrainskii narod v proshlom i nastoiashchem,* vol. 1 (1916), *Ukraïns'ka istoriia dlia serednikh shkil* (1920). Many of the belletristic works are republished in *Predok* (Kyiv, 1990). See also the historical discussion in Hrushevs'kyi's pamphlet *Khto taki ukraïntsi i choho vony khochut'* (Kyiv, 1917).

13. It was published in *Literaturno-naukovyi visnyk* 1(2) 1898: 1–26. The short story takes place against the events of the first year of the uprising, Khmel'nyts'kyi is the powerful and caring matchmaker who overcomes the opposition of Father Kyrylo Ivanovych to give his daughter Nastia in marriage to the former seminarian and now Cossack, Hryts'ko Pishchenko.

14. Hrushevs'kyi, "Khmel'nyts'kyi i Khmel'nychchyna: istorychnyi eskiz," *Zapysky Naukovoho tovarystva im. Shevchenka* 24 (1898): 1–30, reprinted in the anthology *Z politychnoho zhyttia staroï Ukraïny* (Kyiv, 1917), pp. 50–77.

15. On the individual in Hrushevs'kyi's writings, see Natalia Iakovenko, "Osoba iak diach istorychnoho protsesu v istoriohrafii Mykhaila Hrushevs'koho" in *Mykhailo Hrushevs'kyi i ukraïns'ka istorychna nauka: Materialy naukovykh konferentsii prysviachenykh Mykhailovi Hrushevs'komu,* ed. Iaroslav Hrytsak and Iaroslav Dashkevych (Lviv, 1999), pp. 86–97.

16. The article includes the traditional assertions that Khmel'nyts'kyi was in the ranks of the rebels in 1637 and that his son was killed in Daniel Czapliński's raid, views that Hrushevs'kyi later modified (pp. 3–4).

17. The problems of translating the word *narod* are formidable. In Ukrainian it embodies both the concept of a people as a nation and of the people or the masses. In early twentieth-century texts the use of *narod* and *natsiia* for "nation" at times was a conscious decision to make distinctions between different types of national communities but often was not. This article will provide the original after translation of *narod* and other similar terms.

18. "Ein interessanter Jahrestag. Ein geschichtliche Rückblick," *Ruthenische Revue* 1 (1904): 11–16; "250 lit," *Literaturno-naukovyi visnyk* 25(7) 1904: 1–6. (Citations here are to the Ukrainian version.) Reprinted in *Z politychnoho zhyttia.*

19. In his 1898 "Khmel'nyts'kyi i Khmel'nychchyna," he used the word "revolution" only in his assertion that the leaders of the Cossacks did not aim for a "social revolution" (p. 21).

20. See Maksymovych's "Pis'ma o Bogdane Khmel'nitskom" (1857–1859) in *Sobranie sochinenii M. A. Maksimovicha,* vol. 1 (Kyiv, 1876), pp. 395–474.

21. On the controversy over the monument, see Orest Levyts'kyi, "Istoriia budovy pamiatnyka B. Khmel'nyts'komu u Kyievi," *Literaturno-naukovyi visnyk* 16 (June 1913): 467–83; and M. G., "Istoriia odnogo pamiatnika," *Golos minuvshego* 1913 (7): 284–85.

22. Published in Lviv in 1905. Also see his booklet *Bohdan Chmielnicki i jego polityka* (Warsaw, n.d.).

23. Mykhailo Hrushevs'kyi, "Bohdanovi rokovyny," *Literaturno-naukovyi visnyk* 10 (1907) vol. 39: 207–212, reprinted in *Z politychnoho zhyttia.* Appearing to refer to the commemorations of 1898, Hrushevs'kyi called the attitude of Galician Ukrainians to the events of the mid-seventeenth century more straightforward, since they represented the struggle against the Poles. He maintained that for the Russian-ruled Ukrainians the depiction and the marking of the event presented more problems, presumably because of their different relations with the Poles and the role of the revolt in bringing them under Russian rule.

24. Adherents of views similar to those of Mykhailo Iuzefovych, who became a ukrainophobe and argued in the 1880s that the Khmel'nyts'kyi monument must be erected against "Ukrainian separatism."

25. (Kyiv, 1909). The edition of 1993 published in Dnipropetrovsk is used here.

26. Hrushevs'kyi was writing for a Ukrainian reader in the Russian Empire in the early twentieth century, who almost assuredly had received his or her education in Russian and had been denied access to Ukrainian printed texts for 50 years. Hrushevs'kyi demonstrated his concern for these problems by providing the Russian names for months next to their Ukrainian equivalents. He also felt obliged to explain to his readers who were used to the pejorative connotation of *zhid* in Russian that *zhyd*, not *ievrei*, was the proper, neutral form for "Jew" in Ukrainian (p. 20).

27. *Iliustrovana istoriia Ukraïny* (Kyiv–Lviv, 1913), reprinted in Kyiv in 1992. The volume has "tenth thousand" on the title page, presumably the run to that time.

28. Hrushevs'kyi, "Na ukraïns'ki temy: 'Mazepynstvo' i 'Bohdanivstvo,'" *Literaturno-naukovyi visnyk* 15(57) 1912: 94–102, reprinted in *Z politychnoho zhyttia*, pp. 117–26.

29. For Hrushevs'kyi's views on Mazepa on the occasion of the 200th anniversary of the Battle of Poltava, see his "Shveds'ko-ukraïns'kyi soiuz 1708," *Zapysky Naukovoho tovarystva im. Shevchenka* (henceforth *ZNTSh*) 92 (1909): 7–20, reprinted in *Z politychnoho zhyttia*, pp. 102–116, and "Vyhovs'kyi i Mazepa," *Literaturno-naukovyi visnyk* 12(46) 1909: 417–28.

30. Rawita-Gawroński, vol. 1: *Bohdan Chmielnicki do elekcyi Jana Kazimierza* (Lviv, 1906); and vol. 2: *Bohdan Chmielnicki od elekcyi Jana Kazimierza do śmierci* (Lviv, 1909). Ludwik Kubala, *Wojna moskiewska: Szkice historyczne, seria III* (Warsaw, 1910), pp. 1–46 (pp. 7–18 on Khmel'nyts'kyi).

31. V'iacheslav Lypyns'kyi (Wacław Lipiński), ed., *Z dziejów Ukrainy* (Kyiv and Cracow, 1912). Much of the material in *Z dziejów Ukrainy* was written by Lypyns'kyi, including the monograph *Stanisław Michał Krzyczewski: Z dziejów walki szlachty ukraińskiej w szeregach powstańczych pod wodzą Bohdana Chmielnickiego (rr. 1648–1649)*, pp. 147–513. Khmel'nyts'kyi is discussed on pp. 147–50 (evaluation) and pp. 253–61 (issue of noble descent).

32. For historians outside Soviet Ukraine who saw Khmel'nyts'kyi as a state builder, see Ivan Kryp'iakevych, "Studiï nad derzhavoiu Bohdana Khmel'nyts'koho," *ZNTSh* 138–40 (1925): 65–81; 144–45 (1926): 109–140; 147 (1927): 55–80; 151 (1931): 111–50; and Myron Korduba, "Der

Ukraine Niedergang und Aufschwung." The only exception to this tendency among members of the statist school was Stepan Tomashivs'kyi. After the failure to establish Ukrainian independence and the revolutionary events of the period, his conservative politics resulted in his questioning whether Khmel'nyts'kyi was an appropriate hero. He advocated heroes of the earlier princely epoch. He also argued for seeing the Zaporozhians who followed Mazepa—rather than the hetman and elite of the Hetmanate, whom Lypyns'kyi praised—as the heroes of 1709. His negative evaluation was strengthened by his Catholic convictions that caused him to disapprove of Khmel'nyts'kyi's attack on the Uniates. He entered into a bitter historical polemic with his fellow conservative thinker Lypyns'kyi over these questions. See Stepan Tomashivs'kyi, *Pro ideï heroïv i polityku: Vidkrytyi lyst do V. Lypyns'koho z dodatkamy* (Lviv, 1929), especially pp. 29–35. On the influence of the statist school on historians in Soviet Ukraine, see Lev Okinshevych, "Heneral'na rada na Ukraïni-Het'manshchyni XVII–XVIII st.," *Pratsi Komisiï dlia vyuchuvannia istoriï zakhidno-rus'koho prava* 6 (1929): 253–425; idem, "Tsentral'ni ustanovy Ukraïny-Het'manshchyny XVII–XVIII st. Ch. II. Rada starshyny," *Pratsi Komisiï dlia vyuchuvannia istoriï zakhidno-rus'koho prava* 8 (1930): 1–349; idem, "Rada starshyns'ka na Het'manshchyni," *Ukraïna* 4 (1924): 12–26 (these studies are reworked in his *Ukrainian Society and Government [1648–1782]* [Munich, 1978]); and Mykola Petrovs'kyi, "Do istoriï derzhavnoho ustroiu Ukraïny XVII v.," *Zapysky Nizhens'koho pedlahohichnoho instytutu* 11 (1931): 87–97.

33. Mykhailo Hrushevs'kyi, *Istoriia Ukraïny-Rusy,* vol. 8, pt. 2 (reprint: New York, 1956), p. 223.

34. Hrushevs'kyi, *Istoriia Ukraïny-Rusy,* vol. 8, pt. 2, pp. 162–63.

35. On Hrushevs'kyi's life and career in Soviet Ukraine, see R. Ia. Pyrih, *Zhyttia Mykhaila Hrushevs'koho: Ostannie desiatylittia (1924–1934)* (Kyiv, 1993).

36. On Hrushevs'kyi as a "historian-sociologist," see Leo Bilas, "Geschichtsphilosophische und ideologische Voraussetzungen der geschichtlichen und politischen Konzeption M. Hruševśkyjs. Zum 90. Geburtstag des ukrainischen Historikers (29 September 1956)," *Jahrbücher für Geschichte Osteuropas* N.S. 4 (1956): 262–92; Illia Vytanovych, "Uvahy do metodolohiï i istoriosofiï Mykhaila Hrushevs'koho," *Ukraïns'kyi istoryk* 3(1–2) 1966: 48–51; Omeljan [Omelian] Pritsak, "Istoriosofiia Mykhaila Hrushevs'koho," in Mykhailo Hrushevs'kyi, *Istoriia Ukraïny-Rusy,* vol. 1 (reprint: Kyiv, 1991), pp. xl–lxxiii.

37. Hrushevs'kyi, *Istoriia Ukraïny-Rusy,* vol. 9, pt. 2 (reprint: New York, 1956), pp. 1497–1506, including criticism of Lypyns'kyi's views.

38. It was in the notes to this section that Hrushevs'kyi mentioned the importance of Lypyns'kyi in studying at least the noble colleagues of Khmel'-nyts'kyi (p. 1485).

39. *Ukraïna na perelomi: Zamitky do istoriï ukraïns'koho derzhavnoho budivnytstva v XVII-im stolittiu* (Vienna, 1920), pp. 145–51, and also p. 121 on the goal of building a European state. On Hrushevs'kyi's scholarly and political contacts with Lypyns'kyi, see Pavlo Sokhan and Ihor Hyrych, "V'iacheslav Lypyns'kyi i Mykhailo Hrushevs'kyi u dorevoliutsiini chasy," in *V'iacheslav Lypyns'kyi: Studiï*, vol. 1: *Istoryko-politolohichna spadshchyna i suchasna Ukraïna*, ed. Iaroslav Pelens'kyi (Kyiv and Philadelphia, 1994), pp. 53–59; and Ihor Hyrych, "Derzhavnyts'kyi napriam i narodnyts'ka shkola v ukraïns'kii istoriohrafiï (na tli stosunkiv Mykhaila Hrushevs'koho i V'iacheslava Lypyns'koho)," in *Mykhailo Hrushevs'kyi i ukraïns'ka istorychna nauka*, pp. 47–64.

40. For Hrushevs'kyi's views on the need for the intelligentsia to work among the peasant masses, see his speech of 3 October 1926 at the celebration of his sixtieth birthday, *Mykhailo Hrushevs'kyi mizh istoriieiu ta politykoiu*, doc. 52, pp. 72–77.

41. For a discussion of the Khmel'nyts'kyi uprising as a revolution by the major Ukrainian Marxist historian of the 1920s, see Matvii Iavors'kyi, *Narys istoriï Ukraïny,* 2 vols. (Adelaide, 1986), vol. 2, pp. 65–139. For a discussion of the concept and use of the term "revolution" for the Khmel'nyts'kyi uprising, see Frank E. Sysyn, "War der Chmel'nyćkyj-Aufstand eine Revolution? Eine Charakteristik der "grossen ukrainischen Revolte" und der Bildung des kosakischen Het'manstaates," *Jahrbücher für Geschichte Osteuropas* 43(1) 1995: 1–18.

42. For the Marxist attack on Hrushevs'kyi, including his terminology, see the review article by F. Iastrebov, "Tomu dev'iatoho persha polovyna," *Prapor marksyzmu* 9: 133–48.

43. See Frank E. Sysyn, "Cossack Chronicles and the Development of Modern Ukrainian Culture and Identity," *Harvard Ukrainian Studies* 14(3–4) 1990: 593–607.

44. V. A. Smolii and V. S. Stepankov, *Bohdan Khmel'nyts'kyi: Sotsial'no-politychnyi portret* (Kyiv, 1993); and their *Bohdan Khmel'nyts'kyi: Khronika zhyttia ta diial'nosti* (Kyiv, 1994). See also the special issue of *Ukraïns'kyi istorychnyi zhurnal,* 1995, no. 4, especially the lead article by V. A. Smolii.

Ernest Gellner and the "Constructivist" Theory of Nation

ANDRZEJ WALICKI

The late Ernest Gellner (1925–1995) formulated one of the most widely known and influential theories of the nation and nationalism. His concept has become very popular, mainly because of his thesis that nations are products of nationalism, and not vice versa. It concurs with the current "constructivist" perspective which claims that nations are not anything real, objective, or indispensable; they are only "constructs," contingent and artificial, deliberately created by various elites. Thus we cannot speak of the process of "awakening" nations to conscious life, as such an approach is defined as "preconstructivist simple-mindedness" which presumes that nations did exist in the objective sense and just waited to be "awakened."

The opponents of "constructivism" are usually referred to as "primordialists" or "essentialists." It is, however, evident that although the term makes argument much easier, it largely distorts the essence of the dispute. In order to oppose "constructivism," one does not have to go so far as to claim that nations are "perennial" and possess "invariable essence"; it is enough to recognize that they have a sociological reality as permanent products of objective and spontaneous historical processes.

In order to understand the specific nature of Gellner's views, as well as the intellectual climate in which his views have been received, it is worthwhile to examine contructivism in its consistent and extreme form. It is well exemplified in an article by the American author Rogers Brubaker, "Nation as Institutionalized Form, Practical Category, Contingent Event."[1]

According to Brubaker, nations are not by any means "enduring components of social structure"; they are constructed, contingent and fluctuating, they are "illusory or spurious communities," and an "ideological smoke-screen." The very question "What is a nation?" is not innocent, as it assumes, quite mistakenly, "substantialist belief" in the existence of nations. What is real is nationalism, but it is not a product or function of nations.[2] If it proved to be a powerful force in the period of the collapse of the USSR, it was not because nations had survived on its territory. The reason was that the communist regime had provided ready-made forms for nationalism by having divided the state into national republics and introduced nationality as a category in identity papers for its citizens.

I would not claim that Brubaker's evident aversion to the concept of nation is typical of "constructivist" literature. What is typical of it, however, is the profound skepticism and apprehension with which strong national identities are viewed.

The skepticism of the "constructivists" concerning clearly defined and unquestionably accepted national identities follows mainly from the fact that they describe this phenomenon from the outside, and have no personal internal experience of it. The most prominent constructivists (including Gellner, who was brought up in Czechoslovakia) are mainly either migrants, who know more about changing identity than about inherited identity, or Americans—that is, members of a nation that consists of migrants and easily gives up a specific national and cultural identity (which is best manifested in the U.S. by the mainstream endorsement of the philosophy of "multiculturalism").[3] The experience of such people is in some respects richer, and in some respects more restricted than the experience of "naive nationalists" from the "backward" parts of Europe. It is not surprising, therefore, that when they confront a Pole, for example, who is deeply convinced that the division into nations is obvious and natural, they ask themselves a question about who lacks what: Do they themselves lack an experience of some essential dimension of human existence, or does that Pole lack criticism, reflection, and knowledge? It is only human, if certainly regrettable, that in such a situation they choose a biased answer that favors their own position, and do not attempt any emphatic understanding and weighing up of arguments.

Apprehension of national identity as something "given" which defines an individual automatically, is, on the other hand, characteristic of the postmodern frame of mind, shared by many Western intellectuals. This frame of mind values mostly the autonomy of the individual and the ability to make various choices, so it must be apprehensive of an identity that is deeply rooted and that provides one with certainty, but at the same time does not leave any room for free self-determination. It prefers an identity which is "constructed," "made up," "contingent," and "fluctuating," an identity which can be deliberately shaped and changed, and which is therefore incompatible with the concept of a nation as an inevitable "commonly shared fate."

However, to return to Gellner: on closer examination we can see that the reception of his views is often superficial, selective, and contrary to his intentions. After all, he was very critical of postmodernism, to say nothing of the doctrine of "political correctness." It will be demonstrated that his views on nationalism were in fact fairly distant from the stereotypes of anti-nationalist liberalism. It seems that his position has been increasingly better understood; recently, the attitude of the typical representatives of "constructivist consensus" to Gellner's works has become demonstrably reserved and much more reticent than in the 1980s.

The most important differences between Gellner's theory and the prevalent version of "constructivist consensus" concerning research on nations and nationalisms may be formulated as follows:

First, his questioning of the real character of nations and his claim that no definite nation can demonstrate that its existence is determined by inner objective necessity do not lead, in Gellner's view, to questioning the objective necessity and historical validity of *nationalism*, which is a process that accompanies the transformation of agrarian societies into industrial ones. Just the opposite: specific nations are, according to Gellner, *contingent*, constructed in a more or less arbitrary way, while nationalism—defined as a force shaping homogeneous and centrally directed social cultures and striving to establish political boundaries congruent with cultural boundaries—is a *necessary* aspect of the modernization process. Belief in the sociological reality as well as in the natural and perennial character of a nation is an ideological illusion; nevertheless nationalism is a necessary phenomenon as it expresses "the inevitable process of mutual adjustment of state and culture." It does not result from ideological aberration but from the specific structural needs of industrial society.[4]

In other words, although Gellner strikes a blow at nationalist mythologies, he does not consider it to be tantamount to the de-legitimization of nationalism itself. On the contrary, he emphasizes the fact that those mythologies are only a fallacious apprehension on the part of nationalists, which has very little in common with the actual historical function of nation-forming movements. He defines nationalism in a different way from nationalists, yet—contrary to the prevailing version of liberal anti-nationalism—he legitimizes nationalism in recognizing it as one of the necessary factors that create "a more homogenous humankind."[5] He firmly opposes the illusion that nationalism is in fact an intellectual aberration that can be eliminated by appropriate pedagogical procedures.

Second, contrary to appearances, Gellner does not support the popular opinion which holds as relevant Renan's "voluntarist" concept of nation, which defines a nation as an expression of conscious self-identification and the continually renewed will to co-exist in a particular community. He considers this definition too broad, as it may be applied to all types of associations, such as clubs, parties, and even gangs.[6] The volition factor plays an important role in shaping each particular nation, yet volition appears in the circumstances defined by general rules that govern the modernization process. Nations are not social realities, they do not emerge from "natural" preexisting ethnic differences, and are not deeply rooted in the human mental makeup; but this does not mean that they are products of freely associated individuals, independent from the general rules of "the epoch of nationalism."

It seems that Gellner emphasizes his objection to one-sided voluntarism in comprehending nation more in his later works. Defying the illusion of democratic voluntarism, he declares clearly that institutions and cultures, and thus nations as well, are rather our fate than our choice. Also, he explains that the thesis that nationalism creates nations is not tantamount to the statement that the formation of nations is the result of nationalist propaganda; in fact, nationalists do not create nations, for they are actually created by nationalism, which is a historical process and an essential aspect of the transformation from agrarianism to industrialism.

Third, Gellner's theory cannot be reconciled with the ideology of multiculturalism which is very fashionable with the "constructivists" and widely accepted in the United States. Gellner dismisses the thesis formulated by Elie Kedourie which argues that the homogenization of culture is artificial and imposed by the perfidious and power-hungry nationalists;[7] he challenges it with the opinion that what is reflected in nationalism is "the objective need for homogeneity."[8] This need results from the fact that the modern state requires its population to be mobile, standardized in the cultural sense, and internally interchangeable. Thus, if its boundaries do not correspond with the area of a fairly homogeneous national culture, either they should be changed or cultural assimilation should be deliberately imposed on ethnic minorities.[9]

As we can see, Gellner's concept concurs with the argument of the Polish integral nationalist Roman Dmowski, who claimed that the modern state "always assimilates tribes which are alien in the political and cultural sense," and that always and everywhere, it aims more or less deliberately at "creating a culture of unity."[10] On the other hand, Gellner's concept is firmly opposed to the view that an exclusively political and culturally neutral nationalism is possible—a nationalism which may be reconciled with programmatic multiculturalism. Such a view is promoted by Liah Greenfeld, who presents the United States as a model of "civic nationalism."[11] It is worth mentioning here that Gellner's theory of nationalism does not consider the United States at all, and does not even attempt to explain it.

Fourth and lastly, Gellner deliberately distances himself from moralism, adopting an attitude which the younger generation of academics has associated with the morally questionable Victorian scientism. This is pointedly demonstrated by the philosophical equanimity with which he discusses ethnic cleansing and forcible population transfers. "To conform to the nationalist imperative," he argues, "was bound to take more than a few battles and some diplomacy . . . In many cases it was also bound to involve population exchanges or expulsions, more or less forcible assimilation, and sometimes liquidation, in order to attain that close relation between state and culture which is the essence of nationalism. And all these consequences followed, not from some unusual brutality of the nationalists who in the end employed these measures (they were probably no worse and no better than anyone else), but from the inescapable logic of the situation."[12]

If we assume "the objective need for homogeneity"—with the resulting view that "nationalism as such is fated to prevail"[13]—it sounds pessimistic indeed, if not sinister.

However, why should we regard cultural homogeneity as an objective need for the purposes of development, a kind of historical necessity? In answering this question, Gellner lists characteristic differences between the traditional agrarian society and modern industrial society. In the former, people are assigned specific social roles and bound to specific local communities; therefore it is a society segmented, diversified as far as language and culture are concerned—a society which does not have any need for intensive social communication. On the other hand, the industrial society requires a mobile and literate population, culturally standardized and internally interchangeable. Indispensable to it is the equal access of the whole population to a homogeneous high culture, disseminated by schools, and the national written language which serves to formulate precise statements understandable beyond the immediate situational context. Yet each high culture which permeates a whole population needs political support and reinforcement. According to Gellner, nationalism and its historical legitimacy result from this fact.

Developing this concept further, Gellner formulates a thesis that the emergence of homogeneous national societies is largely tantamount to the process of forming a modern civil society. This is obviously contrary to the view (which is particularly popular in Germany and Poland) that the ideal civil society excludes all forms of nationalism. Gellner maintains, however, with deliberate provocation, that members of the civil society must be nationalists up to a point[14]—for civic equality requires cultural equality, and thus it requires that all language and cultural differences be erased. If we want equal opportunity, equal access to jobs, and thus liberation from being assigned specific social roles in life, we must accept the situation in which the population of a state consists of anonymous citizens, comparable as far as their basic cultural assets are concerned, and not of culturally diverse social groups and static local communities.[15]

Thus Gellner's theory of nationalism is a part of his general theory of social modernization. It is both its great advantage and its weakness; it helps to understand the broadly defined "modernity," yet it is of little use in explaining particular nation-making processes. Gellner is a theoretician who employs categories too broad to deal with the history of specific societies and countries.[16] When he discusses transformation from agrarian society to industrial society, he pays no attention to peasant emancipation and enfranchisement, a fact of crucial significance for shaping modern nations which was hardly ever the direct result of industrialization. He does not appreciate the continuity between modern nationalism and territorial patriotism, as well as the historical consciousness of agrarian societies, or at least of their elites. Having defined different "time zones" in Europe, he regards all countries in East Central Europe as lacking their own "high cultures" and political traditions;[17] he displays thereby total ignorance of Polish history, and passes over the traditional division of the nations of that region into "historical" nations (i.e., those which had their own "upper class," fully shaped literary language, and strong traditions of functioning as a state) and "non-historical" nations (which lacked all of these assets).[18]

However, the theory of nationalism as a function of modernization in fact provides little support for the "constructivist" theories of nation. It completely disregards the importance of nationalist ideologies and, by the same token, the role of nationalist intellectuals.[19] It points out the connection between nationalism and the processes of cultural homogenization, but does not explain why those processes have often resulted in the victory of weaker cultures which had eliminated or marginalized stronger ones. It attempts to interpret the origin of nations without considering the ethnic factor, yet in fact it tacitly assumes that this factor exists.

Let us examine, for example, the process of forming the modern Czech nation. In the late eighteenth century, Czechs lacked not only their own state, but also their own "historical class" and their own "high culture." Thus it was only natural that the reforms of enlightened absolutism aimed at making German the only language of state administration and at homogenizing education by making it German, at least above the local level. If we assume that nations are "contingent" and invented, we are unable to explain why the inevitable cultural homogenization, emphasized so forcefully by Gellner, did not result in the complete Germanization of the Czech lands. It can be explained, however, if we assume that the Czech people did exist in the objective sense, which was not yet a nation but which possessed a kind of collective identity and therefore was able to resist Germanization. In spite of the great role which historical fiction played in the process of forming Czech national consciousness, the emergence of the Czech nation was an impressive process of grass-roots social evolution (*vide* Hroch),[20] and not the result of ideological manipulations by a handful of influential philologists, historians, and literary men. German theoreticians and writers (including Marx and Engels) persisted in disregarding that process and maintained that the Czech nation was the invention of eccentric Slav scholars, and had no place in the modern world anyway. The doubtful validity of such theories, which were presented with amazing confidence as late as the Spring of the Nations (1848),[21] should caution us against regarding nations as ideological "constructs" that lack sociological reality and their inner dynamics of growth.

What is particularly valuable in Gellner's model is that it has presented nationalism and liberalism as historical forces that are complementary and which both shape the reality in which we live—the reality of a civil society in a national state. This cognitive perspective does not support the stereotypes of liberal anti-nationalism which dominate in the *reception* of Gellner's theory. It provides arguments for the possible emergence of *liberal nationalism*, clearly different from the nationalist fundamentalisms that now pose the most serious threat to the liberal societies. Yet even such a possibility demonstrates how the strong points of Gellner's theory are organically bound to its numerous weaknesses. The most important of these weaknesses is its total inability to explain national identity as a spiritual phenomenon, rooted in centuries-old history and irreducible to the process of social and economic modernization. Therefore,

Gellner's theory does not facilitate our comprehension of those forms of nationalism which are a very real problem indeed in the modern world: religious nationalism and, naturally, anti-liberal integral nationalism. Moreover, Gellner's theory has no predictive value as it does not answer the question: What will nationalism be like in circumstances of economic globalization and the expansion of supranational communities, and particularly, of the European Union?

It is worth noticing that Gellner kept modifying his theory and did not rule out any serious revaluations. Toward the end of his life he became increasingly doubtful about the symbiosis of nationalism and liberalism within national states. In 1964, he recognized nationalism as an ally of liberalism,[22] yet in the 1990s he was unenthusiastic about the multiplication of national states in the aftermath of the collapse of the USSR. Quite the opposite: in a lecture on nationalism given in 1994 at the Moscow School of Politics, he argued that it would be much better if aspirations for national self-determination were expressed not in terms of separatism, but in terms of extraterritorial autonomy.[23] It was an unexpected turn back to the ideas with which the Austro-Marxists tried to preserve the multinational Habsburg Empire. As it is easy to see, it had no justification in the theory which claims that nationalism is an inseparable part of modernization, and that the only solution to the problem is the congruence of the cultural and political borders.

NOTES

1. Rogers Brubaker, "Rethinking Nationhood: Nation as Institutionalized Form, Practical Category, Contingent Event," *Contention: Debates in Society, Culture, and Science* 4(1) Fall 1994: 3–14.

2. Ibid., pp. 3–5.

3. See Michael Lind, "Are We a Nation?" *Dissent* Summer 1995: 355–67.

4. Ernest Gellner, *Nations and Nationalism* (Ithaca and London, 1983), p. 39.

5. Ernest Gellner, *Plough, Sword and Book: The Structure of Human History* (Chicago, 1988), pp. 262–63.

6. Gellner, *Nations and Nationalism*, pp. 53–54.

7. In fact, Gellner's theory was adequately described as a theory of *monoculturalism.* See Damian Tambini, "Explaining Monoculturalism: Beyond Gellner's Theory of Nationalism," *Critical Review: An Interdisciplinary Journal of Politics and Society* 10(2) Spring 1996: 251–70.

8. Ibid., pp. 39, 46.

9. In his *Conditions of Liberty*, Gellner presented cultural assimilation as a voluntary choice—to diminish the "discomfort" which arises from the lack of cultural homogeneity. See Ernest Gellner, *Conditions of Liberty: Civil Society and Its Rivals* (New York, 1994), p. 108.

10. Roman Dmowski, "Podstawy polityki polskiej" (1905) in *Narodowa Demokracja: Antologia myśli politycznej "Przeglądu Wszechpolskiego"1895–1905*, ed. Barbara Toruńczyk (London, 1983), p. 230.

11. See Liah Greenfeld, *Nationalism: Five Roads to Modernity* (Cambridge, MA, 1992), p. 484.

12. Gellner, *Nations and Nationalism*, pp. 100–101.

13. Ibid., p. 47.

14. Gellner, *Conditions of Liberty*, ch. 13.

15. Ibid., pp. 104–105.

16. In a polemic with Roman Szporluk, Gellner did not hesitate to assert that in order to understand nationalism, "the nature of industrialism contains all the premises we need." This amounted, of course, to a conscious defense of a crudely reductionist standpoint. See Ernest Gellner, *Encounters with Nationalism* (Oxford, 1994), p. 11.

17. Ibid., p. 30.

18. The term "non-historical" is, admittedly, unfortunate and misleading, but the distinction between nations with or without their own upper classes, developed literary languages, and state tradition is, nevertheless, empiri-

cally valid and very important. See Ivan L. Rudnytsky, "Observations on the Problem of 'Historical' and 'Non-Historical' Nations," in Ivan L. Rudnytsky, *Essays in Modern Ukrainian History*, ed. Peter L. Rudnytsky (Cambridge, MA, 1987), pp. 37–48. A good summary of the differences between the two types of nations is contained also in Konstantin Symmons-Symonolewicz, *Nationalist Movements: A Comparative View* (Meadville, PA, 1970), pp. 22–23. See also Miroslav Hroch, *Social Preconditions of National Revival in Europe* (Cambridge, 1985), pp. 8–10.

19. This aspect of Gellner's theory of nationalism has been subject to a thorough criticism by Roman Szporluk. See Roman Szporluk, *Communism and Nationalism: Karl Marx Versus Friedrich List* (New York and Oxford, 1988), chs. 6 and 10 (direct reference to Gellner on p. 79).

20. Hroch, *Social Preconditions*, ch. 9.

21. See Roman Rosdolsky, *Engels and the "Non-Historical" Peoples: The National Question in the Revolution of 1848*, ed. and trans. John-Paul Himka (Glasgow, 1987).

22. See Ernest Gellner, *Thought and Change* (London, 1964).

23. See Ernest Gellner, "Lektsiia o natsionalizme," *Vestnik Moskovskoi shkoly politicheskikh issledovanii* 1995 (4): 47.

Old-Fashioned Slavs at Carnival in Venice:
The Dramatic Dilemma of Eastern Europe

LARRY WOLFF

At the Teatro Sant'Angelo in Venice, during the carnival season of 1793, a drama was performed entitled *Gli Antichi Slavi,* about the "ancient" or "old-fashioned" Slavs. The author Camillo Federici, born in 1749 under the name of Giovanni Battista Viassolo, was not Venetian, but came from the other side of northern Italy, from Piedmontese Liguria. In 1787 he established himself in Padua, and during the remaining 10 years before the abolition of the Venetian republic, Federici had a successful career as a dramatist on the stages of Padua and Venice.[1] In *Gli Antichi Slavi* he set his drama in the Dalmatian mountains, a scenario of particular interest to the Venetian public, for Dalmatia was the most significant remnant of Venice's overseas empire, the *oltremare,* beyond the Adriatic. Venice had ruled over an empire of Slavs in Dalmatia continuously from the early fifteenth century, and intermittently from the early eleventh century; during the eighteenth century, under the aegis of the Venetian Enlightenment, purposeful political attentions were applied to the problems of creating a modern imperial administration and a profitably integrated national economy that made the most of Dalmatia's subjects and resources. At the same time, the European Enlightenment discovered the Slavs as a category of classification that gave anthropological and ethnographic coherence to the idea of Eastern Europe. The intellectual landmark for this discovery of the Slavs was Herder's *Ideas for the Philosophy of the History of Mankind,* whose first part appeared in 1784. The fourth part was published in 1791 and identified the "Slavic peoples" living in an area "from the Don to the Elbe, from the Baltic to the Adriatic," which constituted "the most monstrous region of earth which in Europe one nation for the most part inhabits still today."[2] This monstrous region touched on the Venetian republic at its Adriatic corner, and Herder's anthropological interest also touched upon the theme of Federici's drama of 1793: the survival of ancient customs among the old-fashioned Slavs of contemporary Dalmatia. This coincidence of concerns between philosophy in Weimar and carnival in Venice testified to the important role of the Venetian Enlightenment in the cultural discovery of the Slavs and the philosophical delineation of Eastern Europe.

The most important dramatic representation of Dalmatians in eighteenth-century Venetian theater was Carlo Goldoni's play, *La Dalmatina,* performed at the Teatro San Luca in 1758. The Dalmatian hero Radovich rescued the

Dalmatian heroine Zandira from Moroccan captivity by Barbary corsairs. Radovich was a valorous Venetian patriot—"I have my Lion in my breast" (*ho il mio Leone in petto*)—and Goldoni made his Dalmatians proud to be among "the fortunate peoples of the Adriatic empire" (*dell'Adriaco impero popoli fortunati*).[3] The pioneering research on the Slavs of Dalmatia was presented to the public of Venice in the *Viaggio in Dalmazia*, written by Alberto Fortis about his voyage in Dalmatia, and published in 1774. Fortis wrote anthropologically about the customs of the Morlacchi, the inland pastoral inhabitants of the mountains who lived along the border between Venetian Dalmatia and Ottoman Bosnia. He rejected the common conception of the Morlacchi as ferocious barbarians, and wrote instead in sensitive appreciation of their primitive customs, which, in the enlightened spirit of Rousseau, he found to be sometimes superior to those of "the society that we call civilized." He also recognized that the Morlacchi, who spoke a Slavic language, belonged to a larger community of Slavs, together with "so many other nations resembling them in customs and in language in such a manner that they can be taken for one sole nation, vastly extended from our sea to the glacial ocean," from the Adriatic to the Arctic. Fortis found resemblances of custom that linked Dalmatia to Ukraine. He discussed, for instance, the marital customs among the Morlacchi, the general interest in the sexual consummation of the marriage, which was sometimes announced with a pistol shot, and the communal concern if the bride were discovered not to be a virgin. Fortis remarked: "They do not make as much noise as in similar cases the Ukrainians, from whom our Morlacchi are in this instance a little different, although in general they have between them a very great conformity of clothing, of customs, of dialect, and even of orthography."[4] In this perceived "conformity" Fortis found an anthropological pattern that made Slavdom the key to contemplating Eastern Europe as a coherent geographical region.

Fortis's recognition that the Morlacchi of inland Dalmatia were related to other Slavic peoples by language and customs received further elaboration in a novel that appeared in 1788, *Les Morlaques*, written in French by the Venetian writer Giustiniana Wynne, the countess of Orsini-Rosenberg. Her anthropological novel was also a sentimental love story, which took its details of custom from Fortis's account. She described the Morlacchi in love, as well as the Morlacchi in a crisis of identity, suddenly recognizing themselves as Slavs, in fraternal relation to the Russians, and therefore implicated in the military victories of Catherine the Great against the Ottoman Empire. Fortis in his travel account, as well as Wynne in her novel, appreciated that the Slavs of Dalmatia were anthropologically linked to a larger Slavic domain, and such concerns thus anticipated and paralleled those of the German Enlightenment. Herder was definitely interested in Fortis's transcriptions and translations of Slavic folk poetry; Goethe read Wynne's novel with interest. Federici's drama of 1793, *Gli Antichi Slavi,* was thus composed and performed in the context of enlightened Venetian interest in the significance of Slavic customs.

*　　*

*

The Morlacchi were recognized as an ethnographic category in the eighteenth century, and became, in fact, well known to the European Enlightenment as Fortis was translated into English, French, and German. Over the course of the nineteenth century the Morlacchi were reclassified according to the ongoing ethnographic sorting of the South Slavs, until today they may be considered completely extinct. In the Habsburg censuses of the nineteenth century they were identified as Serbo-Croatian by language, and in twentieth-century Yugoslavia they seem to have been separated into Serbs and Croats according to religious affiliation. In Federici's drama the Morlacchi were already being reconceived simply as Slavs, the most primitive sort, characterized by their tenacious preservation of ancient customs. Indeed, the dramatist claimed a certain anthropological authenticity for his work, and the preface to Federici's published edition remarked that, in the performance of *Gli Antichi Slavi*, "the national customs and character were exactly maintained." The setting was geographically precise: mountain cliffs, caverns, and streams, in the region of the Cetina River.[5] The character and customs of the ancient or old-fashioned Slavs were none other than the character and customs of the Morlacchi, as investigated by the Venetians during the eighteenth century.

The main characters were romantic rivals: an old-fashioned Slav named Dusmanich, from the mountains, with his sword in hand, and a new-fashioned Slav named Serizca, from the Adriatic coast, in Italian clothes with Italian manners. (These appellations, "Dusmanich" and "Serizca," were Federici's Italian selection and spelling of Slavic names.) Both were in love with the same Dalmatian heroine, Elena, costumed in a red cap as a token of her virginity, a detail that would have been familiar to the public from Fortis's account of customs. The old-fashioned Slavs, like Dusmanich, despised foreign customs and influences. He slept outdoors, on the ground, and did not covet greater comfort: "Our fathers had no better or more delicate bed. Now commerce with foreigners has enervated the posterity of the strong, and degraded the nation." Federici had no doubt that these Slavs constituted a sort of "nation," and that the coherence of their national community was consolidated by their old-fashioned customs. Dusmanich was even proudly illiterate, and rejected the notion that reading is a "necessary" science: "This [indicates sword] is the science of the Morlacchi. There is none other among us, except to obey our sovereigns and defend our country."[6] Dusmanich thus combined the Dalmatian patriotism of Goldoni's Radovich with the primitive customs of Fortis's Morlacchi. The obligatory patriotic flourish naturally referred to San Marco, when it was recited on the Venetian stage in 1793; by the time the play was published in Venice in 1819, however, Dalmatia was ruled by a Habsburg sovereign in Vienna, and the unelaborated reference could be interpreted accordingly.

The critic Arturo Cronia has described *Gli Antichi Slavi* as "the boldest interpretation of Fortisian *morlacchismo*," appealing for its success to the *morlaccomania* of the Venetian public.[7] It was Fortis's publication of *Viaggio in Dalmazia* in 1774 which had sparked this "mania" of interest in the Morlacchi, and Federici appeared to be familiar with the principal themes of that work. Dusmanich proclaimed himself an old-fashioned Slav from the very beginning of the play by his ungallant attitude toward women, an attitude that Fortis had found among the Morlacchi 20 years before. The old-fashioned Slav had never set eyes upon the woman he was supposed to marry, and explained himself to his friend: "You, Slav, you who are like me of noble descent from the Geti and the Scythians, you ask me if I have lowered myself to the weakness of contemplating a woman?" He believed that to set eyes upon his promised spouse would make him "effeminate," and, when told that all other men gaze upon their brides before the wedding, he declared them all "degenerate." *Morlacchismo* was most emphatically *machismo*, as Dusmanich defined himself on the Venetian stage:

> Shall I imitate the custom of the Italians and the French, who make idols of their women, who basely bend the knee and adore their own slaves? For me it is enough to know that she is the daughter of a robust and fertile mother and of a valorous father. I marry to immortalize my posterity. If not for that I would live free, friend only of my name and my sword. The daughter of such parents will perpetuate the heroes of my descent, with arms always in hand in the service of my prince.[8]

While Fortis philosophically called into question the customs of "the society that we call civilized," Federici ultimately flattered the Venetians by representing their own civilized gallantry from the perspective of a primitive Morlacco. Of course, it is possible that Venetian men and Venetian women interpreted the misogyny of Dusmanich differently, according to the divergent perspectives of the gendered public.

The female public, at least, must have sympathized with the heroine, Elena, in her reluctance to marry Dusmanich in spite of the recommendation of her father, Marcovich:

> Marcovich: You are near to becoming the wife of the most valorous man of our nation. Our country is proud of his name, and its enemies tremble within.
>
> Elena: That means I shall be the slave of a ferocious man.
>
> Marcovich: No, love will make him gentle and humane with you. I told you he was valorous, not barbarous (*valoroso, non barbaro*).[9]

The Venetian ideal of the loyal and valorous Dalmatian subject was complicated by the ferocious reputation of the Morlacchi. At the same time, this alleged ferocity gave the Adriatic empire a civilizing mission which was elaborately articulated within the Venetian Enlightenment. In this context, *Gli*

Antichi Slavi dramatized the proposition that love might bring about a transformation of the barbarous male Morlacco, civilize him, endow him with humanity. The valorous-not-barbarous Dalmatian was the model Venetian subject.

Dusmanich, however, despised the civilized coastal Dalmatian even before meeting him, even without realizing that Serizca would turn out to be his romantic rival. Marcovich informed Dusmanich that they were awaiting a visitor:

> Dusmanich: Who is this man?
>
> Marcovich: Someone who has Italian clothes and Italian manners.
>
> Dusmanich: Enough. And this is the friend you boast of? A weak man, the slave of pleasures, a foreigner?
>
> Marcovich: Do not condemn so freely the apparent softness of our neighbors. We despise them wrongly. They have virtues different from ours, but their own virtues, of their climate and education . . . Let me add that he was born in this glorious country, and has only the appearance of a foreigner . . . [10]

So when Dusmanich, the mountain Morlacco, finally came face to face with his coastal counterpart, Serizca, the Dalmatian with Italian manners and clothes, the antithesis was already established. Dusmanich still pretended to suppose that his rival was a foreigner—but Serizca replied, "Your country is my country. I was born here, and I too share the honor of your nation."[11] Federici thus staged a public debate about what constituted a true Dalmatian, between the old-fashioned Slav and the newly fashionable Slav. Both parts were, presumably, taken by Italian actors.

Dusmanich spoke first, making the case for the primitive virtues of the Morlacchi, comparing his own stage costume to that of his rival:

> Look at you and me, from head to toe. Where are your native clothes, the glorious insignia of a valorous people? . . . Oh my country, look upon a son who disfigures you, who renounces the hair that nature gave him and adorns his head with ornaments of women, of barbarous and dishonest habits. His hair, his countenance, announce the softness and slavery of pleasure. The heavy, shining sword no longer hangs at his side . . . Oh my prince, shining star, my defense, my deity, remove if you can this shame from my country; make the degenerate sons put on again the insignia of their elders, and strike down these rebels. I pray you with my head prostrate in the dust, in the name of your justice and the glory of my nation.[12]

The old-fashioned Slav was thus recognizable on stage by his old-fashioned costume, and presented the case for clinging to old customs in the face of modern fashions. He sustained the ideology of the Adriatic empire by his insistent synthesis of the glory of his Slavic nation with reverent loyalty to Venice. Indeed, he appealed to his Venetian prince on behalf of the nation, just as he presented his case to the Venetian public in the audience.

Serizca, however, was unintimidated by the insults of Dusmanich, and defended his own Dalmatian identity by affirming his extravagant loyalty to Venice.

> I will not blush before you at such an accusation. I want to have the strength to pity you, because you, restricted within the confines of these horrible crags, do not know that this respectable uniform is dedicated like yours to the service of the same government . . . Ask the most courageous enemies of my country, and they will tell you that they have seen me the first in every intrepid encounter to oppose my own breast to their desperate blows, in defence of my just and beloved prince.[13]

In an age of Venetian neutrality it might have been difficult to determine just when Serizca found the opportunity to engage in such valiant combat against the enemies of San Marco. Federici, however, clearly affirmed before the Venetian public that Venice still commanded the absolute loyalty of both primitive Morlacchi and civilized coastal Dalmatians. Indeed, Serizca's speech seemed to suggest that Venice could confidently decide to civilize the Morlacchi without fear of attenuating their ferocious patriotism. Federici proposed the formula of "valorous-not-barbarous" to sum up Venice's civilizing mission in Dalmatia.

"If you call yourself a Slav, put your valor to the test," cried Dusmanich, challenging his rival, and, at the same time, addressing the fundamental issue of identity concerning Venetian Dalmatia. Fortis studied the Morlacchi and called them Slavs; Wynne wondered what it might mean for them to call themselves Slavs, to discover a Slavic identity that transcended the borders of the Republic. Federici explored divergent representations of Slavdom, but limited his reflections to Venetian Dalmatia, virtually insisting that loyalty to Venice was the defining characteristic of the Slav. Elena, the heroine, did not call them Slavs, but gave them another name, as they prepared to fight each other for her sake: "Ah, barbarians!" Perhaps the public in Venice was gratified to suppose that even the seemingly most civilized Slav could lapse into violent barbarism. The occasion of the rivals' combat, however, offered an opportunity to an evil Bosnian Moslem, Orcano, who had been lurking and plotting since the beginning of the drama. He now kidnapped Elena with the intention of delivering her to his master, Osman Ogly, "the richest and most effeminate Moslem in Bosnia." Dusmanich and Serizca had to bury their differences in order to rescue Elena from "a troop of Bosnians" in the name of "Illyrian glory." Ultimately, though, she killed Orcano with her own hand. "Let's massacre them all!" (*trucidiamoli tutti*), cried Marcovich, Elena's father, in pursuit of the Bosnians; but this was the eighteenth, not the twentieth century, and the play was a comedy, so in the end the Moslem prisoners were spared: "Morlacco valor knows how to pardon even the enemy."[14] The Bosnians, after all, were also Slavs, though the play did not take note of that. As in Goldoni's *La Dalmatina*, in Federici's *Gli Antichi Slavi* the drama of Dalmatia lay in its relations with the Orient, the danger of Dalmatians exposed to Moslem depradations, and the prurient redemption of Illyrian glory from the menacing shadow of the harem.

In Federici's drama, as in Wynne's sentimental novel, the plot turned on a romantic rivalry between more and less civilized Slavs over a red-capped Dalmatian heroine. In presenting these Slavic alternatives—violent primitives versus more refined fellows—Federici posed the dilemma of Dalmatia within the Adriatic empire; that same dilemma—between barbarism and civilization—defined the domain of Eastern Europe as a whole, according to the philosophical values of the Enlightenment. Federici had no doubt about which of the brave deserved the fair, and, at the end of the comedy, he had Dusmanich concede the hand of Elena to Serizca: "Enjoy the prize of your virtue, and may you have children who emulate the heroism of their parents, increase the number of loyal subjects of our good prince, and crown the glory of this fortunate nation." Serizca accepted the prize with a gracious nod to his rival: "Generous friend, worthy Dusmanich, you are the hero who honors these climes. Your friendship is dear to me and completes my happiness." Thus Federici represented the friendly reconciliation of the more and less civilized Slavs, and reaffirmed the ideal of Dalmatian loyalty on the basis of Venice's civilizing mission among the Slavs. At the conclusion of the drama, Serizca promised to lead Elena to the Adriatic so that she might contemplate the administrative base of Venetian rule in Dalmatia: "that throne, surrounded by splendor, majesty, and glory, on which reposes the security of your prince, among the applause of his fortunate vassals." Such was the refurbished vision of Goldoni's "fortunate peoples of the Adriatic empire," celebrated by Federici in full awareness of their divergent levels of refinement. Marcovich, Elena's father, summed up the civilizing message in an enlightened philosophical coda: "Courage and strength are common to men and beasts. But friendship, equity, and reason are the virtues that distinguish us, and form the delight and concord of humanity."[15] Such civilized reconciliation between coastal Dalmatians and inland Morlacchi suggested that different degrees of civilization constituted the only obstacle to common identity between old-fashioned and up-to-date Slavs.

*   *

*

In 1802, the year of Federici's death in Padua, *Gli Antichi Slavi* was performed there as a musical "farce" about marriage among the Morlacchi, under the title *Le Nozze dei Morlacchi*, with a libretto by Giulio Artusi and music by Vittorio Trento.[16] The title, of course, was reminiscent of Mozart's masterpiece *Le Nozze di Figaro*, with comic opera reconceived as anthropological farce. Also in 1802, *Le Nozze dei Morlacchi* was staged as a ballet with choreography by Giacomo Serafini and (presumably exotic) costumes by Francesca Piatoli. The ballet was performed in Bergamo, another city of the former Venetian republic, and, with the subtitle "The Kidnapping of Elena," appeared on the same program as an opera by Domenico Cimarosa. The corps de ballet were identified, female and male, as "Morlacche" and "Morlacchi" respectively, though the program gave no intimation of the savage dances by which they would have expressed their barbarous natures. The denouement of the plot, however, was reversed from the Federici play, and the civilized suitor from coastal Split generously surrendered the hand of Elena to the primitive Morlacco, whose leading role was danced by the choreographer Serafini himself. Dusmanich was now named "Friderich" and Serizca was "Baliso," according to the account of the characters in the program. Elena and the old-fashioned Friderich truly loved one another, and it was he who ultimately rescued her:

> Friderich carries the unconscious Elena in his arms, and presents her to Baliso, who generously cedes her to her savior, admiring in him not only valor and courage, but also the more intense love. This act of generosity and philosophical virtue touches everyone and makes them happy, since the constant and sublime love of Elena and Friderich is to be rewarded and satisfied, and the virtue of Baliso is to be glorified.[17]

The Venetian revaluation of primitive virtues among the Morlacchi was consummated in the spirit of early Romanticism, when the civilized Dalmatian thus philosophically ceded his place to the barbarous Morlacco.

For several decades into the nineteenth century the ballet continued to be performed, ending one way or the other, with the title later simplified as *I Morlacchi* (*The Morlacchi*); anthropological fame survived in the form of theatrical entertainment. In 1812, *I Morlacchi* was performed at carnival in Novara, with new choreography by Antonio Biggiogero, and a geographical note that "the action is supposed to occur in Morlacchia on the border of Turkish Bosnia." In 1830 *I Morlacchi* was performed in Bologna, together with a Rossini opera, *La Donna del Lago*, and in 1831 the ballet was staged in Milan, on the same program with a drama about Peter the Great.[18] Fortis had, in fact, watched the Morlacchi in Dalmatia, dancing in a circle (*kolo*), with high leaps, according to custom, and had observed "the transport that the Morlacchi feel for this savage dance."[19] In the nineteenth century, in the aftermath of anthropological discovery and sensation, the Morlacchi became a folkloric curiosity, an exotic entertainment, an exercise in the choreography of barbarism, on the way to eventual effacement and oblivion.

Federici made use of Italian costume to make his ardent Dalmatian, the fashionable Slav Serizca, appear acceptably civilized before the Venetian public. Yet, Dusmanich's disapproval of his rival's clothing was also consistent with an authentic Dalmatian perspective articulated since the middle of the eighteenth century. In 1729 Filip Grabovac wrote a poem about Dalmatian disdain for Italian clothing, and he published it in Venice in 1747 in his anthology of verses and stories concerning the legendary and historical past of Dalmatia, *Cvit razgovora naroda i jezika iliričkoga aliti rvackoga* (The Flower of Conversation of the Illyrian or Croatian Nation and Language).[20] In 1776

Giovanni (Ivan) Lovrich published a book of reflections on Dalmatia, generally critical of Fortis's recent account, and remarked upon the attachment of the Morlacchi to their clothing: "They think there is no clothing in the world more noble. The Morlacco who changes clothing receives the opprobrium of the nationals." Lovrich even included a "song" about "the contempt that the Morlacchi have for the clothing of the Italians," which turned out to be an Italian translation of the poem by Grabovac, mocking Dalmatians in Italian clothes: "Who having just arrived from Italy on our shores/ Made themselves Italians, and blushed/ To call themselves Slavs."[21] Lovrich represented this as a contemptuous Morlacchi perspective on Italian clothes, though in fact it defined the dilemma of his own condition as an educated Dalmatian, studying at the university of Padua, and uncomfortably familiar with the difference between the customs of the Slavs and those of the Italians.

Giulio (Julije) Bajamonti, an educated coastal Dalmatian from Split—who was also a graduate of the university of Padua, a doctor, a composer, and a philosophe—ultimately made his peace with the customs of the Morlacchi when he published an article called "Il Morlacchismo d'Omero" in Venice in 1797. He argued that the customs of the Morlacchi were tellingly similar to those of the ancient Greeks, as described by Homer in the *Iliad* and the *Odyssey*. Though he himself, no doubt, preferred to sleep in a bed, Bajamonti embraced the heroic virtue of primitive customs. He addressed himself to Homer "to make him become a Slav (*farlo diventare schiavone*)," so as "to make myself related (*imparentarmi*) to him in a certain manner."[22] Overcoming the ambivalence of an educated Dalmatian, Bajamonti reconciled himself, through Homer, to *morlacchismo*, to the customs of the old-fashioned Slavs. He even cited the story of Achilles at the funeral of Patroclus, offering as prizes to the athletes a tripod worth 12 oxen and a female servant worth only 4. "Can you imagine anything more Morlacco?" asked Bajamonti, assuming familiarity with the subject on the part of the Venetian public.[23] Indeed, only a few years before, the public might have heard Dusmanich disparaging women from the stage of the Teatro Sant'Angelo. Federici concluded his drama with a mutually appreciative Slavic amity achieved between Serizca and Dusmanich, the civilized and the primitive protagonists. A similar resolution was tentatively undertaken offstage when a Dalmatian intellectual like Bajamonti dared to identify himself with the Homeric customs of the Morlacchi.

Considering the characters of Dusmanich and Serizca 200 years after their appearance at carnival in Venice in 1793, one can not help noting some meaningful relevance to matters concerning Eastern Europe across the centuries. In the contemporary global carnival—the extended season of celebration that has followed the collapse of communism—the dilemma of Eastern Europe is still represented as a choice between civilization in Western dress and the bankrupt values and visions of the former Eastern Bloc, where some misguided, old-fashioned Slavs might still prefer to sleep outdoors on the rubbish heap of history. In the eighteenth century Voltaire saw Russia poised between the alternatives of civilization and barbarism, and this fateful crossroads came to characterize the Enlightenment's evolving view of Eastern Europe as a whole. Serizca and Dusmanich were dramatic manifestations of the same dilemma. At the end of the twentieth century, in the postcommunist consensus that has so notably enhanced the ideological hegemony of market capitalism and constitutional democracy, the customs and values of presumptive civilization may seem more universally valid than at any time since the age of Enlightenment. Federici's eighteenth-century comedy of Eastern Europe, *Gli Antichi Slavi*, may serve as a reminder that clear-cut alternatives are also sometimes dramatic simplifications. The dilemma of Eastern Europe, compelled like Elena to choose between importunate rivals, was first formulated in the Enlightenment, and has been repeatedly restaged since that time according to the dramatic values of a public that sporadically shows interest, whether amused or alarmed, in the customs of the old-fashioned Slavs.

NOTES

1. "Camillo Federici," *Biografia degli Italiani illustri nelli scienze,* ed. Emilio de Tipaldo, 10 vols. (Venice, 1834–1845), vol. 5 (1837), pp. 346–52.

2. Johann Gottfried Herder, "Ideen zur Philosophie der Geschichte der Menschheit," in *Herders Werke,* ed. Regine Otto, 5 vols. (Berlin and Weimar, 1982), vol. 4, p. 393. Larry Wolff, *Inventing Eastern Europe: The Map of Civilization on the Mind of the Enlightenment* (Stanford, 1994), pp. 284–331.

3. Carlo Goldoni, "La Dalmatina," in *Tutte le opere di Carlo Goldoni,* ed. Giuseppe Ortolani, 14 vols. (Milan, 1935–), vol. 9 (1960), pp. 943, 953; Larry Wolff, "Venice and the Slavs of Dalmatia: The Drama of the Adriatic Empire in the Venetian Enlightenment," *Slavic Review* 56(3) Fall 1997: 428–55.

4. Alberto Fortis, *Viaggio in Dalmazia,* ed. Jovan Vuković and Peter Rehder, 2 vols. (Munich and Sarajevo, 1974), vol. 1, pp. 44, 58, 77. Fortis's work was originally published in Venice in 1774.

5. Camillo Federici, "Gli Antichi Slavi," in *Collezione di tutte le Opere Teatrali del Signor Camillo Federici,* 17 vols. (Venice, 1818–1819), vol. 16 (1819), pp. 3–5.

6. Ibid., pp. 3–5, 9, 20–21.

7. Arturo Cronia, *La Conoscenza del mondo slavo in Italia: Bilancio storico-bibliografico di un millennio* (Padua, 1958), pp. 331–33; see also Marijan Stojković, "Morlakizam," *Hrvatsko Kolo,* 26 vols. (Zagreb, 1905–1946), vol. 10 (1929), pp. 254–73; Grga Novak, "Morlaci (Vlasi) gledani s mletačke strane," *Zbornik za narodni život i običaje* 45 (1971): 579–603; Andrei Pippidi, "Naissance, renaissances et mort du 'Bon Sauvage': à propos des Morlaques et des Valaques," in *Hommes et idées du Sud-Est européen à l'aube de l'âge moderne* (Bucharest, 1980), pp. 1–23; Barbara W. Maggs, "Three Phases of Primitivism in Portraits of Eighteenth-Century Croatia," *Slavonic and East European Review,* 67(4) October 1989: 546–63; Valentina Gulin, "Morlacchism between Enlightenment and Romanticism," *Narodna umjetnost* 34(1) 1997: 77–100; Mate Zorič, "Croati e altri slavi del sud nella letteratura italiana del '700,'" *Revue des études sud-est européennes* 10(2) 1972: 301–312; idem, "Hrvat, Skjavun, Dubrovčanin, Morlak i Uskok—kao stereotipi i pjesnički motivi u talijanskoj književnosti," *Književna smotra* 24(85) 1992: 47–55;

8. Federici, "Gli Antichi Slavi," pp. 11–14.

9. Ibid., pp. 31–32.

10. Ibid., p. 15

11. Ibid., pp. 51–52.

12. Ibid., pp. 52–53.

13. Ibid., p. 53.

14. Ibid., pp. 8, 54–55, 70–71, 78, 84–85.

15. Ibid., pp. 85–86.

16. Cronia, *La Conoscenza del mondo slavo in Italia*, p. 332.

17. "Le Nozze de' Morlacchi, ossia il Rapimento d'Elena. Ballo eroicomico composto dal Serafini Giacomo" (Bergamo, 1802), Walter Toscanini Collection, *libretti di ballo*, Library for the Performing Arts, The New York Public Library.

18. "I Morlacchi. Ballo di Carattere in tre atti, composto e diretto da Antonio Biggiogero" (Novara, 1812); "I Morlacchi. Ballo di Carattere in quattro atti, d'invenzione di Gaetano Gioja, composto da Ferdinando Gioja" (Bologna, 1830); "I Morlacchi, ossia Le Nozze Interrotte. Ballo Serio, composto e diretto dal Signor Giovanni Fabris" (Milan, 1831), Walter Toscanini Collection, *libretti di ballo*, Library for the Performing Arts, The New York Public Library.

19. Fortis, *Viaggio in Dalmazia* , vol. 1, pp. 92–93.

20. Filip Grabovac, *Cvit razgovora naroda i jezika iliričkoga aliti rvackoga* (Split, 1986), pp. 260–66.

21. Giovanni Lovrich, *Osservazioni sopra diversi pezzi del Viaggio in Dalmazia del signor abate Alberto Fortis* (Zagreb, 1948), pp. 116–19; Grabovac, pp. 290–92.

22. Giulio Bajamonti, "Il Morlacchismo d'Omero," *Nuovo giornale enciclopedico d'Italia* March 1797: 77–78; Franco Venturi, *La Repubblica di Venezia*, vol. 5, pt. 2 of *Settecento Riformatore* (Turin, 1990), pp. 411–13.

23. Bajamonti, pp. 85–96.

The Diminishing Burden of the Soviet Past:
Russian Assessments of Russian-Ukrainian Linkages

WILLIAM ZIMMERMAN

A central feature of the collapse of the Soviet Union was the emergence of Ukraine as an independent country. Whether Ukraine will remain independent is problematic and contingent on a number of factors. It depends significantly on what citizens of Ukraine do and think, and it depends significantly on the foreign policy of Russia and the attitudes of Russian elites and mass publics. In a recent paper, I argued that an analysis of national surveys conducted in European Russia in 1993, in all of Russia in 1995–1996, and in Ukraine in 1994 showed that there was some evidence of an emerging Ukrainian political community.[1] Regional differences in Ukraine concerning orientations to the political economy are, to be sure, pronounced. Nevertheless, it turns out that for most foreign policy items and with regard to notions about the preconditions for citizenship, the mean scores of respondents for the obvious Ukrainian regions—western Ukraine, central Ukraine, and southern and eastern Ukraine—differ systematically from the mean scores for mass publics in Russian regions.

In this brief paper, my focus is on Russia. Here, I wish to explore Russian assessments of the Russian-Ukrainian divide. I attempt to identify the factors that define which Russians most wish to see Ukraine as once again part of the same country as Russia, and to extract from survey data[2] some sense of the extent to which those Russians who wish for union are willing to pay for it with blood and treasure. I advance four arguments.

The first is that in comparison with other foreign policy issues, Russians who know anything about the outside world attach enormous importance to Ukraine. (Foreign policy issues are far down virtually all Russians' lists of important matters. Mass publics in Russia, moreover, are every bit as ignorant of the outside world as are Americans; a sizable proportion of Russians do not even know that Crimea is part of Ukraine.)

Second, in the aggregate, Russians have a reasonably accurate intuition about eastern and southern Ukrainians' preferences with respect to ties between Russia and Ukraine.[3] They are also in the ballpark with respect to citizens of Ukraine dwelling in central Ukraine, but as a whole they completely fail to appreciate the intensity of nationalist sentiments in western Ukraine. However, those Russians who do not seek the union of Ukraine and Russia, do get the views of Ukrainians—even including western Ukrainians—on Ukraine's links to Russia about right.

The third point is that for Russian mass publics, certainly, and very likely for elites as well, the impetus for regarding the two countries as one stems largely from views that might best be described as *perezhitki proshlogo*, or "vestiges of the past," with the past here referring to the erstwhile Soviet Union, the Soviet system, and a Cold War-based fear of the American threat. Among mass publics, what identifies those who support union is nostalgia for the Soviet Union and the Soviet system and a continued view of the United States as a threat. Among mass publics at least, it is not some diffuse sense of the distinctiveness of Russian civilization that impels support for union, but attitudes that we would all regard as characteristically Soviet.

Finally, the Russian elite and mass surveys on which this paper draws provide some indication that elites who favor union with Ukraine are more disposed than others to use force in the context of scenarios that could involve a conflict between Ukraine and Russia. On balance, though, the Russian data do not support the proposition that there exists an a priori consensus either among elites or among mass publics that the use of force would be legitimate in settling those issues that are likely to seize Russian-Ukrainian relations in the policy-relevant future.

Although I have shown elsewhere that broad-ranging dispositions toward the relation of Russia to the international political system are important politically for Russians,[4] it would be professional deformation of the worst kind to argue that quotidian foreign policy problems are of great moment to ordinary Russians. They are not fools. In a January 1997 omnibus survey based on a national sample of the Russian Federation and conducted by the survey research company ROMIR, 92 percent of the respondents elected "overcoming the economic crisis" or "solving the problem of delays in payments" as the most serious problem confronting Russia. Fewer than 3 percent of the respondents identified the restoration of the USSR, preventing an external threat, and strengthening the international status of Russia *in total* as constituting the most serious issue.

Foreign policy matters are viewed by a somewhat larger number as the second most serious problem. Still, in the same survey, only about one in six respondents mentioned a foreign policy concern as the second greatest problem confronting Russia. Of these, 12 percent elected the restoration of the USSR, slightly more than 1 percent referred to preventing an external threat of some kind, and 4 percent said "strengthening the international status of Russia" when asked to name the second most serious problem confronting Russia. Given four alternatives ("yes"; "more yes than no"; "more no than yes"; and "no"), fully 43 percent of the respondents in the same survey answered "no" when queried about whether they had heard of the West's plans for NATO expansion, and an additional 9 percent answered "more no than yes"—whatever that means. Foreign policy matters are of secondary concern to Russian citizens.

Table 1. Regional Priorities, 1995. Russian Elites and Mass Publics *(1 = very low; 5 = very high)*

	Mass Publics	Elites
Africa	1.39	2.05
Asia	2.32	3.90
Baltic States	2.82	3.27
Central Asia and Kazakhstan	3.74	4.11
Europe	2.54	4.14
North America	1.70	3.13
Ukraine, Belarus, and Moldova	4.17	4.62
(valid n listwise)	2097	176

When, however, the respondents were asked to attach priority to various locales outside Russia, Ukraine overwhelmingly took pride of place. Table 1 shows the mean responses given by foreign policy elites and the Russian mass publics in 1995 to a battery of questions asking the respondents to assess the importance of various regions for Russian foreign policy. An item mentioning the three non-Baltic European states—Ukraine, Moldova, and Belarus—constitutes a cue that is far more salient than items referring to anywhere else within or outside the former Soviet Union. These means are basically unaffected by the respondent's level of knowledge about Ukraine: the mean scores on the importance of Ukraine, Moldova, and Belarus for those who knew that Crimea was a part of Ukraine and that it became a part of Ukraine in the 1950s, those who said Crimea was a part of Ukraine but were wrong on when this had occurred, and those who thought Crimea belonged to Russia or otherwise had a status separate from Ukraine, were all within less than a tenth of a point of the overall mean reported in Table 1.

Table 2 explores Russian assessments of Ukrainian views about the links between Ukraine and Russia. It shows two things. The first is the mean responses that citizens of Ukraine from the southern and eastern, the central, and the western regions gave in a 1994 national survey when asked to locate themselves on a seven-point scale where 1 meant "Russia and Ukraine should be absolutely independent countries" and 7 meant "Russia and Ukraine should be united into one country."[5] The second is the mean scores that Russian foreign policy elites and a national sample of Russian mass publics gave when asked in 1995 where they thought citizens of Ukraine would place themselves on such a scale.

Table 2. Russian Elite and Mass Evaluations of Ukrainian Preferences Concerning Links Between Russia and Ukraine, 1995 *(1 = should be completely independent; 7 = should be one country)*

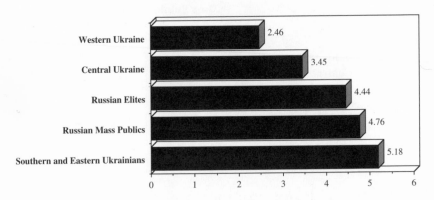

The way I interpret these data is that, in the aggregate, Russians have a fairly accurate sense of the views of those Ukrainian citizens who live in the regions of Ukraine that were part of the Soviet Union from its inception in the 1920s after the Bolshevik seizure of power in Russia in 1917. On average, they accord a somewhat greater penchant for the independence of Ukraine than one in fact finds among the heavily Russian or Russian-speaking population of southern and eastern parts of Ukraine. They underestimate somewhat the dispositions on this score in central Ukraine. Their assessment of the views of Ukrainians from the western regions of Ukraine is however quite faulty; their ascribed scores (4.76 for the masses and 4.44 for the elites) are far from the measured views of Ukrainians in the western part of Ukraine (i.e., the part of Ukraine that was annexed only in 1939).

Cognitive dissonance and attribution error seem to explain the discrepancy in assessments, as Table 3 underscores. Russians wishing for a close relationship between Ukraine and the Russian Federation attribute beliefs to citizens of Ukraine that are far more supportive of the two countries' uniting than others attribute to them. Among elites who themselves are highly disposed to answer that Russia and Ukraine should be a single country, the mean placement of Ukrainians along the seven-point scale was 5.06. Those Russians for whom union of the two countries is not a high priority[6] generate a mean score for Ukrainians of 3.75. The tendency to project was even greater among mass publics, with their mean placement of Ukrainians being 5.59 and 2.98 respectively. Both Russian elites and Russian mass publics who favor the union of Ukraine and Russia attribute to Ukrainians a greater disposition to prefer that Russia and Ukraine be a single country than do the mean scores for the entire samples of Russian mass publics and elites.

Table 3. Russian Estimates of Ukrainian Preferences Concerning Links Between Ukraine and Russia, Controlling for Preferences of Russians, 1995 *(1 to 7 scale)*

	Should Be One Country	Other Substantive Answer[a]
Elite	5.06	3.75
Mass	5.59	2.98

a. Includes those who positioned themselves at a place between 1 and 5 on a 7-point scale.

Those among Russian foreign policy elites and the Russian mass public who are not supportive of the notion that Russia and Ukraine should be a single country also apparently project their own views onto Ukrainians. In doing so, however, they actually have rather good aggregate intuitions about Ukrainian preferences. Russian elites who are not strong supporters of Ukrainian-Russian unity ascribe to Ukrainian citizens a position of 3.75, which is relatively close to the mean response of residents of central Ukraine. Ordinary Russians for whom union of Ukraine and Russia is not a high priority ascribe views to Ukrainians that are situated exactly in between the mean scores for Ukrainians from the western and central regions.

In general, disputes between states occur because "there is a 'there' there": tangible interests compete. It is easy to imagine, though, a coalition in power in Moscow, more desirous of closer links between Russia and Ukraine than is the case currently, pressing for something approximating unity in the belief that such efforts would be viewed favorably in Ukraine, only to be rebuffed—in a way that would exacerbate relations between the two states—by a Ukrainian governing coalition that would view such efforts as anything but solicitous.

Who, then, are the Russians who favor Russian-Ukrainian unity? For mass publics the answer is relatively straightforward. A number of attributes that might be hypothesized as distinguishing advocates from those to whom something less than union appeals turn out not to matter, or to be statistically significant but exceedingly weak predictors, or to co-vary in bivariate analysis but not in multivariate analysis. There is, for instance, substantially no difference between men and women in their disposition to endorse the proposition that Ukraine and Russia ought to be a single country. In bivariate analysis, university attendance and a scale measuring which respondents knew something about the world outside Russia[7] (regardless of educational attainment) correlate with a disposition toward close Ukrainian-Russian linkages. Those with university attendance and those who are knowledgeable about the outside world are noticeably more likely *not* to favor Ukraine and Russia becoming a single country. Those who respond well to the notion that Russia should pursue its own separate path rather than drawing on Western experience tend, in bivariate analysis, to be more disposed to support unification.

Employing multivariate analysis, however, we find that for mass publics, none of the above factors retains its statistical significance. Table 4 divides the respondents into two groups depending on where they placed themselves on the Ukraine-Russia scale (to which reference has been made already), the end points of which were that Russia and Ukraine should be entirely separate countries and that Russia and Ukraine should be a single country. It turns out that one can predict approximately 70 percent of the responses by a combination of variables, all of which relate to the Soviet era and as such may be thought of as part of a package. They are: attitude toward liberal or market democracy; views about whether the Soviet system before perestroika, the current political system in Russia, or "democracy of a Western type" is most suitable for Russia; intensity of regret regarding the demise of the Soviet Union; fear of the United States; and membership in the CPSU. (Age does not have a statistically significant separable and direct effect but is included here because it approaches $p < .10$ and because it does predict well the attitudinal variables in the model that predict attitude toward Russian-Ukrainian linkages.) The impact of these variables is summarized in the logistic regression found in Table 4.

Table 4. Who Among Russian Mass Publics Favors Ukraine and Russia Being One Country?

Variable	B	S.E.	Probability	R	Odds/Exp(B)
Member CPSU?	.4329	.2397	.0709	.0351	1.5418
Age 50 or >?	.2685	.1724	.1195	.0204	1.3080
Not a Liberal Dem.	.4682	.1698	.0058	.0740	1.5971
Soviet System Preferred?	.4773	.1917	.0128	.0641	1.6118
US a Threat?	.4503	.1720	.0089	.0689	1.5687
Should not have broken up USSR.	.5639	.1782	.0015	.0886	1.7575
Constant	-4.8277	.5932	.0000		

N = 799
Correct predictions 68.7%
Initial log likelihood function: -2 log likelihood. Goodness of Fit: 790.46

Logistic regression is a preferred regression technique when the outcome variable (Does respondent favor unity of the two countries or not?) is dichotomous. Unfortunately, the coefficients (column 1) are not readily interpretable. Rather, the Odds/Exp (B) makes more sense intuitively, since it represents the change in the odds of an event occurring if a dichotomous predictor variable (CPSU membership or no) has a value of 1 rather than 0. Recall how the odds of getting tails on a particular flip of a coin are 1 (.5/.5).

A brief elaboration of each of the predictor variables is appropriate here. One variable divides those who are liberal or market democrats, more or less as the terms are commonly understood in the West, and those who are not. It draws from a typology, described elsewhere, that I have developed for sorting orientations to the political economy that distinguishes liberal democrats, market authoritarians, social democrats, and socialist authoritarians.[8] For the purposes of this analysis, it proved best to divide the respondents into those who supported liberal democracy and those who did not. (For the explanation that I am developing, it would have been better if the model provided a better fit by dividing the respondents into those who were socialist authoritarians—and these people have genuinely Leninist values—and those who were not. Dividing them in that way is statistically significant at the $p < .10$ level, but the model in Table 4 which separates liberal democrats from others provides a slightly better fit with the data.)

The second variable is straightforward: respondents were asked whether they thought the Soviet system before perestroika, the current Russian political system, or "democracy of a Western type" was most suitable for Russia. The variable simply contrasts those who chose the old pre-perestroika system and those who did not. The USSR variable, likewise, was constructed by distinguishing those who agreed or strongly agreed with the proposition that "The Soviet Union should not have been destroyed under any circumstances" and those who did not. The fourth variable differentiates between those for whom the Cold War lingers on and those for whom it does not by dividing the respondents into persons who gave affirmative and negative answers when asked "Do you think the United States constitutes a threat to the security of Russia?" Finally, I included in the model both CPSU membership and age—dividing respondents into those who were 50 or above and those who were not. Their inclusion makes conceptual sense and at $p < .10$, CPSU membership is statistically significant. Being over 50 is close to that threshold, the presence of variables related to preference for the Soviet system, the Soviet Union, a Cold War outlook vis-a-vis the United States, and nostalgia for the Soviet Union notwithstanding.

As Table 4 shows, there are independent effects for each variable. CPSU membership, being 50 or over (although not statistically significant by conventional criteria), not supporting liberal democracy, favoring the old Soviet system before perestroika, agreeing or strongly agreeing that under no circumstances should the Soviet Union have been destroyed, and continuing to regard the United States as a threat to Russian security—all of these *perezhitki proshlogo* independently contribute to the proclivity to favor Ukrainian-Russian union. What drives the impetus to unification among Russian mass publics is not some Huntington-like sense of Slavic civilization, and it is certainly not a belief that a counterpart to the European Union would be beneficial. Rather, these are people who were socialized into a set of beliefs about the political economy and about the Soviet competition with the United

States—beliefs which have shown remarkable resistance to change despite or because of more than five years of perestroika and another five years of experience in post-Soviet Russia.[9]

What this means in practice is captured in Table 5. This table shows the proportion of respondents locating themselves at or near the "united-in-one-country" end of the scale ranging from "completely independent" countries to "united in one country" for various groups of respondents. To simplify what would be an otherwise hopelessly convoluted table I have omitted the two items in the multivariate model—CPSU membership and age 50 or over—that were not statistically significant at the .05 level. The table permits the reader to ascertain, for instance, the proportion—88 percent—of respondents favoring the union of Ukraine and Russia among those who are not liberal democrats, are nostalgic about the Soviet Union, regard the Soviet system before perestroika as suitable for Russia *and* who view the U.S. as a threat. Having done so, one can then compare the views of such people concerning the links between Ukraine and Russia with the views of those, say, who are *not* liberal democrats, but nevertheless are *not* nostalgic for the USSR, do not agree that the old pre-perestroika Soviet system is appropriate for current-day Russia, and do not regard the United States a threat (only 59 percent favoring union).

Table 5. Mass Public Orientation to Ukraine-Russia Unity

Liberal Democrats? V = Not X = Yes	USSR Nostalgia? V = Yes X = No	Suitable System for Russia? V = Soviet Mold X = Current or Western	US Threat? V = Yes X = No	Proportion Favoring Unity of Ukraine and Russia
V	V	V	V	88%
V	V	X	V	66%
V	X	V	V	68%
V	X	X	V	63%
V	V	V	X	72%
V	X	V	X	67%
V	X	X	X	59%
X	V	V	V	87%
X	V	X	V	61%
X	X	V	V	33% (n = 1)
X	X	X	V	50%
X	V	V	X	62%
X	V	X	X	63%
X	X	V	X	50% (n = 3)
X	X	X	X	38%

Data limitations and the nature of Russian foreign policy elites precluded an exactly parallel analysis of foreign policy elites. In terms of elite values, no question was asked, unfortunately, concerning the intensity of regret for the demise of the Soviet Union, nor did the survey instrument include an item relevant to the respondents' notions about the political system that best suits Russia. The absence of the latter is not of great concern because the construction of a measure defining orientation to the political economy for the 1995 elite and mass surveys is based on exactly the same questions. The absence of an item concerning nostalgia for the Soviet Union, however, means that the finding (below) that there is an independent effect for believing that Russia should follow its own unique path rather than learning from the West might not hold up were a Soviet nostalgia variable of the type incorporated in the mass public analysis included in the multivariate analysis.

Moreover, the kind of demographic analysis typical of analyses of mass publics is virtually pointless in assessing the dispositions of Russian foreign policy elites. Examining issues about the relevance of gender and university education on attitudes makes no sense, for the simple reason that there is, with respect to these attributes, a sameness to the Russian foreign policy elites that precludes analysis. There is no variance. Almost to a man, so to speak, Russian elites are male. Likewise, virtually all are university educated.

It is of greater interest, though, that neither age nor membership in the CPSU is a statistically significant predictor in multivariate analysis of orientations to Ukrainian-Russian unity. In the case of age, a natural explanation would be that the age profile is considerably more truncated than it is for the Russian mass public—which it is. Almost two-thirds (64 percent) of the foreign policy elites interviewed in 1995 were born between 1936 and 1955 whereas 38 percent of the mass public had been born in those years. But closer inspection reveals no consistent pattern. Those born before 1936 were more likely to support unification than were those born between 1936 and 1945. The latter, though, were also less prone to support unification than those born between 1946 and 1955, who were in turn more likely to favor unity than were those born after 1955.

The fact that erstwhile CPSU membership does not correlate with orientation to Ukrainian-Russian links among foreign policy elites requires some comment. As my book in progress will show, CPSU membership among foreign policy elites correlates with very few orientations either to foreign policy concerns or to issues of domestic policy. Those who were members of the Party when it was "The Party" are systematically more likely to consider the United States a threat to Russia and systematically less likely to favor the teaching of religion in the schools than are others. On the other hand, one can make a long list of items dealing with the political economy and Russia's relations to the outside world where CPSU membership and respondents' answers do not correlate or correlate weakly in bivariate analysis and have no independent effects in multivariate analysis. One of these is orientation to Ukrainian-Russian unity. Why is this so? My instinct tells me that what we are finding is that membership in the CPSU in the 1970s and 1980s describes a multitude of sins and that those who joined the Party did so for a variety of ideological and careerist reasons. Consequently, they entertained a range of views on joining, and an even more diverse set of views once the Soviet Union had collapsed.

This, though, is only to assert that knowing that someone in the Russian foreign policy elite had been a member of the erstwhile CPSU is not terribly informative in general and in particular about that person's orientation to links between Ukraine and Russia. As with members of the Russian mass public, elites evidencing a Soviet and Cold War mentality, regardless of whether they had or had not been members of the former CPSU, are disproportionately inclined to favor the proposition that Ukraine and Russia should be a single country. Of those I code as authoritarians, 89 percent adopt that stance. With regard to those coded as either liberal or social democrats, 48 percent respond that Ukraine and Russia should be one country ($tau_c = -.15$, $p < .001$). Among those who regard the United States as a threat to Russian security, 70 percent maintain the two states should be one country. By contrast, only 32 percent of those who do not consider the U.S. a threat favor unity ($tau_c = .39$, $p < .001$).

Table 6. Elite Orientations to Russian-Ukrainian Unity

Variable	B	S.E.	Probability	R	Odds/Exp(B)
Democratic or Not?	1.9197	.8001	.0164	-.1328	6.8189
Follow Unique Path?	.8448	.4061	.0375	.1045	2.3276
US a Threat?	1.1586	.4019	.0039	.1721	3.1853
Constant	-6.6917	1.6878	.0001		

N = 154
Correct predictions 71%
Initial log likelihood function: -2 log likelihood 177. Goodness of Fit: 149.

The predictive power of authoritarian tendencies and Cold War orientation is shown in Table 6. Three variables—whether the United States is seen as a threat, whether the person is coded as democratic, and whether the person thinks Russia should follow its own unique path—correctly predict 70 percent of the cases. (The individual variables have been recoded so that the expected relationships—Russia's unique path, U.S. a threat, and nondemocratic political orientation—all generate positive coefficients.) As noted above, lacking a Soviet nostalgia variable, I am not confident as to whether the model has conflated regretting the collapse of the Soviet Union and believing strongly in Russia's cultural distinctiveness. But the powerful role that fear of the U.S. plays in explaining orientation to Ukrainian-Russian linkages hints strongly at the proposition that for Russian elites, as for Russian masses, those for whom values about the Soviet political economy and the USSR's relation to the outside world continue to be policy-relevant are among the most prone to endorse the unity of Ukraine and Russia.

But would they do anything about it? Russian-Ukrainian relations in the 1990s have dealt with several complex and disputatious issues, and each side has shown an ability, when push comes to shove, to compromise or defer decisions. Russian elites are largely in agreement that the use of armed force is legitimate to protect the Russian state (86 percent) and to maintain Russia's territorial integrity (91 percent). They are almost as clear that the use of force would *not* be legitimate to extricate Russia from its economic crisis (90 percent saying it would not be a legitimate use of force), to aid countries friendly to Russia (84 percent saying not legitimate), or to aid Russians not in the former Soviet Union (82 percent saying not legitimate).

Where they divide is in their response to two questions: coming to the "defense of the economic interests of the country" and "defense of the interests of Russians (*russkie*) in the former republics of the USSR." Foreign policy elites interviewed in 1995 were thoroughly divided on these matters, with 46 percent saying the use of armed force would be legitimate in the former case and 42 percent in the latter and, correspondingly, 54 percent and 58 percent disagreeing.

Where matters become worrisome—especially when combined with the finding above that Russians who favor unity ascribe to the Ukrainians the same view—is that those who answer that Ukraine and Russia should be one country are more disposed to view the use of military force as legitimate than are other elites. Table 7 shows the distribution of responses among those who think Ukraine and Russia should be one country and those who do not endorse that proposition with respect to the legitimate use of force to protect Russian economic interests, to defend Russians in former republics of the USSR, and to defend Russian territorial integrity. A slight majority of the supporters of Ukrainian-Russian unity regard as legitimate the use of force to protect Russian economic interests and to defend Russians in former republics of the USSR, while only about a third of the remaining foreign policy elites are so disposed. Likewise, while consensus about the legitimacy of force to defend Russian territorial integrity exists among Russian foreign policy elites, there is a modest but statistically significant difference between those who think Russia and Ukraine should be one state and those who think otherwise.

Table 7. Legitimacy of Use of Force, 1995, Russian Elites

	Ukraine and Russia:	
Military Force Legitimate to:	**Should be One Country**	**Should be Independent**
Defend Economic Interests	55% N = (51) tau$_c$.20, p < .01	36% (29)
Defend Russians in ex-USSR	53% N = (48) tau$_c$.22, p < .05	31% (25)
Defend Territorial Integrity	96% N = (89) tau$_c$.10, p < .05	85% (70)

It is readily possible to envisage scenarios in Russian-Ukrainian relations in the next decade that could be cast as defense of Russia's economic interests or protection of Russian citizens (*rossiiane*) abroad. Indeed, such incidents have already occurred.[10] This might result in a substantial fraction of pro-unity elites asserting that resort to military force would be appropriate and indeed legitimate, especially if in such scenarios the status of Crimea became viewed as a matter of Russian territorial integrity. Were it then also the case that the composition of the governing coalition had altered in favor of those wishing to see Russia and Ukraine a single country, one could spin out the scenarios in ways that would imply grisly consequences for Ukrainian-Russian relations.

It is important to emphasize, though, that even elites who favor the unity of Ukraine and Russia are almost evenly divided on the legitimacy of the use of force to defend Russia's economic interests or to defend Russians in the former Soviet Union. Among Russian mass publics, support for use of force in such instances is still less. Those favoring unity are evenly divided on the legitimacy of the use of force to defend Russia's economic interests, with those answering in the affirmative constituting a slight minority, and only roughly a third of those in the mass public (36 percent among those favoring unity, 30 percent of those not) regarding it legitimate to use force to aid Russians in former republics of the Soviet Union.

Such response patterns are scarcely cast in stone. They could be altered one way or another by shifts in the political context. It is manifestly the case that many Russians, especially those who are cognitively and emotionally Soviet, wish Ukraine and Russia united in one fashion or another, and believe that Ukrainians think this way as well. What on balance does not appear to be evident is the kind of consensual resolve on the part of either Russian elites or, especially, on the part of Russian mass publics to spill the blood or spend the treasure needed to bring about unity by force. I doubt it will happen otherwise—at least as regards the bulk of Ukraine. Rather, a more plausible scenario would envisage the growth of a sense of political community in Ukraine coupled with the growth of a Russian identity increasingly lacking the Soviet coloration it has had for those Russian citizens, mostly over 50, who attach high priority to the unity of Ukraine and Russia.

* *

*

Roman Szporluk's work over more than a third of a century has focused on the grand themes of nationalism and communism.[11] At times when Soviet power seemed a permanent feature of the East European and Eurasian landscape, he reminded us repeatedly of the role of nationalism as a political idea and as a political force. The data in this paper have shown that Soviet ideas about the political economy and East-West relations continue as core political concepts for many Russians, and as such are a factor to be reckoned with when assessing Russia's relations with Ukraine. But within the former Soviet Union, it is these ideas at century's end that on balance are appropriately seen as the remnants of the past, and not the idea of national identity, harnessed as it is with the state in both Ukraine and the Russian Federation.

NOTES

1. "Is Ukraine a Political Community?" *Communist and Post-Communist Studies* 31(1) 1998: 43–55. The Ukrainian survey consisted of face-to-face interviews with 1,203 respondents selected in a national sample conducted by Sotsinform and directed by Evgenii Sinitsyn.

2. The surveys in this instance are two: The first is a panel study initially composed of 2,841 respondents and based on a national sample of the Russian Federation. All areas of Russia except Kaliningrad, Chechnya, Sakhalin, and the extreme northern parts of Siberia were included. The survey was administered by Demoscope, a firm led by Polina Kozyreva and her colleagues at the Institute of Sociology of the Russian Academy of Sciences. The surveys were conducted before and after the December 1995 Duma election and after the July 1996 presidential election. The second survey is one of 180 foreign policy elites with 30 persons drawn from each of 6 sectors of Russian society: the media—editors and commentators of major newspapers, television commentators, and the like; the foreign policy-relevant institutes of the Academy of Sciences, the government, including members of the foreign policy committees of the Duma and comparable officials in the Ministry of Foreign Affairs and the Office of the President; major figures in the ministries and in state owned enterprises; leading figures in private enterprises with large foreign dealings; and senior officers (usually colonels) in the military whose responsibilities had major foreign policy or national security dimensions. The elite survey was conducted by ROMIR (Rossiiskoe obshchestvennoe mnenie i rynok) under the direction of Elena Bashkirova.

3. Except where otherwise noted, in this paper "Ukrainians" refers to citizens of Ukraine, regardless whether they are ethnic Ukrainians who speak Ukrainian at home, ethnic Ukrainians who speak Russian at home, or ethnic Russians.

4. "Foreign Policy, Political System Preference, and the Russian Presidential Election of 1996," Paper presented at the American Association for the Advancement of Slavic Studies Annual Meeting, Boston, MA, 1996.

5. This question was asked in the 1994 Ukrainian survey as well as in the Russian elite and mass surveys. In the 1995–1996 Russian panel survey, a five-point scale was used. In the Russian elite and Ukrainian mass surveys, a seven-point scale was used. In attempting to compare responses across the three surveys, I recoded the responses in the Russian mass survey from 1 . . . 5 to 1, 2.5, 4, 5.5, and 7 respectively. This retained the interval nature of the scale and resulted in the extremes and the mid-point being precisely comparable, while treating a 2 and a 4 on the five-point scale as equidistant between a 2 and 3, and a 5 and 6 respectively on the seven-point scale.

6. Here defined as those who answered 1, 2, or 3 on a five-point scale and 1 through 5 on a seven-point scale.

7. The scale is based on ability to associate five Western leaders with their proper countries, whether the respondent knew that Crimea was part of Ukraine and when this occurred, and whether the respondent knew that Russia was part of the IMF and when that occurred. In practice few knew when Crimea had been ceded by the RSFSR to the Ukrainian SSR or when the Russian Federation had joined the IMF. As a result, the highest scores went to those who could locate all five foreign leaders and knew that the Russian Federation had joined the IMF and that the USSR had transferred Crimea to Ukraine.

8. Judith Kullberg and William Zimmerman, "Liberal Elites, Socialist Masses, and Problems of Russian Democracy," *World Politics* 51(3) April 1999: 323–58; William Zimmerman, "Markets, Democracy, and Russian Foreign Policy," *Post-Soviet Affairs* 10(2) April 1994: 103–127.

9. In a paper written with Judith Kullberg, "*Perezhitki proshlogo* and the Impact of the Post-Soviet Transition" presented at the 1999 Midwest Political Science Association Annual Meeting, we found that a strong predictor of orientations to the traditional Soviet model was the respondent's personal economic experience during the 1990s. Neither in multivariate nor cross-tabular analysis does this factor play a statistically significant role in explaining orientation to Ukraine-Russian linkages. I presume the reason for this discrepancy is that for respondents, the connection between these linkages and experience in the 1990s is too remote.

10. Karen Dawisha and Bruce Parrott, eds., *Russia and the New States of Eurasia* (Cambridge, 1994) contains a good survey of Russian-Ukrainian relations in the first years after the collapse of the USSR.

11. See especially *Communism and Nationalism: Karl Marx Versus Friedrich List* (Oxford, 1988).